Encyclopedia of Indie Rock

Encyclopedia of
INDIE ROCK

KERRY L. SMITH

Foreword by Marcus Congleton of Ambulance LTD

GREENWOOD PRESS
Westport, Connecticut • London

Library of Congress Cataloging-in-Publication Data

Smith, Kerry L., 1975–
  Encyclopedia of indie rock / Kerry L. Smith ; foreword by Marcus Congleton.
    p. cm.
  Includes bibliographical references and index.
  ISBN 978–0–313–34119–9 (alk. paper)
1. Alternative rock music—Bio-bibliography—Dictionaries. I. Title.
ML102.R6S63 2008
781.6603—dc22   2008004529

British Library Cataloguing in Publication Data is available.

Library of Congress Catalog Card Number: 2008004529
ISBN: 978–0–313–34119–9

First published in 2008

Greenwood Press, 88 Post Road West, Westport, CT 06881
An imprint of Greenwood Publishing Group, Inc.
www.greenwood.com

Printed in the United States of America

The paper used in this book complies with the
Permanent Paper Standard issued by the National
Information Standards Organization (Z39.48–1984).

10 9 8 7 6 5 4 3 2 1

To those for whom Music is the language of the soul

Contents

List of Entries

Bands

Adams, Ryan
The Afghan Whigs
Air
The Album Leaf
Alice Donut
Ambulance LTD
. . . And You Will Know Us By the Trail
 of Dead
Apollo Sunshine
The Apples in Stereo
Arab Strap
Arcade Fire
Archers of Loaf
Arctic Monkeys
Art Brut
Atom and His Package
At the Drive-In
Au Revoir Simone
Aztec Camera
Azure Ray

Babyshambles
Bad Brains
Banhart, Devendra
Barlow, Lou
Bearsuit
Beat Happening
Beck
Belle and Sebastian
Bellini
The Beta Band
Beulah
Be Your Own Pet
Big Black
Black, Frank
Black Eyes
Black Flag
Black Mountain

Bloc Party
Blonde Redhead
The Blood Brothers
Blunt, James
Boatzz
The Bravery
The Brian Jonestown Massacre
Bright Eyes/Conor Oberst/Saddle Creek
 Records
British Sea Power
Broken Social Scene
Built to Spill

CAKE
Calexico
Calla
Camper Van Beethoven
Cansei De Ser Sexy
Cat Power
!!! (Chk Chk Chk)
Clap Your Hands Say Yeah
Comets on Fire
Cursive

The Dandy Warhols
Danzig/Glenn Danzig
Death Cab for Cutie
The Decemberists
Del Rey
Denali
dEUS
DiFranco, Ani
dios (malos)
The Dirtbombs
Dirty on Purpose
The Dismemberment Plan
The Dresden Dolls
Dressy Bessy

Foreword

I knew some indie rockers in high school. I did not know what that term meant exactly, but I understood it to imply flamboyantly nerdy guys who could not really play but used that to their advantage somehow. They had better girlfriends. For these reasons we tended to mock them, my musical friends and I. Issues of independence vs. dependency aside, it seems to be generally agreed that **Pavement** and maybe **Built to Spill** are what best represent indie rock—1990s groups, whimsical sort of prettyish, sometimes noisy rock not aimed (presumably) at commercial successes. In the good ol' present 2K8, indie rock has evolved to mean, "Didn't sell shit," or so my manager tells me. But I would amend it to read, "Flamboyantly nerdy guys who didn't or don't sell shit." It is therefore alarming to learn that my own musical efforts will be noted in this book. But if I'm in there with **Pavement**, I'll take it.

Marcus Congleton
Ambulance LTD
May 2007

Preface

Fists may fly on indie rock stages, but the biggest debate, it seems, is not usually fueled by fashion or interband feuds (although those are frequent causes)—it is often a heated debate over whether a certain well-loved band has "sold out." Built on a solid foundation of blood, sweat, and tears, countless brave, resourceful bands of this genre have struggled to adhere to the **DIY (Do-It-Yourself)** aesthetic despite all obstacles. The **DIY (Do-It-Yourself)** movement (which is covered in more detail in the Introduction) is an ideal that indie rock and punk bands have upheld in order to retain more control over their lives, their careers, and their music. Choosing to record, produce, release, and manage their own music rather than have all of the decisions made by major labels who could impose creative control—or worse, reap the monetary benefits the bands felt they solely deserved—independent (or "indie" as it has become known) rock is, by its very definition, a genre of music that is made with the salt and vinegar of a band's labor of love.

For over 40 years, indie bands have prided themselves on the back-breaking efforts of self-promotion, self-produced albums, homemade album cover art and even, for the stalwart artist, self-run record labels that are often operated in the lead singer's dingy mold-filled basement or drafty furniture-less loft apartment. Still, that work, as it may seem to some, is in fact the only way many of these artists know how to survive. They live, breathe, eat, and drink music—and it would not be the art it has become without the lack of sleep and tiresome efforts that it requires.

Like many political and social movements, indie rock was spurned out of the fires of necessity. And although no official date can be tied to the birth of the genre and movement, certain moments along the indie rock timeline have exhibited the feeling and passion behind what drove indie rockers to soldier onward despite the monetary and countless other speed bumps within the music business that lay on their path to grasp true artistic freedom.

Nirvana front man Kurt Cobain summed up his feelings when he appeared on the April 1994 cover of *Rolling Stone* magazine wearing a homemade T-shirt that read "Corporate magazines still suck." He was sending a universal gesture for indie mainstream rockers everywhere by giving corporate America—big magazines, major labels, radio stations, and popular culture—the middle finger. In true indie rock fashion, Cobain was expressing his feelings toward the suffocating norms of conformity, controlling major labels, programmed radio stations, and all of the other business executives who would have loved the opportunity to work with him, which, in Cobain's eyes, would have been a death sentence under which corporations could have told him and his bandmates how to play, what to wear—or even worse, what to sing.

In the 1960s, **Frank Zappa** was one of the first musicians to do it all himself—write, record, produce, perform, and release his music. A true original, Zappa produced over 60 albums. The fact that one person could do what a whole record label promised was certainly no small feat, but it clearly makes sense to musicians who feel no need to share the fruits of their labors with opinionated executives who could neither play an instrument nor sing. Indie rock in the 1960s was an extension of the political and social upheaval that everyone was feeling at the time. Personal freedom was becoming increasingly important and trust in and of the government was waning. Music was a way for artists to express themselves and indie rockers figured it was only logical and fair that they control their own lives.

The success of indie rockers like **Frank Zappa** soon spread and indie rock bands started cropping up across cities all over the United States. In the late 1960s and 1970s, such bands as **The Velvet Underground**, the **Ramones**, and the **Talking Heads** were forging an underground indie rock scene in places like New York City. Independent record labels and independently owned record stores were popping up everywhere and the indie rock community was growing into a web of bands, musicians, and music business pioneers who were unable to resist the contagiousness of the power and personal ownership of the **DIY (Do-It-Yourself)** movement.

Indie rock in the 1980s became increasingly important as the popularity and powerful reach and impact of MTV grew; indie rockers strove to stay true to their ideals and remain steadfast against the temptations of "selling out" to corporate entities like chain stores, clothing companies, and other merchandisers who wanted to make a quick buck off of their art. Popular culture and indie rock art were dangerously close to blending together, but true **DIY (Do-It-Yourself)** bands united together to fight unfair practices by labels who wanted complete ownership, including the licensing and copyright of their music.

Throughout the 1990s, the same issues played over and over again like a looped mix tape. A few bands that were unable to resist that Garden of Eden apple of a record contract with a major label gave in and, in turn, "sold out." Indie rock throughout the 1990s and into the 2000s, though, was essential to the anticorporate, **DIY (Do-It-Yourself)** movement in that bands sang and played even louder about their personal struggles and strife. They were using their music as a means to unite, stay strong, and educate their fans about the importance of staying independent, proving that not everything could be bought or sold.

They say a star is born every second, but if the research and labor of love that went into this work proves anything, it is that another indie band sprouts even quicker—it takes nanoseconds—or one full swoop of a heart-pounding riff—for a fan to fall in love with a band. Because of the hands-on nature of this blue-collar genre and the ever-changing lineups, the closing and opening up of the flocks of labels, and the pin-the-tail-on-the-donkey game of naming the "it" band, indie rock lacks a proper tome of its history, influence, and scope. This encyclopedia aims to uncover the histories, legends, and pioneers of indie rock to better explain their motivations and methods. This comprehensive reference defines the bands, labels, and icons who shaped the genre, from the humble beginnings in the 1960s and **Lo-fi** homemade records by bands that played long and hard in dingy basements up through the history of seasoned veterans who mastered the fine art of staying afloat despite every obstacle that the cutthroat music industry threw at them.

Organized in an easy-to-use A–Z format, with a timeline and a list of the top indie records and the most influential bands, including a Resource Guide that includes books and additional references, this encyclopedia started out at as an account of a few hundred bands and labels. But not even an army of **DIY (Do-It-Yourself)** bandmates and street teams could manage to pump out a clear, concise work on such a hefty number. As the work progressed, the number of bands, labels, genres, and movements grew and I struggled to decide which bands to cut. The elimination process, which felt very much like an A&R representative's horrific duty to maintain the "bottom line" by trimming bands from a record label's roster, was painful and difficult. Bands that have just started out and have not logged enough tour mileage or released enough material (their continued valiant efforts notwithstanding) to warrant a full entry were cut.

It was a difficult elimination process, but the 150+ bands included in this encyclopedia truly represent the hard work, determination, and ambition of all indie rock bands. Many of the bands covered in this book also laid the groundwork for indie bands that have formed in recent years (including those who are shouting "Let's start a band" even as you read this). These bands paid the price for indie bands through years of sleeping in beat-up, old tour busses and living off next to nothing so that indie rock could survive and thrive. Documenting how indie music has shaped and has been shaped by youth and culture, the entries in this encyclopedia feature the most significant musicians, songs and songwriters, record labels, producers, genres, publications, and concerts. This encyclopedia aims to uncover high-interest topics, including socially aware bands that wrote politically charged songs and instilled values like the **DIY (Do-It-Yourself)** movement that are intrinsic to the history, the foundation, and the evolution of indie rock.

Deciding who among the wide spectrum of indie rock artists should hold court in the top ranking spots in terms of the "best indie rock artists of all time" was quite a hair-pulling event. Still, a select few indie rock artists have carved their own niches out in the genre, making indelible and lasting impressions on the scene that help them to stand out among the crowd. So if one were to take on the task of devising a list of the "Top 10 Influential Indie Rock Artists," there would indeed be a lot of erasing, crossing out, circling, and rewriting. But in the end, ten acts would stand apart, boldly marking the page with their **DIY (Do-It-Yourself)** triumphs, pioneering sounds, and overall iconic stance within the realm and spectrum of that seemingly indefinable genre of indie rock. Such a list, which you will find conveniently located in the back of this book as Appendix A, has been printed neatly and legibly in black and white, with all evidence of any hair-pulling, hemming and hawing, or overall internal dialogue removed from the page. These artists, listed in no particular order, have been included in this list for the simple purpose of highlighting their contributions to the sonic, visual, and oral histories of indie rock, which they helped to write with every opening riff. The list has also been supplied in order to give you, the reader, ample ammunition should you ever find yourself involved in a debate over the best indie bands of all time. This list, combined with a towering collection of indie rock albums, and your carnal knowledge of the genre itself should serve as the arrows in your quick, should an honorable debate over indie rock ensue.

The explanation behind Appendix B, "Most Significant Indie Rock Albums," on the other hand, has a much more succinct purpose and explanation. Also located conveniently at the back of this encyclopedia, Appendix B is a running list of albums that are considered the epitome of indie rock music. Each album was carefully chosen to represent the climactic work of top indie artists. Select albums may even serve as a band's single-handed achievement as indie rock pioneers, while other albums simply sum up a band's signature sound and, therefore, should be studied with the same passion and determinism with which they were created. In short, Appendix B should be considered a starting point for the reader's next few consecutive Christmas wish lists.

This work is designed to meet the needs of students, general readers, and even those of you who have adorned your locker, backpack, or car with a band name and/or logo by offering you the stories, triumphs, and failures of the hundreds of bands in this book—and the records that resulted from their labors of love. These works have been left behind as sonic journals that serve to chronicle the lives of these musicians who have paved, and still are paving, the way for that next big thing that may very well be, at this moment, rehearsing in one of the band member's parents' basement.

Acknowledgments

I would like to thank my friends and family for all of their support and encouragement: Kelly, Richie, Beth, Chris, Jason C., and Erik. I also want to thank the "hipsters" of Williamsburg, Brooklyn, and the various venues and hangouts where I had the opportunity to see many of the bands in this tome play: Mercury Lounge, The Living Room, North Six, Arlene's Grocery, Bowery Ballroom, Brownies, CBGB, Continental, Galapagos, the Knitting Factory, Luna Lounge, Pete's Candy Store, and the Warma Café, where they serve the best coffee and hangover-curing seviche. I also want to thank my best friend, Missy, for her endless patience while I toiled away in front of my computer on so many nights like a frantic grad student making a midnight dash to complete a thesis paper. Most of all, I want to thank my mother for instilling in me a lifeblood love of music (even if her preference for the songs of Barbra Streisand, which she plays at the highest volume, forces me to put on my noise-canceling headphones). My thanks also go to my editor, Kristi Ward, for giving me the opportunity to write this book.

Introduction: How Indie Rock Shaped and Inspired Generations of Do-It-Yourselfers

B.Z. (BEFORE ZAPPA)

A decade before indie rock artist **Frank Zappa** started wailing on his guitar, writers and editors spotted a wave of change in the music industry. Magazines such as *NME (New Musical Express)* and underground publications like *The Village Voice* were founded in the 1950s during what seemed like an innocent decade. Peppered by rosy-cheeked teenagers and bubble-gum-popping music fans who could hardly wait for the release of Broadway and movie musicals and who fawned over Elvis and The Beatles, American music in the 1950s was polished, proper, and, above all else, "popular," as in pop music that catered to mainstream listeners. In fact, the music business was so predictable that someone had to come along and shake things up.

A.Z. (AFTER ZAPPA)

Rebellious rockers like Chuck Berry, Elvis Presley, and Buddy Holly were making music that heeded the call of youths' anticonformist desires in the 1950s, but it was not long before their music became the mainstream that parents also enjoyed and the indie spirit had all but lost its edge. R&B acts such as Chuck Berry and Fats Domino slowly wooed fans with their youth-oriented lyrics, cool ways, and smooth guitar rhythms, but it was not until the 1960s that music became edgy again and the future of music showed a different side of the coin. Artists began blending genres together, and bands were soon playing odd-sounding hybrids like folk rock, jazz-rock, and even psychedelic rock. Acid and other hallucinatory drugs were the popular hobby now, and artists such as **Frank Zappa** emerged like the Wizard who lived in Emerald City in *The Wizard of Oz,* bringing with him surrealist, experimental, guitar-heavy rock that was not easily identifiable or categorized.

Frank Zappa, a true individual, was perhaps the first true independent (or "indie") artist who multitasked as a producer, a songwriter, a performer, and a musician. An underground scene was slowly growing under the cement-like layer of rock 'n' roll that had captured the attention of the general population. Indie rock—or rock that is made by the musician without the help or influence or funding from a controlling record label—was, in a way, a weed that started growing and spreading its seeds long before it was officially defined. By simply designing and forging his own path, Zappa helped to pave the way for what is now referred to as the "independent" rock, or music that is made by the musician who fights to retain most of the creative control over his or her songs. By standing on his own, Zappa was defining the **DIY (Do-It-Yourself)** attitude that indie rockers share today: an anticorporate stance that maintains that the artist should be the major decision maker who maintains the rights to his or her music. This independent ideology maintains that the musician is able to write, record, and produce music that is free from the financial constraints of record labels that might otherwise put creative limitations on a song or album, so that the music is free (or independent) of any corporate or money-driven interests. Today's modern "indie rock" artists, though they may share little musical commonalities with Zappa, have him to thank for setting the waves in motion for the headway he made in the music industry for independent artists.

Frank Zappa was also an outspoken advocate of free speech. In 1985, the mustached musician appeared before the U.S. Senate in an effort to educate the Commerce, Technology, and Transportation Committee about the dangers of the censorship efforts of Tipper Gore, who founded the Parents' Music Resource Center (PMRC). Boldly going where no artist had gone before, Zappa explained the importance of the freedom of speech, a constitutional right that he felt should be upheld at all costs. Through communal efforts by musicians and public figures, the PMRC's goals were not fully realized. Even though the Recording Industry Association of America agreed to paste "Parental Advisory: Explicit Lyrics" stickers on explicit albums, it did not follow through with the PMRC's demands to create a heavily monitored media watch sector that would pressure broadcasters not to air "questionable-talent."

EAST COAST AMBITION

Teenagers like the NYC-based act the **Ramones**, who are considered the "first punk rock group in America," started playing in basements, locals clubs, and neighborhood parties in the early 1970s, where teenager crowds were hungry for a loud, rule-free environment in which they could make their own rules. In nearby New Jersey, the **Misfits**, a "horror punk" band whose skull-like face makeup would cause any parent to worry, were culling from rockabilly bands and playing a mix of punk, rock, and metal. Just a few states away in Washington, D.C., bands such as the politically charged rock band **Fugazi** were further splintering the indie rock genre by mixing it with the aggressive, angst-filled elements of hardcore music that had taken over the city in the 1980s. Such bands as **Fugazi** were among the first acts to publicly and wholly declare their allegiance to the **DIY (Do-It-Yourself)** aesthetic, an ideal that sprouted from such punk bands as **Iggy and The Stooges** and the ever-unpredictable 1970s guitarist Ted Nugent whom they idolized. **DIY (Do-It-Yourself)** artists were similar to **Frank Zappa** in that they did it all themselves—writing, producing, recording, and distributing their own music and even forming their own record labels.

Indie rock's ties to the **DIY (Do-It-Yourself)** movement are deep and strong. The **DIY (Do-It-Yourself)** movement itself, however, is a term that was originally used to define grassroots political movements. The **DIY (Do-It-Yourself)** movement was popularized in the 1960s by various activists and artists who wanted to work free from the rules and confines of the government and self-interest groups like big corporations. The indie rock concept of **DIY (Do-It-Yourself)** originated from the artists' desire to create music that they had complete control over—creatively, politically, and monetarily. This **DIY (Do-It-Yourself)** ideal is defined by the very nature of independent artists who strive to pay for music with their own money and find their own means to record, release, and distribute their music so that they do not have to conform to the desires or restrictions of a record company that would otherwise be able to tell them how to do things.

WEST COAST ATTITUDE

On the West Coast in the mid-1970s, bands such as the politically and socially aware hardcore act **Black Flag** were declaring their independence even louder by forming their own record labels, touring incessantly, and spreading their angst-filled music and autonomous attitude to teens around the country. Meanwhile, hardcore music fans who did not play in a band but wanted to support local musicians and bands who lived in cities near them founded record labels in order to support bands the best way they could—by harvesting their talents and handling the production and distribution so the bands could continue touring and making music. Pioneers of this effort, including Rick Harte, a diehard music fan and native Bostonian who founded **Ace of Hearts Records**, simply strove to support bands he loved by helping them get the funding they needed to make records, tour, and distribute their music to riff-seeking fans.

Record labels in the 1970s were not focused on the financial rewards of the music; in fact, at the very core of "indie" rock is an understood belief in the artistic benefits of making music. The lines between the music business and the music itself blurred years later when executives and CEOs saw profits in the guitar-strumming hands and decibel-blowing voices of up-and-coming musicians.

MAINSTREAM ATTACKS!

The British press caught on to the wave of indie rock much faster than many stateside publications. In the 1980s, such bands as **The Jesus and Mary Chain** and **The Smiths** in the United Kingdom were already being branded as "alternative" for their overall boldness and steadfast commitment to the **DIY (Do-It-Yourself)** ethics and experimental ambitions they exhibited as loudly as they played their instruments. The line that differentiates alternative music from indie rock can be difficult to draw because alternative (or "alt" rock, as it has been called) can be indie, and indie rock can be considered alternative simply because the defining characteristics of alternative are shared by indie acts—antimainstream lyrics and attitudes that call their anticonformist fans to action. Yet while some alt rock can be considered "anticommercial," many alt rock acts are played on mainstream radio stations, and their albums are sold in record stores that may not otherwise carry smaller, or lesser known, indie acts.

In many circles, alt rock is simply a subgenre of rock 'n' roll that is a bit more daring and envelope pushing in nature, but alt rock does not veer too far off the mainstream spectrum that it would be considered underground (or the other way around—hence, the source of the confusion). Much of indie rock is by nature underground music that is not readily available in popular record stores, and until recently you were not likely to hear many indie bands over the speakers in a shopping mall. Alt rock, on the other hand, hovers so close to the mainstream that it is simply an offshoot of popularized rock 'n' roll, while indie rock is an acquired taste that is developed by seasoned fans who are seeking music that others may consider too "out there" for their tastes.

Early indie rock in the United States was not by nature a loud, in-your-face aural attack with strictly political ambitions. Acts such as **Hüsker Dü**, Dinosaur Jr., and **R.E.M.** shared the same kind of peaceful change-mongering ideals as many U.K. acts. But as indie rock evolved over the 1970s and the 1980s, the **DIY (Do-It-Yourself)** ideology, message, and attitude became more socially and politically charged and the music got louder. When the Dead Kennedys sang, "You've turned rock and roll rebellion . . . into Pat Boone sedation" in their 1985 song, "M.T.V.—Get Off the Air," they were not worried about backlash from listeners, the press, or the law. In fact, the disorderly punk denizens did not care much about anything—except their music. In the early 1980s, punk and indie rock artists shared more than a closet full of ripped homemade shirts, pants, and mussed-up haircuts; they possessed a collective hope to carve a new niche in the music world so that independent rock artists could own and maintain complete creative control over their music.

Some of these indie artists shared a common disdain for "poseurs," or artists they felt did not exactly live or exhibit the antiestablishment ideals—wore punk clothes and tried to dress in the same fashion as punks who were living off of little means and just trying to survive so they could play the music they loved. Others shared a mutual hostility toward the overproduced music being played on the radio and "poseurs" shown on MTV. And the rest, while they may not have subscribed to the extreme principles that were considered dear to acts like the San Francisco–based Dead Kennedys (the band spent a lot of time in court over politically charged lyrics that openly criticized public leaders and album art that was considered "obscene"), who would most certainly never be caught shopping in Hot Topic store. Because part of the criteria of being considered an indie band (if there ever was such a checklist) goes deeper than the material realm—it is an adherence to the **DIY (Do-It-Yourself)** mentality and a staunch opposition to following anyone's rules. Indie rockers ultimately have become unlikely heroes simply by making the type of music and scene they could not find—so they made it themselves.

ONE NATION, UNDERGROUND

Over the years, indie rock artists spliced the genre by developing new sounds, off-shoots, and subgenres such as the following:

- **post-punk,** an experimental version of punk that often involves few chords. It is best exhibited by bands like **Echo & the Bunnymen**;
- **indie pop,** a style of experimental pop music that **Belle and Sebastian** claim influenced them;
- **shoegazing,** a subgenre of music that emerged in the United Kingdom in the 1980s. It is exhibited by the stance a musician takes while playing it;
- **emo,** or emotionally charged music played by bands like Dashboard Confessional;
- **math rock,** which incorporates complex set of rhythms and angular sounds;
- **Lo-fi,** a highly recognizable subgenre that is characterized by a style of recording and production that highlights feedback and distortion;
- **post-rock,** which is often characterized by bands that make instrumental music;
- **pop punk,** or pop-inspired punk music that is played by the likes of the **Ramones**;
- **dance punk,** a fusion of new wave, punk, and dance music that emerged in the 1970s and is played by such bands as **LCD Soundsystem**;
- **Twee pop,** which is also referred to as "Bubblegum pop," is a more "innocent" version of punk rock;
- **freak folk,** a subgenre of folk music that is difficult to define since the term was coined by **Devendra Banhart** out of a necessity to define his music;
- **Baroque pop,** a darker, more pessimistic form of pop, it is often considered to be the antithesis to "sunshine pop" made by the likes of The Beach Boys;
- **sadcore,** a more melodramatic form of **emo,** and other wordplay combinations.

Indie rock, while it is a subgenre of alternative rock, encompasses all subgenres that fall under the **DIY (Do-It-Yourself)** aesthetic. Oftentimes, bands are cross-influenced by each other, generating new subgenres with each new band.

PUNK BANDS EXPRESS THEIR "HARD" FEELINGS

In the late 1970s, hardcore punk (harder, faster, and more politically charged punk music) and indie rock bands began to write more introspective lyrics that, despite the tough male persona that punk rockers flashed, showed their sensitive side. This subgenre became known as **emo,** a derivative of the word "emotional." Even further splinters of **emo** like **sadcore**—slower tempo music played by acts like **Cat Power** (page 101)—and **emocore**—more emotionally driven hardcore music made by such bands as **Rites of Spring** (page 305)—have developed since **emo**'s inception in the 1980s. **Emo** bands such as **Sunny Day Real Estate** and Texas Is the Reason maintained a more indie approach to **emo,** while such full-on **emo** bands as Dashboard Confessional went on to pioneer the genre and morph it even more. **Emo** rockers wore their hearts bravely on their sleeves—and just about as much black as a funeral procession.

While **emo** was washing over the scene in Washington, D.C., fans in Seattle, Washington, during the 1990s were experiencing **grunge** music, a hybrid of alternative, hardcore, and heavy metal for the first time. **Grunge** gods like Kurt Cobain of **Nirvana** and Eddie Vedder of Pearl Jam donned loose-fitting, dirty-looking flannel shirts and ripped jeans. They turned the feedback up again and created ear drum–bursting, fuzzy guitar riffs, heavy distortion, and incoherent lyrics that served as the voice of teen angst and frustration.

From the humble beginnings of their quiet, left-wing Pacific Northwest city, Vedder and Cobain became overnight sensations, leading packs of teenagers like rough-around-the-edges pied pipers. Moshing, an aggressive expression by fans who slam into one another at hardcore or punk concerts, became a frequent occurrence at **grunge** shows, as did crowd surfing and head banging. This new form of music seemed to inspire kids who were frustrated with authority and the social and peer pressures being thrust upon them, giving youths idols who detested everything they detested—rules, curfews, and parents.

Pearl Jam and **Nirvana** went from playing parties and grimy basements to performing in sold-out arenas. **Grunge** helped indie rock break into the mainstream, and soon, preppy kids in high school hallways who always got straight A's were bopping their heads to "Smells Like Teen Spirit" on their Walkmans. Kids were ripping their jeans and shopping at places where loggers would buy their red and black flannel shirts. MTV even jumped on the bandwagon, seeing dollar signs in Kurt Cobain's blue eyes and disaffected attitude.

Music magazines like *Rolling Stone* also made plans to capitalize on indie rock's popularity by placing such bands as **Nirvana** and **Green Day** on its covers. But stalwart indie fans claim *Rolling Stone* catered to the corporations and big-money companies that placed their advertisements in its pages and opted instead to read *SPIN* magazine, which selected bands for its covers based on an act's ability to define indie rock at that moment in time rather than by record sales or appearances on MTV. Still, **Nirvana**, which appeared on the cover of *Rolling Stone* on more than one occasion, managed to one-up the magazine when Cobain wore a self-made T-shirt on an April 1994 cover that read "Corporate Magazines Still Suck."

FROM ON STAGE TO ONLINE

When Northeastern University student Shawn Fanning's brainchild, the file-sharing Web site Napster, made headlines in the summer of 1999, record labels viewed it as a blessing—and then a curse. Several labels that had planned to get involved with the file-sharing site pulled the plug, and Fanning experienced a windfall of lawsuits, legal battles, and headaches.

But bands recognized the concept as a new opportunity to reach fans. Groups such as the Brooklyn-based band **Clap Your Hands Say Yeah** (CYHSY) started marketing themselves online with such sites as MySpace.com, building bigger and more solid fan bases that spread quicker than any record company's snail mail campaign could have achieved. After the band sold 200,000 copies of their 2005 debut album, the indie rock group knew it did not need the help of a major record company. "The question that we asked record companies was essentially, 'What can you do for us that we can't do for ourselves?' "[1] CYHSY told CBS News. Today online fanzines like TrouserPress.com and blogs like the trendy Gothamist.com have served as news outlets for up-and-coming bands; they are among the first stops fans visit when looking for news about "it" acts or their favorite bands.

Social networking sites like MySpace, Facebook, and Friendster have helped bands reach out and find new fans and spread their music through word of mouth. These sites have been instrumental in helping indie acts showcase their music and spread word of mouth about live shows, news, and new records. It is free to set up a MySpace Web page, and bands can post songs on their site, enabling them to reach indie rock fans who live hundreds—or thousands—of miles away. Sites like MySpace are key to a band's success nowadays, as labels often monitor a band's success rate (a rating that is often gauged by the band's number of "friends" on its page) when they scout and decide which acts to sign.

INDIE LABELS SET UP SHOP

As a large number of the major record labels have merged into what is referred to as "the Big Four" (a grouping of labels that are all combined under four major labels, all of which seek to control the majority of the industry's music), independent labels have both fallen and prospered in the changing landscape. A few of the labels that withstood all of this earthquake-like activity have seen bands on their roster sell just as many records as mainstream artists; their groups have topped the charts and even rivaled popular acts for magazine covers and slots on bills at major music festivals. Indie labels, with their eclectic names and loft- and apartment-based headquarters, have spread all over the United States and the United Kingdom. Bigger name labels, such as Jetset Records, **Saddle Creek Records**, **Kill Rock Stars**, spinART Records, **Sub Pop Records**, and StarTime International Records have all made headlines as breeding grounds for successful indie bands.

Indie bands with shoestring budgets have often opted to record anywhere they could. The **Lo-fi** movement, in fact, was born out of this practice of home recording, which was popularized in the 1980s more out of a need to save money than to gain certain sounds. But as the hiss, buzz, and crackle of distortion, feedback, and background noise became something most bands aspired to include it in their music (it gave the songs a more natural, laid-back, "just recorded" feel), musicians began building home recording studios. Such bands and musicians as Sebadoh, **Pavement**, **Guided By Voices**, and **Lou Barlow** pioneered the **Lo-fi** movement.

The popular music-editing program Pro Tools proved useful for many solo artists, self-employed producers, and bands. The user-friendly program (which was made available to the public in the late 2000s) costs upwards of $10,000, but the long-term benefits of being able to cut, edit, and even conduct post-production work on songs was a necessity for bands that wanted full creative control over their music. Even popular recording artists started building home recording studios, spending bulk sums to customize vocal booths, drum rooms, and engineering equipment. Home studios built by indie artists like **Elliott Smith** and **Arcade Fire** became hang out areas for their musician friends, and acts often shared the space and pooled their money to invest in equipment.

STICKS AND STONES

As the temptation of mainstream paychecks, glossy magazine cover shoots, and freebie swag grew harder and harder to resist, several indie bands fell from grace and committed the worst crime of all by "selling out" to sign with major labels. In an ironic twist of oxymoronic fate, bands like **Nirvana** and **Sonic Youth**, which opted to ink deals with big name labels, did not suffer the fate of becoming outcasts in the indie world. Fans had developed a deep respect for these acts, which had struggled throughout their early years, and that respect lasted throughout the acts' internment with major record labels, which made them impervious to the "sell out" label that caused many a band's downfall. Several theories abound as to why these acts were granted immunity to that reputation-damaging label, but the most logical reason seems to be that these bands have logged enough miles on poorly equipped tour buses, visited remote cities full of loyal fans, and played by their own rules long enough that they have been given a "Get out of jail free" card to serve as waivers for any discerned improprieties like selling a song for use in a TV commercial.

Others, though, suffered ill repute when they decided to make mainstream deals. Singer-songwriter **Liz Phair** suffered this wrath to the nth degree when she teamed up with megastar production team The Matrix, which had produced records by Avril Lavigne (whom many indie fans consider a fake or "poseur" punk rocker). Phair, who had taken a hiatus since her career shot her to stardom in the 1990s, had made plans to return to the music business. A music critic for the *New York Times* accused the indie princess of committing "career suicide" and continued to lash at her with accusations that Phair had attempted to "remodel herself as a contemporary Avril Lavigne."[2]

A media debate ensued over the *Times'* articles' excessive attacks on **Liz Phair**. Fans divided into two camps—those supporting Phair for branching out to work with a skilled team with proven songwriting credits and those on the other side, an angry mob who was ready to crush Phair's guitar for her mainstream sins. Phair's album notably sold well, moving 400,000 copies[3] and producing a few radio hits. The indie rock icon and single mom, it seemed, did not exactly have the last laugh—the press helped give the singer newfound media exposure, and, although her career was not destroyed over the debacle, but Phair endured months of criticism and she had to work doubly hard to prop herself back up to a point where she was regularly touring and working on new material.

The sell-out debate is still one of contention, however, with bands such as **The Killers** and **The Bravery** staging indie rock cat fights and accusing the other of copying each other or catering to the masses (they are ironically both signed to the very same major label Interscope Records, which pays the bills and signs their checks). Such bands as **The Bravery** and **The Killers**, while they tout the indie rock "look," do not exactly adhere to the **DIY (Do-It-Yourself)** ethic and aesthetic that forged their pathways to major radio stations. Many indie rock fans who believe in the strains of the genre that helped build it up to what it is today may not consider these acts to be indie acts. Still, the fact that **The Killers** and their rivalries **The Bravery** have been dubbed "indie" acts is no fault of theirs. Critics and media outlets toss the term around loosely, and the very definition of indie itself can become tangled.

THE FUTURE OF INDIE ROCK

Contemporary indie acts walk a thin line when it comes to the term "independent." Acts such as **Modest Mouse** and **Arcade Fire**, both of which started out as underground acts, have broken through to the mainstream much in the way **Nirvana** did a decade ago. They are playing MTV events, winning awards, cashing large checks signed by big labels, and selling out tours. Still, bands like these have managed to make their indie forefathers proud; by selling countless albums and building solid fan bases who have proven loyal, major labels who court the bands are mindful of the artistic integrity of their music and realize that it is not something to be tampered with. So by towing their own line and making their own rules (and toughing it out in cramped tour vans and less than desirable living or working conditions), a few select bands are calling the shots, earning big paydays, while manning the creative controls.

In 2007, independent labels banded together to form what many are calling the "virtual fifth major" record label, which will give the Big Four record labels an uneven count—and a run for their money. This "fifth" label, which may be the biggest of all in size and scope, has inked a deal to sell songs by its bands to the popular social networking Web site MySpace. The "fifth," which is licensed as "Merlin," is being led by Charles Caldas, the former head of Australia's largest independent music distributor, and it is a grouping of labels from across the globe. The future of indie rock may yet depend on the blood, sweat, and tears of pioneers like those involved in Merlin and their abilities and passionate willingness to join forces with the very bands whose careers they will work to protect.

Notes

1. "Internet Challenges Musician's Traditional Longing to Be Signed by a Label," CBSnews.com, May 28, 2007.

2. Meagan O'Rourke, "Liz Phair's Exile in Avril-ville," *New York Times,* June 22, 2003.

3. http://www.google.com/search?hl=en&q=liz+phair+album+400%2C000 +copies&btnG=Search.

Timeline: 1952–2007

1952 The first issue of *NME* (*New Musical Express*), a weekly U.K.-based music publication, is published.

1955 Dan Wolf, Ed Fancher, and playwright/novelist Norman Mailer start the underground newspaper *The Village Voice* in an apartment in the East Village neighborhood of New York City.

1964 **Frank Zappa** joins the group The Soul Giants; he becomes the band's leader and renames the group The Mothers.

1967 The **Ramones** sign to **Sire Records** and release their self-titled debut album, which cost around $7,000 to record.

The Velvet Underground releases its debut album, *The Velvet Underground & Nico,* the cover of which features one of Andy Warhol's most famous paintings of a peeled banana. The album is considered one of the most important—and accomplished—debut albums.

1970 **Fugazi**'s Ian MacKaye forms Dischord Records. The label puts out its first release, an EP (extended play) by The Teen Idles called *Minor Disturbance*.

1974 Three Rhode Island School of Design students form the **Talking Heads** in Providence, Rhode Island.

1977 Former UCLA economics major Greg Ginn and his pal Chuck Dukowski form the hardcore band **Black Flag**.

Glenn Danzig forms the **Misfits**.

With a little help from David Bowie, Iggy Pop pursues a solo career.

The Go-Go's front woman Belinda Carlisle plays drums for **The Germs** under the stage name "Dottie Danger."

1978 Robert Haber founds *CMJ*. Haber is regarded as an authority on college radio; he establishes CMJ in 1978 after having served as the Music Director for WBRS, the radio station at Brandeis University. The company owns *CMJ New Music Monthly* and *CMJ New Music Report* and hosts the annual **CMJ Music Marathon**.

Black Flag guitarist/founder Greg Ginn forms **SST Records** in Long Beach, California.

Rick Harte starts **Ace of Hearts Records**. The label's first-ever release was the 7-inch "Where'd You Get That Cigarette" by the raucous Boston quartet the Infliktors in 1979.

Geoff Travis founds the Rough Trade Shop record store on Kensington Park Road in the West End of London in 1976; the outfit evolves into **Rough Trade Records** two years later.

1979 Dead Kennedy's Jello Biafra founds **Alternative Tentacles Records**, releasing recordings by the Dead Kennedys, Butthole Surfers, and D.O.A.

1980 **R.E.M.** plays its first-ever gig at a birthday party in a local church in Athens, Georgia. But during a gig on April 5, 1980, at the 11:11 Club in Athens, Georgia, police raid the event during their set and close the venue's doors forever.

Acts such as **Beat Happening**, **Beck**, Sebadoh, **Liz Phair**, and **Elliott Smith** popularize the **Lo-fi** subgenre releasing low quality, home recordings that are heralded as works of high art. The Lo-fi sound incorporates the "accidental" live background sounds—hiss, distortion, and feedback—that are recorded along with the music.

Mission of Burma releases its debut 7-inch single, "Academy Fight Song," on **Ace of Hearts Records**.

The Dead Kennedys release their first EP, *In God We Trust, Inc.*, on Manifesto Records.

Pere Ubu's 25-year-old Peter Laughner passes away from pancreatitis.

1981 The first **CMJ Music Marathon** is held in New York City; for every year after, 10,000 music professionals, 1,000 artists, and more than 50,000 music fans attend the event.

1982 The Smiths form in Manchester, England.

1983 Mission of Burma goes on an indefinite hiatus when front man Roger Miller develops tinnitus, a ringing in the ears caused by years of listening to loud music.

Aztec Camera puts out its first full-length album, *High Land, Hard Rain,* when the group's front man, Roddy Frame, is only 19 years old.

The "Elvis of Rock," **Glenn Danzig**, publicly announces his plans to form a band called Samhain, subsequently bringing the **Misfits**' reign as punk pioneers to a halt.

1984 Sub Pop Records signs its first band, the first official **grunge** band, **Green River**.

Music critic Kurt Loder gives the **Meat Puppets**' sophomore album, *Meat Puppets II,* four stars in a *Rolling Stone* review.

Hüsker Dü releases its double-disc concept album, *Zen Arcade*.

1985 The **emo** subgenre becomes known as the "D.C. sound," and its official entrance into pop culture is marked by a *Flipside* magazine interview with the band **Rites of Spring**.

The Jesus and Mary Chain releases its breakthrough album, *Psychocandy*.

1986 Lou Barlow and Eric Gaffney form the band Sebadoh in their kitchen in Amherst, Massachusetts.

C/Z Records puts out the indie compilation *Deep Six,* featuring acts like the **Melvins**.

1987 The first **South by Southwest (SXSW)** music conference and festival is held in Austin, Texas. The event, which was originally titled the New Music Seminar Southwest, attracts 700 people, and over 200 bands perform.

The Smiths announces its breakup; Morrissey embarks on a solo career.

Sub Pop Records releases the debut EP *Dry to the Bone* by the first-ever **grunge** act, **Green River**.

1988 Producer Rick Rubin starts **American Recordings**, a label that will kick-start the careers of bands like **The Jesus and Mary Chain**, Slayer, **Danzig**, and Madonna.

1990 Camper Van Beethoven breaks up while mid-tour in Europe.

Ani DiFranco starts her own label, **Righteous Babe Records**.

1991 The first **Lollapalooza** kicks off at the Shoreline Amphitheatre in Mountain View, California. Performers include Jane's Addiction, **Nine Inch Nails**, Siouxsie & the Banshees, Ice-T/Body Count, Living Colour, Butthole Surfers, and Rollins Band.

The International Pop Underground Convention (IPU), a **Riot Grrrl Movement**–inspired concert, is held at the Capitol Theater in Olympia, Washington.

Nirvana releases its seminal album, *Nevermind,* which goes on to sell 10 million copies.

Darren Walters and Tim Owen form **Jade Tree Records** in Wilmington, Delaware.

Robert Schneider teams up with musician friends to form **The Elephant 6 Recording Company**/Music Collective.

Slim Moon starts the **Kill Rock Stars** record label. The roster includes acts such as **The Decemberists**, Deerhoof, and **Elliott Smith**, among others.

Rhino Records releases the famous **shoegazing** album *Loveless* by the Irish/British rock quartet group **My Bloody Valentine**.

1992 **PJ Harvey** appears nude on the cover of *NME (New Musical Express)*.

Robert Schneider starts the band **The Apples in Stereo** in Denver, Colorado.

1993 **Frank Black** (aka Black Francis) of the band the **Pixies** tells a reporter for BBC Radio that the band is breaking up. The rest of the group finds out later, via fax.

Nine Inch Nails' album *Pretty Hate Machine* becomes the first indie album to sell over a million copies. It remains on the *Billboard* charts for two years.

In an interview on MTV, Natalie Merchant of **10,000 Maniacs** announces she's leaving the band to start her solo career.

Frank Zappa is found dead in his Los Angeles, California, home. He endured a brief battle with prostate cancer.

Lydia Hutchinson founds *Performing Songwriter* **Magazine** in the guest bedroom of her home in Nashville, Tennessee.

1994 Kurt Cobain, the 27-year-old lead singer of the group **Nirvana**, is found dead in his Seattle home. Police inform the public that the cause of death was a single gunshot wound to the head, and his death is ruled a suicide.

Longtime friends Jason Reece and Conrad Keely form . . . **And You Will Know Us By the Trail of Dead** in Olympia, Washington.

1995 Vocalist Aidan Moffat and multi-instrumentalist Malcolm Middleton form the group **Arab Strap**.

David Bazan becomes the one-man band **Pedro the Lion**.

Recent high school graduate Ryan Schreiber creates and launches **Pitchfork Media**.

1996 **CAKE**'s song "The Distance" reaches #4 on the Modern Rock charts and hits the Top 40 in the United States and the Top 30 in the United Kingdom.

The **Ramones** plays its 2,263rd (and final) show at the Palace Nightclub in Los Angeles.

1997 Jello Biafra becomes an adversary of his own group when he refuses to allow the Dead Kennedys' song "Holiday in Cambodia" to be used in a Levi Jeans TV ad. His former bandmates sue him and are awarded $200,000 in damages.

Lilith Fair kicks off at The Gorge Amphitheatre in George, Washington.

1999 A professor of criminal justice from the University of North Carolina authors a paper about the social spin-off of **emo** known as "Straight Edge" (Minor Threat had coined the term on its debut studio album back in 1981), marking its official birth date.

The first **Coachella Valley Music and Arts Festival** takes place at the Empire Polo Fields in Indio, California. **Beck**, The Chemical Brothers, Tool, Rage Against the Machine, DJ Shadow, Underworld, and Jurassic 5 are among the acts that perform at the event.

dEUS' third full-length album, *The Ideal Crash* (Island Records), garners support from bands such as **Radiohead** and **R.E.M.**, resulting in sold-out shows across Europe and a plethora of festival dates.

2000 **Ben Folds Five** breaks up; **Ben Folds** launches his solo career.

Radiohead's fifth studio album, *Kid A,* sells 55,000 copies in its first day in stores.

The Smashing Pumpkins plays its final show at the metro club in Chicago, Illinois, the exact place where its career started 12 years before.

Snow Patrol's album *Final Straw* skyrockets, topping charts and selling over 2 million copies in the United States, becoming the in 26th most popular album that year in Britain.

Jello Biafra launches an unsuccessful campaign for president of the United States.

TV on the Radio brings something completely new to the indie rock scene with its experimental blend of atmospheric **post-punk**, electronic, free jazz, trip hop, and **post-rock**, kicking off an indie rock resurgence in the "hipster" borough of Williamsburg, Brooklyn, New York.

2001 At the Drive-In calls it quits; the band members form spin-off groups Sparta and The Mars Volta.

Joey Ramone passes away after a six-year-long battle with lymphoma.

Dee Dee Ramone dies of a drug overdose.

2002 The White Stripes releases its third album, the critically acclaimed *White Blood Cells*.

The band the **Ramones** is inducted into the Rock and Roll Hall of Fame.

2003 Atom and His Package play its final show in Philadelphia.

Elliott Smith is found dead in his apartment in Los Angeles, California, of an apparent suicide.

The White Stripes' Jack White engages in a bar brawl with The Von Bondies' Jason Stollsteimer.

The Dismemberment Plan disbands, cementing the end of a decade-long indie reign with a sold-out show at the 9:30 Club in its home city of Washington, D.C.

DFA Records/LCD Soundsystem founder James Murphy remixes **The Rapture**'s single "House of Jealous Lovers."

Belle and Sebastian's album *Dear Catastrophe Waitress* sells over 280,000 copies in the first few months of its release (Sanctuary Records).

The **Yeah Yeah Yeahs**' debut album, *Fever to Tell*, is released; it sells approximately 750,000 copies worldwide.

BLENDER magazine tags **Art Brut** the "Best unsigned band in the world."

Paz Lenchantin writes a news post indicating that **Zwan** will soon break up.

2004 Green Day releases its controversial, politically charged album *American Idiot*.

Actress Natalie Portman's character in the film *Garden State* name-drops **The Shins**, claiming, "The Shins will change your life."

Johnny Ramone dies after a battle with prostate cancer.

Nirvana's Krist Novoselic and Dave Grohl reach a short-lived peace accord with Courtney Love, and the pair put together a four-disc (including three CDs and one DVD) box set called *With the Lights Out* (Geffen Records) in 2004 in an attempt to have closure on Kurt Cobain's death.

The Beta Band announces its breakup.

Filmmakers pay tribute to **MC5** with the documentary *MC5: A True Testimonial*.

Franz Ferdinand's single "Take Me Out" hits #3 on the British music charts, selling over 3 million copies worldwide and ultimately earning the group a $1-million-dollar label deal with the Sony BMG imprint Epic Records.

The Palm Pictures independent film *Dig!* makes a ruckus at the Sundance Film Festival for capturing the rivalry between **The Brian Jonestown Massacre** and the group's former pals, **The Dandy Warhols**.

Beulah plays its final show in New York City's Battery Park.

2005 Media across the world plaster photos of Pete Doherty's former fiancée (and then girlfriend), supermodel Kate Moss, snorting cocaine during a **Babyshambles** studio recording session.

SPIN magazine calls **Death Cab for Cutie**'s Ben Gibbard "the poet laureate of the young and hopeful."

Modest Mouse walks away with the "Woodie of the Year" and "Silent But Deadly Woodie" awards for the song (and video for) "Float On" at the mtvU Awards.

The Bravery's debut album hits the Top 20 in the United States and the Top 5 in the United Kingdom; the band enters a nasty name-calling feud with label mates **The Killers**.

Clap Your Hands Say Yeah's debut album sells roughly 110,000 copies; **Pitchfork Media** gives both the album and the single a 9-out-of-10-star rating.

2006 Cat Power cancels its U.S. tour, citing "health issues" following a bout of live gigs at which the singer-songwriter mooned the audience, had a conversation with a squirrel, and told fans to leave the club, insisting that they should sue her.

Boston's nearby city, Providence, Rhode Island, paid tribute to **The Dresden Dolls**.

Touch and Go Records celebrates its 25th anniversary in Chicago, Illinois, featuring such bands as **Ted Leo and the Pharmacists**, **Big Black**, **Girls Against Boys**, and more.

The Dandy Warhols open for classic rocker Tom Petty at The Greek Theater in Los Angeles, California, before sharing the stage with the Rolling Stones for one show.

Underground legend **Alice Donut** plays its 20th anniversary show at New York City's Knitting Factory club. The group broadcasts the event live on its Web site, www.alicedonut.com.

An eccentric TV battle ensues between comedian/actor Stephen Colbert (an alumni of *Saturday Night Live* and Comedy Central's *The Daily Show*) and **The Decemberists'** Chris Funk.

Johnny Marr, the former guitarist for **The Smiths**, becomes an official member of the band **Modest Mouse**.

2007 Sebadoh kicks off its reunion tour at WOW Hall in Eugene, Oregon.

Dinosaur Jr. kicks off its reunion tour, playing together for the first time in 20 years, at Slim's in San Francisco, California.

My Morning Jacket opens for Bob Dylan at the Red Rocks Amphitheatre in Morrison, Colorado.

Patti Smith, Debbie Harry of Blondie, and **Bad Brains** play at CBGB in New York City one last time before the club closes its doors forever.

The Jesus and Mary Chain and **Green River** announce reunion gigs.

ACE OF HEARTS RECORDS

Founded in the late 1970s, this Boston, Massachusetts–based rock/punk label's rich history begins with Rick Harte, a steadfast music fan who got hooked on music after he attended a Beatles concert with his father. Harte, whom many credit with creating the sound of the Boston rock club scene of the late 1970s and the early 1980s, began recording jazz bands and collecting 45s before finally producing the early recordings of punk and rock bands **Mission of Burma**, the Neighborhoods, the Lyres, the Nervous Eaters, the Infliktors, and the Neats.

Surprisingly enough, though, Harte did not start out with any intention of becoming a producer. "I never wanted to be a producer or have a record label, but there was a great scene here in the wake of the punk rock revolution and nobody was making records with these bands that had something important to say," Harte told the *Boston Phoenix* in 2006.

Ace of Hearts' first-ever release was a 7-inch single by the raucous Boston quartet, the Infliktors, "Where'd You Get That Cigarette," which came out in 1978. Ace's second release, the full-length album *Prettiest Girl* by the Neighborhoods (a band that Thurston Moore of **Sonic Youth** felt was ahead of its time), was the label's first album to be recorded in a studio; it sold 10,000 copies. Sparked by the success of that release, Ace of Hearts (AOH) released the debut 7-inch single by the **post-punk** band **Mission of Burma**, "Academy Fight Song," in 1980. The B-side to that release, "Max Ernst," was an homage to the surrealist painter/collage artist of the same name, and it kicked off Ace's long-winded history of punk rock recordings.

Harte, however, never really rested his laurels on the punk genre; he felt that record labels and salespeople used punk rock as a way to tap into youth culture. "Academy Fight Song" broke records by selling out the 7,500 copies from the first printing. Harte's vision was clear and focused. The chance-taking label head repeatedly signed bands on instinct after catching their live shows. On the signing of **Mission of Burma**, Harte said, "They had strong, gutsy material with a progressive, slightly angry/punk feel" (Drozdowski, 2002). Harte's main concern was not just making records to make sales—it was putting out good music he believed in.

Ace continued to release a steady stream of records by **Mission of Burma** (MOB), a band that would go on to become what many believe was one of the most important rock bands of the last 20 years. Ace maintained a long-standing relationship with MOB, releasing its "Signals, Calls and Marches" EP in 1981, which featured what would become the band's signature song, "That's When I Reach for My Revolver" (future bands to cover the anthem included electronic musician Moby and Icelandic singer/songwriter Björk's first band, the Sugarcubes). Ace of Hearts released "Trem II"/"OK-No Way" by **Mission of Burma** a year later, the *Vs.* LP came out in 1982, and finally, the *The Horrible Truth About Burma* LP was released in 1985. Rykodisc reissued several of MOB's recordings in 1997. Another of AOH's star acts, the Nervous Eaters, was the house band for the popular Boston nightclub, The Rat. This quartet's raw, edgy sound attracted Harte, who appreciated their British guitar inflections and no-frills rock mentality.

The label's rich history is partially captured on the 1993 Rhino/WEA compilation, *DIY: Mass. Ave.: The Boston Scene (1979–83),* which features tracks from several Ace recording artists such as MOB, the Lyres, the Nervous Eaters, and the Classic Ruins. The compilation captures that fragmented moment in Boston history—right before the tattered basement nightclub the Rathskeller (aka The Rat, which many consider to be the location of the birth of punk in Boston) had closed and The Channel, a Boston music venue located on Necco Street that featured underground artists, had yet to open, and the rock club Paradise started showcasing bigger, more nationally recognized up-and-coming talents.

The Lyres have long been considered one of the all-time most popular Boston rock acts. The band, which played regularly at The Rat, also had one of the most turbulent and frequent lineup changes in Boston's underground rock history. Harte bestowed his infamous patience on the Lyres, as he did with most all of his bands; in an attempt to get the most quality recordings from them, Harte would simply stick around until what he considered the "magic" unfolded. He prided himself on the fact that he did not pressure bands to deliver on a time frame that hinged on money and budgets.

The Neats, surprisingly, started out playing nouveau folk rock before finding their true calling in edgier rock 'n' roll. AOH also released a few solo albums by **Mission of Burma** front man Roger Miller, whose poor hearing was a direct cause of the ultimate demise of the band in 1983 (Miller suffered from what is known as aggravated tinnitus, which is a constant, high-pitched ringing sound in the ears that is caused by long-term exposure to loud volumes).

Famed comic artist Frank Rowe fronted the Classic Ruins, a Boston-based quartet that was ranked highest among Boston's rock crowd. One of the first artists signed to the Ace of Hearts' roster, many of the Classic Ruins' members were also members of the Boston new wave band, The Real Kids. The Classic Ruins' 45, "1 +1/Nyquil Stranger" (1980), was their standout release; their sound blended garage rock, punk, and a bit of roots rock.

The Del Fuegos was a Boston-based four-piece garage rock outfit (which consisted of brothers Dan and Warren Zanes, who later became the Vice President for the Rock and Roll Hall of Fame in Cleveland, Ohio, and Tom Lloyd, and Steve Morrell) that was eventually lured away from AOH by a deal from the Los Angeles–based label Slash Records. Chaotic Past, one of the more recent bands to join the AOH roster, released *Yer-In* in 1999, which was produced by Harte; it placed the band on the verge of rock stardom. The now New York City–based trio's music is reminiscent of music by AC/DC and Black Sabbath.

Harte had been talking about a self-proclaimed "Ace of Hearts Story" for years, but it was years until the discs actually saw the light. Featuring never-before-released tracks by MOB, the Neighborhoods, the Del Fuegos, and more, the compilation served as more of a greatest hits collection of 23 songs by many of the same Ace artists. The long-awaited Ace of Hearts compilation made its debut in 2000; donned "The Wasted Years," the compilation was heralded by critics and hailed as an important historical snapshot of Boston's music scene from that long-gone era. It was also considered Harte's salute to a time when Ace experienced its greatest highs—and it served as his closing statement to the end of an era.

Ace of Hearts records continues to thrive, releasing records, LPs, and EPs by Boston-based bands. Harte is still an active member of both the Boston music scene and anything produced by **Mission of Burma**. He was hired as a consultant for MOB's comeback album (2004) *OnOffOn,* which was released by the band's new home, Matador Records, which is also home to such indie bands as **Cat Power**, **Pavement**, **Arab Strap**, and **Belle and Sebastian**. Harte also provided archive footage and soundtrack music for *Inexplicable,* the documentary that covers their 2002 reunion shows, which debuted at Boston's famed Somerville Theatre. Most recently, Harte produced the *Out Trios* CD by a band consisting of drummer William Hooker, **Sonic Youth**'s Lee Renaldo, and Roger Miller.

Ace of Hearts released another collection, *12 Classic 45s,* in March 2006, featuring 25 classic tracks from 12-inch EPs by celebrated AOH bands like the Classic Ruins, **Mission of Burma**, Tomato Monkey, Chaotic Past, the Infliktors, the Neighborhoods, and more.

Further Reading: Andersen, Mark, and Mark Jenkins. *Dance of Days: Two Decades of Punk in the Nation's Capital.* New York: Soft Skull Press, 2001; Gimarc, George. *Post Punk Diary: 1980–1982.* New York: St. Martin's Griffin, 1997; Keithley, Joe, and Jack Rabid. *I Shithead: A Life in Punk.* Vancouver, BC, Canada: Arsenal Pulp Press, 2004; McNeil, Legs, and Gillian McCain. *Please Kill Me: The Uncensored Oral History of Punk.* New York: Penguin, 1997; http://www.aceofheartsrecords.com.

ADAMS, RYAN

Donned the "new Neil Young" by the press, Ryan Adams achieved mainstream success while in his twenties, crooning his unique brand of alt-country rock that is tinged with a punk-like passion and roots rock feel. Born in 1974 and raised on country music in his home state of North Carolina, Adams began writing songs at a young age. The singer formed his first band, the Patty Duke Syndrome, at the age of 15 before moving to Raleigh, North Carolina, in search of fame.

Adams formed the alt-country group Whiskeytown with musicians Steve Grothman (bass), Eric "Skillet" Gilmore (drums), Phil Wandscher (guitar), and Caitlin Cary (violin) in the mid-1990s. Whiskeytown released a well-received debut album, *Faithless Street* (Mood Food Records) in 1997. The group's sophomore release, the twangy guitar rock of *Strangers Almanac* (Outpost Records), followed the next year, and the band underwent a series of lineup changes before the band was stripped nearly bare—with Adams and Wandscher as the last standing members. Whiskeytown signed to major label Geffen Records before putting out its final album and disbanding because of interband quarrels and unrealized sales expectations.

Bent on making it big, Adams recorded a solo album with songwriters David Rawlings and Gillian Welch. Critics and fans alike immediately praised *Heartbreaker* (Bloodshot Records, 2000), and even celebrity rockers like Elton John extolled Adams's praises. Adams relocated to New York City for his 2001 album, *Gold,* which featured the song "New York, New York," which was considered a tribute to the country's strength in the wake of the 9/11 attacks. *Gold* was certified Gold and earned Adams three Grammy nominations for Best Country Vocal Performance–Male, Best Rock Vocal Performance–Male, and Best Rock Album.

Meanwhile, Adams opened a bar in New York City's Lower East Side with his musician friend Jesse Malin; the two collaborated on Malin's debut album as well as on their side project, a punk group called The Finger. Adams appeared alongside John on Country Music Television's *Crossroads* program, during which John claimed Adams helped inspire his 2001 album, *Songs From the West Coast.*

The prolific singer-songwriter had soon penned enough songs for four albums —a collection of unheard demos called "Demolition" (2002), the concept album *Rock 'n' Roll* (2003), and the double EP *Love is Hell.* Adams parted ways with his longtime squeeze, singer-songwriter Leona Naess, before he began dating actress Parker Posey, who appeared on 2003's *Rock 'n' Roll*—along with musicians such as former Hole bassist Melissa Auf Der Maur and **Green Day**'s Billie Joe Armstrong. Adams's cover of the song "Wonderwall" by the rock duo Oasis earned him a Grammy nomination for Best Solo Vocal Performance in 2005.

Adams continued to pair up with his newly found friends in the music world— Grateful Dead bassist Phil Lesh, his new backing band The Cardinals, and jazz singer Norah Jones, with whom he dueted on a track from his 2005 album, *Jacksonville City Lights* (with The Cardinals). Adams's 2005 solo album, *29,* featured Adams on solo acoustic guitar and piano. Adams befriended a super friend of sorts—country star Willie Nelson, who produced his 2006 album.

He released his ninth album, 2007 album *Easy Tiger,* a powerful, lyrically charged album that critics likened to his breakthrough album and his early days as a poignant up-and-coming alt-rocker with a broken heart on his sleeve. Adams continues to garner rave reviews from critics. While fans clamor to catch his live show, he is sometimes remembered as the guy who kicked a fan out of his show for asking him to play the song "Summer of '69" by Bryan Adams. Adams toured through the end of 2007 with his backing band, The Cardinals, with whom he worked on his 2007 record, *Follow the Lights.*

Further Reading: Heatley, Michael. *Ryan Adams.* London: Omnibus Press, 2003; Zimmerman, Keith, and Kent Zimmerman. *Sing My Way Home: Voices of the New American Roots Rock.* Milwaukee, WI: Backbeat Books, 2004; http://www.bloodshotrecords.com; http://

www.leonanaess.com; http://www.losthighwayrecords.com; http://www.myspace.com
/ryanadams; http://www.phillesh.net; http://www.ryan-adams.com.

THE AFGHAN WHIGS

Having spent "the bulk of their career on the cusp of stardom," as a February 2001
Rolling Stone article chimed (Baltin, 2001), this Ohio-based band dabbled in
guitar-heavy rock and seedy lyrical topics. Although the **post-punk** quartet reportedly started out as a garage rock outfit, The Afghan Whigs, who formed in 1986,
cultivated a cult following as they hovered just at the precipice of the glass ceiling
to mainstream success. Fans were drawn to the group as much for their critically
acclaimed music as they were for front man/vocalist/rhythm guitarist Greg Dulli
(a former film student at the University of Cincinnati) and his self-loathing, dark
side–infused sensibilities.

Dulli formed the group with fellow undergrads drummer Steve Earle and attri-
bution lead guitarist Rick McCollum. The trio teamed up with bassist John Curley,
then a photography intern at the *Cincinnati Enquirer,* after Dulli met him at a
friend's apartment. The quartet officially birthed The Afghan Whigs as an aggressive, garage punk band akin to The Replacements and Dinosaur Jr., playing in
and around their hometown's club circuit, including regular gigs at local lesbian
bar The Squeeze Inn, before pooling enough money to self-fund an album. *Big
Top Halloween* was released in 1988 on their own Ultrasuede label, and it did well
on college radio. The Afghan Whigs followed with a song on the local compilation
Where the Hell Are the Good Scissors? and a respectable buzz in the underground
press ensued, garnering the attention of Seattle's **Sub Pop Records**. Looking to
expand its roster beyond Pacific Northwest bands, the label signed The Afghan
Whigs in 1989 (the original purpose was just to contribute the song "I Am the
Sticks" to the Sub Pop Singles Club, a service where subscribers received band singles in the mail on a monthly basis).

That contribution, however, soon became a full-fledged contract, and the indie
rock quartet's first **Sub Pop Records** album was the searing, guitar noise of April
1990's *Up in It.* Though not **grunge**, the band's sound (and label affiliation) was
such that critics pegged it as part of the Seattle pack, a brand that would inhibit
its ability to grow as **Sub Pop Records** itself took off. The Afghan Whigs toured
heavily in the early 1990s, leading up to the early 1992 release of its third album,
Congregation. That album featured what would become The Whigs' signature aesthetic: a dark, swaggering, and soulful **post-punk** sound with elements of R&B
and country complementing Dulli's literate and often self-loathing lyrics. Critical
praise greeted *Congregation,* and major labels came knocking.

Uptown Avondale, an EP of soul and R&B covers, and a split single with fellow
Cincinnati band Ass Ponys, appeared before The Whigs inked a deal with Elektra
Records in 1993. Elektra was so eager to sign the guys that Dulli was even allowed
control in directing the band's videos and producing its records. The Afghan
Whigs' major label debut arrived that year; 1993's *Gentlemen* was highly praised
by fans and critics alike, though Dulli almost scrapped the album thinking it was
too personal. The first single off the album, "Debonair," became a hit on

MTV, and the band made its national television debut on NBC's *Late Night with Conan O'Brien*.

Despite receiving overwhelming praise, The Afghan Whigs were unable to catch their so-called "big break." The band's summer 1994 EP *What Jail Is Like* coincided with an American tour, but off the road and back at home that fall, the band went on an extended break to work out internal issues that had interfered with touring and recording. Earle left the band in the spring of 1995 and was replaced by drummer Paul Buchignani, with whom the group recorded its fifth album, *Black Love*. Issued in spring 1996 through Elektra, it peaked at #79 on the U.S. charts, but once again, positive reviews did not earn the band highly expansive acceptance, and that was taking a toll on the band.

The Afghan Whigs made a cameo appearance as a bar band in the 1996 movie *Beautiful Girls* and toured with Neil Young before effectively breaking up. Dulli pursued a solo career and went on to form the Twilight Singers in 1997, recording an album whose release was later canceled when The Whigs got back together the very next year. Armed with a new label (Columbia Records) and a new drummer (Michael Horrigan), The Afghan Whigs released the 1998 album, *1965* (named for the members' birth years). Subsequent singles "Somethin' Hot" and "66" were successful, and the band toured with rockers Aerosmith in April 1999.

However, *1965* was The Afghan Whigs' final release. The quartet officially announced its dissolution in February 2001, citing the geographic strain caused by band members living in different states. In the fall of 2006, The Afghan Whigs temporarily reunited to record two new songs—"I'm a Solider" and "Magazine"—for a band retrospective entitled *Unbreakable (A Retrospective)* that came out in June 2007 on Rhino Records. According to the Web site summerskiss.com, the former bandmates are staying busy with various side projects.

Further Reading: Erlewine, Stephen Thomas. *Afghan Whigs*. Ann Arbor, MI: All Music Guide (database), 4th edition, 2001; Thompson, Dave. *Alternative Rock*. San Francisco: Miller Freeman Books, 2000; http://aerosmith.com; http://afghanwhigs.com; http://columbiarecords.com; http://neilyoung.com; http://rhinorecords.com; http://subpop.com/artists/afghan_whigs; http://www.summerskiss.com.

AIR

Air's ambient pop-infused, Moog synthesizer–flowered sound captured fans with complex compositions that seemed to simply transcend time as it teeters within the realm of both retro and modern sensibilities. The French ambient pop and electronica duo Air got together in 1995 in Paris, France. Founding members Nicolas Godin and the classically trained Jean-Benoît Dunckel both grew up in Versailles, but they did not meet until their college years when mutual friend Alex Gopher brought Godin into the band Orange, which he was playing in with Dunckel. Gopher later left to work on solo material, and in 1995, the two began operating together under the identity of Air.

For the project, Godin and Dunckel combined influences from French singer Serge Gainsbourg, new wave, and the synthesizer sounds of the 1970s that were used by artists like celebrated French composer Jean-Michel Jarre and pioneering Japanese synthesizer maestro Tomita. After scoring a deal with France's Sourcelabs label and Britain's trip-hop label Mo' Wax, Air released some early singles such as "Modular," "Casanova 70," and "Le Soleil Est Prés de Moi." "Modular" especially became an impressive U.K. club hit and brought Air to the attention of the European dance scene.

In 1997, Air remixed tracks by artists such as Depeche Mode and Swedish pop singer Neneh Cherry, and the duo paired up with French "musique concrete" artist Jean-Jacques Perrey for a track on the Source compilation *Sourcelab, Vol. 3.* This collaboration led to the duo's first American release, the summer 1997 compilation *Singles.* Eventually, Air's critically acclaimed debut album, *Moon Safari,* surfaced in early 1998 through Virgin Records/Astralwerks. The record was an exceptional display of French electronic pop with layers of synths and atmospherics, and critics and fans alike quickly embraced it.

Air scored hits in the United Kingdom with singles "Sexy Boy" and "Kelly Watch the Stars"; the former song did exceptionally well in the United States and earned the guys heavy rotation on MTV. Though the duo had previously decided against performing live, Air launched an ambitious tour of Europe and the United States that same year to support the album. Additional early singles were then collected into the 1999 EP compilation, *Premiers Symptomes.*

Air's next project appeared in early 2000, not as a regular album, but as the soundtrack to the Sofia Coppola film, *The Virgin Suicides.* Air's second proper studio effort, *10,000 Hz Legend,* was not issued until the spring of 2001. Due to the album's darker themes and experimental direction, it was not as enthusiastically received as prior efforts, though it was not perceived as a failure by any means. More touring followed its release, and in January 2004, Air released its third album, *Talkie Walkie,* which found a happy medium between the first two records. The album sold well, and for the next two years, Air remained busy touring and collaborating with various artists like Pulp singer Jarvis Cocker and the Divine Comedy's Neil Hannon on French actress/singer/daughter of Serge Gainsbourg Charlotte Gainsbourg's 2006 album, *5:55.*

In 2006, Dunckel released an album of solo material under the name Darkel. This preceded Air's fourth full-length album, *Pocket Symphony* (Astralwerks, 2007), a collection of "soundtrack"-worthy songs and instrumentals that was recorded with English producer and longtime collaborator Nigel Godrich (who has worked with artists such as **Radiohead** and **Beck**). Air stayed on the road for the rest of the year, touring Europe with supporting act **Au Revoir Simone** in 2007.

Further Reading: Thompson, Dave. *Alternative Rock.* San Francisco: Miller Freeman Books, 2000; http://depechemode.com; http://sergegainsbourg.com; http://www.astralwerks.com; http://www.jeanjacquesperrey.com; http://www.mowax.com; http://www.nenehcherry.de; http://www.pocket-symphony.com; http://www.thedivinecomedy.com/framebiog.htm.

THE ALBUM LEAF

Taking its name from a piece by Chopin, The Album Leaf was essentially the solo project of Jimmy LaValle. Best known as the guitarist for the San Diego instrumental rock act Tristeza, LaValle was a classically trained multi-instrumentalist who, through the years, also took part in other projects including noise rockers the Locust, indie act GoGoGo Airheart, and the dark rock of the Black Heart Procession. As The Album Leaf, LaValle created ambient indie rock with a rotating cast of collaborators.

Combining elements of **post-rock**, classical, and jazz, he often used field recordings, ambient noise, radio transmissions, and compositional atmospherics inspired by the likes of Brian Eno to achieve his dreamy results. 1999's *An Orchestrated Rise to Fall* was his first full-length album; it was released through a collaboration between Music Fellowship and Linkwork Records, the latter label run by an artists and repertoire (A&R) representative for New York upstart Tiger Style Records. The EP *In An Off White Room* followed in early 2001 via New Jersey–based Troubleman Unlimited, which preceded The Album Leaf's second album, *One Day I'll Be on Time,* issued through Tiger Style the next May. The record was supported with an opening spot on Icelandic experimentalists Sigur Rós' fall U.S. tour, which brought added exposure to The Album Leaf and sparked a friendship between both groups.

In 2003, The Album Leaf appeared on two splits: one with post-rockers On!Air!Library! entitled *A Lifetime of More* and one with electronic **indie pop** act Her Space Holiday. For album number three, LaValle headed to Iceland's Western coast to record with members of Sigur Rós (and the band's string section Amina) in their studio, Sundlaugin. The album also included collaborations with Pall Jenkins of the Black Heart Procession. The resulting *In a Safe Place* appeared in June 2004 on **Sub Pop Records** in North America and City Slang in Europe. Various songs from the record later appeared in multiple episodes of the popular FOX TV teen drama *The O.C.,* as well as on various shows on CBS, NBC, and Showtime. The next year, the EP *Seal Beach,* which was originally issued in 2003 through Spain's Acuarela Discos, was re-released stateside through Better Looking Records.

The subsequent *Red Tour* EP was available only at shows in 2005, and in September 2006, The Album Leaf's fourth full-length album, *Into the Blue Again,* surfaced on record shelves. It resulted from six straight months of writing in LaValle's San Diego home and was recorded partly in a studio outside of Seattle and for three weeks in Iceland. LaValle handled most of the instrumental duties, but once again, also worked with various collaborators, including Telefon Tel Aviv's Josh Eustis, Pall Jenkins, violinist Matt Resovich (who had previously performed on *In A Safe Place*), Drew Andrews, and Brigir Jon Birgisson, the engineer at Sundlaugin studio. Shows with New York neo-**shoegazing** act **Dirty on Purpose** followed. The Album Leaf's gigs incorporated projection art and live strings, and by that point, LaValle's live band included Drew Andrews (guitar, keys, and bass), Timothy Reece (drums), Matthew Resovich (violin) and Andrew Pates (live visuals).

Further Reading: http://thealbumleaf.com; http://www.musicfellowship.com.

ALICE DONUT

Emerging from the punk underground scene in New York City's Lower East Side in the 1980s, Alice Donut earned a following for its off-kilter sense of humor and musical risks—both of which fit right in at Dead Kennedys's front man Jello Biafra's raucous label, **Alternative Tentacles Records** (ATR), which Alice Donut signed to just three months after its first live show in 1988. The quintet's "subversive" music has thrived for nearly a decade—and, in true indie rock fashion, the eclectic band managed to survive without the support (or bankroll) of a major label. Alice Donut was comprised of front man Tomas Antona (vocals/lyrics), Stephen Moses (trombone/drums), David Giffen (guitars/vocals), Sissi Schulmeister (bass/banjo), and Michael Jung (guitars, keyboard, and vocals), who replaced original member Richard Marshall (guitars) when he reportedly left to join the U.S. Space Program.

Other Alice Donut members included Ted Houghton (guitars), who was kicked out of the band shortly after its third LP. Alice Donut received extensive airplay on indie and alternative radio stations, and punk fans clamored to see the group's decadent live stage shows and to hear firsthand Antona's sneerish warble. Fans also aligned with the Donut's shrouded political sarcasm, which the band's members shared with their ATR label mates, the Dead Kennedys.

Alice Donut's debut album, *Donut Comes Alive,* was released by ATR in 1988, and the band stayed busy, releasing subsequent albums nearly every year afterward. *Bucketfulls of Sickness and Horror in an Otherwise Meaningless Life* came out in 1989, *Mule* followed in 1990 along with the unabashedly in-your-face album *Revenge Fantasies of the Impotent,* which preceded the equally abrasively titled full-length *The Untidy Suicides of Your Degenerate Children* in 1992 and 1994's *Dry Humping the Cash Cow* (recorded live at New York City's legendary East Village underground rock/punk nightclub CBGB). 1994's *Chicken Door,* which blended punk, hard rock, and jabs of free jazz and even country, was followed by 1995's psychedelic-infused *Pure Acid Park.*

Alice Donut's albums ping-ponged across the **pop punk** genre—stretching the thin line between crude and clever, and bungeeing between offensive and informative whenever the group tackled the arduous task of using its music to forward its members' own social positions (opponents of the group included censorship advocate Tipper Gore, horror queen Linda Blair of *The Exorcist* fame, and TV evangelical ministers). Still, Alice Donut's fan base remained loyal, carrying the group along a decade of wild stage shows and seven albums.

The troublesome group called it quits, though, in 1995, each member citing desires to pursue his or her own individual projects and/or musical pursuits (Schulmeister and Antona's project, however, was of the familial kind). But, after much coaxing by Schulmeister, Moses, and Jung—who had begun playing together again around 1999—Antona agreed to resurrect Alice Donut. Successfully reunited, Alice Donut played a private reunion show at its old haunt, CBGB, in 2003, the result of which became its first album in almost a decade—the *Three Sisters* full-length, which was released on the New York City–based indie label Howler Records. Still, despite the tamely named album that crowned its return to the punk scene, Alice Donut returned to form with an appropriately inappropriate title for the DVD that captured its live London reunion concert, *There's a Curious Lump in My Sack* (Punkervision, 2004). Howler Records put out Alice Donut's 2006 studio album, *Fuzz,* for which the group added former band-mate Dave Giffen.

Further Reading: Byrne, David, and Hilly Kristal. *CBGB and OMFUG: Thirty Years from the Home of Underground Rock.* New York: Harry N. Abrams, Inc., 2005; Salyers, Christopher D., and Richard Hell. *CBGB: Decades of Graffiti.* New York: Mark Batty Publisher, 2006; Sinker, Daniel. *We Owe You Nothing, Punk Planet: The Collected Interviews.* New York: Akashic Books, 2001; http://www.alicedonut.com; http://www.alternativetentacles.com; http://www.cbgb.com; http://www.howlerrecords.com.

ALTERNATIVE TENTACLES RECORDS
Reigning as the current heavyweight champion of indie rock labels for being the longest running underground record label, Alternative Tentacles Records (ATR) is home to the recordings by hardcore and punk acts like the Dead Kennedys, the Butthole Surfers, and D.O.A. Founded in 1979 amid a hotbed of political activism and social unrest in San Francisco, California, by free speech advocate/spoken word artist/vocalist Jello Biafra, ATR developed a reputation not only for the inflammatory bands on its roster but for the long-term impact that the record label made on the underground music scene and the role it played in the development of the **DIY (Do-It-Yourself)** mentality that is inherent to indie rock.

Alternative Tentacles Records' founder Jello Biafra. [AP Wide World Photos/Erin Lubin]

Biafra, who fronted the politically charged hardcore punk outfit the Dead Kennedys, started the label after the band faced extensive difficulties surrounding the release of its music on its debut album *Fresh Fruit for Rotting Vegetables*. The roadblocks the Kennedys encountered, however, also stemmed from a backlash that resulted from Biafra's city mayoral campaign in 1979 (at the age of 21, he launched his campaign after accepting a bet from a friend).

Alternative Tentacles Records released the Dead Kennedys's first EP, *In God We Trust, Inc.,* in 1981. And, in true Kennedys fashion, the track "Too Drunk to F- - -" was banned from radio play. The Kennedys continued their antiestablishment tradition in 1982 with the release of the full-length LP *Plastic Surgery Disasters* before going on hiatus and ultimately disbanding in 1986. Meanwhile, Alternative Tentacles Records gained momentum on the underground scene, releasing LPs and EPs by bands such as the Butthole Surfers, Winston Smith, NOmeansno, D.O.A., Neurosis, Voice Farm, 7 Seconds, **Alice Donut**, and the Beatnigs.

Biafra's original intent for the label was to have it based solely in England, but the *Let Them Eat Jellybeans* compilation album that ATR put out in 1982 (which was designed to introduce Europe and the world at large to D.O.A., **Black Flag**, Flipper, **Bad Brains**, Half Japanese, and even Voice Farm, among others) was gaining popularity in the United States, so Biafra and company set up shop in San Francisco.

Noise rock/punk band the Butthole Surfers released its first 12-inch EP, *Brown Reason to Live,* in 1983 on ATR followed by the live EP *PCPPEP* a year later. Known for their "shock rock" antics and hardcore sound, the Texas-based **post-punk** band fit right in when it signed with Alternative Tentacles Records in 1981. The Surfers, like the Dead Kennedys, attracted fans and foes for their controversial lyrics and in-your-face band name. But the Butthole Surfers pushed the envelope even further by playing a string of unforgettable live shows that included pyrotechnics, nude dancers, backdrop films depicting grotesque sex-change operations, and overall disjointed mania. The Butthole Surfers recorded two albums on ATR before congenially parting ways with Biafra and his label in 1983 to join the roster of the Chicago-based indie label Touch and Go Records.

The "punk kings of Canada," D.O.A. (which stands for Dead on Arrival), also found a home at Alternative Tentacles Records in 1981, launching a 25-plus-year-long career that influenced more recent bands like Rancid, the Red Hot Chili Peppers, the Offspring, and **Green Day**. D.O.A.'s debut release on ATR, *War on 45* (1982), was re-released in 2005—and it remains as popular and feather ruffling as it was the year it debuted. But contrary to the fears of the parents of the group's followers, the quartet wore their civil duties on their sleeves as much as they did their political angst, playing benefit shows for the likes of Rape Relief and Oxfam International, standing up against censorship, and playing to earn money in support of several non-profit environmental organizations. The rebellious punk group continues to release albums on ATR and through its own imprint, Sudden Death Records, which was founded by the group's vocalist/guitarist, "Canada's godfather of punk," Joey "Sh- -head" Keithley (the label was an upstart back in 1978 on which D.O.A. released its first-ever 7-inch record).

ATR currently has over 100 artists on its roster, including one of its earliest-signed bands, **Alice Donut**, a punk quintet that made a splash on New York City's East Village scene in the late 1980s. The band released its first album, *Donut Comes Alive,* on ATR in 1988.

Alternative Tentacles Records' catalog, which now spans more than two decades, includes CDs/LPs, vinyl, EPs, and spoken word recordings by Biafra (in 1990, he launched a spoken word tour of college campuses across the country to spread his antiestablishment, antigovernment gospel) and people like Noam Chomsky; it also is filled out by Biafra's many musical incarnations with such groups as the **Melvins**. After running an unsuccessful 2000 campaign for president of the United States, Biafra teamed up with guitarist Charlie Tolnay of Grong Grong to record songs under the moniker Tumor Circus. Throughout its lifetime, ATR has added bands in the following genres to its roster: Brazilian hardcore, bent pop, and faux country.

Biafra and Alternative Tentacles Records faced an onslaught of uphill battles, and, notably, ATR survived various court trials and governmental speed bumps time and time again. Obscenity charges were bought against the Dead Kennedys when they included an offensive poster of artist H. R. Giger's painting Landscape #20 (Penis Landscape) with their 1985 album, *Frankenchrist.* Thanks to a hung jury, the obscenity charges against the Dead Kennedys were eventually dropped, but Biafra, who surprised many with his uncanny ability to survive nearly every legal battle he faced, suffered an unforeseen and utterly ironic fate when skinheads, who claimed he was a "sellout," attacked him in San Francisco in 1994. Biafra suffered various injuries and both of his legs were broken.

Biafra became an adversary of his own group when he refused to allow the Dead Kennedys's song "Holiday in Cambodia" to be used in a Levi Jeans TV ad in 1997. His former bandmates sued and were awarded $200,000 in damages. Divided by these disputes, the Dead Kennedys canceled their contract with ATR in 1998.

Surprisingly today, several albums released by Alternative Tentacles Records can be purchased at select Wal-Mart stores. But, despite this ironic distribution guffaw, bands signed to ATR have always had a knack for giving the establishment the middle finger—and attracting trouble. Biafra and ATR were summoned back in court because of the cover of The Crucifucks' album *Our Will Be Done,* which showed a photograph of an allegedly deceased Philadelphia police officer. Despite the fact that Biafra and ATR claimed that the photo was printed in an effort to raise awareness during a 1986 union contract dispute between the city and the police union, the court awarded a $2.2 million default judgment to the Fraternal Order of Police on behalf of the police officer depicted in the photo.

Biafra faced his toughest fight in the twentieth century when he fought to maintain the rights to release the Dead Kennedys' music under the Alternative Tentacles Records label. In 2003, hordes of fans signed an online petition in support of Biafra, stating, "By signing this petition I am supporting Jello Biafra in his ongoing efforts to bring the Dead Kennedys' music catalog back under the protection of Alternative Tentacles Records (ATR). This will ensure that the Dead Kennedys will continue to be known as an independent, underground band on a **DIY (Do-It-Yourself)** record label, holding true to the original spirit and ethics behind the Dead Kennedys music and to the principles that made the Dead Kennedys such a unique and special group of musicians." The court ruled against Biafra, and the ruling spurred an even more unpleasant situation when, in 1997, the remaining Kennedys members filed a suit claiming that Biafra had underpaid his bandmates for a total of $76,000 in royalties. After a three-week trial a few years later, the court ruled in favor of Biafra's former bandmates and stated that "Alternative Tentacles Records engaged in fraudulent conduct" and that Jello Biafra "breached his contractual and fiduciary obligations to plaintiff [Dead Kennedys]" (www.deadkennedysnews.com, 2000).

In the latter half of its tenure as a figurehead of punk and hardcore music, ATR became known for its reissues and compilations. The 2002 *Apocalypse Always* LP features a recording of Biafra paying tribute to the **Ramones** front man/vocalist and songwriter Joey Ramone, who passed away in 2001 from lymphatic cancer. The album includes songs by M.I.A., The Flaming Stars, Half Japanese, and D.O.A., as well as exclusive material like a recording of Mumia Abu-Jamal speaking from prison in December 2001.

More recent recording artists added to the ATR roster include the eccentric (and schizophrenic) rapper Wesley Willis, who waxed poetic about topics such as Northwest Airlines, McDonald's, Tom Petty and the Heartbreakers, mullets, termites, and Spider-Man. Willis released 4 of his 50-odd albums on ATR; he even wrote a song called "Jello Biafra" in tribute to the label's head honcho. Willis passed away in 2002 after being diagnosed of chronic myelogenous leukemia. Biafra was one of Willis's biggest fans; ATR currently distributes three of his Greatest Hits albums.

ATR has also garnered attention for its "Re-Issues Of Necessity Series," a collection of "obscure classics" by bands such as The Dicks, B.G.K., The Fartz, and the False Prophets; it also includes the 1982 Bay Area compilation *Not So Quiet on the Western Front*. Alternative Tentacles Records is still alive and running, employing four staffers in Emeryville, California. ATR maintains a healthy reputation as a label and a mail order company, selling and distributing DVDs, CDs, and merchandise.

Further Reading: Biafra, Jello, Camille Paglia, and Ursula Owen. *Index on Censorship: Smashed Hits The Book of Banned Music.* London: Index on Censorship, 1998; Biafra, Jello, Lawrence Ferlinghetti, and Christian Parenti. *Mob Action Against the State: Collected Speeches from The Bay Area Anarchist Book Fair* (Audio CD). Oakland, CA: AK Press (AK Press Audio), 2002; Kester, Marian. *Dead Kennedys: The Unauthorized Version.* Edited by F-Stop Fitzgerald. San Francisco: Last Gasp, 2004; Rollins, Henry, Jello Biafra, Lawrence Ferlinghetti, and Billy Childish. *Real Conversations, No. 1 (Henry Rollins, Jello Biafra, Lawrence Ferlinghetti, Billy Childish).* San Francisco: Re/Search Publications, 2001; True, Everett. *Hey Ho Let's Go: The Story of the Ramones.* London: Omnibus Press, 2005; http://

www.alternativetentacles.com; http://www.buttholesurfers.com; http://www.ramones.com; www.deadkennedysnews.com.

AMBULANCE LTD

Combining dream pop, indie rock, and the sounds of the British **shoegazing** sub-genre, this Brooklyn, New York–based band quickly signed to the New York City–based independent label TVT Records in the early 2000s amid buzz that circulated about their live performances. Originally known simply as Ambulance, Ambulance LTD was formed by front man/guitarist Marcus Congleton, who joined forces with guitarist Benji Lysaght, bassist Matt Dublin, drummer Darren Beckett, and keyboardist Andrew Haskell in 2000. Their eponymous five-track 2003 EP earned the group comparisons to the trailblazing, **shoegazing** outfits Ride and **My Bloody Valentine** for its music's melodic pop sensibility, mesmerizing waves of rhythm, and Congleton's soft-spoken, near-whisper vocal style. The EP received rave reviews from the press, who praised the group's pretty melodies, hypnotic vocals, and cascading guitar riffs.

Ambulance LTD toured with American alt rock band Placebo before releasing its self-titled LP in 2004 on TVT Records. The album revealed the group's influences and earned it comparisons to the likes of groups such as **The Apples in Stereo** and Sea and Cake, but the album remained a standout record that critics applauded. Ambulance LTD built a solid fan base in and around its home base of Brooklyn before heading out on the road in 2004 as the opening act for groups such as **The Killers** and **Guided By Voices**, before the group hit the "it" music event **South by Southwest (SXSW)** in Austin, Texas, in 2005, and before the group appeared on the popular late night television programs *Tonight Show with Jay Leno, Late Show with David Letterman,* and *Late Night with Conan O'Brien* as

Ambulance LTD's Marcus Congleton and his crew. [Roger Sargent]

the featured musical act. The group's 2004 LP went on to become a "Best Of" album for critics nationwide and one of the most acclaimed indie releases of that year.

In 2005, Ambulance LTD hit the road as the opening act for **R.E.M.** on its European tour, played with indie darlings The Dears, and went on the road with Scottish alt/indie rockers The Cinematics before returning stateside to gain new fans at that year's **Lollapalooza** and Austin City Limits music festivals. Ambulance LTD put out two singles in 2005—"Primitive" and the slow-moving, ethereal "Stay Where You Are."

Haskell left the band that year on the eve of the release of Ambulance LTD's next LP, *New English,* which featured the new title track, the new song "Arbuckle," a cover of the famed English psychedelic rock act Pink Floyd's song "Fearless," an original eight-track recording of the demo "Heavy Lifting," the original demo "Sugar Pill," the track "Country Gentleman" (which appeared on a compilation by Brooklyn, New York's StarTime International Records), as well as the bonus hidden U.K. LP track, "Straight A's."

Three-quarters of the group disbanded to form the group The Red Romance, leaving Congleton to carry on the Ambulance LTD flame alone. Congleton teamed up with John Cale, a founding member of the 1960s glam rock band **The Velvet Underground** in 2006 to record new material for Ambulance LTD's sophomore release. Meanwhile, The Red Romance (which consists of Lysaght, Dublin, Beckett and musician/bassist Adam Chilenski) toured with **The Killers** and made plans to release its debut EP in late 2006. Music from Ambulance LTD's upcoming record was featured on the Donna Karan New York (DKNY) Web site in early 2007. Congleton, however, posted an announcement on the band's Web site in an attempt to explain the band's prolonged absence from "the musical map." The messy-haired singer claimed that drama and legal battles are to blame, citing a likeness to a segment of VH1's *Behind the Music* program.

Further Reading: http://www.ambulancenyc.com; http://www.myspace.com/ambulanceltd; http://www.startimerecords.com; http://www.thecinematicsmusic.com; http://www.theredromance.com; http://www.tvtrecords.com.

AMERICAN RECORDINGS

If **SST Records** was the hard rocking, tattooed, punk rock label of the late 1980s, then the Los Angeles–based American Recordings was its black T-shirt-wearing, bling-toting, indie and rap-music-loving cousin. Producer Rick Rubin, who has since gained notoriety for his work with mainstream acts like Pink, Linkin Park, and even Justin Timberlake, was adept at managing the label that became famous for balancing the yin and the yang of music—indie acts as well as rap artists. Rubin is also the mastermind behind Def Jam Recordings, which he co-founded in 1984 while studying for his undergraduate degree; Russell Simmons is the label's other co-founder.

Originally named Def American when Rubin started the label in 1988, American Recordings was the result of Rubin's years of experience working at Def Jam

Recordings as well as his passion for rock music. The label's roster was a potpourri of acts—comedian Andrew Dice Clay, **The Jesus and Mary Chain**, hard rockers Slayer, theatrical metal rockers **Danzig**, the New York City–based rock group Masters of Reality, and the English group Wolfsbane (the members of which would later form the famous act Iron Maiden). Rap acts on the roster included Sir Mix-A-Lot and Dirty Southern rappers the Geto Boys. Rubin reportedly came up with the name Def after hearing it used as a slang term in the rap culture he was immersed in, but when he spotted the term in a dictionary, the eccentric producer/label head held an impromptu funeral for the word and retired it from the label's name. The label's name was officially changed to American Recordings in 1993.

Rubin's scouting talents paid off quickly; the debut record by a new band, The Black Crowes, went platinum in just a short period of time. The chart topping and record sales kept climbing in both the indie and rap divisions—Sir Mix-A-Lot's 1992 single "Baby Got Back" hit #1 on the *Billboard* music chart and became one of the most popular rap songs of that decade. Rubin's artists may not all have been indie acts by nature, but his independent thinking and the fact that he had the heart of a true music fan proved flawless—and profitable—for the label's investors.

American Recordings grew and Rubin, who produced almost all of the bands on the roster, continued to make magic. Albums by both Slayer and **Danzig** went Gold while the acts were signed to the American Recordings roster. American Recordings eventually splintered off into subset labels and inked a distribution deal with Geffen Records. Some of the rap albums released through American bore the Def Jam label, though. American prospered under Geffen, but it was not long before Rubin switched gears to work with Columbia Records and then finally settled on Warner Bros. Records Inc. for the label's distribution.

True to record label fashion, legal entanglements ensued when the American Recordings catalog was split up in the late 2000s. Artists such as Johnny Cash, Slayer, and **Danzig** joined the Warner Bros. catalog while the rest of the bands' works were absorbed into major label Sony/Columbia's catalog. Rubin was caught up in the legal throes as well as he struggled to find his place amid the paperwork and the court-related chaos. The American Records label's Web site—which lists Tom Petty, The (International) Noise Conspiracy, Luna Halo, Dan Wilson, System of a Down, Johnny Cash, The Vacation, and Slayer as its artists—is "temporarily under construction" as are many of the label's releases, which have been put on hold until all of the legal details have been ironed out and all of the dotted lines have been signed.

The eccentric, Buddha-looking Rubin, who has often been called a "guru," has since become the co-head of Columbia Records. He continues to scout for promising up-and-coming acts and sign unconventional artists to the Columbia label. In 2007, *Time* magazine ranked Rubin #8 on its list of the "100 Most Influential People in The World." And although Rubin's paycheck is signed by the big whigs at mega-label Columbia, his methods and instincts, which stem from a pure **DIY (Do-It-Yourself)** indie aesthetic, make him stand apart from the rest of the corporate glitterati. In fact, Rubin (who was described by *Rolling Stone* magazine as "the most successful producer in any genre" [Freedom du Lac, 2006]) is the man credited with coming up with the idea to pair rockers Aerosmith with rappers Run-D.M.C. for the smash 1986 hit "Walk This Way."

Further Reading: Farinella, David. *Producing Hit Records: Secrets from the Studio.* New York: Schirmer Books, 2006; Ogg, Alex. *The Men Behind Def Jam: The Radical Rise of Russell Simmons and Rick Rubin.* London: Omnibus Press, 2002; http://www.americanrecordings.com
.

... AND YOU WILL KNOW US BY THE TRAIL OF DEAD

This Austin, Texas–based band's brand of "apocalyptic rock" is an in-your-face blend of rock, noise, and the type of heyday punk music that broke social barriers (and eardrums). Heralded for their explosive live shows, this high-octane foursome formed in the late 1990s in Olympia, Washington. Comprised of founding members and singers/guitarists/drummers/longtime friends Jason Reece and Conrad Keely, guitarist Kevin Allen, bassist Neil Busch (who was later replaced by Danny Wood) and newer members drummer Doni Schroeder and keyboardist David Longoria, ... And You Will Know Us By the Trail of Dead (a line taken from an ancient Egyptian burial text), the band circulated a demo tape via a local label called Golden Hour before it released its self-titled debut on an imprint of the Chicago-based label Southern Records called Trance Syndicate in January 1998. The group's wild, out-of-control live shows (at one show, a falling monitor bruised one of the singer's ribs, and blood has been known to spill on the stage on more than one occasion) had already generated buzz about the group within the indie circuit, but when the group began hearing earshot comparisons to The Who and **Sonic Youth**, success was not far off. Following Trance's sudden demise, ... And You Will Know Us signed with the North Carolina–based indie label Merge Records, which was founded by members of the band **Superchunk**.

Merge Records put out the group's sophomore release, *Madonna,* in 1999, a work that revealed the group's darker side. Fans clamored to buy the album and catch the group live. Naysayers claimed the group was unable to capture the energy and rawness of their live performances on disc, but sales of their albums soared. Jimmy Iovine, the president of Interscope Records, was so intrigued by the band after he read an article about it in the U.K. music publication **NME (New Musical Express)** that he signed the band for their third and most talked-about release, *Source Tags and Codes* (2002). The band's star had not yet risen as high in the United States as it had soared in the United Kingdom, but that did not stop critics worldwide from lauding it as "well thought out indie rock" that exhibited the group's raw energy, while showcasing an **emo** factor that drew fans in without making the band seem "soft."

...And You Will Know Us drew heavy criticism after signing to Interscope Records for the simple fact that the label is home to musician Fred Durst of Limp Bizkit. But the group stood by the major label's promise to grant it complete artistic freedom over its music. And, despite the occasional "suggestion" from upper management, the band claims it has been able to have complete control over its music, lyrics, and album art. The band's argument was that several prominent punk bands—The Clash and the Sex Pistols, for instance—found homes on major labels and that those bands would not otherwise have gotten the distribution and backing they needed to make their songs and albums into the legendary works they have become.

A film student at Emerson College in Boston, Massachusetts, got a lucky break in 2005 by winning the chance to direct the music video for "Caterwaul," the single off *Worlds Apart,* at the Middle East music club. The band's fascination and affinity for Buddhism were reflected in the more introspective nature of subsequent album titles and album art on records such as *The Secret of Elena's Tomb* (Interscope, 2003). The group's next record, *Worlds Apart* (Interscope, 2005), which features a touch of psychedelica, was allegedly delayed for release by six weeks before being leaked online and ultimately getting branded a minor failure by many critics, who cited poor album sales. Keely consequently entertained the idea of disbanding the group, but he and the rest of the band found inspiration and marched on. The result of their struggles was the full-length LP *So Divided* (2006), which had originally been planned to be an EP.

So Divided demonstrated the band's harmonious prowess, which further supported its claim that it is influenced by The Beach Boys. Several musicians made guest appearances on the album—drummer Pat Mastelotto of the English prog rock group King Crimson, piano player/vocalist Amanda Palmer of the Boston-based cabaret/punk act **The Dresden Dolls**, guitarist Daniel Wilcox and a few members of fellow Texans Brothers & Sisters.

In late 2006, . . . And You Will Know Us played a series of free in-store performances at select Virgin Megastores, launched a fall tour with Seattle rock group **The Blood Brothers**, and were subsequently added to the bill for Miami's underground music and art event, the Anti-Pop Music Festival. The group's on-the-edge live shows took a turn for the worse in November 2006 when Conrad Keely shoved guitarist Kevin Allen into an amplifier at a show at the Jannus Landing Courtyard in Florida. The crowd noticed Allen had repeatedly collapsed and was unable to play his instrument before he was pushed into the drum set. Allen was carried off stage and a few band members continued playing before the group cut the gig short.

In early 2007, rumors abounded about the group's impending breakup, but the band quelled all worry with the launch of both U.S. and European tours. The persistent quartet toured with new member Aaron Ford, who replaced former drummer/percussionist Doni Schroader, and made plans to record its next album following the cessation of the final fall 2007 tour dates.

Further Reading: http://www.antipopmusicfest.com; http://www.mergerecords.com; http://www.nme.com; http://www.thebloodbrothers.com; http://www.trailofdead.com.

APOLLO SUNSHINE

Three former Berklee College of Music students—Jesse Gallagher (vocals, bass, and keyboards), Sam Cohen (guitars, vocals, and pedal steel), and Jeremy Black (drums and percussion)—brought to indie rock a kaleidoscope of hooky and colorful pop/rock tunes that was the result of their unique take on chaotic and quirky neopsychedelic, idea-packed songs that seem to be filtered through a barrage of influences dating back to the 1960s.

Apollo Sunshine quickly drew comparisons to such indie rock acts as The Flaming Lips, **The Elephant 6 Recording Company** collective (which included such acts as Neutral Milk Hotel and **The Apples in Stereo**), They Might Be Giants, and The Kinks, yet they managed to sound like all and none of these bands at any given moment. Apollo Sunshine built up a local following with gigs in and around Boston, including a residency at T.T. the Bear's Place in Cambridge, Massachusetts, while also hitting up the East Coast on shows with **emo**-rockers Piebald, indie rock band the **French Kicks**, and Sweden's Sahara Hotnights. Apollo Sunshine's modest fan base grew steadily thanks to a fiery live show that included off-beat humor and members playing different instruments simultaneously or swapping them out among themselves mid set.

In 2003, Apollo Sunshine signed with Berklee's student-run label, Heavy Rotation Records, appearing on the first in a series of compilations called *Dorm Sessions.* The band's song "I Was on the Moon" served as the first volume's lead track. That same year, the band also inked a higher profile deal with New York–based indie spinART Records, after label president Mark Price caught one of the group's Brooklyn gigs and was thoroughly impressed with its musicianship. Apollo Sunshine's full-length label debut, *Katonah,* was recorded in a converted barn and released in October 2003. Full of frenetic energy, three-part vocal harmonies, shifting instrumental arrangements, and unexpected twists and turns within every song, *Katonah* garnered rave reviews from publications such as the *New York Times,* the *Boston Herald,* and *Alternative Press* magazine, scoring the band an appearance on NBC's late-night talk show *Last Call with Carson Daly.*

The vivacious trio went on to share bills with rockers **Sonic Youth**, indie darlings **The Decemberists**, and hip-hop outfit The Roots. Guitarist and longtime friend Sean Aylward was added to the fray in 2004 to help round out the sound. Apollo Sunshine returned in September 2005 with an eponymous sophomore effort, which was issued as a joint release between spinART Records and Heavy Rotation. The band's affiliation with Berklee's label continued to help spread Apollo Sunshine's name on a grassroots level, primarily through the use of online networking sites and blogs. A live album (recorded on January 29, 2005, at the Paradise Rock Club in Boston) also appeared in 2005 via iTunes. Eventually, Apollo Sunshine wanted to return to its roots as a trio and amicably parted ways with Aylward in 2006. The band toured the West Coast that year with New York jam band Benevento/Russo Duo before taking a well-deserved break.

Apollo Sunshine performed snippets of its third full-length album, *Great Mysteries of the Old Soul,* on the road during a brief fall 2007 tour, during which it traveled in a blue-painted school bus nicknamed "the Blue Buffalo." Meanwhile, band member Sam Cohen unleashed his solo side project "I Am the Bison," the name under which he had been performing in subway stations in Brooklyn, New York.

Further Reading: Schmeling, Paul. *Berklee Music Theory Book 1.* Boston: Berklee Press, 2005; http://www.apollosunshine.com; http://www.beneventorussoduo.com; http://www.hrrecords.com; http://www.spinartrecords.com/site/index.php.

THE APPLES IN STEREO

A central component of **The Elephant 6 Recording Company** collective (the group's lead vocalist/guitarist is the organization's co-founder), The Apples in Stereo is an electro-pop indie rock group from Denver, Colorado. Banding together in 1993, front man and Louisiana native Robert Schneider, guitarist John Hill (of the group **Dressy Bessy**), and bassist Eric Allen released four full-length studio LPs before signing to actor Elijah Wood's independent label, Simian Records, in 2007, for the release of *New Magnetic Wonder* by way of Yep Roc Records/Redeye Distribution.

Known for its triumvirate combination of upbeat, melodic, and eclectic (yet edgy) pop music, a la The Beach Boys, of whom Schneider is a self-confessed fan, The Apples in Stereo was originally comprised of Schneider (vocals, guitar, and keyboards), Hilarie Sidney (drums and vocals), Jim McIntyre (bass and backing vocals), and Chris Parfitt (guitar). Together, the trio released the EP *Tidal Wave,* the first record to be released on Schneider's brainchild, **The Elephant 6 Recording Company**: a collective of bands that share ideas, musicians, and sentiments—to many, he is the glue that holds this musical web together. Schneider has produced albums by bands within the collective, such as with **Lo-fi** band The Olivia Tremor Control.

In 1994, after Parfitt's departure, The Apples in Stereo released its second EP, *Hypnotic Suggestion,* on Bus Stop Records. Hill, who had been brought on board temporarily to record a few tracks, became a permanent member of the band. The Apples in Stereo released a string of split singles with bands such as The Olivia Tremor Control, the Heartworms, and Sportsguitar, all of which belong to the Elephant 6 collective.

The psych-pop band's first full-length album, *Fun Trick Noisemaker,* was released in 1995, but McIntyre, who left midway through the recording, left the band and appears only on part of the record. Pressing onward, the group released *Science Faire* in 1997. The band constantly seems to revert to a musical chairs game of gaining and losing band members; bassist Eric Allen and Chris McDuffie joined the trio for its second full-length album, *Tone Soul Evolution* (spinART Records, 1997).

Amid an ambitious spread of singles and 7-inch releases, The Apples in Stereo released its third and fourth full-length LPs, *The Discovery of a World Inside the Moone* in 2000, followed by *The Velocity of Sound* in 2002. In addition to releasing their own albums, Schneider and his crew remained busy by recruiting countless musical guests to their own recordings, appearing on albums by fellow **Elephant 6 Recording Company** bands' records, opening for acts such as The Strokes, and dabbling in various projects, e.g., the group's contribution to the soundtrack *Heroes and Villains: Music Inspired by The PowerPuff Girls* in 2000, which includes the group's cover of The Beach Boys' song of the same name. Schneider produced the *New Magnetic Wonder* album, notoriously using over 90 separate tracks for some of the songs off the new record, which was recorded at Trout Studios in Brooklyn, New York. The fuzzy album *Velocity of Sound* emerged in 2002.

The band's original name was simply the Apples; the group lengthened its moniker (and went hi-fi) and changed it to The Apples in Stereo to avoid confusion with other similarly named groups.

Further Reading: http://www.applesinstereo.com; http://www.elephant6.com.

ARAB STRAP

This Scottish post-funk indie rock outfit did not need the attention its tongue-in-cheek name, synonymous with a certain sexual device, garners to help its career, but the band's members seem to enjoy it. Created by vocalist Aidan Moffat and multi-instrumentalist Malcolm Middleton, Arab Strap formed in the mid-1990s, releasing its first full-length album, *The First Big Weekend,* on the Scottish indie label Chemikal Underground (Matador Records is the label's U.S. counterpart), which was formed by fellow Scottish indie rockers The Delgados.

Moffat and Middleton added drummer David Glow and bassist Gary Miller to the lineup soon after joining forces; the band attracted fans for the honesty in its songs, which touch on topics as personal as its namesake. A track from that demo secured the band a record deal, sufficient airplay on the radio, and served as the backdrop for a Guinness commercial. Moffat and Middleton, who bonded over a mutual disdain for the dreary atmosphere of their small town of Falkirk, Scotland (which angered the town's residents) and an affinity for local pubs, left bands they had been playing in to join forces and form Arab Strap.

Arab Strap released the LP *The Week Never Starts Round Here* in 1997, singing about its affinity for supermodel Kate Moss, love lost, and lonely towns. Fans who related to the band's intimate musings reveled in Arab Strap's off-kilter stage shows, which finally came to a head after a 1997 show with **post-rock** Scots Mogwai that reached a chaotic climax when fans rushed the stage, tearing whatever they could to pieces. Critics lauded Arab Strap, however, comparing them to long time famed English post-punkers Joy Division. Arab Strap released the EP *Girls of Summer* in 1997 and the single, "Holiday Girl" (a remixed cover of David Holmes's song "Don't Die Just Yet"), entered the U.K. charts. Focused on channeling chaotic energy into their music, Arab Strap recorded its second album, *Philophobia,* in 1998; the album hit the U.K. Top 40 charts without pause. Arab Strap released the EP *Cherubs* and almost immediately afterwards put out its third LP, *Elephant Shoe,* which proved the band could be serious about its art. Both releases were later distributed in the United States by the New York City–based label Jetset Records. Arab Strap launched a North American tour and held a live recording of a performance at Queen Elizabeth Hall in London, which was entitled *Mad For Sadness.*

In true indie rock fashion, Arab Strap was able to stave off hefty financial offers from potential major label suitors, that was until Go! Discs Records' subsidiary Go! Beat Records agreed to grant the band full creative control over its music and the band signed on to the London-based label around 1999. But when Go! Beat cried foul at the band's "artful" product and demanded mainstream money-making music, Arab Strap fought back; Go! Beat attempted to freeze the band's efforts, but the band won out, allowing it to leave with the rights to its music in tow.

Proud and with its "rejected" music in tow, Arab Strap returned to its original home at Chemikal Underground to release *The Red Thread* in 2001, the first album the band released at the same time on both sides of the pond, followed by the 13-track *Monday at the Hug Pint* (2003) and the 10-track *The Last Romance* (2005). In 2006, as a celebration of the ten-year anniversary of its first musical endeavor, Arab Strap released *Ten Years of Tears,* a compilation of its early demos, B-sides, and previous unreleased tracks, which it called an "audio rockumentary." Arab Strap toured the United Kingdom before disbanding in late 2006/early 2007. Moffat and Middleton have since joined the Scottish supergroup The Reindeer Section. Arab Strap's Web site, however, is still up and running, with updated posts about news, reviews, MP3s, discography, and videos.

Further Reading: http://www.arabstrap.co.uk; http://www.chemikal.co.uk; http://www.delgados.co.uk; http://www.neworderonline.com.

ARCADE FIRE

Leading the pack for the indie rock renaissance of the mid-2000s, Canadian artists in the band Arcade Fire became a "band to watch" with the release of their first full-length album, *Funeral,* which made its debut on October 5, 2004, via the Chapel Hill, North Carolina–based independent record label Merge Records. Arcade Fire gained as much attention for its seemingly oxymoronic combination of euphoric music, somber lyrics, and a highly coiffed wardrobe (they religiously don waistcoats and formal attire, even when playing outdoor shows in 90 degree weather) as they did for the subject matter of their first album—death.

Formed in 2003 in Montreal, Quebec, Arcade Fire is comprised of husband and wife duo Win Butler and Régine Chassagne, who met at an art opening at college (where Régine was singing jazz standards until Butler asked her to start a musical venture with him), and members Richard Reed Parry, Win's brother William Butler, Tim Kingsbury, Sarah Neufeld, Jeremy Gara, and drummer Howard Bilerman. After Bilerman left the band to pursue other projects, Arcade Fire added Pietro Amato (horns) and Owen Pallett (violin).

After playing several shows in Canada and selling countless copies of its *Us Kids Know* EP at shows, Arcade Fire signed to Merge Records in 2004, bringing its stage-filling lineup and post-modern musical ambitions (band members are well skilled at playing a gamut of instruments—guitar, drums, bass, piano, violin, viola, cello, xylophone, keyboard, French horn, accordion, and harp) to the United States, where the group became an instant hit. The majority of Arcade Fire's songs are written by husband and wife Régine and Win, both of whom sing on the album. Additionally, Régine sings and plays a spectrum of instruments—piano, guitar, accordion, mandolin, flute, drums, and harmonica.

Taking its name from a seemingly believable fable about an arcade that caught on fire, Arcade Fire, with its pitch-black wardrobe and morbid inspirations, seemed to revel in its position on the thin line between reality and the "hereafter." In fact, the inspiration for that successful *Funeral* LP was, in fact, death. Several songs from the album—"Une année sans lumière" ("A Year without Light"), "In the Backseat," and "Haiti"—were all influenced by or spawned from many of the band members' experiences of the loss of close relatives, all of which occurred in a very short period of time. ("Haiti" is an homage to Chassagne's lost homeland, and, quite possibly, the resting place for a "wounded mother I'll never see.") In essence, Arcade Fire was the phoenix that rose from the ashes of death—Chassagne lost her grandmother in the summer of 2003, the Butlers' grandfather passed away in mid-2004, and Richard Parry's aunt passed away soon after. Chassagne and Win Butler married in the midst of it all in 2003, and the band decided to name its album *Funeral* in light of all that darkness.

Funeral immediately shot to the top of the charts in the United States; it sold over a half a million copies, catapulted to #5 on the Billboard Heatseekers Chart, sold out rapidly on nearly every online outlet, and was endlessly lauded by critics. The editors of *Rolling Stone* magazine ranked the album #3 on their Top 50 Records of 2004 list, calling Butler a "mastermind." Consequently, Merge Records sold out of the first inventory run of the album. *Funeral* received a 9.7 rating from the hard-to-please critics at **Pitchfork Media**.

To top off the album's successes, Arcade Fire received nods of approval and support from its celebrity fans—glam rock icon David Bowie, Chris Martin (of Coldplay), and David Byrne (of **Talking Heads** fame), to name a few—which did much to spark the album's rocket-fueled success. *Funeral* also ended up on the Top 10 Lists of critics all across the country. **Pitchfork Media** voted *Funeral* the best album of 2004, while ***The Village Voice*** added it to the higher ranks of its annual Pazz & Jop list. A media frenzy then ensued, with features and "buzz" articles popping up in print and online media across the United States—including prominent news organizations such as the *New York Times* and the *Los Angeles Times,* which featured lengthy interviews with the band.

Suddenly, the tour bus–filling Canadian outfit had gone from Canada's icy temperatures and the interiors of depressing funeral parlors to playing a nearly over-booked tour schedule in 2005 that included the **Coachella Valley Music and Arts Festival** in Indio, California, the resurrected **Lollapalooza** festival at Grant Park in Chicago, Illinois, the Sasquatch! Music Festival at The Gorge Amphitheatre in Washington state, the c/o Pop Festival in Germany, the Download Music Festival at the Shoreline Amphitheater in Mountain View, California, and New York City's **CMJ Music Marathon**. Arcade Fire also appeared on the popular PBS series *Austin City Limits,* played at the **South by Southwest (SXSW)** music festival in Austin, Texas, and graced the stage at the West Coast's version of National Public Radio (or NPR), KCRW's World Music Festival.

Burning up the music scene, Arcade Fire was the featured cover story for the Canadian edition of *Time* magazine on April 4, 2005, which claimed Arcade Fire "helped put Canadian music on the world map." That same year, Arcade Fire recorded the song "Cold Wind" for HBO's hit series *Six Feet Under;* the song was released on the show's second soundtrack, *Six Feet Under: Vol. 2: Everything Ends.* Fittingly enough, the show revolves around a family that owns and operates a morgue and funeral home out of its house.

Arcade Fire received a golden stamp of approval on its rock credentials certificate on September 9, 2005, when, during a performance for VH1's *Fashion Rocks* concert, David Bowie joined the group on stage for a rendition of the song "Wake Up." That fall, Arcade Fire and Bowie teamed up again, this time for a concert at the Central Park SummerStage in New York City. Arcade Fire later performed on CBS's *Late Show with David Letterman,* and the group cemented its status in the United Kingdom by appearing on the popular BBC's music series *Top of the Pops.*

Moving even higher in the echelons of rock stardom up toward the rock gods, Arcade Fire was surprised to hear that Irish rock gods U2 played the group's song "Wake Up" at the opening of nearly every performance on their 2005 "Vertigo" tour. Arcade Fire subsequently opened for Bono and crew for three dates on that tour before finally joining them on stage for a cover of Joy Division's hit song "Love Will Tear Us Apart."

Having played on stage with some of rock's greatest legends, Arcade Fire was due for yet another rock rite of passage—the Grammys. At the 2005 awards ceremony, *Funeral* was nominated for Best Alternative Rock Album, and the single "Cold Wind" received a nod for Best Song Written for Television, Film, or Other Media categories. In early 2006, Arcade Fire was awarded a Juno Award for Songwriter of the Year for three tracks off of the *Funeral* LP. The band was also nominated for three BRIT Awards, including Best International Group, Best International Album, and Best International Breakthrough Act. In 2006, the song "Cold Wind" earned Arcade Fire a nomination for best song written for motion picture, television, or other visual media.

Arcade Fire decided to give back to society at large after having ridden a roller coaster of successes since the release of *Funeral.* In 2006, the group participated in a poster auction organized by Merge Records, for which the record label sponsored a series of eBay auctions benefiting Oxfam International and the North Carolina Food Bank. Arcade Fire was among 14 Merge bands to donate autographed silk-screened tour posters for the cause. Proceeds from a live recording of the band's "Wake Up" performance with David Bowie (released as a 7-inch and via iTunes) were donated to Katrina relief efforts.

Good karma added more wind to the group's sails and the accolades continued. That same year, Arcade Fire topped MTV2's "50 Greatest Albums of the Year" list and received five nods from mtvU's Woodie Awards. Following the deluge of success with *Funeral,* Arcade Fire released a strong string of singles, which included a cover of the **Talking Heads**' song "This Must Be the Place (Naive Melody)" featuring David Byrne, and a cover of a song by Win Butler's grandfather. Merge Records released a 7-inch of "Cold Wind" and, to much acclaim, Merge Records reissued the band's self-released, self-titled 2003 debut EP.

In 2006, Arcade Fire purchased an old church outside of Montreal, which the group converted into a studio to record its follow-up album to *Funeral*. Material for the album *Neon Bible* included several live tracks as well as a song that the band wrote for David Bowie. Arcade Fire completed shooting the music videos for several songs from *Funeral;* the video for the track "Neighborhood #3 (Power Out)" featured animation and **Yeah Yeah Yeahs**, and **Pavement** video director Lance Bangs shot the video for the song "Neighborhood #1 (Tunnels)."

Fans can view photos of the band and read online diaries written by each band member on Arcade Fire's Web site. A 2007 DVD featured live performances from Arcade Fire's 2006–2007 tour dates. In May 2007, the band joined the likes of other handpicked acts such as **Air**, Deerhoof, **The Polyphonic Spree**, and Secret Machines for the High Line Festival. Organized by Arcade Fire fan David Bowie, the ten-day High Line Festival took place at venues nearby the High Line, a defunct, 1.45-mile elevated rail line in Manhattan. Portions of the event were donated to the nonprofit organization that is working to transform the area into a public park. The band played as part of a free concert at Stuart's Opera House in Nelsonville, Ohio, on March 2, 2008, in support of Democratic hopeful Barack Obama.

Further Reading: http://www.arcadefire.com; http://www.hob.com/tickets/festivals/sasquatch; http://www.kcrw.com; http://www.mergerecords.com.

ARCHERS OF LOAF

Chapel Hill, North Carolina, native Eric Bachmann's versatile voice and the jagged edges guitar riffs of Eric Johnson helped this indie/guitar rock band gain sufficient radio play in the early 1990s. Archers of Loaf's brand of accessible noise pop became a landmark sound for college rock in the early 1990s, and the intensity of the group's sound earned it repeated comparisons to **Pavement**. The group's nonsensical name is just that; not wanting to have to explain the inspiration and meaning behind the band name repeatedly in countless interviews, Bachmann and his bandmates simply attempted to create the most senseless name they could devise.

Formed in 1991 at the University of North Carolina, Archers of Loaf, which also included Mark Price on drums and bassist Matt Gentling, followed the **DIY (Do-It-Yourself)** mantra, using **Lo-fi** recording techniques to capture the rawness of their post-modern pop music. Signs of their musical influences—bands such as **Sonic Youth** and The Replacements—were evident in their music. Archers of Loaf self-released its debut single, "Wrong," before signing to the California-based independent label Alias Records for its follow-up single, "Web in Front," which received heavy radio play.

Leveed by the success of its singles, Archers of Loaf released its highly anticipated full-length debut album, *Icky Mettle,* a collection of high-octane, catchy songs that helped it become one of the landmark indie rock albums of all time. *Mettle* made its way onto countless mix tapes created by indie fans, and word quickly spread about the group's ability to raise the bar for indie rock standards.

Its rock and punk roots elevated Archers to new heights—and the stage was set for a successful and prolific, yet short-lived, career that would leave an indelible mark on the indie rock genre.

Archers kicked off a national tour, which was followed by its 1994 EP, *Greatest of All Time.* The band became a magnet for major labels such as Madonna's Maverick Records, which attempted to court the band as its star rose higher and higher. College radio made an even bigger success story out of the group's 1995 album, *Vee Vee,* an edgier release that garnered the group widespread press coverage and even topped the college radio charts.

The group recorded a series of five tracks at DJ John Peel's radio show on the BBC's Radio 1 station in the United Kingdom in 1994; the tracks made their way onto a tribute to the legendary DJ as well as the group's 1996 album *The Speed of Cattle,* a collection of rare tracks, B-sides, and live tracks. Archers of Loaf ended the major label battle for the band when it signed to Elektra Records for its unpredictable, melodic album *All the Nation's Airports* (1997). Bachmann, meanwhile, worked on his side project, Barry Black, while the group worked on its fourth full-length album, the introspective, yet heavy rocking album *White Trash Heroes* (1998). Archers of Loaf toured in support of that album, but on the tail end of that tour, citing rigorous tour schedules and a mutual feeling that the band had hit a plateau creatively, the group disbanded in 1999. The live album *Seconds before the Accident* was released after the group's split in 2000. Bachmann focused his efforts on his new group Crooked Fingers and the pursuit of a solo career.

Further Reading: Goldberg, Justin. *Ultimate Survival Guide for the New Music Industry: A Handbook for Hell.* Los Angeles: Lone Eagle, 2004; www.aliasrecords.com/archersofloaf.htm.

ARCTIC MONKEYS

This English quartet released one of the most successful indie albums of 2006, its debut album, *Whatever People Say I Am, That's What I'm Not* (Domino Records), and sold almost 120,000 copies just days after its release. *Whatever* outsold releases by every other indie band out there, save for the experimental indie/Brit pop band **Snow Patrol**, moving more albums than every record on the Top 20 combined.

Formed in 2002 in Sheffield, England, by lead vocalist/guitarist Alex Turner, bassist Andy Nicholson, guitarist Jamie Cook, and drummer Matt Helders, the Arctic Monkeys took the United States by storm, making critics' Best Of and Bands to Watch lists and selling out shows on both sides of the pond. The group, whose influences range from **The Smiths** to The Clash and English punk/mod revival band The Jam, started out playing hits by such groups as The Vines and **The White Stripes** and honed its punk-infused, Britpop/indie/alt rock sound until the group found itself at the center of a bidding war between major labels; the group eventually signed with London's Domino Records in 2004.

The group released its debut EP *Five Minutes with the Arctic Monkeys* on its own Bang Bang Records in 2005, which hit the Top 40. "I Bet You Look Good on the

Dancefloor" was released in late 2005; the single debuted at #1 on the U.K. singles chart. The group toured extensively in 2005, but its career shot off like a rocket in 2006 when *Whatever* became the fastest-selling debut album in the history of British music, helping the group to win the coveted Mercury Prize that year.

Much of the album's success can be attributed to the band's **DIY (Do-It-Yourself)** efforts; the group handed CDs out at gigs and spread news and music online through file sharing, social networking sites such as MySpace.com, and blogs, building a large fan base that would eventually show up at the record stores, money in hand. The group's second single, "When the Sun Goes Down," was a hit single as well, and *Whatever* had quickly sold over 350,000 copies just a few weeks after its release. Record chain HMV compared the group's success and impact to that of The Beatles.

Now a household name, the Arctic Monkeys (a name that Cook came up with) was being heralded as "one of the greatest U.K. rock groups of all time" (www.npr.org/templates/story/story.php?storyId=5293452). The group toured extensively again in 2006, combing North America, hitting all the big stops like the Sasquatch! Music Festival and appearing on the cover of *NME* (*New Musical Express*) magazine that March. Nicholson, however, sat out on a few gigs due to fatigue; by the end of 2006, he was officially out of the group. Bassist Nick O'Malley, who had substituted for Nicholson while he was ill, became a permanent member of the band soon after, helping the group to complete the rest of its world-crossing tour dates in the United Kingdom and Europe, Australia, New Zealand, and Japan. The Arctic Monkeys lined up a slue of openers and co-headliners for the group's 2006 tour dates (solo gigs and festivals)—including We Are Scientists, **Clap Your Hands Say Yeah**, **Death Cab for Cutie**, **Serena-Maneesh**, **Franz Ferdinand**, **dEUS**, and more.

The group, whose lyrics often contain sentiments about working-class life, released two singles—"Who the F- -k Are the Arctic Monkeys" and "Leave Before the Lights Come On"—in the fall of 2006; the singles contained covers of the group The Little Flame's "Put Your Dukes Up, John" and Barbara Lewis's soul classic "Baby I'm Yours." The DVD "Scummy Man," a dramatic short film inspired by the group's music, followed that same year. The Arctic Monkeys joined the likes of **Franz Ferdinand**, Quincy Jones, Coldplay, and Kaiser Chiefs to contribute to a collaboration album by the Cuban supergroup Buena Vista Social Club (Hip-O Records, 2006) entitled *Rhythms del Mundo: Cuba*.

The Arctic Monkeys entered the ranks of the likes of indie groups such as **Clap Your Hands Say Yeah** and **Bloc Party** by avoiding the feared sophomore slump with their follow-up 2007 full-length album, *Favorite Worst Nightmare*. The year 2007 was a busy year for the Monkeys—so busy, in fact, that the group was unable to appear in person to accept its prizes at the BRIT Music Awards. Instead, the group sent a video clip in which the members were dressed in full costume as the characters from the film *The Wizard of Oz* and as the 1970s disco music group the Village People. The Arctic Monkeys accepted the BRIT Awards (the U.K. equivalent to the Grammys) for Best British Group and Best British Album for its debut full-length LP. The Arctic Monkeys toured in 2006, hitting the Reading Festival in the United Kingdom; by popular demand, the band went out on the road again the next year hitting the 2007 **Coachella Valley Music and Arts Festival**. The group also made some eclectic musical alliances, teaming up with rapper Dizzee Rascal, who made a cameo on the group's single "Temptation Greets You Like Your Naughty Friend," and the U.K. female pop duo Girls Aloud. Turner also announced plans to collaborate with Simian Mobile Disco's James Ford.

The Arctic Monkeys walked away with two **NME (*New Musical Express*)** Awards for Best Album (*Whatever People Say I Am, That's What I'm Not*) in 2006 and Best DVD (*Scummy Man*) before announcing additional tour dates with supporting acts Supergrass, Amy Winehouse, and The Coral. Drummer Matt Helders showed his entrepreneurial ambitions when he launched his own clothing line later that year. Each piece of clothing from the "Supremebeing" collection, Helders revealed, would include a mixed Arctic Monkeys CD. The band experienced a sequence of highs and lows throughout 2007; the group toured relentlessly and was the recipient of seven nominations at the British Music Awards. The band's successes, however, were not impressive enough to convince bouncers outside an **NME (*New Musical Express*)** after-party hosted by Kate Moss because the bouncers did not deem them "famous enough" to let the bandmates into the party.

Further Reading: http://www.arcticmonkeys.com; http://www.dominorecordco.us; http://www.myspace.com/arcticmonkeys; http://www.snowpatrol.com; www.npr.org/templates/story/story.php?storyId=5293452.

ART BRUT

Tagged as the "best unsigned band in the world" by *BLENDER* magazine (Dverden, 2004), this U.K. outfit redefined the "avant-garde" tag by combining art, punk, and indie rock when it formed in 2003. Taking its name from the 1970s art term (it literally translates into "rough" or "raw art") used to describe the work of the French painter Jean Dubuffet—who was inspired by art created by inmates and people admitted to insane asylums—Art Brut is fronted by the outspoken, hell-raising singer Eddie Argos. Art Brut is known in various musical circles by several aliases—AB0, AB3.14/Pi, and AB197. Art Brut is Argos (lead vocals), Freddy Feedback (bass), Jasper Future (guitar), Chris Chinchilla (guitar), Ian Catskilkin (guitar), and Mikey Breyer (drums).

Art Brut's demo, "Brutlegs," ended up in the hands of an A&R (Artists and Repertoire) representative at London's **Rough Trade Records**. **Rough Trade Records** released the demo as a single before putting out the group's follow-up single, "Formed a Band" in 2004. **NME (*New Music Express*)** named the release Single of the Week and hailed the group as pioneers of the new wave movement in the United Kingdom. "Band" was also a featured song for Sony's PlayStation 2 game system. Argos and his cast of characters toured in 2004, joining **Babyshambles**' front man Pete Doherty's side project Wolfman & Pete and gigging at the Rock Against Racism concert before releasing another set of the popular

"Brutlegs." The "Band" single wound up selling 5,000 copies, hitting #52 on the Billboard charts.

Claiming to have earned the enamoration of fans such as actor Daniel Radcliffe (of *Harry Potter* fame), the indie group **British Sea Power**, and bands such as The Libertines, Hope of the States, and musician Graham Coxon, Art Brut released three subsequent singles, "Modern Art/Little Brother" (2004), the three-track single, "Emily Kane" (2005), and "Good Weekend," all on another London independent label, Fierce Panda Records.

In 2005, Argos, a former member of the band the Art Goblins, stirred up some trouble when he told a *SPIN* online music journalist that **Bloc Party** (to which Art Brut had often been compared) lead singer Kele Okereke and his group were not very good, which resulted in a fisticuffs between the two lead vocalists.

Art Brut's debut album, *Bang Bang Rock & Roll,* turned the attention back on the music when U.S. and U.K. critics alike hailed the album for its Britpop sensibilities. Art Brut toured Europe in support of *Bang Bang* for the remainder of 2004 before heading to the United States to tour through 2005. *Bang Bang,* which was produced by Dan Swift (who has worked with groups such as **Franz Ferdinand**, Kasabian, and **Snow Patrol**) quickly made its way to the crest of several year-end Best Of lists including **Pitchfork Media**, *BLENDER*, and *SPIN*. The crafty Art Brut also received dual releases for *Bang Bang*—it was distributed in the United Kingdom by Fierce Panda and in the United States by the American independent label/publishing company Downtown Records. *Rolling Stone* German Edition featured the group on its cover in 2005.

In 2006, Art Brut hit the stage at three major music festivals—**Coachella Valley Music and Arts Festival**, Siren, and the **Pitchfork Media** Music Festival—before seeing the release of its fall 2006 single "Nag Nag Nag Nag," which featured live tracks and rare recordings (London's Mute Records—the first in Britain to have an Internet presence). Art Brut also put out its Wild Animus "storytelling project," combining fine art, music, and book in one. But while Art Brut was exploring the lengths of its artistic freedom, band member Chris Chinchilla was ready to explore a musical life on his own. Revealing a personal account of his decision to leave the band on his LiveJournal weblog, Chinchilla claimed he needed "a break to sort a few personal issues out." Chinchilla formed the group MaMu soon after his departure; he also started a solo art project simply known as the "Arts Project."

Art Brut soldiered on, releasing a split 7-inch with American **post-punk**/rock trio We Are Scientists, touring with English indie act Maximo Park in 2007, performing at the three-day Great Escape festival in Sydney, Australia, receiving a nod for the 2007 Shortlist Music Prize, and helping to launch a new radio show series in conjunction with XM Radio. Art Brut showed its true colors that same year when it was included in an elite group of artists and bands (such as Bob Dylan, **Cat Power**, Gnarls Barkley, and the **Yeah Yeah Yeahs**) participating in a painting-music collaboration produced by an Ohio State University professor.

Art Brut headlined its own tour and released its second record, *It's A Bit Complicated,* on Mute Records in June 2007. The band was entangled in a feud with its label, EMI, in 2008 when the major label released a single for the band's song "Pump Up the Volume" without its consent.

Further Reading: http://www.artbrut.org.uk/; http://www.myspace.com/artbrut; http://www.roughtrade.com/; http://www.thegreatescape.net.au; http://www.toofar.com.

ATOM AND HIS PACKAGE

This Pennsylvania-based duo is Bronx, New York, native Adam Goren and his beloved synthesizer, a Yamaha QY700 music sequencer that Goren donned with the moniker "package." Armed also with a Yamaha RM1X music sequencer and a B. C. Rich guitar, Goren performs comedic "geek" rock, writing, and performing synth-pop-punk songs as his alter ego, Atom.

Goren created Atom and His Package in the mid-1990s after Fracture, the punk band he had been playing with, disbanded. Using music sequencers, synthesizers, and a guitar to write songs, Atom and His Package released its first recording, *The First CD,* in 1995 on Bloodlink Records. Atom and His Package quickly attracted fans with Goren's self-effacing banter (Goren was well known for making bold, opinionated comments about political and public figures and for lightly poking fun at his Jewish heritage), awkward keyboard playing, and tracks that unabashedly combined comedy with political satire, such as the track "Tim Allen Is Not Very Funny" off of the debut album. One of the group's signature songs, "Pumping Iron for Enya" playfully pokes fun at Goren's less-than-statuesque frame and his attempts to lift weights to gain the affections of the Irish singer.

Many of Goren's songs, however, earned him negative criticism and even hate mail; Goren has even devoted a section of his official Web site to such submissions. In the 1997 track "If You Own the Washington Redskins, You're a Cock," Goren attacked the owners of the football team for using Native Americans as their symbol. Other songs, like the in-your-face title track "Mission 1: Avoid Job Working with Assholes" further exhibited Goren's disdain for adhering to the norm. Several of Atom and His Package's songs inspired Goren to post commonly misinterpreted lyrics on the group's Web site. Some of those misinterpreted lyrics include "I'm always armed with a burrito," which fans have misinterpreted as "and in my arm, there's Judge Ito."

Atom and His Package released two EPs in 1998—*Gun Court* and *Behold, I Shall Do a New Thing. A Society of People Named Elihu* followed in 1999 on Mountain Records, and the EP *Making Love* (No Idea Records, 1999) featured tracks such as "(Lord It's Hard to be Happy When You're Not) Using the Metric System" and "It's a Mad Mad Mad Mad Mad Mad Mad Mad Lib." Atom and His Package came under fire for the album's controversial track "Hats Off to Halford," in which Goren discussed Judas Priest front man Rob Halford's sexual orientation (Judas Priest is a metal band, a genre that seemed, to Goren, to be the poster child for all things homophobic). Tracks such as "The Palestinians Are Not the Same As the Rebel Alliance, Jackass" exhibited Goren's political furor.

Goren teamed up with showy indie rock/dance artist Har Mar Superstar for the EP *Shopping Spree* in 2001 (Sub City Records). Atom toured relentlessly during that time, often funding his tours by himself—and his fan base continued to grow. Fans collected albums, T-shirts, and anything Atom-related they could get their hands on. The full-length *Redefining Music* (Hopeless Records, 2001) bore the labels "Explicit Lyrics' and "Parental Advisory," and Atom and His Package continued to gain new fans, eventually earning cult status in the indie rock world.

The 2002 *Hamburgers* EP featured songs that shed some light into Goren's real life; the track "Sebastian in Nigeria" tells the story of a friend of Goren's who, at the age of 19, drove across the Sahara Desert, and "Wonderman (Hammer Smashed Ball)" was Goren's outcry response to his friend's decision to vote for George W. Bush for president in 2000. Atom's final official full-length album of all original material, *Attention, Blah Blah Blah,* was released in 2003 on Hopeless Records.

Following his recent marriage and the birth of his first child and after having been diagnosed with diabetes in 2003, Atom and His Package played its final show in Philadelphia on August 29 that same year. A sort of "Best Of" collection, *Hair: Debatable,* featuring 27 tracks (Hopeless Records, 2004), was combined with a DVD that featured Atom and His Package's final live performance as well as documentary footage and various videos. Goren, who continues to manage the record label File-13 Records, maintains the Atom and His Package Web site, but his time is now devoted to his current project, a band titled Armalite.

Further Reading: Cleveland, Barry. *Creative Music Production: Joe Meek's Bold Techniques.* Emeryville, CA: Artistpro, 2001; Schwartz, Daylle Deanna. *I Don't Need a Record Deal! Your Survival Guide for the Indie Music Revolution.* New York: Billboard Books, 2005; Spellman, Peter. *The Self-Promoting Musician (Music Business).* Boston: Berklee Press, 2000; http://www.atomandhispackage.com; http://www.hopelessrecords.com; http://www.noidearecords.com.

AT THE DRIVE-IN

This El Paso, Texas, quartet's explosive, unpredictable, heart-racing, punk-metal-indie/post-hardcore music shone brightly on the indie rock soundscape, burning out after seven years of high-octane performances, unforgettable live shows, and extensive touring. Formed in 1994, At the Drive-In (acrobatic front man/vocalist Cedric Bixler, guitarists Jim Ward and Omar Rodriguez-Lopez, drummer Tony Hajjar, and bassist Paul Hinojos), which was named after a line in the hit song "Talk Dirty to Me" by the 1980s hair metal group Poison, gigged locally, appealing to the local kids with its high charged music, eccentric look, and eardrum-shattering live shows. The group released its debut EP, the ironically titled *Hell Paso,* on its own Western Breed label before self-releasing its second EP, *Alfaro Vive, Carajo!* and touring across the United States. Soon enough, the eclectic group caught the attention of record label execs, but at a particular gig (perhaps its smallest) in Los Angeles, California, the group played for a staffer from the Virginia-based independent label Flipside Records; At the Drive-In signed with Flipside in 1996.

The energetic band's debut full-length album, *Acrobatic Tenement* (Flipside, 1996), exhibited the group's **emo** side, proving it was a group worth noting. Though not exactly comprised of the most technically skilled musicians, the group's rawness, punk edge, and real emotive abilities captured the harts of indie fans and critics alike.

Word of mouth spread quickly about the group, and soon Bixler was hanging from stage supports in front of thousands of admiring fans. At the Drive-In released its follow-up EP, *El Gran Orgo,* in Orange County, California's punk label, Fearless Records, before putting out its sophomore effort, *In/Casino/Out* (Fearless), in 1998. *In/Casino/Out,* which the band recorded live in the studio, further conveyed the group's earnestness, and its music became an elixir to hordes of indie and punk fans who could not get enough of the spry, passionate quartet.

At the Drive-In released a staggering amount of singles, EPs, and split albums (with bands such as Sunshine, Burning Airlines, the Murder City Devils, and Aasee Lake) throughout the course of its years as a group, but the band's third full-length album made At the Drive-In bigger than the explosive, politically charged groups **Fugazi** and Rage Against the Machine, to which the band has often been compared. At the Drive-In (ATDI) released its 1999 EP, *Vaya,* and soon after, the band signed to the label the Beastie Boys called home, Grand Royal (a new division under the Capitol Records umbrella), for its third LP, *Relationship of Command* (2000), which catapulted the group into superstardom. *Rolling Stone* called the group "hard-boiled brigands" and the head-banging-inspiring record sold over 1 million copies worldwide, making it a must-have for record collectors and rock fans alike. The album's standout song, "One Armed Scissor" received heavy rotation on MTV and won over any remaining critics who were holding out on jumping on the At the Drive-In bandwagon. The group performed the single on several hit TV shows, including *Late Show with David Letterman* and *Late Night with Conan O'Brien.* In 2000, ATDI postponed a number of shows after its tour bus hit a patch of ice; Bixler and Hajjar received minor injuries.

In 2001, the band performed at the Big Day Out music festival in Australia; during a set by rap/metal rockers Limp Bizkit, a fan passed away after being crushed by the surging crowd. During At the Drive-In's set, Bixler called the crowd a bunch of "sheep" and continued to make sheep noises at them while asking them to calm down. The group toured extensively in 2001, so much so that it soon announced the cancellation of the European leg of one of its biggest tours because the group reportedly suffered from complete mental and physical exhaustion. Then, suddenly it seemed, the group went on an "indefinite hiatus," citing irreconcilable musical ambitions for its next album. Various theories circulated, though, that the group was feeling the pressure of its newfound success and was admittedly feeling asphyxiated by the media and press, for which the band's members did not feel they were ready.

Certain that the group was actually headed for RIP (rest-in-peace) status, Rodriguez-Lopez and Bixler teamed up to form the intense modern group Sparta, which experienced an unexpected level of success. Sparta's debut 2002 album, *Wiretap Scars,* sold approximately 144,000 copies. Ward, Hajjar, Hinojos, and bassist Matt Miller (from the group Belknap) formed the spin-off group, The Mars Volta, a highly charged punk band that rose from the ashes of At the Drive-In's

Omar Rodriguez-Lopez (from left), Cedric Bixler-Zavala, and drummer Jon Theodore of the band The Mars Volta perform. [AP Wide World Photos/Susan Walsh]

infinite energy and songwriting ambitions (some of their tracks are more than eight minutes long). The Mars Volta toured with **Radiohead** and U2, releasing four albums to date. The Mars Volta's debut album, *Comatorium,* was co-produced by the legendary Rick Rubin (the famed producer who brought together Aerosmith and Run-D.M.C. for the 1986 hit "Walk This Way"). The band has featured rock star musical guest band members such as the Red Hot Chili Peppers' John Frusciante.

The ever-prolific Rodriguez-Lopez and Bixler continued work on a reggae/dub side project, De Facto, which they had been working on during their ATDI days. De Facto released its debut album, *Megaton Shotblast* on DSL Recordings in 2001. The group, however, disbanded after its sound engineer/vocalist, Jeremy Ward, passed away of a drug overdose. Bixler also joined a group called Phantasmagoria.

Fearless Records re-released the group's signature albums *Acrobatic Tenement* and *Relationship of Command* in 2004. At the Drive-In released its career retrospective album/anthology, *This Station is Non Operational,* on Fearless Records in 2005, which consisted of 18 tracks including B-sides, BBC sessions, covers of the Pink Floyd song "Take Up Thy Stethoscope and Walk" and **The Smiths**' song "This Night Has Opened My Eyes," rare recordings as well as a companion DVD with live concert footage, and a mini booklet of 20 previously unreleased photographs of the band.

Further Reading: http://www.bigdayout.com; http://www.fearlessrecords.com/atdi; http://www.flipsideweb.com; http://www.hollywoodrecords.go.com/sparta; http://www.

themarsvolta.com; http://www.myspace.com/atdi; http://www.myspace.com/sparta; http://www.spartamusic.com.

AU REVOIR SIMONE

The Williamsburg, Brooklyn, New York City–based **indie pop** outfit Au Revoir Simone formed a solid fan following long before its song "Through the Backyards" was featured in the 2006 finale of the popular ABC drama *Grey's Anatomy*. The Casio keyboard–loving trio formed in late 2003, taking its name from a line in Tim Burton's 1985 comedy *Pee-Wee's Big Adventure*. Vocalists and keyboardists Erika Forster and Annie Hart met while on a train back to New York from Vermont, both heading home from weekend getaways with friends. They bonded over the shared desire of one day starting an all-keyboard band and quickly developed a friendship that led into writing songs together once they returned to the city. At the time, Forster was still a member of the local shoegaze-inspired indie rock act **Dirty on Purpose**; she ultimately left the group following the release of **Dirty on Purpose**'s 2004 album, *Sleep Late for a Better Tomorrow,* to concentrate fully on her newfound musical endeavor.

After some time spent jamming as a duo, Heather D'Angelo (vocals, drum machine, and keyboards) and Sung Bin Park (keyboard and vocals) started sitting in on various practice sessions, ultimately joining the Casio-loving crew. Together, Au Revoir Simone based its attack around the simple formula of a heavy dose of keyboards, melodious voices, and electronic drum beats to make warm and elegant pop songs that draw their influence from a variety of acts, including alt rockers Stereolab, The Beach Boys, **Lo-fi** act **Pavement**, and quirky indie rock band **Modest Mouse**.

The quartet started playing local shows around town before Park decided to leave in January 2005 to pursue other projects. Au Revoir Simone pressed on as a trio and continued honing its skills, eventually self-releasing an eight-song mini-LP in June 2006 called *Verses of Comfort, Assurance & Salvation*. The album, which was recorded in a friend's basement apartment using a rigged-up shower stall as a makeshift vocal booth, appeared that fall in Europe through London-based indie Moshi Moshi Records. Due in part to the label support overseas, the band began fostering a respectable international audience, in addition to steadily working the indie rock crowds back home.

As already states, Au Revoir Simone's song "Through the Backyards" was included in the second season finale of *Grey's Anatomy,* which aired in May 2006. The group played shows at home and abroad with fellow Brooklynites We Are Scientists, including a sold-out run of overseas dates in late 2006. Touring continued throughout 2007, making a stop at Austin's **South by Southwest (SXSW)** music festival that spring and sharing gigs with Texan **indie pop** group Voxtrot into the summer. The single "Fallen Snow" surfaced in February 2007 in the United Kingdom, preceding the release of its formal debut album there that March, *The Bird of Music*. The album did not appear stateside until the spring when Au Revoir Simone issued it through its own label, Our Secret Record Company. Written and recorded over the previous year, *The Bird of Music* was a more organic recording that expanded on Au Revoir Simone's past arrangements by using strings, vibraphone, cymbals, and more to create its memorable songs. In 2007, Au Revoir Simone performed live on stage with Hollywood director David Lynch (who was interviewed while the trio played) before setting out on an extensive tour, during which the trio was the opening act for the band **Air**.

In 2008, the trio's music was included in Barnes & Noble's new multimedia upstart called "Barnes & Noble Studio," an online feature that showcases up-and-coming musicians. That same year, the girls teamed up with **The Shins** and **Devendra Banhart** for their charity project, Yellow Bird Project, which sells T-shirts designed by musicians to benefit a charity of the group's choice.

Further Reading: http://wearescientists.com; http://www.aurevoirsimone.com; http://www.dirtyonpurpose.com; http://www.modestmouse.com; http://www. moshimoshimusic.com/artists/au-revoir-simone; http://www.stereolab.co.uk.

AZTEC CAMERA

Members came and went from this dream pop/new wave outfit, but founding member—essentially the heart and soul of the group—Roddy Frame, remained through the thick and thin, often being the one to pick up the pieces and put it all together again to release full albums worth of material himself. Frame, a Scottish singer/songwriter with noteworthy guitar skills and a gift for lyric writing (he cites English musician Elvis Costello as one of his major influences and inspirations), created acoustic-driven music that garnered the attention of Glasgow-based Postcard Records, a label credited with creating and cultivating the **indie pop** genre.

Formed in the early 1980s, Aztec Camera—Frame and founding members drummer Dave Mulholland and bassist Campbell Owen and the part-time member guitarist Malcolm Ross—released a couple of singles on Postcard before signing to **Rough Trade Records**. Aztec Camera's debut full-length album, *High Land, Hard Rain,* was released in 1983; it showcased Frame's guitar chops and skills for playing jazz-style riffs, cementing the group as purveyors of high-energy, catchy indie guitar rock that helped it stand apart from the rest of the indie rock pack of that era. During the time of the release of *Rain,* Frame (who had long been a favorite of the British music press) was just 19 years old; consequently, several critics claimed he was "ahead of his time."

Aztec Camera released an album nearly every year afterward, for a total of six albums throughout its career. Each and every release seemed to be, though, the result of one person's blood, sweat, and tears—Frame, who played on and wrote nearly every track on the group's releases in the wake of the revolving door of departing band members. *Knife*'s (1984) emotive, poetic lyrics were a fitting juxtaposition to *Love* (1987), a mature album that showed Frame drawing on soul music and experimenting with keyboard sounds.

The turn of the century released a pensive, more sensitive than ever Frame with *Stray* (1990), an album that featured lush guitar sections and reconfirming fans' theories that Frame would indeed leave a timeless mark on the indie genre.

Dreamland (1993) was not necessarily one of Aztec Camera's standout releases, but, like the rest of the group's discography, it was worthy of a few spins—even just to step inside Frame's eclectic mind for a few songs. *Frestonia* (1995) (named for the tiny London neighborhood in Notting Hill), however, was considered Aztec Camera's best release; the deep, captivating album had fans up in arms, claiming Frame was one of the decade's most unappreciated artists.

After years of going it alone, Frame decided to make his solo efforts official. He parted ways with the group's label in 1998 for his debut solo album, *North Star,* an acoustic record on which Frame stepped out from behind the lens of Aztec Camera and stood out on his own. The Clash guitarist Mick Jones made a cameo appearance on the group's 1999 record, *The Best of Aztec Camera,* a compilation of tracks from the group's career that included Frame's cover of the 1980s Van Halen (during the David Lee Roth days) hit "Jump."

Frame's first solo EP, *Surf,* was released in 2002, and his sophomore album, *Western Skies* (2006), showcased an even deeper Frame playing his signature acoustic soulful songs. In 2005, Aztec Camera's final release surfaced in the form of the live album *Live at Ronnie Scotts.* Frame released a record he recorded at the Blue Note Jazz Club in Japan, *Live at The Blue Note, Osaka* in 2006.

Further Reading: Roberts, David. *British Hit Singles and Albums (Guinness 18th Edition).* London: Guinness World Records Limited, 2005; http://www.myspace.com/theroddyframe; http://www.roddyframe.com.

AZURE RAY

Saddle Creek Records recording artists Azure Ray's brand of dream pop attracted fans, among them electronica giant Moby, with whom the duo collaborated on the track "The Great Escape" on his 2002 album, *18.* Bandmates Orenda Fink and Maria Taylor originally met at the tender age of 15 at a fine arts high school in Birmingham, Alabama, where the two became fast friends and musical collaborators. The duo performed as an acoustic duo before later adding drummer Louis Schefano and bassist Greg Nobles under the band name Little Red Rocket, whose sugary alternative pop was strikingly similar to other female-fronted acts like Belly or Veruca Salt.

Together the quartet released two albums, but at some point during Little Red Rocket's life, Fink and Taylor were determined to play an acoustic gig together in Athens, Georgia. Loving what he heard, Brian Causey of the Athens-based label Warm Records urged the two to release an album of their material. Meant to be only a side project, their first album as Azure Ray for the label was released by the two friends in 2001. The stripped-down and self-titled record found the newly formed Azure Ray crafting naturally warm and understated indie rock with the help of producer Eric Bachmann of Crooked Fingers and **Archers of Loaf** fame. Not only were their confessional songs well received by critics, but the gals also found Azure Ray to be a much better fit than Little Red Rocket, which fizzled while Azure Ray blossomed.

Azure Ray's eponymous album made a fan out of **Bright Eyes**' mastermind **Conor Oberst**, who invited Fink and Taylor to open for his indie rock band. They accepted, eventually going so far as to join **Conor Oberst** on stage as part of **Bright Eyes**' rotating lineup of musicians. Over time, Fink and Taylor would continue playing with **Bright Eyes** as well as performing in other outside projects like the moody pop of Now It's Overheard and the improvisational rock of Japancakes. Unsurprisingly, though, Azure Ray's connection to **Conor Oberst** did not stop with live gigs, and the two ultimately signed with **Conor Oberst**'s Omaha-based imprint **Saddle Creek Records**.

The gorgeous six-song EP *November* was released through the label in January 2002, featuring collaborations with producer Andy LeMaster of Now It's Overheard. Azure Ray's sophomore album, *Burn and Shiver,* followed that spring through Warm Records, and by working again with Bachmann, Azure Ray achieved a record where the breathy vocals were complemented with added instrumentation and slightly slicker production. Outside of the indie rock scene, Azure Ray collaborated, as previously stated, with techno figurehead Moby on the song "The Great Escape" from his 2002 album, *18,* and Azure Ray later shared the stage with him and the dream pop group Her Space Holiday in support of *Burn and Shiver.*

Azure Ray played at the 2002 **CMJ Music Marathon** in New York City, later touring with **Cursive** front man Tim Kasher's side project the Good Life. The pair soon relocated from Athens to Omaha, where they could be active members of the area's growing musical scene, not to mention living closer to their friends and home base of their new label. Azure Ray's third album, *Hold on Love,* appeared in the fall of 2003, mixing the ethereal aspects of the band's past work with a slightly more upbeat approach. Critics celebrated the album's emotional depth and the "cinematic" quality of the songs, which proved that the group has more talent up its sleeves than previously anticipated.

The talented duo's members branched out on their own in 2004, with Maria releasing her first solo effort, *Lynn Teeter Flower,* on **Saddle Creek Records** and Orenda putting out her debut solo album, *Invisible Ones,* in 2005. Orenda also formed another group called Art in Manila that same year.

Further Reading: http://azureraymusic.com; http://herspaceholiday.com; http://moby. com; http://www.nowitsoverhead.com; http://www.saddle-creek.com; http://www. thewarmsupercomputer.com.

B

BABYSHAMBLES

This British rock 'n' roll band is more than a former side project for ex-Libertines singer Pete Doherty. The act has produced music that has not only topped the U.K. charts, it has also produced songs (with clever, drink, drug, and down-and-out experience-heavy lyrics) that have critics heralding the group's Clash-inspired sounds and musical chops. The group's overall talent, it seems, might just be good enough to top references to Doherty's other career as a tabloid regular. Despite having been in and out of both jail and rehab numerous times, Doherty (who has been referred to as Mr. Kate Moss) has managed to tour endlessly and front the indie quartet, which formed in 2004. The Libertines, in which Doherty had been a member since its inception in 2001, disbanded under Doherty's increasing drug abuse and repeat legal and jail troubles.

Named for the U.K. beverage Babycham and a nickname given to Doherty by his musician friends, Babyshambles—Doherty (vocals/guitar), Drew McConnell (bass), Mick Whitnall (guitar), and Adam Ficek (drums)—released its self-titled debut single in the spring of 2004 on High Society Records. Only 1,000 copies of the single (which hit #8 on the U.K. charts the first week of its release) were made available; the rare single currently goes for upwards of a $100 on online auction sites. The raucous quartet released its follow-up single, "Kilimanjaro," later that same year on the London-based independent label **Rough Trade Records**.

As the success of the band gained momentum, so did Doherty's drug habit. "Kilimanjaro" entered the U.K. charts, and the group appeared on the popular U.K. TV music program *Top of the Pops*. Yet while the group attracted accolades and planned extensive tours, Doherty attracted the attention of the law and the band underwent extensive lineup changes.

Babyshambles toured relentlessly in 2004, and rumors abounded that the need for the lengthy tour schedule was related to Doherty's expensive drug habit. A riot broke out during a gig at the Astoria in London, and during another gig in Blackpool, Babyshambles was forced to leave the stage because Doherty was too intoxicated to perform. Original member Gemma Clarke left the band after expressing her concerns over the label's inability to control Doherty's drug addiction. She was replaced by new member Adam Ficek, while another founding member of the group, Doherty's one-time Libertines bandmate, Steve Scarborough, eventually left the band as well.

On the eve of the release of Babyshambles' successful 2005 EP, *F- -k Forever* (the single reached #4 on the U.K. charts and topped out at #10 on the BBC Radio

1 Album charts), Doherty and musician Alan Wass were arrested on charges they assaulted documentary filmmaker Max Carlish, who had made an unauthorized documentary about Doherty called *Stalking Pete Doherty*. Doherty was forced to pay a hefty fine, and he spent a few days in jail. The charges against Doherty were eventually dropped, but while on tour that year (during which the group played the U.K. Wireless Festival, the Shockwaves NME Awards, and a Tsunami benefit with opening act Littl'ans), police raided the Babyshambles tour bus and Doherty was charged with class A possession; the wide-eyed, svelt singer claimed the drugs were prescribed to him by a physician to help him overcome alcoholism. Following the incident, Sir Elton John reportedly told the press, "Addiction is a horrible thing, it's nothing to be laughed at. I look at Pete Doherty and I just want to put my arm round him" (Virgin Radio, 2005).

Freshly released from jail in August 2004, Doherty and the band began work on their debut album, *Down in Albion,* which was released on **Rough Trade Records** in late 2005. Doherty, who has published several works of poetry, also started releasing books of collections from his personal diaries; the collections, which he titled *The Books of Albion: The Collected Writings of Peter Doherty,* are available for sale on the band's Web site (Albion is the ancient name for Great Britain). Doherty, however, was arrested again—this time for being involved in a street fight with a stranger who called him a "crackhead." Mick Jones, the famed guitarist and founding member of the London punk group The Clash, mixed and produced the album, which charted in the Top 10 in the United Kingdom. The album was a mash of Babyshambles's out-of-control rock 'n' roll, which, because of the combination of Doherty's unintelligible, warbled vocals, speedy guitars, and edgy sounds, sounded more like a late-night recording session the band had made while intoxicated. Despite charting at #8, the album, which, like Doherty, seemed to represent the heyday of unpredictable rock 'n' roll, sold poorly, causing **Rough Trade Records**, which was already tiring of Doherty's antics, to drop the band from its roster.

The public and the press, however, maintained their interest in Doherty, whom many have compared to infamous punk troublemaker Sid Vicious. A photo exhibit of the group was featured in the largest photo gallery in the United Kingdom in the fall of 2005; the media, meanwhile, featured photos of Doherty's then girlfriend Kate Moss reportedly doing cocaine in the studio where Babyshambles was recording its next album. The event cost Moss a substantial modeling contract, and she was arrested, though she avoided jail time for the incident.

Doherty appeared on the BBC news program *Newsnight* soon afterward to discuss cocaine and heroin possession charges, music, and the band; he performed solo gigs that same year. Babyshambles soldiered on, though, playing a few select secret gigs around London; surprisingly, though, the rough and tumble band members performed without guitarist Patrick Walden. Walden left the band soon afterward, with Babyshambles claiming he did so to pursue other projects. Babyshambles joined the likes of singer Jessica Simpson and the Pussycat Dolls when the band was awarded with the Worst Live Act Award at the 2006 Naomi Awards, a parody of the highly acclaimed BRIT Awards that gives accolades to the poorest music acts of that year.

By 2006, Doherty had been arrested roughly a dozen times in just two years. Doherty's antics hit a climax when he squirted a syringe that was allegedly filled with his own blood at MTV reporters; that same year, he was booted from an airplane when airline personnel found a syringe in his possession. Babyshambles put out the EP *The Blinding* (Regal Recordings); the video for the single was directed by Julien Temple, who directed the videos for the Sex Pistol's song "The Filth and the Fury." Babyshambles also released the single "Janie Jones (Strummerville)," a cover of The Clash's song, "Janie Jones" (B-Unique Records) by Babyshambles and 22 other musicians, including former Libertines' lead guitarist Carl Barât's new group Dirty Pretty Things. Strummerville is the name of the music charity that was set up in Joe Strummer's name after The Clash front man passed away after a heart attack in 2002.

Babyshambles performed for 20,000 fans alongside bands like Buzzcocks, De La Soul, **British Sea Power**, The Slits, and more at the Get Loaded in the Park festival in London. That fall, however, Doherty was arrested for five counts of drug possession. Moss made her musical debut when she sang a duet with Doherty onstage in Ireland during the band's gig at The Music Factory in Carlow.

Things started to look up for both the group and Doherty in 2007, though, when Babyshambles inked a deal with EMI Music Group's Capitol Records (the first release was a five-song EP) in the United States and a lucrative, three-album deal with EMI label Parlophone Records in Europe for a reported $2 million to $4 million. Doherty also reunited with his on-again, off-again girlfriend, Kate Moss. The two entered rehab together in January that year before announcing weddings plans in March (Doherty named Barât as his best man). Rumors abounded that Moss was pregnant, but to date, Doherty's only child is the one he had with Lisa Moorish of the **pop-punk** band Kill City back in 2003.

Babyshambles was nominated for two awards at the 2007 NME Awards—Best Live Band and Best British Band. Moss and Doherty were kicked out of the awards show, however, when the overtly physical duo was caught trying to sneak into a bathroom at the event. Babyshambles performed as part of the V and Glastonbury festivals, and rumors circulated about a possible Libertines reunion when Barât told a major U.S. publication that he would "be happy to work with [Doherty]" (http://news.bbc.co.uk, 2007). However, 2007 was not all roses and fanfare for the group. Trouble found its way to the group again when police found a gun on the group's tour bus (the group claimed the gun was a prop), and Doherty's license was suspended after he was caught driving without insurance. Moss and Doherty eventually split, and Babyshambles made plans to release an album of all-new material in late 2007. The album, entitled *Shotter's Nation,* was released in October 2007 via Astralwerks Records. It mixed sounds from indie rock of the 1980s with punk and Brit pop and with insight into the band's own personal experiences via emotional lyrics.

Further Reading: Doherty, Jacqueline. *Pete Doherty My Prodigal Son.* London: Headline Book Publishing, 2006; Hannaford, Alex. *Pete Doherty: Last of the Rock Romantics.* London: Random House UK, 2007; Kendall, Katherine. *Kate Moss: Model of Imperfection.* London: Publisher, 2004; Samson, Pete, and Nathan Yates. *Pete Doherty: On the Edge: The True Story of a Troubled Genius.* London: John Blake, 2006; Welsh, Pete. *Kids in the Riot: High and Low with The Libertines.* London: Music Sales, 2006; http://www.babyshambles.net; http://www.highsocietyrecords.com; http://thelibertines.org.uk; http://www.myspace.com/wearebabyshambles; http://www.strummerville.com.

BAD BRAINS

Fueled by the raucous musings of the Sex Pistols and inspired by the reggae vibes of Bob Marley, this Washington, D.C., foursome played as fast and furious as they lived, leaving behind an indelible legacy on the indie scene, as Bad Brains was crowned one of the first—and possibly most important—American hardcore acts. Bad Brains, whose members were proud, self-proclaimed Rastafarians, captured the interest and attention of local music fans in the Washington, D.C., area not just because of the simple fact that it was made up of four Afro-wearing African-Americans who played the mostly Caucasian-dominated genre of punk music, but because those four played it extremely well—and with as much (if not more) emotion and raw power than their lighter-skinned peers.

Bad Brains underwent a series of various incarnations, changing members faster than its spike-haired fans could tear through jars of hair gel. Fronted by the dreds-donning H.R. (aka Paul D. Hudson/Human Rights/Ras Hailu Gabriel Joseph I), a volatile, yet strikingly emotive singer who replaced founding Bad Brains member Sid McCray (who led the group back in 1975 when it was a jazz fusion known

Bad Brains appears on a poster for the 2006 film *American Hardcore*. [Sony Pictures Classics/Photofest]

as Mind Power), Bad Brains led the charge to develop the first-ever hybrid of reggae and punk that eventually paved the way for the genre known as hardcore punk, a subgenre of punk music in which bands like Bad Brains rocked harder, lived harder, and made bolder political statements than its previous incarnation.

The name Bad Brains was reportedly inspired by a song of the same name that was performed by the 1970s New York City punk act the **Ramones**, which held the title of "the first punk rock group" during its 20-something reign over the underground scene in New York City. The longest standing Bad Brains lineup—H.R. (vocals), Dr. Know (guitarist), Earl Hudson (drummer and younger brother of H.R.), and Darryl Jenifer (bass)—impressed the music community with its musical chops, which far outperformed the struggling sounds of the hordes of other emerging punk bands in the D.C. area.

The unpredictable quartet's 1980 debut recording, "Pay to Cum," further proved that its fast-paced, unapologetic hardcore punk sound was too big to be contained on tape—however, fans had to wait nearly 16 years for the cassette-only recording to be released on CD. As it turns out, the band's sound was not the only thing that was growing in size and scope—the band's popularity soared, but the Afroed quartet faced difficult circumstances when its members were caught in the middle of their first political entanglement when D.C.'s city council members enforced legislation banning minors from bars and nightclubs. This legislation limited the amount of shows the group was able to book—not to mention the amount of fans it could reach, so the frustrated foursome relocated to New York City, where they worked with the cassette-only record label ROIR (Reach Out International Records, which is pronounced "Roar") for their self-titled full-length debut album. *Bad Brains* featured the original recording of the group's hard-to-ignore debut track, as well as the hard-rocking track "Banned in D.C.," which described the band's political experience and resilience.

Bad Brains's milestone 1983 album, *Rock for Light,* which was produced by the former front man for the American punk/new wave act The Cars, Ric Ocasek, served as a megaphone for the band's political positions and an even bigger stage for its glass-shattering, bicep-flexing punk music. Split apart by H.R.'s hot-blooded behavior, though, the group took a brief hiatus in 1984. H.R. meanwhile, turned to his softer side for two solo albums. Bad Brains band members were able to put a Band-Aid on their feud though, and in 1986, **Black Flag**'s singer/songwriter/guitarist Greg Ginn's California-based label, **SST Records**, put out the band's back to basics album *I Against I,* which many critics and longtime fans considered its finest work to date. *I* featured more metal-heavy tracks, and the song "Sacred Love" featured an in-cell vocal recording by the then-incarcerated H.R.

MTV featured the album on the channel's popular alternative music TV program *120 Minutes,* giving the band mainstream reach and catapulting its sound to millions of teenage bedrooms across the nation. Still, in the wake of arduous touring and incessant in-group struggles, Bad Brains disbanded for a second time in the late 1980s. Never ones to go down for the count, Bad Brains members patched up their wounds again and teamed up for their 1989 album, *Quickness* (via the New York–based distributor Caroline Records), an even rougher metal-heavy album that featured the group's poorly received antigay sentiments. Relativity Records released the band's first-ever cassette-only recordings on LP in 1989 via the album *Attitude: The ROIR Sessions,* which punk fans clamored to get their tattooed hands on it for its true punk spirit and rawness.

Bad Brains left H.R. at home following the tour for *Quickness,* replacing him on the mic with Chuck Mosley, the singer for funk metal/rock band Faith No More. Bad Brains supported its musician friend Henry Rollins for his cover of the Detroit hard rock band **MC5**'s song "Kick Out the Jams" for the 1990 film *Pump Up the Volume,* starring Christian Slater and Winona Ryder.

Youth Are Getting Restless: Live in Amsterdam, a high-octane live recording released in 1990, exhibited what throes of fans who were lucky enough to see Bad Brains live had known all along—that the band was and would remain one of the most potent live acts in the history of the hardcore scene. The stage diving, unpredictable H.R. took his homophobic rantings with him when he departed the band before the group signed a deal with major label Sony Records for its 1993 album, *Rise.* The album, which featured H.R.'s replacement, singer Israel Joseph, was received with mixed reviews by fans that either reveled in Joseph's fresh vocal style or despised him simply for being "the guy who replaced H.R." Hardcore Bad Brains critics claimed the band was simply "cashing in" on the name that made it famous by releasing an album with only a portion of the group's original lineup.

Bad Brains pulled the plug again after H.R., who had returned to the group, pummeled a fan (with a microphone to the head) at one of its shows in Kansas in 1995, the same year the band was busted for possession of drug paraphernalia while crossing the Canadian border. H.R.'s irresponsible behavior hit a new high when he attacked the group's manager, which resulted in the cancellation of a co-headlining show with the Beastie Boys at Madison Square Garden in New York City.

Legal woes stripped the band of its name after H.R.'s return for the group's 1995 album, *God of Love* (Maverick Records); the feral foursome was ultimately left without a label as well, leaving the group with no choice but to soldier on as its newest incarnation, Soul Brains. (Bad Brains had broken up and reunited several times, finally reemerging as the band Soul Brains in 2001.) The new name, the band reportedly told the media, was inspired by H.R.'s "spiritual" transformation, which well served the loss of the word "bad" and the addition of the word "soul."

The *Omega Sessions* (Victory Records) EP surfaced in 1996, reminding the music community that Bad Brains was a force to be reckoned with—and that its talent far outweighed all of the controversy, legal trouble, breakups, and jail time the band had logged over the years. Caroline Records reissued the band's 1979 Don Zientara–produced LP, *Black Dots,* in 1996, leaving behind an indelible impression on listeners within hearing distance who felt that Bad Brains was one of the best hardcore/punk acts of all time.

Bad Brains' musical output was put on hold until 2002 when Reggae Lounge released the band's first recording since the mid-1990s, an LP of re-recorded versions of classic songs for an enhanced version of *I Against I* that captured the group's classic fusion of punk and reggae. Another blast from the past, the career-spanning *Banned in D.C.: Bad Brains Greatest Riffs* emerged via Caroline in 2003, further proving why the group was such a fitting influence for bands such as No Doubt, In Living Colour, and Beastie Boys, all of which have covered the group's songs at one point in their successful careers. The 2002 album *I & I Survived* tapped into the group's love of dub music, a collection of its classic songs that were re-recorded by the original lineup.

Its 2002 album *I & I Survived* was a mix of reggae and dub music. The band continued to release an amalgam of reggae-inspired works throughout its career, including the acclaimed 2007 record *Build a Nation*.

In 2006, Bad Brains released its official reunion album, *A Bad Brains Reunion*, via 2b1 Records. The group's 1982 celebrated (and much talked about) live show at New York City's birthplace of punk, CBGB, was captured on the 2006 live album *Live at CBGB: 1982*, which featured over four hours of footage of the uncontainable band and its frenetic live performances. The album's release date also marked the club's final days, which commenced with a star-studded performance in October 2006 by Bad Brains, alongside the likes of Patti Smith and Blondie's platinum lead singer Debbie Harry. CBGB closed after over 30 years of business after having failed to win a court case over years of unpaid rent bills.

The year 2006, which seemed to be a year of celebrating the past, marked the release of the soundtrack to the film *American Hardcore: The History of American Punk Rock: 1980–1986*. The film, which premiered at the Sundance Film Festival, captures the rich history of groundbreaking punk such as Bad Brains and its peers, such acts as **Black Flag**, Minor Threat, and Gang Green. Bad Brains perfected its return to the spotlight with the group's first studio album in ten years, the Adam Yauch–produced (of the Beastie Boys) album *Build a Nation* (Megaforce Records, 2007), a "raw-sounding album" featuring the band's original lineup and the very same rawness that pierced the hearts of fans around the world.

Fans were outraged, though, when the band was featured as the "Artist of the Week" on an episode of the MTV program *Headbangers Ball* in an effort to promote its new album.

Further Reading: Connolly, Cynthia, Sharon Cheslow, and Leslie Clague. *Banned in DC: Photos and Anecdotes from the DC Punk Underground (79–85)*, 1st ed. Washington, DC: Sun Dog Propaganda, 1988; Hurchalla, George. *Going Underground: American Punk, 1979–1992*. Stuart, FL: Zuo Press, 2006; http://www.badbrains.com; http://www.roir-usa.com.

BANHART, DEVENDRA

Freak-folk icon Devendra Banhart—a native of Texas who spent his childhood in Los Angeles and in such far-flung places as Venezuela—left art school to create surreal, stream-of-consciousness songs on his own until his friends convinced him to release the material as demos. Michael Gira of the experimental industrial group Swan supported Banhart and released his music, which has been tagged with such oddball genres as New Weird America and Psych Folk, on his own Brooklyn, New York–based Young God Records.

A well-traveled vagabond, Banhart released his debut album, *Oh Me Oh My . . . ,* in 2002. The **Lo-fi** recording revealed Banhart's ability to tap into the core of human emotion, creating emotive, soulful music using just a guitar and a four-track recorder. Some of the album's tracks were created from excerpts of phone messages that Banhart had left on his friends' answering machines while he was living in Paris.

Banhart became a success on the college circuit, and he released the 2003 EP *The Black Babies,* an intimate album recorded in a **Lo-fi** style that helped to amplify the background noise as much as his raw guitar playing and tender vocals. Banhart's unique vocals stood out on his 2004 album, *Rejoicing in the Hands,* a timeless album that earned the scraggly-haired singer/songwriter comparisons to soft-spoken English musician Nick Drake and even American folk artist Daniel Johnston.

XL Recordings signed Banhart for the release of his 2005 full-length album, *Cripple Crow,* a warm accessible album that showed Banhart emerging from his cozy shell. The album art itself even alluded to Banhart's abandonment of his image as the loner musician walking the railroad tracks—it featured a Sgt. Pepper–style photograph of Banhart surrounded by his musician pals in a lush green forest. The 1970s-infused album was recorded with an army of Banhart's pals at a studio in Woodstock, New York. Critics have often said Banhart shares a gift to connect with listeners that only the likes of Jeff Buckley had possessed.

Banhart's leading role in the pysch-folk genre was solidified when he curated the CD compilation *The Golden Apples of the Sun,* a celebration of bands and songs of the genre, for *Arthur* magazine that chronicled the publication's run from 2002–2007. In 2005, the instinct-following Banhart and his pal Andy Cabic founded Gnomonsong Records, a small boutique-like San Francisco–based label that has become home to a handful of artists like Jana Hunter, Papercuts, Feathers, and Rio en Medio. In 2007, Banhart released the album *Vasu deva kutumbam* and toured, hitting the newly established Green Man Festival in Wales, with acts like Clinic and Six Organs of Admittance. Banhart contributed to the 2007 compilation *Guilt by Association,* a collection of covers of songs by female artists such as Mariah Carey, Destiny's Child, and the Spice Girls. Banhart's tour crew usually consists of his full band—which he refers to as Power Mineral. Banhart channeled musicians from the 1960s for his September 2007 album, *Smokey Rolls Down Thunder Canyon,* which was released by XL Recordings.

Further Reading: Banhart, Devendra, Johan Rench, and Karl Lagerfeld. *Karl Lagerfeld: Room Service.* Paris, France: Edition 7L, 2007; Weissman, Dick. *Which Side Are You On? An Inside History of the Folk Music Revival in America.* New York: Continuum International Publishing Group, 2006; http://www.cripplecrow.com; http://www.gnomonsong.com; http://www.myspace.com/devendrabanhart; http://www.younggodrecords.com.

BARLOW, LOU

One of the most respected and prolific songwriters to emerge from the 1990s indie rock scene, Dayton, Ohio–born Lou Barlow was a founding member of some of the most notable underground rock bands of that same decade—Dinosaur Jr., Deep Wound, The Folk Implosion, and Sebadoh. Barlow was also a leading pioneer of the **Lo-fi** movement during the 1990s, when bands were incorporating a "less is more" mentality into music. **Lo-fi** music typically involves using a low fidelity or lower quality recording style that includes raw outside noise and distortion from electric guitars. Barlow was a fan of **Lo-fi** music's sound, in which background noise heard behind the music often became part of the song's appeal. The **Lo-fi** sound originated in the **DIY (Do-It-Yourself)** way of doing things, and by recording his own music, Barlow had created a whole new subgenre of indie rock.

Barlow's first musical incarnation, Deep Wound, was a hardcore act the singer-songwriter/guitarist formed with pal J Mascis, with whom Barlow formed the hardcore/new wave/rock act Dinosaur Jr. (with Barlow handling the bass responsibilities) when Deep Wound disbanded in 1983.

However, years of personal tension between the two musicians took its toll and Mascis and Barlow had a falling out—the result of which was the end of Mascis's involvement in Dinosaur Jr. in 1988. The split, however, sparked in Barlow another musical incarnation—the **Lo-fi** trio Sebadoh, a side project that Barlow had started with multi-instrumentalist Eric Gaffney. Mascis and Barlow's relationship took years to heal—Mascis's infamous antisocial tendencies had taken their toll on Barlow (he even allegedly sang about the drama for Sebadoh's 1991 single "Gimme Indie Rock" and the even less subtly titled "The Freed Pig"), though Barlow remained in the band with Mascis a full two years after their friendship was officially over. The pair eventually smoothed things over almost ten years later when Barlow ran into Mascis at one of his former bandmate's shows.

Formed in 1987, Sebadoh's first two self-released cassette-only recordings, *The Freed Man* and *Weed Forestin'*, were put out by Barlow. A few years later, the cassettes were remixed and re-released as a full-length debut album on Homestead Records by the insistence of the label's founder, Gerard Cosloy, who had become a fan of Barlow's work. For its first tour, Sebadoh was the supporting act for **Fugazi** and Firehouse, during which the group was forced to play an acoustic show when Gaffney decided not to join Barlow and Jason Loewenstein. Fans were attracted to the honesty of the song lyrics and the band's punk rock spirit. The online review site All Music Guide tagged the group "the quintessential lo-fi band of the '90s" (www.allmusic.com).

Barlow's musical prowess was seemingly uncontainable, and he began work on yet another side project around 1991, which he dubbed Sentridoh. Sentridoh put out several cassette-only recordings, including the standout *Losers* recording and a collection of albums called *Winning Losers: A Collection of Home Recordings, The Original Losing Losers,* and *Lou Barlow and His Sentridoh* (Smells Like Records, 1994). Barlow joyously released another set of his homemade recordings in

1995 under the title *Lou Barlow & Friends: Another Collection of Home Recordings,* which featured Gaffney's replacement, Bob Fay.

Barlow relocated to the West Coast in the late 1990s, settling in Los Angeles where he formed The Folk Implosion around 1994 with musician/singer-songwriter John Davis. That same year, Sebadoh released *Bakesale,* its first record without Gaffney, which yielded the hit song "Rebound." Sebadoh went on a brief hiatus and The Folk Implosion contributed to the soundtrack of the hit underground film *Kids,* which featured the Top 40 track "Natural One." The Folk Implosion's 2003 album, *The New Folk Implosion* (ARTISTdirect Records), however, was a complete departure from the group's tried and true sound—harnessing a more melancholic sound.

Sebadoh put out its critically acclaimed 1996 album, *Harmacy,* which marked Sebadoh's first entry into the Billboard charts. As Barlow somehow managed to stay on top of all of his musical endeavors, The Folk Implosion put out its 1997 album, *Dare to Be Surprised,* on Communion Records. Sebadoh's drummer, Bob Fay, was replaced by Russ Pollard for the group's 1999 album *The Sebadoh.*

Barlow let The Folk Implosion fizzle out around 2000 so he could focus on other musical pursuits, but he formed a seemingly unlikely partnership in 2004 with his old pal Jason Loewenstein for a Sebadoh reunion tour (featuring just Barlow and Loewenstein) that kicked off at T.T. the Bear's Place, a nightclub in Boston, Massachusetts. The long-awaited reunion was inspired in part by an invitation that was extended to Barlow to play at the 10th Anniversary of Domino Records. Because the London-based label's first-ever release was the group's 1993 album, *Bubble and Scrape,* Barlow felt it was only fair that he revive the band for the big event. That single show eventually led the pair across Europe and North America through 2006 and 2007. Domino Records put out the re-release of *III,* which now contained two discs—the original full 1991 recording of the same name and a disc's worth of new material in 2006.

Barlow put out his first solo EP, the five-track *Mirror the Eye,* on the Spanish record label Acuarela before putting the finishing touches on his first proper solo album, *Emoh,* which was released by the North Carolina–based independent label Merge Records in 2005. Barlow recorded the album in Massachusetts, Los Angeles, and Nashville, and while the album's sheer presence harkened back to Barlow's **Lo-fi** days, the high-quality production of it leads straight to the future of Barlow's long-anticipated solo career. Ever the workaholic, Barlow also managed to have time to play in additional bands such as The 6ths and Lou's Wasted Pieces.

In 2006, Dinosaur Jr. members Barlow and Gaffney (and the newly added Lowenstein) saw the reissue of the 1991 Sebadoh album, *III* (Domino Records); the remastered album featured the 23 original tracks as well as 18 new tracks and never-before-released songs, demos, and remixes. Dinosaur Jr. eventually jumped on the reunion trail when the original lineup performed together at the Avalon nightclub in Boston in 2005. Dinosaur Jr.'s three albums were remastered and re-released that same year. Mascis and Barlow, however, had played together for the first time in almost 15 years when the two reunited for a benefit show at Smith College on stage in 2004—Barlow probably would never have played the event had it not been for the fact that it was organized by his mother. Dinosaur Jr. released its first album of all-new material, *Beyond,* in 2007, featuring the group's original lineup of guitarist Mascis, bassist Barlow, and drummer Emmett "Patrick" Murphy. Gaffney released his 70-minute solo album *Uncharted Waters* via Old Gold Records in 2007. The band released a 52-song reissue album that same year titled *The Freed Man,* put out by Domino Records. The effort contains all tracks from the group's definite **Lo-fi** recordings on just one disc.

Further Reading: Erlewine, Stephen Thomas, Vladimir Bogdanov, and Chris Woodstra. *All Music Guide: The Expert's Guide to the Best Recordings (All Music Guides).* 4th ed. Milwaukee, WI: Backbeat Books, 2001; Thompson, Dave. *The Music Lover's Guide to Record Collecting.* Milwaukee, WI: Backbeat Books, 2002; http://www.acuareladiscos.com; http://www.dinosaurjr.com; http://www.fatpossum.com; http://www.myspace.com/loubarlow.

BAROQUE POP

The word baroque was used in seventeenth century Rome to describe a style of art. These works of art—painting, drama, and especially music—involved a certain amount of tension through dissonance and varied pitches, which resulted in highly dramatic works that exuberated high emotion and usually included various themes.

Baroque pop, therefore, is a style of music that is considered the antithesis (or the yin to the yang of) sunny pop. This style of music emerged in the 1960s as a counterpoint to the sun and surf–style smiley music of the likes of The Beach Boys. Baroque pop is usually dramatic, theatrical, and even "melodramatic." As ironic as it seems, though, The Beach Boys' later works were considered baroque pop, as the group broke away from the shiny innocence that had made it famous. In the 1960s, producers such as Phil Spector (who is known for his creation of "the wall of sound") and Burt Bacharach became known for their experimental music that later led to the birth of baroque pop. In the 1970s, bands like the Bee Gees carried on the baroque pop torch.

This subgenre of rock also includes music that uses orchestral compositions. These complex arrangements are sometimes called chamber pop or chamber rock, and many modern baroque pop musicians utilize these full string, horn, or woodwind section sounds to add a dramatic feel to their music. This union of pop music and orchestral sonics makes baroque pop an innovative subgenre that helps these artists stand out for their emotive appeal and clever songwriting and even arranging abilities.

Baroque pop sort of stayed low in the 1980s while disco and Top 40 hits ruled the airwaves. But it was refueled in the 1990s with acts like the psychedelic rockers Mercury Rev and the synthesizer-loving English band Tindersticks. Modern indie bands and acts that are often considered baroque pop include **Belle and Sebastian**, the **Arcade Fire**, The Dears, Antony and the Johnsons, **Cat Power**, Augie March, **Feist**, **The Decemberists**, **The Hidden Cameras**, **Sufjan Stevens**, Neutral Milk Hotel, Final Fantasy, **Joanna Newsom**, Rufus Wainwright, **The**

Polyphonic Spree, Teenage Fanclub, Regina Spektor, Mercury Rev, **The Shins**, and Matt Pond PA. Acts such as **Radiohead** have further developed baroque pop for their computer-generated orchestral arrangements, which sound as lush and alive as if they were played with real instruments. More mainstream purveyors of baroque pop include Tori Amos, Fiona Apple, and Björk.

In some ways, baroque pop artists are outwardly and openly staving off the stripped down, bare bones practices of **Lo-fi** acts by adding flourishing sounds to their music and carefully (and even didactically) creating complex parts to their songs. Baroque pop artists, therefore, can fill the arched dome ceilings and vaulted rooms of concert halls with their full, lush sound. Indie labels that have catered to and cultivated baroque pop artists include Not Lame Records, Parasol Records, and the labels that baroque pop artists are signed to, such as Geffen Records, Merge Records, and Matador Records.

Further Reading: Brend, Mark. *Strange Sounds: Offbeat Instruments and Sonic Experiments in Pop.* Milwaukee, WI: Backbeat Books, 2005.

BEARSUIT

Bearsuit, a U.K.–based indie rock collective, played its first gig as a group in 2001, showing off its trademark sound—a turbulent fusion of rock, dance, noise, electronics and **Twee pop**. Bearsuit's unique "chaotic art" approach was enough to inspire legendary BBC Radio DJ John Peel to say, "In an era when almost everything is quite like something else, Bearsuit are not quite like anything" (www.myspace.com/bearsuit). Even so, for journalistic purposes, Bearsuit was often compared to a combination of acts such as British **Riot Grrrls** Huggy Bear, **Twee pop** outfits **Belle and Sebastian** and Architecture in Helsinki, American eccentrics Deerhoof, and even the influential New York rock act **Sonic Youth**.

Bearsuit's band members—Iain Ross (vocals and guitar), Cerian Hamer (keyboard, violin, percussion, cornet, and vocals), Lisa Horton (vocals, keyboards, and accordion), Matt Hutchings (drums and percussion), Jan Robertson (guitar, keyboards, flute, vocals, and percussion), and Matthew Moss (bass)—were also known to wear flamboyant, strange costumes like prom dresses soaked in blood and silver "bear-bot" outfits at gigs. Initially, Bearsuit released five singles and the EP *The Bearsuit Jesus Will Spear You Through the Heart* through a variety of record labels including the United Kingdom's Sickroom GC, its own Bearsuit imprint, the Michigan-based Microindie Records, and Brixton's Fortuna Pop!

Bearsuit was invited to play the Swedish noise-pop festival Emmaboda in 2004, where the group played a set alongside acts such as Deerhoof and fellow Norwich, England, outfit KaitO. Later that year, Bearsuit also gigged in Amsterdam with another hometown act, the alt rockers Magoo. Finally, Bearsuit's debut album, *Cat Spectacular,* was released in Europe and the United Kingdom in mid-2004, and a North American release followed in early 2005. Response to the album's off-kilter melodies was generally positive.

Moss, however, left the band in 2004 and was replaced on bass by Richard Squires. Bearsuit embarked on a full U.K. tour in 2005 along with appearing at several European festivals and hitting America for the first time. That October, Fantastic Plastic Records released what Bearsuit termed its "long lost" true debut album *Team Ping Pong,* which was apparently supposed to have been issued prior to *Cat Spectacular,* but was delayed due to various issues. The gang's vivacious sound continued to make a fan out of John Peel, and by mid-2005, Bearsuit had done four Radio 1 sessions with him on his famous show.

Since its inception, Bearsuit snagged three of Peel's Festive 50 Top 5 hits, which was his annual list of the year's best songs as voted on by his listeners. "Hey Charlie, Hey Chuck" hit #4 in 2001, "Chargr" hit #2 in 2004, and "Itsuko Got Married" peaked at #5 in 2005. Bearsuit's single "Steven F- - -ing Speilberg" came out via Fantastic Plastic in April 2006. Bearsuit proved to be ambitious in 2007, releasing two albums on the Fantastic Plastic Label—*Cat Spectacular!* dropped in May, and *Oh: Io* was released in November.

Further Reading: Schwartz, Daylle Deanna. *I Don't Need a Record Deal! Your Survival Guide for the Indie Music Revolution.* New York: Billboard Books, 2005; http://architectureinhelsinki.com; http://deerhoof.killrockstars.com; http://www.bearsuit.co.uk; http://www.fantasticplasticrecords.com/homenews.htm; http://www.fortunapop.com /artists/bearsuit/index.html; http://www.kaito.co.uk; http://www.microindie.com/records; http://www.thesickroom.co.uk.

BEAT HAPPENING

This bare bones trio was a cornerstone of the indie rock scene in Olympia, Washington, in the 1980s. Famous for its **Lo-fi** recording style and experimental ways, Beat Happening's last name–less band members Calvin, Bret, and Heather (who met while the three were students at The Evergreen State College) took turns on the band's staple trifecta of instruments—drums, vocals, and guitar—singing cheeky **indie pop** music that helped them become pioneers of the **post-punk** movement of that era. Bands such as Bikini Kill, **Nirvana**, and the Vaselines even considered the group a heavy influence.

Beat Happening stolidly subscribed to the **DIY (Do-It-Yourself)** ethic, releasing music on Calvin's very own K Records, a label that is now home to over 100 artists, including **Modest Mouse**, Kimya Dawson, and Chicks on Speed. The label was even heralded by **Nirvana** front man Kurt Cobain, who went so far as to get a "K" tattooed on the inside of his forearm. Calvin (who is also a member of the band The Go! Team), consequently, was also one of the founding members of the Sub Pop fanzine, which helped lay the foundation for the **Sub Pop Records** label. Several of the group's albums were either released by K Records, or split between K and labels like **Sub Pop Records** and **Rough Trade Records**.

The three-chord-loving trio released a series of EPs (one of which was a collaboration with the Seattle-based rock group the Screaming Trees) that launched its career and solidified its reputation in the indie scene. Beat Happening toured Japan, and in 1985 the group released its self-titled debut album, a minimalist record that presented the group's talent for making big sounds with little equipment or embellishments. The group stood by its antiestablishment mantras, but it was Calvin who went just a few steps further when in 1991, he created the

International Pop Underground Festival, an event that showcased about 50 bands that united against corporations' ownership—and monopoly—over music.

By the time the group had released its sophomore album, *Jamboree,* it was one of the most popular indie bands around. Critics lauded praise on both albums, celebrating Calvin's simple, yet profound lyrics. Beat Happening released *Dreamy* (1991) and *You Turn Me On* (1992), two albums that showcased the band's growing maturity and advancements as musicians. Several reviews cited *You Turn Me On* as a "masterpiece," calling upon the group's groundbreaking multitrack recording techniques and nine-minute-long tracks.

Despite the fact that the group never officially announced a breakup, the group sort of dissolved as each of the members pursued various musical prospects—Bret continued to play with the band D+ while running his record label Know Your Own, and Calvin joined the groups The Halo Benders and Dub Narcotic Sound System until Beat Happening released its first record in a decade in 2002: *Crashing Through,* a seven-disc box set featuring rare tracks, live recordings, classic songs, out-of-print music, and live footage from the International Pop Underground Festival.

In 2003, Beat Happening put out *Music to Climb the Apple Tree By,* a mishmash of singles, compilation tracks, and recordings that were previously made available only on its box set. Live footage of Beat Happening was featured in a 2007 DVD, *Rockin' on Paper,* a release by the pop underground scenesters at Vera Club, who compiled a collection of rock posters and concert footage by groups such as **Sonic Youth**, Dinosaur Jr., The Jon Spencer Blues Explosion, and Sebadoh, among others.

Further Reading: Spencer, Amy. *DIY: The Rise Of Lo-Fi Culture.* London: Marion Boyars Publishers, 2005; http://www.knw-yr-own.com; http://www.krecs.com; http://www.subpop.com; http://www.vera-groningen.nl.

BECK

One of rock's most innovative **Lo-fi, DIY (Do-It-Yourself)** performers and songwriters, Beck (the son of a musician and an artist, born Bek David Campbell in Los Angeles, California, in 1970) became a household name with his early 1990s breakout hit, "Loser," a catchy, folk-rap track that combined self-deprecating lyrics (half of which were sung in Spanish) delivered in a lackadaisical, free-flowing, oddball rap style laid over a mishmash electronica sound and loose, hip-hop style drum machine beats. The off-kilter track, which was recorded in just a few hours in a living room, was produced by former Geto Boys collaborator Karl Stephenson; it became an instant hit that earned Beck a cult following and helped pave the way for the svelt singer's career.

Before Beck became a well-known "Loser," however, the scraggly haired singer/songwriter had been working odd jobs, living in a shed, and playing local gigs in coffeehouses. Soon after Beck relocated to New York City, he met Tom Rothrock and Rob Schnapf, the owner of the local indie label called Bong Load Records;

with Bong Load's support, Beck began recording in a proper studio. Oddly enough, Beck had been playing in a side project known as Loser; he wrote the song as a joke, naming it with the nickname that his friends often used for him. Beck used samples from his friend Steve Hanft's feature film *Kill the Moonlight* and snippets from the track "I Walk on Gilded Splinters" by New Orleans pianist/performer Dr. John in the song. Hanft directed the award-nominated video, which featured surreal dream-like sequences of the singer and a cast of characters that included the grim reaper working as a windshield washer at a gas station.

"Loser" had been sitting on the shelves until Bong Load released it as a 12-inch. Bong Load could barely keep up with demand for the track, and even self-described Beck fan Thurston Moore of **Sonic Youth** helped to create a buzz about Beck until the word of mouth spread like wildfire, creating a major label bidding war over the singer, who eventually signed with Geffen Records (home to such acts as **Nirvana**, **Sonic Youth**, and Weezer). The contract with Geffen, however, was the first of its kind—the agreement allowed Beck to release his music on smaller indie labels, with the help of Geffen's distribution muscle.

"Loser'" was added to the unpredictable singer's 1994 debut album, *Mellow Gold*. Thanks to copious radio play, *Gold* was also an instant hit and "Loser" became a seminal track of early 1990s rock, with Beck leading the fold as a creator of a collage of musical sounds no one else had mixed together before—indie rock, noise rock, jazz, hip-hop, folk, blues, R&B, psychedelica, country, and even blues. Beck's earlier recordings—a track called "MTV Makes Me Want to Smoke Crack" and a cassette recording called "Golden Feelings"—have since been made available through bootlegged copies.

With "Loser" reaching fans nationwide, *Mellow Gold* went to #1 on the modern rock charts, went platinum, and peaked on the top ten. "Loser" became an emblematic song for the "slacker" generation, and Beck was a bona fide star. Still, some critics dragged their feet and claimed the singer was a one-hit wonder. But Beck (who toured in 1995 and was added to the bill for 1995's **Lollapalooza** tour) delivered quality, groundbreaking music with every release, starting with a string of hit singles from the follow-up album, 1996's *Odelay*. The experimental album featured two of Beck's signature songs—"Devil's Haircut" and the track that coined the popular phrase "I got two turntables and a microphone," "Where It's At"—both of which featured freestyle lyrics that seem to have been put together in a manic free association-style cut-and-paste session. Beck enlisted famed production team The Dust Brothers for the double-platinum selling *Odelay,* which scored two Grammy's for the blond-haired singer.

In 1998, artwork that Beck had created with his late grandfather was displayed at a gallery, and he turned his musical focus toward a folkier sound, enlisting **Radiohead** producer Nigel Godrich for *Mutations* (Geffen Records). A brief legal scuffle ensued between Geffen and Bong Load, however, since the Grammy-winning *Mutations* was originally slated to be released by the smaller label. But the two parties settled the dispute amicably. In 1999 *Midnite Vultures* saw Beck letting loose and coveting R&B and funk sounds. Songs from *Vultures* appeared in the 2004 acclaimed film *Eternal Sunshine of the Spotless Mind*. On a personal note, Beck married Marissa Ribisi in 2004; he announced his affiliation with the Church of Scientology in 2005. Several of his songs have appeared in countless films, and he has performed on *Saturday Night Live* a half dozen times.

Beck reteamed with Godrich for his 2002 album, *Sea Change*, a softer, slower-paced (but no less potent) confessional album that featured string arrangements by Beck's father. Beck launched an acoustic tour in support of the album and contracted the band The Flaming Lips as his backing band. The second-time's-a-charm Beck teamed up with The Dust Brothers again for his 2005 album, *Guero* (Geffen Records), a work that seemed to encompass all of his varied sounds in one package. *Guero* featured bass lines from **The White Stripes**' Jack White. On the heels of *Guero*, Beck put out *Nintendo Variations*, an EP of four remixed *Guero* tracks featuring Nintendo sound effects.

Beck revealed his artistic side even more with his seventh studio album, *The Information*, which came with stickers for fans to create their own album art. Produced by Godrich, *The Information* (Geffen Records, 2006) became Beck's third top-10 album, a collection of fuzzy hip-hop sounds and funky pop that furthered some people's view of Beck as one of the most creative musicians of modern rock.

Beck toured throughout 2007 and ushered in 2008 with the release of a deluxe edition of his seminal album *Odelay*. The two-disc edition features tracks from the original album, as well as remixes by The Dust Brothers. **Pitchfork Media**, however, reported that the lyric booklet included with the deluxe edition was rife with errors.

Further Reading: Souvignier, Todd. *Sampling: The Real Sound Revolution*. Milwaukee, WI: Hal Leonard, 2006; http://www.beck.com; http://www.bongload.com; http://www.drjohn.org; http://www.geffen.com.

BEGGARS BANQUET RECORDS/BEGGARS GROUP

In its 25+ years of business this London-based record label has withstood the tumultuous changes of the music industry, riding the highs and lows of bankruptcy and hit records to become one of the preeminent independent record labels of the last decade.

Founded by Martin Mills, a London native who at the time was working at the Office of Population Census and Surveys on reforming abortion laws in the early 1970s, Beggars Banquet was forged out of a partnership between Mills and friend of his with whom he ran a "mobile discotheque" (that is British for a nightclub that rotates venues) called Giant Elf. The two merged with some friends of theirs who ran a similar operation under the name Beggars Banquet and, after quitting his government job, Mills found employment at a record shop before opening his own store, where he hoped to do something most record stores did not do—sell new and used records alike under the same roof.

Around this time in the 1980s, Mills and his partners dabbled in side work as booking agents, scoring gigs for local acts such as Tangerine Dream, Southside Johnny, Dory Previn, and the Crusaders. However, in the wake of the explosion of punk music and the rising popularity of bands like the Sex Pistols in London, the concerts Mills had been promoting were losing money, so Beggars Banquet turned its focus on this new genre and began promoting punk acts.

Ever the entrepreneurs, Mills and company transformed the basement of their record store into a rehearsal space for acts like the Billy Idol–worshiping four piece punk act Generation X and the band whose single "Shadow/Love Story" would mark the first 7-inch release by Beggars Banquet—The Lurkers (who would go on to be tagged the "British Ramones" for the level of influence they held over future punk acts). Beggars Banquet secured a distributor and from there the label pretty much learned everything on its own, as there were no small indie labels whose lead or example it could follow.

Punk fans clamored to buy every album of short, hard, and fast music their spikey-haired, skinny-jeans-wearing idols put out in record stores, so Mills and his partners took things to a new level by distributing a punk compilation called *The Streets,* followed by the Lurkers' second release, which entered the Top 20. Beggars signed the coifed English singer-songwriter/electropop pioneer Gary Numan soon after, releasing the composer's material just as fast as he could record it. Numan's self-titled debut release sold out of its first pressing and his band Tubeway Army's 1989 single, "Are 'Friends' Electric," reached #1 on the charts, giving the label exposure that stretched all the way to the United States, where it secured a distribution deal with Island Records. Legal developments with the EMI Music Group forced Island to part ways with Mills, though, leaving him in the lurch, with a pile of debts and no choice but to seek another distributor. Luckily, though, Warner Music showed interest in Beggars Banquet and the major music umbrella wrote a check to Mills for upwards of $100,000, with which the groundbreaking record founder claims to have been able to pay some long unpaid bills.

Beggars experienced an unprecedented high in the late 1970s with hit singles and charting albums by the likes of Numan, and in the early 1980s, Beggars broke new ground by signing the British jazz funk group the Freeez, whose debut album served as the predecessor to the formation of 4AD, an innovative label within the Beggars Group that would do things the way Beggars did before; it exploded in size, scope, and commercial reach—concentrate on signing small, unknown acts, that, with a little support, could become big-name bands with dedicated fans.

Founded by producer/musician Ivo Watts-Russell, 4AD developed its own identity apart from its parent company by signing such acts as the Australian duo Dead Can Dance, Nick Cave's new wave band the Birthday Party and the Scottish dream pop/alt-rock group the Cocteau Twins. 4AD gained momentum —and widespread success—by jumping on the house music wave in the late 1980s with the release of the #1 single "Pump Up the Volume" by the British group M.A.R.R.S.

The former director of dance music for EMI, Rick Halkes, set out to sign rave and dance music acts on yet another Beggars imprint, XL Recordings, which soon took center stage at the whole Beggars operation in the 1990s with newly signed acts the **Pixies** and Throwing Muses. Over the years, XL has gone on to sign some of the most inventive indie bands of the 1990s—Lemon Jelly, **Devendra Banhart**, Basement Jaxx, **The White Stripes**, Peaches, Dizzee Rascal, M.I.A., Ratatat, Adele, **Be Your Own Pet**, Jack Peñate, RJD2, and the English band Prodigy that crossed over to the mainstream with its accessible hardcore techno and theatrical live shows. Beggars, on the other hand, went the route of "gothic" bands, buttering its bread with the likes of such bands as Bauhaus, which is often referred to as "the founding fathers of goth rock" (Harrington, 2005), and the goth-influenced London rock group Gene Loves Jezebel.

Situation 2, another Beggars imprint, was started in 1981 as a means to directly reach the indie fans who were out of reach now that Beggars had such a solid working relationship with its mainstream distributor, Warner Bros. Situation 2 signed the English dance and 1960s psychedelica-influenced act The Charlatans, whom Mills admitted was one of the most commercial bands the label had signed. Situation 2 folded in 1992, with Beggars taking over the dissolved label's roster; Beggars continued to flourish, though, thanks to Mills's unabashed risk taking and willingness to follow new musical trends that could have turned out to be just that—wavering trends that may have lost the company millions. Instead, that fore-sightedness paid off for Beggars. Meanwhile, across town, **Rough Trade Records** was floundering, and filing for bankruptcy, which Mills said was due mostly in part to the label's lack of risk taking and unexplored genre development.

Beggars signed bands across the spectrum including GusGus, Thievery Corporation, and Mark Lanegan, while XL excelled with acts like The Avalanches, Basement Jaxx, and Badly Drawn Boy. The newest member of the Beggars family, Mo'Wax Records, became more of an underground operation, signing acts like UNKLE, DJ Shadow, Money Mark, and Blackalicious (to name a few) in the jazz, electronic, hip-hop, reggae, rock, funk, and soul genres.

Mills and company grasped the opportunity to branch out in the online world via a partnership with the online music site Playlouder, with which they inked a deal in 2000, which allowed fans even faster and more convenient ways to hear and download music by Beggars' artists.

As the twentieth and twenty-first centuries turned time, Beggars signed even more bands, expanding and growing in size as the label experienced a steady stream of success with modern acts like Biffy Clyro, **Calla**, Devestations, The Early Years, Film School, iLIKETRAiNS, Mark Lanegan, The National, Oceansize, St. Vincent, and Tindersticks. Beggars continued to see the wealth of opportunity in online deals; in 2007, Beggars joined several other indie labels by inking a partner-ship with the popular New York City–based independent record store Other Music for its digital download store in 2007 that offers DRM-free MP3s from a seemingly unlimited array of bands and artists. DRM-free (DRM stands for digital rights management) music was the result of a controversial decision by EMI to release downloads of songs that would allow fans to copy and share them across all digital music devices—without having to purchase them a second time. And while naysayers feared the move might "hurt" the iPod or inspire fans to share music rather than purchase it at the record store, EMI's executives felt it was the only way to try to curb the increasing occurrences of illegal downloading.

Beggars Banquet proudly announced its release of the latest album by alt rocker pioneer and **Hüsker Dü** man Bob Mould in 2008. Beggars is also home to Mo'Wax Records, Nation Records, and Mantra Recordings, among others.

Further Reading: Bacon, Tony. *London Live: From the Yardbirds to Pink Floyd to the Sex Pistols.* Milwaukee, WI: Backbeat Books, 1999; Southall, Brian, and Chris Wright. *A–Z of Record Labels.* 2nd ed. London: Sanctuary Publishing, Ltd., 2003; http://www.beggars.com; http://www.4ad.com; http://www.mowax.com.

BELLE AND SEBASTIAN

A talented troupe of musicians, the **Lo-fi** indie rock collective from Glasgow, Scotland, has constructed an impressive career of majestic 1960s-inflected songs, intelligent lyrics, and a blue-collar-like reputation for working hard and playing soft (although their songs are nothing short of powerful). Named for a popular children's TV series, Belle and Sebastian is comprised of founding members Stuart Murdoch (lead songwriter/guitars/keyboards/vocals), Stuart David (bass), Sarah Martin (vocals/violin), Isobel Campbell (vocals/cello), Chris Geddes (keyboards/ piano), Richard Colburn (drums), Mick Cooke (trumpet/bass/guitar), Bob Kildea (guitar), and Stevie Jackson (guitar/vocals).

Signed to Matador Records, which is also home to such indie acts as **Cat Power**, Pretty Girls Make Graves, and **Pavement**, Belle and Sebastian gained

Belle and Sebastian's Stevie Jackson (right) and Stuart Murdoch perform at the 2006 South by Southwest (SXSW) music festival in Austin, Texas. [AP Wide World Photos/Jack Plunkett]

momentum as a band following the release of its debut album, *Tigermilk,* in 1996 (the album began as Murdoch's school project; Matador re-released the LP in 1999). Although the album was made available only on vinyl and only 1,000 copies were printed, it nonetheless catapulted the group onto a long path that eventually led to its status as a staple of the indie rock scene. Just as noteworthy are the group's eccentric—and constant—aversion for being interviewed, its few and far between gigs, and the lifeblood of its cult following, which disillusioned critics have referred to as "The Gospel According to Stuart Murdoch," following the release of the band's 1996 album, *If You're Feeling Sinister.*

In 1997, Belle and Sebastian released an EP of its early demos called *Dog on Wheels;* it reached #59 on the U.K. singles chart. The EP includes a raw version of one of Belle and Sebastian's signature songs, "The State I Am In," which showcases Murdoch's former aspirations of becoming a poet. A collection of the group's three 1997 EPs called *Lazy Line Painter Jane* came next, causing band member Geddes to lose a bet to an executive at Jeepster Records over whether it would enter the U.K. singles Top 40 chart (it just missed the mark). *Painter,* which featured guest vocalist Monica Queen, gave the group the opportunity to tour for a short while.

In America, Virgin Records distributed *If You're Feeling Sinister* via the imprint The Enclave. Belle and Sebastian crossed the Atlantic to play one of its most memorable shows ever—a stint at the **CMJ Music Marathon**—which cemented the success the group would experience into the next decade. The group released its final EP of that year, *3..6..9 Seconds of Light.* The group's subsequent release, *The Boy with the Arab Strap* (Matador Records, 1998), which is named for the indie band of the same name and not the sexual device, earned the group comparisons to the soft-spoken crooning of English singer/songwriter Nick Drake. Several Belle and Sebastian band members were given the opportunity to take the wheel and do some songwriting on the record. Belle and Sebastian was the winner of the Best Newcomer Award at the 1999 BRIT Awards.

For its fourth album, *Fold Your Hands Child, You Walk Like a Peasant* (Matador, 2000) Belle and Sebastian returned to its old homestead, CaVa Studios in Glasgow. A number of the songs on the record were written by bassist Stuart David, who later left the band to pursue other interests. The album cover features a haunting image of a young girl facing her more sinister reflection; some consider the introspective nature of the album to be a crossover into the **Twee pop** subgenre.

The prolific group took a brief songwriting hiatus before putting out two singles in 2001 titled "Johnathan and David," on which member Stevie Jackson handled lead vocals. The single "I'm Waking Up to Us" served as a precursor to the band's soundtrack for the indie film *Storytelling* by eccentric film director Todd Solondz. The album (Matador, 2002) included a 34-minute instrumental track that was written for the film. Always ones to keep busy, Belle and Sebastian members Bob Kildea, Mick Cooke, and Richard Colburn joined Scottish supergroup The Reindeer Section with members of such bands as **Snow Patrol**, Mogwai, and **Arab**

Strap. The Reindeer Section's debut album, *Y'all Get Scared Now, Ya Hear,* was recorded in Glasgow in just ten days, receiving a statewide release via PIAS America; Bright Star Recordings handled all U.K. distribution.

During the band's 2002 U.S. tour, Isobel Campbell left the band, and Belle and Sebastian picked up where it left off, releasing what many critics claimed to be its most diverse album to date. Produced by Trevor Horn, who has worked with more commercial acts like t.A.T.u. and the Pet Shop Boys, *Dear Catastrophe Waitress* sold over 280,000 copies in the first few months of its 2003 release on Sanctuary Records.

The group launched a tour soon after, with even more dates packed into 2004, which included the **Coachella Valley Music and Arts Festival** in Indio, California. In 2005 Belle and Sebastian appeared on the bill for the All Tomorrow's Parties Festival, which was created by promoter Barry Hogan, alongside such groups as The Kills, Les Savy Fav, **Blonde Redhead**, and more.

In 2006, Belle and Sebastian released its sixth album, *The Life Pursuit,* which became the group's first-ever record to hit the Top 10 in the United Kingdom. Produced by Tony Hoffer, who has worked on several of **Beck**'s records, *Pursuit* featured some of the group's best harmonies and call-and-response vocal stylings, highlighting the flute, horns, and even a clarinet. That same year, Belle and Sebastian contributed a song to a children's compilation, *Colours Are Brighter,* benefiting the Save the Children nonprofit organization.

Belle and Sebastian also launched a tour with fellow Matador recording artists and Canadian indie band **The New Pornographers** in support of *Pursuit,* a high note of which was an instrumental appearance at the Hollywood Bowl where the group was backed by the Los Angeles Philharmonic. Matador later released a CD/DVD package of *Pursuit,* featuring live performances from that tour. Earlier that year, the group was the focus of a comic book entitled *Put It Back on the Shelf: A Belle and Sebastian Anthology* (Image Comics) in which a collection of artists drew stories inspired by various Belle and Sebastian songs.

The band's rich history has been collected in the unauthorized 2006 biography *Just a Modern Rock Story*. While its lineup has not changed drastically in some time, the group added a cellist, who also played keyboards and contributed some vocals while joining the group on its 2006 North American tour. While on tour, the group also prominently featured a string section. Long-time band member Stevie Jackson also began work on a side project called NADFLY, for which he created music to complement art exhibited at an art festival in Glasgow.

Belle and Sebastian's music has been featured on the Fox hit drama *The O.C.* and The WB's *Gilmore Girls*. In 2008 the group released a calendar entitled "Toast to Glasgow" featuring a veritable tour of the city, with the band members serving as tour guides. That same year, Murdoch appeared in a documentary about Postcard Records.

Further Reading: Kielty, Martin. *Big Noise: The History of Scottish Rock 'N' Roll as Told by the People Who Made It*. Edinburgh, Scotland, United Kingdom: Black & White Publishing, 2007; Whitelaw, Paul. *Belle and Sebastian: Just a Modern Rock Story*. New York: St.

Martin's Griffin, 2005; http://www.atpfestival.com; http://www.belleandsebastian.
co.uk; http://www.jeepster.co.uk; http://www.matadorrecords.com; http://www.
sanctuaryrecords.com.

BELLINI

Experimental **post-rock** outfit Bellini was formed in the summer of 2001, following the dissolution of the instrumental **math rock** group Don Caballero earlier that
year, of which drum virtuoso Damon Che and guitarist Agostino Tilotta (also of
the Sicilian noise rock act Uzeda) were both members. Uzeda and Don Caballero
had shared a label home at Chicago's Touch and Go Records, and the duo had
previously jammed together on the side, but it was not until the two met up to
write at Che's Pennsylvanian farm with Tilotta's wife, Giovanna Cacciola (vocalist,
also of Uzeda), and bassist Matthew Taylor that Bellini officially came alive.

Taking its name from the Italian classical composer Vincenzo Bellini who was
born in Uzeda's hometown of Catania, Italy, Bellini began building its fan base
with a series of local shows in July 2001. Bellini's heavy, rhythmic, and brilliantly
aggressive sound was more structured and accessible than Che's previous work
with Don Caballero, but it was still challenging enough for the group's **math rock**
fans. The quartet signed to Baltimore imprint Monitor Records in 2001, touring
North America and Italy the next year. Bellini released its debut album, *Snowing
Sun,* in 2002, which it recorded with Steve Albini of **Black Flag**, who had previously worked on albums by both Don Caballero and Uzeda. *Sun* received a positive critical response, and Bellini played a seemingly endless stream of shows to
support the album; while the foursome was out on the road, tensions between
the notoriously difficult Che and the rest of the band were increasing by the day.
This friction came to a head one night in a much publicized onstage incident at
an Athens, Georgia, show at which Che dramatically exploded in an alcohol-
induced tirade directed at his bandmates. He promptly left the group that night,
taking with him the band van and leaving the rest of Bellini stranded in Georgia.

Che returned to Pennsylvania where, in 2003, he resuscitated Don Caballero
with a completely new lineup. Down but definitely not out, Bellini quickly
rebounded from Che's departure and finished the remaining tour dates by replacing Che with ex-Soulside and **Girls Against Boys** drummer Alexis Fleisig. This
lineup wrote new material for the band's sophomore effort, and in August 2004,
Bellini entered the studio for five days (again with Albini) to record the limited
edition 7-inch single (only 500 copies were pressed) "The Buffalo Song/Never
Again" (Radio Is Down Records, 2005).

"Buffalo" served as a precursor to the fall release of Bellini's third release, *Small
Stones,* which was released by the Brooklyn-based imprint Temporary Residence
Limited. *Stones* was again greeted with praise from critics and fans alike, and the
band headed out on the road for tours of North America and Japan with Japanese
instrumental post-rockers Mono. Tilotta and Cacciola returned to Uzeda's ranks
for the 2006 release of its album *Stella,* and though Bellini never officially broke
up, the band remained largely inactive through late 2006 and into 2007 as Uzeda
and **Girls Against Boys** played out gigs. The band, however, announced a series

of tour dates and plans for a new album in a 2007 posting on its Web site.

Further Reading: Spellman, Peter. *The Self-Promoting Musician (Music Business).* Boston: Berklee Press, 2000; http://www.monitorrecords.com; http://www.mono-jpn.com; http://www.radioisdown.com; http://www.snowingsun.com; http://www.southern.com/southern/band/UZEDA; http://temporaryresidence.com.

THE BETA BAND

Formed in 1996 by Scottish musicians Steve Mason and Gordon Anderson, The Beta Band was a self-described "folk hop" group. In fact, the group's blend of rock, folk trip hop, and jam band music earned it far more musical classifications than it had hoped. The group drew an almost cult following and received critical acclaim for almost a decade before disbanding in 2004.

Still, its history is that of indie rock fantasy, but not without the commonplace pitfalls of other indie rock bands—shuffling band members, label pressure, and ultimately, a dramatic split. After the addition of bandmates John Maclean and Robin Jones (on DJ/sampler/keyboards and drums, respectively), Anderson fell ill and also left the band, making room for bassist Richard Greentree.

The Beta Band recorded its debut EP, *Champion Versions,* in 1997, and it was well received for both its musical ambitions as well as for the cover design, which the multitalented Maclean had created. The quartet brought Brain Cannon on board as its manager and Nick McCabe, the guitarist for the British pop group The Verve, mixed part of that first EP. The band released two EPs the next year, *The Patty Patty Sound* and *Los Amigos del Beta Bandidos,* both of which, along with the tracks from *Champion,* became the material for The Beta Band's first full-length album, *The Three E.P.'s* (Regal/Parlophone, 1998). The group then attempted to tell its oral history on the track "The Beta Band Rap" on its sophomore effort, the self-titled album *The Beta Band,* which was released in 1999.

While busy at work on its 2001 release, *Hot Shots II*, the band was the opening act for **Radiohead**'s U.S. summer tour. The Beta Band was now shrouded in enough buzz that it caught the attention of the bigwigs at the New York City–based dance/electronica label, Astralwerks Records, a major label that claims on its MySpace profile to be "the home of uncompromising music" (www.myspace.com/Astralwerks). Having been given the freedom to spread its wings, The Beta Band self-produced its next effort, *Heroes to Zeros* (Astralwerks Records, 2004), handing the final mixing control over to famed producer Nigel Godrich, who has worked with such big name acts as **Radiohead**, Travis, and **Beck**. The Beta Band's long history of experimentation, however, was a practice that, in its early days, did not always pay off.

During the band's early days, when Mason and his crew first emerged on the British music scene, the band was signed to the U.K. label Regal Recordings. Pressured by limited budgets and stringent recording deadlines, The Beta Band's early efforts were so constrained that it limited the output of what the band considered to be its best work. Nonetheless, several of The Beta Band's songs from that time, "Brokenupadingdong," "The Cow's Wrong," and "The Hard One" (all of which appear on the self-titled LP), found success, inevitably ending up on TV series, soundtracks to films (such as the 2002 drama *Igby Goes Down*), and **NME (New Musical Express)**'s annual best singles lists.

Around 2000, The Beta Band was awarded the coveted opportunity to have one of its songs featured in the 2000 cult hit film *High Fidelity,* which centered around the life of an obsessed music fan/indie record store owner. Based on the Nick Hornby book by the same name, the film became a cult hit among indie rock and music fans everywhere.

The Beta Band announced its breakup toward the end of 2004. The band released its final effort, *The Best of the Beta Band,* a two-disc collection of its greatest hits on Astralwerks in 2005. Mason continues to make it into the news often while working as a DJ and playing with his latest musical project, Black Affair.

Further Reading: Budnick, Dean. *Jambands: The Complete Guide to the Players, Music, and Scene.* Milwaukee, WI: Backbeat Books, 2003; http://www.astralwerks.com; http://www.betaband.com/gotflash.html; http://www.regal.co.uk.

BEULAH

One of the most significant (and groundbreaking) bands crammed under **The Elephant 6 Recording Company** umbrella, Beulah consisted of two unlikely people—office mates Miles Kurosky and Bill Swan, both sharing an equal and seemingly unyielding dislike for one another—who formed this **Lo-fi** indie rock duo in 1996. The pair put away their differences, however, when they discovered a communal love of music and they released their debut 7-inch "A Small Cattle Drive in a Snow Storm" in 1997, recording more and more music anywhere and any way they could—in the bathroom, in the office, and even on cassette tapes.

Beulah's 1997 album featured newly acquired member Anne Mellinger (backup vocals/violin) for its follow-up EP, *Handsome Western States,* a collection of catchy pop songs that was mastered by Robert Schneider of fellow **Elephant 6 Recording Company** band **The Apples in Stereo**. *States,* which earned the group comparisons to the Dayton, Ohio–based **Lo-fi** band **Guided By Voices** and **Pavement**, quickly sold out of its first press run; it was repressed in 2005. Inspired by the success of *States,* Kurosky (lead vocalist/guitar) and Swan (vocals/guitar/trumpet) decided to make the outfit a full-on band, adding members Steve St. Cin (drums), Pat Noel (guitar/keyboard), and Steve La Follette (vocals/bass).

The English indie label Shifty Disco released a few of Beulah's singles on the cusp of the new millennium. Swelling in size with about 18 members, Beulah turned to Chicago's Sugar Free Records, with its more aggressive marketing campaigns and wider reaching distribution offerings, to put out the bright, multi-instrumental album *When Your Heartstrings Break,* which the group claims was inspired by the layered orchestral-type musings of such contemporaries as **Belle and Sebastian**, The Olivia Tremor Control, and the Brooklyn, New York–based **indie pop** group The Ladybug Transistor. The band headed out on the road with roster mates **The Apples in Stereo** and Neutral Milk Hotel in support of *Break,* and Beulah's music became increasingly popular with indie fans in both the United States and the United Kingdom for its skilled songwriting and accessible 1960s-style pop-inflected music.

Things were on an upswing for the group until, on the release of Beulah's debut album for the Atlanta, Georgia–based independent label Velocette Records, *The Coast is Never Clear,* newer band members Ana Pitchon (French horn) and St. Cin left the group citing exhausting tour schedules, among other reasons. Beulah rebounded by adding new members Eli Crews (bass), Pat Abernathy (keyboards), and Danny Sullivan (drums) for its new lineup and Beulah's fourth album, the dark, melancholic *Yoko* (Velocette Records, 2001). Beulah shone at that year's **CMJ Music Marathon** and embarked on a tour of the United States with the American indie rock duo Mates of State.

Amid certain personal splits each of the band members was experiencing (several members got divorced and one member broke off a potential engagement), rumors circulated of a breakup if the release was not successful, but *Yoko,* which critics hailed as one of the group's best, helped ticket sales to soar at tours held stateside and in Europe. Pretty soon the hype and success ran out of fumes. Beulah broke up in 2004, topping off its career with one final, complimentary show in Bryant Park in New York City. The group released the posthumous DVD *A Good Band Is Easy to Kill* the following year, featuring an 89-minute tour documentary and live footage.

Kurosky prepped for the release of his debut solo album in 2007. The release of the record, however, was delayed by a series of kidney surgeries he had to undergo to treat a large intestine/colon disease.

Further Reading: http://www.beulahmania.com; http://www.matesofstate.com; http://www.velocetterecords.com.

BE YOUR OWN PET

This Nashville-based **post-punk** band caught the attention of London-based indie label **Rough Trade Records** after much-raved-about performances at two of indie rock's biggest events—the **CMJ Music Marathon** in New York City in 2004 and the **South by Southwest (SXSW)** music festival in Austin, Texas, in 2005. The underaged band (most of the members had yet to graduate from high school) were also the victors of Nashville School of the Arts's Battle of the Bands.

Be Your Own Pet (BYOP)—Jemina Pearl Abegg (vocals), guitarist Jonas Stein, Jamin Orrall (drums), and Nathan Vasquez (bass), who replaced BYOP founding member Jake Orrall—was formed in 2003 in the Orrall basement, the home base of Orrall's other project, the indie label Infinity Cat Recordings. Jamin Orrall eventually left the band to finish college and tour with his other band, JEFF; John Eatherly subsequently replaced him.

Fronted by Abegg, who has since been known as Jemina Pearl, BYOP started out playing local pizza parlors and coffee shops. The group recorded its debut single, "Damn Damn Leash," in Orrall's basement and released it in March 2005. The band did not have to wait long to see the light after BBC Radio 1's Zane Lowe got wind of the track—success followed, as did the three-track EP *Fire Department,* which came out on **Rough Trade Records** in June 2005, the single "Extra Extra" (Infinity Cat), and the opportunity to record a cover of the classic track "Bicycle Race" for the album *Killer Queen: A Tribute to Queen* (Hollywood Records, 2005).

BYOP signed to XL Recordings. In 2006, the London-based label released the singles "Let's Get Sandy (Big Problem)" and "Adventure," and Universal Music imprint Ecstatic Peace put out the EP *Summer Sensation,* all of which served as appetizers to the group's first full-length album, the eponymously titled *Be Your Own Pet.*

Suddenly, what had started out as a spark had officially transformed into a full-fledged fire when BYOP played the Leeds Festival in Europe and then opened for **Sonic Youth** for a few select dates in the fall of 2006. BYOP launched its first-ever North American tour, combing the United States and Canada along with such bands as Whirlwind Heat, the Black Lips, Awesome Color, and Tall Firs for alternate dates.

Garnering attention for Abegg's off-center, unpredictable on-stage style, and the group's blend of garage rock edginess and energetic, catch-me-if-you-can rhythms, BYOP enjoyed the spotlight, performing on *Late Night with Conan O'Brien,* appearing on the cover of *NYLON* magazine, being featured on AOL Music's top "21 Under 21" bands, and appearing in the *New Yorker* and *Rolling Stone* magazines.

BYOP's members happen to have unique pedigrees. Abegg, who has earned the band comparisons to the New York City female-led indie rock outfit the **Yeah Yeah Yeahs**, is the daughter of famed rock photographer and videographer Jimmy Abegg; Jonas Stein's father is manager Burt Stein, whose clients include Mötley Crüe's Vince Neil, Ronnie Milsap, and Nancy Griffith; and Nathan Vasquez is the son of Latin Jazz guitarist Rafael Vasquez.

Lead singer Pearl starred in the independent film *The South Will Rise Again* in 2007. BYOP released its second full-length album, *Get Awkward,* in 2008 on Ecstatic Peace, which is run by **Sonic Youth**'s front man/lead guitarist Thurston Moore, touring in support of the album shortly thereafter.

Further Reading: Bond, Sherry. *The Songwriter's and Musician's Guide to Nashville.* New York: Allworth Press, 2000; Kosser, Michael. *How Nashville Became Music City, U.S.A.: 50 Years of Music Row.* Milwaukee, WI: Hal Leonard, 2006; http://www.beyourownpet.net.

BIG BLACK

No band's noise rock burst more speakers or split more eardrums than Chicago's Big Black, a five-piece punk band that left an indelible mark on the punk scene in the mid- to late-1980s. Fronted by Steve Albini, who later in his career would go on to become a big-name producer, working with such acts as **PJ Harvey**, **Nirvana**, and the **Pixies**), Big Black played by no one's rules but its own—and the group even managed to break a few of its own rules along the way.

Bursting onto the indie scene when the group formed in 1982, Big Black's machine gun–like drum machine sounds, depraved lyrics, and searing guitars laid the ground work for industrial rock music that would spawn the likes of **Nine Inch Nails**. Big Black achieved cult status, though the band was never embraced by the mainstream (the feeling seemed to be mutual, however), maintaining the **DIY (Do-It-Yourself)** work ethic to a length that only the most fervent, hardworking bands could achieve. The group handled its own publicity and management and even served as its own booking agent. But whatever attracted fans—be it the controversial lyrics or the shocking subject matter of its songs—Big Black seemed hell-bent on staying its course, with or without the support of the album-purchasing public.

A self-taught musician, Albini had been pursuing an undergraduate degree in journalism when he decided to form a band. But when the challenges of finding living, breathing bandmates proved a task too difficult to surmount, Albini holed himself up in his abode and, armed with a drum machine he had nicknamed "Roland," began recording a series of songs under the moniker Big Black. Albini, who had at this point begun writing cantankerous articles for local fanzines, had gained a following. He soon released Big Black's early recordings as the EP *Lung* on the Los Angeles–based label Ruthless Records.

Anxious to bring his songs to life on stage, Albini recruited some of his musician friends from a local band he had long admired called Naked Raygun—Jeff Pezzati, who was later replaced by Dave Riley, and Santiago Durango—to join Big Black. Complete with a filled out lineup, Big Black released three EPs on the experimental, New York City–based Homestead Records label. Big Black released its first full-length album, *Atomizer,* in 1986; the album became an overnight underground success, and when it was subsequently released on CD, Albini insisted on retitling the record *The Rich Man's Eight Track,* a name that fell in line with Albini's disdain for the digital format of music.

Displeased with the distribution deal the group had secured with Homestead, Big Black signed with Touch and Go Records in 1987. Big Black's popularity continued to rise, as did the number of people who vowed to ban the group based on its sexist and offensive lyric choices. The group put out the *Headache* EP in 1987; the general consensus within the group was that the album was an inferior recording compared to its previous efforts, so Big Black slapped a label on it that read "Not as good as *Atomizer,* so don't get your hopes up, cheese!"

Worried that their egos and thirst for the spotlight may had gotten too big for their britches, the members of Big Black made plans to call it quits. Albini managed his own recording studio Electrical Audio and moved on to become a "sound engineer" for various acts, and Durango planned a career in law and played with an act called Arsenal. Riley, however, suffered a stroke; while working on his recovery, he released a CD and book. Big Black released its final album together, *Songs About F- -ing,* in 1992, which, ironically, went on to become the group's most successful release to date.

Further Reading: Albini, Steve, Art Chantry, and Greg Kot. *100 Posters, 134 Squirrels: A Decade of Hot Dogs, Large Mammals, and Independent Rock: The Handcrafted Art of Jay Ryan.* San Jose, CA: Punk Planet Books, 2005; Azerrad, Michael. *Our Band Could Be Your Life: Scenes from the American Indie Underground 1981–1991*. New York: Back Bay Books, 2002; http://www.electrical.com; http://www.ruthlessrecords.com.

BLACK, FRANK

If indie rock had superheroes, singer/songwriter/guitarist Frank Black would be "Captain Black," a bald-headed, guitar-wielding musical pioneer who would help give indie rock its long-awaited break into the mainstream. Black fronted the Boston, Massachusetts–based pop-heavy foursome the **Pixies** from the group's formation in the mid-1980s until its unfortunate (and unpleasant) breakup in the early 1990s. Together they inspired college kids with their discord-fueled pop songs, which caused the mainstream to beckon for them instead of the usual other way around.

Black, who also served as the band's principal songwriter, crafted lyrics that seemed to require a decoder ring that only **Pixies**' fans possessed; he wailed about such topics as sex, politics, religion, and pop culture with his signature "yowl" of a voice that helped the **Pixies** to become one of the most influential indie rock bands of the 1990s—and perhaps even of all time. The noisy band, though, experienced resistance from the dominant music channel MTV, which was hard-pressed to air the group's videos. Still, fans flocked to the group's shows, helping it outsell venue after venue during its decade-long career.

Black's tumultuous relationship with **Pixies**' band member Kim Deal wore on the singer, helping to fuel the band's split in 1993. Black became famous for his statue-like on-stage persona, which was as unwavering as his strong personality, which sometimes clashed with the three other big personalities with whom he was sharing a tour bus and the stage.

During the **Pixies**' hiatus in 1990, Black took the opportunity to pursue a solo career, for which he toured the United States. Black's love of surf rock continued to grow, as did the tension between him and Deal, and when the group met again on stage after its brief break the reunion did not last long. The **Pixies** announced the cancellation of its tour citing "exhaustion" as the main cause (as if tiring of one another could be categorized that way), and Black sealed the split by officially changing his stage name Black Francis to Frank Black.

Black released his eponymous debut in 1993 to rave reviews, for which he clung to his addiction to surf rock and crafty pop. Black branched out musically on his sophomore album, *Teenager of the Year* (Elektra Records, 1994) which, in the signature style of Black's penchant for comedy, featured a caricature-like photograph of the plump Black clutching a bouquet of roses and wearing a golden tiara. The 22-track album featured the hit single "Headache," which hit the charts, causing fans to compare the well-crafted song to the **Pixies**' standout signature song "Here Comes Your Man." Nevertheless, a successful record, high chart positions, and catchy pop tunes were not enough to satisfy Elektra Records, which dropped Black once the album's sales started to slag.

Black reemerged on record store shelves with his follow-up 1996 album, *The Cult of Ray,* via **American Recordings** and Sony Records. Despite Black's cult following, the album sold poorly. Black's musical career hit a record low when

American Recordings went out of business sinking the musical ship and taking Black's record contract with it down to the depths of music business bankruptcy. Unable to wrangle free of the heavy anchor of a contract he had inked with **American Recordings**, Black walked away from a recording he had made with the band who backed him on *Ray,* which he then referred to as the Catholics. Black found respite in the English label Play It Again Sam on which he released an album named none other than *Frank Black and the Catholics.*

The New York City–based independent record label spinART Records picked Black and the Catholics up for their 1999 album, *Pistolero,* a complex recording that fans claimed featured Black's best vocals—and his best album—since the **Pixies** disbanded. Black steadied his course, releasing album after album with the Catholics as his backup—2001's *Dog in the Sand* (What Are Records?), 2002's *Black Letter Days* and *Devil's Workshop,* and 2003's *Show Me Your Tears*—all of which seemed to represent Black's expounding of the toxic dark past that trailed behind the **Pixies**' breakup (*Tears* was reportedly said to have been inspired by Black's stint in therapy).

After the weight of years of inner turmoil had been lifted, the **Pixies** found a way to meet on mutual ground in 2004, touring North America and hitting the **Coachella Valley Music and Arts Festival** in Indio, California, for a much-advertised reunion show that attracted throes of **Pixies** fans from what seemed like another lifetime. The strangely dual personality title of the 2004 album, *Frank Black Francis,* which was officially released by a mysterious pair of performers named Black Francis and Frank Black, was a fitting name for this collection of demos and reinterpreted **Pixies**' songs recorded by Black himself. Black enjoyed a lengthy reunion tour with the band through 2005, releasing yet another solo effort, the sweetly titled album *Honeycomb* (Back Porch Records), which Black had recorded in Nashville on the eve of the **Pixies**' reunion.

Black reteamed with the cast of character musicians he had recruited for *Honeycomb* for his 2006 double-disc solo album, *Fast Man Raider Man,* a more mellow recording from a man who had faced his demons—and lived to tell the tale. Black opened for Seattle alt rockers the Foo Fighters in support of the album through 2007. The U.K.–based Cooking Vinyl Records released Black's first-ever best of album, a two-disc collection of his songs culled from his first year without the **Pixies** (1993) through 2003. Black, who toured Europe in support of the historical album in the spring of 2007, released the first single off the album under the name Black Francis.

Further Reading: Mendelsshon, John. *The Pixies and Frank Black.* London: Omnibus Press, 2005; http://www.cookingvinyl.com; http://www.foofighters.com; http://www.4ad.com /frankblack; http://www.spinartrecords.

BLACK EYES

Black Eyes was a short-lived experimental **post-punk** outfit that formed in August 2001. Its members were based out of Washington, D.C., and most of the band had already logged time playing together in various other local acts such as Trooper and the No-Gos. Coming out of the D.C. scene, with its rich musical history, Black Eyes looked to such well-respected hometown acts as **Fugazi**, **Q and Not U**, and **Girls Against Boys** as influences for the framework of its discordant and jagged, yet rhythmic sound. Black Eyes' off-kilter rhythms and dark lyrical sentiments, however, which were combined with the band's penchant for free jazz and no wave music, also found certain inspiration in such various U.K. bands as The Slits and Gang of Four.

The driving forces behind Black Eyes were Dan Caldas (drums, bass, and vocals), Daniel Martin-McCormick (guitar and vocals), Hugh McElroy (bass, keyboards, and vocals), Jacob Long (bass, guitar, and vocals), and Mike Kanin (drums and vocals). Despite their individual instrumental assignments, all of the members of Black Eyes contributed to the hearty racket with some form of percussion. Prior to Black Eyes, Long had been a brief member of the New York–by-way-of-D.C. indie rock band **The Rapture**. Initially, Black Eyes released a two-song 7-inch through McElroy's Ruffian Records, which included the songs "Some Boys" and "Shut Up I Never," which was followed by a split EP with art punks Early Humans through a different hometown indie, Planaria Recordings.

At Black Eyes' first official gig, the band was lucky enough to count D.C. figurehead Ian MacKaye, the man responsible for such influential groups as straight-edge pioneers Minor Threat and **post-punk** icons **Fugazi** and the founder of the preeminent D.C. label Dischord Records, as a member of the audience. MacKaye was so impressed with the group's performance that he invited Black Eyes to record at one of the free sessions he often conducted with producer Don Zientara. After a few sessions together Black Eyes's debut eponymous full-length recording was complete. The ten-song set surfaced in April 2003 via Dischord Records, and, by that point, the band's live show had become known for its uniquely chaotic approach.

The five-member crew often took the stage boldly, standing in a symmetrical shape, with two drummers sitting on either side of the stage, a bassist in the front and back, and one lone guitarist in the middle. It was hardly a rigid setup, however, as Black Eyes was not one for the separation of band and audience. Spectator participation was key—the band often went so far as to pass out drums for fans to play—and their shows turned into notorious frenzied jam sessions with fans rushing the stage. Following the 2003 release of its debut album, Black Eyes toured extensively with local underground heroes **Q and Not U** before eventually hitting the studio in January 2004 to record its follow-up album. The resulting *Cough* was recorded with the intensity of a band on the verge of collapse, its cacophonous proceedings overlaid with brass instruments (most notably a squawking saxophone) in the spirit of free jazz. Black Eyes incorporated more of the improvisational work and dub influence that its earlier music had only hinted at, and the album's tone of imminent self-destruction ultimately foreshadowed what would become fact soon after its completion. Black Eyes broke up in 2004 shortly before the release of its final album *Cough*, playing its final show together at the D.C. club the Black Cat.

Further Reading: Horgan, Susie J. *Punk Love.* New York: Universe, 2007; http://bornbackwards.com/black%20eyes; http://dischord.com/band/blackeyes; http://www.planariainc.com; http://www.ruffianrecords.com/Index2.html.

BLACK FLAG

This four-piece hardcore punk act worked hard, touring relentlessly (often on a shoestring budget) across the United States, pollinating the country with its **DIY (Do-It-Yourself)** mentality and antiestablishment music. Black Flag won the hearts of fans by hitting the smaller cities that most bands would not even stop in to fuel up on gas, brandishing its mosh pit-inspiring live shows, experimental adrenaline-firing punk music, and extreme social and political viewpoints. Black Flag's legacy stands strong as the band retains its reputation as the first hardcore punk band.

Formed in 1977 by former UCLA economics major Greg Ginn and his pal Chuck Dukowski, Black Flag entertained a rotating lineup of band members, the most streamlined of which included drummer Brain Migdol and guitarist Dez Cadena. The most recent and infamous member, Henry Rollins, joined on the departure of then-singer Keith Morris, who experienced personal troubles stemming from cocaine and speed abuse and who later went on to form the punk act the Circle Jerks. Rollins, the group's new front man, a 20-year-old Washington, D.C. native, joined the band after he leapt on stage with the group and gave an impromptu performance with the group during one of its gigs in New York City. Bald, brash, and flailing his tattooed body through crowds at live shows, Rollins fronted the L.A.–based hardcore/punk act throughout its decade-long career that eventually ended in 1986 due to intraband and monetary problems the bandmates could no longer withstand or endure..

Rollins summed up the band's mentality and sound best when he said, "Normal people do not listen to hardcore. And we like it that way" in the 2006 documentary *American Hardcore.* Black Flag independently released its 1980 debut recordings, the four-song, 7-inch *Nervous Breakdown,* a roller-coaster flagship of pure punk rock, and the 12-inch *Jealous Again,* which were released on Ginn's own **SST Records**. Not surprisingly, the music on Black Flag's debut album was deemed "too dangerous and vulgar" by the group's previous label Unicorn Records, to which the group had inked a deal in 1981. Despite all the odds—and there were many—Black Flag found even bigger success when it took matters into its own hands.

Nevertheless, no true punk act's history would be complete without a pending lawsuit. When Unicorn attempted to put a gag order on the album and the band's use of its own name and logo (designed by Ginn's brother, artist Raymond Pettibon, the logo's series of four rectangular black columns resembled a flag), Black Flag fought back by releasing the record as part of a double-disc retrospective called *Everything Went Black.* The band's clever handling of the **SST Records** release saved the day; only the names of the band members—minus the logo and the band name—were featured on the album's cover.

Karma seemed to catch up with Unicorn, however, when the label filed for bankruptcy in 1983. Consequently, Black Flag was awarded all legal rights to its name, and Rollins and crew celebrated by entering into their most prolific period in the group's life span. From 1984 to 1986, Black Flag released an LP a year, salivating its fans' appetites with its four-chord-style, high-speed songs, which further certified famed music critic Ira Robbin's claim that the group was America's first hardcore band.

Black Flag's 1984 LP, *Slip It In,* showcased more than Rollins's tenacious, throaty snarl; it served as a platform for his developing songwriting skills. The abrasive, intense album, though, also showcased the group's affections for heavy metal, a musical direction that displeased many of its fans. *Slip* featured vocal effects from 15-year-old Suzi Gardner, who would grow up to front the brash all-female punk group L7. Black Flag released three additional full-length albums that year—a "live" cassette-only recording, *Family Man,* featuring for the first time Rollins's poetry, which would serve as a precursor to his later spoken word albums, and *The First Four Years*—and the group managed to play over 150 performances despite its near-empty bank accounts. In 1985, Black Flag put out the LP *My War,* an explosive punk rock album that represented the band's best attributes—an uncompromising band that could care less about what other people thought, Rollins's screeching vocals, Ginn's glass-shattering riffs, and, above all else, a group that thrived not in spite of but because of the fact that it was widely hated along with the genre it proudly cultivated.

A new band member joined the explosive fold that same year—Kira Roessler, the younger sibling of Hollywood punk rocker Paul Roessler, who played with renowned punk acts Twisted Roots and the Screamers. Tension within the group, however, grew with the expansion of Black Flag—Roessler happened to be Rollins's ex-girlfriend, and the split had apparently been a downright awful experience for all involved. Rollins, consequently, threatened to leave the group, and rumors circulated that the whole thing was a well-concocted plan by Dukowski to oust the hulky front man. The pair eventually made peace, and Rollins even went so far as to take his new bandmate to get her official Black Flag logo tattoo.

Black Flag re-released the *Everything Went Black* LP, proudly plastering the band's name and logo on the new cover. In 1985, Black Flag put out *In My Head,* a more cohesive album that would sadly become its final studio recording together. *Head* featured drummer Bill Stevenson, who went on to join the punk act the Descendents. Black Flag's other 1985 recordings, the EP *The Process of Weeding Out* and *Loose Nut,* showcased the group's improvisational and technical chops. Its 1986 release *Who's Got the 10½?* was a live collection of songs that included the scathing "Gimme, Gimme, Gimme," a track that poked fun at the "me" generation the group so despised (it was later covered by the alternative rock supergroup A Perfect Circle) and other tracks recorded with the band's then-drummer Anthony Martinez.

Black Flag's standout songs—"TV Party" (a speedball song that contained the word TV in almost every line) and "Six Pack" (an oddball cover of the popular

1950s song "Louie Louie")—remain its signature songs to this day. The band's legacy, however, was not enough to keep the group together. Ginn's growing creative ambitions were pulling him in opposite directions until the founding member phoned in his exit to the band in 1986, noting his plans to start a side project called Gone.

The hardcore scene mourned the loss of the band that defined the hardcore genre in the 1980s. Black Flag, which had been hailed as heroes by its fans and as destructive, poor role models by the police (the group was banned from playing several Hollywood clubs by the Los Angeles Police Department), continues to influence such modern acts as My Chemical Romance, The Mars Volta, The Ataris, and Pennywise to name a few. Black Flag played its final show at Club Soda on June 28, 1986, in Detroit, Michigan.

Rollins and Ginn seemed to make the best of their careers in the posthumous days of Black Flag. Rollins went on to front the Rollins Band and has since released books of poetry and spoken word albums, and he has even launched a few comedy tours. Two albums of material surfaced after the band dissolved—1987's *Wasted... Again* and 1989's EP *I Can See You*—both of which featured a retrospective of Black Flag's essential songs. Ginn continued to run **SST Records**, eventually releasing albums in the mid-1990s under the name Poindexter Stewart. Rollins, meanwhile, continues to be an icon in the world of alternative music. He launched yet another spoken word tour in 2008, spouting his opinionated rants and controversial jokes and opinions.

Further Reading: Azerrad, Michael. *Our Band Could Be Your Life: Scenes from the American Indie Underground 1981–1991.* New York: Back Bay Books, 2002; Rollins, Henry. *Get in the Van: On the Road With Black Flag.* 2nd ed. Los Angeles: 2.13.61 Publications, 2004; http://www.descendentsonline.com; http://www.sstsuperstore.com.

BLACK MOUNTAIN

The Canadian indie rock outfit Black Mountain was a part of the Black Mountain Army, a Vancouver, British Columbia, arts collective that featured various musicians and friends freely collaborating together in a supportive and creative environment in the mid-2000s. Alongside Black Mountain, additional bands that resulted from this communal atmosphere included Pink Mountaintops, Jerk With a Bomb, Sinoia Caves, the Black Halos, Dream on Dreary, Orphan, and Blood Meridian, all of whom tinged their individual rock sounds with various flavorings of blues and country.

As with most collectives, members were often shared between multiple bands, and the roots of Black Mountain come from this principle. Front man Stephen McBean founded the group Jerk With a Bomb in the late 1990s with Joshua Wells, and together they issued a few releases of rock music that often earned them comparisons to such singer-songwriter acts as Palace and Nick Drake, their career culminating with the critically acclaimed 2002 album *Pyrokinesis*. Over time, the group had slowly grown into a four-piece band, and by 2004, Jerk With a Bomb had effectively transformed into a new band called Black Mountain. McBean simultaneously held a spot in the **Lo-fi** classic rock act Pink Mountaintops, but with Black Mountain, McBean and crew mixed psychedelic blues and acid rock into a groove-based rock sound that alluded to the influence of such bands as New York's influential art rockers **The Velvet Underground**, British metal gods Black Sabbath, Bay Area heavy metal pioneers Blue Cheer, and The Animals–era Pink Floyd.

The band, though, felt that art, music, and learning in general could not—and should not—be made distinct from the problems of the world. To Black Mountain, art and music were always political and personal, and the group's mantra revolved around the theory that a little bit of madness never hurt anyone. The group's first release was a 12-inch called *Druganaut* that was issued through the Indiana-based label Jagjaguwar in October 2004. The release eventually went out of print and was later reissued in the CD format.

Black Mountain's subsequent full-length debut was recorded during the winter and spring months of 2004 and gained its release as an eponymous album in January 2005. The self-titled record was equal parts cultural protest, sludge rock, stoner grooves, and heartfelt balladry. For the record, Black Mountain found McBean's vocals being rounded out by the work of musicians Matthew Camirand, Jeremy Schmidt, Joshua Wells, and Amber Webber. Four of Black Mountain's five members worked day jobs as social workers in Vancouver's Downtown East Side; McBean worked in a needle-exchange center for drug addicts. The band spent time in the fall of 2005 opening for British alternative rockers Coldplay, and the following year, Black Mountain released the "Stormy High/Voices" 7-inch single through Seattle-based indie label Suicide Squeeze Records.

The band kicked off a nationwide tour in 2008 and made its national television debut on the *Late Night with Conan O'Brien* show. Black Mountain's latest release, *In the Future,* was put out by Jagjaguwar Records in January 2008; it featured both male and female vocals on the 17-minute-long epic song "Bright Lights."

Further Reading: Borg, Bobby. *The Musician's Handbook: A Practical Guide to Understanding the Music Business.* New York: Billboard Books, 2003; http://jagjaguwar.com/artist.php?name=blackmountain; http://suicidesqueeze.net; http://www.hivestudios.net/artists/blackmountain.php;

BLOC PARTY

A self-described "nu skool Brit guitar band," this indie band's debut album, *Silent Alarm,* sold a whopping 1 million copies, remained on the U.K. album charts for 69 weeks, and was proclaimed 2005 Album of the Year by **NME (New Musical Express)**—all without the support of a major label. *Alarm* was released by the Brooklyn, New York–based Vice Records, a popular music label and magazine that holds substantial sway in the underground indie scene.

Comprised of four London youths—front man/guitarist/singer Kele Okereke, drummer Matt Tong, bassist Gordon Moakes, and guitarist Russell Lissack—Bloc Party's nostalgia for the 1980s shines through its high energy, dance-inducing **post-punk** rock. Some of the British foursome's tracks, however, skew too far on the political side for many fans who simply want to enjoy the music for its surface value, but for a group that many suspected would never be courted by the United States, Bloc Party seems to always outperform the expectations.

Bloc Party's roots stretch back to 2003 when the group, which was then known simply as Union, released demo tapes that quickly made their way around the British club scene and into the hands of fellow U.K. rockers **Franz Ferdinand**, who invited the frenetic foursome to join them on stage for the Domino Records party that same year. The band's 2004 self-titled album was a clear indicator of the group's influences—Gang of Four, the Smashing Pumpkins, The Cure, and three decades of guitar rock.

For a group that thinks nothing of touring relentlessly, Bloc Party spent nearly two years on the road from 2005 to 2007, along the way releasing its debut full-length album in the United Kingdom while streaming singles across the pond to the United States. Word of mouth spread around the band, creating a deafening buzz that laid the platform for the success of *Alarm*. Bloc Party remixed the album the same year it was released, capitalizing on fans' insatiable desire for more. A few thousand copies of the album contained bonus acoustic tracks; tracks on the record were remixed by the likes of Nick Zinner of the **Yeah Yeah Yeahs**, Ladytron, Mogwai, and Pretty Girls Make Graves.

Bloc Party released the 2006 EP *Helicopter,* before putting out its sophomore album, *A Weekend in the City* in 2007. *Weekend* proved the group was a band apart from the wave of indie bands swarming the scene in the early 2000s; its art rock compositions and jagged edge rock helped the group avoid the dreaded curse of the "sophomore slump." And while *Alarm* failed to break the U.S. charts, *Weekend,* which many compared to the ambitious efforts of **Radiohead**, had little trouble: the album quickly sold almost 50,000 copies within the first few months of its release and it hit #12 on the Billboard 200. Bloc Party cut its 2006 gig schedule short when Tong's lung collapsed; the group refueled its tour bus after his recovery, though, and picked up where it had left off, trekking across the world for its 2007 tour.

The year 2008 was a busy year for Bloc Party. The band played the 2008 NME Awards, covered pop singer Nelly Furtado's track "Say It Right," and broke up a brawl at a hotel following the awards ceremony that involved an angry musician from another band and a journalist.

Further Reading: Lanham, Robert. *The Hipster Handbook.* New York: Anchor, 2003; Malloy, Merrit. *The Great Rock 'N' Roll Quote Book.* New York: St. Martin's Griffin, 1995; http://www.blocparty.com; http://www.dominorecordco.com; http://www.franzferdinand.co.uk; http://www.myspace.com/blocparty; http://www.vicerecords.com.

BLONDE REDHEAD

This New York City–based indie rock/alternative rock trio permeated the underground rock scene with its fusion of noise rock and strong-willed experimentalism when it emerged in the early 1990s. Japanese art student Kazu Makino (the group's lead vocalist and wife of Simone) and Italian twin brothers Amadeo Pace (guitars) and Simone Pace (drums) could not help it when they channeled the guitar fuzz and raw **Lo-fi** sounds of their heroes **Sonic Youth** (although fans claimed

Kim Gordon's wails could not hold up to Makino's unabashed screams) when they put out their eponymous debut album in 1995 via Youth's drummer Steve Shelly's own Smells Like Records. The group took its name from a song by the 1970s no-wave group DNA.

Blonde Redhead's signature sound is the result of Makino's eerie, high-pitched voice, framed by the Pace brothers' wall of guitars and precision-like drum beats. The triangle of musicians (the group was originally comprised of four members —Maki Takahashi was a short-lived member who left the band after 1993) gigged around Manhattan before releasing an album that would become a mix tape favorite—the chaotic 1993 debut self-titled album. Blonde Redhead's 1995 sophomore album, *La Mia Vita Violenta,* preceded the group's move to the Chicago-based label Touch and Go Records. *Violenta* marked the group's entry into more sophisticated production and greater alignment of vocals and instruments.

The band evened out its lineup with guest bassist Vern Rumsey, who contributed to the 1997 album, the distortion-rich *Fake Can Be Just As Good.* But it did not take long for the band to strip down again for its 1998 album, *In An Expression of the Inexpressible. Expression* was created in the wake of the group's move away from its initial sound (and its departure from featuring a bass within the mix); *Expression* also marks the point at which critics and fans started to move away from the standard **Sonic Youth** comparison. The group's 2000 album, *Melody of Certain Damaged Lemons* went on to sell over 50,000 copies, helping the group to reach even more fans who hungered for its strangely haunting sounds.

The band made a creative leap for its first album in nearly four years (and its debut on **Beggars Group**'s 4AD Records), 2004's *Misery Is a Butterfly,* a more focused and tender album that featured rich instrumentals and mellowed out arrangements. *Butterfly,* which outsold *Melody,* featured more subdued recordings that inspired some to say that the group had chilled out as a result of a brief hiatus the band took after Kazu sustained injuries after being thrown from a horse. Blonde Redhead smoothed out its edges with synthesizers and strings for its seventh album, the dream pop record the band had titled *23* (4AD, 2007), for which it kicked off a world tour. The album *23* convinced critics and fans alike, not to mention any naysayers who claimed the group admired its idols too closely, that Blonde Redhead had finally come into its own.

Blonde Redhead performed at the 2007 **South by Southwest (SXSW)** music festival and the **Coachella Valley Music and Arts Festival**. The band was forced to cancel the remaining dates on its 2007 tour when Amadeo fell sick in the fall of that year.

Further Reading: http://www.blonde-redhead.com; http://www.4ad.com/blonderedhead; http://www.myspace.com/blonderedheadislove.

THE BLOOD BROTHERS

Offending—and informing—fans with its political and social mindfulness, this Seattle, Washington–based experimental punk/hardcore/post-hardcore band formed in 1997 amid the **grunge** music movement of the 1990s. Front man/lead vocalist Jordan Billie, joined by bassist Morgan Henderson, drummer Mark Gajad-har, keyboardist/vocalist Johnny Whitney, and guitarist Cody Votolato, delivers with a vocal style that borders on the bizarre as he makes his way through the group's often grotesque lyrics, while the music rises and falls in temper tantrum–style from disturbingly quiet bouts of pop and in-your-face, off-the-dial punk.

Consequently, the general populous may have developed a love/hate relationship with the band, with The Blood Brothers winning out on many an occasion for its untapped passion and experimental instrumentation. Drawing from the new wave movement of the 1980s, the ear-splitting quintet released its debut full-length album, *This Adultery Is Ripe,* on the Kansas City, Missouri independent record label Second Nature/Sound Virus in 2000. On *Adultery,* the Blood Brothers brought new meaning to chaos and explosive music, hitting fans with a pungent album possessing a raw energy unequaled by many save for the explosive El Paso, Texas indie/rock group **At the Drive-In**.

On 2002's *March on Electric Children* (Three One G Records) The Blood Brothers delivered a double dose of vocal action with Billie's and Whitney's glass-shattering voices careening through the band's aggressive wall of hardcore sound. The Blood Brothers signed to ARTISTdirect Records for the group's third proper full-length, *. . . Burn, Piano Island, Burn* (2003), a critically acclaimed release that satiated its increasingly growing (and loyal) underground fan base. For *Burn,* The Blood Brothers teamed up with producer Ross Robinson, who has fine-tuned albums by KoRn, Slipknot, and Limp Bizkit.

Always striving to stretch the hardcore genre and sound (and possibly to create a ripple effect from the shock or awe affect their striking album art incurred), The Blood Brothers released a string of notable EPs and 7-inches before putting out its most notable album to date, 2004's *Crimes* on dance, electronica, hip hop, rock and pop label V2 Music. The success of *Crimes* helped the band—the members had plans to write songs that would be fun to play live when they started working on the album—cast an even wider net, with gigs stretching far across the United States with the likes of modern prog/hard rock act Coheed and Cambria. *Crimes* was recorded with producer John Goodmanson, who has worked with such bands as **Blonde Redhead** and **Sleater-Kinney**. The album's standout single, "Trash Fla-vored Trash," served as the band's mud-slinging homage to its much-abhorred topic, the nightly news.

The Blood Brothers toured with noise/indie act **. . . And You Will Know Us By the Trail of Dead** from 2006 through 2007 before heading over to Europe in 2007 in support of the group's most recent release, *Young Machetes* (V2), which the band worked on with **Fugazi**'s songwriter/guitarist Guy Picciotto. With *Machetes,* the Blood Brothers sang straight to the heart of the subculture of modern youth, switching gears like a high-strung teenager with attention deficit disorder, proving, however, that the band did not falter by putting the cart (experimental-ism) before the horse (song construction).

The Blood Brothers officially announced the group's breakup in November 2007; each member is working on various side projects—Whitney runs the

Crystal City Clothing company and has played in the group Neon Blonde, a musical collective that includes members of the **Yeah Yeah Yeahs**. Other Blood members have collaborated with Neon Blonde, too, as well as bands like hardcore supergroup Head Wound City, of which Billie and Votolato are members.

Further Reading: http://www.myspace.com/headwoundcity; http://www.myspace.com/thebloodbrothersband; http://www.secondnaturerecordings.com; http://www.thebloodbrothers.com; http://www.v2music.com.

BLUNT, JAMES

British singer-songwriter James Blunt (originally spelled "Blount") became the first British performer in over a decade to top the U.S. charts with his hit song, "You're Beautiful." His songs transcended the indie world and his blend of pop, folk, and rock music sustained his popularity and helped increase the airplay of his songs on college and mainstream radio.

Blunt was born in a military hospital in Tidworth, Wiltshire, England, on February 22, 1974. His family had such a long enough tradition of military service that it would have been a stretch for James's parents to think that their son would grow up to be a chart-topping musician. In fact, early on, it would have been a far-fetched proposition even to James himself. Growing up, popular music was not a welcome part of the family's household, as his father felt that all music was just frivolous and unnecessary noise. About the only exposure James had as a child to anything resembling songs on the radio was a handful of Beach Boys albums and American folk singer Don McClean's classic song, "American Pie."

But even if a young James was quite out of tune with the popular music that his friends enjoyed, his mother still felt it was important for him to learn how to play instruments. She started his musical education early, and at age 3 James picked up the recorder. Violin lessons followed at age 5, and after being sent away to boarding school two years later (he attended the famed Harrow School in North London), James began playing piano. At school, he excelled in the subjects of math and science, but following his participation in a school musical, James was hooked on music. He knew he wanted to grow up to be a musician, and he immersed himself in as much of it as possible. Outside of the classroom, James's buddies at school helped to begin his education in the world of popular music, introducing him to such big-name artists as Pink Floyd, the Rolling Stones, and Queen.

At age 14, James picked up a friend's guitar and began teaching himself to play by playing along to famed Seattle **grunge** band **Nirvana**'s classic album *Nevermind*. He wrote his first song soon after, and in no time at all, James had become something of a nuisance to his teachers, since they knew that any music heard drifting around the halls at night was invariably coming from him. At age 16, James earned his pilot's license, which meant he was able to fly single engine aircrafts. Later, he received an army-sponsored place at Bristol University, which meant that though music was definitely a part of his future, so would the military. James concentrated on aerospace manufacturing, engineering, and sociology in his studies, and he ultimately completed his education at the Royal Military Academy Sandhurst.

Though he had no real interest in going into the army, James joined up following graduation at his father's insistence and out of obligation; his prior academic scholarships ensured that James would be in the service for at least four years. He eventually reached the rank of captain and served in Kosovo as part of the Household Cavalry of the British Army. Leading 30,000 peacemaking troops, he was the first British officer to enter the country's capital of Pristina in the aftermath of a bloody civil war.

Along with his gun, James took his guitar with him to pass the time (bolting it to the outside of his tank when not in use); several years later the song "No Bravery" would appear on his debut album, which he wrote while on duty in Kosovo. Aside from his service overseas, James's military career also included his participation as one of the guards standing over the Queen Mum's coffin following her death in 2002; he took part in her funeral procession that spring as well.

The budding songwriter left the army later that year, much to the dismay of his father, and set off to realize his dream of breaking into the music industry. Though he had only a few of what he considered mediocre demos under his belt, the songs were still enough to show off James's haunting voice and highly personal subject matter. Within months, he had landed a management and publishing deal. James's neatly disheveled hair, clean-cut appearance, and handsome face presumably did not hurt matters either. His publishers gave some of his songs to songwriter, producer, and former 4 Non Blondes singer Linda Perry, who had previously found success working with such American pop stars as Christina Aguilera and Pink. She was so intrigued by what she heard at Blunt's set at the 2003 **South by Southwest (SXSW)** music festival in Austin, Texas, that she quickly signed him to her Custard label, which was distributed by Atlantic Records.

Blunt set off for Los Angeles in September 2003 to record his debut record with Tom Rothrock, a producer who had made a name for himself working with such artists as singer-songwriter **Elliott Smith** and multifaceted rocker **Beck**. Through some connections, James wound up staying with actress Carrie Fisher (*Star Wars* trilogy) during his time in Los Angeles, even recording the starkly poignant "Goodbye My Lover" in her bathroom where an old piano was kept. When he was not in the studio, James spent his nights navigating through the intimidating local club scene. He moved back to England following the completion of his record, which had come to life as an airy collection of adult contemporary rock songs built around Blunt's gentle voice, often dark imagery, and simple arrangements of piano and guitar.

Back to Bedlam was released in the United Kingdom in the fall of 2004, and Blunt served as the support act for Sir Elton John on his tour that year; the iconic British singer had only high praise for the young songwriter. Blunt's first single, "High," did moderately well upon its October 2004 release, and he followed up in March 2005 with "Wisemen," which sent *Back to Bedlam* into the U.K.'s Top 20 album chart. However, it was not until the release of his smash hit single "You're Beautiful" that James Blunt became a certified household name. It was a tender yet sorrowful pop ballad written about randomly seeing an ex-lover with her new boyfriend on the subway. The song spent five weeks at #1 on the U.K. singles chart and made equally big splashes upon its release in mainland Europe and the United States that summer.

Back to Bedlam surfaced stateside in October 2005, and it sold well based on the strength of "You're Beautiful." The album peaked at #2 on the Billboard Top 200 and #1 on the Heatseekers chart. Meanwhile, the song itself hit #1 in both 2005 and 2006 on various charts, including Adult Contemporary, Adult Top 40, and the Billboard Hot 100. But for all of the glowing reception and words of praise directed toward him, Blunt also handled his fair share of criticism and hatred, largely due to the incessant playing of "You're Beautiful" on radio. Though it began innocently enough, the song came to saturate the airwaves and people grew weary of its gentle strumming and sentiments of vulnerability. Furthermore, there were also many critics who termed his music inoffensive or claimed that it lacked substance, and they were quick to toss him aside as simply playing commercially "disposable" soft rock instead of being a genuine songwriter.

Consequently, Blunt had turned into a polarizing character whom people either loved or hated. Blunt, however, took it all in stride and simply kept touring, including 2005 dates all over the United Kingdom and Europe. Blunt ended the year with North American shows opening for the slightly funky alternative rocker Jason Mraz, while his fourth official single, "Goodbye My Lover," appeared back home and, once again, soon worked its way into the Top Ten. The song did not formally appear in the United States until the end of the following year, where its naked emotions, buoyed by little more than affecting piano notes and Blunt's compelling tenor, were met only with lukewarm reception.

The CD and DVD set *Chasing Time: The Bedlam Sessions* was released in February 2006; it included live renditions of the ten tracks on *Back to Bedlam* alongside interviews, documentary footage, and videos. That year, his equal amounts of praise and condemnation were glaringly evident as Blunt won awards for Best Male and Best Pop Act at the BRIT Awards and Best Male Video at the MTV Video Music Awards, but he also picked up the award of Worst Album at the NME Awards that same year. As many before him (and certainly after him), 2006 also found Blunt a victim of America's premiere parody singer, Weird Al Yankovic. Originally with Blunt's permission, "You're Beautiful" was reworked into the deprecating song "You're Pitiful" and was meant to go on Weird Al's 2006 album, *Straight Outta Lynwood*. Regrettably though, Atlantic Records went back on its agreement and forbade the song's inclusion, so Weird Al released it for free on his Web site mid-year instead.

Meanwhile, Blunt's first full North American headlining tour in 2006 resulted in many sold-out shows and the inescapable qualities of "You're Beautiful" remained intact, as Blunt went on to be nominated for Best Song and Record of the Year at the 49th annual Grammy Awards. He performed live at the February 2007 ceremony held in Los Angeles, but the straggly-haired singer ultimately lost both awards to country pop act the Dixie Chicks. Atlantic Records and Custard

Records co-released Blunt's 2007 *All the Lost Souls,* which has helped him earn comparisons to such singers as Damien Rice and David Gray. Blunt kicked off a U.K. tour in 2008.

Further Reading: http://custardrecords.com/flash.html; http://www.jamesblunt.com.

BOATZZ

Though the indie rock quartet Boatzz was technically conceived in a Spanish Harlem apartment, the band's career did not really get off the ground until after a move from New York back to its members' hometown of Cleveland, Ohio, in 2003. Michael Di Liberto was a founding member of the New York dream pop group **Ambulance LTD** in the early 2000s, but he ultimately left before the band released anything of substance. Di Liberto's friend Matt Jauch (formerly of Cleveland hardcore band Chalkline) was visiting him in the city in 2003 when he heard some of the post-Ambulance songs Di Liberto had been working on; Jauch loved what he heard so much that he told his friend that as soon as he moved back to Ohio, they needed to start a band together.

Soon enough, after four years of living in the Big Apple, Di Liberto (vocals, keys, and guitar) made the move; he and Jauch (guitars and vocals) rounded out their sound with drummer Eric Mzik and bassist Dave Gibian. Meanwhile, Cleveland rock group Solo Flyer, of which Jauch and Mzik were once members, had slowly begun to fade out around 2004, and Boatzz soon became their top priority. The band's name came from the result of Di Liberto's doodling over the word "Beatles," as he covered up various letters. The word that surfaced was Boatzz, and it ultimately stuck.

The quartet worked on creating music that mixed soulful, artsy rock with bouncy punk into catchy and jangly pop/rock tunes, which seemingly took influence from the likes of Welsh alt rockers Super Furry Animals, 1960s melodic rock act The Zombies, British punks Buzzcocks, and influential London rock and rollers The Kinks. Boatzz earned itself a respectable local following by playing shows at such popular local venues as the Grog Shop and Beachland Ballroom, and the group quickly managed to score opening slots for such bands as Vegas rock act **The Killers**, teenaged British rockers The Subways, and **emo** act Rainer Maria, among others. Along the way, Boatzz almost signed a deal with an established record label, but the arrangement ultimately fell through when the band and the label could not reach a compromise concerning the design layout and track sequencing of Boatzz's first album.

Undeterred, Boatzz simply decided to release the album on its own imprint, which was dubbed Council of Forward Minds Media. The group's debut LP, *Peacock Blood,* was subsequently released in October 2005, and the foursome toured around the Midwest and East Coast sections of the United States in 2006 to spread Boatz's music and name, even playing a spot at the summer's installment of the **CMJ Music Marathon**, which was held in Cleveland. That October, Boatzz was also chosen to complete a two-week tour of the Netherlands, which was sponsored by the helpful musician Web site http://www.Sonicbids.com. The group's overseas jaunt coincided with the release of their four-song EP, *Uzi*, again issued through the band's own label. Boatzz supported the record with widespread promotion on college radio and various music publications, all the while playing regional shows whenever it could.

Further Reading: http://www.boatzz.com.

THE BRAVERY

This New York City (via the Lower East Side) indie rock quartet's music is more new wave than neaveau. Born out of the post-9/11 atmosphere, The Bravery is comprised of front man/guitarist and Washington, D.C. area native Sam Endicott, guitarist Michael Zakarin, bassist Mike "H" (Hindert), keyboardist/synthesizer programmer John Conway, and drummer Anthony Burulcich.

The Bravery's name, claims Endicott, was the result of the singer's oppositional reaction to his peer's communal fears of the future and that "the sky is falling" mentality that seemed to hover over New York City in the wake of the aftermath following the terrorist attacks. The Bravery played its first show in 2003 in a former strip club located in the up-and-coming neighborhood of Williamsburg, in the Brooklyn borough. After a memorable show at Arlene's Grocery, a legendary indie rock showcase/nightclub located in the Lower East Side neighborhood of Manhattan, the band gained local notoriety and recognition and it was offered a residency at the club.

Endicott, who was inspired by the **DIY (Do-It-Yourself)** mentality of bands he idolized when he was younger—Washington, D.C.'s seminal rock band **Fugazi** and the D.C.–based post-hardcore group **Jawbox**—took a staunch stance on the bands seen on such music outlets as MTV, claiming that the music his contemporaries were making was tired, uninspired, and often a carbon copy of other bands' music. The Bravery's self-titled debut album was mostly recorded in Endicott's bedroom with **Lo-fi** equipment, which he purchased at such places as Radio Shack, analog keyboards, and his computer. The 2005 album (Polydor Records) reached the top five on the U.K. music charts, resulting in a string of soldout gigs. The album exhibits the band's darker side and its penchant for the sounds of such bands as The Cure, the English alternative rock/electronica act New Order, and the English synthpop group Human League, to which the band is often compared.

The Bravery released its first EP, the four-track *Unconditional* in 2004 on Polydor Records, an imprint under the Island Def Jam umbrella. The Bravery's subsequent 2005 EP, the three-track *Honest Mistake* (Polydor Records), which is featured on its self-titled 2003 debut full-length album, has become the band's signature song. The catchy track captures the band's electro-pop and rock sound—replete with new wave swagger and pomp—and it practically personifies the group's aesthetics (worn leather jackets, "skinny" black jeans, and Endicott's jet black coif, which some say resembles the famed mop-top of the popular 1980s British **indie pop**/alt rock group **The Smiths**' front man, Morrissey).

The Bravery signed to Def Jam/Island Records in 2005, and its debut album hit the Top 20 in the United States and the Top 5 in the United Kingdom. Amid all of its success, though, the band experienced a snag within its very own label. Label mates **The Killers**, a band that had shared a similar timeline and the level of success, launched a verbal attack on Endicott and his crew, stating in a radio interview that **The Killers** were the reason that The Bravery had any success at all. The Bravery issued a rebuttal, refuting **The Killers**' insulting claims that The Bravery was riding on **The Killers**' coattails (**The Killers**' lead singer, Brandon Flowers, also claimed that because Endicott was once in a ska band, he was not a true rock 'n' roller).

Endicott's efforts to differentiate his band from **The Killers**, and to diffuse the situation, were futile, however, because the feud only seemed to escalate once the media caught wind of it. But what the media did not seem to focus on was the one thing that both bands *did* have in common—a mainstream presence via heavy video rotation on MTV and record deals with an imprint that falls under a major recording company, all while both bands were enjoying the attention and reaping the rewards of having been cast within the indie rock genre.

Despite the negative press surrounding the verbal battle between the two bands, The Bravery pressed on, touring the United States with the Irish alt rock band Ash that same year and receiving accolades from media outlets *The Village Voice, Rolling Stone,* and the very same outlet that Endicott had criticized during the band's early days—MTV. The Bravery appeared on the bill for one of California's biggest music events, the **Coachella Valley Music and Arts Festival** and the Glastonbury Festival, the largest music and performing arts festival in the world, which is held annually in England.

The band remained busy in 2005 and 2006, performing at the **South by Southwest (SXSW)** music festival in Austin, Texas, on the NBC talk/variety show *Late Night with Conan O'Brien,* and at the Austin City Limits Music Festival. The Bravery opened for the influential English electronic band Depeche Mode on its U.S./U.K. tour. Following 18 months of nonstop touring, The Bravery began work on its 2007 release, which was produced Brendan O'Brien, who has worked with Stone Temple Pilots, Pearl Jam, KoRn, Rage Against the Machine, and more. Released in May 2007, *The Sun and the Moon* received favorable reviews from critics. The group showcased its monetary success by appearing on a 2008 episode of MTV's show *Cribs,* which gave a tour of the house owned by bandmate and drummer Anthony Burulcich.

Further Reading: http://www.arlenesgrocery.net; http://www.thebravery.com; http://www.thekillersmusic.com.

THE BRIAN JONESTOWN MASSACRE

Gaining inspiration for its name from the untimely death of the Rolling Stones' lead and rhythm guitarist Brian Jones, this San Francisco, California–based indie/psychedelic rock quintet has experienced a constant flux of bandmates since its formation in 1990 (over 60 members have reportedly passed through the fold). The Brian Jonestown Massacre (BJM) gained notoriety not only for its music, but for the on- and off-stage shenanigans that made the kind of headlines that would make Dr. Phil's head spin. The group, however, openly expressed its disdain for journalists who attached "wild child" labels to it so quickly, even though the group has made little effort to curtail its long history of barroom fights, drug-induced performances, and out-of-control live shows, at some of which fans have demanded refunds.

The Brian Jonestown Massacre's supercharged blend of classic and modern rock has earned the group comparisons to such bands as the Rolling Stones, the 1960s–1970s American rock group **The Velvet Underground**, and English pop rockers The Zombies. The group's playful song titles have caught the attention of pop culture fanatics, too—sample titles include "God Is My Girlfriend," "Not If You Were the Last Dandy on Earth," and "Ballad of Jim Jones," which revealed Anton Newcombe's fascination with the infamous 1970s cult leader. The current lineup consists of front man and songwriter Anton Newcombe (lead vocals and guitar), returning member Ricky Rene Maymi (guitar), Rob Campanella (keyboards), Collin Hegna (bass), Frankie "Teardrop" Emerson (guitar), and Daniel Allaire (drums). Former BJM members have gone on to such form bands as **The Dandy Warhols**, Black Rebel Motorcycle Club, and The Warlocks. Newcombe is the only remaining founding member.

BJM released its debut album, *Methodrone,* in 1995 on Burbank, California's Bomp! Records. *Methodrone* exhibited the group's **shoegazing** sound, spreading its Stones-like attitude and pomp to fans nationwide. A steady stream of releases followed—the title of its 1996 sophomore album, *Their Satanic Majesties' Second Request,* is a play on the title of the the the Rolling Stones' 1967 album, *Their Satanic Majesties Request.* And that same year, BJM released *Thank God for Mental Illness,* which was reportedly recorded in just one day; the album also features rarely heard acoustic tracks. BJM's follow-up album, *Take It From the Man!* (recorded live in a studio) followed a year later. In 1997, BJM released *Give It Back!* on its own Tangible Records label before signing to New York City–based independent record label TVT Records, which put out the 1998 three-track EP, *Love.*

TVT and BJM's front man, Newcombe, came head-to-head on several issues (including Newcombe's personality and demeanor), so the band was subsequently dropped from TVT's roster. As it turns out, though, Newcombe's antics were the cause of the majority of the group's ups and downs. The 1998 self-destruction-filled LP, *Strung Out in Heaven,* was the subject of critical acclaim (it was frequently featured on critics' Best Of lists, and it has been deemed "timeless" by music industry gurus), but despite the recent success, several members departed—Matt Hollywood, Dean Taylor, and Joel Gion left the group, leaving BJM in search of new band members who could stay on board for at least an album, and a label that would grant the group full artistic freedom. Consequently, BJM signed to another New York City–based indie rock label; this time, the group worked its way farther down the island to team up with Tee Pee Records. Amid the label shuffling and lineup turmoil, BJM released the LP *Bringing It All Back Home—Again* on Which? Records in 1999.

In 2000, Newcombe founded the indie label "Committee to Keep" (an abbreviated title for the label's full name, The Committee to Keep Music Evil), a project he was able to get off the ground with a little help from Bomp! Record's Greg Shaw. Their creed, "The Committee stands for everything the music industry doesn't: the artists, the music, the revolution" (http://www.bomp.com/Committee.html), seemed to mirror Newcombe's hell-bell approach to life. Through Committee to Keep, BJM released its most recognized work to date, its tenth full-length album, the six-track album, *Zero,* which featured high-quality production and showcased the group's abilities to modernize the sound and feel of the 1960s rock BJM's members so admired in their own unique way. *Bravery Repetition and Noise* followed the next year, featuring 12 introspective tracks that challenged Newcombe's reputation for being a troublemaker.

On BJM's 6-track EP *Bring It All Back Home Again* (2001) Newcombe channeled the Stones's front man Mick Jagger's vocal stylings via a collection of folk/blues infused songs that were later featured in the controversial documentary *DIG!* (Palm Pictures). The film, which made a ruckus at the 2004 Sundance Film Festival, was a documentary of two bands—the Brian Jonestown Massacre and former pals **The Dandy Warhols**—that was shot over a span of seven years. A collection of over 2,000 hours of footage, *DIG!* was a box office success and the recipient of the coveted Grand Jury Prize. At the film's center was the rivalry that developed between former friends Newcombe and Courtney Taylor-Taylor, the lead singer of the group **The Dandy Warhols**. The film, which started out as a documentary of two similar bands on similar paths, documenting live gigs, tour footage, and more, entered a downward spiral when the bands turned into foes—amid arrests, on-stage brawls, off-stage battles, and down paths of self-destruction—as BJM experienced a downturn in its career and **The Dandy Warhols** were in a commercial upswing.

DIG!'s beginnings captured a friendship that was formed out of a mutual desire to stand up against the "profit-driven [music] business" (www.deconstructingsundance.com) (Newcombe had previously played on a **Dandy Warhols** record before the pair had a falling out), but the very thing the groups strove for seemed to drive them apart. The film features countless hours of live footage of BJM and candid interviews with Newcombe. The film, however, portrayed Newcombe in a dark light—as a heroin user and tortured artist; he was arrested during filmmaking, and the film reveals a tale of a gig at which he reportedly kicked a fan in the face. *DIG!,* however, caused a jump start in BJM's career—and despite the lack of major label support and quality distribution, the buzz created around Newcombe and the band's eccentric antics increased their exposure, which ironically nearly surpassed the success level of their rivals, **The Dandy Warhols**.

In 2003, the Committee to Keep released only 500 vinyl copies of BJM's rare album *Spacegirl and Other Favorites,* which featured six never-before-released bonus tracks. In 2003, Tee Pee Records put out BJM's follow-up release, *And This Is Our Music,* which featured contributions from musicians such as the Lilys's Kurt

Heasley, singer-songwriter Ed Harcourt, and several Los Angeles area musicians. The title for the album was yet another tribute to BJM's musical heroes; this time, the album title paid tribute to the **indie pop** trio **Galaxie 500** and its 1992 album, *This Is Our Music. Music* remains one of BJM's most popular recordings to date.

Keeping the pace (BJM released over 40 albums in just a decade), BJM released the four-track EP *If Love Is the Drug I Want* in 2004 and the LP *Virtual Heavy Pet* (M-Theory Records) later that same year. BJM's 2004 two-disc greatest hits album, *Tepid Peppermint Wonderland: A Retrospective* (Tee Pee Records), featured 38 well-loved BJM tracks. The album does not include the title track to "Heaven" because of legal and copyright issues.

BJM's 2005 five-track album, *We Are the Radio: Mini Album,* was, despite its length, considered a mini album, simply because of the near conceptualism of its contents. BJM toured in the summer and fall of 2005 in support of *Mini,* playing such events as **Lollapalooza** music festival in Chicago, Illinois. But things took a turn for the worse when the band was robbed one night before its **CMJ Music Marathon** performance in New York City. A long list of the group's equipment was stolen along with its tour van and trailer; among the items stolen were a 1960s Gretsch drum kit bearing the BJM logo, a 1960s Fender guitar, and several amps and microphones. Mahogany, another group that was playing that night, had a large amount of gear stolen as well. Newcombe released an online plea to fans to keep an eye out in local pawnshops for the items; the whole of their gear was never recovered. BJM played the gig nonetheless, but it failed to complete a song on stage.

BJM performed at the 2006 **South by Southwest (SXSW)** music festival, and fans have since launched the BJM Fan's Covers Project. Newcombe offered his full support for the effort, for which BJM fans cover BJM songs and post them online to share. The Brian Jonestown Massacre played gigs on select dates in 2006 and 2007; however, the band had to bow out from playing a music festival in Hong Kong in early 2007 when Newcombe developed walking pneumonia. That same year, Anton created his own label "a records," through which all of the band's future recordings would be released. The group prepped for the April 2008 release of its newest album, *My Bloody Underground.*

Further Reading: Rough Guides. *The Rough Guide to Cult Pop (Rough Guide Sports/Pop Culture).* London: Rough Guides, 2004; Thompson, Dave. *Alternative Rock: Third Ear—The Essential Listening Companion.* Milwaukee, WI: Backbeat Books, 2000; http://www.brianjonestownmassacre.com; http://www.digthemovie.com; http://www.hellospaceman.com; http://www.myspace.com/brianjonestownmassacre; http://www.myspace.com/926016; http://www.tvtrecords.com.

BRIGHT EYES/CONOR OBERST/SADDLE CREEK RECORDS

Bringing forth music as vulnerable as a vinyl album laid bare in a punk nightclub replete with spike boot heels and tossed off still-lit cigarettes butts, Bright Eyes is the music project of Nebraska native Conor Oberst, who helped put the midwestern city of Omaha, Nebraska, on the music map when he began making music, which he released through his own Saddle Creek Records. Oberst, who has been called the "next Bob Dylan" by the music press (Ross, 2002), had captured the attention of the indie rock community in the early 1990s and formed his own record label—all by the time he was just 14 years old.

Oberst was formerly the guitarist and singer/songwriter for a group called Commander Venus before he formed Bright Eyes, a six-person large group of rotating musicians from the Omaha area (although Oberst sometimes also performs solo as Bright Eyes). The doe-eyed singer/songwriter attended Omaha Creighton Preparatory School before launching his music career and forming Saddle Creek Records, which currently has almost 20 bands on its roster. The first bands signed to the label were Bright Eyes and the bands **Cursive** and Lullaby for the Working Class.

Fans were attracted to Oberst for his overtly sensitive music, articulate lyrics, quivering voice, and flair for bringing talented musicians together. Bright Eyes (of which Oberst and his musician friend/guitarist/engineer Mike Mogis are the only static members; other frequent members include Saddle Creek musicians Andy LeMaster and Maria Taylor) released its first official release, *Letting Off the Happiness,* in 1998, a recording that introduced the music world to Bright Eyes' fragile sounds and enigmatic songwriting. The five-track EP *Every Day and Every Night* followed a year later; fans and critics alike feted the EP and hailed the docile-looking young man's music as deeply "poetic," honest, and complex.

Bright Eyes (whose real name is Conor Oberst) performs at the 2005 Newport Folk Festival in Newport, Rhode Island. [AP Wide World Photos/Joe Giblin]

The very antipoetically titled *A Collection of Songs Written and Recorded 1995–1997* followed in 2000. The 20-track retrospective, most of which included songs that had been written by a 15-year-old Oberst, served Bright Eyes' as-yet-unreleased songs well, helping the band to forge its way into the **emo**-folk genre, with its bare-all mentality and **Lo-fi** recording quality.

The more focused though heavily depressive album *Fevers and Mirrors* emerged that same year, pushing Oberst's now caricature-like persona and his introspective music into the mainstream. Consequently, the media started wagging their tongues about the musician's penchant for aural masochism, and for the first time in his unsoiled career, Oberst was as a person overwrought with dark thoughts and too-deep emotions whose formerly fresh views were now scrutinized—such as the comment the tousle-haired singer made about **Nirvana**'s 1993 album *In Utero* being the best produced album of the 1990s.

Bright Eyes teamed up with the Canadian alt rock band Son and the dream pop indie rock quartet **Ambulance LTD** for the 2001 album, *Oh Holy Fools: The Music of Son, Ambulance and Bright Eyes,* a collection of fervent melodic songs from three of indie rock's emerging stars. Bright Eyes received widespread attention and praise for its 2002 release, *Lifted . . . or the Story Is in the Soil, Keep Your Ear to the Ground,* a folk-heavy work that many considered a masterpiece—not only for Oberst's raw honesty, but for Magis's skilled production on the record. The 2002 EP *There Is No Beginning to the Story,* preceded the beginning of Oberst's debut in gossip-based media and tabloid attacks when he was reportedly spotted on the arm of pixie-haired actress (and re-offending rock start magnet) Winona Ryder in 2003. A photo capturing the thin singer and the Academy Award–nominated actress locking lips appeared in supermarket checkout magazines and on-line until the two split that same year. The split may have spurned material for Bright Eyes's 2005 album, *Digital Ash in a Digital Urn,* for which Oberst, who had by now become known as "rock's boy genius" (www.saddle-creek.com/bands/brighteyes), turned to a more electronic-oriented sound. *Urn* also featured the guitar chops of **Yeah Yeah Yeahs** member Nick Zinner, whose presence alone upped the album's rock wattage.

Oberst's country roots permeated the band's next release, *I'm Wide Awake, It's Morning,* the second release for the highly prolific Oberst in 2005. Country chanteuse Emmylou Harris contributed vocals to the haunting album, which many considered his best work. Oberst offered fans a taste of Bright Eyes history, a sort of time capsule of early basement recordings, rare covers, collaborations, and singles in the form of 2005's *Noise Floor (Rarities 1998–2005).* The effort proved that Oberst was not only a talented musician with a knack for scoring Hollywood starlets, but a shrewd businessman as well, who was well aware of the historical significance (and cash cow potential) of the legacy he had been building since his early teens.

Saddle Creek experienced a significant low, though, in the spring of 2005 when Oberst insulted President George W. Bush on late-night TV during a Bright Eyes performance on the *The Tonight Show with Jay Leno* on which the group played the protest song "When the President Talks to God." Angered viewers assaulted the label with criticizing phone calls and flooded the offices with harsh letters.

Bright Eyes did its best to keep its head high and, supported by its left-wing fans, the band put out two EPs in 2006 and 2007 before heading into the studio to record its sixth studio album, *Cassadaga,* in 2007. The album, which was named for a Floridian town that several psychics call home, featured the talents of country singer Gillian Welch and Portland musician M. Ward. The folk-indie record was an instant success, debuting at #4 on the Billboard chart and making Saddle Creek history as the group's highest charting album. *Cassadaga* quickly sold 58,000 copies, helping Bright Eyes to rise even higher than it had on its constantly elevating career. Bright Eyes headed out on the road and toured the United States and the United Kingdom in support of *Cassadaga,* which would go down in the record books for Oberst and company for being the top-selling Internet record, the #2 digital album, and the #2 indie release.

Cassadaga knocked off the previous Saddle Creek record holders for best-selling album, outperforming *Digital Ash in a Digital Urn,* which debuted at #15 on the charts and sold 56,000 copies, as well as *I'm Wide Awake, It's Morning,* which debuted at #10 on the Billboard Top 200 charts. *Cassadaga* was set apart from the deluge of Bright Eyes' releases for another reason—the fact that the seemingly simple album cover, a plain gray background featuring a flag-like seal depicting what looks like a comet careening between two pyramids, is actually a riddle. But, when the record's transparent cover is moved across the sleeve, various words and images appear on the album art, which was designed by Zach Nipper, a graphic designer who is employed by the Saddle Creek Record label.

In 2007, the band contributed songs to the soundtrack of actor/writer Ethan Hawke's independent film *The Hottest State,* alongside the Canadian singer-songwriter Leslie Feist (known simply as **Feist**) and singer-songwriter Jesse Harris (who penned the Norah Jones hit "Come Away with Me"). Bright Eyes experienced its first copyright tangle when the wholesale store Costco reportedly sold acoustic guitars bearing Oberst's signature for upwards of $900; the guitars were removed from the stores immediately. Bright Eyes also performed with the Los Angeles Philharmonic Orchestra at the Hollywood Bowl in October 2007, after enduring a lengthy tour of Canada and the United States. Saddlecreek put out the 2007 EP *Four Winds;* sessions from the recordings of it and *Cassadaga* featured such performers as **Sleater-Kinney**'s Janet Weiss.

Further Reading: Gray, Michael. *The Bob Dylan Encyclopedia.* London: Continuum International Publishing Group, 2006; http://www.myspace.com/brighteyes; http://www.saddle-creek.com/; http://www.sonambulance.saddle-creek.com/; http://www.thisisbrighteyes.com/.

BRITISH SEA POWER

This Brighton, England, quartet's conceptual **post-punk**/new wave indie rock has earned it comparisons to the celebrated 1970s English rock group Joy Division, while the group's offbeat dress (military-style uniform) and theatrics (stuffed birds) have created a big enough buzz to inspire curiosity from fans and critics alike. The group originally called itself the British Air Powers.

Formed in 2000, British Sea Power's (BSP) members are former school friends who are simply known as Hamilton (bass, vocals, and guitar), Yan (vocals and guitar), Wood (drums), and Noble (guitars)—band member Eamon was added in 2002 (keyboards). **Rough Trade Records**' founder Geoff Davis signed the band after seeing the explosive group perform live. **Rough Trade Records** released BSP's first singles, the self-released "Fear of Drowning" (Golden Chariot Records, 2001) and "Remember Me" before the group headed off to the 18th annual **South by Southwest (SXSW)** music festival, where it won over the hordes of fans, music journalists, and just about everyone who is anyone on the music scene.

World of mouth helped British Sea Power's debut album, the ironically titled *The Decline of British Sea Power* (Sanctuary Records), sell over 60,000 copies over the next few years, and the group began selling out shows regularly. The album featured the 13-track "Lately" and proved that the group's pop prowess and musical maturity far exceeded those of its musical contemporaries. British Sea Power brought its epic-proportion-sized music all over the world on its 2004 international tour (a far cry from its early beginnings, when the quartet would host an eclectic fashion show/club night known as "Club Sea Power" at a now defunct night spot back in Brighton). That same year, BSP was awarded the "Band of the Year" award by Time Out London.

BSP's 2005 full-length release, *Open Season,* was well received, hitting #13 on the U.K. Albums Chart and the single from the album, "It Ended On an Oily Stage," reached #18 on the U.K. Singles Chart. BSP made plans to commemorate the release of its single "Remember Me" by offering fans the chance to nominate the name of a long lost loved one to be inscribed on each of the 7-inch albums' sleeves. Jarvis Cocker, the front man for the English Britpop group Pulp, was among the list of names that the BSP members personally submitted.

Yet, amid the band's success, Hamilton decided to leave the band to pursue a solo effort called Brakes. BSP sailed onward, prepping the release of a DVD and heading to Canada to work on its third full-length album (Howard Bilerman, the former drummer for the Canadian indie rock band **Arcade Fire**, who has worked with such bands as Godspeed You! Black Emperor, worked with the band on the record.

The group was interviewed for a 2006 BBC documentary about the life and works of the English poet/writer/broadcaster John Betjeman. Hamilton made a brief return to the group for its 2007 show as the headliners of the famed Glastonbury Festival in England, before Brakes toured with fellow English rockers the **Editors** and **Belle and Sebastian**. BSP toured extensively in support of its 2008 album, *Do You Like Rock Music?,* which was released by **Rough Trade Records**.

Further Reading: http://www.britishseapower.co.uk; http://www.roughtrade.com.

BROKEN SOCIAL SCENE

This Canadian indie group's blend of unpredictable, atmospheric pop/rock helped Canada earn its reputation for being a hotbed for talented, groundbreaking musical acts. Officially formed in Toronto, Ontario, in 1999 by Kevin Drew (who had played in the group K.C. Accidental) and Brendan Canning (formerly of the band By Divine Right), who fused their musical vision with musicians Charles Spearin (formerly of the band Do Make Say Think), Evan Cranley (of the Canadian supergroup Stars), and Emily Haines (from the band Metric), Broken Social Scene (BSS) was at the forefront of the wave of indie bands to experiment with a more electronic, melodic blend of rock in the early 2000s. The group helped pave the way for Canadian bands that strove to make it big in the United States—like Wolf Parade and Constantines, although **Arcade Fire** had already set some of the groundwork.

BSS wowed fans and critics alike with its ambient debut release, *Feel Good Lost* (originally put out on Paper Bag Records, Arts & Crafts officially released the album in 2001), creating a nail-biting anticipation for its 2002 sophomore album, *You Forgot It in People,* a rich, orchestral album that quickly sold approximately 100,000 copies worldwide and helped the group to win the "Alternative Album of the Year" award at the 2003 Juno Awards. BSS was not an instant smash hit in the United Kingdom, though; a distribution deal with Mercury Records fell through after just six months, leaving the band to establish itself as an indie rock band to reckon with all on its own from across the Atlantic.

By the end of 2003, BSS had toured both North America and crossed the Atlantic, having experienced a growth spurt, expanding to upwards of 15 members by adding musicians Andrew Whiteman, Justin Peroff, Leslie Feist, and Jason Collett to the fold. BSS pleased salivating fans eager to hear more of its music with the B-side and rarities collection *Bee Hives* (Arts & Crafts) in 2004 before the group gigged at **Coachella Valley Music and Arts Festival**.

For the group's self-titled album (its second in 2005, which featured the ironically titled track "Major Label Debut") BSS teamed up with producer David Newfeld (the project was put on hold, however, when Newfeld suffered from depression and the group was forced to finish it with Do Make Say Think producer/multi-instrumentalist Ohad Benchetrit), further pushing the envelope with contributions by the group's musician friends in the bands Raising the Fawn, the Dears, the Stars, Metric, and more. BSS swept North America with a 2005 tour (taking along the solo act **Feist**) in support of the album, which included the bonus EP, *EP To Be You and Me.* BSS's self-titled third album (Arts & Crafts, 2005) earned the band comparisons to such groups as **Beulah**, Super Furry Animals, and even New Order with its remarkable harmonies and cleverly crafted, yet ethereal dream pop. Produced by Tony Hoffers (who has worked on albums by **Beck** and Granddaddy), *Fire* proved the band's uncanny ability to make better, more intricate music with each release.

In 2006, BSS contributed to the soundtrack for the film *Half Nelson,* starring actor Ryan Gosling, and the Canadian film *Snow Cake.* The group's previous film soundtrack contributions included adding songs to the 2004 film *Wicker Park,* and BSS's music was used in a 2003 episode of the Showtime TV drama *Queer As Folk.* BSS was nominated for the 2005 Canadian Polaris Music Prize (the equivalent of the Mercury Prize in Britain) for making the best album in the country. The indie scene paused before sending out an S.O.S. distress call amid rumors of a split in 2006, but BSS quickly quelled those rumors by explaining that the group was actually planning a simple break from so much touring (as the headliners for the Virgin Festival, as well as stints at such high-brow festivals as the Glasgow Music Festival, **Lollapalooza**, and Voodoo Music Experiencet in New Orleans).

Dubbed a "collective" for its magnetic qualities and penchant for regularly collecting new members, BSS preformed energetic, captivating live shows that helped its fan base grow exponentially. BSS was named the "Best Live Act" at the 2006 PLUG Awards before the group crowded the stage at the 2007 **South by Southwest (SXSW)** music festival. The group's members continued to work on each of their own side projects while the band toured and wrote and recorded music for its forthcoming album. Dinosaur Jr. alum J. Mascis was among the special guests who joined BSS on stage during select shows on its brief 2007 tour. BSS's most current lineup includes the following members: Justin Peroff, Brendan Canning, Kevin Drew, Charles Spearin, Andrew Whiteman, **Feist**, Jason Collett, Evan Cranley, Emily Haines, James Shaw, Amy Millan, Dave Newfield, John Crossingham, Ohad Benchetrit, Julie Penner, and Lisa Lobsinger. The band released the 2007 album *Broken Social Scene Presents: Kevin Drew Spirit If . . .* , a solo debut by BSS member Kevin Drew, on Arts & Crafts.

Further Reading: http://www.arts-crafts.ca/bss; http://www.myspace.com/brokensocial scene.

BUILT TO SPILL

This Boise, Idaho rock quintet made indie rock history when it bartered with major label Warner Bros. Records, which signed the group in the mid-1990s, to do something many artists have waged mini battles to do—retain the majority of creative control over its music. Built to Spill, which was formed by local musician Doug Martsch after his band, Treepeople, disbanded, was formed around Martsch's idea to maintain an ever-changing band lineup while keeping himself as the centrifugal force holding the group together. But that idea did not stick after the group's first album, and after it released its debut album on C/Z Records (home to the **Melvins**), the group was solidified.

While Martsch aspired to become a guitar hero along the lines of **Pavement**'s Stephen Malkmus and Dinosaur Jr.'s J. Mascis (he also idolized legendary singer/songwriter/guitarist Neil Young), Built to Spill as a whole gained popularity on the college circuit and indie scene as one of *the* acts to see at **Lollapalooza**, and releasing a compilation album that captured the group's many incarnations, *The Normal Years*. Built to Spill consisted of permanent members Scott Plouf and Brett Nelson, former members Jim Roth and Andy Capps, sometimes member Sam Coomes, and a few stragglers from the defunct Treepeople. Martsch's guitar chops and Built to Spill's smart lyrics (not to mention the group's unpredictable on-stage antics) helped the group become one of the most popular indie rock acts of the

1990s. Yet while the group's notoriety forever wavered on the precipice of the underground scene, it never broke big—save for its most commercially successful album, 1999's *Keep It Like a Secret,* on which the group mixed pop sensibilities with meandering guitars and Martsch's distinct yawl of a voice.

Built to Spill found success with its deal with Warner Bros., and the group continued to make records. Its 2000 live album, produced by Phil Ek, who has worked with such groups as **Modest Mouse** and **The Shins**, captured the group's energy and melodic skills like a true studio album. Built to Spill's popular fifth studio album, *Now You Know,* featured touches of blues and funk, but its 2001 release, *Ancient Memories of the Future,* was received with lukewarm reviews. In 2002, the band took a hiatus from working on the album while fame-hungry Martsch started working on solo material for his debut acoustic album, *Now You Know.* Fans feared the band was destined to dissipate in the wake of Martsch's personal ambitions, but the group resurfaced in 2006 with its first studio album in five years, *You In Reverse,* which proved the band was still on the top of its game, putting Martsch on the indie rock pedestal he had long been seeking.

Built to Spill, however, was forced to cancel its 2006 **South by Southwest (SXSW)** performance when Martsch injured his retina. The group resumed touring after Martsch healed, celebrating its bandmate, Andy Capps, who had recently passed away. Built to Spill continued to work on its follow-up to *Reverse* and toured through 2007. Warner Bros. Records re-released several of the group's early recordings on vinyl that same year.

Further Reading: Mcdonough, Jimmy. *Shakey: Neil Young's Biography.* New York: Anchor, 2003; http://www.builttospill.com; http://www.czrecords.com; http://www.neilyoung.com; http://www.philek.com.

C

CAKE

A year before Weezer came along, the group CAKE was the quintessential essence of geek rock. Founded in 1992 in Sacramento, California, by goatee-donning and cowboy hat-wearing singer/guitarist John McCrea, these purveyors of college and guitar rock created a unique fusion of so-called "white-boy" funk and hip-hop, with country sounds, ska, new wave pop, and a bit of jazz. CAKE was, however, branded "one-hit wonders" (www.mtv.com/music/artist/cake/artist.jhtml) after its satirical song "The Distance" became a hit in 1996, reaching #4 on the Modern Rock charts and reaching the Top 40 in the United States and the Top 30 in the United Kingdom. CAKE's offbeat music has earned the group comparisons to the oddball American alt rock group They Might Be Giants, the 1980s new wave band The Cars, and, more often, the 1990s indie act **Camper Van Beethoven**.

CAKE defied the one-hit wonder brand by producing a short string of minor hits soon after, and "The Distance" became a staple on mainstream radio. Band member Sean McFessell (bass) left the band to attend college, but the other original members—Greg Brown (guitars), Vince DiFiore (trumpet), Frank French (drums)—and McCrea remained. Gabe Nelson soon replaced McFessell, and CAKE released its self-produced single "Rock 'n' Roll Lifestyle" before following suit with its self-released album *Motorcade of Generosity,* which the group also distributed in 1993.

Soon, CAKE's music, rife with pop culture references and sardonic irony, reached the ears of the bigwigs at Phil Waldon's (who, after managing Otis Redding's career for many years, was responsible for launching the career of the Allman Brothers Band) Georgia-based Capricorn Records, and *Motorcade* received an official, nationally focused release. On the eve of the group's first national tour, members Nelson and French, possibly overwhelmed by the massive set of closely packed tour dates, departed the band, only to be replaced by Victor Damiani (bass) and Todd Roper (drums).

The song "Rock 'n' Roll Lifestyle" became a hit on the college radio circuit, and CAKE released its cover version of the Dolly Parton classic "Jolene." Although the group's politics were never fully revealed in its music, CAKE never shied away from criticizing those it felt abused power—such as the members of Congress, the U.S. Navy, the Bush administration, and even First Lady Laura Bush, whom the group has quoted on its official Web site.

In 1996, CAKE released its sophomore album, *Fashion Nugget,* which featured that well-known song "The Distance" (it was written by band member Greg

Brown). The song became a favored anthem at sporting events ranging from bocce to NASCAR. *Nugget* hit the Top 40 charts and sold over 1 million copies. CAKE continued its playful streak of releasing cover songs by putting out a version of the 1970's Gloria Gaynor disco club hit "I Will Survive." But the effort backfired enormously, and the song succeeded only in earning the group harsh criticism by fans and critics who thought the track to be a crude joke.

Brown and Damiani departed the group to form their own band, Deathray, in 1997, and the duo secured a deal with the band's alma mater, Capricorn Records, that put out Deathray's first recordings. McCrea, on the other hand, who was being hit from all sides with criticism for his "flat" tonal quality and speak-sing vocal approaches, briefly considered giving CAKE the chopping block, but decided against it. Instead, McCrea recruited former bandmate Nelson for the group's next album, the ambitiously titled *Prolonging the Magic* (Volcano Records, 1998), on which five different guitarists were used for each of the record's tracks. The band experienced yet more tumultuous drama, though, at a 1998 gig at Bowery Ballroom in New York City that was briefly interrupted when bassist Gabe Nelson spotted a fire, which was safely put out.

Magic, which ultimately went platinum, produced another smash hit for CAKE, "Never There," which reached #1 on the U.S. Modern Rock charts. CAKE planned a tour in support of the album, and one of the guitarists who had appeared on *Magic,* Xan McCurdy, joined the group as an official member. A few select dates from CAKE's 1999 tour schedule in Germany were canceled when McCrea injured a metacarpal bone in his hand while moving furniture. CAKE inked a deal with Columbia Records in 2000, and in 2001, the group put out its fourth record, *Comfort Eagle*. The album became the group's highest charting record to date, and the single from the album, "Short Skirt/Long Jacket," received heavy rotation on MTV. Shortly after, Roper left the band and was replaced by drummer Pete McNeal. In 2000 an instrumental version of the CAKE song "Italian Leather Sofa" became the theme song of the WB cartoon series *Mission Hill.*

CAKE performed for approximately 200,000 fans alongside such acts as Ween, **Cat Power**, **Guided By Voices**, and Jurassic 5 for the 31st annual Bumbershoot festival in Seattle, Washington in September 2001. McCrea, it turns out, is not a fan of gigs at stadium-size arenas—and the singer/songwriter is also extremely picky when it comes to the acoustic quality of the venues where CAKE plays. McCrea, who insists that the band's music was meant to be played in venues with capacities of 50,000 or less, insisted that CAKE play a string of surprise gigs at smaller venues in the summer of 2001 as a sort of dress rehearsal for its bigger live shows.

McCrea, who directed the *Short Skirt/Long Jacket* video, also got behind the lens for the video for the track "Love You Madly," in which the group spoofed the popular Food Network cooking competition *Iron Chef.* CAKE also released several versions of the *Short Skirt/Long Jacket* video, in which various people wearing headphones critique the song while listening to it. The video was shot by friends of the band and then edited by McCrea.

In 2002, CAKE toured extensively, joining mainstream rockers Nickelback, former Hole member Melissa Auf Der Maur, and a long list of other bands to play at Canada's annual Edgefest music festival; performing at the **Coachella Valley Music and Arts Festival**; and headlining the Unlimited Sunshine Tour music festival, playing alongside such acts as Kinky, The Flaming Lips, and **Modest Mouse**. CAKE released its fifth album, the aptly titled *Pressure Chief* in 2004 on Sony Music.

CAKE joined the likes of singers/songwriters Sarah McLachlan and Tom Waits for a children's music charity compilation benefiting VH1's Save the Music Foundation in that same year. In a 2004 National Public Radio interview, McCrea described the **Lo-fi** sound of CAKE's music and explained "that his songwriting is often inspired by the frustrations and sadness of romances gone wrong" (Norris, 2004). McCrea and his bandmates, oddly enough, admitted they prefer writing and recording songs to touring. In a 2004 interview with MTV, McCrea described relentless on-the-road jaunts as "rootless and depressing" (Wiederhorn, 2005), citing them as the direct cause of drug and alcohol addictions that befall many a rock star.

CAKE performed at 2005's two-day music extravaganza **Lollapalooza**, joining the likes of **Death Cab for Cutie**, **The Killers**, and Dinosaur Jr. on the indie rock star–studded bill. CAKE's satirical song "Frank Sinatra" was featured on the soundtrack for the second season of the HBO hit drama *The Sopranos*. A CAKE live album, *Live at the Crystal Palace,* was slated for release by Upbeat Records in 2007, but the band's perfectionist ways stalled the release until 2008. CAKE instead self-released its sixth album, the rare tracks compilation album *B-Sides and Rarities,* in October 2007. The album features the group's live cover of the Black Sabbath song "War Pigs."

Further Reading: Bogdanov, Vladimir, Chris Woodstra, and Stephen Thomas Erlewine. *All Music Guide to Rock: The Definitive Guide to Rock, Pop, and Soul.* 3rd ed. Milwaukee, WI: Backbeat Books, 2002; http://www.cakemusic.com.

CALEXICO

Calexico is essentially an eclectic Tucson, Arizona–based collective of musicians centered around the core duo of musicians Joey Burns and John Convertino. Their Mexican- and Southwestern-flavored indie rock was the result of a diverse pool of musical styles and influences, including Americana, Afro-Peruvian, composer Ennio Morricone's spaghetti westerns, Portuguese Fado, country, Gypsy, 1950s jazz, and 1960s surf twang. The band was even sometimes loosely described as being an alternative country/indie mariachi band.

The roots of Calexico can be traced to Los Angeles in 1990 when Burns, who had studied classical music at the University of California–Irvine, first met Convertino. Convertino was then playing with Howe Gelb's experimental rock group Giant Sand, and Burns joined them as an upright bassist for a European tour. Though the two continued playing together in Giant Sand, they eventually began writing songs as a duo on the side. The budding musical partners ultimately moved to Tuscon in 1994 where they began working with the local neo-lounge act, Friends of Dean Martinez. Burns and Convertino soon took up various instruments like marimba, cello, accordion, and vibraphone, expanding their musical repertoire.

Calexico recorded a split record with Friends of Dean Martinez's founder Bill Elm in 1996, and soon they began doing session work, providing the rhythm section for such various musicians as Barbara Manning, Richard Buckner, Victoria Williams, and more. Calexico finally marked its arrival as a separate entity in 1976 with the release of its **Lo-fi** debut, "*Spoke,*" through German label Hausmusik. Calexico then signed with Chicago-based Touch and Go/Quarterstick Records, which released Calexico's dramatic and sprawling sophomore album, *The Black Light,* in 1998. The album earned Calexico excellent reviews, which continued with the release of May 2000's *Hot Rail.*

Calexico continued to build its reputation and fan base with a wide variety of tours, while also performing spots at various festivals such as Montreux Jazz Festival, North Sea Jazz Festival, Bonnaroo Music & Arts Festival, and Germany's Hurricane Festival. The EP *Even My Sure Things Fall Through* appeared in 2001, compiling outtakes from *Hot Rail* along with B-sides and remixed and previously unreleased material from the band's European label, City Slang Records. The EP also employed the skills of longtime members Martin Wenk, Volker Zander, and Jacob Valenzuela, along with members of Mariachi Luz de Lune, who often played with Calexico live.

The live album *Scraping* surfaced in 2002, and in 2003, Calexico released the well-received *Feast of Wire,* which touched on ambient electronica and jazz. It charted in 14 European countries and cracked into Billboard's Independent Album chart in the United States. The next two years Calexico remained busy, issuing a live DVD in early 2004, which was recorded at the Barbican in London, and releasing an EP of covers called *Convict Pool.* Along with its continued friendship with Giant Sand, Calexico contributed to recording sessions with such artists as Neko Case and Nancy Sinatra and even made a cameo appearance as a bar band in the 2004 Michael Mann–directed film *Collateral* starring Tom Cruise.

Calexico performed at the Sundance Film Festival in 2005 and completed the album *In the Reins,* a collaborative effort between Calexico and Iron & Wine's Sam Beam. The groups toured together in the United States to support the album during the second half of 2005. Calexico eventually started work on its fifth official album (though the band issued many tour-only releases over its career) with producer J. D. Foster, who had previously worked with such acts as Richmond Fontaine and Green on Red. The resulting *Garden Ruin* appeared in 2006 as the band's most song-oriented record to date. It included more studio contributions from its touring band of Valenzuela, Wenk, and Zander, and former Lambchop pedal steel player Paul Niehaus. The group kicked off a series of tour dates in Germany in 2008.

Further Reading: http://casadecalexico.com/about; http://friendsofdeanmartinez.com.

CALLA

The roots of the Texas-based indie rock band Calla go back to 1993 in Denton, Texas, when Aurelio Valle and Wayne B. Magruder began playing together in the band Factory Press. In 1995, following a 7-inch and EP release through Austin's ND Records, the Texas outfit relocated to New York City, where it recorded the album *The Smoky Ends of a Burnt Out Day*. But upon the record's early 1998 release, Factory Press broke up and its members moved on to other things.

Once in New York, the band reunited as Calla in 1997 and started to gain popularity in the underground scene as it logged more and more gigs in and around the city. Performing live allowed the group to sharpen its skills and develop its sound. As Calla, Valle played guitar and sang, Magruder handled percussion and programming, and Sean Donovan capped things off on bass, keyboards, and some programming touches; its members' experience with electronics and samples ultimately resulted in Calla's songs growing out of a different framework than typical rock and creating dreamier and more atmospheric arrangements. However, there would remain a particular sense of rock grit in Calla's music that its harmonious nature could not mask. A certain ethereal darkness also permeated much of the band's sound, partly due to a mixture of such moodier influences as **post-punk** bands **The Smiths**, Joy Division, and Nick Cave and the Bad Seeds, as well as trip-hop pioneers Massive Attack and Portishead.

Calla recorded a four-track demo in 1998, stirring interest from the Brussels-based label Sub Rosa, which wound up releasing the band's debut album in mid-1999. That eponymous album was completed over the course of the previous year in Calla's Fort Greene, Brooklyn home; critics received it with high praise for its elegant electronic soundscapes that did not depend on normal song structures. However, once the band began playing live in support of the album, the approach it would take on future recording work was impacted, as stage performing was much different than the studio environment, so the band members subsequently became less reliant on using effects.

As Calla began fostering a fan base, its music caught the ear of Michael Gira, who signed it to his experimental imprint, Young God Records. Calla set to work on its next album in June 2000, again recording in Brooklyn. The resulting *Scavengers* was released in January 2001, featuring a slightly more traditional approach to songwriting, but one that still embodied an atmospheric feel; electronics still played a key part to the mix, but never overtook the actual songs. Again, Calla earned accolades from such publications as *Alternative Press* music magazine and the *New York Times*. This new approach was further developed and solidified into Calla's uniquely droning **indie pop** on January 2003's *Televise,* which was released through Arena Rock Recording Company and Rykodisc. Calla played U.S. shows that year with indie outfit Interpol and launched an ambitious bout of world tour dates that spring to France, Italy, Austria, and Britain.

Arena Rock reissued Calla's self-titled album in early 2004 with three appended live tracks, and the band played shows with England's The Cooper Temple Clause around the same time. Prior Factory Press bandmate Peter Gannon came on board in 2003, with Donovan parting ways with his bandmates the next year. The new lineup entered the studio in late summer with producer Chris Zane, who had previously worked with the group on *Televise*. Dates with the **French Kicks** and a spot at the 2005 **South by Southwest (SXSW)** music festival led to the release of Calla's next album, *Collisions* (Beggars Banquet). *Collisions* met with a positive response, though it sparked some comparisons to fellow New Yorkers Interpol. The next year, Calla went overseas for a string of European dates, writing and practicing between gigs. Consequently, the group's travels were what inspired much of its fifth album, February 2007's self-produced *Strength in Numbers,* which was recorded in New York and Austin. Calla toured as the supporting act for the band Interpol in the summer of 2007.

Further Reading: Koster, Rick. *TexasMusic*. New York: St. Martin's Griffin, 2000; http://www.arenarockrecordingco.com/calla/recordings.htm; http://www.beggars.com/us/calla; http://www.callamusic.com.

CAMPER VAN BEETHOVEN
This Santa Cruz, California quintet band helped to craft the signature sound of mid-to-late-1980s indie rock—melodic, genre-crossing (punk, folk, and even ska), experimental music festooned with ironic lyrics and a hopefulness expressed by the unmistakable vocals of the group's front man, David Lowery, who would later go on to form the early-1990 hit-producing group Cracker.

Camper's signature sound, rooted not only in Lowery's distinctive voice, was anchored by the dramatic swells created by violinist Jonathan Segel, creating the never-before-heard union of violins and indie rock that helped the band stand out among the throes of emerging indie bands of that bygone era.

Camper Van Beethoven, consisting of front man/lead vocalist/guitarist Lowery, drummer Chris Pedersen, guitarist Greg Lisher, bassist/vocalist Victor Krummenacher, violinist/guitarist/keyboardist Jonathan Segel, and guitarist David Immerglück, released its debut album, *Telephone Free Landslide Victory* (Independent Project Music/**Rough Trade Records**, 1985), highlighting the group's penchant for humor through such songs as "Take the Skinheads Bowling" and the track "ZZ Top Goes to Egypt" off its sophomore album, *II & III* (Pitch-A-Tent Records, 1986).

Camper's catchy songs, with their two-sided coin quality of maintaining a humanistic aspect on one side while poking fun at anything they could, permeated college radio throughout the mid-1980s, helping the group to become one of the most influential acts of the 1980s/1990s. The group managed to cross over into the mainstream with its 1989 album, *Key Lime Pie* (Virgin Records), an ambitious effort that featured two of the group's hallmark songs, "Pictures of Matchstick Men" and "Jack Ruby," which became instant classics.

The group added multi-instrumentalist Eugene Chadbourne for its 1993 self-titled album, a country and folk-tinged work that featured a cover of Pink Floyd's classic song "Stairway to Heaven." Camper moved up to the major ranks by inking a deal with Capitol Records in 1993 before releasing its most accessible album to date, *Our Beloved Revolutionary Sweetheart* on which the group followed a straighter and narrower line than on its previous releases. Fans accepted the more mainstream work, nonetheless, and went on to praise Lowery's pop "genius" as a songwriter.

Despite almost a decade free of band disputes and the kind of drama that tears apart most groups, Camper Van Beethoven was ultimately torn at the seams in 1990 when Lowery continued his pursuits for a solo career with the roots/rock group Cracker. Lisher, Krummenacher, and Camper's recently added drummer Pedersen pushed on together to work on their side project the Monks of Doom.

The original lineup of Camper Van Beethoven reunited a decade after its breakup for the 2000 album *Camper Van Beethoven is Dead. Long Live Camper Van Beethoven* via the group's own Pitch-A-Tent Records. The album, which was forged from a conversation that Lowery and Camper's original members had about how to release an album of their classics, features radio broadcasts, live recordings, demos, and rare songs among reworked signature songs that launched their careers. The newly (yet temporarily) formed team also put out the 2002 album, *Tusk,* a two-disc collection of songs, videos, live footage, and photographs of the band. The album was reportedly a nudge against Fleetwood Mac, which released an album by the same name in 1979; Camper had actually recorded the album back in the 1980s while it was working on *Key Lime Pie*.

Camper's main focus during the 2000s was its first studio album in 15 years, 2004's *New Roman Times*. The group topped 2004 off with a live album, *In the Mouth of the Crocodile,* and a reunion performance in Seattle, Washington. Lowery focused his energies on Cracker, while Chadbourne and select members of the group collaborated on a series of albums by a group they donned Camper Van Chadbourne. Camper Van Beethoven played a series of shows alongside Cracker through 2007.

Instead of focusing on making a reunion album, the bandmates announced their focus on "getting used to each other and figuring out that we could still make music together" on a posting on the band's Web site in 2008. Camper Van Beethoven also happily announced its 25th anniversary show at The Fillmore venue in San Francisco, California, on June 28, 2008.

Further Reading: Sullivan, Denise.*Rip It Up!: Rock 'n' Roll Rulebreakers*. San Francisco: Backbeat Books, 2001; http://www.campervanbeethoven.com; http://www.crackersoul.com; http://www.myspace.com/campervanbeethoven; http://www.pitchatent.com.

CANSEI DE SER SEXY

Translated literally, "Cansei de Ser Sexy" is Portuguese for "tired of being sexy." As one of the few Brazilian rock bands to find success in the United States, Cansei de Ser Sexy claims to have gotten its name after hearing Beyoncé use the phrase in conversation. Despite the joke inherent in the band's name, the Cansei de Ser Sexy bandmates, many of whom are former art school students, have proven fashionable in their own sense. The group's 2006 song "Meeting Paris Hilton" appeared in a promo for the South-American airing of FOX's reality series *The Simple Life*. In song and dress, Cansei de Ser Sexy's dress recalls the early 1980s— short shorts, tube socks, kitten heels, and Rick-Springfield-style headbands. While the band's songs often elude categorization—veering toward Blondie, Peaches, and glitchy dancehall—a tongue-in-cheek humor pervades its music. Cansei De Ser Sexy's songs are often about nothing more than the occasional pop-culture parody, partying, and all that happens afterward. Three years into its young career, Cansei de Ser Sexy became the first Latin American band to sign to the legendary indie/**grunge** label **Sub Pop Records**.

Cansei de Ser Sexy formed in 2003 in Sao Paulo, Brazil, without the members entirely knowing how to play their instruments, but responsibilities fell into place seemingly on accident. Lead vocalist Lovefoxx did not assume her role in the band until she forgot to bring her guitar to practice, and the other five members' musical roles, drummer/guitarist/backing vocalist Adriano Cintra, guitarists Ana Rezende (who doubles on the harmonica), Carolina Parra (who also plays drums), Luiza Sá (who also plays keyboards), and bassist Iracema Trevisan, seemed to fall into place around her.

The career trajectory of Cansei de Ser Sexy reflected the greater role the Internet has played as a means of music promotion as the group utilized online resources to attract listeners—all before the group had finished a song. The ambitious quintet developed publicity to connect with younger audiences through its artist profile on the Trama Virtual fotolog, a Brazilian visual-diary Web site used for social networking. Eventually, through word-of-mouth and **DIY (Do-It-Yourself)** marketing, Cansei de Ser Sexy began playing in small clubs, which met with positive reviews in Brazilian newspapers.

With that positive reception, the band continued to use the Internet for inexpensive marketing, adding a profile on the networking Web site MySpace.com and uploading songs while its fans supplied homemade live footage to the video Web site YouTube.

Cansei de Ser Sexy's first self-titled album was released on **Sub Pop Records** in 2006, which the band worked hard to self-promote through efforts by the likes of Lovefoxx, a graphic designer who designed the album's artwork, and Trevisan, a former fashion designer, who designed T-shirts for the band. Standout songs from the album such as "Off the Hook" and "Let's Make Love and Listen to Death from Above," showcased the band's ability to alternate effectively between sneering garage-pop and electroclash.

In 2007, Cansei de Ser Sexy launched the international "It's Already a Sensation" tour with Tilly and the Wall and Ratatat, playing the **Coachella Valley Music and Arts Festival** in Indio, California, that spring. In 2008, the group toured the United Kingdom, playing several big music festivals.

Further Reading: http://www.csshurts.com; http://www.myspace.com/canseidesersexy; http://www.peachesrocks.com; http://www.subpop.com.

CAT POWER

Crippling stage fright and a heavy addiction to drugs and pills were not enough to keep this eccentric indie rock singer-songwriter down. Instead, her combination of introspective, story-like lyrics, an ethereal—borderline haunting—stage presence, and hopeful, yet sad and longing-filled vocal stylings quickly outshone the rumor mill surrounding this Georgia native's odd stage antics. Fans claim she played entire shows with her back to the audience, cursed at stage hands, constantly changed songs mid-tune, and even canceled shows mid-performance by simply leaving the stage.

Born in Atlanta in 1972, Charlyn "Chan" Marie Marshall, who grew up in the households of several relatives after her parent's divorce, began playing music and writing songs at age 12. Leaving the South behind, Marshall dropped out of high school and moved to New York City in 1993, where she immersed herself in the indie music scene and collaborated with the likes of Steve Shelley, the drummer for the legendary indie rock outfit **Sonic Youth**, and guitarist Tim Foljahn of Two Dollar Guitar and Half Japanese before releasing her first single, "Headlights," and opening for indie rock queen **Liz Phair** in 1994 on the basis of a recommendation by one of Marshall's friends.

Marshall donned the moniker Cat Power; she reportedly got the name after spotting a hat with a "Cat Diesel Power" logo on it. Cat Power promptly began capturing the attention—and hearts—of indie rock fans and rock stars (such as former **Nirvana** member Dave Grohl, who played drums on her 2003 album, *You Are Free,* and Pearl Jam's Eddie Vedder, who added vocals to a track on that album). Armed only with a guitar or piano and always hiding behind a solid wall of those signature chocolate brown bangs, Cat Power played the circuit of New York's smaller clubs to eager indie fans who would later be unable to tear themselves away from her shows—despite her penchant for wrecking a domino-like line of performances after buckling under her own crippling stage fright and a swarm of paralyzing insecurities.

Offstage, where she was able to hide behind the protective walls of an isolation booth, Marshall recorded a barrage of albums and singles. Her debut 7-inch, "Headlights" (The Making of Americans, 1993), was followed by the LP *Dear Sir* two years later, and in 1996, she released the full-length CD *Myra Lee* and two 7-inches, "Undercover" and "Guv'ner In Catpowerland/Catpower Goes To Guvnerville," which she recorded with Merge Records artists/indie rock trio Guv'ner. But unbeknown to many, Marshall had been recording quality music since she was in her early teens. In 1974, one of her songs was included in the film *Rockets,* in which she reportedly played a bit part.

The world, however, did not embrace Marshall and her eccentricities until, after bouncing around among such small labels as the San Francisco, California–based boutique label Runt, New Jersey–based label Smells Like Records, which was formed by **Sonic Youth** member Steve Shelley, Undercover, Inc., and Wiija. Marshall eventually found a home at the New York City–based indie rock label Matador Records. In 1998, she recorded the full-length LP *Moon Pix,* which, claimed Matador, "was heralded 'round the world as a paragon of modern song-writing" (www.matadorrecords.com/cat_power/biography.html). Then in 2000, Marshall, who had earned a reputation for breaking the rules of musical pomp and for prodigality, released her fifth album, *The Covers Record,* a collection of her personal takes on a dozen classic songs such as The Rolling Stones' "(I Can't Get No) Satisfaction," Bob Dylan's "Kingsport Town," Moby Grape's "Naked, If I Want To," **The Velvet Underground**'s "I Found A Reason," and even Nina Simone's "Wild Is The Wind." Marshall, who accompanied herself on only piano or guitar, added her token slice of melancholic grandeur to the songs. The album has become one of her catalog's biggest sellers.

Renting a tiny room in New York City's West Village, this daughter of a Southern hippie and an accomplished blues pianist succumbed to her addictions, and she began drinking excessively and taking pills. In 2003, Marshall put out her most acclaimed record, *You Are Free.*

Marshall had been managing to forge her way through the occasional performance, but for the most part, things fell apart and her shows ended unannounced and rather abruptly. Surprisingly though, her poor on-stage etiquette failed to damage her career, nor did it manage to water down her growing fan base. Instead, fans who may have been annoyed by her live show antics chose to purchase her albums so they could hear her songs all the way through without dramatic interruption and others who chose to stick around seemed to marvel at the strange songstress's odd behavior, which simply increased their curiosity.

Marshall's shows may have been fodder for bets based on how long she would last on stage after sound check, but clubs remained full nonetheless. Marshall started on the path toward sobriety and her songwriting improved, as did her sales figures. The ironically titled *You Are Free,* which Chan recorded during her travels, has sold more than 100,000 copies, and the album found a secure spot on Top 10 and Best Of lists across the country. The album was also a finalist for the Shortlist Music Prize in 2003.

In 2004, Marshall managed to squelch her stage fright long enough to perform at benefit shows for The Bereaved Israeli and Palestinian Parents' Circle and The Jackie Farry Fuck Cancer Benefit at New York City's Bowery Ballroom. And while engulfed in what seemed like an uphill battle with her on- and off-stage demons, Marshall somehow managed to record her most celebrated and critically acclaimed album, *The Greatest,* in just three days in August 2005 in Memphis, Tennessee.

In a 2006 interview with the *New York Times,* Marshall said, "Even playing all my shows I was always intoxicated, always kind of not there, which led to the depression. It was more about the uncomfortableness with just being in my own skin, and that's why the alcohol was always with me" (Miller, 2006). The *Times* reported that two weeks before the release of *The Greatest* the singer locked herself inside an apartment in Miami, "turned off the phone, played Miles Davis on repeat, stopped eating and sleeping, drank to oblivion and prayed to die" (Miller, 2006).

Discovered by a friend, Marshall left her apartment and was admitted into Mount Sinai Medical Center for psychiatric treatment. Marshall also revealed to the paper that, before the crux of her addiction and downward spiral that eventually led her to sobriety, her standard breakfast consisted of "a mini bar's worth of Jack Daniel's, Glenlivet and Crown Royal" (Smith, 2006), upon which point she would move onto a brunch that included "a bottle of Scotch, which she nursed throughout the day," and, "on nights [that] she performed, the anti-anxiety drug, Xanax" (Smith, 2006), which she usually topped off with a consistent chain of cigarettes. An article in *The New Yorker* depicted her "as [a] schizophrenic and as [a] genius" (Als, 2003).

Along the path to sobriety, Cat Power experienced a series of highs: in 2006, Cat Power was added to the bill for a Bob Dylan tribute at the Music for Youth Benefit Concert "The Music of Bob Dylan" at New York City's Avery Fisher Hall on November 9. Marshall was also the subject of the 2005 documentary *Speaking for Trees,* which included a two-hour solo performance in the middle of a forest and a bonus CD with Cat Power's previously unreleased 18-minute track "Willie Deadwilder" (an outtake from the *You Are Free* sessions). Marshall took her lone step toward mainstream in 2006 when she was asked to be the new face of Chanel after Karl Lagerfeld spotted the singer enjoying a cigarette outside a hotel in New York City while sitting atop a pile of Louis Vuitton luggage. Her participation in the lavish ad campaign somehow did not sour her fans' view of her.

Cat Power prepared for an upswing with a tour in support of *The Greatest,* but, due to "unspecified health issues" (Cohen, 2006), it was canceled; the stint included a date at the **South by Southwest (SXSW)** music festival in Austin, Texas, and a gig at which she was supposed to perform with The Memphis Rhythm Band. *The Greatest* debuted at #34 on the Billboard 200 Chart and sold 23,000 copies in its first week, making it her highest ranking album and her biggest debut sales ever.

Marshall had recruited a string of top-notch musicians for *The Greatest*—1970s soul singer Al Green's former guitarist and songwriting partner, Mabon "Teenie" Hodges, bassists Leroy "Flick" Hodges and David Smith, guitarist Doug Easley, keyboardist Rick Steff, saxophonist Jim Spake, trumpeter Scott Thompson, and drummer Steve Potts.

Fresh out of rehab, Marshall expressed interest in pursuing an acting career, and rumors abounded that she coveted plans for another cover album. *The Greatest* marked another new beginning for Marshall; a simple lyric change reflected the singer-songwriter's resolve to keep her demons locked away: for the song "Hate," she reportedly contemplated adding the words "don't" and "do not" to the song's despairing declaration, "I hate myself and I want to die."

Marshall's rise from her self-destructive past was crowned by her victory at the 2007 Shortlist Music Awards in 2007. Cat Power is the first woman to win the honors. Her 2008 follow-up to her first covers album, the two-disc release *Jukebox* (Matador Records), is a collection of covers of popular songs by the likes of Bob Dylan, the Rolling Stones, and **Pavement**.

Further Reading: Goode, Michael I. *Stage Fright in Music Performance and Its Relationship to the Unconscious.* 2nd ed. Marina Del Rey, CA: Impression Publishing, 2003; http://www.matadorrecords.com/cat_power; http://www.runtdistribution.com; http://www.shortlistofmusic.com; http://www.smellslikerecords.com.

!!! (CHK CHK CHK)

This bicoastal (California and New York City)-based **post-punk**, funk-rock band's music, like its name, avoids all rhyme and reason. Inspiring skinny jeans-wearing hipsters to dance since the group formed in 1996 at a dance party in Sacramento, California, !!! (or, as some refer to them, "Chk Chk Chk," "Pow Pow Pow," or some such monosyllabic words chimed three times in a row) released its self-titled debut on the San Diego–based indie label Gold Standard Laboratories (GSL). The band name, it turns out, was actually inspired by the sounds a group of bushmen made with their tongues in the 1980 film *The Gods Must Be Crazy.*

Sharing members with the New York City (NYC) dance band **Out Hud**, the septet's aural cocktail of funk, ska, disco, and indie rock caught the attention of the founder of GSL Recordings, Sonny Kaye (of Angel Hair, The VSS, and Subpoena the Past fame), who signed the band in 2000. !!! experienced heightened success with its 2003 single, "Me and Giuliani Down by the School Yard," the title of which was yet another play on a famous title (Paul Simon's 1972 hit "Me and Julio Down by the School Yard") and the subject of which was then-NYC Mayor Rudy Giuliani. The song represented the band's feelings about New York City's strict cabaret laws, which still enforce a ban on dancing in most NYC nightclubs. Several bands have joined the fight against the measure, most notably through the organization Metropolis in Motion.

Known for its sweaty live shows and dance-inducing tracks, !!! then signed to the prominent Chicago-based indie label Touch and Go Records (home to such groups as The Black Heart Procession and **Ted Leo and the Pharmacists**), on which the group released its second full-length album, "Louden Up Now." !!!, which does not lend itself too often to political commentary like the majority of indie rock bands, stayed true to its **DIY (Do-It-Yourself)** mentality by never signing to a major label and managing to push the boundaries of music by mixing various styles and genres with seemingly little effort.

Touch and Go released !!!'s 2004 LP, *Hello? Is This Thing On?* and the 12-inch "Pardon My Freedom" before the band's 2005 EP, *Take Ecstasy with Me,* for which it covered the same-titled track by The Magnetic Fields. "Pardon My Freedom," however, includes a lyric that is clearly a direct derogatory comment about U.S. President George W. Bush.

In 2005, !!!'s founding member (and drummer), Anthony Mikel Gius, was killed by a motor vehicle while he was riding his bicycle. The remaining members John Pugh (drums and vocals), Mario Andreoni (guitars), Dan Gorman (keyboards and percussion), Nic Offer (vocals), Tyler Pope (guitars and vocals), Justin van der Volgen (bass), and Allan Wilson (keyboards, percussion, and horns), and former member Jason Racine, who played percussion, pushed onward, attempting to honor their fallen bandmate by keeping the band intact.

!!! performed at Touch and Go's 25th Anniversary Celebration in September 2006 alongside 25 of its fellow label mates at the 10th Annual Hideout Block Party in Chicago. !!! released *Myth Takes* in 2007 and toured as the opening act for California's funk rock band, the Red Hot Chili Peppers on that group's U.K. tour.

Further Reading: http://www.brainwashed.com/!!!; http://www.brainwashed.com/outhud/; http://www.goldstandardlabs.com; http://www.metromo.org; http://www.metropolisinmotion.org; http://www.tgrec.com.

CLAP YOUR HANDS SAY YEAH

The indie rock resurgence in New York City hit a high note in 2005 with Clap Your Hands Say Yeah, a five-piece band that managed to accomplish a feat that will go down in the annals of indie rock history by selling roughly 110,000 copies (in the United States alone) of its 2005 self-titled debut album through the mail, by using the power of online presence through such sites as MySpace.com, self-promotion, and word of mouth.

The Brooklyn-and-Philadelphia-based group, which is comprised of front man Alec Ounsworth, guitarists Lee Sargent and Robbie Guertin, bassist Tyler Sargent, and drummer Sean Greenhalgh, took matters into its own hands and decided against pursuing the holy grail of music, the coveted major label deal. Instead, the band ran as online publicity campaign to create enough buzz around its debut album to get noticed.

A series of news blasts about the album that were posted on the Bierne's MP3 blog spurned an online frenzy that caught the attention of **Pitchfork Media**—the same music Web site that was responsible for launching the career of the Canadian indie rock band **Arcade Fire**—which gave both the album and the single "In This Home on Ice" the rarest form of complement—a 9-out-of-10-stars rating. Soon after, a trendy New York City (NYC) blog that covers the arts/music/literary scene, Gothamist.com, conducted an interview with the band—and the band left its humble beginnings behind. The buzz level became down right deafening when that same Web site later posted a news story covering David Bowie's cameo appearance at the band's show at the downtown NYC music venue, the Knitting Factory.

In order to deal with all of the incoming attention, Clap Your Hands Say Yeah (CYHSY) hired a former college friend, and Atlantic Records publicist, Nick Stern, as its manager. National Public Radio featured the band in a November 2005 article about the success of its **DIY (Do-It-Yourself)** approach, reporting on the band's success following the stream of online chatter that led all the way to its ultimate success. The noise on the Internet was turned up even higher and even more blog posts went live following the band's much raved-about record release party in June 2005. Clap Your Hands continued to press its own CDs, selling out of copies at the group's live shows.

Clap Your Hands launched brief European and stateside tours in support of the album in September 2005 with opening acts Cold War Kids, an indie rock act from Culverton, California, folk rock singer Elvis Perkins, the Australian music ensemble Architecture in Helsinki and fellow NYC indie rockers Takka Takka. Clap Your Hands worked with each band to compile an exclusive EP of a sampling of their songs, selling them only at live shows.

2005 was a busy year for Clap Your Hands—the scruffy quintet shared the stage with indie rock heavyweights **Sonic Youth**, played the Osheaga Music and Arts Festival in Montreal, Canada, and wowed fans in its home base at the Central Park Summerstage concert series. Clap Your Hands played a standout show at 2005's indie rock showcase, the **South by Southwest (SXSW)** music festival in Austin, Texas, before crossing the Atlantic to play select European festivals. That same year, Mr. Brownstown, a Guns N' Roses tribute band that Clap Your Hands' Greenhalgh, as well as the group's former manager, had been playing in, called it quits.

Clap Your Hands received mainstream exposure performing on *The Tonight Show with David Letterman* in 2006 and NBC's *Late Night with Conan O'Brien*. The group garnered several awards at the annual PLUG Independent Music Awards, a music event sponsored by and celebrating the independent music community, including Artist of the Year and Album of the Year. Clap Your Hands toured with its Brooklyn neighbors, the indie rock outfit The National, in 2006.

Ounsworth lost his voice in July 2006; the group canceled its Japan and Australia tour dates to avoid further damage to his vocal chords. CYHSY's Robbie Guertin designed a T-shirt for the Yellow Bird Project, a Montreal-based nonprofit Montreal organization that donates proceeds from the money made selling T-shirts designed by musicians to charity.

Clap Your Hands revealed tracks from its 2007 sophomore album, *Some Loud Thunder* (V2 Records) at NYC's Hammerstein Ballroom a few weeks before it hit stores. Singer/songwriter Bob Mould (of the 1980s alt rock group **Hüsker Dü**) and the one-man Canadian violin/pop outfit Final Fantasy opened for CYHSY for the group's 2007 New Year's Eve show. The group played a concert in New York City in early 2007 to benefit the Willie Mae Rock Camp for Girls. CYHSY, as the group has often been referred to online, single-handedly managed the distribution of the album in the same way it promoted its first album. Wichita Recordings distributed the record in the United Kingdom and Virgin Records' global dance/electronica/hip-hop/rock/pop conglomerate V2 Records handled it worldwide. The album, which the band promised would consist of "more complex" songs, was produced by Dave Fridmann, who has worked with such bands as Low, The Flaming Lips, and **Sleater-Kinney**.

With the help of Stern, CYHSY secured a distribution deal with Warner Music's Alternative Distribution Alliance (ADA) to ship a second pressing of its highly acclaimed debut album. However, he negotiated a deal that allowed CYHSY to deal with ADA directly—without any input or meddling from a major label. The group, however, was involved in talks of a deal (reportedly worth up to $1 million) with one of the world's biggest record labels, Columbia Records, in January 2007.

CYHSY's self-released album, *Some Loud Thunder* (Wichita Records, 2007), received mixed reviews, but the record reached #47 on the Billboard charts the week after its release. The band launched a North American tour in support of the album that spring. One track from the album, "Love Song No. 7" was leaked early online, receiving rave reviews on blogs and music review Web sites. CYHSY toured through 2007 and performed live on *Late Night with Conan O'Brien*.

In 2007, the members of CYHSY, still working day jobs and working in a make-shift distribution office that doubles as a band member's bedroom, were consider-ing bankrolling the group to fund its artistic endeavors full time. But for now, having sold over 25,000 copies of its debut album (through the mail) without major tour support or any funding from a major label, CYHSY members continued to handle the business side of music themselves. The band also entertained talks with Seattle's Barsuk Records in 2007. The band toured through 2007, playing gigs and benefit concerts across the United States.

Further Reading: MacKaye, Ian, Richard Kern, Mike Watt, and Jim Rose. *Diy Or Die: How to Survive As Independent.* documentary, 2002; Mewton, Conrad. *All You Need to Know About Music & the Internet Revolution.* New York: Sanctuary, 2005; Spellman, Peter.*The Musician's Internet: Online Strategies for Success in the Music Industry (Music Business).* Boston: Berklee Press Publications, 2002; http://www.clapyourhandssayyeah.com.

CMJ MUSIC MARATHON

The longest-running music industry event, the annual CMJ Music Marathon, attracts an estimated 100,000 music industry types, musicians, and fans, present-ing thousands of bands at hundreds of venues across New York City in just four or five days.

Sponsored by the weekly music business trade magazine *CMJ New Music Monthly,* which tracks emerging bands and college radio charts, the CMJ Music Marathon began back in the early 1980s by the magazine's founder/CEO and Pub-lisher, Robert Haber. Recognized as a pioneer in the music realm, Haber is regarded as an authority on college radio; he founded CMJ in 1978 after having served as the Music Director for WBRS, the radio station at Brandeis University (he received his undergraduate Bachelor of Arts degree there), where he discov-ered the rend-making importance, broad-reaching power, and sales influence of college radio.

Consequently, Haber and his new company were the first to feature The Police on the cover of a music magazine, and *CMJ* was among the first in the national media to write about then up-and-coming acts such as **R.E.M.** and U2. *CMJ New Music Monthly,* which originally printed the play lists of college radio DJs, continues to cover underground acts and underrepresented, independent musicians; the weekly print publication usually includes a CD featuring music by emerging bands.

Leading the pack of successful music industry showcases, CMJ is followed closely only by Austin, Texas's **South by Southwest (SXSW)** music festival, and it has influenced several other festivals of its kind like the NXNW festival in Toronto, Canada, and the Macintosh Music Conference. The indie music show-case is the place to be for emerging bands that want to become the next buzzed-about band on the scene. CMJ earned a reputation for the sheer number of up-

and-coming bands that get their shot to play at the most prominent music venues in the city, and where the majority of unsigned bands only dream of landing a gig; bands on the verge have played at CBGB, the Knitting Factory, Hammerstein Ballroom, Irving Plaza, Webster Hall, Bowery Ballroom, Mercury Lounge, and the Living Room—all before they even entertained the possibility of landing a record deal.

Historically, CMJ has attracted unsigned bands that have gone on to the big time—such groups as James Brown, Patti Smith, **R.E.M.**, the Beastie Boys, **Radiohead**, Johnny Cash, and even Eminem have graced the CMJ showcase stages. Other indie acts who have played at CMJ include **The Decemberists**, Tapes 'n Tapes, **French Kicks**, The Black Keys, Hot Chip, and singer-songwriter Suzanne Vega, to name a few.

Music industry insiders and the press typically attend the packed event for free, leaving their record company or radio station to foot the bill, but loyal music fans shell out upwards of $500 to score a CMJ pass (students pay around $300). The pass, however, gains one entry to a number of nonmusic events that have been added over the years—a series of hundreds of music industry discussion panels that have been presented by journalists, pop culture icons, famous musicians, record label executives such as Public Enemy founder Chuck D, electronica artist Moby, CBGB founder Hilly Kristal, comedian/actress Janeane Garofalo, Grammy-winning musician Steve Earle, and funk music icon/musician George Clinton. These interactive panel discussions have touched on topics such as A&R (the artist development department at major labels, which is responsible for signing new bands), digital media, radio, indie labels vs. major labels, music activism, and the state and the future of independent retail.

The CMJ Music Marathon has grown exponentially since its inception, having expanded into the realm of film in recent years. The three-day film portion of the festival showcases independent films made by indie filmmakers looking for their big break. Past films that have showcased more high caliber talent include 2006's *F-ck,* which starred the likes of famed *Rolling Stone* scribe Hunter S. Thompson, indie director Kevin Smith, comedian/political commentator Bill Maher, and actor/comedian Drew Carey. Other films shown at CMJ include the controversial comedy film *Borat* starring newcomer and 2006 Golden Globe winner Sascha Baron Cohen, as well as films that featured actress Rachel Weisz and actor Hugh Jackman. The film portion of CMJ showcases dozens of films each year that have been selected from a vast pool of films from all over the country.

CMJ celebrated a milestone event when the festival marked its 25th anniversary in 2005. Having come a long way from the "College Radio Brainstorm" it once was, interestingly enough, no bands performed at the first CMJ Music Marathon in 1981—it was simply a series of panels and discussions intended to "analyze" the music business and college radio. CMJ marked its 25th year by heralding the top 25 bands that have helped shape the future of music—and, more specifically, that helped shape the path and carve the course for college radio—acts such as (and in this order) **Nirvana**, **Sonic Youth**, the **Pixies**, Public Enemy, **Pavement**,

The Smiths, Violent Femmes, They Might Be Giants, Slayer, **Black Flag**, New Order, Jane's Addiction, U2, De La Soul, Aphex Twin, Uncle Tupelo, **Fugazi**, Mike Watt, Bikini Kill, **Hüsker Dü**, **Ani DiFranco**, The Replacements, **Radiohead**, and **Superchunk**.

Donned with the tag "the Sundance of rock 'n' roll," meaning the showcase is the music industry's equivalent to the film industry showcase, the Sundance Film Festival in Park City, Utah, CMJ Filmfest has often showcased premieres and screenings of Academy Award–nominated films since its launch 12 years ago. CMJ Filmfest is also known for having shown screenings of cult classics such as *Boogie Nights* and *Fight Club,* and it often features panels with such prominent filmmakers as Quentin Tarantino, Trey Parker, Michael Moore, and David Cronenberg, among others. CMJ Filmfest has woven music into the fold by adding retrospectives, behind-the-scenes footage, and by showcasing live performances by such acts as The Dust Brothers, The Beach Boys' Brian Wilson, and artists who have contributed music to films' soundtracks as part of the screenings.

Bands showcased at the 2006 CMJ Music Marathon included **The Shins**, Medeski Martin & Wood, **The Album Leaf**, Madlib, The Black Keys, Mixel Pixel, AM Syndicate, Bling Kong, and The Honorary Title, among approximately 1,000 other acts that performed at over 50 venues all over the city. Other current acts that have played the CMJ showcase include the **Yeah Yeah Yeahs**, **Modest Mouse**, and the Foo Fighters. The 2006 festival was a standout for many reasons—among them the fact that the festival stretched far uptown to the highly regarded halls of Lincoln Center at Avery Fisher Hall, and it included a memorable panel about the closing of the birthplace of punk, NYC's CBGB nightclub, which shut its doors after losing a legal battle over several years of unpaid rent. That panel featured a who's who of speakers including Chris Stein, founding member and guitarist for the legendary 1970s/1980s act Blondie; Tommy Ramone, the founding member and drummer of the **Ramones**; Hilly Kristal, CBGB's founder; Joey Ramone's brother Mickey Leigh; Pat DiNizio, front man for the group The Smithereens; and Darryl Jennifer, the bassist for the hardcore punk act **Bad Brains**. Legs McNeil, the founder of *Punk* magazine and a former editor for *SPIN* magazine, left a resounding impact on the crowd attending the panel when he invited the aspiring musicians in attendance to support the local music community.

The 2007 lineup included such bands as ... **And You Will Know Us By the Trail of Dead**, **British Sea Power**, Counting Crows, The Hourly Radio, The Ladybug Transistor, Mickey Hart, The Ponys, Sahara Hotnights, Serendipity Project, **The Walkmen**, Xiu Xiu, and Zerobridge. The 2008 CMJ Marathon & Film Festival was slated for October 21–25 in New York City.

Further Reading: Beall, Eric. *Making Music Make Money: An Insider's Guide to Becoming Your Own Music Publisher.* Boston: Berklee Press, 2003; Boot, Adrian, and Chris Salewicz Boot, *Punk: Illustrated History of a Music Revolution—Sex Pistols, The Clash, Patti Smith, The Chelsea Hotel, CBGB's, Kurt Kobain & Nirvana, Green Day, & More . . . Illustrated with Photographs.* New York: Penguin Studio, 1997; McGuirk, Mike, and Jon Pruett. *The Music Festival Guide: For Music Lovers and Musicians.* Chicago: Chicago Review Press, 2004; Turofsky,

Diane. *CMJ 10: The First Decade 1979–1989*. New York: Robert K. Haber/College Media Inc, 1989; http://www.cmj.com; http://www.cmj.com/marathon.

COACHELLA VALLEY MUSIC AND ARTS FESTIVAL

The Coachella Valley Music and Arts Festival, which takes place annually at the Empire Polo Fields in Indio, California, was started in 1999 by concert promoter Paul Tollett of the promotion company Goldenvoice. Since then, Coachella has grown in size (just over 35,000 people attended the event in its first year, and attendance for 2005 was estimated at over 120,000 in two days) and scope (the event was anticipated to be a weak competitor to **Lollapalooza** in 1999, while the lineup was overflowing with over 100 "must-see" bands performing on the five stages and various dance tents in 2006)—making it one of the biggest and most anticipated events in the music scene. Fans can opt to camp out at the festival on the lawn adjacent to the main grounds of the event; on average, 10 to 15 percent of the attendees camp out at the site. Passes are available on a single-day or three-day basis. Bands on the bill at Coachella typically perform for approximately 50 minutes; bigger name headliner acts get about 110 minutes of on-stage time.

Coachella is especially known for showcasing obscure and up-and-coming bands; unlike most music festivals, where fans clamor to the main stage, ignoring the side stages, visitors to Coachella often find it difficult to organize their schedule between all of the stages so they do not miss any of the bands on the bill. Tollett and his team's pet project has been going strong for almost eight years, but in that first year, there was doubt surrounding Coachella's success because the festival was announced the very same week the media were reporting on the violence and vandalism that took place at the Woodstock music festival in upstate New York. Consequently, the show went on, but the 2000 Coachella festival was canceled due to poor ticket sales.

Since becoming a must-see attraction for music fans and critics across the country (not to mention the celebrity guests who have been spotted meandering from the VIP tents and out into the main area through the crowds), Coachella has also earned a reputation for playing host to some monumental moments in rock history, the first of which occurred during its premiere year—in 1999, when American progressive/hard rock acts Tool and Rage Against the Machine shared the closing night's credit. Other memorable stage shows included a 2005 reunion performance by **Nine Inch Nails**, which had been on a long hiatus, and an appearance in one of the festivals' dance tents by Madonna in 2006. English rock act The Cure and indie/alt rock kings the **Pixies** have also performed reunion shows at the festival.

Despite Coachella's broadened mainstream recognition and success, Tollett has strived to keep corporate sponsors to a minimum—while balancing bigger name acts with bands on the rise. The desert backdrop has become part of the festival's draw—despite the fact that temperatures in the desert valley in Indio have been known to reach past 100 °F (38 °C). The 2001 lineup included performances by Weezer, Fatboy Slim, the Chemical Brothers, DJ Paul Oakenfold, **Iggy Pop**, **Blonde Redhead**, **The Dandy Warhols**, and **Pedro the Lion**, and, for the first

Spectators watch Arcade Fire perform at the main stage at the Coachella Valley Music and Arts Festival in Indio, California, on April 28, 2007. [AP Wide World Photos/Branimir Kvartuc]

time, the bill featured such hip-hop and electronica acts as The Roots, Gang Starr, Tricky, the Orb, and more. The 1990 rock act Jane's Addiction, which is fronted by Perry Ferrell, who created **Lollapalooza**, also performed that year; it was the group's first live show since 1997. URB Music released live albums of the 2001 concert a few years later. Virgin Records released a live album of the concert in 2002.

The event, which was modeled after such European festivals as the annual Leeds and Reading Festivals, has also become famous for the 40-acre, wide open space where it is held. VIPs and musicians typically hang out in their campers backstage, commiserating under beer tents until set time. Late-night parties by the likes of *SPIN* magazine have become regular events at Coachella, and independent film screenings were added to the festival in 2000 by way of the Coachella Independent Film Festival. The film festival, which celebrated its seventh year in 2007, attracts 20,000 concertgoers and showcases shorts, music videos, documentaries, animation, feature films, and concert and performance footage. The festival also features large-scale interactive art installations, a beer "garden," PlayStation tents, and brief theatrical performances by eclectic artists who may walk a tight rope or be part of a freak show.

In 2002, the British rock group Siouxsie and the Banshees reunited for a main stage set at Coachella, sharing the bill with Björk, Oasis, Queens of the Stone Age, Foo Fighters, and more. The 2003 set list included California rockers the

Red Hot Chili Peppers and the Beastie Boys. Attendance continued to grow, and, in 2004, Coachella sold out for the first time with approximately 50,000 people for each day in the two-day lineup. Attendees were lucky enough to see a reunion performance by the **Pixies** and sets by **Radiohead**, Depeche Mode, Daft Punk, and The Cure.

Coachella's lineups continued to impress fans, and the festival garnered worldwide attention, drawing fans from all over the world. In 2006, Tollett expanded the festival to three days and the addition of an Oasis Dome to the festival's five stage lineup—the Coachella Stage, the Outdoor Theatre, the Gobi Tent, the Mojave Tent, and the Sahara Tent. That same year a live DVD of the festival, *Coachella: The Movie,* was released by Epitaph/WEA Records. Directed by Drew Thomas and produced by Goldenvoice, the DVD featured performances by **Arcade Fire**, The Flaming Lips, **The Polyphonic Spree**, and **Iggy and The Stooges**. Bonus features on the DVD consist of interviews with previous Coachella performers such as ... **And You Will Know Us By the Trail of Dead**, Tenacious D, **The Bravery**, Muse, Mos Def, **Belle and Sebastian**, Ben Harper, and a photo gallery of the festival's previous incarnations.

Tollett released plans for a country music–inspired festival in 2006, which he claimed would kick off the day after the 2007 festival. The weeklong concert series, which has yet to be named, would feature performances by country acts Willie Nelson, Lucinda Williams, Kenny Chesney, George Strait, and others.

Acts for the first day of the 2007 lineup included headliner Björk and main stage acts Interpol, **The Jesus and Mary Chain**, the **Arctic Monkeys**, **Sonic Youth**, Faithless, DJ Shadow, Jarvis Cocker, Peeping Tom, Brazilian Girls, Peaches, Felix da Housecat, Rufus Wainwright, Stephen Marley featuring Jr. Gong, Nickel Creek, We Are Scientists, Gogol Bordello, Digitalism, Tokyo Police Club, The Comedians of Comedy, El-P, Julieta Vengas, Circa Survive, Silversun Pickups, Gillian Welch, Benny Benassi, Tilly and the Wall, David Guetta, Amy Winehouse, Noisettes, Evil Nine, Busdriver, and Brother Ali.

Acts for the second day of the 2007 festival included the Red Hot Chili Peppers, **Arcade Fire**, Tiësto, **The Decemberists**, Travis, the Good, the Bad & the Queen, Gotan Project, **Blonde Redhead**, Kings of Leon, **The New Pornographers**, **The Rapture**, **LCD Soundsystem**, The Black Keys, Regina Spektor, Ghostface Killah, Fountains of Wayne, Sparklehorse, Girl Talk, The Cribs, !!! **(Chk Chk Chk)**, Hot Chip, MSTRKRFT, Ozomatli, Jack's Mannequin, Peter Bjorn and John, VNV Nation, the Nightwatchman, Roky Erickson & the Explosives, Cornelius, CocoRosie, Andrew Bird, the Fraines, The Fratellis, Justice, Bojones, Pharoahe Monch, Fields, Mike Relm, DJ Heather, Pop Levi, and Yeva.

The Grammy Award winning politically minded rock/punk/hard rock Los Angeles–based Rage Against the Machine, which played together from 1991 until it disbanded in 2000, reunited for one night as the headlining act for the last day of the 8th annual Coachella festival in April 2007. The group's performance was intended to showcase the group's solidarity against the Bush administration. The group told several media outlets that its performance was a representation of the group's acknowledgment that during its absence, "the country has slid into right-wing purgatory" (Harris, 2007).

Additional acts for the third day's lineup included Manu Chao, Willie Nelson, **Air**, Happy Mondays, Paul van Dyk, The Roots, Crowded House, Kaiser Chiefs, Damien Rice, Placebo, Explosions in the Sky, Konono N°1, Richie Hawtin, Soulwax, Infected Mushroom, Lily Allen, Amos Lee, José González, Spank Rock, Rodrigo y Gabriela, Against Me!, Ratatat, Junior Boys, The Feeling, The Kooks, CSS, Klaxons, Tapes 'n Tapes, Teddybears, Lupe Fiasco, **Mando Diao**, Grizzly Bear, The Coup, The Avett Brothers, Anathallo, and Fair to Midland.

Tickets to the 2008 festival went on sale in January of that year. The April 25–27 festival featured headliners Roger Waters performing "The Dark Side of the Moon." Other bands topping the bill included Portishead, The Raconteurs, **Death Cab for Cutie**, and **My Morning Jacket**, among others.

Further Reading: http://www.coachella.com; http://www.coachellafilmfestival.com; http://www.myspace.com/coachella.

COMETS ON FIRE

Neopsychedelic indie rock group Comets on Fire came together in the last days of 1999 in Santa Cruz, California. Conceived by two longtime friends, Ethan Miller (guitar and vocals) and Ben Flashman (bass), the act was formed out of their mutual desire to create a hard-hitting rock band that simply delivered the goods with bombast and intensity, one that did not necessarily pay attention to the constraints of a specific genre.

The dark and damaged soul of Comets on Fire was noisy, rhythmically solid, and boasted an inherent love of anthemic choruses, dense riffs, and, of course, psychedelica. The group's acid-soaked and keyboard-driven rock could often evoke images of such bands as progressive metal outfits Blue Öyster Cult, Led Zeppelin, Hawkwind, and Pink Floyd. Comets on Fire eventually expanded past the initial duo of Miller and Flashman to include the talents of Utrillo Kushner on drums and Noel Harmonson on the Echoplex and analog electronics.

The quartet debuted in 2001 with a self-released eponymous album, which was recorded on a four-track and was available only on vinyl. The record, a powerfully distorted psychedelic garage workout, quickly sold out of its first pressing and was later reissued in 2003 through Jello Biafra's **Alternative Tentacles Records** as a CD with six appended tracks. After that album's initial release, Comets on Fire quickly became staples in the underground jam rock scene and was extolled as an impressive act on which to keep an eye.

Comets on Fire hooked up next with the New Jersey record label Ba Da Bing Records for the 2002 release of its thunderous follow-up, *Field Recordings from the Sun.* Gone were any of the band's prior punk rock tendencies, and massive riffs and trippy chaos were heard taking their places. The album further boasted various guest musicians, including guitarist Ben Chasny of Northern California's experimental rock group Six Organs of Admittance and Tim Green of Bay Area indie metalheads the F- -king Champs; the album was recorded in the latter musician's San Francisco studio.

A year after the release of *Field Recordings,* Chasny became the official fifth member of Comets on Fire, handling second guitar duties. The group's third album, *Blue Cathedral,* was issued in 2004, and it stood as the group's debut for Seattle-based indie **Sub Pop Records**. *Blue Cathedral* proved to be a richly textured and dynamically layered album and the band's most mature effort to date, drawing on the best elements of the band's earlier work. By now, Comets on Fire played live gigs only infrequently, but it had still over time managed to score successful shows playing alongside such bands as New York rock act **Sonic Youth** and Cleveland proto-punk outfit Rocket from the Tombs. The band's next album arrived in August 2006; *Avatar* was a relatively calmer effort that was the group's most accessible—yet still forceful—album to date. Despite the slight change in sound, the album was greeted with mostly positive response, and Comets on Fire played various live gigs in support of it, including spring 2007 dates in Europe.

The band celebrated lots of events in 2008—Utrillo had a baby, Ethan kept busy with the band Howlin Rain, and Chasny focused on his new release with Six Organs.

Further Reading: Wolff, Carlo. *Cleveland Rock & Roll Memories.* Cleveland, OH: Gray & Company Publishers, 2006; http://alternativetentacles.com; http://badabingrecords.com; http://www.subpop.com.

CURSIVE

The moody and fractured indie rock of Cursive originally materialized in 1995 around compelling vocalist and guitarist Tim Kasher, drummer Clint Schnase, bassist Matt Maginn, and guitarist Stephen Pedersen. Based out of Omaha, Nebraska, the members were all friends from around town with three of the four bandmates having worked together in the local indie act Slowdown Virginia.

Cursive debuted in 1996 with the 7-inch EP *The Disruption* via local imprint **Saddle Creek Records**, which was run by local musician **Conor Oberst** and the band's friends who were heavily involved in the area's independent music scene. Shortly after, the 7-inch "Sucker and Dry" surfaced through New York–based Zero Hour, sufficiently orienting fans with Kasher's emotionally powerful voice. These early releases culminated in Cursive's September 1997 debut full-length album, *Such Blinding Stars for Starving Eyes,* which was released on Crank! A Record Company. The well-received album featured the band's aggressive and volatile penchant for wavering between delicate breaks and swollen choruses dotted with jagged guitars, driving rhythms, and a wholly anxious yet exuberant sound.

In 1998, the Omaha crew released a split with Austin **indie pop** outfit Silver Scooter before returning to **Saddle Creek Records** for November's follow-up LP *The Storms of Early Summer: Semantics of Song,* which described the story of a man's complete breakdown. It was the first concept album for the band, and its creation would leak over into the band's future work. Unfortunately for all parties involved, however, Cursive broke up around the album's release, and since no touring would thus occur, many fans did not even know of the group's existence.

Band members went off to pursue other projects—some playing with local acts Commander Venus and **Bright Eyes**—effectively leaving fans hanging and wanting more. Cursive eventually reunited in April 1999 with vocalist/guitarist/songwriter Ted Stevens, formerly of Lullaby for the Working Class, on board in replace of Pedersen, who had gone back to law school. The newly minted quartet began turning heads all over again, especially following the June 2000 release of its next album for **Saddle Creek Records**, *Domestica,* which was essentially a record of failed love and relationship that paralleled Kasher's own recently messy divorce. The divorce would also serve as the driving force behind the first record for Kasher's solo project The Good Life, whose 2000 debut, *Novena on a Nocturn,* explored the topic in softer indie rock terms.

Cursive issued the EP *Burst and Bloom* (**Saddle Creek Records**) in 2001, which featured the addition of cellist Gretta Cohn. Cursive followed up the next year with a split with Japanese indie rockers Eastern Youth. The group's most ambitious and challenging album yet, *The Ugly Organ,* surfaced in 2003 to high critical acclaim; it was named one of the year's best albums by rock magazine *Blender* and received further accolades from such publications as the *New York Times* and *Rolling Stone.* Cursive played countless shows in support of the record over three continents, even opening for famed British alternative rockers The Cure on the 2004 Curiosa tour. After building all of this momentum and high expectation for its next record, instead of hitting the studio, Cursive next went on an ambiguous hiatus.

A year passed with no activity coming from the band's camp, but in the meantime, in August 2005, **Saddle Creek Records** issued *The Difference Between Houses and Homes,* a compilation of the group's out-of-print 7-inches (with two previously unreleased tracks) to tide over fans. Cursive eventually resurfaced in mid-2006 minus Cohn and her cello, but with a new album, *Happy Hollow,* the group's most adventurous recording to date; it augmented the band's melancholy dissonance with richer instrumentation (including brass and piano) to confront religious paradoxes within the context of a fake western town.

In 2007 the band added a feature on its Web site that allowed fans to submit remixes of its songs. Cursive toured the United States in 2008. Band member Schnase left the group; the rest of the band started work on new material.lineup

Further Reading: Carr, Daphne, and Mary Gaitskill. *Da Capo Best Music Writing 2006.* Cambridge, MA: De Capo Press, 2006; http://www.crankthis.com/cursive.html; http://www.saddle-creek.com/nf_home.html; http://www.thestoryinthesoil.com.

D

DANCE PUNK

Modern bands and groups such as **LCD Soundsystem**, Radio 4, the Liars, **The Rapture**, **Q and Not U**, **!!! (Chk Chk Chk)**, Klaxons, BHS or Beta, Test Icicles, and **Out Hud** helped revitalize and breathe new life into dance punk, a subgenre of music that started around the early 1980s.

The fusion of dance music and punk rock created a completely original, groundbreaking subgenre of music that originated with rock bands that experimented with disco and funk-fueled dance sounds. Such bands as Konk, Public Image Ltd., A Certain Ratio, Liquid Liquid, and Pigba were among the first groups in the 1980s to play around with such experimental sounds and make waves as indie rock fans slowly and gradually accepted dance music into their cassette players.

Dance punk's roots lie in New York City (NYC) and Europe, where bands experimented heavily with this new fusion. Disco and funk were also making their way into clubs that normally catered only to guitar-based rock groups. Later dance punk acts such as **LCD Soundsystem** were more obvious about the dance/funk fusion and wore their disco-ball-style beats openly on their sleeves. Famed NYC music producer James Murphy, who fronts the act, works closely with dance punk acts to germinate the beat-heavy and club-ready side of their sound. Murphy's remix of **The Rapture**'s 2003 song "House of Jealous Lovers" created a wave of buzz, and the hit song went straight to the play lists of club DJs everywhere.

!!! (Chk Chk Chk), Radio 4, and **Out Hud** strove to make a mark with their music, utilizing dance-club-style electronic beats and computerized loops as the building blocks of their songs. Such acts as **Q and Not U**, on the other hand, stand out for their use of dance punk music in a different way that causes many to consider their music to be more post-hardcore than straightforward dance punk.

Indie rockers, meanwhile, poked fun at other indie rockers who refused to dance despite the inspirational sounds that were pumping from the loudspeakers. The dance punk music had a political influence as well. Ironically, what divided indie rockers who loved to dance from those who thought they were "too cool" to shake a leg actually united the two sides. When The City of New York began enforcing the blue law-style Cabaret Law that prohibited dancing in clubs around the city, musicians and music lovers banded together around 2005 to fight the good fight. Everyone from roadies to managers to singers and even patrons who held 9–5 jobs aligned together to petition the city to strip the law from their favorite establishments. However, despite several attempts, the issue remains in the court in 2008, where dance-loving club patrons are still fighting to have the law dismissed.

Dance punk, meanwhile, continues to grow in popularity. The catchiness of tracks like **The Rapture** remix caused critics to applaud dance punk's sound and herald its acts. Bands such as **Le Tigre**, which has been categorized as dance punk, have taken the subgenre to a new level by adding the socio and political stance inherent in their lyrics to the mix.

Further Reading: Brown, Roger James, and Martin Griese. *Electronica Dance Music Programming Secrets.* Upper Saddle River, NJ: Prentice-Hall, 1999.

THE DANDY WARHOLS

This Portland, Oregon–based quartet's sense of humor shines through in just about every aspect—its lyrics ("Heroin is so passe"), its song names ("Lou Weed"), and, most notably, its name, which was inspired by the 1960s eclectic pop art painter Andy Warhol. Front man/singer/guitarist Courtney Taylor, aka Courtney Taylor-Taylor, as he refers to himself, founded the band in the mid-1990s with high school pal Peter Holmström (guitar), friend Zia McCabe (keyboards and backup vocals), and his cousin, Brent DeBoer (drums), who replaced founding member Eric Hedford.

The **indie pop**/rock/psychedelica group's debut EP, *Little Drummer Boy* (Tim Kerr Records, 1995) earned the band comparisons to the iconic 1970s American art rock group **The Velvet Underground**, with its inherent 1980s keyboard inflections. The group's major-label debut, *. . . The Dandy Warhols Come Down,* followed in 1997 via Capitol Records. It was replete with the hit single "Not If You Were the Last Junkie on Earth," which resulted in the group being compared to a collage of musicians, including **The Velvet Underground**'s front man Lou Reed, who enjoyed a successful and lengthy solo career, English groups The Verve and Oasis, and even American singer-songwriter Neil Young. Famed celebrity photographer David LaChapelle shot the video for the track.

The Dandy Warhols' rare 1995 album, *The Dandys Rule, OK?* (EMI), features material that some fans and reviewers claim is better than anything the group released on a major label. On the album, the band also manages to simultaneously fly the 1980s flag via a retro feel that mixes **grunge** and pop seamlessly while parading its 1990s decadence like a glowing lava lamp. The group's third full-length LP, *Thirteen Tales from Urban Bohemia* (Capitol Records, 2000) proved that being signed to a major label did not change things much for the group, although the group's first record for the label never saw the light of day; tracks from that never-released album are allegedly floating around on the Internet in a form known as *The Black Album.* That record, however, was officially released in 2004 as part of a double CD called *The Black Album/Come On Feel The Dandy Warhols,* which was put out by Dandy Warhol Music.

Thirteen Tales from Urban Bohemia clearly showed the group's influences— Iggy Pop and The Rolling Stones—while convincing critics that the group had some depth to it after all. The single "Horse Pills" from that album included three mixes by the trip-hop group Massive Attack's Robert "3D" Del Naja. Taylor-Taylor reportedly called the *Thirteen Tales* the last classic rock album, and despite its apparent success in America, the record reached Gold status in Europe and Australia.

The Dandys, as they are often called, kicked off a mostly sold-out European tour in 2001, and the single "Bohemian Like You" sold 65,000 copies in just two weeks, charting in the Top 10 in the United Kingdom and reaching #2 on Top 40 radio in the United States. The album quickly sold over 50,000 copies just weeks after its release. The Warhols performed at the Shortlist Music awards in Los Angeles that year. Meanwhile Taylor-Taylor fielded accusations by local bands that the Warhols had "sold out" because the group attained a certain level of fame and success before it logged too many hours on the road and stage.

The Dandys released its most well-known album, *Welcome to the Monkey House* (Capitol, 2003) (which shared the same name as a 1973 Kurt Vonnegut novel), the cover of which was pop artist Ron English's take on the classic Andy Warhol banana painting—but adhering to the Dandy style, this banana donned a zipper. Co-produced by Nick Rhodes of the 1980s pop supergroup Duran Duran and producer Tony Visconti, who has worked with David Bowie, critics claimed the album was a "must have" for music aficionados. Of course, The Dandys still managed to balance the group's favor for humor with its musical efforts—sample tracks on the album were titled "The Dandy Warhols Love Almost Everyone" and "Insincere." The single for the album included an acoustic cover of the David Bowie track "The Jean Genie," a video for the track "Plan A," and a mix of the track "You Were the Last High" by the British house music trio Dirty Vegas.

In 2004, The Dandys participated in the popular cult hit documentary *Dig!*, which revealed to the world the group's penchant for onstage nudity and offstage decadence. What started out as a simple documentary about a local band turned into a media fiasco when the group's rivalry with the Californian psychedelic rock group **The Brian Jonestown Massacre** hit full tilt on screen. Yet again, The Dandys's sense of humor crept in surreptitiously when Taylor-Taylor described the band as "the most well adjusted band in America" (Diaz, 2005). The film went on to win the Grand Jury Prize at the famed Sundance Film Festival in Park City, Utah, and the band members' unaware "don't care if you like us or not" personalities shone through on film, causing the group's popularity to soar even higher.

The Warhols' trail of tongue-in-cheek titles continued with its next album, *Odditorium or Warlords of Mars* (Capitol, 2005), which was, in part, named after the group's recording studio. The Dandys performed on Fox TV's comedy/skit show *MadTV* that same year after having toured North America in support of *Odditorium* and appearing on the **Lollapalooza** stage that summer. The band also participated in a relief concert to benefit the victims of Hurricane Katrina along with such bands as the melancholic indie group **The Decemberists**. Courtney Taylor-Taylor also made a cameo appearance on the popular CW television network drama *Veronica Mars*. The Dandys also had a song featured in the first season of FOX TV's hit drama *The O.C.*

In 2006, The Dandys opened for classic rocker Tom Petty at The Greek Theater in Los Angeles, California, before sharing the stage with The Rolling Stones for one show in Portugal in September (Mick Jagger fell ill and the remainder of the gigs were subsequently canceled), after having played with indie "it" boys The Strokes in Mexico City. In 2007, The Dandys performed at the 15th annual Noise Pop Festival in San Francisco, California, alongside over 100 bands such as **CAKE**, **dios (malos)**, Sebadoh, and more.

Despite rumors that the band was dropped after the merger of Capitol Records and Virgin Records, it is still signed to EMI's roster. The merger was a result of profit losses; bands rumored to get the axe included The Vines, Fischerspooner, Shout Out Louds, and Moby. The group made plans to reveal a large chunk of new material, as well as a one-night event retrospective of its 12-year-long career in the spring of 2007 at the Wiltern Theatre in Los Angeles. The band was also added to the bill for the 2007 Sasquatch! Music Festival at the Gorge Amphitheatre in Seattle, Washington, in May.

The Dandys welcomed 2008 with aplomb—Holmström was asked to remix a song for The Raconteurs' new album, and the band worked on remixing its new record.

Further Reading: Warhol, Andy. *The Philosophy of Andy Warhol: (From A to B and Back Again).* Fort Washington, PA: Harvest Books, 1977; http://www.brianjonestownmassacre.com; http://www.dandywarhols.com.

DANZIG/GLENN DANZIG

Born in 1955, Glenn Danzig is well known as "the Father of Horrorpunk." This goth-inspired genre of hardcore/metal/punk music incorporated theatrical makeup, dramatic hairstyles, and lyrics that explored such dark topics as death, evil, the devil, and over-the-top, gory violence. Rarely seen wearing a shirt, the stocky Danzig brandished his signature look—werewolf and bat tattoos, long and sweaty jet-black hair, and a black wristband—both on and off stage. The New Jersey–born singer/songwriter/musician openly discussed his obsessions with evil; fans were uncertain whether his ruminations were pure or whether it was all an act.

Danzig formed the group the **Misfits** in 1977, a band that defined the Horrorpunk genre and forwarded Danzig's romanticized obsession with all things dark and evil. After the **Misfits** disbanded in 1983, Danzig delved deeper into the gloomy depths, using his new band, Samhain, as a platform with which to present himself as a dark lord of heavy metal. Danzig, who formed the group with then-**Misfits** roadie and photographer Eerie Von, was more than the lead vocalist for the group—he played piano, drums, guitar, and bass. The cover of Samhain's debut 1984 album, *Initium,* showed the band drenched in sweat and what was supposed to appear to be blood.

A series of band members rotated through the lineup, and Samhain disbanded in 1988 after just four albums, although a box set surfaced in 1999. Not taking much time to breathe, Danzig immediately formed his most famous group to date, the eponymous Danzig, which was signed to Rick Rubin's Def American Recordings. One of the first acts to be inked to the burgeoning label, whose roster has included acts such as Johnny Cash, Slayer, **The Jesus and Mary Chain**, and System of a Down), Danzig crossed over into the mainstream, thanks in part to the ever-popular late-night MTV program *Headbangers Ball,* which showcased heavy metal acts. The show, which many fans flocked to like loyal Satanic churchgoers, showcased road-trip episodes, of which Danzig was a regularly featured band.

Danzig's self-titled 1988 album is considered a classic metal must-have; it contains the group's seminal hit "Mother," a track that, amid the flurry of expletives, light-speed-fast guitar riffs, and pounding drum beats features Danzig's own signature snarl. The video for the track, a black-and-white endeavor that spliced together live performances by the band and brief snippets of a miniature horror film starring Danzig himself, was a hit on MTV. The album, which many claim eschews early Black Sabbath songs, revealed Danzig's talents as a songwriter. Oddly enough, though, like the **Misfits**, Danzig did not soar into success until several years after the original release of the song. The 1993 release of the live version of "Mother" helped the album to sell millions of copies worldwide.

The strain of bands that were influenced by the band's music and mentality is evidenced today, with the music and garb of such groups as My Chemical Romance, AFI, Type O Negative, and even Metallica, which are self-proclaimed Danzig fans. In 1998, Danzig expanded his resume by appearing in the 1998 film *The Prophecy II* as a fallen angel known as Samyael. Danzig's far-reaching influence even earned the group a spot on the Billboard charts. In 2000, Danzig spread his experimental wings even wider when he composed the instrumental *Black Aria.* Danzig's songs were played in heavy rotation on MTV, and Danzig even contributed to the song "Thirteen" on Johnny Cash's 1994 album *American Recordings.*

Following the release of Danzig's studio LP (the group would release eight in total), internal strife caused founding member Chuck Biscuits to quit the group, though some say he was fired, in 1988 during the group's tour with Metallica. Danzig quickly filled out the lineup, but subsequent albums somehow seemed forced, and they fared poorly in terms of record sales and reviews. Danzig went on to fill the void by forming the record label Evilive, which was named after a **Misfits**' song, and he worked on another one of his lifelong passions—comic books—by founding the creepy adult comic book company Verotik.

A Japanese toy company revealed the first of three Danzig dolls in stores in 2005. Since then, like the rock group KISS, Danzig has capitalized on the sale of **Misfits**' and Danzig-inspired and related merchandise. Danzig headed out on the road that same year for the group's so-called "final" tour, the "Blackest of the Black," a 20-plus date trek across the United States that featured a handpicked lineup of musicians and former **Misfits** guitarist Doyle Wolfgang Von Frankenstein, who appeared on stage with Danzig for 30 minutes of **Misfits** material.

In 2005 Danzig told the press that he had aspirations to work with Alice in Chains' guitarist Jerry Cantrell, who guest starred on the 1996 album *Danzig 5: Blackacidevil,* on a possible forthcoming Danzig album. Danzig said he and

Cantrell would work together on a "dark Southern blues kind of record" (Lorenzo, 2005).

Ever the overachiever, in 2006 Danzig released *Black Aria II,* the sequel to his dark instrumental. In 2007, Danzig's Evilive Records released *The Lost Tracks of Danzig,* a two-disc collection of previously unreleased solo material. The album featured a booklet with rare photos and Danzig's personal stories about each track. The album art is a throwback to the ambitious musician's roots—it features an eerie illustration of what resembles a half-man, half-werewolf man who looks a lot like Danzig himself. The blood, gore, and death-obsessed 50-something-year-old musician brought his dark fantasies to life when he wrote and directed the 2008 film *Ge Rouge,* a zombie-filled horror film set in New Orleans.

Further Reading: Weinstein, Deena. *Heavy Metal: The Music and Its Culture.* Cambridge, MA: Da Capo Press, 2000; http://www.americanrecordings.com; http://www.danzig-verotik. com; http://www.misfits.com.

DEATH CAB FOR CUTIE

Since forming in 1997, this **indie pop** quartet from Bellingham, Washington, has become one of indie rock's biggest acts. The group's front man, Ben Gibbard, who formerly played under the moniker All-Time Quarterback, formed the group after gaining notoriety for a cassette recording he had titled "You Can Play These Songs." *SPIN* magazine called Gibbard "the poet laureate of the young and hopeful" (*SPIN* Staff, 2003).

Frontman and lead vocalist Ben Gibbard of Death Cab for Cutie performs at the Orpheum Theater in Boston, on October 17, 2005. [AP Wide World Photos/Robert E. Klein]

Gibbard soon brought on bandmates Chris Walla (organs and guitars), Nathan Good (drums), and Nick Harmer (bass). Death Cab for Cutie released its debut LP, *Something About Airplanes,* in 1998 on Seattle's Barsuk Records; in the weeks preceding the release, Good departed the group. The LP garnered local and online buzz and earned the group comparisons to such bands as **Modest Mouse**; critics heralded *Something* for the catchy pop hooks and **Lo-fi** aesthetic of the tracks.

Death Cab's follow-up LP, *We Have the Facts and We're Voting Yes* (Barsuk Records, 2000), preceded the addition of new band member Michael Shorr. *Facts* exhibited Gibbard's emotive vocal stylings and the guitarists' high energy. *Facts* was followed up by 2000 EP *The Forbidden Love,* which featured alternative versions of the standout tracks from the album.

The Photo Album, Death Cab's third full-length album (Barsuk, 2001), cemented the group's place in the hearts of indie rockers everywhere with its literary rock ambitions and engaging combination of upbeat rhythms and emotionally jarring lyrics. *Photo* earned the band comparisons to such bands as **Beulah** and **Built to Spill** and even the tenderhearted crooner **Elliott Smith**. Death Cab also toured that year with the groups Trembling Blue Stars, Shiner, and the Swords Project.

Death Cab's 2002 EP, *Stability* (Barsuk), was a clever combination of a cover of two of Björk's songs—"20th Century Towers" and "All Is Full of Love," as well as the hard-to-skip title track. The year 2002's *You Can Play These Songs with Chords* (Barsuk), a collection of 18 rare and never-before released tracks, became a collector's item for Death Cab fans. Death Cab toured in support of the release that spring with newly added drummer Jason McGerr, a Seattle Drum School instructor and former member of the band Eureka Farm.

Death Cab's fourth LP, *Transatlanticism* (Barsuk, 2003), featured polished production by the group's very own Chris Walla. The group launched a (fittingly) transatlantic tour in 2004, hitting Europe, the United Kingdom, and Japan in support of the album. Early sales tracking of the album tallied sales of approximately 300,000 copies. The band also received a thumb's up from a star on FOX TV's hit drama *The O.C.,* which catapulted the band's popularity among teens.

On the road, Gibbard and company wrote material for their next release, the seven-track *The John Byrd E.P.* (Barsuk Records, 2005), which the group named in honor of its sound engineer of the same name; the EP featured contributions by vocalist/pianist James Mendenhall, Harvey Danger's Sean Nelson, and musician John Vanderslice. Walla put on his producer cap again for this release, which was recorded by Byrd himself. The release featured live tracks, a never-before-heard cover of the Massachusetts indie rock group Sebadoh's song "Brand New Love," and the band's between-songs banter.

Gibbard teamed up with electronic artist Jimmy Tamborello, who also plays under the name Dntel while playing in such groups as Strictly Ballroom and Figurine) to form the group The Postal Service around 2003. The serene electronica/ **indie pop** duo released its debut album, *Give Up,* in 2003 on Seattle's **Sub Pop Records**. Even though The Postal Service soared in popularity and sales—*Give Up* has surpassed sales totals for any Death Cab album, having sold approximately

700,000 copies—Gibbard stayed true to Death Cab, playing in both bands simultaneously. Gibbard made an appearance as the Guest List editor for **Pitchfork Media** in 2003, for which he presented his own "My Favorite Ten Songs by the Rock Group Hall & Oates" (http://www.pitchforkmedia.com/article/feature/ 31372-guest-list-death-cab-for-cutie-my-favorite-ten-songs-by-the-rock-group-hall-oates).

Death Cab teamed up with rock musician Ben Kweller for a 46-date tour in the summer of 2004; that same year, the group contributed songs to the soundtrack for the 2003 film *Wicker Park,* along with such bands as **Broken Social Scene** and **The Shins**. Death Cab contributed to a one-man musical project, Cex's 2006 album, with members of the bands Mogwai and **The Dismemberment Plan** before appearing on the holiday compilation *Maybe This Christmas Tree* with the likes of **The Polyphonic Spree** and **Pedro the Lion**. Death Cab let its true colors show when the band contributed songs to Barsuk's political fund-raising compilation *Future Soundtrack for America* with such bands as **R.E.M.** and **Yeah Yeah Yeahs** before going out on the road to join acts such as Pearl Jam for 2004's Vote for Change tour, which benefited online political organizations. Increased demand for tickets forced Death Cab to extend its 2004 home and abroad fall tour schedules, which resulted in the live EP *John Byrd*.

Later that same year Death Cab parted ways with Barsuk Records, after releasing a steady stream of four successful albums, to sign with major label Atlantic Records, on which the group released its first official full-length album, *Plans,* in 2005. The album went on to sell over 400,000 copies in the first week of its release and charted #4 on the U.S. Billboard charts, proving that indie stalwarts do not have to "sell out" to make quality music. One of the first singles from the album, "Soul Meets Body," reached the Billboard Top 100 singles chart and topped out at #5 on the modern Rock Charts. Atlantic Records allowed Death Cab to take the lead, and the band never lost its penchant for experimentalism. Death Cab launched a North American tour in the fall of 2005 in support of the album with such opening acts as the Canadian supergroup Stars and Youth Group. Fans' votes nominated Death Cab for an mtvU Woodie Award in 2005, and the group walked away with top honors in the "Live Action Video" category. Later that same year, the group performed on *Late Night with Conan O'Brien* and *The Tonight Show with Jay Leno*. Death Cab played a special concert in Seattle, Washington, in September 2005 at the Shadowbox club alongside such bands as Harvey Danger to benefit Hurricane Katrina victims.

Death Cab performed on *Saturday Night Live* and *Jimmy Kimmel Live!* in December 2005. The group was mentioned briefly in an article in *ESPN The Magazine* for its song "Marching Bands of Manhattan" in a 2005 article by writer John Buccigross, who said the song inspired his top hockey picks for the year. The award nominations started rolling in for the group when Death Cab was nominated for "Best Alternative Music Album" for the 48th Annual Grammys in 2006, but the award was given to **The White Stripes**. The group was given a second shot at Grammy stardom when it were nominated in two categories for the 2007

Awards—"Best Pop Performance By a Duo or Group with Vocal" for its song "I Will Follow You into the Dark" and "Best Long Form Music Video" for "Directions." The band lost to the Black Eyed Peas for the Pop Award, and Bruce Springsteen won the video honors.

The Death Cab tribute album *Ghost: The String Quartet Tribute to Death Cab for Cutie* came out in 2006 via Vitamin Records, and the group contributed to three compilations in 2006: *Smack! 2006* featuring The Raconteurs, Muse, the **Ramones**, and more; *End Sessions (Volume 4)* featuring Jet, Gorillaz, **Franz Ferdinand**, and others; and *Live at KEXP (Volume 2)* featuring Gang of Four, **Bright Eyes**, **Sleater-Kinney**, among others. The busy indie quartet toured North America with **Franz Ferdinand** in the spring of 2006 and later that same year the group was added to OK Go's North American tour with **French Kicks**. Atlantic Records released the 2006 DVD *Directions*, which featured an anthology of 11 short films that were inspired by the songs off the *Plans* album.

Chris Walla, having yet to decide on a moniker, posted a cover of a song by the English band Clinic and released his debut solo album, *It's Unsustainable* (Barsuk Records) in 2007. Gibbard went his own way in August 2006 at Park West in Chicago, Illinois, for a solo acoustic performance as part of the "Revenge of the Book Eaters" event in support of the educational/tutorial program for young writers, Valencia 826, which was created by literary wunderkind/author Dave Eggers.

Death Cab contributed to a CD compilation accompanying publisher Chronicle Books' *Every Day Is Saturday* by rock photographer Peter Ellenby. The CD featured music by other acts such as Grandaddy, **Beulah**, American Music Club, John Vanderslice, and John Doe.

Death Cab performed its own version of the theme song for a 2006 episode of the Showtime original series *Weeds;* other acts to get the reinterpretation treatment on the drama included Jenny Lewis and Elvis Costello. Death Cab performed in a September 2006 benefit gig to raise money for kidney transplant surgery for the drummer of the San Francisco indie quartet band **Rogue Wave**. For its fall 2006 tour, Death Cab for Cutie took along musicians **Ted Leo** and Rilo Kiley's Jenny Lewis.

The Starz Cinema channel aired the debut of *Drive Well, Sleep Carefully,* a 2006 documentary that featured interviews, live performances, and candid behind-the-scenes footage of the band. Death Cab band members donated their old, used guitar strings to a benefit project organized by *Relix* magazine and AZU Studio jewelers in 2006. The two companies transform the strings into bracelets to raise money for nonprofits such as the voter registration project HeadCount and Rock and Wrap It Up, which donates leftover food from the backstage of rock shows to the homeless.

Death Cab racked up the tour miles in 2006, hitting **Lollapalooza**, the Sasquatch! Music Festival, and VH1 Classic and World Productions' "Decade Rock Live" concert alongside such acts as Fiona Apple and **Green Day**'s Billie Joe Armstrong. Death Cab's DVD *Directions* was nominated for a Grammy for Best Long Form Music Video in 2006. Gibbard landed a role in the 2008 film adaptation of author David Foster Wallace's short story collection *Brief Interviews With Hideous Men.*

Death Cab's members continued to work on their solo projects in 2007. Gibbard collaborated with Steve Fisk on the score to the film *Kurt: About a Son,* a movie exploring the personal life of the **Nirvana** front man. Gibbard followed up his first-ever solo musical tour by being honored by the Rock and Roll Hall of Fame by being featured on its 2007 artist interview series *The Craft.* Death Cab entered the studio to record its as-yet untitled 2008 Atlantic Records album. Walla released the solo album *Field Manual* on Barsuk Records in January 2008.

Further Reading: Sellers, John. *Perfect from Now On: How Indie Rock Saved My Life.* New York: Simon & Schuster, 2007; http://www.barsuk.com; http://www.deathcabforcutie.com; http://www.johnvanderslice.com; http://www.postalservicemusic.net.

THE DECEMBERISTS

This risk-taking, theatrical indie rock quintet managed to pull off a seismic indie rock feat by maintaining indie rock credibility among fans while remaining on the good side of the hard-to-please music critics at the music Web site **Pitchfork Media**, who boasted to stand by the band, nonetheless, declaring, "As long as your records are good, we'll like them, Colin. Don't worry" (Phillips, 2005) when the group signed to major label Capitol Records for its fourth full-length album in 2006.

Founded by front man Colin Meloy around 2000, the band's eclectic lineup is comprised of Meloy, who writes the majority of the songs, drummer John Moen (former drummers include Ezra Holbrook, Steve Drizos and Rachel Blumberg), upright bass man Nate Query, accordionist/pianist Jenny Conlee, pedal steel guitarist/theremin expert Chris Funk, and occasional member violinist Petra Hayden.

The Decemberists self-released a five-song EP before indie label Hush Records, which is located in the group's home base of Portland, Oregon, put out its debut album, *Castaways and Cutouts,* in 2002. The Seattle, Washington–based punk/indie rock label **Kill Rock Stars** reissued the album later that same year after the group's fan base began to swell. The cover of the album features artwork by Portland, Oregon artist Carson Friedman Ellis, who along with having designed covers for the California alt rock band Weezer, continued to draw the artwork for several more of the group's album covers, giving them a consistent feel that allowed the records to stand out among the overflowing indie rock bins at local CD stores.

Castaways proved to be a noteworthy pop debut, and it garnered the attention of the indie rock world. Meloy and company, who have proven to be religiously ambitious, have released a full-length album every year since. In 2003, they put out *Her Majesty,* an album that critics lauded for its literary inspiration (Meloy was a creative writing major during his collegiate days). The record also saved the band from the ill-fated "sophomore jinx" that tragically quells the careers of many a fledgling band.

The Decemberists gained an impressive online presence through exposure on such sites as Myspace.com, which boosted the group's popularity even further, and a few months later, the group released a five-part EP called *The Tain*, the title being taken from a Celtic eighth-century poem of the same name. *The Tain* exhibited the group's romantic sense—and the ability to pull off the astronomical musical feat of creating a Floyd-like indie rock opera that had fans salivating for more.

The year 2004 saw the release of the "Billy Liar," a four-song single featuring two songs from the album *Her Majesty,* which proved to be a fit preview to the band's third full-length album, *Picaresuqe,* which **Kill Rock Stars** put out in March 2005; the album reached #128 on the Billboard 200 Chart. Produced by **Death Cab for Cutie**'s Chris Walla, the album cover features an old-fashioned photograph of the band poised on stage. The Decemberists' next single, "16 Military Wives" was released by London's **Rough Trade Records** in November 2006, and in 2006, The Decemberists made the leap across the great indie rock divide when the group signed to major label Capitol Records for its fourth full-length album, *The Crane Wife,* which sold 26,000 copies and landed at #35 on the Billboard 200 Chart in its first week.

The band toured in 2006 in support of *Crane Wife,* which is based on a tragic Japanese folk tale, and appeared on the *Late Show with David Letterman*. The band stayed on Capitol's roster, grasping tightly to the promise that the label would allow the band members to have creative control over their music. Meloy announced plans to a record an EP's worth of cover songs by the 1960s British folk artist Shirley Collins on the **Kill Rock Stars** label.

The band was featured on the live 2006 compilation *Live at KEXP (Volume Two)* alongside fellow indie bands **Ted Leo and the Pharmacists** and **Death Cab for Cutie**. The Decemberists performed the tragic love song "O Valencia!" on *Late Night with Conan O'Brien* that same year. The band performed at Washington D.C.'s popular 9:30 Club in October 2006; the concert was streamed live on NPR.org. The Decemberists also hosted its first-ever Halloween contest at a gig in the Calvin Theatre in Northampton, Massachusetts.

National Public Radio named *The Crane Wife* Album of the Year for 2006, and the group playfully invited mtvU viewers to create an animation segment that appeared as the ending to the video for "O Valencia!" Sony Music's online music store, Connect, featured exclusive downloads of a digital EP by The Decemberists that featured live tracks from *The Crane Wife* and a cover of the country song "Please Daddy (Don't Get Drunk This Christmas)."

An eccentric TV battle ensued between The Decemberists and comedian/actor Stephen Colbert, alumnus of Comedy Central's *The Daily Show* and the star of the NBC dramedy *The Office,* after Colbert accused the group of copying a "green lightsaber" challenge involving fans rocking out in front of a green screen that was aired on his show. Colbert then asked fans to superimpose their own green screen creations onto the group's video as their entry for the "O'Valencia!" contest; The Decemberists countered by challenging Colbert to a guitar duel to settle the feud. The heated battle between Colbert and The Decemberists's member Chris Funk aired on a December episode of *The Colbert Report*, with Colbert (who claimed to have performed with a fictional group he belonged to in the 1980s called Stephen and the Colberts) showcasing his axe chops while English guitar legend Peter Frampton emerged on Colbert's behalf, executing a show-stopping performance.

The Decemberists released the single "O'Valencia" in 2007. The group gave its songs the orchestral treatment during a gig in July 2007 at the Hollywood Bowl with the Los Angeles Philharmonic. The Decemberists also announced details of the group's first-ever DVD, *A Practical Handbook* (**Kill Rock Stars**), featuring live footage from a 2005 performance, as well as behind-the-scenes clips, a mini documentary that was shot during the making and recording of *The Crane Wife,* candid interviews, illustrations by artist Carson Ellis, whom the band has collaborated with on numerous occasions, and short films that were made during photos shoots for the *Picaresque* album cover.

The group embarked on a North American tour along with the group My Brightest Diamond in the spring of 2007 in support of its new music. The Decemberists performed as part of the first Summer Camp Festival at the Les Schwab Amphitheatre in Bend, Oregon, alongside such bands as **Pedro the Lion**, **Built to Spill**, **Death Cab for Cutie**, and Vive Voce. The group also played the 2007 Bonaroo Music Festival in Manchester, Tennessee, with such acts as **The White Stripes**, The Police, and Tool.

The Decemberists' Tucker Marine contributed to singer-songwriter Laura Veirs's third album, *Saltbreakers* (Nonesuch Records, 2007). The Decemberists's front man, Colin Meloy, kicked off his solo tour in January 2007 in Seattle, Washington. Meloy also guested on The Minus 5's self-titled 2007 full-length album, aka "The Gun Album" (Yep Roc), by lending his vocals to a few tunes. Albums by Meloy's first band, Tarkio, were reissued in early 2007 by the **Kill Rock Stars** label. The band canceled the rest of its fall 2007 tour in November of that year after the band members fell ill.

Meloy's first solo LP, *Colin Meloy Sings Live!,* was released via the band's Web site in February 2008. He kicked off a solo tour that spring.

Further Reading: Strong, Martin C. *The Great Indie Discography*. 2nd ed. Edinburgh, Scotland, United Kingdom: Canongate Books, 2003; http://www.comedycentral.com; http://www.decemberists.com; http://www.hushrecords.com; http://www.killrockstars.com; http://www.pitchforkmedia.com; http://www.roughtraderecords.com.

DEL REY

Playing with a double-barrel force, this Chicago-based band's strictly instrumental songs lurch with overcast, militaristic gloom. Often categorized as a **post-rock** or space-rock band, Del Rey combines labyrinthine song structures with a loud, galactic rhythm section that finds itself on the same orbital plane as bands such as Mogwai, Isis, and Godspeed You! Black Emperor.

The band that would become Del Rey began to take shape in 1997 when friends Eben English, Damien Burke, and Brendan Daly moved from the East Coast to Chicago's Ukrainian Village. With the addition of Michael Johnson, a former North American snare-drum competition champion, Del Rey began to practice and play gigs.

Unlike many bands, though, none of the four members had been trained to or had a desire to play just one instrument. In fact, each band member contributes on keyboards, and every member save Johnson shares bass duties, while Johnson and English play drums with English and Burke playing guitar. Even more unlikely, no one took over vocal duties.

Noise complaints from neighbors resulted in the Del Ray band members being evicted from their first apartment, but after relocating, the band was able to refocus on music. Del Rey released its first four-song EP, *dlry,* in 1999 on its own label, Dirigible Records. In September 2001, Del Rey recorded its first full-length album, *Speak It Not Aloud,* on My Pal God Records. The group recorded the album in Engine Music Studios with producer Jason Ward, who had worked with bands such as Paul Newman and Rhythm of Black Lines.

The absence of a lead vocalist allowed Del Rey's music to be big and cavernous, yet also introverted. Those qualities appealed to listeners who liked the earplug-penetrating heaviness of hardcore with the atmospherics of electronica. In 2003, Chris Cowgill replaced Brendan Daly and assumed bass and keyboard duties. That same year, Del Rey released its second full-length album, *Darkness & Distance,* off My Pal God Records.

Though *Darkness & Distance* clocked in at a mere seven songs, Del Rey managed to build touring efforts around the album. In 2004, Del Rey's music was featured in the DC-Shoes's sponsored skating video *The DC Video,* which compiled the stunt work of a variety of popular professional skaters.

Following this flux of increased exposure, Del Rey headed back into the studio to record *A Pyramid for the Living* (My Pal God Records, 2006), featuring such songs as "Olympus Mons"—with its tom-heavy drum line and spacious guitar fuzz, which saw the band in full exploration mode. *Pyramid* was warmly received by critics.

In September 2006, Del Rey played for the Rock For Kids fund-raising event in support of Chicago's homeless children or children otherwise in need. In 2007, Del Rey planned limited tour gigs at locations in Pittsburgh and New York City with such bands as The Impossible Shapes and Oxford Collapse.

Further Reading: http://www.mypalgodrecords.com/delrey.shtml; http://www.myspace.com/delrey.

DENALI

These purveyors of atmospheric, ambient pop/indie rock formed in 2000, generating a fair amount of buzz long before the release of a five-track demo, which, in turn, led to the release of the group's 2002 self-titled debut on the Wilmington, Delaware–based independent label **Jade Tree Records**. Fielding comparisons to the chaotic sounds of the alt rock group the Smashing Pumpkins and the droned-out qualities of the English trip-hop group Portishead, Denali, which took its name from the Athapascan word for the highest mountain in North America, Mount McKinley in Alaska, is comprised of lead vocalist/pianist/guitarist Maura

Davis, her brother bassist/synthesizer player/sampler Keeley Davis, guitarist Cam DiNuzio, and drummer/sequencer Jonathan Fuller.

Davis's soulful soprano and the group's unique sound brought the band the attention of major labels, but the group, which admired **Jade Tree Records** for its distribution successes and impressive roster (the group also had friends in other bands that were signed to the label) had actually contacted the label before it even had a chance to attempt to court the young quintet.

Denali's 2002 self-titled debut album sold over 10,000 copies, catching the attention of critics and fans alike—partly due to the group's front woman's strong stage presence and mesmerizing vocals. Davis, who started the band with her brother after becoming an admirer of his band, Engine Down, was only 19 at the time. Produced by Mark Linkou, who fronts the melodic indie group Sparklehorse, *Denali* possesses a trip-hop sound that quickly set the group apart from any tag listeners attempted to put on it. *Denali* was recorded at Cracker/**Camper Van Beethoven**'s front man David Lowery's Sound of Music Studios. Denali spurned a tour with Domino Records recording artists Clinic in 2003 before kicking off yet another set of dates with the Madison, Wisconsin indie rock group Rainer Maria and a sling of gigs with the Grammy-winning alt metal/rock band Deftones, who hand-selected the group for the slot. A tour across Europe with singer-songwriter **Pedro the Lion** was rescheduled, though, when the group decided to stick around long enough to complete its long-awaited sophomore LP.

Work on the LP was briefly stalled, though, when "technical difficulties" the band experienced at Mark Linkous's Static King Studio forced the group to team up with engineer Peter Kasin's Tarquin Studios to complete the record; Kasin has tweaked songs by indie kings Interpol. *The Instinct* (**Jade Tree Records**) hit record stores in October 2003; despite the absence of the type of top-notch ballads that appeared on the group's debut album, fans and critics alike were pleased with the effort, though they may have felt uneasy about the band's future amid rumors of an impending breakup. Sure enough, the magic did not last very long and Keeley Davis and Fuller departed the group in order to put their efforts back into their long-neglected group, Engine Down.

Denali soldiered on though, adding former Pinebender member Stephen Howard on bass and keyboards and former Euphone member Ryan Rapsys on drums. Armed with the new lin-up, Denali gigged for just a few months (hitting **South by Southwest [SXSW]** among other gigs) before the group released its official "breakup" statement online in 2004. The amicable split marked the end of a career that hardly had the time or the chance to properly get off the ground. Denali contributed the song "Normal Days" to the 2004 *Rock Against Bush Vol. 1* compilation (Fat Wreck Chords) to benefit the political Web site, PunkVoter.com.

In 2006, however, Denali released a DVD entitled *Pinnacle* (Lovitt Records) that featured concert footage, videos, a hidden Easter egg, exclusive home videos, and over 150 photographs of the band. In the wake of Denali's finale, Maura focused her attention on the bands Bella Lea and Ambulette, while Keeley joined the band

Sparta, DiNuzio continued his work at RCA Records, and Fuller recorded continued music for commercials.

Further Reading: http://enginedown.com; http://www.bellalea.com; http://www.denalimusic.com; http://www.jadetree.com; http://www.myspace.com/denaliband; http://www.soundofmusic.org.

DEUS

Formed in Antwerp, Belgium, in 1994, dEUS (pronounced "day-us") arrived on the U.S. indie rock scene on the heels of its debut album, *Worst Case Scenario* (Polygram Records) and a string of extensive European tour dates. The standout single from that album, "Suds & Soda," exhibited the group's hybrid of **pop punk** sensibilities and an experimental sound that set it apart from the deluge of other indie rock bands from that era for its blend of folk, punk, jazz, and prog rock influences. Originally formed as a Bohemian-style covers band that sang in English, dEUS band members earned a reputation for their creative endeavors having designed their own album cover art and directed their own videos.

dEUS signed to Island Records soon after the label got ahold of its first EP, *Zea* (1993), and the band immediately hit the road. dEUS member Rudy Trouvé departed the band amid a demanding tour schedule before the release of the band's EP *My Sister = My Clock,* which followed in 1995. The eclectic group released its sophomore album, *In a Bar, Under the Sea,* in 1996 by way of Universal Music imprint Polygram Records. *Bar,* which was produced by former **Pixies** and **PJ Harvey** band member Eric Drew Feldman, added to the loss of yet another founding member—Stef Kamil Carlens, who left to focus on his own group, Moondog Jr.

dEUS's third full-length album, *The Ideal Crash* (Island Records, 1999), garnered support from such bands as **Radiohead** and **R.E.M.** and resulted in sold-out shows across Europe and a plethora of festival dates. Guitarist Tim Vanhamel (former band member of the groups Millionaire and Eagles of Death Metal) joined the group for a string of live shows later that year, along with a stage full of fire eaters, dancers, and new band member violinist Klaas Janzoons.

A singles collection, *No More Loud Music,* followed soon after in 2001; the group, however, felt that *No More,* which came with the DVD *No More Video,* was its least creative endeavor to date. Interested in pursuing solo music projects, the members of dEUS took a five-year hiatus before returning to the indie rock scene in 2005 with a new lineup that consisted of front man/guitarist/lead vocalist Tom Barman, former member/drummer Danny Mommens and former member Jules de Borgher, drummer/vocalist (and former Soulwax member) Stéphane Misseghers, bassist/vocalist Alan Gevaert (who replaced Craig Ward, who had replaced Trouvé), and guitarist/vocalist Mauro Pawlowski (formerly of Evil Superstars). dEUS did, however, play a few brief concerts in Europe, including its home base of Belgium, in support of its singles/DVD collection.

News quickly circulated of the group's recent return as did work on a fourth studio album, and the group played sold-out shows amid positive reviews. The long-awaited recording, *Pocket Revolution* (V2 Records, 2005), eventually went Platinum, proving that dEUS's musical chairs lineup game had finally paid off. dEUS generated online chatter about its return with the download only release of the single from that album, "If You Don't Get What You Want." dEUS played over 100 concerts in support of *Pocket,* including a performance at Belgium's 0110 Festival, which featured a record number of Belgian acts and bands.

Barman has since pursued additional opportunities, which included writing and directing his first film, *Any Way the Wind Blows.* The self-described "avant grunge" group has since become known as one of the most important and influential Belgium rock bands to date. dEUS began writing and rehearsing material for its next album, releasing such select tracks as "What We Talk About (When We Talk About Love)" and "Bad Timing" in 2006.

dEUS released its single "The Architect" in 2008 and kicked off a string of tour dates that same year with a show at the Melt! Festival in Germany in June.

Further Reading: http://www.deus.be; http://us.v2music.com.

DFA RECORDS/LCD SOUNDSYSTEM

Indie rock's most well-connected man, James Murphy, formerly of the bands Speedking and Pony and who also leads/founded the **dance punk** outfit LCD Soundsystem, founded the **dance punk** independent label DFA Records with engineer Tim Goldsworthy, founder of Mo-Wax Records. The two run DFA with label manager Jonathan Galkin. The New York City–based label, which earned its chops producing remixes for such bands as **The Rapture**, **Le Tigre**, N.E.R.D., **Nine Inch Nails**, The Chemical Brothers, Gorillaz, and Radio 4, entered a heated legal battle with the Canadian duo Death From Above 1979 when DFA Records emerged on the scene, forcing the group to change its name so the two musical entities were not too similar in name.

Bearing a logo in the shape of a lightening bolt, DFA made a splash in the music industry with its highly successful 2003 remix of **The Rapture**'s "House of Jealous Lovers." The 12-inch **post-punk** disco track helped catapult the group to stardom, making DFA a household name in indie circles. DFA remixed the track "By the Time I Get to Venus" by one of the first bands signed to DFA, The Juan MacLean, Murphy's longtime friend and former musical partner.

DFA and Murphy's calendar quickly filled up once the label signed a distribution deal with Capitol/EMI/Astralwerks, allowing Murphy to focus more time on his band, the 1980s-tinged LCD Soundsystem, a collective that includes New York City area musicians Nancy Whang (keyboard and synthesizer), Pat Mahoney (drums), Al Doyle (percussion and guitar), and sometime live members Phil Mossman (percussion and guitar) and Tyler Pope (bass)—who is also a member of the groups !!! (**Chk Chk Chk**) and **Out Hud**.

LCD's 2002 debut single, "Losing My Edge," remains one of the group's standout songs, prefacing the single "Give It Up/Tired," which quickly sold out of the first 1,500 copies pressed in the United Kingdom after being named the single of the week by **NME** (**New Musical Express**) when it came out in 2003. LCD became

LCD Soundsystem front man/producer James Murphy. [AP Wide World Photos]

a hit across the pond, too, where hardcore music fans were swooping up the singles as quickly as LCD could make them. Murphy capitalized on the group's long stream of successful singles in 2005 by re-releasing them on LCD Soundsystem's self-titled, two-disc compilation, which featured one of its most successful tracks, "Daft Punk Is Playing at My House," which name-calls the French techno collective Daft Punk.

The year 2005 became a smash hit year for DFA and LCD Soundsystem when the group was awarded two Grammys for Best Dance Recording for "Daft Punk Is Playing at My House" and Best Electronic/Dance Album for *LCD Soundsystem*. Amazon.com named the album one of its Top 100 Picks of 2005, and the album peaked as the group's highest charting in the United Kingdom when it hit #29.

Murphy claimed he left the indie rock world behind, though, when he remixed pop superstar Justin Timberlake's hit single "My Love" in 2006; the track was available online as an MP3 only. DFA Records produced LCD Soundsystem's 2006 disc, *Introns,* which featured B-sides and remixes of the group's hits; the album was exclusively available online. Murphy immediately headed back to the studio to work on the group's 2007 sophomore album, *Sound of Silver*. That same year, iTunes aired a promotion for the shoe company Nike, Inc. featuring the 45-minute long, Murphy-made track *45:33*. LCD performed at the 2007 **Coachella Valley Music and Arts Festival** during a densely packed spring/summer tour.

DFA is also home to the Brooklyn, New York–based indie rock/noise rock/electronic group Black Dice. The group's third album, 2005's *Broken Ear Record,* was its first to be released by the DFA/Astralwerks partnership. Formed at the Rhode

Island School of Design, Black Dice relocated to New York City; the group, which has been known to jump out into the crowd at lives shows, has earned screamo and **shoegazing** tags.

The one-man dance-punk/electronica outfit (and synthesizer player/guitarist) The Juan MacLean released his first full-length album, *Less Than Human* on DFA in 2005. MacLean joined the rest of the DFA crew on the 2006 *The DFA Remixes: Chapter 2* before heading out on the road with fellow DFA artist Shit Robot in support of his recent releases.

DFA's credibility spread quickly in the underground indie scene in New York City, with Murphy being hailed as a production mastermind. DFA's roster includes the acts Booji Boy High, Prinzhorn Dance School, Delia Gonzalez & Gavin Russom, and Hot Chip.

LCD Soundsystem released a split tour single with **Arcade Fire** in 2007. On December 1 of that same year, the group performed as part of the Corona Music Festival in Mexico alongside acts such as **Iggy and The Stooges** and !!! (**Chk Chk Chk**).

The year 2008 was another busy year for the label; LCD Soundsystem continued to tour in support of its two 2007 albums, *45:33* and *Sound of Silver*.

Further Reading: http://www.blackdice.net; http://www.daftpunk.com; http://www.dfarecords.com; http://www.lcdsoundsystem.com; http://www.myspace.com/dfarecords; http://www.thejuanmaclean.com.

DIFRANCO, ANI

No other woman in rock has played harder, inspired more fans, or made more of an impact on indie rock than Ani DiFranco. The multicolored dreadlock-donning singer who was born in Buffalo, New York, in 1970 has enjoyed a career that has spanned over 30 years, overcoming many obstacles to become a renowned musician, feminist icon, and pioneer of women's rights. DiFranco's trademark guitar-playing style—at times Flamenco inspired, percussive, and edgy—has become highly influential within the indie rock community.

Flaunting her "it's my prerogative" attitude, the tomboyish singer-songwriter, who tapes fake acrylic fingernails on her fingers to pluck guitar strings, has released almost one album for every year of her prolific career. DiFranco, who started her own record label, **Righteous Babe Records**, in the late 1980s when she was just a teenager, has developed a cult following. The multi-instrumentalist who plays guitar, bass, piano, and percussion had started out performing with a drummer and working with her then-husband sound engineer Andrew Gilchrist—until divorce ended their five-year-long union and her drummer parted ways to pursue a solo career.

DiFranco, who learned to play the guitar at the tender age of 9, started writing songs and playing gigs around age 14 with the help of musician friends Suzanne Vega, known for the hit songs "Luka" and "Tom's Diner," and Texas singer-songwriter Michelle Shocked. The ever-resilient DiFranco left a troubled home soon after, gigging in and around the Buffalo area as much as she could until the

Ani DiFranco performs at Kleinhans Music Hall on April 4, 2001, in Buffalo, New York. [AP Wide World Photos/Harry Scull Jr.]

determined singer moved to New York City. There, DiFranco's popularity, thanks in part to her rebel appearance—tattoos, body piercings, and unruly hair— soared. In an effort to protect the artistic integrity of her music and to retain all legal and creative rights over it, DiFranco followed the **DIY (Do-It-Yourself)** path and founded **Righteous Babe Records** in 1990.

The album art for DiFranco's eponymous debut album (**Righteous Babe Records**, 1990) probably best exhibited the playful singer-songwriter's antiestablishment demeanor—the black and white image of the singer and her freshly shaven head has become an iconic image from indie rock history. DiFranco toured relentlessly, touting her vast catalog of songs; she had reportedly written over 100 songs by the time she was 19. She put out a string of releases from 1991 to 1994— *Not So Soft*, *Imperfectly*, *Puddle Dive*, and *Like I Said: Songs 1990–91*.

It was her 1994 album, *Out of Range*, though, that catapulted DiFranco to cult status; reviews of the album and profiles of the eclectic singer appeared in all major news outlets including CNN and the *New York Times*. Fans were enamored by the singer's honest lyrics (her songs often tackled such difficult topics as sex, rape, war, poverty, sexual abuse, reproductive rights, and homophobia) and funky style, not to mention her outspoken nature and **DIY (Do-It-Yourself)** attitude.

Major labels attempted to court DiFranco, but the unpredictable singer remained steadfast, working tediously to build **Righteous Babe Records** and decrying the "industry" that she felt did not have artists' best interests in mind. Her 1995 album, *Not a Pretty Girl,* demonstrated DiFranco's true-blue nature and the vast scope of her musical abilities; 1996's *Dilate* debuted on the Top 100 Billboard charts—a feat unaccomplished by the vast majority of indie rock releases, especially those by bisexual, politically minded singers who publicly decried the music industry.

DiFranco released the long-awaited live album *Living in Clip* in 1997. And *Little Plastic Castle* (**Righteous Babe Records**, 1998) proved DiFranco was a musical force to be reckoned with, demonstrating her versatility as a musician and songwriter. The chart success and sales of *Castle* (on which she questioned her public persona) paved the way for her next album, the introspective, energy-charged *Up Up Up Up Up Up*. DiFranco called upon a group of musicians to help her create 1999's *To the Teeth,* which featured vocals contributed by the Artist Formerly Known as Prince. DiFranco surprised people yet again by putting out the funk, jazz, and Latin-infused 2003 album *Evolve*.

In 2001, the National Organization for Women (NOW) bestowed DiFranco with the Woman of Courage Award for her work and contributions to the feminist movement. The influential singer-songwriter continued to keep time with her one-album-a-year record, releasing a string of albums as the years passed—*Educated Guess* (2004), *Knuckle Down* (2005), and a bootleg of her live performances at Carnegie Hall (2006). Distraught by the death of her father in 2005, the tough-on-the-outside, tender-on-the-inside DiFranco toured in tribute of the man who helped raise her.

Tendonitis sidetracked the singer from touring and playing in 2005, but she quickly returned to the stage to finish out the year and start the new one doing what she did best—play live. DiFranco gave birth to her first child in 2006; the child's father, Mike Napolitano, was also the producer of her 2006 album, the aptly titled, politically charged *Reprieve*. DiFranco, who had reportedly played more than 100 shows a year, took a brief hiatus to spend time with her newborn baby before setting dates for select gigs in 2007.

DiFranco kicked off North American and European tours and released a new book of poetry along with the 2007 career retrospective album, *Canon*. The sprightly singer performed at the **Righteous Babe Records** headquarters—a revitalized old church called The Church—in support of the album. She continues to sell albums through her own distribution company, which is appropriately titled, 1-800-ON-HER-OWN. DiFranco toured again in 2008.

Further Reading: Quirino, Raffaele. *Ani DiFranco: Righteous Babe Revisited.* Los Angeles: Fox Music, 2004; Rodgers, Jeffrey Pepper. *Rock Troubadours: Conversations on the Art and Craft of Songwriting with Jerry Garcia, Ani DiFranco, Dave Matthews, Joni Mitchell, Paul Simon, and More.* San Rafael, CA: String Letter Publishing, 2000; http://www.righteousbabe.com.

DIOS (MALOS)

This southwestern California-based experimental indie rock outfit has already experienced reincarnation. The group released its debut EP, *Arboles,* which is Spanish for trees, in 2003 and its first full-length album arrived in 2004 on the Brooklyn, New York–based independent label StarTime International Records, home to the **French Kicks** and **The Walkmen**. The group was originally simply called dios, but wsd forced to change its name to dios (malos) following a possible legal injunction by the 1980s hair metal band Dio, which was fronted by Ronnie James Dio.

dios (malos) formed in 2002 and began making 1960s-inspired "sunny" pop music that earned the group comparisons to The Beach Boys. dios (malos) is Kevin and Joel Morales, bassist John Paul Caballero, keyboardist Jimmy Cabeza DeVaca, and drummer Jackie Monzan. The Santa Monica, California–based label Vagrant Records released the group's debut full-length album under its new moniker in 2005; the recording exposed the group's experimental side and proved it could rock hard.

NME (*New Musical Express*), *Rolling Stone* magazine, and the BBC called the group a "band to watch" (Philbrook, 2005); one of its tracks was featured on an episode of the FOX drama *The O.C.,* but the group has stayed true to its indie roots, maintaining its **DIY (Do-It-Yourself)** ethic and often choosing to record songs in Caballero's basement than record in an expensive studio. dios (malos), which grew up rocking on the same stomping grounds as the hardcore punk group **Black Flag** and the label that Greg Ginn founded, **SST Records**, has become known for its unpredictable rhythmic changes and improvisational feel that is rooted in catchy, melodic rock.

The group toured the United States and Europe with acts Grandaddy and **The Shins**, picking up a solid fan base along the way. In 2005, the group played for a packed audience at **South by Southwest (SXSW)** music festival in Austin, Texas, and the Austin City Limits Festival. dios (malos) branched out from its tell-tale samples and shiny pop for the group's third release, tentatively titled *Life Between the Tides*, for which it reteamed with producer Phil Ek. dios (malos) fine-tuned the record while hitting the road in 2007 with the Brooklyn, New York indie rock group **The Fiery Furnaces** and The Spinto Band; the grouped toured in an eco-friendly vegetable-oil-powered van. The group continued to tour in 2008.

Further Reading: Rollins, Henry. *Get in the Van: On the Road With Black Flag.* 2nd ed. Los Angeles: 2.13.61 Publications, 2004; http://www.ronniejamesdio.com; http://www.spintoband.

com; http://www.sstsuperstore.com; http://www.startimerecords.com; http://www.wearedios.com.

THE DIRTBOMBS

An influential and iconic figure on the Detroit rock scene, Mick Collins played in a plethora of bands throughout his career, including primal rockers The Gories and forward-thinking garage punks King Sound Quartet. Another such band to include on his impressive resume was The Dirtbombs. He originally just formed the band as a side project in 1992, putting himself in charge of vocals and guitar and adding a rotating lineup of two drummers and two bassists.

Though on the surface The Dirtbombs seemed simply like another loud and noisy garage punk band driven on dirt, sweat, and cheap beer, the group's rock actually contained a certain soulfulness to it that incorporated a spectrum of styles, including punk, glam rock, classic soul, and R&B. Whenever asked, Collins insisted that The Dirtbombs were not a garage rock act at all. Unsurprisingly, he was the band's primary songwriter and, as such, claimed such influences as British **post-punk** band Wire, underground Cleveland art-rockers **Pere Ubu**, and **post-punk** indie rockers **Mission of Burma**.

After various delays and false starts, The Dirtbombs began setting their sound to wax in 1995, and touring commenced about a year after that. Very much a singles-oriented band at the beginning, The Dirtbombs released five 7-inch singles before Larry Hardy of Los Angeles–based In the Red Records convinced the group to issue an actual full-length record. The result of this agreement was 1998's punk-oriented *Horndog Fest*. More singles followed, of course, before The Dirtbombs's excellent sophomore effort, *Ultraglide in Black,* appeared in May 2001. The album mostly consisted of vintage R&B covers such as Marvin Gaye's "Got to Give It Up" and Stevie Wonder's "Living for the City," but the songs were so well done that the album drew the band high accolades from music critics all around the country. The album also increased profile of The Dirtbombs in Europe, which was growing at a larger rate than in America, helped in part by the band's frequent overseas tour dates.

The Dirtbombs even enjoyed one stint across the pond with fellow Motor City rockers **The White Stripes**. The much more rock-oriented and tougher sounding third album *Dangerous Magical Noise* surfaced in 2003, and two years later, the Dirtbombs appeared on a split called *Billiards at Nine Thirty* alongside garage punk-indebted R&B revivalists King Khan & The Shrines. May 2005 further found In the Red issuing a 52-track singles compilation called *If You Don't Already Have a Look* that contained six new Dirtbombs songs among 29 originals and 23 cover songs.

Boasting a rotating lineup over the years that resulted in over 13 different incarnations since the group's inception, the Dirtbombs' membership had finally settled down by the mid-2000s with Collins, drummers Ben Blackwell and Pat Pantano, and bassists Ko Shih and Troy Gregory. Though still very much flying under the mainstream radar, The Dirtbombs were not going completely unnoticed and even made it into the Top 10 of *SPIN* magazine's mid-2006 list of the "25 Greatest Live Bands Now," coming in right under renowned singer Prince.

The group released the LP *We Have You Surrounded* (In the Red Records) in early 2008, kicking off tour dates in the United States, Australia, New Zealand, Canada, and other places in 2008.

Further Reading: Abbey, Eric James. *Garage Rock and Its Roots: Musical Rebels and the Drive for Individuality.* Jefferson NC: McFarland & Company, 2006; http://www.intheredrecords.com; http://www.thedirtbombs.net.

DIRTY ON PURPOSE

This **shoegazing** indie rock four-piece band started out as a larger cluster of friends who started out making music in each other's home recording studios, using bathrooms for vocal booths, and sharing brunch hangouts with local stars the **Yeah Yeah Yeahs**. Dirty on Purpose (DOP) formed in 2002 in the cultural hotbed of the Williamsburg neighborhood of Brooklyn, New York, often referred to as "hipster central," amid run-down warehouse lofts, bustling independent shops and cafes, and an arts scene that spawned throes of artists, musicians, and wannabe stars.

DOP generated buzz in its neighborhood, playing local venues with such acts as **Clap Your Hands Say Yeah**, **Say Hi to Your Mom**, **The Album Leaf**, and **Arcade Fire**, among other parties until the group garnered enough material to put out a self-released, self-produced four-track EP in 2003. DOP, which features alternating male-female vocals (former keyboardist/singer Erika Forster left the group to form her own trio, **Au Revoir Simone**), consists of lead singer/guitarist Joe Jurewiz, drummer Doug Marvin, bassist DJ Boudreau, and guitarist George Wilson.

Dirty on Purpose's debut full-length album, *Sleep Late for a Better Tomorrow*, caused waves in the local indie scene, receiving praising write-ups on popular blogs and scenester Web sites like Gothamist.com and publications such as *Entertainment Weekly,* NPR (National Public Radio), and *SPIN* magazine, which credited its music as having a certain "potency" (Grose, 2005). When Forster left the group, DOP entertained various guest singers, such as Brooklyn-based singer Jaymay, to fill the XX chromosome component and continued on making dreamy pop music as a quartet.

DOP put out its sophomore effort, 2006's *Hallelujah Sirens,* on the New York City–based independent label North Street Records. *Hallelujah* showcased the group's delicate harmonies and orchestrated guitars, with a few tricks thrown in the mix—a horn section, strings, and smart lyrics. DOP performed at the 2006 Siren Music Festival, an annual event on Coney Island, where sky-scraping roller coasters, cotton candy booths, and noisy rides serve as the backdrop for a summer showcase of local acts. DOP also played a stint at the 2006 **South by Southwest (SXSW)** music festival. *Hallelujah*"garnered the band a nod from the PLUG Independent Music Awards for Best Indie Rock Album, and the artsy foursome was invited to host an episode of MTV2's music show *Subterranean*.

Further Reading: Warner, Jay. *On This Day in Music History: Over 2,000 Popular Music Facts Covering Every Day of the Year.* Milwaukee, WI: Hal Leonard, 2004; http://www.dirtyonpurpose.com; http://www.northstreetrecords.net.

THE DISMEMBERMENT PLAN

The Dismemberment Plan lists among its influences some polar opposite bands such as 1980s English rock group **The Smiths** and the Long Island, New York–based hardcore/political rap outfit Public Enemy. The **emo** quintet, though, managed to accomplish underground success that has reverberated throughout the indie scene like no other band before it. One of the first bands to arrive on the **emo** map, The Dismemberment Plan has become influential to numerous modern acts that have attempted to capture the group's passion, emotive power, sense of humor, and unique combination of punk, pop, new wave, and even funk. The melancholic lyrics, paired with the band's legendary drummer, left an impact on the indie world that has yet to be duplicated.

Consisting of members Jason Caddell (guitar, keyboard, and vocals), Steve Cummings, who was later replaced by Joe Easley (drums), Eric Axelson (bass and keyboard), and Travis Morrison (lead vocals, guitar, and keyboard), The Dismemberment Plan was formed in 1993 while all of the band members were studying at different colleges in the Commonwealth of Virginia. Taking its name from a phrase uttered in the 1993 Bill Murray film "Groundhog Day" The Dismemberment Plan left a legacy behind that has yet to be rivaled in the indie spectrum. With the group's fusion of punk, rock, funk, and new wave all with a bit of hip hop, samples, and tongue-in-cheek pop tossed into the mix for good humor, The Dismemberment Plan's members were pioneers not only for their forward-thinking musical ambitions, but they were also heralded for having brought a long-absent dance element back to rock. **Pitchfork Media** reportedly gave the band the coveted title "the fathers of the late 1990s/early 2000s dance-punk movement" (http://www.informationdelight.info/encyclopedia/entry/The_Dismemberment_Plan).

The group also gained favor with its fans by repeatedly touring cities outside major metropolitan areas where few bands ventured, proving the band's long-lasting loyalty to its fans that was reciprocated for years to come. The steadfast quartet also earned a reputation for staying true to its D.C. hardcore roots that were laid down by such bands as Minor Threat, **Rites of Spring**, and **Jawbox**, which The Dismemberment Plan also cited as influences while embracing the mainstream scene but not bowing to mainstream pressures and trends. The Dismemberment Plan band members quickly became role models for youths by standing up for their beliefs, and they managed to pull off a then-unprecedented feat by disbanding at the apex of the group's career and by having made an album on a major label's dime before walking away with the content intact after being dropped from the roster. The group later released the material on DeSoto Records, an indie label to which the group remained loyal for the remainder of its reign.

The Dismemberment Plan's debut album, the simply titled *!*, was released in 1995 by DeSoto Records, an independent label that is run by former members of the D.C. hardcore band **Jawbox**. The raw quality of the 12-track album became a must-have for fans of the hardcore genre, and it remains one of the group's most reveled recordings to date, having earned it comparisons to hardcore legends **Fugazi**. The Dismemberment Plan (or The Plan or D-Plan as the group is often called) released its sophomore album, *The Dismemberment Plan Is Terrified* (DeSoto Records), in 1997; it exuded the high energy and spontaneity of the band's live shows. This noisy indie rock album showcased the group's transition from simple angst-ridden punkers to musicians who were capable of making complex, experimentalist music. The record also proved Easley's top-notch drumming chops, and it included one of the group's most significant songs, "Do the Standing Still," in which they mocked fans who refused to dance at live shows. Morrison, however, repeatedly encouraged fans to dance although he was vocal about his opposition to moshing.

The Dismemberment Plan topped off 1998 by inking a major-label deal with Interscope Records, which released the group's now out-of-print EP, *The Ice of Boston*. Soon after, however, the band was faced with the realization of an indie band's greatest fear—being signed to and then being dropped by a major label. Interscope, which later sponsored the group's third album, *Emergency & I* (Desoto Records, 1999), parted ways with the band, but allowed the group to exit the building with the material it had recorded while the group was under contract. D-Plan, however, saw this happenstance as a blessing in disguise and the quartet reunited with Desoto Records, to which the group would remain loyal for the long haul. *Ice* contained the demo tracks for a record that has become a must-have for indie music collectors. *Emergency,* which showcased the group's songwriting skills, quickly sold 20,000 copies and caused an influx of soldout shows nearly every time the band played a gig. The success of *Emergency* led to an opening slot for the Seattle, Washington–based **grunge**/alternative rock band Pearl Jam in 2000 on the European leg of Pearl Jam's tour.

In 2001, the Plan put out a split four-track EP with the Seattle, Washington indie rock band Juno. That same year, DeSoto released its fourth full-length album, *Change,* which seemed to smash all preconceived notions of the **emo** and indie rock genres in one full swoop with its emotionally charged, complex tracks. The Plan toured the United States and Europe through 2001 in support of that album before touring Japan for a second time in 2002. The Dismemberment Plan's fifth album, *A People's History of the Dismemberment Plan* (DeSoto Records, 2003), is a collection of remixes by friends and fans such as the metal/hip-hop group Deadverse, the one-man electronica outfit Cex, and the indie/electro act Parae, among others. The 27-track album contains tons of extras in the form of music videos,15 bonus tracks, and more. To remind fans of the Plan's penchant for humor, the album even features a bonus track recording of the often satirized song "Let the Eagle Soar," which was sung by former U.S. Attorney General John Ashcroft in 2002. The Plan co-headlined a string of gigs with **Death Cab for Cutie** in 2002 for the "Death & Dismemberment Tour."

Feeling worn out by endless touring and having experienced a lack of collaboration in their musical efforts, the Plan's members, who were now in their 30s, began contemplating the end of the road for the group. The Plan posted news of the split online and played its final show in July 2003. As sort of parting gift to its fans, though, The Dismemberment Plan made all of the material from its four studio albums as well as MP3s and exclusives to the then-not-yet-released album, *A People's History,* online for free on its Web site.

After disbanding, Axelson and Easley formed the group Statehood, while Easley returned to school to study aerospace engineering. Axelson formed the band Maritime with two former members of the D.C. hardcore legends The Promise Ring, and Morrison released a solo record. Maritime has since signed with The Dismemberment Plan's alma mater, Desoto Records; Maritime's debut full-length album, *Glass Floor,* emerged in the spring of 2004 and the follow-up *We, the Vehicles* came out in 2006 (Flameshovel Records). Caddell began producing albums for bands such as the Illinois group Troubled Hubble. The Seattle, Washington-based label Barsuk Records (home to **Death Cab for Cutie** and Rilo Kiley, among others) released Morrison's 2004 debut solo album, *Travistan.* Morrison had help recording the album—Chris Walla (a member of the indie groups **Death Cab for Cutie**, **The Decemberists**, and The Velvet Teen) co-produced the album with Don Zientara, the founder of D.C.'s famed Inner Ear Studios. Morrison made a cameo on Cex's 2004 album *Invisible Sidis.*

Though the Washington, D.C.–based quartet disbanded in 2003, cementing the end of a decade-long indie reign with a soldout show at the 9:30 Club in its home city, The Dismemberment Plan's influence has stretched far and wide in the indie worldi, and its albums are considered blueprints for aspiring indie musicians.

Further Reading: Wimble, David. *The Indie Bible 7th Edition (Indie Bible).* 7th ed. Ottawa, Ontario, Canada: Big Meteor Publishing, 2005; http://www.barsuk.com; http://www.deadverse.com; http://www.desotorecords.com; http://www.dismembermentplan.com; http://www.innerearstudio.com; http://www.jasoncaddell.com; http://www.southern.com/southern/band/JUNO0/biog.html; http://www.statehood.us; http://www.travismorrison.com.

DIY (DO-IT-YOURSELF)

A commonly used term for grassroots activism, DIY (Do-It-Yourself) gradually played a bigger part in the music industry when bands that had once dreamed of securing that holy grail of the music business—the major recording contract—decided they would be much better off doing it all themselves. Distraught by the record labels' desire to exhibit creative control over their music and outraged by labels that wanted to take a bigger cut of their profits, bands were fed up with record labels—so many of the bands started forming their own.

Indie bands, by their very definition, are usually those that make experimental music that most labels would want to "mold" into something more commercially viable, meaning profitable, for the company. Indie bands also felt the need to maintain creative control over their music—which many major labels tried to tone down or change so that it fit in with mainstream music heard on the radio.

Instead, many DIY bands forged their own paths. In the 1970s, punk bands, whose artistic integrity was too great to be held under the thumbs of label execs, were the first to adhere to the DIY aesthetic. They were also the ones able to hold out the longest—making their own cassette demos, selling albums at shows, playing all over the underground scene for little or no money, and living on next to nothing.

The DIY mentality has changed over the years, though. Many bands that have the legal and business savvy their predecessors did not are able to strike deals with record labels so that they have creative control over their music. In short, these artists are able to convince the label that they are profitable only if they make and play music their way—and only certain labels have taken that gamble. **Nine Inch Nails** and **Talking Heads** are key examples of bands that have been able to convince labels to invest their money, marketing, and distribution efforts in the band without letting the corporate partners have a say in the music itself. **Nine Inch Nails** successfully formed the imprint Nothing Records at Interscope Records, but Trent Reznor learned how to deal with labels the hard way—he was engulfed in a lengthy battle with TVT Records so that he could get out of his restrictive deal. **Talking Heads**, on the other hand, proved so viable that label execs hardly ever tried to sway the band from its their nerd-art-rock ways.

DIY by nature is an indie ideal that transcends independent bands and the community surrounding them. DIY spread even wider in the 1980s when bands started publishing fanzines and educating each other about their rights as artists. The artists-corporation struggle has waged on ever since. Artists have fought against censorship, while labels have attempted to strip songs of curse words and offensive material in order to sell more records—and artists have fought back. The DIY movement is also a group effort in which bands unite against unfair label practices and other restrictions.

The rise of the Internet has made DIY efforts a bit easier; fans and musicians connect through such networking Web sites as MySpace.com, and bands continue to produce their own music and post samples online. Musicians have also learned how to use production software and built home studios in order to be able to create their music in their own time—on their own terms.

The DIY effort has led to bands setting up their own distribution, and it has even spawned online grassroots efforts. Artists such as **Ani DiFranco** continue to maintain all creative control over their music. **Ani DiFranco**, who owns and runs her own record label, took a chance when she ventured out on her own. And she has been able to manage her music as a business and enjoy it as an artist, but not everyone has had those successes. Money is often a key reason that bands sign deals with major labels, but the indie bands that have worked hard to go it on their own know that their hard work and sacrifice have made all the difference.

Further Reading: Spencer, Amy. *DIY: The Rise of Lo-Fi Culture.* London: Marion Boyars Publishers, 2005.

THE DRESDEN DOLLS

This Boston-based duo gained acclaim for its unique blend of cabaret theater aesthetic and dark punk music. Formed in 2001, members Brian Viglione and Amanda Palmer (who met, fittingly enough, at a Halloween party) developed The Dresden Dolls from a combination of a few of their favorite things—1920s/1930s German cabaret, Kabuki-like makeup, showy stage outfits, pop-rock music, and theatrical nuances. Palmer, the principal songwriter, sings lead vocals and plays piano, while Viglione plays the drums and, on occasion, sings vocals and plays guitar.

The band name is also a combination of a few of their favorite things—having been influenced by both an earlier song of the same name by the English

Amanda Palmer and Brian Viglione of the Boston-based band The Dresden Dolls. [AP Wide World Photos]

post-punk band The Fall, the German city of Dresden, and porcelain-faced dolls whose pale faces are painted with the same dramatic makeup the duo dons for its shows.

The Dresden Dolls released its self-titled debut in 2003, and the duo steadily gained a following in and around its home base of Boston, Massachusetts, thanks mostly in part to its memorable live shows at which fans are encouraged to get involved in the theatrics. The New York City–based record label Roadrunner Records signed the duo soon after and re-released that LP in 2004, further spreading The Dresden Dolls eccentric-yet-spellbinding stage shows and punk piano rock kitsch nationwide.

A live DVD of a Dresden Dolls's performance at the Boston nightclub the Paradise emerged in 2005. The concert DVD included two hours of bonus footage, a full-length concert, and a documentary of the traveling sideshow-like pair. 8ft. Records released The Dresden Dolls's 2005 EP, *A Is for Accident,* which featured such tracks as "Coin-Operated Boy" that further elevated the duo's dramatic element. The EP, which is a collection of a sampling of some of the group's live performances from 2001 to 2003, became a coveted collector's item for Dresden Doll fans. The band's success rose like mercury—and culminated when it was asked to open for Trent Reznor's industrial rock band, **Nine Inch Nails**, on an American tour later that same year.

The Dresden Dolls' second full-length record, *Yes, Virginia,* was released in April 2006 (Roadrunner Records) to widespread acclaim. The standout single "Sing" from that album was a huge success—and, despite the fact that the video for the song was in heavy rotation on MTV, the group did not suffer any casualties of the loyal indie rock fan kind.

Viglione and Palmer brought their visually appealing act to various staple indie concerts in 2006, including **South by Southwest (SXSW)** music festival in Austin, Texas, **Lollapalooza** in Chicago, Bonnaroo Music Festival in Manchester, Tennessee, and the Leeds and Reading festivals in the United Kingdom. The duo's **South by Southwest (SXSW)** performance was included on the 2006 compilation *Wild Wild SXSW Affair, Vol. 3,* and the duo was given a coveted spot as the opening act for 2006's "it" **pop punk** band Panic! At the Disco.

Boston's nearby city, Providence, Rhode Island, paid tribute to The Dresden Dolls in 2006 with a musical featuring several songs from the duo's catalog. Written by a fan, *The Clockwork Waltz* was performed at the East Providence Community Theatre in August. Cambridge, Massachusetts staged its own homage to the band in December 2006 with the production *The Onion Cellar* at the American Repertoire Theatre's Zero Arrow Theatre, which also prominently featured music by The Dresden Dolls.

The group kicked off its participation in the True Colors Tour 2007 alongside Debbie Harry, Cyndi Lauper, The Gossip, and more.

Further Resources: Butcher, Jim. *Death Masks (The Dresden Files, Book 5).* Cincinnati, OH: Roc, 2005; Butcher, Jim. *Fool Moon (The Dresden Files, Book 2).* Cincinnati, OH: Roc,

2001; Dresden Dolls, The. *The Dresden Dolls Companion.* New York: Cherry Lane Music, 2006; http://www.dresdendolls.com.

DRESSY BESSY

The story of Dressy Bessy is, in many ways, the story of indie rock's **Twee pop** movement in the mid-1990s. Dressy Bessy's music was sweet and effete, favoring the sugary harmonies of The Shangri-Las over soaring guitar licks. The group's fans were more likely to bring horn-rims and teddy bears to concerts than Mohawks and drugs, more likely to have at most a fey sneer than second-rate tattoos. The band's passions include Archie comic strips and vintage clothing—the group once claimed to have visited nearly every vintage clothing store in the United States. Belonging to **The Elephant 6 Recording Company** collective, most of the band's work has been released on the Kindercore Records label, one of the largest purveyors of feminized rock. With so many bands rocking out around them, Dressy Bessy represented all things cute and antiheroic about mid-90s **indie pop**.

Dressy Bessy formed in 1996 outside of Denver, Colorado. Singer Tammy Ealom and **The Apples in Stereo** guitarist John Hill had been dating for two years when Hill taught her some basic guitar chords. Ealom began cobbling songs together on a four-track recorder, hopping from failed band to failed band until she met drummer Darren Albert at a record store. New York City native Albert and his friend Rob Greene had been traveling cross-country when their van broke down in Colorado, and they were working to accumulate enough money to get home. Instead, after one extended conversation about music, a friendship formed among the three, and eventually, a band.

With Ealom's shoestring-budget four-track, Dressy Bessy recorded its first 7-inch single, "Ultra Vivid Color," in 1997 on the Little Dipper label. The EP *You Stand Here* followed in 1998 on Drug Racer Records. Dressy Bessy's first full-length album, 1999's *Pink Hearts Yellow Moons* was released on Kindercore. Ealom grew up listening to everything from classic rock to **Pavement** to Edison Lighthouse, and *Pink Hearts Yellow Moons* wove those roots into a catchy, bubble-gum garage pop. Tracks off that album, such as "Jenny Come On" (about a girl named Jenny and her brand new dress) and "Big Vacation," stuck to the simple, unthreatening lyrics characteristic of the 1950s and the early 1960s.

After *California EP* emerged in 2000, Dressy Bessy released its second full-length album, *SoundGoRound* (Kindercore, 2002). Like their previous efforts, *SoundGoRound* struck the same balance between diner-jukebox balladry and garage-pop messiness. That same year, Dressy Bessy's music appeared on the *Powerpuff Girls: Heroes & Villains* compilation in the form of a cover of the song "Bubbles" by the 1960's pop outfit the Free Design. In 2003, Dressy Bessy's self-titled full-length album (Kindercore) continued to reinterpret the sound of its 1960's influences for a broadening audience.

In 2004 the band found itself in one of the most rewarding and most challenging points in its career. That year, the *Denver Post* named Dressy Bessy "The Best of the Underground"; however, the band found itself label-less and drummer-less, as

Kindercore went out of business and Albert left Dressy Bessy. Resisting discouragement, the band quickly recruited new drummer Craig Gilbert and released its fourth full-length, *Electrified,* in 2005 (Transdreamer).

While Dressy Bessy managed to release both EPs and LPs regularly, the group always successfully managed to schedule playing time around John Hill's endeavors with **The Apples in Stereo**. Despite increased attention, Dressy Bessy maintained its innocent charm. Ealom worked a day job through many of the band's releases, and, unlike most musicians, readily admitted so; her mother framed many of the news articles written about her. In 2006, the band launched a U.S. tour. The band worked through 2007 on its forthcoming fall 2008 album.

Further Reading: Sellers, John. *Perfect from Now On: How Indie Rock Saved My Life.* New York: Simon & Schuster, 2007; http://www.elephant6.com; http://www. transdreamer.com.

E

EARLIMART

Sharing a sound strikingly similar to its indie rock contemporaries **Elliott Smith**, **Pedro the Lion**, **Sonic Youth**, Sparklehorse, and the **Pixies**, this influential Los Angeles–based band managed to develop a following in its hometown, which is located just miles from the town that inspired the band's name—Earlimart, California.

Front man Aaron Espinoza has performed and recorded with a dozen or so musicians since its inception in 1999. Espinoza has also earned praise for his work as a producer for albums by such acts as the popular American rock group The Breeders, helping the group tweak its 2002 comeback album, The Meeting Places, **Elliott Smith**, and The New Folk Implosion.

Espinoza's songwriting earned him classic accolades from the likes of the *New York Times,* which claimed that "their music empowers the misunderstood and encourages the underachiever" (Corcoran, 2004). Espinoza teamed up with musician/bassist/backing vocalist Ariana Murray, guitarist Solon Bixler, keyboardist/drummer Davey Latter, and drummer Brian Thornell for the band's first official release, *Filthy Doorways* in 2000 on Devil in the Woods Records.

Earlimart revamped its sound a bit later that year with the sped-up album *Kingdom of Champions* (Devil in the Woods Records, 2000), which mixed a revival of the heyday of 1970s punk rock and the height of 1990s indie rock. Earlimart's ever-shifting lineup continued to morph as singer/keyboardist/guitarist Jim Fairchild, front man for the "indietronica" group Grandaddy, joined the fold for Earlimart's slowed-down, more melodic 2003 EP *The Avenues,* which was released by the group's new label, Palm Pictures. A string of tour dates ensued with **Pedro the Lion**, **Denali**, and even comedian David Cross in 2004 in support of the group's 2003 full-length album, *Everyone Down Here,* which was produced by Grandaddy's Jason Lytle. Shifting its musical focus yet again, *Everywhere,* which featured Espinoza's rich, textured voice, received an 8.5 out of 10 rating from **Pitchfork Media**.

Earlimart paid tribute to Espinoza's late friend, neighbor, and musical pal **Elliott Smith** in *Treble & Tremble* (Palm Pictures, 2004), a ballad-heavy, piano-driven album that ends with an even more haunting track entitled "It's Okay to Think about Ending." The album, which Fairchild and Espinoza produced at Earlimart's studio, the Ship, received critical acclaim for its orchestral arrangements and Espinoza's warm, emotive vocals. Los Angeles area bands Silversun and Irving also record at the Ship.

Earlimart toured extensively in 2007, taking along supporting acts Clinic and Sea Wolf for select dates, while working on the band's forthcoming fifth studio album. Espinoza joked with the media saying the self-produced LP would be titled "Untitled Album." Espinoza previewed the album, which was eventually titled *Mentor Tormentor* (2007), with a 2006 limited edition 7-inch featuring two tracks from the album on Suicide Squeeze Records. *Mentor Tormentor,* which was released by Majordomo Records, an imprint formed by Earlimart and the Shout! Factory entertainment company, was well received by critics. Earlimart's most recent album, *Mentor Tormentor,* came out in August 2007 via Majordomo Records.

Further Reading: http://www.earlimartmusic.com; http://www.grandaddylandscape.com; http://www.myspace.com/earlimart; http://www.palmpictures.com.

ECHO & THE BUNNYMEN

Long before **Nirvana**'s music smashed through the mainstream force field wielding a megaphone of indie rock, this British **post-punk** group captured the hearts of fans in the 1980s before resurging in the **Lollapalooza** generation's CD players. Echo & the Bunnymen, comprised of front man/lead vocalist Ian McCulloch, Will Sergeant (who replaced original member Pete Wylie) Les Pattinson, and a drum machine they had named Echo (which was swiftly replaced by drummer Pete de Freitas, earned cult status; the group's debut album, the moody stripped down *Crocodiles* (Warner Bros. Records, 1980) reached the charts almost immediately after its release.

Hit songs and records did not get the Liverpool-based band kicked out of the indie rock circle—in fact, as the artful musicians continued to improve upon their signature sound and write more intriguing, insightful songs, their popularity soared. Finicky indie fans continued to buy their albums, and Echo & the Bunnymen returned the favor by producing gorgeous, haunting music.

Echo & the Bunnymen bounced from record label (Warner Bros.) to record label (Euphoric) to yet two more labels (London Records and Cooking Vinyl) and back again (Warner Bros.) throughout the group's lengthy career. The band's 1984 album, *Ocean Rain,* was touted as the best album; *Rain* topped the U.K. charts, and many considered the record to be the group's "masterpiece," marking the group as the most underrated British band in hearing distance. Meanwhile, in 1988–1989 the group was experiencing inner turmoil—McCulloch left the band and experienced success with a solo recording, and de Freitas was killed in a motorcycle accident. The band dissolved one member at a time, with McCulloch's replacement, Noel Burke, causing mixed feelings among fans. The new lineup forged on, but the group fell into discord with its label; in a display of rebelliousness, Echo & the Bunnymen toured playing only covers of songs by the likes of Television, The Doors, and The Rolling Stones.

The newly recruited members made a feigned attempt at resurrecting the group, only to have it dissolve around them. McCulloch and Sergeant, however, who had started working together on another musical project, recruited Pattinson and released their first album in almost a decade. 1997's *Evergreen* was a slow start on the band's return to the road it had been on for years, but the painful accuracy of the title of the group's 1999 album, *What Are You Going to Do with Your Life?* proved the band was unable to revive the past. The band issued the 2001 album *Flowers,* but soon Pattinson left the group due to issues in his personal life. McCulloch and Sergeant took another stab at their second chance in the spotlight after almost a dozen albums with the live album *Me, I'm All Smiles,* which preceded the group's 2005 record, *Siberia* (Cooking Vinyl), a recording that proved that indie music still flowed fervently through the group's veins.

Further Reading: Adams, Chris. *Turquoise Days: The Weird World of Echo & the Bunnymen.* New York: Soft Skull Press, 2002; http://www.bunnymen.com; http://www. cookingvinyl.com; http://www.zoorecords.com.

EDITORS

This English rock quartet brandished its indie rock feathers when it turned down a deal with several major labels to sign with the U.K.–based Kitchenware Records label in 2004.

Formed at Staffordshire University in England while studying music technology, the Editors is comprised of vocalist/guitarist Tom Smith, guitarist Chris Urbanowicz, bassist Russell Leetch, and drummer Ed Lay. Online presence bolstered the band's success, and, after shopping its debut around for what seemed like an eternity, the band hit pay dirt when its October 2005 debut single "Bullets" sold out of its initial print run.

While critics may have been impressed by the band's guitar prowess, fans flocked to the band for the band's emotionally charged fervor, which likely stemmed from the angst Smith and crew developed while working at dead-end jobs in Birmingham, England, where they relocated shortly after graduation around 2003.

Briefly known as Snowfield, the Editors have earned comparisons to the 1980s/1990s British **post-punk** group **Echo & the Bunnymen**, the 1970s English rock group Joy Division, and New York City indie darlings **Bloc Party**. The Editors' sophomore single, "Munich," which featured a cover of the 1960s Moog synthesizer-loving band Stereolab's song "French Disko," reached the Top 10 in the United Kingdom and was lauded by critics, helping to spark a nonstop tour in 2005. Prior to that, though, the band had released the subsequent singles "Blood" and "Blood Pt. 2" on Kitchenware.

The Editors released its debut album, *The Back Room* in 2005 via the Fader label (a subsidiary of the music magazine of the same name), and it went Gold. The band toured North America with the New York City–based new wave/**pop punk** group stellastarr at the same time the album was released stateside. In 2006, *Back Room* was nominated for the prestigious Mercury Prize, which celebrates the best album of the year made by a British or Irish act. Having lost the top honors to the U.K. act **Arctic Monkeys**, the Editors kicked off its North American tour at that year's **South by Southwest (SXSW)** music festival in Austin, Texas; the tour lineup included a gig at that summer's **Lollapalooza** festival in Chicago, Illinois. *Rolling Stone* listed the Editors among its 2006 "Artists to Watch"; on the eve of that tour, *The Back Room* went Platinum.

The Editors's five-track EP *All Sparks* came out in May 2006 on Play It Again Sam Records. Sony Records released the import version of that single, which included an enhanced version of the reissued track from *The Back Room* album, never-before-seen artwork, the single's video, a cover of the song "Orange Crush" by the American alt rock band **R.E.M.**, a remix of London record producer/DJ Paul Oakenfold's track "Camera," and never-before-released B-sides.

Far, far away from dreary dead-end jobs and seemingly out-of-reach dreams, the Editors had been catapulted from playing small shows to touring sold-out stadiums in just about a year, proving that the steadfast **DIY (Do-It-Yourself)** indie mentality is a foolproof formula. The Editors kicked off a 2007 tour and released its 2007 album, the Joy Division–inspired "An End Has A Start" on Fader Records. The group toured Europe in 2008.

Further Reading: http://www.editorsofficial.com; http://www.kitchenwarerecords.com.

EISLEY

To this melodic **indie pop** quintet, music is all in the family. Hailing from Tyler, Texas, Eisley is sisters Sherri, Chauntelle, and Stacy, brother Weston, the siblings' friend Jon Wilson, and their cousin Garron. The DuPree siblings (and cousin) were originally named after a town mentioned in the *Star Wars* sequels—Mos Eisley—but the "Mos" was later dropped due to legal and copyright issues. The DuPrees founded Eisley together in 1997, after having played together after church for years until they realized that Eisley was more than just an after-prayer hobby.

Citing **Radiohead**, **Sunny Day Real Estate**'s Jeremy Enigk, Pink Floyd, and The Beatles as their influences, two of the Eisley sisters, Sherri and Chauntelle, began writing and recording songs in their bedroom. Stacy joined the group at the young age of 8 as a songwriter, and Weston was later added to the fold as the band's drummer. Eisley, which originally took the name The Towheads, is comprised of Chauntelle on guitar, Sherri on guitars and vocals, Stacy on keyboards and vocals, Weston on the drums, and Garron on bass, taking over for founding member Jon Wilson.

After years of recording on its own, Eisley began performing locally in and around the greater Dallas, Texas area until 2003, when the *Dallas Observer* newspaper awarded the group its coveted Best New Act Award and Eisley was catapulted into the public eye. Soon after, Eisley garnered the attention of major labels, and the group signed to the Warner Bros. Records imprint, Reprise Records, that same year. Eisley's debut five-track EP, *Laughing City,* which was put out by the Santa Monica, California–based label, Record Collection Music, home to such bands as **The Walkmen**, showcased the group's song-writing abilities and its knack for surreal imagery.

That summer, Eisley toured with pop superstars Coldplay (with which Eisley once shared a manager) and the Canadian singer-songwriter Ron Sexsmith. Eisley released its 2003 follow-up EP, *Marvellous Things,* on Reprise Records, on which the group revealed a slightly darker side. Two years later, Eisley put out its debut LP, *Room Noises* (Reprise, 2005), cementing its categorization under the pop rock umbrella and earning the group comparisons to 1990s Swedish band The Cardigans. *Noises*'s melodic tones have earned the group comparisons to the wistful English alt rock group band The Sundays.

Eisley logged serious miles soon after, hitting the road with their tour manager/father, Boyd Dupree, in tow in 2004, with the **indie pop** band **Snow Patrol**; in 2005 as the supporting act for the alt rock group Switchfoot and the Canadian indie/garage rock group Hot Hot Heat; and in 2006, as the opening act for the emo band Taking back Sunday before headlining its own *Final Noise* tour. The track "Telescope Eyes," off of the group's debut EP went into heavy rotation on the radio and the band launched an online marketing campaign to publicize the videos for several of the songs from *Noises.*

Eisley's Sherri got engaged to guitarist Chad Gilbert of the punk rock group New Found Glory shortly after Eisley opened for the band on its 2005 tour.

Eisley's second full-length album, *Combinations* (Warner Reprise Records), which was produced by Richard Gibbs (former member of the 1980s new wave group Oingo Boingo), came out in early 2007. Eisley earned a slot at **South by Southwest (SXSW)** music festival in its home state of Texas that same year. Eisley launched its "Combinations" tour in the spring of 2008 in support of the album *Combinations*

Further Reading: Koster, Rick. *Texas Music.* New York: St. Martin's Griffin, 2000;http://www.eisley.com/journals;http://www.myspace.com/eisley;http://www.recordcollectionmusic.com.

THE ELEPHANT 6 RECORDING COMPANY

Four Louisianan high school friends—Robert Schneider, Bill Doss, Will Cullen Hart, and Jeff Mangum—who shared a passion for music, the **DIY (Do-It-Yourself)** aesthetic, and for such bands as The Beach Boys, The Beatles, and **The Velvet Underground** formed this Athens, Georgia, and Denver, Colorado–based music collective in the early 1990s. This label/music collective is split into two offices—E6 East and E6 West. The name Elephant 6 was a suggestion of Hart; it was chosen from an array of other animal-number combinations such as Rhinoceros 12 and Hummingbird 19. Elephant 6 is less of a label and more of a collective of interconnected musicians who collaborate on various projects. The E6 musicians are often considered **Lo-fi** artists because of their **DIY (Do-It-Yourself)** recording practices—almost all of the E6 albums are recorded in Schneider's home studio.

Elephant 6 really got its legs, though, when Schneider, who moved to Colorado to attend college, met Jim McIntyre and Chris Parfitt, who shared his passion for music. Schneider began playing music with Parfitt, and the two wrote songs together until Hart and Mangum also soon relocated to Colorado. Along with Schneider's other new acquaintance, Hilarie Sidney, Schneider, Parfitt, and Mangum formed the indie outfit **The Apples in Stereo**.

The E6 family was featured in a 1998 issue of *Rolling Stone* magazine, which highlighted the universality that ties together all of the bands on the roster—a collective indie rock **DIY (Do-It-Yourself)** approach and mentality, a penchant for "classic psychedelica and oddball instrumentation" (Hermes, 1998). Schneider engineers a large majority of the albums released by Elephant 6.

The Apples in Stereo recorded an EP and released 500 copies (along with a 12-page illustrated CD booklet) of it in 1993 as the first official release from the Elephant 6 Recording Company. **The Apples in Stereo**'s albums, which were distributed by the New York–based independent label spinART Records, had sold approximately 20,000 copies each by the year 2001. **The Apples in Stereo** also did something most indie bands would turn their noses up at—the band licensed the use of its song "Strawberryfire" to a New York City advertising agency for use in a Sony commercial. Instead of viewing the sale of the song as "selling out," the group told the *New York Times* that the band members saw it as an opportunity to earn more money in one short period of time than they did in a whole year of touring and selling albums. Plus, Schneider, who had married Sidney, was worried about providing for their son, Maxwell, who was born in 2000 (Schneider and Sidney divorced a few years later).

The oft-described "patriarch" of Elephant 6, Schneider also records music under bands known as Orchestre Fantastique. As Orchestre Fantastique, Schneider contributed songs to the soundtrack for the 2000 film *Dean Quixote*. He also records music as Marbles, the moniker for his solo work. Marbles's early recordings were released as cassettes; on these, Schneider sang about his friends, family, and even his cats on a four-track recorder.

The next band signed to the Elephant 6 roster was the **indie pop** group The Olivia Tremor Control, formerly known as Synthetic Flying Machine, of which Doss, who still records music under the moniker The Sunshine Fix for his solo work, and Hart, the group's front man, were members. The Olivia Tremor Control's first release, *California Demise,* came out in 1994. Doss also worked on his solo project, Neutral Milk Hotel, which also became part of the Elephant 6 music collective. These three bands—**The Apples in Stereo**, The Olivia Tremor Control, and Neutral Milk Hotel—and the group Of Montreal are considered the heart center of The Elephant 6 Recording Company.

The Olivia Tremor Control's members all have ties to or share members with other E6 bands such as The Sunshine Fix; Circulatory System; Frosted Ambassador; Pipes You See, Pipes You Don't; Black Swan Network; and Elf Power. Black Swan Network, which is the experimental side project of The Olivia Tremor Control, released its first full-length album, the eight-track opus *The Late Music Volume One,* in 1997 on the Australian independent label Camera Obscura. After The Olivia Tremor Control called it a day, a few of the group's members formed the sextet Circulatory System, with some of their E6 pals. Circulatory System self-released its debut album in 2001 on the group's own Cloud Recordings; the band is currently at work on its sophomore release.

Neutral Milk Hotel's early cassette-only recordings were released by E6 in the mid-1990s. The Athens, Georgia–based group put out its debut album in 1994 with help from Schneider. After a change in the lineup, Neutral Milk Hotel recorded its sophomore album in Schneider's Pet Sounds Studio; the group took a brief hiatus from 1998 to 1999 so each of the band members could pursue solo efforts. Neutral Milk Hotel made plans to release a B-side/rarities collection on the Athens, Georgia–based indie label Orange Twin Records. Neutral Milk Hotel's critically acclaimed 2003 sophomore album, *In the Aeroplane over the Sea* in which Mangum sang about the fate of Anne Frank, beat out **Nirvana** in the ranking of the top 60 albums of the past decade by *Magnet* music magazine. *Aeroplane* ranked #15 on the reputable Pazz & Jop poll by *The Village Voice*.

Sharing members with the groups Elf Power and Circulatory System, the indie band Of Montreal, created by front man Kevin Barnes, formed in the late 1990s. The Athens, Georgia–based band has deep roots in the E6 equation—using basic pop guidelines mixed with experimental multi-instrumentalism.

Will Westbrook, Scott Spillane, and John D'Azzo formed The Gerbils back in 1992 during their college years. Several of the group's releases featured contributions by members of The Olivia Tremor Control, Neutral Milk Hotel, and the band Marta Tennae. London's Earworm Records and Orange Twin Records released a string of the group's releases. The band disbanded after the death of Westbrook in 2006.

The indie quartet Elf Power formed in 1993, starting out with a series of four-track recordings and its **Lo-fi** debut album, *Vainly Clutching at Phantom Limbs,* which was released by the Portland, Oregon–based Arena Rock Recording Co. in 1995. Several of Elf Power's recordings feature contributions by musicians who belong to other bands on the E6 roster, and a few of its recordings have been released jointly by E6 and Arena Rock, which was initially formed in New York City's Lower East Side. Elf Power shares members with the all-female "art performance" group Dixie Blood mustache.

The **Lo-fi** trio Chocolate USA was formed pre-E6 back in 1989 when the group was known as Miss America. The band, however, was forced to change its name after Miss America Pageant officials expressed their disdain at the band's name. Chocolate USA's first release was a self-released cassette; the group also ran the popular "Chocolatey Good Smash Hit of the Month Club," a tape exchange club, for several years. The pop/folk/indie label Bar/None Records released the band's albums before the group disbanded in the mid-1990s. Chocolate USA, which is fronted by Julian Koster of the Music Tapes and Neutral Milk Hotel, however, is still considered part of the E6 collective. Chocolate USA's members are also part of The Olivia Tremor Control, The Music Tapes, and Neutral Milk Hotel.

Frosted Ambassador, which was formed back in 1977, is yet another group that has a rich history predating the E6 collective; Frosted Ambassador shares members with The Olivia Tremor Control and The Music Tapes. Another mysterious band signed to the E6 roster is Major Organ and the Adding Machine, which was originally believed to be Neutral Milk Hotel's Jeff Mangum and Julian Koster's side project, but the ensemble has grown in size to include members of the Elephant 6 Orchestra and contributors from such bands as Circulatory System, Elf Power, The Olivia Tremor Control, The Music Tapes, and the band Of Montreal.

Beulah's six members joined forces in 1994, but did not formally release an album until 1997, when E6 put out the group's EP *A Small Cattle Drive in a Snow Storm*. Schneider mastered the group's 1997 LP, *Handsome Western States,* but its sophomore 1999 album, *When Your Heartstrings Break,* was released by Sugar Free Records. **Beulah** played its final show in 2004 before the group disbanded so each member could pursue solo projects.

Dressy Bessy's front woman, Tammy Ealom, was inspired to learn to play the guitar after her boyfriend, John Hill (of **The Apples in Stereo**), gave her one for Christmas. Named for an actual doll, **Dressy Bessy** put out its first official release, the single, "Ultra Vivid Color," in 1997 via the group's own Little Dipper Records. In 2005, **Dressy Bessy** released its fourth full-length album, *Electrified.*

The Brooklyn, New York–based trio Essex Green released its debut album, *Everything Is Green,* on the Athens, Georgia–based label Kindercore Records in 1999. Merge Records put out the group's 2003 sophomore album, *The Long Goodbye*. Essex Green shares members with groups outside the E6 collective.

The Olivia Tremor Control and Circulatory System's Peter Erchick's solo project, Pipes You See, Pipes You Don't, put out his debut album, *Individualized Shirts,* in 2001. Orange Twin Records re-released the album in 2003.

Schneider's home studio, Pet Sounds, was forced to relocate in 2001 when new developers purchased the building it occupied. That same year, Schneider teamed up with Andy Partridge, the front man for the 1970s English new wave group XTC, on some music for Schneider's Orchestre Fantastique project. Partridge had become a fan of Schneider's work after hearing some of **The Apples in Stereo** recordings put out by SpinART Records.

In 2001, **The Apples in Stereo** contributed a song to an episode of the Cartoon Network program *The Powerpuff Girls,* and the song appeared on the soundtrack to the movie. Schneider, who was a big fan of the show, was delighted to have the opportunity to contribute a song for the show.

During a hiatus of **The Apples in Stereo**, Schneider launched a second label, Optical Records Manufacturing, in Lexington, Kentucky, in 2003, which he ran with pal Amanda Burford, of the group Elf Power. Optical's first releases were 7-inches by groups such as Oranger, Von Hemmling, High Water Marks (Sidney's project with members of Palermo, Von Hemmling, and Oranger; its debut album was released in 2003 by Eenie Meanie Records), ulysses, Palermo, and Hair Police. Schneider and Sidney also formed a new band, ulysses, which he said was influenced by the music of such bands as The Cars, **My Bloody Valentine**, and **The Velvet Underground**. Ulysses, which Schneider formed in 2003 while living in Lexington, Kentucky, played the 2003 **CMJ Music Marathon** in New York City.

That same year, the indie label Isota Records released a series of vinyl-only copies of three albums from bands signed to the Orange Twins Records roster, including one by Elephant 6 founder Jeff Mangum. Mangum was also a member of the hodge-podge music project Major Organ and the Adding Machine, which featured a number of his fellow Elephant 6 compatriots. Von Hemmling is the side project of Jim McIntrye, the former bassist of **The Apples in Stereo**. A collection of Von Hemmlings's singles from 1995 to 2004 is compiled in the *Wild Hemmling* anthology.

Toward the end of Elephant 6's decade anniversary, though, things started to wind down. Fewer and fewer of the records put out by the collective featured its signature logo, which Hart had designed (an artist, Hart has released books of his artwork), and Schneider informed the media that Elephant 6 was indeed running out of gas by alluding to a final as-yet-to-be-determined Elephant 6 compilation album. Schneider, though, remained busy, operating Pet Sounds Studio and making plans with **The Apples in Stereo** to return to the studio to record new music and possibly tour in 2004.

Sidney's side project, High Water Marks, released its debut album, *Songs About the Ocean,* on the Los Angeles–based Eenie Meanie label in 2004. Sidney, who played drums for **The Apples in Stereo**, also records music under the name Secret Squares. She left **The Apples in Stereo** in 2006 after her divorce from Schneider.

The Olivia Tremor Control's catalog was back in print in 2004, a few years after the group's former label, Flydaddy Records, went bankrupt. *In the Aeroplane Over the Sea,* a book in the 33-1/3 series of books about classic albums about the making of Neutral Milk Hotel's album, was published in 2005.

The Elephant 6 Recording Company experienced a sad event in late 2006 when its long-time friend and musical collaborator, Will Westbrook, who was a member of Neutral Milk Hotel as well as The Olivia Tremor Control and the guitarist for The Gerbils (a band signed to Elephant 6 affiliate label Orange Twin), passed away. Westbrook suffered from an undisclosed long-term illness. His death gripped the music community in Athens, Georgia.

The Apples in Stereo's 2007 album, *New Magnetic Wonder* (the group's first in five years), was the first album to be released by actor Elijah Wood's Yep Roc Records label (in conjunction with Simian Records). Schneider created an E6 reunion of sorts by recruiting members of The Olivia Tremor Control and Jeff Mangum for the effort. Schneider has since remarried and has been working on yet another musical installation, the acid rock band The American Revolution. **The Apples in Stereo** performed on *Late Night with Conan O'Brien* in 2007, made an appearance at the 2007 **South by Southwest (SXSW)** music festival, and played on the bill of the 2007 "All Tomorrow's Parties Vs the Fans" festival in Minehead, England, before kicking off a North American tour with the band Casper & the Cookies in support of *New Magnetic Wonder*. Schneider created buzz for the new album by appearing on a highly publicized episode of Comedy Central's

The Colbert Report during which host Stephen Colbert engaged in a guitar battle with Chris Funk of **The Decemberists**.

Bands signed to the Elephant 6 Recording Company roster include the following:

The Apples in Stereo	Frosted Ambassador	Neutral Milk Hotel
Beulah	The Gerbils	The Olivia Tremor Control
Black Swan Network	High Water Marks	Orchestre Fantastique
Chocolate USA	Major Organ and the Adding Machine	Pipes You See, Pipes You Don't
Circulatory System	Jeff Mangum	Secret Square
Dixie Blood mustache	Marbles	The Sunshine Fix
Dressy Bessy	Minders	ulysses
Elf Power	The Music Tapes	Von Hemmling
Essex Green		

Further Reading: Cooper, Kim. *The Aeroplane Over the Sea.* New York: Continuum International Publishing Group, 2005; http://www.arenarockrecordingco.com; http://www.bar-none.com; http://www.earwormrecords.com; http://www.eeniemeenie.com; http://www.elephant6.com; http://www.e6townhall.com; http://www.heratyhall.com/kindercore; http://www.neutralmilkhotel.net; http://www.oliviatremorcontrol.com; http://www.orangetwin.com; http://www.recordcollectionmusic.com/; http://www.sugarfreerecords.com.

EMO/EMOCORE/SADCORE

The emo indie rock subgenre, which is also sometimes referred to as "emocore," emerged in the 1980s in Washington, D.C., after such bands as the influential hardcore group Minor Threat disbanded, leaving behind a dry spell of new, innovative sounds and music. Emo was therefore born out of a desperate need for honest music with the same kind of edge that the D.C. scene had grown accustomed to; thus, on the precipice of the impending death of hardcore, emo was born. Sadcore, a slower, more emotional version of hardcore music, is yet another offshoot of the subgenre.

Emo, which refers to sensitive music made by often tattooed, black T-shirt-wearing, and even eyeliner-wearing musicians, was actually a derivative of "hardcore" punk music, a genre that incorporates palpable angst and nearly unintelligible lyrics that are screamed more than they are sung. The 1984 album "Zen Arcade" by the Minneapolis, Minnesota–based hardcore/punk outfit **Hüsker Dü** is credited with being the significant album that set the stage for this new sound. Emo's official birth date, however, harkens back to 1985, which is often referred to as "Revolution Summer."

Emo now encompasses a wide range of both rock and punk music that has a softer side (hence the use of the prefix from the word, "emotional"); in other words, emo bands are typically comprised of singers who proudly fly the punk flag while wearing their hearts on their sleeves, paving the way for rough-around-the-edges musicians to show their emotions through their music. Emo has even morphed off into yet another subgenre known as "screamo," in which song lyrics are emoted through vocal-chord ripping screams.

This sound, therefore, became known as the "D.C. sound," and its official entrance into pop culture is marked by a 1985 *Flipside* magazine interview with **Rites of Spring** in which the band used the term. The 1980s Maryland-based band, Moss Icon, is highly regarded as one of the most influential emo bands to incite other groups to focus on the emotional aspect of their music more than the punk side. Other significant emo bands include Embrace, One Last Wish, Beefeater, and Gray Matter. **Fugazi** front man Ian McKaye's own label, Dischord Records, is credited with releasing the biggest chunk of emo releases in the early 1980s before the genre fizzled out around the time D.C. post-hardcore band Hoover disbanded.

Early emo bands such as **Rites of Spring**, One Last Wish, and Embrace, all of which were at one time signed to the punk label Dischord Records, added melodic sounds to heavier punk music, singing about more personal topics and even discussing themes that would otherwise be taboo in the punk world—meaning one's true innermost feelings. Other D.C. area bands on the scene—Fire Party, Marginal Man, Shudder to Think, and Soulside—all stretched the hardcore punk sound by lending this new vocal sound to the mix. A blend of slightly ambiguous, soul-searching, yearning vocal stylings and softer lyrics helped to set the tone for the next generation of bands that would be handed the emo baton.

The **DIY (Do-It-Yourself)** mentality swept through D.C., expanding across the United States to San Diego, California, where like-minded bands and musicians were making and releasing emo music on such labels as Gravity Records and Ebullition Records. Such groups included Swing Kids, Mohinder, Heroin, Indian Summer, Drive Like Jehu, Angel Hair, Antioch Arrow, Portraits of Past, Still Life, and more—all of which shared a similar mentality as well as political and social themes that rang true with and further influenced their fans.

The first wave of emo slowly died out in the early 1990s, except for such groups as **Fugazi** and Texas Is the Reason that added an indie spin to emo, pioneering the sub-subgenre known as indie emo. After **Fugazi**, though, next-generation indie emo bands seemed to embrace the mainstream by touting the roots of indie emo. This dichotomous marriage seemed like a blasphemy to truehearted emo fans, but the MTV crowd embraced it full on, thinning the subgenre to the point that any band touting a frown or angst-ridden lyrics would then be categorized as "emo."

A social spin-off of emo known as "Straight Edge," the term for which was coined from a song by Minor Threat, got its legs in the California Bay Area. Influencing teens to abstain from alcohol and drugs and to live a pure lifestyle, the straight-edge community blossomed, sprouting such straight-edge bands as Teen Idles (which Ian McKaye formed before Minor Threat). Members of the straight-edge subculture often mark the backs of their hands with black Xs; some of them are vegans.

The emo sound continued to find it voice and it was occasionally thinned out, but many bands that struggled to represent it in its purest form worked hard to keep emo's roots intact. Groups such as Funeral Diner, A Day in Black and White, and Circle Takes the Square were particularly popular for their efforts in this regard.

The Midwest eventually got on the emo bandwagon, resulting in such groups as Kansas City's Boy's Life and Chicago's Cap'n Jazz. **Fugazi** continued to be a major influence on newer bands, and emo scenes popped up in unlikely places such as Phoenix, Arizona. Punk still has its place in the emo world, though, with bands such as **Hüsker Dü** and Boston's **Mission of Burma** selling out shows and influencing kids even more. The band **Sunny Day Real Estate** (SDRE) experienced a high in the mid-1990s, emerging as a leader in the emo scene and the **DIY (Do-It-Yourself)** movement until the group disbanded in 2001. SDRE is often tagged "emo-core," which helped indie emo to gain even more popularity in the music world and online.

Indie music was woven intricately into emo in the 1990s by such hardcore bands as **Sub Pop Records** recording artists **Sunny Day Real Estate**, New York City band Texas Is the Reason, which was signed to **Jade Tree Records**, San Francisco punk band Jawbreaker, and the influential **Fugazi** (whose name is an acronym used during the Vietnam War). Mid-1990s bands such as the Kansas City **pop punk** band The Get Up Kids, the Arizona band Jimmy Eat World, and the Milwaukee, Wisconsin–based band The Promise Ring, which went on to attain national exposure and success, skewed the genre even further by mixing an **indie pop** sensibility into the mix. Tried and true hardcore fans argue that bands like these have strayed from the emo sound so far that they can hardly be classified as such, but the media, hard-pressed to label them with a genre, have otherwise branded them with the "emo" tag.

Emo's biggest stars, such as Florida's Dashboard Confessional, helped to introduce emo to the mainstream—and the genre exploded. The press took the aesthetic of emo and ran with it, causing a tidal wave of confessional, intimate songwriting that was ultimately spread a bit thin in the eyes of the genre's early fans who felt that emo had been stretched to span the **pop punk** genre they so detest; meanwhile, adding salt to the wound, Confessional's front man Chris Carrabba has since become a poster boy for emo.

This thinning out of the genre paved the way for modern bands such as the Long Island–based "rockemo" quintet Brand New and nearby pop punkers Taking Back Sunday, Chicago's Fall Out Boy, and New Jersey band Thursday, which have thinned the genre to the point that it is unrecognizable to its early supporters. Additionally, after bands like these inked deals with major record labels, the marketing and advertising industries ultimately designed a way to get into the fold by offering them sponsorships and endorsement deals. Stores like Hot Topic, which markets and sells clothes based on the original punk aesthetic to suburban kids, started popping up in shopping malls over the country, and emo bands started licensing their songs for use in TV commercials.

Even bands that were not necessarily emo groups were categorized that way by the media. Perhaps the best example of this is the 1990s band Weezer, whose nerd-like persona and "woe is me" lyrics meant the band would be deemed emo, even though the group's roots are deeply rooted in pop and alternative rock.

Eventually, a few indie labels emerged to stave off the eradication of emo. Labels such as Omaha, Nebraska's **Saddle Creek Records**, **Jade Tree Records**, England's **DIY (Do-It-Yourself)** label Crank! Records, and Boston's Big Wheel Recreation put out albums and compilations by indie emo bands and emo pioneers alike, such as The Promise Ring, Mineral, Knapsack, and more. And bands such as Texas' **At the Drive-In**, whose high-octane melodies, speedy punk edge, and angsty guitar riffs harkened back to emo's early days in ways the group's contemporaries could only dream of, emerged on the scene.

Seeing the earning potential of marketing, sales, and lengthy tour itineraries, major labels started scooping up emo bands that had been barely making ends meet, but bands such as Jawbreaker and D.C.'s **Jawbox**, which took the bait, complained of major-label bullying and mistreatment that affected their music in ways they did not anticipate. Several emo bands that were approached with major-label deals disbanded over disagreement about whether to sign, which in their eyes, was seen as "selling out." Groups such as Texas Is the Reason and Mineral disbanded around this time in the late 1990s as emo was transforming into a trendy subgenre made by bands that had jumped on the mainstream bandwagon in hopes of becoming stars on MTV. In the eyes of their early comrades, however, they were sellouts, which was the worst kind of fate to befall a true punk rocker. Still, modern bands such as Pennsylvania band The Juliana Theory, California's Sparta (a spin-off of **At the Drive-In** that is comprised of its former members), and the Irish/English group Jetplane Landing strive to keep emocore's roots alive, and kicking.

The genre now spans so far as to encompass modern acts that may not have been part of the emo subgenre such as **Bright Eyes**, My Chemical Romance, **Death Cab for Cutie**, Hawthorne Heights, Panic At the Disco (the band decided in 2008 to drop the "!" from its name), Story of the Year, Senses Fail, The Used, The Starting Line, Something Corporate, and more. Popular culture's adoption of the term emo has seemed to strip all of the subgenre's original meaning—and intent—from it, reducing the subgenre to nothing more than a marketing ploy used by major labels to make a buck.

The emo genre still remains difficult to define, with publications such as *USA Today* pondering the equation, stating that even bands and musicians themselves are hard-pressed to explain it fully: "emo pop-rockers concoct abstract and ungainly song titles that are often clever and self-referential but rarely correspond to lyrics and may have only a peripheral relationship to the song's meaning" (Gundersen, 2006). Other newspapers and magazines claimed that emo rockers are even tiring of the emo tag.

Further Reading: Emond, Steve. *Emo Boy Volume 1: Nobody Cares About Anything Anyway, So Why Don't We All Just Die?* San Jose, CA: SLG Publishing, 2006; Greenwald, Andy. *Nothing Feels Good.* New York: St. Martin's Griffin, 2003; http://www.dashboardconfessional.com; http://www.dischord.com; http://www.fightoffyourdemons.com; http://www.thegetupkids.com.

F

THE FAINT

Resurrecting 1980s new wave music with a unique blend of danceable music that infused certain angst-filled, dark qualities, The Faint was one of the flagship bands signed to **Saddle Creek Records** in the late 1990s. **Saddle Creek Records** founder **Conor Oberst** was a brief member of this indie rock/synthesizer pop quintet that hails from Oberst's hometown, Omaha, Nebraska, a locale that became a most unlikely hotbed of musical pioneers in the late 1990s and early-2000s.

The Faint—Joel Petersen, Clark Baechle, and Todd Fink, who had taken his wife's last name when they were married in the spring of 2005—released a selection of singles before becoming a testament to the burgeoning music scene in the group's hometown when it released its 1998 debut album, *Media,* a ballsy, edgy album that helped put The Faint on the map beyond the circumference of the group's historical city. Leaving Omaha and the band's original name behind— the group was formerly known as Normal Bailer, a tongue-in-cheek reference to the American novelist/journalist and playwright Norman Mailer, under which it recorded the lone album *Sine Sierra*—The Faint toured the United States on the success of *Media;* a change of lineup ensued shortly thereafter, but with the addition of new member Jacob Thiele, the group developed a more techno-heavy sound.

Inciting indie fans to lift their "Chucks" (aka Converse sneakers) and dance, The Faint's sophomore album, *Blank-Wave Arcade* (**Saddle Creek Records,** 1999) helped the band expand into the underground scene, where it gained even more fans. The Faint's lineup underwent yet another change in makeup with the addition of a death metal guitarist known as Dapose during the making of its next album—2001's electronica and house music–influenced recording, *Danse Macabre* (**Saddle Creek Records**, 2001), which catapulted the group into the realm of commercial success and critical applause, resulting in a lengthy tour for the group [Astralwerks released a remix of the album in 2003 and **NME (New Musical Express)** gave the album an 8 out of 10 rating]. Along the way, The Faint released quite a few singles on such record labels as Gold Standard Laboratories, City Slang Records, and Fierce Panda Records, along with a split 7-inch with pop rockers Ex-Action Figures, on **Saddle Creek Records** and a remix of the group's 2001 album in 2003 entitled *Danse Macabre Remixes.*

In 2004, The Faint released the intense, zealous *Wet From Birth* **Saddle Creek Records,** an album title that the band created to describe the cliché "wet behind the ears," which the band members felt aptly titled their habit for genre-jumping and their penchant for penning tongue-in-cheek lyrics. The Faint celebrated its recent successes by vacating the empty warehouse the group had been recording in (the band referred to the space as the Orifice) and moving into a new space where the band recorded its follow-up effort, the single "I Disappear," before heading out on the road for select tour dates with **TV on the Radio**. Rumors circulated that the experimental group was in talks regarding the record with big-time producer Rick Rubin, who has worked with acts such as the Red Hot Chili Peppers, Metallica, and Justin Timberlake. Members of The Faint dabbled with the production end of music by remixing songs by groups such as **Yeah Yeah Yeahs** and **Azure Ray** in 2004.

Over the years, The Faint's lineup has experienced a game of musical chairs—having entertained such members as Matt Champagne, **Conor Oberst**, and Matt Bowen. The current lineup consists of Fink (lead vocals and keyboards), Jacob Thiele (backing vocals and keyboards), Dapose (guitar), Clark Baechle (drums), Paul Mackenzie Braden (keyboards and synthesizer), and Joel Petersen (bass). Founding member Oberst rejoined the band onstage for the first time in years when his group, **Bright Eyes**, toured with his former bandmates for select dates in 2005 when they played gigs in the United States, Japan, Australia, and Europe.

Saddle Creek Records rounded up The Faint and several other bands on its roster to contribute songs for a 2005 compilation to benefit victims of Hurricane Katrina.

The Faint hit the road after two years of not touring with a mini tour in 2006 for which the electro band Ratatat joined the group as the supporting act. That same year, Dapose continued work on his side project, Precious Metal, before the group auctioned off a guitar he had autographed to raise money to contribute to a friend's lung transplant operation.

In 2007, The Faint contributed to the compilation *At the Crossroads: A Benefit for Homeless Youth,* which features rare tracks by other indie bands such as **Calexico** and **Rogue Wave**. Also in 2007 the band kicked off a brief tour before playing its first **South by Southwest (SXSW)** performance in seven years in Austin, Texas; the group continued work on its follow-up album as well.

Further Reading: Azerrad, Michael. *Our Band Could Be Your Life: Scenes from the American Indie Underground 1981–1991.* New York: Back Bay Books, 2002; http://www.myspace.com/thefaint; http://www.saddle-creek.com; http://www.thefaint.com.

FEIST

Cast among the new crop of indie rock "all stars" that has popped up on the underground music scene in the last few years, this Canadian singer-songwriter has been an on-again, off-again member of the indie conglomerate **Broken Social Scene**. Feist, who was born Leslie Feist in 1976, self-produced a demo recording in 2001 called "The Red Demos," which earned her a major-label contract, several Juno Awards, and the opportunity to have her song "The Reminder" featured on the ABC hit drama *Grey's Anatomy* and in a commercial for the much buzz about iPod Nano.

Born into a musical family, Feist played guitar in bands called Placebo and By Divine Right. While playing with Placebo, the group won a Battle of the Bands contest that earned Feist and her crew the opportunity to play in a festival that featured the **Ramones** on the bill. Feist went solo and released her self-produced solo album, *Monarch (Lay Your Jewelled Head Down)* in 1999. The singer, who was once told she would "never sing again" (Rule, 2008) after severely damaging her vocal chords in the mid-1990s, became roommates with electro-shock rocker Peaches and began touring with the performer in the late 1990s.

In between extensive touring with **Broken Social Scene** (BSS), Feist recorded her sophomore release, *Let It Die,* for BSS's record label, Arts & Crafts Records in 2004. The home recording, which was made with the help of pianist/electro artist Gonzales, helped Feist gain more exposure and notoriety as a songwriter. Feist soon moved to Paris, France, where she collaborated with the group Kings of Convenience. In 2005, Feist was awarded two Juno Awards for "Best New Artist" and "Best Alternative Album." *Let It Die* has sold over 85,000 copies, and the album went straight to the Top 30 in Europe (http://www.musicianguide. com). Feist stands apart from most indie artists with her sound: atmospheric music that is layered with her whimsical vocal stylings and hypnotic, yet ethereal electronic beats. Feist's music shares similarities with BSS's music for its clever use of electronic music that sounds natural and even undeniably organic despite its partially computer-generated origins. The accomplished torch singer writes, performs, and records all of her own music with her backing bandmates Julian Brown, Bryden Baird, and Jesse Baird.

In 2006, Feist released an album of remixes entitled *Open Season* on Arts & Crafts Records. She reentered the recording studio to record her 2007 release, *The Reminder* (from Santa Monica, California–based indie label Cherrytree Records), which features the hit song "1234," hitting #8 on the U.S. Billboard charts. The track has since been referred to as the "iPod Nano song" on the blog circuit. Still, Feist's hard work, drive, and self-producing work in her early days as a musician have managed to stave off any whispers of "sell out" in the wake of the success—and heavy TV rotation—of the iPod Nano commercial. *BLENDER* magazine heralded the album by ranking it #80 on the magazine's list of "The Best 100 Indie Albums Ever," which appeared in the December 2007 issue (http:// www.blender.com/guide/articles.aspx?ID=2974).

Feist performed at the 2008 Grammys, though she did not win in any of the categories in which she was nominated. She did, however, walk away with the 2008 Shortlist Music Prize. Feist kicked off 2008 with select tour dates in the United States.

Further Reading: Reddington, Helen. *The Lost Women of Rock Music,* Ashgate Popular and Folk Music Series. London: Ashgate Publishing Co., 2007; http://www. cherrytreerecords.com; http://www.enotes.com/contemporary-musicians/feist-biography; http://www.listentofeist.com; http://www.myspace.com/feist.

THE FIERY FURNACES

The primary players in this Brooklyn, New York–based indie group is brother-sister duo Matthew and Eleanor Friedberger. Their experimental, enigmatic rock easily caught the attention of the hipster clientele in the borough—not to mention the ears of the execs at **Rough Trade Records**, who signed the band in the mid-2000s for its debut album, *Gallowsbird's Bark* (2003), a 16-track effort that spanned the sounds of alt-country, psychedelica, dreamy pop, and no-holds-barred indie rock.

The Fiery Furnaces, whose name is reportedly inspired by a combination of things including poet William Blake and the 1960s children's book *Chitty Chitty Bang Bang,* attracted acclaim for the group's clever lyrics and surreal storybook-like tales they weave, not to mention its stripped down sound, which has earned The Fiery Furnaces comparisons to that other "brother-sister" duo **The White Stripes**. Entertaining a rotating lineup of drummers and sound engineers, The Fiery Furnaces released its sophomore effort, *Blueberry Boat,* in 2004. On this record, the Friedbergers spin a kaleidoscope of songs in which they sing about abstract things and surreal activities like having "tea time at Damascus computer café."

On the duo's 2005 complex, off-beat *EP,* The Fiery Furnaces proved the duo was more than just a pair of Brooklynites who enjoyed standing out in a crowd; this 41-minute epic compilation featured rare tracks, B-sides, and singles, including a prelude to the duo's follow-up album, *Rehearsing My Choir.* Setting the artistic bar even higher, *Choir* is a well-planned concept album that literally spans decades—pairs of tracks represent various decades from the 1920s up through the 1990s. The Friedbergers, who dedicated the album to their grandmother Olga Sarantos, who is featured lovingly on the cover art, allowed their matriarchal idol to take the artistic direction helm on the album as she narrates various fable-like stories about her eclectic life on each track.

The duo's 2006 album, *Bitter Tea,* which came out on the Mississippi-based Fat Possum Records label (home to mostly Mississippi blues artists), was reportedly influenced by the 1970s synthesizer pop act Devo, the red foam hat-wearing harbingers of the hit "Whip It." *Tea* is a more centered release that appeased fans who criticized the siblings for dabbling too extremely in vaudevillian waters for their last record. *Tea* brought back what fans of The Fiery Furnaces love best—dance-inducing pop, hard-rocking indie, and even a bit of electronica. Meanwhile that same year, Matthew put out two solo albums, a pop-infused album and a noise rock effort that earned the musician comparisons to The Magnetic Fields' Stephin Merritt; *Winter Women* and *Holy Ghost Language School* (859 Recordings) came packaged together, although the set was not meant to be a double release.

The duo toured as the opening act for the San Francisco–based experimental/improv rock group Deerhoof later that year, surprising fans by looping the songs on *Tea* into one long singular song that lasted over 30 minutes. The duo's 2008 album, *Widow City,* was released by the Chicago, Illinois–based independent label Thrill Jockey.

Further Reading: Pollack, Neal. *Never Mind the Pollacks: A Rock and Roll Novel.* Reprint ed. New York: Harper Paperbacks, 2004; http://www.859recordings.com; http://www.fatpossum.com; http://www.myspace.com/fieryfurnacesfolife; http://www.thefieryfurnaces.com; http://www.thrilljockey.com.

FLYLEAF

Formed in Temple, Texas, the name Flyleaf comes from the dedication page that often appears before the beginning of a book. Crediting such mid-1990s influences as the Smashing Pumpkins, Rage Against the Machine, and even The Cranberries, Flyleaf's music—rife with scathing guitars and jabbing drum lines—honors those roots musically with a lyrical departure that explores a positive path leading away from the ambivalence and angst that often overcame the group's predecessors.

Flyleaf's upbringing, though, does not have the simplicity of a mere dedication. Lead singer Lacey Mosley grew up living from paycheck to paycheck, as one of six children raised by a single mother. By age 16, Mosley was already battling drug addiction, resisting suicidal urges, and ultimately taking to writing songs that reflected the bleakness of her life.

Amid the turmoil, Mosley eventually moved in with her grandparents in Mississippi. Her grandparents took her to church, and Mosley's life, and her songwriting, changed forever. While she initially aspired to be a schoolteacher, Mosley soon moved from Mississippi to Temple, Texas, where she met drummer James Culpepper. Working with Culpepper, along with bassist Pat Seals, and guitarists Sameer Bhattacharya and Jared Hartmann, Mosley's songwriting found renewed ambition While many bands with a crunch distortion pedal used anger as their core emotion and selling point, the band—which played under such names as Listen, Sporos, The Grove, Passerby, and, finally, Flyleaf—was intent on infusing a weighty, often funereal sound with a sense of hope and religious discovery.

After gigging aggressively and developing a fan base throughout Texas, the band, still playing under the name Passerby, pursued broader ambitions. In 2004, living on meager concert earnings and money offered by members of the church the band attended, the band drove to New York and played a show for the president of RCA Records in hopes of a record deal. While feedback was encouraging, RCA hesitated to sign the band. However, Hartmann's and Bhattacharya's gravelly, cascading riffs, combined with Mosley's helium-induced vocals, piqued the interest of the president of New York–based indie label Octone Records, who was present at the show. Octone released the band's first self-titled EP later that year, and the band toured with Staind and 3 Doors Down to promote its release.

The year 2005, though, was Flyleaf's breakout year and the year during which the bandmates finally settled on their current namesake. Collaborating with music producer Howard Benson, whose resume included such metal staples as Sepultura, as well as My Chemical Romance, The All-American Rejects, and Papa Roach, Flyleaf recorded its self-titled full-length debut. Guitarist Dave Navarro of the Red Hot Chili Peppers happened to be in the studio at that time. After overhearing Flyleaf's song "There For You," he volunteered to record a guitar part for it.

Several tracks on Flyleaf's self-titled full-length debut such as "I'm So Sick" and "Fully Alive" found themselves at home on the airwaves. In 2006, both tracks landed in the Top 40 on the U.S. Modern Rock Chart and within the Top 20 on the U.S. Mainstream Rock Chart. Flyleaf's lyrics, which often ruminate on themes of abandoned and rediscovered religion, also found favor with Christian listeners.

After the success of its full-length debut, Flyleaf embarked on the 2006 Family Values Tour with the likes of KoRn and the Deftones. In 2007, Flyleaf embarked on its first-ever headlining tour; for the "Justice and Mercy" tour, Flyleaf brought supporting acts Kill Hannah, Sick Puppies, Resident Hero, Skillet, Fair to Midland, and Dropping Daylight.

In 2008, Flyleaf toured in support of the hard rock act Korn on that band's European tour. The group also celebrated sales of 1 million copies of its self-titled debut album, which was certified Platinum.

Further reading: http://www.flyleafmusic.com; http://www.flyleafonline.com; http://www.myspace.com/flyleaf; http://www.octonerecords.com.

FOLDS, BEN/BEN FOLDS FIVE

This Chapel Hill, North Carolina, native's rule-breaking, jazz-influenced pop piano rock is as unpredictable as some of the milestones that stand out in his storied life—from a tumultuous childhood moving from state to state with his carpenter father; to his multi-instrumental talents as a piano player, drummer, and even bass; to his brief stint as an actor in various theater groups in New York City; to earning a full scholarship for percussion to the University of Miami; Folds's several feigned attempts at discovering himself were the perfect backdrop to the illustrated lyrics of his songs—and the various musical incarnations he was involved in until he branched out on his own in 2001.

After playing bass in his first group, Majosha, which released a few obscure recordings before winning the Battle of the Bands at Duke University in the late 1980s, Folds played drums in the short-lived group Pots and Pans before the brown-haired singer-songwriter relocated to Nashville, where he attempted to secure that holy grail of the music industry—a deal with a major label. Nashville proved itself to be just a pit stop along Folds's musical career, though. Folds's scholarship at the University of Miami, though, ended on a sour note when he was failed for being unable to play at his final recital (his hand was broken from a tussle he had been involved in the night before).

Folds played several shows at the popular New York City nightclub Sin-é, the very place made famous by musician Jeff Buckley, until he eventually relocated back to his home state. Back in North Carolina in 1994, Folds teamed up with drummer Darren Jessee and bassist Robert Sledge to form the trio Ben Folds Five. Their upbeat piano-driven rock served as a welcome alternative to the dark, sometimes narcissistic, music of emerging **grunge** artists. Local independent label Carolina Records signed the group, releasing its self-titled debut full-length album in

1995. The album showcased the guitarless group's high energy and Folds's songwriting talents, paving the way for a lengthy career that would change the way fans and critics viewed—and listened—to piano-driven pop music.

Ben Folds Five released a steady stream of albums in the mid- to late-1990s, among them the album *Whatever and Ever Amen,* a collection of catchy, irony-infused songs, among them the hit tracks "Song for the Dumped" and one of the group's signature songs, "Battle of Who Could Care Less." *Whatever* was the band's best selling album, charting in the Top 50 on the Billboard charts and selling over 1 million copies. It included the track "Brick," a cleverly crafted song that dealt with the controversial topic of abortion. "Brick" became a hit song that people continue to talk about; rumors circulated that Folds had written the song about an intimate personal experience of his, but that rumor was never confirmed.

Ben Folds Five's music continued to soar up the charts, and the group maintained intense tour schedules. And in 1998, the group's former label (it had by now signed to Sony Records) put out a collection of rare tracks called *Naked Baby Photos.* Meanwhile Folds, who had been contemplating branching out on his own and writing more personal songs, had been working on his solo debut, *Volume 1,* which featured vocals by Star Trek's William Shatner. In an effort to stave off the aftereffects of leaving his trio behind, Folds released the album under the pseudonym Fear of Pop.

Folds reteamed with his trio for 1999's *The Unauthorized Biography of Reinhold Messner,* a more introspective album on which the group tackled such topics as death, relationships, regret, and hope, among other deeper subjects, proving that the group had matured. Citing a loss of drive to keep the magic of Ben Folds Five alive, the group disbanded in 2000.

In 2001 Folds released his first solo album after the break up, *Rockin' the Suburbs,* on which he played nearly all of the instruments himself (including guitar). *Suburbs* elevated the recognition for Folds's songwriting skills with such songs as "Fred Jones Part 2" and "Mess"; this album remains his most well-known release to date. Folds's 2005 album, *Songs for Silverman,* featured the tribute "Late" to singer **Elliott Smith**. Folds's solo career blossomed; he booked tours with Tori Amos, Rufus Wainwright, and Weezer. And by 2006, the prolific singer-songwriter had released five albums, a live album, and a handful of EPs. Folds formed a supergroup of Bens called The Bens with musicians Ben Lee and Ben Kweller around 2004. In 2007, Folds toured as the opening act for John Mayer, a self-proclaimed fan of Folds, who told the media that Folds was among his inspirations and a guitar hero for Mayer when he was starting out as a guitar player and songwriter. He also accepted a coveted spot as the featured performer at the opening night of the Boston Pops in June 2007 at Symphony Hall. That same year, Folds celebrated the release of the concert DVD, *Live at My Space,* which was filmed at Folds's studio in Nashville, Tennessee, in 2006 to kick off the release of the LP *Supersunnyspeedgraphic,* which was part of MySpace.com's first-ever live webcast. Folds was also one of the featured acts at the 2007 Bonnaroo Music Festival in Manchester, Tennessee.

Further Reading: Hal Leonard Corp. *Pop/Rock Piano Hits for Dummies: A Reference for the Rest of Us!* Milwaukee, WI: Hal Leonard Corporation, 2006; Hal Leonard Corp. *VH1's 100 Greatest Songs of Rock and Roll: Piano/Vocal/Guitar Edition.* Milwaukee, WI: Hal Leonard Corporation, 2003; http://www.benfolds.com; http://www.benfoldsexperience.com; http://www.carolinarecords.net.

FRANZ FERDINAND

Formed in 2001 by four students from Glasgow, Scotland, this dance-inspiring art-rock quartet is named after an archduke whose murder was the impetus for World War I. Comprised of front man/guitarist Alex Kapranos, drummer Paul Thomson, bassist Bob Hardy (who had never played an instrument before joining the group), and guitarist Nick McCarthy, Franz Ferdinand cemented its place as an "it" indie band after the stateside success of its catchy, hard-to-forget 2004 single "Take Me Out."

After a brief lineup change, Franz Ferdinand set up shop in an abandoned warehouse the bandmates called the Chateau, where they rehearsed and hosted all-night parties, which eventually landed them in trouble for breaking several fire hazard and noise regulations. Franz Ferdinand band members scrapped plans to release their debut EP themselves when—after approximately 40 labels attempted to snag the band for their rosters—the U.K. independent label Domino Records, home to such groups as the British electronica act Four Tet and indie group **Arctic Monkeys**, signed the group in 2003. The EP *Darts of Pleasure* earned the band opening slots for the American indie rock group Interpol and the Canadian garage rock group Hot Hot Heat, so Franz Ferdinand was soon a household name in the United States, where word of the group's catchy music spread nationwide.

The success of "Take Me Out" catapulted the group to another level—hitting #3 on the British music charts, selling over 3 million copies worldwide, and ultimately earning the group a $1 million label deal with the Sony imprint Epic Records. The video (directed by Swedish film and video director Jonas Odell) for "Take Me Out," which features intricately designed segments of the band performing in an avant-garde style that harkens back to print ads from the 1930s, earned Franz Ferdinand the coveted Breakthrough Video award at the 2004 MTV Video Music Awards. Prefacing its 11-track, 2004 self-titled debut album (which hit #32 on the Billboard 200 Chart just a few months after its release), Franz Ferdinand released two singles—"Dark of the Matinee" and "Take Me Out/All For You, Sophia/Words So Leisured."

Franz Ferdinand was forced to tour without its bassist Bob Hardy on a few select dates of the 2004 world tour when he was briefly hospitalized for a serious case of the stomach flu. The group kicked off the North American portion of that tour with the English rock group the Futureheads. Franz Ferdinand released the follow-up single "Michael" in 2004; that same year the group was awarded the reputable Mercury Prize, competing against English piano rock group Keane, which is often compared to U2, and English rapper Mike Skinner, who is known as The Streets.

The Scottish band Franz Ferdinand perform at the 2004 Glastonbury Festival in England. [AP Wide World Photos/Yui Ul Mok]

Franz Ferdinand's self-titled debut album went Platinum in late 2004, and the band's follow-up album was predicted to have even more substantial sales. Franz Ferdinand released DVDs of two of its singles in 2004, "Matinee" (the third single) and "Take Me Out," both of which featured live performances and videos of the songs, along with interviews with the band. Franz Ferdinand walked away with an emerging talent award at the 2004 **NME (New Musical Express)** Music Awards.

On a sour note, the band's label, Sony, was forced to pay a $10 million fine for offering radio deejays payola for spinning the group's single "Take Me Out." The group's label, however, did not seem to squawk at Franz Ferdinand's involvement in the British erotic film *9 Songs,* which featured explicit sex scenes spliced between performance clips of the group and such bands as **The Dandy Warhols** and Black Rebel Motorcycle Club.

Franz Ferdinand's 2005 single, "Do You Want To, Pt. 2" (Domino Records) was inspired by a party that was held in the group's hometown of Glasgow, Scotland. A string of singles prefaced Franz Ferdinand's 2005 sophomore album, *You Could Have It So Much Better* and the group's 2006 LP, *Eleanor Put Your Boots On,* included a bonus track that was not on the album called and a remix of the track "Fade Together" by Scotland's largest independent record store, Avalanche and the single "Fallen" featured several additional non-album tracks. Franz Ferdinand was the featured musical act on "Saturday Night Live" in October 2005.

The band's 2005 sophomore full-length album, *You Could Have It So Much Better* (Sony) showcased the group's **pop punk** sound, earning it the nickname "the

Scottish Interpol." The album also featured a cover of the track "Sexy Boy" by the French musical duo **Air**. The U.K. version of *Better* featured videos, interviews, and a featurette documenting the making of the album. *Better* debuted at #1 on U.K. charts, and the first single from the album, "Do You Want To," hit #14 on Billboard's Modern Rock Chart a month after its release.

The group performed as part of the *Austin City Limits* PBS series in 2005. Rapper/singer Kanye West, who met Franz Ferdinand at the 2005 MTV Europe Music Awards, tagged the group with the term "white crunk" and claimed that the group was a big influence on his 2005 album, *Late Registration*. Kapranos and crew told MTV in a 2005 interview that fans that played their albums backwards could hear hidden messages. The band took its cue to apply the backward messaging, a process called "backmasking," on its LPs from bands such as The Beatles and Pink Floyd that did it in the 1960s and 1970s, but Franz Ferdinand's plans differed in that the band planned on putting strictly positive messages on the LPs. In the summer of that same year, Franz Ferdinand was awarded several songwriting awards at the 50th Annual Ivor Novello Awards, which are presented by the British Academy of Composers & Songwriters.

Franz Ferdinand contributed a song to the 2007 indie film *Hallam Foe* by British director David Mackenzie. Front man Alex Kapranos, who once worked as a chef, proudly released a collection of food columns he had written about the band's food choices on the road for *The Guardian* newspaper titled *Sound Bites: Eating on Tour with Franz Ferdinand* (Penguin Books, 2007). Franz Ferdinand released a two-disc live DVD that year featuring karaoke versions of a few of the group's tracks as well as interviews, live footage, and a documentary titled *Tour de Franz*.

The Scottish foursome participated in a string of nonprofit music events and collaborations in 2006, including the www.StarsAuctions.com event in England, for which musician's belongings were sold to raise money for a disabled children's charity. The group also contributed songs to the *Colours Are Brighter* compilation to benefit the Save the Children nonprofit organization and a compilation to benefit the Susan G. Komen Breast Cancer Foundation along with indie acts **Yeah Yeah Yeahs**, **Cat Power**, **The Walkmen**, and more. Kapranos performed the group's signature song "Take Me Out" at the 2006 "Ridiculously Early Xmas Party," which was sponsored by Canada's Mint Records; he was backed by members from the English indie trio The Cribs and the Canadian indie supergroup The Evaporators, which is comprised of musicians from such bands as **The New Pornographers** and The Smugglers.

The quintet was also featured on the November 2006 collaboration album *Rhythms Del Mundo* (Hip-O Records/Universal Music) by the Cuban music collective Buena Vista Social Club alongside such bands as **Arctic Monkeys**, **Radiohead**, and U2. In March 2006, Franz Ferdinand toured with indie kings **Death Cab for Cutie**; later the group turned down the opportunity to have one of its songs featured in a TV commercial, a deal reportedly worth $50 million.

Subsequently, the band's label dropped the group just three weeks before its next album was due out.

In 2007, however, Franz Ferdinand stayed busy; Kapranos busily worked on producing an album by The Cribs and promoted his food book, and the group turned its focus on the next release, which Kapranos told **NME** (**New Musical Express**) would be more experimental, in hopes the group would veer away from its signature art-punk sound. Franz Ferdinand got even more creative in 2007, when it covered **LCD Soundsystem**'s song "All My Friends," and the group released its own annual, a 50-page indie rock and fun-loaded booklet of puzzles, photos, crosswords, fact pages, and more.

In 2008, the band came back into the news after a brief hibernation-like break with its 2008 single "What She Came For," which the group described as having been influenced by African music.

Further Reading: Artsrunik, Nicholas. *Franz Ferdinand.* London: Artnik, 2005; Harvey, Hamilton. *Franz Ferdinand: And the Pop Renaissance.* Kew Gardens, Richmond, Surrey, United Kingdom: Reynolds & Hearn Limited, 2006; Kapranos, Alex. *Sound Bites: Eating on Tour with Franz Ferdinand.* New York: Penguin, 2006; http://www.dominorecordco.com; http://www.epicrecords.com; http://www.franzferdinand.co.uk; http://www.myspace.com/franzferdinand; http://www.pbs.org/buenavista.

FREAK FOLK

Freak Folk (or Indie Folk or Psychedelic Folk, as it is also known) is not easily defined by simply saying it is "Bob Dylan on acid." This modern form of folk music is an extension of the antifolk movement of the 1980s and 1990s—but with a twist. Led by the "pied piper" of the pack, **Devendra Banhart** (as he has been called by the *New York Times*), freak folk is a unique subgenre in that it fuses the spirit of punk rock and the aesthetic of folk music. This hard outer edge and soft inner core combination made freak folk an underground phenomenon for its fervor and spirit. In other words, freak folk artists are not New Age hippies; they are riled up artists who attract swarms of fans with honey *and* vinegar.

Artists who have been described as participants in the freak folk subgenre include solo acts and bands such as Josephine Foster, Sir Richard Bishop, Iron & Wine, Feathers, Espers, Vetiver, Six Organs of Admittance, Animal Collective, CocoRosie, **Joanna Newsom**, and even soft-spoken crooner Nick Drake. Freak folk, which is also coined as "naturalismo" for its adherence to naturalism or making music from the perspective that everything has its roots in nature, is a growing genre that was first categorized and coined in a 2003 article in the British publication *The Wire* called "New Weird America" in which the magazine profiled a collection of freak folk artists and identified the subgenre as a trend.

Combining whimsical sounds with **Lo-fi** sonics, acoustic recordings, experimental electronic tracks, loaded instrumentals, and fantastical and surreal yet idealistic lyrics, freak folk music spread like a weed, causing the media to latch on to the new movement and subsequently appoint **Devendra Banhart**, who emerged as an unexpected icon and involuntary pioneer of the subgenre. Outwardly denying the soft-hearted singer-songwriter persona, **Devendra Banhart** led the pack of bold artists who sang about mushy topics without seeming like the wilted flowers they may have waxed poetic about. But soon after **Devendra Banhart** was plastered with the "poster boy" label; he publicly rejected it, denying his association with such a term that he felt was put upon him by the trend-craving media. **Devendra Banhart** instead claimed that the artists who have been collected under the subgenre's umbrella are merely part of a collective he calls "The Family," a union of musicians with similar musical styles and sonic approaches.

David Byrne, front man of the **Talking Heads**, on the other hand, whose own band was categorized into multiple subgenres, did not seem to mind the term's trend-building potential. Byrne hosted a night of performances by freak folk artists in 2007 at Carnegie Hall that featured acts such as CocoRosie, Adem, Cibelle, **Devendra Banhart**, Vetiver, and, most notably, Vashti Bunyan, a pioneer of the psych-folk movement of the 1960s.

Freak folk's roots are imbedded in the **DIY (Do-It-Yourself)** aesthetic, as the community of artists have banded together and formed a sort of unspoken union. As a celebration of their nonverbal pact, **Devendra Banhart** curated the first-ever unofficial 2004 freak folk compilation album *The Golden Apples of the Sun*.

Further Reading: Lornell, Kip, and Linda Ronstadt. *The NPR Curious Listener's Guide to American Folk Music.* New York: Perigee Trade, 2004; Weissman, Dick. *Which Side Are You On? An Inside History of the Folk Music Revival in America.* London: Continuum International Publishing Group, 2006; http://naturalismo.wordpress.com.

FRENCH KICKS

Childhood friends Nick Stumpf (lead vocals and keyboards) and Matt Stinchcomb (guitar) formed this Brooklyn, New York–based experimental **indie pop** group with Nick's younger brother, Lawrence (bass), in the late 1990s. Josh Wise (vocalsand guitar) was added to the fray around 1998.

The French Kicks released their debut full-length album in 1999 via Chicago's My Pal God Records. The album's wide range of musical sounds and influences had fans and critics throwing darts at several musical genres until the release of the French Kicks's 2000 EP, *Young Lawyer* on the Santa Monica, California–based punk/**emo**/rock label, Vagrant Records, which revealed a penchant for danceable rock 'n' roll. Still, the group experimented further with its sound, and it was tough for critics to pigeonhole the group into one genre. The French Kicks also contributed to *The My Pal God Holiday Record Volume 2* collection that same year.

In 2001, following extensive touring, the group contributed to the compilation *This is Next Year: A Brooklyn-Based Compilation* (Arena Rock), which featured fellow indie New York City (NYC) acts **Calla** and **The Walkmen**. The French Kicks's sophomore effort, *One Time Bells* (Vagrant Startime, 2002), was both panned and praised for its **Lo-fi** recording style, and critics heralded the French Kicks's intelligent lyrics.

In 2003, the French Kicks made waves at the **South by Southwest (SXSW)** music festival, and the group released *Close to Modern Remixes* (Stifle/StarTime), which was a collection of various remixes of the tracks by the likes of such acts as Manic Panic and Eucho. Stumpf, who had originally sang lead vocals from behind the drum kit, was able to focus on being the front man when the group brought Aaron Thurston on board.

The NYC label StarTime International Records, which helped launched the band's career—the group was actually the first act signed to its roster, released one of the group's most acclaimed albums, *The Trial of the Century* in 2004. The album caught on quickly, appealing to people beyond the local "hipster" crowd; Stinchcomb departed the band amid the added pressure and rigorous recording schedule, making room for new member Kush El Amin (guitar and percussion). Sales of *Trial* surpassed the numbers for almost every other band on the StarTime International Records roster in just about two weeks. and the French Kicks were soon playing a residency at the hip downtown NYC music venue the Mercury Lounge.

Critics claimed the French Kicks' long-awaited third album, *Two Thousand* (Vagrant Records, 2006) sounded ironically similar to the group's NYC indie rock peers, such as The Strokes, but the French Kicks managed to stand apart with its songwriting chops and melodic abilities. Nick and Josh composed the majority of the material for the album, which was recorded in Los Angeles with producer Doug Boehm. The band gave the album a tongue-in-cheek title, which was a loose reference to the Y2K phenomenon that swept the country in 1999.

The French Kicks toured extensively in 2006, playing the Noise Pop Festival in San Francisco, California, and touring with the power pop group OK Go and indie rock quartet **Death Cab for Cutie**. **Pitchfork Media** reported that tickets to a few of the group's 2007 shows with the group Phoenix were available for $5 on Ticketmaster, but as part of a promotion for the gigs, anyone wielding a Camel cigarette could gain entry. The French Kicks stopped in at the ten-day long, second annual *PASTE* magazine's Rock 'n' Reel Festival in Atlanta, Georgia, before touring with the groups The Little Ones and Sound Team. The video for the track "So Far We Are" featured actress Olivia Wilde of the FOX TV drama *The O.C.* The group also performed the single on the CBS TV show *Late Late Show with Craig Ferguson*.

In 2007, the French Kicks played the Tomorrow Never Knows Festival in Chicago. The group's 2007 *Roller EP* featured songs the group had written while recording *Two Thousand*. The group toured the northeast section of the United States in 2008.

Further Reading: http://www.cookingvinyl.com; http://www.frenchkicks.com; http://www.mypalgodrecords.com; http://www.myspace.com/frenchkicks.

FUGAZI

This quartet is credited with leading the charge for the post-hardcore scene in the late 1980s. Fans of Fugazi favored the band for more than its musical pursuits and political endeavors—the Washington, D.C., foursome had become icons for the punk culture and a whole generation of youths who held art as a lofty ambition above all else—proving that commercialism and all things mainstream were not the formidable foes they attempted to be.

Formed in 1987 by four local musicians who remained steadily active in their community—Joe Lally (bass), Guy Picciotto (vocals), Brendan Canty (drums), and front man Ian MacKaye (guitars and vocals)—Fugazi further proved that its artful noise rock was more art than noise—and that the group's political rantings were warnings of which the establishment need take heed.

MacKaye, who founded the legendary punk label Dischord Records in 1970, and his bandmates had already cut their teeth in the local punk scene—MacKaye was a former member of the groups Minor Threat, Embrace (as was Picciotto), and the Teen Idles before forming Fugazi; Canty had been a member of the D.C. punk group **Rites of Spring**.

Cheap shows and CDs—and the bandmates' publicly anticommercial stance—helped the group stand out, but it was their **DIY (Do-It-Yourself)** mentality, non-stop gigging, eardrum splitting music, and songwriting chops that convinced fans to stay loyal for the duration of Fugazi's reign over the D.C. punk scene. Fugazi—which is a Vietnam War era slang term for "f- -ked up, got ambushed, zipped in"—released its self-titled debut album in 1988. An amp-tearing anthemic album, the vinyl-only album *Fugazi* tore the lid off all expectations fans had as to this emerging band's greatness—the album featured songs that shocked fans and critics alike for the group's depth and musical prowess.

The 13-track debut, which was released on MacKaye's own Dischord, was combined with the band's second EP and was subsequently re-released in 1990 on the LP *13 Songs*. In the song "Suggestion," MacKaye sang from the point of view of a woman who decries sexism and the objectification of females, while another, *Fugazi,* went on to inspire guitar bands into the 1990s.

Fugazi, which often performed at D.C.'s renowned 9:30 Club, insisted that its shows be open to people of all ages. Consequently, the group—which has since been synonymous with the concept of all-ages shows—refused to grant interviews to publications that featured ads for alcohol or cigarettes. The group's guitar heavy songs also lent themselves to a reggae feel, with catchy rhythms and insightful, inciting lyrics that were often screamed rather than sung, helping cement what became known as the "hardcore" sound.

The band's debut full-length *Repeater + 3 Songs* emerged in 1990 showcasing the power of the group's dual vocal sound and guitar chops. As Fugazi's anticommercialism campaign grew, so did its fan base; the shows got bigger and the crowds got wilder. Soon, Fugazi's on-stage antics were tame performance art compared to the bloody uncontrollable mania created by the fans below. MacKaye, who stopped the show on more than one occasion to beg fans to calm down, offered to refund fans' money if they would vacate the premises.

With the band's refusal to do interviews, the press countered by forging stories about the group, resulting in rumors circulating about the band and its mysterious ways. More and more time seemed to elapse between releases—*Steady Diet of*

Nothing (1991), *In on the Kill Taker* (1993), and *Red Medicine* (1995)—and rumors about a split spread throughout the punk scene.

With 1998's *End Hits,* fans complained the group was losing its edge. Ten years into their careers, Fugazi bandmates seemed to be running out of musical steam, but the group toured nonetheless. Filmmaker Jem Cohen, who has done films on **Elliott Smith** and **Sonic Youth**, collaborated with the band to produce the video *Instrument,* a documentary spanning ten years that features live studios footage, short films, live performance footage, interviews, tour footage, bonus tracks, and even profiles of diehard fans from around the country.

Staying true to their perseverant nature and tough-as-nails reputation, Fugazi bandmates soldiered on, releasing the album that reaffirmed fans' faith in their heroes—*The Argument* in 2001 (Dischord), which featured contributions by some of their musician friends, simply raised the bar in terms of what people considered skillful songwriting and explosive rhythms.

Fugazi took a much-needed hiatus in 2004, clearly stating that the break was not a breakup, and played a handful of live dates after that, while band members branched off to focus on their respective side projects—Picciotto tried his hand at filmmaking, MacKaye grew Dischord, and Canty co-directed a documentary about the band Wilco and worked on producing albums by such musicians as guitarist Mary Timony and **Ted Leo and the Pharmacists**; Lally, on the other hand, joined a side project group called Ataxia with John Frusciante of the Red Hot Chili Peppers. The group worked to keep its live shows, which the bandmates admitted to recording purposefully throughout their career, intact as sort of an ongoing time capsule by offering 20 full concerts online via the Fugazi Live Series service.

In odd news, in 2007 MacKaye assisted police investigators who were looking into the 1970 shootings that occurred at a protest at Kent State University in Ohio; MacKaye aided the officers by enhancing audio of the event.

Further Reading: Klosterman, Chuck. *Sex, Drugs, and Cocoa Puffs: A Low Culture Manifesto.* New York: Scribner, 2004; http://www.dischord.com; http://www.fugaziliveseries.com; http://www.jemcohenfilms.com.

G

GALAXIE 500

This 1980s–1990s dream pop/shoegaze group's musical legacy lives on through the music of modern bands that continue to be influenced by the Boston trio's inventive sounds. Formed by Harvard University students in the mid-1980s, Galaxie 500's music was ahead of its time, predating the **shoegazing** and slowcore movements that the band helped pioneer. Galaxie 500's trio—front man and guitarist Dean Wareham, drummer Damon Krukowski, and bassist Naomi Yang—all met when they were in high school in New York City before the three of them moved to Boston to attend one of the country's most prestigious Ivy League schools, but their musical ambitions soon proved more fruitful than studying for exams.

Taking the name of a 1960s Ford car, Galaxie 500's minimalist music gigged in and around Boston and New York City before the group started shopping around a self-made demo that eventually made its way into the hands of Mark Kramer (aka Kramer), the founder of Shimmy Disc Records.

Known for its ambitious and clever covers, which included tracks by The Beatles, Yoko Ono, and New Order), Galaxie 500 signed to Rykodisc for its 1988 debut album, *Today,* which was made for a reported $750. The album made a fan of **Sonic Youth**'s Thurston Moore, who claimed the record was "my favorite guitar record of 1988" (Moore, 2005). Standing out among the hair metal wave that was engulfing the music scene in the late 1980s, Galaxie 500 made lifelong fans with its jazz influenced, fuzzy pop, lush harmonies and Wareham's rich vocals, all of which had critics crooning.

British music magazine *Melody Maker* said the LP was "an astonishing debut by anybody's standards" (www.rykodistribution.com). *Today* remains one of the top indie releases of that decade and a must-have for music collectors, featuring the "masterpiece" track "Tugboat." Kramer served as producer on the album. Galaxie 500 signed to **Rough Trade Records** for its sophomore album, 1989's *On Fire* (the U.K. release included the critically acclaimed companion EP *Blue Thunder*), which elevated the band up a whole tier in the music world. *Rolling Stone* gave the album 3.5 out of 5 stars.

Galaxie 500 toured the United States and Europe, and in 1990, the indie label Rykodisc put out the group's lesser-received follow-up album, *This Is Our Music.* Shortly after the album's release, the group made plans to tour the United Kingdom, and just when the group seemed perched on the edge of superstardom, Wareham announced his plans to part from the group and moved back to New

York City. In the wake of his departure from Galaxie 500, Wareham released a solo EP before forming a sort of "supergroup" with former members of the bands The Chills and The Feelies called Luna.

Left to their own devices, the remaining Galaxie 500 members forged ahead as Damon & Naomi and the Magic Hour while also forming a publishing house called Exact Change Press, on which they published a collection of Gertrude Stein's work entitled *Everybody's Autobiography*. With the band separated and no sign of Wareham reuniting with his old pals, Galaxie 500's reign as one of the top slowcore/**shoegazing** bands of the late 1980s/early 1990s was over. What is worse, the band members never recouped royalties for the full-length albums Galaxie 500 recorded with **Rough Trade Records** when the label filed for bankruptcy. Krukowski, however, was able to purchase the group's master tapes when **Rough Trade Records** auctioned off its assets. He released the material in a four-disc box set in 1996 on Rykodisc. Wareham experienced success with Luna, while Krukowski resurfaced as Pierre Etoile before reteaming with Yang as the group Damon & Naomi.

Further Reading: http://www.grange85.co.uk/galaxie; http://www.rykodisc.com.

THE GERMS

For a group of musicians who could hardly play their instruments, The Germs's brand of intense, haphazard punk rock spread rather quickly across Los Angeles in the mid-1970s. The group's founding members were inspired by the likes of glam rocker David Bowie and the Sex Pistols.

The bad attitude–toting foursome—front man Darby Crash (whose real name was Paul Beahm; aka Bobby Pyn), guitarist Pat Smear (whose real name is Georg Ruthenberg), bassists Dinky and Lorna Doom, and later drummers Michelle Baer, Dottie Danger, and Don Bolles—played parties in the glittery city, building a reputation as stage-destroying, art-defying, nonsensical artists.

The punk band was so cool, in fact, that it managed to attract two up-and-coming punk scene starlets—Belinda Carlisle, the front woman for the 1980s rock outfit the Go-Go's, who played drums as Dottie Danger in the group; and Nicky Beat of the innovative 1970s punk band the Weirdos.

Garnering attention for his "Sid Vicious–like persona," Crash personified the band's music—hard, fast, and loud. The Germs' live shows involved Crash flailing himself across the stage, breaking glasses, and often bleeding as a result of his antics; one show even involved the wild front man tossing peanut butter at the crowd. The Germs released its debut single, "Forming" on What? Records in 1977. The band's sole release that was produced by Germs fan and punk icon Joan Jett, the LP *GI* (Slash Records, 1979), was the group's sole full-length release.

The Germs bandmates eventually sharpened their chops as musicians, but their all-over-the-map music proved too mighty a challenge for anyone who dared keep a beat; The Germs entertained various drummers throughout its short-lived career. Priding themselves on the fact that they never set foot in a rehearsal studio, the bandmate played a showcase of "terrible" bands for a mock talent show at The Roxy nightclub in a scene for Cheech and Chong's 1978 movie, *Up In Smoke*.

The Germs disbanded in the wake of Crash's increasing drug abuse and personal struggles with his own homosexuality. Darby returned to England with Smear to pursue a solo career with the Darby Crash Band. True to form, The Germs went out with as loud a bang as when the group entered the rock scene when, just three days after a reunion show in December 1980 at the Starwood Club in Los Angeles, Crash died of a heroin overdose at the age of 22. Bolles joined the lineup of such groups as Celebrity Skin and 45 Grave, and guitarist Pat Smear later went on to record with **Nirvana** and tour with the Foo Fighters.

A number of Germs compilations appeared in the mid-1990s, most notably *MIA: The Complete Germs Anthology* (Rhino Records), a collection of 30 reckless songs that attracted everyone's attention in the first place. The tribute album *A Small Circle of Friends: A Germs Tribute* (Grass Records, 1996) featured music by such bands as NOFX, L7, and the **Meat Puppets**, who were influenced by The Germs.

The Germs—Shane West, Pat Smear, Lorna Doom, Don Bolles—reformed in the late 2000s for a series of performances, including a live gig at the Los Angeles Film Festival premiere of the film *What We Do Is Secret*. The 2007 biopic, which stars actor Shane West and actress Bijou Phillips, profiles the last few years of The Germs' explosive front man, Derby Crash.

Further Reading: http://www.theweirdos.net; http://www.whatrecords.com.

GIRLS AGAINST BOYS

In a basement in Maryland, **Fugazi** drummer Brendan Canty, bassist Eli Janney, and singer/guitarist Scott McCloud challenged punk rock's testosterone-driven conventions when they formed the punk outfit Girls Against Boys in 1988. Girls Against Boys would ultimately become known for being a surprisingly dance-friendly hardcore band, rising to major-label stardom and, by the late 2000s, falling back into obscurity all over again.

The name Girls Against Boys was the band's joke about the masculine angst that dominated the punk scene for decades. Initially, the post-hardcore band started off as the smallest of side projects. Girls Against Boys recorded three unfinished songs that the group would sit on for two years. When Canty decided to refocus his efforts on **Fugazi**, Janney and McCloud recruited two members from the Dischord-label hardcore band Soulside—drummer Alexis Fleisig and, more unlikely, a second bassist in Johnny Temple—to form the essential core of Girls Against Boys' sound, where the bass guitars stewed angrily and the drums erupted with violent precision.

Unlike many hardcore bands, this noise rock act ventured beyond the stern riffs and mummy-footed arrangements of its D.C. neighbors, reinterpreting rap and funk through a hardcore filter. Girls Against Boys' first album, *Tropic of Scorpio,* was released in 1992 on Adult Swim Records, which was owned by Dischord co-founder and Minor Threat drummer Jeff Nelson. The album was short and uneven, alternating between the growling bass lines of traditional hardcore and the slinkiness of Joy Division. Still, *Tropic of Scorpio* showed a band willing to experiment in a genre that was often preoccupied with mere rebelliousness.

However, in keeping with the frenetic work ethic of punk, Girls Against Boys embarked on aggressive touring campaigns while managing to switch labels and churn out an album a year. The years 1993 and 1996 saw releases of full-length albums *Venus Luxure No. 1 Baby, Cruise Yourself,* and the breakthrough *House of GVSB,* respectively, on the Touch and Go Records label. During the band's Touch and Go years, Girls Against Boys fell into a more consistent sound with often heavier, groove-centric beats with distortion that sometimes swallowed wry, dead-pan vocals. The band rode singles such as "Bullet Proof Cupid" and "Kill the Sex-player" to video exposure. The latter of those two songs was even featured on the soundtrack to the 1994 Kevin Smith–directed movie *Clerks.* In 1994, Girls Against Boys toured the United States and Europe with the likes of The Jesus Lizard and **Jawbox**, and after the release of *House of GVSB,* the band made a brief stint at **Lollapalooza**.

By the late 1990s, *House of GVSB* had cast Girls Against Boys into a dramatically wider arena of exposure, complete with celebrity friends and major-label deals. In 1998, during the recording of *Freak*on*ica,* the band began throwing involved *House of GVSB* parties, often at the 400 Bar in Minneapolis, with such guests as **Nine Inch Nails**, the Wu-Tang Clan, Rage Against the Machine, and the occasional Soul Asylum band member. *Freak*on*ica* was released on major label Geffen Records in 1998, much to the chagrin of some of its original fans. The groove-based panache of the band's previous albums was brought to *Freak*on*ica*'s forefront and mixed to have a more industrial feel. The song "Boogie Wonderland" appeared on the soundtrack for the 1999 indie film *200 Cigarettes.*

After a four-year creative hiatus, Girls Against Boys broke ties with Geffen, retreated from the spotlight, and released what could be called a "come-down" album. The 2002 *You Can't Fight What You Can't See,* which was released by the indie label **Jade Tree Records**, saw the band returning to the guitar and double-bass fuzz that gave the group its original appeal. Girls Against Boys then turned its efforts toward film, serving as Gina Gershon's backup band in the 2004 movie *Rocked with Gina Gershon.* In February 2007, Girls Against Boys launched a tour across Italy.

Girls Against Boys played Europe in early 2008; along the way the band hit Spain's Primavera Sound Festival along with such bands as **The White Stripes** and the **Melvins**. Girls Against Boys' member McCloud put the finishing touches on his semi-solo album *Failure American Style.*

Further Reading: http://www.gvsb.com; http://www.tgrec.com.

GREEN DAY

The faces of these East Bay, California pop punkers may be splashed all over such mainstream media outlets as MTV, *Rolling Stone,* and even in a Pepsi ad (PepsiCo

Green Day: (left to right) Mike Dirnt, Billie Joe Armstrong, and Tré Cool. [Photofest]

used the group's song "I Fought the Law" in one of its TV ads), but their struggle to break beyond the underground scene and see their dreams of rock stardom materialize is certainly matched by the group's efforts to maintain its **DIY (Do-It-Yourself)** roots, punk ethics, and loyalty to fans in the wake of its ever-cresting success.

The band that reportedly pointed the finger at the U.S. president with the controversial single off its 2004 album, *American Idiot,* stayed afloat in the punk realm even after it signed to a major label (but not without any fan base casualties) to become one of the most successful alternative/**pop punk** bands to make it big. Consisting of three core members, singer/guitarist Billie Joe Armstrong, bassist Mike Dirnt, and drummer Tré Cool, who replaced founding member Al Sobrante, Green Day (a name the group reportedly chose in honor of smoking weed) released and marketed its music using grassroots efforts before releasing records on the Berkeley, California–based independent label Lookout! Records (home to such acts as **Ted Leo and the Pharmacists** and The Donnas).

Word of mouth spread quickly about the group's on-stage energy until its popularity soared high enough for the group to gain enough exposure to catch the eye of a major label. Warner Bros. imprint Reprise Records scooped up the spikey-haired bandmates, their college-boy humor, and three-chord songs in the mid-1990s, releasing their much-celebrated debut album, *Dookie,* in 1994. Their meld of ska, punk, and pop culminated in their success as MTV put tracks from *Dookie* into heavy rotation. Miffed hardcore fans who waved the anticorporate flag dismissed the band, but hordes of fans took their places within seconds.

Despite its mainstream success and throughout its career, Green Day has attempted to make waves, utilizing the funds and distribution power of its A-list label as a soapbox for the bandmates' political views—and by the sounds of *American Idiot,* no one seemed safe from the spotlight. Singles from *Dookie* hit the rock charts, and the record sold over 5 million copies. Still, as Green Day's star shot higher, its indie roots seemed to lag farther and farther in the distance —especially when the band performed at the 1994 Woodstock Festival. Green Day earned a Grammy for *Dookie* for Best Alternative Music Performance, so the group that many fans had rebuffed as having "sold out" was credited with shedding light on punk and bringing it the attention and applause it had long deserved.

As of 2005, StubHub reported the group had sold upwards of 50 million albums worldwide (www.stubhub.com/green-day-tickets); Green Day's success, however, has been controversial for fans of the indie genre, especially since the group's success has paved the way for such popular bands as Sum 41 and Good Charlotte, which many believe have diluted the pop-punk/indie genre to forward their own record sales. Green Day continues to sell out venues and collect Grammy Awards. The band with the diehard **DIY (Do-It-Yourself)** ethics hit the jackpot and never turned back, continuing to make inspired fast-paced music in the very same vein it did from day one, but naysayers continue to claim the band has prostituted the punk movement by utilizing major-label assets and connections to forward its messages, which so-called hardcore punks feel is the worst platform to use to promote such political and social commentary.

Green Day performed live on the 2007 *American Idol* finale and prepared for the release of its 2008 album. The band also told **NME (*New Musical Express*)** in a November 2007 interview that it has plans to make a movie along the story in its album *American Idiot.*

Armstrong focused some of his time on his "other" band, Pinhead Gunpowder" in 2008. But Green Day remained intact; in fact, Green Day celebrated a nomination for the 2008 Grammys in the category "Best Rock Performance by a Duo or Group with Vocals." The group also released a live CD/DVD called *Bullet in a Bible* on Reprise Records, featuring its two-night stint at Milton Keynes National Bowl in England.

Further Reading: Myers, Ben. *Green Day: American Idiot and the New Punk Explosion.* New York: Disinformation Company, 2006; Spitz, Marc. *Nobody Likes You: Inside the Turbulent Life, Times, and Music of Green Day.* New York: Hyperion, 2006; http://www.greenday.com; http://www.lookoutrecords.com.

GREEN RIVER

Contrary to popular belief, **Nirvana** was not the first **grunge** band; a little-known quintet called Green River was. Green River, comprised of bassist Jeff Ament, drummer Alex Vincent (his birth name was Shumway), guitarist/vocalist Mark Arm, guitarist Steve Turner, and guitarist Stone Gossard, was the first Seattle-based band to play what is now referred to as **grunge** music.

The first band ever signed to **Sub Pop Records**, Green River played only for four speaker-blowing years from 1984 to 1988, but the group is often credited with recording the first **grunge** album, its debut six-track EP, *Come On Down,* on Homestead Records in 1985. What later became known as the genre that defined the early 1990s, **grunge** was actually, in fact, a messy hybrid of punk, hard rock, metal, and partially inaudible lyrics that pretty much summed up the sloppy sound.

The band, named after the serial killer "Green River Killer" who terrorized the streets of the bandmates' hometown for decades, was a major component of the underground scene in Seattle, along with other up-and-coming acts such as Pearl Jam, Mudhoney, and Mother Love Bone, all of whom would (ironically enough) achieve fame and fortune thanks to the **grunge** groundwork laid down by Green River's hardcore, metal, and punk-loving band members.

Like many rock acts, Green River's history is rife with drama. Band member Steve Turner left Green River, citing his disdain for the band's growing metal influences; he was swiftly replaced by Bruce Fairweather in the months following the release of 1985's *Come On Down*. Green River contributed a few tracks for the first-ever **grunge** compilation *Deep Six* (C/Z Records, 1986), a collection of songs by such acts as the **Melvins** and Soundgarden. In 1986, Green River crisscrossed the United States to head to New York, where it began work on its follow-up EP, *Dry As a Bone* (**Sub Pop Records**, 1987).

Heavy on guitars and, as some claim, a representation of "the epitome of **grunge**," *Bone* revealed the band's 1970s and 1980s influences. It also sounds oddly reminiscent of the early albums by Pearl Jam and Mudhoney, which were formed by various Green River alums. Interband member drama and disagreement, though, started tearing at the band's infrastructure. And while several of the band members wanted to vie for a major-label record deal, the rest of the group felt that remaining indie was essential to the core of the band. Divided, the band members continued to feud over such things as backstage passes and the issue of commercialism. Green River finally imploded in 1988. *Bone* was subsequently combined with an LP called *Rehab Doll,* which was supposed to be the band's final album together; instead, **Sub Pop Records** combined the two albums and named the 16-track album *Dry to the Bone/Rehab Doll*. which includes a cover of the David Bowie track "Queen Bitch."

Turner and Arm joined forces, however, to form Mudhoney; Arm would later also belong to the bands Monkeywrench and Alice in Chains. Ament, who would later join such bands as King's X and Dot Allison, and Gossard, who was in the group Temple of the Dog, started Mother Love Bone before forming Pearl Jam with fellow Seattleite Eddie Vedder.

The original lineup of Green River, however, resurrected the band for a one-night reunion in 1993 at a Pearl Jam show in Las Vegas. Gossard and the original lineup (except Steve Turner, who will be replaced by Bruce Fairweather) made plans for a reunion show at the 20th anniversary of **Sub Pop Records** in the summer of 2008.

Further Reading: Anderson, Kyle. *Accidental Revolution: The Story of Grunge.* New York: St. Martin's Griffin, 2007; Hal Leonard Corp. *Grunge Guitar Bible* Milwaukee, WI: Hal Leonard Corp., 2003.

GRUNGE

Often referred to as the "Seattle Sound," grunge originated from the dingy basements of bored, angst-filled teenagers living in Seattle, Washington, a city that is as well known for being the largest city in the Pacific Northwest region of the United States as it is for its damp climate and unbearable months of inclement weather. Certain teens in the area, however, picked up instruments as a means to escape the loneliness of their isolated locale—or rather, to do something to counteract the drones of pop music they heard on the radio. These youths took it upon themselves to create music that they felt was real, raw, and, as many perceived it to be, reactionary to the stagnancy of the state of social, political, and cultural affairs of the world in the late 1980s and early 1990s.

Forged mainly by such bands as **Green River** and **Nirvana**, grunge was born out of the hearts and souls of young local teens who were simply attempting to combat boredom. Inspired by hardcore punk, heavy metal, and indie rock, these bands inadvertently forged one of the most well-known, pioneering genres of music simply by melding the sounds of the music they loved.

A local label called **Sub Pop Records** started signing grunge bands and helped them to release their debut albums. Grunge soon swept the nation, and kids on the East Coast were blasting songs by **Nirvana** and **Green River** and adopting their style of dress—loose-fitting flannels, unkempt hair, and dirty jeans. Grunge soon became the anthemic sound of what has become known as Generation X. The sound quickly replaced classic rock as the most popular form of music, and teens across America seemed to be hypnotized by the grunge movement, a term that was reportedly coined by the members of the group Mudhoney, **grunge** being slang for "dirt."

Seattle, long ignored by the music scene in favor of such cities as Los Angeles and New York City, was soon becoming a household name. **Sub Pop Records** was gaining attention from the media, and the city was soon connected with the rest of the country through grunge. But local grunge acts already felt connected with other cities because acts they identified with—and admired—were living and playing there. **Nirvana**, for instance, openly celebrated such bands as the **Pixies** and **Sonic Youth**, both of which the group considered to have big influences on its music.

The first real record to feature grunge acts was a 1986 compilation put out C/Z Records called *Deep Six*. That same year, **Sub Pop Records** put out the vinyl compilation *Sub Pop 100,* which showcased the music of bands such as Scratch Acid, Naked Raygun, the Wipers, **Sonic Youth**, Skinny Puppy, Shonen Knife, and The U-Men. Other grunge acts were popping up all over the Seattle area: Blood Circus, Hammerbox, Gruntruck, Love Battery, Screaming Trees, Tad, Skin Yard, Soundgarden, Seven Year Bitch, the **Melvins**, My Sister's Machine, and Alice in Chains to name a few. Grunge had infected bands outside the Seattle area, too: the Minnesota-based band Babes in Toyland, Los Angeles' Hole, which is fronted by Kurt Cobain's former wife, Courtney Love, and L7, Lawrence, Kansas' Paw, Denver's The Fluid, and San Diego's Stone Temple Pilots all experienced various levels of success in the music business.

Soon though, grunge, which basically consists of loud, crunching guitars surrounded by ample distortion and fueled by angst-filled lyrics, was attracting the likes of suburban teenagers everywhere. A 1989 article in the British music magazine *Melody Maker* championed Seattle and grunge music as the next coming of rock trends. All across America and in Europe, **Nirvana** became the "it" band of the early 1990s. Lead singer Kurt Cobain, who struggled with mainstream fame and seemed uncomfortable with the group's instant success, became an icon for a generation that society had labeled as one that lacked the ability to define itself. Grunge music had ironically become the theme music for the "slacker" generation that everyone had believed lacked ambition or interest in anything worthwhile. But all the while many grunge artists and fans were mistakenly labeled as lazy or apathetic, they, in fact, simply refused to conform. Grunge music itself was a protest of the detested social norms that were strict in nature, and these musicians knew well enough to use their music as an outlet for their feelings about the unfairness of society's social roles and expectations of what "good, upholding citizens" should be. Many of the lyrics in grunge music spoke to those ideals, revealing the genre's roots in punk music, which had a more outspoken, up-front attitude toward social and political norms they strove to oppose.

Grunge music was also inherently an outcry for personal freedom. Band members such as **Nirvana**'s felt as though they were artists working to educate the masses about what they felt was social alienation and the suffocating of this freedom. The ironic twist is that such an apathetic band, and a socially awkward, shy, and depressed singer as Cobain was, would become the face of a generation that was labeled as one unable to make a stand on its own could have very well been at the root of the cause of the end of the genre.

Soon, though, marketing and sales departments started seeing dollar signs whenever they looked into Kurt Cobain's ocean-blue eyes. MTV aired the group's reveled *Unplugged* performance in November 1993, and the subsequent album went straight to #3 on the charts and has since sold millions of copies worldwide. But Cobain, despite the fame and fortune and god-like status the music scene had bestowed upon him, was still the shy Seattle teenager who just wanted to play his guitar. The grunge community mourned the loss of the blond-haired singer when he committed suicide on April 5, 1994. At a loss without its patron saint, and with genres like Britpop and post-grunge stealing the spotlight, grunge lost its sheen and the genre fizzled out.

Further Reading: Anderson, Kyle. *Accidental Revolution: The Story of Grunge.* New York: St. Martin's Griffin, 2007; Heylin, Clinton. *Babylon's Burning: From Punk to Grunge.* Edinburgh, Scotland, United Kingdom: Canongate, 2007.

GUIDED BY VOICES

Robert Pollard left school teaching behind to enroll in the school of rock when he formed the **Lo-fi**/indie group Guided By Voices (GBV) in 1985 his hometown of Dayton, Ohio. Often categorized as art-punk, Guided By Voices is well known for making short pop songs with catchy songs surrounded by **Lo-fi** hiss and background noise that is reminiscent of a basement recording studio.

Leading the indie rock underground during the late 1980s, Guided By Voices released a few EPs and self-released LPs in the 1980s, for example, *Devil Between My Toes* and *Self-Inflicted Aerial Nostalgia,* before it finally caught the attention of **Sonic Youth**'s Thurston Moore and then finally grasped listeners' attention with its debut release, *Bee Thousand* (Scat Records/Matador Records) in 1994. Packed with 20 tracks that seem to have been titled during a game of pin-the-tail on the song title—"Her Psychology Today," "Smothered in Hugs," and "The Gold Heart Mountaintop Queen Directory"—the album turned hordes of fans onto the group's kitschy lyrics, short songs that featured hints of strange sound effects, and melodic pop, making it one of the definitive **Lo-fi** albums of the early 1990s.

The band's demanding tour schedule and prolific album-releasing habits, not to mention Pollard's on-stage drinking habits, led to the evacuation of several band members throughout the years; Pollard's brother had even joined the mix at one point, and Pollard created a new manifestation of GBV with the band Cobra Verde in the mid-1990s. The band's current lineup now includes front man and singer/songwriter Robert Pollard, guitarist/backing vocalist Doug Gillard, drummer Kevin March, guitarist/backing vocalist Nate Farley, and bassist Chris Slusarenko. Guided By Voices became a college radio sensation, playing the college circuit along with such bands as **R.E.M.** and **Sonic Youth**.

The general public also caught wind of GBV, and the band were featured in *SPIN* magazine, which gave it even wider exposure. GBV continued to tour, and audiences became increasingly fascinated by the group's on-stage antics—Pollard's high kicks, (former member) Mitch Mitchell's chain-smoking habits, and (former member) Greg Demo's The Who-like black-and-white-striped pants.

At the behest of the group's new label, TVT Records, GBV teamed up with the former front man for the 1970s rock band The Cars, Roc Ocasek who produced the group's TVT debut in the hopes to make its sound more radio-friendly. Meanwhile, GBV released a box set of its older material to appease fans: *Suitcase: Failed Experiments and Trashed Aircraft* featured 100 tracks of classic GBV material spanning 25 years of rits career. Nonplussed by sales, the group left TVT following the release of its 2001 album, *Isolation Drills,* and resigned with Matador for its 2002 album, *Universal Truths and Cycles,* which showed a return to the group's **Lo-fi** roots. Pollard also resurrected his Rockathon Records label, through which the group released merchandise and music it created for various side projects.

Satisfied with the group's 2004 album, *Half Smiles of the Decomposed,* which Pollard called "befitting as a final album" (www.matadorrecodrs.com/guided-by-voices), GBV announced its breakup and a farewell tour. Pollard marched onward though, going so far as to poke fun at his well-reported drinking habits, which had became a topic of conversation within the music community, in true Pollard style with his 2005 solo album, *Relaxation of the A- -hole,* a concept album about an alcoholic who risks losing it all—save for his beloved bottle and booze. The year 2007 saw the release of the live GBV album *Live From Austin, TX,* which captured its final live show at the Austin City Limits Music Festival back in 2004. Matador Records released the GBV album *Half Smiles of the Decomposed* in August 2004.

Pollard amicably parted ways with Merge Records in 2008 after making four albums with the label in two years. In 2008, Pollard announced his new venture, his full-length album *Robert Pollard Is Off to Business,* which was slated for release by his own label, Guided by Voices Inc.

Further Reading: Greer, James. *Guided By Voices: A Brief History: Twenty-One Years of Hunting Accidents in the Forests of Rock and Roll.* New York: Grove Press, Black Cat, 2005; http://www.gbv.com; http://www.matadorrecords.com/guided_by_voices; http://www.robertpollard.net; http://www.rockathonrecords.com; http://www.scatrecords.com.

H

HARVEY, PJ

Of all the women to emerge as indie rock queens in the early 1990s, PJ Harvey seemed to possess the darkest, most enigmatic lyrics—and a mysterious, indefinable persona to match. Born Polly Jean Harvey in 1979 in England, the eccentric (she reportedly ate nothing but potatoes during the recording of her 1993 album), raven-haired singer rose to fame with her 1991 single, "Dress," which earned her media coverage on *Melody Maker* magazine. Harvey originally recorded and performed as part of a trio known as PJ Harvey (with drummer Rob Ellis and bassist Ian Olliver), recording songs that touched on sensitive topics such as religion, sex, love, and even abortion. The group released another popular single, "Sheila-Na-Gig," before putting out its debut EP, *Dry,* in 1992 on Island Records.

Boldly waving the do-it-my-way flag, Harvey was named Best New Female Singer and Best Songwriter by *Rolling Stone*. While Harvey steered clear of detracting herself from the mainstream media or claiming to be a tried and true **DIY- (Do-It-Yourself)**-er, she seemed to enjoy causing a ruckus. A controversy arose when Harvey appeared topless on the cover of **NME (New Musical Express)**, but when the media attempted to label her a "feminist," she plainly denied any association with the movement. The influential singer left the trio behind and branched out on her own for her follow-up album, *To Bring You My Love* (Island, 1995), a collection of bold, on-my-own-feet songs, including the hit track, "Down By the Water," a dark song that seemed to capture Harvey's potential for eeriness. *Love* received heavy rotation on MTV, sold 1 million copies, and topped the rock charts.

Harvey toured in support of *Love*, but amid the fanfare surrounding the album—several major media outlets such as the *New York Times* voted the record Album of the Year—she reverted to seclusion the following year. Harvey emerged from her hibernation period with an even more striking look—blacker-than-black hair, combat boots, and elaborate makeup; her on-stage presence took on a theatrical twist, too. The svelt singer told *SPIN* magazine that her new person was a "combination of being quite elegant and funny and revolting, all at the same time" (*SPIN* magazine, 1996).

Harvey seemed to make a 180-degree turn musically with her 2000 album, *Stories from the City, Stories from the Sea,* a dual concept album on which she sang from both sides of the pond—in the bustling aura of New York City and the quiet calm of the Parisian countryside. The effort won the 2000 Mercury Music Prize and 1 one million copies, proving that Harvey had successfully reinvented herself

British singer PJ Harvey performs in 2001. [AP Wide World Photos/Laurent Gillieron]

as a musician worthy of attention. *Stories,* for which Harvey reteamed with former bandmate Rob Ellis, featured vocals by **Radiohead**'s Thom Yorke.

In 2001, Harvey was listed among the 100 Greatest Women in Rock 'n' Roll by Britain's Q magazine. Harvey returned to the studio for her seventh studio album, *Uh Huh Her* (Island, 2004), on which she played every instrument—save the drums. Over the years, Harvey collaborated with a barrage of musicians including English rapper/trip-hop performer Tricky, English singer/actress Marianne Faithfull, the Australian musician Nick Cave, and the in-your-face California rockers Queens of the Stone Age. Harvey was slated to play the 2004 **Lollapalooza** festival in 2004, but when the tour was canceled, she launched a string of solo dates instead.

In 2006, Island released a collection of songs Harvey recorded with legendary broadcaster John Peel, *PJ Harvey: The Peel Sessions, 1991–2004.* In 2007, Harvey contributed to an exhibition by the eclectic California-born visual artist/musician Captain Beefheart in New York City. Harvey continued to work on her eighth studio album, which was slated for a 2008 release. Harvey returned to the stage in 2008 with select dates in various countries; she announced the release of a previously unreleased track from 1998, which she planned to make into a B-side to her upcoming 2008 single.

Further Reading: Blandford, James R. *PJ Harvey: Siren Rising.* London: Omnibus Press, 2004; http://www.beefheart.com; http://www.mariannefaithfull.org.uk; http://www.nationwidemercurys.com; http://www.pjharvey.net.

HATFIELD, JULIANA

This slender, soft-spoken, New England–born guitarist/singer/songwriter is among the handful of female icons who made lasting impressions and influences on the indie rock genre. Hatfield attended the prestigious Berklee College of Music in Boston, Massachusetts, before she formed the rock band the Blake Babies with friends Freda Boner and John Strohm and later branched out of her own in the early 1990s. Her influences range from Neil Young to the Los Angeles–based punk rock group X, which Hatfield grew up listening to and eventually toured with later in her career in the mid-2000s.

Hatfield's signature songs, a combination of her fragile baby-doll voice backed by loud, catchy guitar riffs, circulated the college radio circuit. While working on her solo debut, Hatfield played bass and sang on the teenage group Lemonheads' (fronted by media darling Evan Dando) album, *It's a Shame About Ray,* a critically acclaimed release that helped shed some light on Hatfield's talent and create a platform for her debut album, *Hey Babe* (Mammoth Records, 1992), a record that showcased Hatfield's playing chops and songwriting capabilities, proving she was more than a pretty bass wielding a pick.

The whispery-voiced singer moved up the ranks to a bigger playing field at Atlantic Records for her follow-up album, *Become What You Are,* released under the moniker The Juliana Hatfield Three, which she had formed with musician friends Todd Phillips and Dean Fisher. *Become What You Are* yielded two of her biggest hits—the tracks "Spin the Bottle" and "My Sister," which received countless air play on the radio. "Bottle" ended up on the soundtrack to the movie *Reality Bites,* a classic film that has become a pop culture relic of Generation X.

Hatfield's persona made her an idol for young girls across the United States; she appeared in fashion magazines and became an icon for the **Riot Grrrl Movement** as a woman who could hold her own in the male-dominated music business. Hatfield continued to release albums and tour nationwide, and her shyness and antiestablishment attitude continued to precede her in interviews and live appearances.

The Blake Babies made a futile attempt to reunite in 2000, but the fleeting effort produced just one album, *God Bless the Blake Babies,* and a brief tour. Hatfield hit a snag in her career when her record label refused to release an album the songstress believed to be a solid piece of work, *God's Foot,* but Hatfield rebounded when she

Juliana Hatfield performs at the Paradise Lounge in Boston on January 8, 2005. [AP Wide World Photos/Robert E. Klein]

formed the group Some Girls with one of her Blake Babies bandmates before refocusing her efforts on her solo career. She also founded her own label, Ye Olde Records, on which she released the self-produced 2005 album *Made in China,* a raw, aggressive record that saw Hatfield returning to her aggressive, guitar-fueled indie roots. She released the EP *Sittin' in a Tree* with musician Frank Smith in 2007.

In 2008, Hatfield's Web site announced that Ye Olde Records would be releasing all of Hatfield's previously unreleased material on a "pay what you want/ what you can afford" basis. Hatfield continues to perform with the band Some Girls. She announced an in-the-works new album, which was produced by Andy Chase of the band **Ivy**.

Further Reading: Unteberger, Richie. *The Rough Guide to Music USA.* London: Rough Guides, 1999; http://www.evandando.co.uk; http://www.julianahatfield.com; http://www.myspace.com/julianahatfield.

THE HIDDEN CAMERAS

The Hidden Cameras' front man, Joel Gibb, an out-and-proud homosexual, has often described his band's music as a "gay church folk music" (www.last.

fm/music/The+Hidden+Cameras). Flamboyance, religion, and sexuality are often seen as the most defining aspects of The Hidden Cameras—and also the most distracting.

Music magazines have zoomed in on the group's sexual politics and the songs that, on the surface, seem to be about enemas and unsanitary bodily fluids. Concertgoers seemed to be both entertained and overwhelmed by the group's busy live shows, which have been held in churches and porn theaters and in which the number of go-go dancers or strippers occasionally outnumber the band. Critics and fans alike have claimed that the Hidden Cameras prove to be a pop outfit with the chipper electricity of **The New Pornographers** and the thick harmonies and breezy simplicity of The Beach Boys and **Belle and Sebastian**.

The Hidden Cameras, initially, was a product of front man Joel Gibb and Joel Gibb only. Gibb had been writing songs since high school, and the band originated from the Ontario, Canada suburbs. On The Hidden Cameras's earliest recordings, Gibb used a 4-track and played everything from guitar to glockenspiel to drum machine. Never one to be coy with opinions, Gibb titled The Hidden Cameras's 2001 full-length debut, *Ecce Homo,* a phrase meaning "Behold the man!" that was used by Pontius Pilate before Christ's crucifixion, which he released on his own Evil Evil label. Such songs as "Ode to Self-Publishing" feature lines such as "Fear of the Bible/has wasted my whole life away"—consequently, The Hidden Cameras have made no effort to conceal its politics.

By 2003, Gibb had nearly a ten-piece band to work with. Among others, that band consisted of Paul Mathew on bass, Maggie MacDonald on glockenspiel and keyboard, David Mez Meslin on bass and percussion, Lex Vaughn on drums, Lief Mosbaugh on viola, Jamie McCarthy on violin, and cellist Mike Olsen.

That same year, The Hidden Cameras recorded its second full-length album, *The Smell of Our Own.* Its sophomore effort's lewd, often politically charged lyrics found a home on the indie label **Rough Trade Records**. The track "Ban Marriage" seemed timely with the controversy surrounding the Constitution and gay marriage in 2003, while aforementioned bodily toxins in "The Man That I Am with My Man" brought the band its hype and fandom.

In 2004, The Hidden Cameras released its third album, *Mississauga, Goddamn,* which was named after the Mississauga Dam, in Canada, near where Gibbs grew up. The album featured more symphonic, sexually drenched pop piled high with graphic imagery. Critics responded to Gibb's talent for crafting such songs as "Music Is My Boyfriend" and "The Fear Is On," which seemed to address Gibb's isolation during his own upbringing, but they responded equally to Gibb's tendencies toward coarse subject matter. While Gibb intended songs like "I Want Another Enema" to be about bodily self-perception, many were mislead by the title.

In 2006, The Hidden Cameras released its third studio album, *Awoo.* In the summer of that same year, Joel Gibb played a variety of collaborative shows. He joined with the Magnetic Fields's Stephin Merritt, among others, to perform at a gay pride concert at Joe's Pub in New York City. Gibb later formed a duo with the critically acclaimed musician Jens Lekman, playing a one-time show together in Sweden. In the beginning of 2007, Gibb made his art-gallery debut in New York City with a series of felt banners, watercolors, and collages.

While the band was on its North American tour in 2007, its song "Music Is My Boyfriend" was featured in a commercial for the Apple iPhone. Gibb made his New York City gallery debut with his art show "Rise Up Thou Earth" in the spring of 2007.

Further Reading: http://www.thehiddencameras.com.

HÜSKER DÜ

Bands seeking to make the leap from an indie label to a major label while keeping their artistic integrity intact have this 1980s American **post-punk** band and its pioneering front man, Bob Mould, to thank for forging the path and casting the mold.

Formed by three record store junkies, Hüsker Dü, named after a 1950s Swedish board game, made music that boldly exuded the angst and anger shed by such bands as **Black Flag**. Influenced by hardcore bands of that era, Hüsker Dü later incorporated pop sounds. It was the first indie **post-punk** band in the 1980s to sign with a major label, and its music laid the groundwork for bands in the late 1980s and the 1990s that sought major label deals that would appease their cravings for creative control.

Hüsker Dü, comprised of founding members Bob Mould (songwriter, guitarist, and lead vocalist), Grant Hart (drummer and background vocalist), and Greg Norton (bassist and background vocalist), stayed true to its edgy sound, making uncompromised music that made the group a cult hero—but the group never struck it rich. Mould's guitar chops and innovative playing helped solidify his reputation as one of the most influential guitarists of the decade.

Formed in Minneapolis, Minnesota, Hüsker Dü put out eight full-length albums in its almost decade-long career. The prolific band pleased fans with its talent and rocked amps with its distortion-fueled, high decibel songs; the group's trademark layers of heavy rock played over catchy pop melodies made fans of habitual record buyers and the band's musician peers. Hüsker Dü has influenced such bands as Soul Asylum, The Replacements, **Superchunk**, the **Pixies**, and, even in some respects, **Nirvana**; the group's existential lyrics often touched on personal topics, bringing fans closer to the group in much the same way early hardcore **emo** music did—by discussing sensitive subjects under a veil of what sounded on the surface to be purely party-worthy rock 'n' roll.

Hüsker Dü rehearsed in Hart's basement prepping songs Mould had written. The group released its debut single, "Statues," on a local label called Reflex Records. New Alliance Records put out the group's debut full-length album in 1981, a collection of songs recorded during its early touring days called *Land Speed Record* (**SST Records** re-released it in 1987). In 1983, Hüsker Dü released *Everything Falls Apart* (Reflex), and the group toured, logging tons of on-the-road miles.

Hüsker Dü's songs aired repeatedly on college radio, and the group gleefully played its songs sloppily—and often without stopping in between songs—for hordes of fans. Its 1983 LP, *Metal Circus* (Reflex/SST) rocked even harder than the band's earlier efforts. Hüsker Dü's signature single, "Eight Miles High," a cover of the Byrds' classic song, has echoed decades after its initial release.

It was not until the band put out the double-disc concept album, 1984's *Zen Arcade,* that tongues started wagging in the music scene. Often referred to as the "White Album of Punk," *Zen Arcade* shattered many conceptions about what punk was and could be with its pop structured punk tracks. The bare bones production quality (the album was reportedly recorded in just 80 hours) adhered to the punk aesthetic, while the songwriting reached to new heights. The 13-minute instrumental track, " Reoccurring Dreams," stands out as an epic achievement in music on which the group combined rock, psychedelica, punk, sound effects, and even bits of jazz. The *Zen* album is often credited as an early precursor of the **emo** genre.

Hüsker Dü put out two albums in 1985, *New Day Rising* and *Flip Your Wig.* Both Mould's and Hart's increasing drug and alcohol abuse put strains on the band, eventually reducing its once-strong personal relationship to rubble. Yet despite increasing tensions within the group, Hüsker Dü inked a deal with Warner Bros. Records, making it the first indie band to sign a deal with a major label. The topic of "selling out" soon emerged, but the band quelled those accusations by negotiating a recording contract that allowed it full creative control over its music. The band's milestone accomplishment (and downright good business sense) helped break the ice for other bands that would later make the same demands of labels that would have otherwise stripped them of their publishing rights or even worse—creative decision making rights. Hüsker Dü started a chain of peer-to-peer advice giving when the group offered to assist **Sonic Youth** with its contract negotiations.

Mould and his cohorts never quite broke the bank; in fact, their deal with Warner Bros. was more of an artistic statement that helped level the playing field for indie bands; plus they received even wider distribution and visibility. The group's 1986 Warner Bros. debut, *Candy Apple Grey,* featured some of the group's best hard-rocking songs, a pair of surprise acoustic tracks, and Mould's increasingly introspective lyrics. The divide between Mould and Hart, however, grew to the point that the band convinced a then-hesitant Warner Bros. to allow them to split the songwriting credits on its next album, 1987's *Warehouse: Songs and Stories.* Both albums placed modestly on the Billboard charts. The bandmates were brought together briefly, however, when their manager, David Savoy, committed suicide in 1986, on the night before they were slated to go on tour. While the bandmates soldiered on despite their mutual loss, Hart's personal demons had gotten the best of him. His heroin habit became an obstacle the band could not survive. Meanwhile, Mould had sobered up; Hart, who had not, was fired from the group.

The band dissolved sometime between 1987 and 1988. Mould and a sobered-up Hart pursued music separately—Hart formed the band Nova Mob, and Mould pursued a solo career. Norton, on the other hand, left music behind for good. Mould also formed a trio called Sugar in the early 1990s. Sugar's albums reached the charts, but Mould returned to his solo endeavors in the mid-1990s.

The band minus Norton, who reportedly became a chef/restaurant manager following the demise of Hüsker Dü, reunited for a brief stint in 2004, when the band played a benefit show for Soul Asylum's bassist Karl Mueller, who had recently been diagnosed with throat cancer. Mould joked about a Hüsker Dü reunion during that gig, but that idea proved to be just folly—he likened a Hüsker Dü reunion to the successful eviction of President George W. Bush from the Oval Office.

Mould's successful solo career continued to bear the fruits of his labors; he revealed a "lighter" side with his most recent album, *District Line* (Anti, 2008), while critics lauded his tour that year.

Further Reading: Marcus, Greil. *In the Fascist Bathroom: Punk in Pop Music, 1977–1992*. Boston: Harvard University Press, 1999; http://www.bobmould.com.

IGGY AND THE STOOGES/IGGY POP

Twenty-year-old Iggy Pop, who was born James Newell Osterberg, Jr., in a small town in Michigan, probably did not know (or would have cared) that rubbing peanut butter or cutting himself on stage and smearing blood all over his bare chest on stage would help make him a bona fide rock 'n' roll icon. The petite, extremely thin singer seemingly had little idea how big his band—The Stooges—would become either. But the band, which is widely recognized for its on-stage mania and hell-will-care garage rock, had few plans—or disillusions—for its future or fame; all the bandmates cared about was their music. In fact, neither did their audiences, who were often as hostile and unwieldy as they were.

Formed in 1967 in Ann Arbor, Michigan, The Stooges (originally known as Iggy and The Stooges, The Psychedelic Stooges, and Iggy Pop & The Stooges)— front man Iggy Pop, brothers guitarist Ron Asheton and drummer Scott Asheton, and bassist Dave Alexander—was a mesh of garage rock, proto punk, and ear-splintering feedback. The band was formed by Pop, who, after having played in such groups as The Iguanas and The Prime Movers, was inspired to start a new band after hearing music by blues drummer Sam Lay and attending a Doors concert. The Stooges' music, though, was pure rock-infused and raw, edgy and often considered borderline dangerous. The Stooges played its debut show on Halloween at the University of Michigan and toured locally before word of Pop's "primitive" performance, during which he almost always dove into the audience, spread throughout the underground.

Much like their Detroit counterparts, **MC5**, The Stooges were signed to Elektra Records after an A&R (Artists and Repertoire) representative for the label spotted the group opening for that very band. Pop and his long-haired brethren released their eponymously title debut album in 1969, which served to be an appropriate year to unleash their chaotic music on the world. The angst-filled album included what has become one of the band's signature songs, "I Wanna Be Your Dog," a sex, drugs, and rock 'n' roll–inspired anthem that epitomized the band's revolutionary, incendiary sound (and Pop's signature aggressive off-center vocal style). Produced by **The Velvet Underground**'s star band member John Cale, *The Stooges* captured the essence of the band—and fans clamored to own a piece of the explosive group. The album hit a high note on the Billboard charts, and even though sales were poor from a label's perspective, the album served to place the band solidly in the rock-loving hearts and dirty minds of teens and indie fans everywhere. It pretty much embodied the unpredictable, uncontrollable spirit of that pivotal year, 1969.

The Stooges second album, 1970's *Fun House,* clearly described the band's state of mind at the time. Unable to play its songs correctly on stage (or without the bandmates tuning their instruments for the amount of time it takes to play another song), the band was losing the battle with drug abuse and sinking deeper into a heroin- and cocaine-induced sort of trance that severely affected Pop. *Fun House* sold even fewer copies than the band's first record, but fans started building a cult-like adoration for the emaciated front man and the band's off-kilter antics. The label, though it may have seen a Doors-like profitable future stemming from potential controversies surrounding the band, decided instead to drop the band from its roster.

Inner band drama and drug abuse eventually split the bandmates apart. Dave Alexander left the band and was subsequently replaced by Zeke Zettner and then James Recca. In the midst of the musical band chairs, Ron Asheton switched to bass and the group added guitarist James Williamson. After beating his heroin addiction, Pop worked various jobs to make ends meet while the band went on a year-long hiatus. Pop's struggle to beat the demons of addiction continued, but along the way, he met a fairy godmother of a different sort—glam rocker David Bowie, who was inspired by Pop and felt a desire to help the struggling musician. With Bowie's help, the band got back together and became known as Iggy and The Stooges. With Pop as the showcased front man, Bowie produced the group's 1973 album, *Raw Power.* And true to form, the record's label served as a psychic precursor to the band's state at the time. The cover art for *Power* featured a very Bowie-esque Pop—shirtless, wearing lots of eye makeup, and dressed in tight, hip-hugging gold pants. The album was a commercial success, and the band's immortal attitude helped to increase its popularity. Bowie had taken a bet that fans would fall in love with Pop's raw, unpredictable character-like persona and the band's chaotic, oversexed music—and he was right. *Raw* is considered a pre-eminent punk rock album, and it has since been reissued, even though it sold scarcely any copies the year it debuted.

With the success, money, and newfound pressure (not to mention the band went without a manager after it had a falling out with Bowie's manager), The Stooges bandmates resorted to copious drug use when they went on the road in support of *Power.* Consequently, Iggy spent a year in a mental health facility in Los Angeles. Upon his release, Pop spent some time with his new friend Bowie in Germany (Bowie later reportedly wrote the song "Jean Genie" about Pop). Freed from his addiction once more, Pop went back to work. In the late 1970s, Bowie produced Pop's debut solo albums *The Idiot* and *Lust for Life,* both released on Virgin Records; their collaboration proved a success. Bowie plastered Pop's ghost-like face on both covers, but the portrait on *Lust for Life* was friendly, wide-eyed, and less menacing than images of Pop on the covers of previous records. Without the Stooges backing him, Pop was free to explore, and his persona seemed freed from the dark, dingy city he hailed from and full of new light.

Songs like the emblematic and poppy "China Girl," which Bowie and Pop co-wrote, and the nonsensical lyrics of "Nightclubbing" showed a lighter side of Pop that made him and his music more accessible.

Meanwhile, albums full of angst-charged Stooges material surfaced—the two-disc *Metallic K.O.* captured the band's last show together in 1974—but The Stooges were on indefinite hiatus. While Pop's solo career skyrocketed, the rest of the bandmates were not having the same kind of luck on their own (Alexander passed away in 1975 from pneumonia). Williamson, however, teamed up with Pop as his songwriter for a few years before retiring from the music business altogether. The Asheton brothers started the band New Order, but their fate—which may have been adversely affected by that *other* band called New Order that was so successful—was sealed when they disbanded in the early 1980s. Ron, how-ever, acted in a few small films and played briefly with various well-known musi-cians from **MC5**, **Sonic Youth**, and Mudhoney who had started various musical side projects.

Branded too "dangerous" for mainstream audiences and too out of line with the current musical trends, The Stooges' music seemed to freeze in time. And while Pop's star soared (his solo career has been a series of successes), the band's moment had passed. Still, 30 years after the group formed in that Great Lake state, The Stooges's music has had a permanent place in the pages of rock history as some of the most reactionary and experimental music of all time. Pop has, by the sheer nature of the irony of his stage name, become a pop culture icon and The Stooges's music has influenced countless bands such as **Mission of Burma**, the Red Hot Chili Peppers, **The White Stripes**, **Sonic Youth**, among others. Pop and the Stooges, though, have no bad blood between them. The band's reunion was reportedly initiated when Pop heard that his former bandmates, the Asheton brothers, were playing Stooges covers during live shows in 2002. Pop returned the honor when he asked his Stooges bandmates to play on his 2003 album, *Skull Ring*. The Stooges played its first concert together in over 30 years at the **Coachella Valley Music and Arts Festival** in Indio, California, in 2003.

Then the bandmates only did what felt natural—they started touring together again. Pop continued to release solo albums, but he toured with The Stooges through 2003, and three years later, **Big Black** alum Steve Albini produced the group's first record in over 30 years—2007's *The Weirdness* (Virgin Records), which was followed by a world tour. *Weirdness* also featured new Stooges member (and former Firehouse and Minutemen band member) Mike Watt. The Stooges received yet another nomination for induction into the Rock and Roll Hall of Fame in 2006, but the group has yet to be inducted. Iggy and The Stooges continued to tour together through 2007, playing various festivals in the United States and Europe, including **Lollapalooza**. The reunited band celebrated Pop's 60th birth-day on stage during that tour. News outlets revealed that a biopic is in the works about Iggy and The Stooges' career; actor Elijah Wood is reportedly in talks to por-tray Pop.

The Stooges received yet another nomination for an induction into the Rock and Roll Hall of Fame in 2008, but the band got no further than the ceremony itself as the bandmates performed for one of the year's inductees, Madonna, whom they had actually opened for on her Re-Invention World Tour 2004.

Iggy Pop's solo career continues on its stalwart path; Pop released his most recent solo effort, the live album *Acoustic KO* in 2008 on Skydog Records.

Further Reading: Rock, Mick, and Iggy Pop. *Raw Power: Iggy & The Stooges.* London: Omnibus Press, 2005; Trynka, Paul. *Iggy Pop: Open Up and Bleed.* New York: Broadway Books, 2007; http://www.iggypop.com.

INDIE POP

Indie pop is not to be confused with **Twee pop**, which has a more innocent angle and blatantly pop-driven sound. Indie pop refers to indie music that sways a bit toward the pop spectrum, with its melodic sound and rhythmic qualities. Indie pop emerged in the early 1980s in Europe when bands played music that was "pretty" sounding, guitar-based, catchy, and synthesizer driven in a similar way to that of pop music from the 1960s. An indie pop artist's focus is on all things sweet and soft; it is often considered the yin to the yang of the **Riot Grrrl Movement**.

Acts such as the Scottish act **Orange Juice**, which formed at the turn of the decade in 1979, played indie pop that repeatedly hit the charts. The band, though commercially focused, remained an indie act for its **DIY (Do-It-Yourself)** sensibilities and label base, but its pop sound was undeniable. Some of the later acts in the indie pop genre swayed even farther into bubble gum pop territory. These "twee" acts made sugary sweet pop that helped music fans to categorize them under the **Twee pop** umbrella.

Indie labels such as Postcard Records, K Records, and the U.K.–based Sarah Records were home bases for several indie pop acts. During the 1980s, however, indie and **Twee pop** were criticized for their "soft" ways, but critics and naysayers later realized that these subgenres helped pave the way for experimentalism in music in Europe.

While the **Twee pop** movement was attributed to the bands included on *NME* (*New Musical Express*)'s C86 tape, the indie pop acts were all grouped together on the magazine's earlier C81 cassette. Zines and indie publications helped spread the word about indie pop acts, and this communication increased their fan bases. Acts included on the C81 tape included John Cooper Clarke, Linx, Essential Logic, **Orange Juice**, The Raincoats, The Red Krayola, Scritti Politti, Josef K, and Subway Sect. **Rough Trade Records** co-released the compilation with *NME* (*New Musical Express*).

Indie pop was an indirect influence on **post-rock** with its melodic sound and what some consider "jangly" guitars. Acts such as the **Ramones** even had some pop inflections in their music, which meant that indie pop had even influenced some punk acts. Indie pop also started to grow in such places as Olympia, Washington, the home base of K Records, and acts with soft-sounding names, such as

Honeybunch and Tiger Trap were put on the musical map. Other indie pop acts include Milksop Holly, Call and Response, Heavenly, Cub, and The Field Mice.

Further Reading: Friskics-Warren, Bill. *I'll Take You There: Pop Music and the Urge for Transcendence.* London: Continuum International Publishing Group, 2006; http://www.indiepages.com.

IVY

In 1989, Ivy front woman Dominique Durand traveled from Paris to the United States to learn English. In 1994, while living in New York City, Durand discovered she could sing and joined up with multi-instrumentalist Andy Chase and Fountains of Wayne pop-whiz-kid Adam Schlesinger to form the **indie pop** group Ivy. Without any formal vocal training, Durand's coolly distant vocals became Ivy's trademark. The band's jet-set appeal and dream-pop sensibilities earned it easy comparisons to Stereolab, Saint Etienne, and, more distantly, Serge Gainsbourg.

Unlike most bands, whose back stories stew with rejection and piecemeal income, Ivy's early efforts found reward quickly. "Get Enough," off of one of the band's demo tapes, was named "Single of the Week" in 1994 by the U.K. magazine *Melody Maker.* In 1995, Ivy released its full-length debut, *Realistic,* on the indie label Unfiltered Records. *Realistic* was a solid, backbeat-driven album, with the icy guitar jangle of The Cranberries and some softer elements of **Juliana Hatfield**, but the album was largely typical of music in the mid 1990s and lacked the atmospheric sophistication of the band's later efforts. Still, *Realistic* garnered enough attention to land Ivy some touring gigs with the likes of Edwyn Collins and Oasis.

However, in 1997, Ivy found a style and locked in on it. That year, the band released its sophomore album, *Apartment Life.* On much of the album, guitars became less of a focal point and played more of a supporting role, gluing songs together rather than driving them entirely. Tracks such as "This Is the Day," "Never Do That Again," and "Baker" navigated lounge and trip-hop with relative confidence.

Before the release of Ivy's third full-length, *Long Distance,* Durand and Chase married. Chase and Schlesinger worked with former Smashing Pumpkins guitarist and longtime friend James Iha to open the Stratosphere Sound recording studio in the Chelsea neighborhood of New York City, but before the band could complete *Long Distance,* the studio was destroyed in a 1999 fire. *Long Distance* was finally released in 2001, and Stratosphere Sound reopened in a new location in 2002.

On the all-covers album *Guestroom,* Ivy applied its French-pop-style ambience to an array of the band's influences. The covers on *Guestroom* ranged from The Cure to Steely Dan to The Ronnettes. In 2005, Ivy released its fifth album, *In the Clear,* on Vancouver-based Nettwerk Records.

Despite the cozily evocative qualities of their music, Ivy bandmates have always been opportunists at heart, never shying away from TV or film to sell their music. Their song "This Is the Day" appeared in the 1998 comedic film *There's Something About Mary.* Ivy's other movie credits include 2001's *Shallow Hal* and 2002's

Orange County and *Insomnia*. Ivy's TV resume is even larger, with songs featured in the 2004 Stephen King–penned miniseries *Kingdom Hospital*, the UPN sitcom *Veronica Mars*, Volkswagen commercials, and even a live performance on the WB show *Roswell*.

In their spare time, Chase, Schlesinger, and Durand stay busy with their respective side projects. Chase and Durand formed the technopop outfit Paco, which released its second album, *This Is Where We Live*, in 2004. Chase maintains solo project Brookville and produces several full-length releases by the band Tahiti 80. In 2007, Schlesinger's other, more well-known band, Fountains of Wayne, released its fifth full-length album, *Traffic and Weather*. Nettwerk Records released Ivy's 2007 album, *In the Clear*.

Further Reading: Carson, Mina, Tisa Lewis, and Susan M. Shaw. *Girls Rock! Fifty Years of Women Making Music*. Lexington, KY: University Press of Kentucky, 2004; http://www.myspace.com/brookville; http://www.thebandivy.com.

JADE TREE RECORDS

Founded by long-time friends and then college students Tim Owen and Darren Walters in 1990, this Wilmington, Delaware–based independent record label is home to over 60 bands, including such notable acts as **My Morning Jacket**, **Pedro the Lion**, **Girls Against Boys**, Hot Water Music, **Denali**, and Alkaline Trio. Owen and Walters pledged to avoid signing bands from only one geographical area or within one genre, and they aimed to sign bands that represented the underground mentality and mind-set above all else. Owen and Walters eventually moved the operation out of their bedrooms and into real offices in the Washington, D.C. suburb, where they were ideally located, sitting front row to witness the birth of "the D.C. scene."

Owen and Walters, who had each founded imprints, Axtion Packed Records and Hi-Impact Records, respectively, before starting Jade Tree, were once advised by a friend that starting a record label was a poor way to make money; but Jade Tree Records, having grown in size and scope over the years, has proven to be a fruitful endeavor nonetheless. The first band signed to the roster, the political hardcore/straight-edge band Four Walls Falling, which has since disbanded, preceded such bands as the alt metal outfit Railhed, of which Walters is a band member, and the Washington, D.C.–based art rock group Pitchblende.

Most of the bands on Jade Tree's roster rock the thin line between hardcore and alt rock (with a tiny pinch of prog rock thrown in for good measure), creating the label's signature genre, which has become known as "post-hardcore." Ironically, though, Swiz, the band that put Jade Tree on the map, had broken up before the label was able to put out its first album. Jade Tree's 1995 release of the debut album by the New Jersey–based melodic hardcore band Lifetime, however, really got the attention of the music scene.

Soon after, Jade Tree signed such groups as New York City's punk rockers Texas Is the Reason, which reunited for two shows in 2006 after splitting in 1997, and Milwaukee, Wisconsin's **post-punk/emo** band The Promise Ring, which already had a steady following. Momentum surrounding the label picked up, and Owen and Walters left their college degrees and careers behind to focus full-time on the label. Jade Tree was the most talked about label of the mid-1990s.

Successful records continued to flow out of Jade Tree by bands such as the rock band Jets to Brazil, which included former Jawbreaker front man Blake Schwarzenbach, the short-lived punk band Kid Dynamite, **emo**/space rock band Joan of Arc, and the two-person instrumental outfit Euphone. Jade Tree is credited with discovering Edmonds, Washington native David Bazan's introspective solo project **Pedro the Lion**; the critical acclaim earned by Bazan's albums catapulted Jade Tree into a level of success Owen and Walters had never anticipated.

Jade Tree continued to sign promising bands to its roster—Richmond, Virginia's indie band **Denali**, the musical collective Milemarker (aka the Milemarker Collective, the Milemarker People's Liberation Army, or the Milemarker Entertainment and Reprogramming Committee), and These Arms Are Snakes.

The majority of the bands that started out on Jade Tree in the mid-1990s continue to record and release albums with the label as it approaches its second decade. The media have taken serious notice of the label, with the prominent music publications claiming that the label is a leader in the underground music scene. Walters and Owen's hands-on/**DIY (Do-It-Yourself)** mentality is the direct cause of Jade Tree's success, mostly because the duo continued to work hard for a label that in the beginning was an endeavor that reaped only passionate results and benefits of the musical kind—meaning they made no money at first.

Jade Tree's founders have reportedly been offered six-figure payments in exchange for their catalog, but the pair has repeatedly turned down such offers. Their mail-order business has more than doubled in productivity and profit margins, and the label's online presence has solidified the label's standing in the indie rock community.

Asked to list the albums that served as turning points for the label, Owen and Walters cited Lifetime's 1995 album, *Hello Bastards,* which sold 20,000 copies that year alone, and The Promise Ring's 1996 release, *30° Everywhere.* Jade Tree's most commercially viable band has been The Promise Ring, which has topped Best Of lists in the likes of *SPIN* magazine, and its videos have been in heavy rotation on MTV. The Promise Ring has remained loyal to Jade Tree simply because the label has been good to it, offering the group what the group views as a fairer system of royalties, artistic freedom, and a hand in the decision making with regards to everything and anything it produces.

British music fans noticed Jade Tree and its impressive roster in the early 2000s, giving the label an even bigger spot on the indie music map. Jade Tree showcased a selection of bands on its roster by releasing the compilation album *Location Is Everything, Vol. 1* in 2002, featuring tracks by Trial By Fire, Milemarker, The Promise Ring, and Jets to Brazil.

By 2003, Jade Tree had collectively sold over a million records. In 2004, Jade Tree released its second compilation album, *Location Is Everything, Vol. 2,* featuring music by such Jade Tree recording artists as Cex, onelinedrawing, Paint It Black, and Challenger. In 2005, Jade Tree's founders parted ways with their distributor, Modam, in favor of Chicago's indie stalwart, Touch and Go Records.

Jade Tree's influence continues to hold court over the indie community, as the label continues to add groundbreaking **emo**, **emocore**, noise rock, **post-punk**, **Lo-fi**, hardcore, Straight Edge, and experimental bands to its lineup. Jade Tree has signed the electro-op group Statistics, punk bands Paint It Black, From Ashes Rise, and Strike Anywhere. In 2006, Jade Tree marked its 100th release with a record by Lifetime called *Somewhere in the Swamps of Jersey*. Jade Tree currently has over 80 releases in its catalog, a solid heaping of bands with videos in rotation on MTV, countless bands touring relentlessly, and a roster of bands that will help define indie music for decades to come. The Jade Tree Web site offers fans tour dates, band pages, and a detailed history of the label, discographies, message boards, mail-order options, digital samples of new music, and more.

The complete Jade Tree lineup includes the following:

Alkaline Trio	Gravel	**Pedro the Lion**
Avail	Hot Water Music	Pitchblende
Breather Resist	J Church	Railhed
Cap'n Jazz	Jets to Brazil	Snowden
Cex	Joan of Arc	Songs: Ohia
Challenger	Jones Very	State of the Nation
Cloak/Dagger	Juno	Statistics
Cub County	Kid Dynamite	Strike Anywhere
Damnation AD	Kill Your Idols	Sweetbelly Freakdown
David Bazan	Leslie	Swiz
Denali	Lifetime	Texas Is the Reason
Despistado	Lords	The Explosion
Edsel	Micah P. Hinson	The Loved Ones
Eggs	Mighty Flashlight	The Promise Ring
Eidolon	Milemarker	These Arms Are Snakes
Ester Drang	**My Morning Jacket**	Trail By Fire
Euphone	New End Original	Turing Machine
Four Walls Falling	New Mexican Disaster Squad	Turning Point
From Ashes Rise	onelinedrawing	Universal Order of Armageddon
Fucked Up	Owls	Walleye
Fury	Paint It Black	Young Widows
Girls Against Boys	Panda & Angel	Zero Zero
Good Riddance		

Further Readings: Blush, Steven. *American Hardcore: A Tribal History*. Los Angeles: Feral House, 2001; Haenfler, Ross. *Straight Edge: Clean-Living Youth, Hardcore Punk, And Social Change*. Rutgers, NJ: Rutgers University Press, 2006; http://www.jadetree.com; http://www.myspace.com/jadetree.

JAWBOX

Look up anything about Jawbox, one of Washington, D.C.'s most utilitarian indie rock bands from the 1990s, and you will find a band whose history is full of more interesting facts than the mere mention that it was "the band that left Dischord Records." Neither the band nor the label in question parted ways with any harsh feelings, but the band's departure from Dischord remains a substantial controversy. Aside from the band's later deal with Atlantic Records and the creation of its own label, DeSoto Records, Jawbox was also a gimmickless band that simply wanted to be known for its music. And yet, it seems, it is Jawbox's impressive post-Dischord success that remains one of the most talked about events in the group's career.

When front man J. Robbins's former punk band, Government Issue, disbanded in 1989, Robbins created Jawbox in its image, recruiting drummer Adam Wade and bassist Kim Coletta. Jawbox's sawtooth guitars, tinny drums, and melodies that never seemed to lack abrasion tinged with a feeling that suggested loneliness amid the noise were reminiscent of the band **Pavement**. The music, along with the band's nose-to-the-grindstone work ethic, which was rooted in both the band's **DIY (Do-It-Yourself)** mentality and Robbins's years with Government Issue, attracted fans, helping Jawbox release its first self-titled EP in 1990 on its own DeSoto Records.

Likewise, the rest of Jawbox's career was spent negotiating its two greatest strengths—the ability to make appealing, forearm-throwing songs, and its uncanny talent for focusing on a principled, music-first approach to recording and managing. Jawbox's first full-length album, *Grippe* (Dischord Records, 1991), weighed in at 14 songs. An exercise in loudness and economy with guitar sprints, drums that alternately raced to the finish or slowed to an uphill climb, and a Replacements-esque cover of Joy Division's "Something Must Break," *Grippe* poised the group in good standing with most critics, who immediately saw potential in the band.

In 1992, with newly conscripted second guitarist Bill Barbot, Jawbox set to work on its second full-length album, *Novelty,* a more diverse and precise album on which deftly accented drums bounced around snaky guitar lines in the breakdown of songs such as "Static" and sludgier psychedelic territory in such tracks as the acoustic "Spiral Fix." Following *Novelty,* Robbins's lyrics became more insular and convoluted, but it was Barbot's additional guitar that finally put the band together and allowed *Novelty* to be both airy and punchy, with long, tracer-like notes often punctuated by the more guttural hardcore riffage of many Dischord bands.

While Jawbox's sound had all the steel screech of its Discord label mates, the band's videos showed its members were armed with relatively conventional, un-fussed-over haircuts, standard-issue jeans, and off-the-rack shirts. More importantly, Jawbox impressed a few industry heavyweights, and, as Dischord's resources proved limited, the group's flirtation with Atlantic Records began in the early 1990s.

Drummer Adam Wade left Jawbox in 1994 to join the group Shudder to Think; soon after, a studious undergrad named Zach Barocas, who attended school in Washington, D.C., and happened to live with Kim Coletta and play drums, was brought in as the group's new drummer for Jawbox's first Atlantic Records release, *For Your Own Special Sweetheart,* in 1994.

Sweetheart alienated some D.C. hardcore music purists, but it opened the band up to a broader fan base, arming it with more promotional muscle and broader distribution. Signing to Atlantic also allowed the band to release two singles, "Motorist" and the sparsely lyricized "Savory," both of which were made into videos. Most importantly, though, *Sweetheart,* and the band's 1996 self-titled follow-up album, showed the band could still be loud and take names—and sell itself without selling out.

Eventually the unpretentious ideals that made Jawbox also broke the group. Jawbox had always been a band of songs, not singles. When Jawbox did not produce significant radio play, Atlantic Records dropped the group in 1997. Barocas left the band to pursue film school, and in 1997, the band called it a career.

Many members of the band quickly rebounded musically, joining other bands, starting careers in the music industry, or playing music with each other. Robbins formed the band Burning Airlines while Coletta and Barbot, who got married in 1997, went on to run DeSoto Records, which has signed such artists as **The Dismemberment Plan** and Edie Sedgewick. Jawbox released a career retrospective, *My Scrapbook of Fatal Accidents,* in 1998. Near the beginning of 2007, DeSoto reclaimed the rights to Jawbox's Atlantic Records releases, which were distributed via iTunes.

The ex-members of Jawbox continued to run the label DeSoto Records through 2008.

Further Readings: Harcourt, Nick. *Music Lust: Recommended Listening for Every Mood, Moment, and Reason.* Seattle, WA: Sasquatch Books, 2005; http://www.burningairlines. com; http://www.desotorecords.com; http://www.dischord.com.

THE JESUS AND MARY CHAIN

A staple of the late 1980s and early 1990s indie scene, this London-via-Scotland group drowned sticky sweet pop in distortion and feedback, the result of which became affectionately known in the music industry as "white noise." Inspired by the 1970s rock group **The Velvet Underground**, The Jesus and Mary Chain succeeded in most part due to the heavy rotation its songs had on college radio, which made the band's members cult heroes and underground stars.

At the nucleus of The Jesus and Mary Chain were the Reid brothers—Jim and William, the group's main vocalists and guitarists—who formed the group in their hometown of Glasgow in the mid-1980s along with bassist Douglas Hart and drummer Murray Dalglish, who leftthe fold soon after he signed up. Entertaining a steady rotation of drummers, for example, Primal Scream front man Bobby Gillespie sat behind a drum kit for a brief period of time, The Jesus and Mary Chain had quickly become as well known for its bandmates' matching split-top mop-like hairdos as for its brief 20-minute sets, which infuriated many a crowd.

The Jesus and Mary Chain released what would become the group's breakthrough single in 1984, "Upside Down," which sparked a tour during which the Reid brothers and company developed a bad habit adopted by many bands within the **shoegazing** genre—a penchant for playing with their heads down and their backs turned toward the audience. Still, despite these live quirks, The Jesus and Mary Chain's popularity climbed steadily. Riots ensued at the group's live shows, particularly when fans felt that the group members played more for themselves than for the crowds. The British press, however, with **NME (*New Musical***

Express) quite often the front runner, boasted of the group's talents, crowning it with the nickname "The Jesus and Mary Chain Riot."

This so-called "bad press," if there really is such a thing in the music business, helped spread the word about the band's follow-up singles "You Trip Me Up" and "Just Like Honey," which proved the band's echoey blend of indie fuzz and smooth pop chords could be undeniably catchy. The Jesus and Mary Chain's debut album, 1985's *Psychocandy* (Blanco y Negro Records), was also received with aplomb. *Pyschocandy* possessed the type of wall of sound that The Beatles' producer Phil Spector made famous; only this group's wall consisted of its signature speaker-piercing feedback squeal, screeching guitars, and well-crafted pop melodies. Critics and fans alike lauded the album a masterpiece; many accredited its genius to the group's other bad habit—recreational drugs such as LSD, which the band members reportedly ingested during the recording of the album.

More "bad press" ensued for the band after one of the Reid brothers was arrested for possession of methamphetamines. The Jesus and Mary Chain became a success almost overnight, and, consequently, the press was right there with its cameras and notebooks when Jim Reid physically attacked an audience member who was giving the band a hard time. The group's antics did not stop there; the group was booted from the popular British music show *Top of the Pops* for singing the controversial lyrics to its song "Reverence" ("I wanna die just like Jesus Christ") despite warnings from the show's producers.

The Jesus and Mary Chain's sophomore album, *Stoned & Dethroned* (Warner Bros., 1994), showcased the group's new mellowed-out side. The group's 1994 **Lollapalooza** gig was a combination of its frenetic past and its newer, softer side. Tracks from the mostly acoustic album featured guest vocalist and Mazzy Star singer Hope Sandoval. The album's first single, which featured Sandoval, "Sometimes Always," was anticipated to be a major hit, but the album resulted in lukewarm sales and reviews. When 1995's ironically titled *Hate Rock 'n' Roll* was deemed nothing more than a "B-sides album," the group took a four-year hiatus. Of course, the single from the album *Hate Rock 'n' Roll* proved the band had the last laugh. On the track, Reid sings boldly and unequivocally about the BBC's schoolmarm attitude toward the group's "questionable" lyrics and MTV's faux positing in the music industry.

The Jesus and Mary Chain signed to Seattle's **Sub Pop Records** for its next release, 1998's *Munki,* which was also unable to stir the waters the way the band's previous albums had. The Reid brothers and crew called it quits in 1999, and the band members pursued other musical endeavors; Jim formed the group Freeheat, and William started an outfit called Lazycane. The growing emotional distance and an increasing number of disagreements that grew among the bandmates during the recording of *Munki* were major contributing factors to teh band's demise, and the album's sonic disparity. Interband quarrels and a highly intoxicated Jim Reid crowned the band's final performance at the House of Blues club in Los Angeles in 1998.

Rhino Records resurrected The Jesus and Mary Chain in spirit by releasing a string of reissues of the band's five albums in 2006; each CD came with a DVD featuring the band's videos. Somehow, though, life was breathed back into the group almost eight years after its breakup. Rumors circulated that the band was slated to perform at the 2007 **Coachella Valley Music and Arts Festival**; the group, along with long-time member and rhythm guitarist Ben Lurie, delivered. Actress Scarlett Johansson joined the band onstage, providing vocals for the "Just Like Honey" single. That show spawned a series of live performances by The Jesus and Mary Chain at festivals across the globe; the group sealed its reunion stint with a performance of the song "All Things Must Pass" on the *Late Show with David Letterman* TV program in May 2007.

In 2007, the band, which proved to be the core influence for such early 1990s bands as **My Bloody Valentine** and Dinosaur Jr., told the press of its plans to record a new album. The Jesus and Mary Chain also released details of a four-disc CD box set of B-sides, demos, bootlegs, and rare tracks via Rhino Records for release that same year.

The band contributed its first new song in a decade to the 2008 soundtrack to the NBC TV series *Heroes*. The group scheduled a two-night stint at the Roundhouse in London on March 11–12, 2008, playing only the second night with no explanation as to why the first night's show was canceled.

Further Readings: Foranow, Wendy. *Empire of Dirt: The Aesthetics and Rituals of British Indie Music.* Middleton, CT: Wesleyan University Press, 2006; http://www.blancoynegro.com; http://ogami.subpop.com/bands/JAMC/website.

K

THE KILLERS

Formed in 2002 in "Sin City," Las Vegas, Nevada, The Killers rose to fame with British-influenced, new wave sounding hit songs "Mr. Brightside" and the single "Somebody Told Me," in which catchy choruses were overlaid with pulsating guitar riffs and 1980s-style synthesizer effects.

Armed with expensive haircuts and stylish outerwear, The Killers fit right in with the modern armada of new wave music-wielding indie rock artists of the 2000s—such acts as **The Bravery**, Interpol, Kaiser Chiefs, and **Bloc Party**—which are currently reigning over the modern indie rock scene. Ironically, The Killers have had public feuds with two bands to which the group has been compared—**The Bravery** and Fall Out Boy—and all three bands share the same label, Island Records. Brandon Flowers of The Killers told MTV.com that **The Bravery** was "riding on the coattails" (Montgomery, 2005) of The Killers' success, and he told **NME (New Musical Express)** magazine that Fall Out Boy was hogging (http://www.nme.com/news/the-killers/21090) the bulk of A&R (Artists and Repertoire) funds at their record label. Dave Keuning of The Killers went on to criticize fellow Nevada band Panic! At the Disco, claiming the group was nothing more than Blink-182 rip-off artists. Flowers and his crew did not stop their tirade there; he later made a public statement that **Green Day**'s 2004 album, *American Idiot* was "calculated anti-Americanism" (http://www.nme.com/news/the-killers/24702).

The Killers's debut album, *Hot Fuss* (Island Records, 2004), immediately put the group on the map with its woven stories and heart-pounding drum beats. Conveniently, *Fuss* also included radio-ready hits, and suddenly this unknown band from the desert was plastered all over mainstream media.

In essence, for a band that releases its debut on a major label, although it was released on the indie label Lizard King Records in the United Kingdom, it is not considered to be in the running for **DIY (Do-It-Yourself)** Band of the Year, but The Killers' clever blend of influences by bands (mostly other "the" bands it seems) that paved the indie/new wave path—**The Smiths**, The Cars, The Cult, and New Order, among others—helped cement The Killers' spot on the indie roster as a band with a mind of its own. The members of The Killers—Brandon Flowers (keyboards and lead vocals), David Keuning (guitars), Ronnie Vannucci, Jr. (drums), and Mark Stoermer (bass)—were all working odd jobs in Las Vegas (Flowers was a bellhop) when Keuning placed an ad in the local paper seeking bandmates. The original drummer and bassist left the group, however, making way for Vannucci and Stoermer.

Brandon Flowers of The Killers sings with the band at the Live 8 concert in Hyde Park, London, on July 2, 2005. [AP Wide World Photos/Lefteris Pitarakis]

With "Mr. Brightside" and "Somebody Told Me" topping the U.K. and U.S. charts, The Killers became unstoppable. The group toured relentlessly, appeared on countless magazine covers, and worked on making theatrical videos for its first record. The Killers were nominated for several Grammy Awards in 2005 and 2006, including Best Rock Album for *Hot Fuss*. The group was also nominated for Group of the Year at the 2005 Billboard Awards. In 2005, The Killers won the award for Best New Artist at the 2005 MTV Video Music Awards. In 2006, the group released its sophomore album, *Sam's Town*. The album produced the radio hit "When You Were Young," and director Tim Burton directed the video for the first single, "Bones."

The Killers performed for the 2006 premiere of *Saturday Night Live*, and *Sam's Town* went on to sell almost 1 million copies worldwide. Flowers and crew performed the circuit of late night television programs as musical guests, and they toured various festivals such as **Coachella Valley Music and Arts Festival** in Indio, California, before opening for U2 on that group's Vertigo Tour in Europe. That same year, though, the band's former manager, Braden Merrick, filed a lawsuit against The Killers over what he claimed was a breach of contract.

In 2007, the group won the Best International Group and Best International Album for *Sam's Town* at the BRIT Awards in England. The Killers was forced to cancel a show mid-performance when Flowers was unable to continue performing because he was suffering from a bout of bronchitis; the group returned to the road in late 2007 upon Flowers's recovery. That same year, the band released a compilation of B-side tracks and rarities called *Sawdust* on Island Records.

The Killers got a friendly reminder from boxer Mike Tyson to thank God on the acceptance of the group's award for Best International Band at the 2008 **NME (New Musical Express)** Awards.

Further Readings: Frew, Timothy. *New Wave Pop Music of the Early 80's (Life, Times & Music)*. Berlin, Germany: Friedman/Fairfax Publishing, 1997; http://www6.islandrecords.com; http://www.mtv.com/bands/m/music_geek/indierock_sissyfights_050905; http://www.thekillersmusic.com.

KILL ROCK STARS

If this Olympia, Washington–based indie rock/punk record label's tongue-in-cheek name indicates anything, it is that the bands on its roster do not take themselves too seriously. More to the point, the Kill Rock Stars (KRS) staff proudly boasts its any-"TRL" stance, as in the popular MTV show *Total Request Live*). Boasting over 45 bands on its roster, including such local groups as the all-girl Olympia, Washington indie/punk trio (and feminist activists) **Sleater-Kinney**, the punk outfit Bikini Kill (which was part of the **Riot Grrrl Movement** in Washington state in the 1990s), and the all-girl punk group Bratmobile, among others.

Kill Rock Stars was founded in 1991 by Montana native and former record store owner, agent, and promoter Slim Moon (his real name is Matthew Moon). KRS's name was inspired by a painting Moon had purchased that happened to bear the words "kill rock stars." Moon called upon those very words after he purchased his business license as the title of his endeavor; coincidentally, the first poem on the first album released by KRS was called "Rock Star." KRS is revered by punk and indie fans nationwide for launching the careers of such bands as **Sleater-Kinney**, Half Japanese, and melancholic, **Lo-fi** singer-songwriter **Elliott Smith**, to name a few. Kill Rock Stars maintains Moon's mission is to release "relevant" music, by either artistic or political means, above all else—meaning that profits and the "bottom line" that are touted by most major labels are not KRS's immediate (or underlying) priority.

Moon has a track record of finding new bands for the KRS roster by word of mouth spread by a friend and from referrals by bands already on board. Kill Rock Stars's initial intention was to serve as an outlet for releases it called "wordcore," spoken word 7-inches made by local acts that Moon felt needed an outlet, and a little help with distribution. Over the years, KRS has grown into one of the most significant labels on the scene—putting out records by punk rock acts and indie stalwarts, and the occasional compilation album and 7-inch, by mostly local artists and the occasional non-Washington state band.

The first Kill Rock Stars release was the split spoken word single titled "Word-core Vol. 1," by Kathleen Hanna, the former lead singer for the bands Bikini Kill and **Le Tigre**, and the label's founder, Slim Moon. The label's first official release was a compilation album that featured music by local groups such as the **post-punk** group Unwound, grunge rock groundbreakers **Nirvana**, the **grunge**/alt metal band the **Melvins**, and Bratmobile, among others.

Unwound, one of the first bands signed to the label and one of the flagship bands on KRS's roster, was signed in 1992. Unwound's first 7-inch, "Caterpillar," and its full-length album, *Fake Train,* were among KRS's first full-length release. The band disbanded in 2002, ironically enough, on April Fool's Day. Moon's friends in the punk band Bikini Kill approached him about signing them to the roster, and as a result, KRS put out Bikini Kill's self-titled debut in 1991. Bikini Kill put out a split LP with the English band, self-proclaimed "boy/girl revolution-aries," Huggy Bear, called *Yeah Yeah Yeah Yeah/Our Troubled Youth* before hitting the road with the group and then returning to the United States to work with singer Joan Jett of "I Love Rock 'n' Roll" fame on Bikini Kill's next release.

Bikini Kill and Huggy Bear were bands that were heavily involved in the **Riot Grrrl Movement** of the 1990s that took place on KRS's turf in Olympia, Washing-ton. The **Riot Grrrl Movement**'s origins date back to the 1970s in the punk scene when female musicians were taking a more abrasive, in-your-face approach to music and life. The 1990s movement was a spin-off from that movement in which female rockers and bands united with writers and friends; this indie rock/feminist movement inspired girls to stand up and be heard. They adhered to the **DIY (Do It Yourself)** aesthetic, which has become a mainstay in the indie music realm, its traditions and creed having been carried on by bands through the 1990s. Kill Rock Stars supported the **Riot Grrrl Movement** by signing local bands and re-leasing compilations featuring Riot Grrrl groups.

KRS released another compilation featuring the all-female **Twee pop** group Tiger Trap, singer/songwriter Mary Lou Lord, the all-female punk trio Slant 6, named after a 1960s car engine, and the noise rock duo godheadsilo before re-leasing the Bratmobile's first LP, *Pottymouth,* in 1993. Bikini Kill's first full-length album, *Pussy Whipped,* emerged in 1993, and in 1995, KRS put out releases by Mary Lou Lord, Excuse 17, and Juliana Luecking's spoken word album, *Big Broad.* KRS put out Bikini Kill's compilation *The Singles* in 1998, featuring some of the group's best songs to date, "Rebel Girl" and "New Radio," which were produced by Jett.

Portland, Oregon native **Elliott Smith**, a melancholic singer-songwriter who pioneered the **Lo-fi** sound in the early to mid-1990s, was a part of the Kill Rock Stars team until his death in 2003. Smith, who reportedly committed suicide, released four releases with KRS, and his music appeared on various KRS compila-tions. Smith had signed in 1995 to KRS for his self-titled solo debut LP; prior to that, Smith had been playing in a group called Heatmiser. Smith's follow-up LP,

Either/Or, garnered him and the label even more attention when film director Gus Van Sant approached the singer about including his music in the 1997 film *Good Will Hunting,* which was nominated for several Oscars.

Bikini Kill and Unwound released LPs on KRS in 1997, and, from then on, the momentum behind KRS was unstoppable and the flow of groundbreaking sounds from local bands was steady. Slim Moon released the spoken word album *Won't You Dance with This Man?* in 1998, the same year he founded the subsidiary record label 5RC (5 Rue Christine) to put out records by punk rockers the Replikants and the experimental rock band Deerhoof. **Sleater-Kinney**'s LP *Dig Me Out* garnered nationwide exposure for the label, achieving an unheard-of-before indie feat of selling 50,000 copies. The cover art for the album was inspired by an album by the 1969 rock group The Kinks.

Amid Moon's claims to release music "that is personal and autobiographical and kinda corny" (www.killrockstars.com/about/timeline.php), KRS put out a hailstorm of releases before the turn of the century by such bands as Julie Ruin, The John Doe Thing, Jad & David Fair, the Frumpies, bangs, Mike "Sport" Murphy, the Mailorder Freak, Unwound, **Sleater-Kinney**, and Tight Bros. In 2000, with the elevation of KRS's reputation, Moon put out an EP by former member of the Ronettes Ronnie Spector (aka "the original bad girl of rock 'n' roll") featuring a duet with Joey Ramone of the New York City punk outfit the **Ramones** and added a spoken word CD collection by 1980s and 1990s writer Kathy Acker to its catalog.

In 1999, Lois Maffeo & Company put out an LP, as did **Sleater-Kinney**, and Sherry Fraser's (who later worked with the post-**grunge** group Marcy Playground) solo project Two Ton Boa's debut EP saw the light of day. Jim Carroll, author of the critically acclaimed book *The Basketball Diaries* (actor Leonardo DiCaprio starred in the film adaptation), put out the rock EP *Runaway* in 1999, which featured a cover of a song by American 1960s rock 'n' roller Del Shannon. KRS celebrated its ten-year anniversary in 2001 by continuing its long-time tradition of releasing records by local bands, most—if not all—of which happened to consist of Moon's friends, such as The Gossip, C Average, Unwound, and LiLiPUT, which was then known as Kleenex, among others.

In 2002, Touch and Go took over the wheel from Mordam Records to handle KRS's distribution. **Sleater-Kinney** took a brief hiatus that year as one of the group's members, Corin Tucker, worked on various side projects and raised her son with her husband, filmmaker Lance Bangs. KRS released the 1999 LP *Tigertown Pictures* by the psychedelic group Comet Gain, and that group's music has become a signature sound of both the label and the Olympia, Washington area. KRS then handled releases by singer-songwriter Jeff Hanson, and with help from 5RC, the label put out CDs by California's rock band Xiu Xiu. KRS released its debut *Fields and Streams* double CD compilation in 2002; the follow-up, *Tracks and Fields,* featured previously unreleased tracks by over 40 KRS bands.

The Portland, Oregon pop outfit **The Decemberists** joined the KRS roster in 2003, putting out two records in the same year, *Castaway and Cutouts* and *Her*

Majesty. KRS added the hamburger-obsessed, Oakland, California quartet Gravy Train!!!! and the **post-punk** band Essential Logic to its fold. KRS also celebrated a victory with the group Deerhoof's 2003 album, *Apple O',* which critics claimed was their best album to date. In 2004, KRS expanded its focus by staging the three-day Yeah! Fest at Eagle's Hall in Olympia, Washington, featuring "Bands Against Bush," an event at which musicians and bands loudly stated their desire for President George W. Bush's removal from office. The event also marked the last live show by KRS band the Bangs. KRS bands Xiu Xiu, **Sleater-Kinney**, **The Decemberists**, and Deerhoof all participated in the debut of KRS's Video Fanzine #3.

The KRS staff worked overtime the next few years putting out albums by **The Decemberists**, punk rock band the Numbers, Portland, Oregon's the Makers, and the debut solo album by former 4 Non Blondes member and producer Linda Perry, who has worked on albums by the pop artist Pink. The staff at 5RC was also burning the midnight oil, with a stream of releases by such bands as The No-Neck Blues Band, The Robot Ate Me, BARR, The Vanishing Voice, The Punks, The Planet The, the Metalux, need new body, and Wooden Wand. KRS celebrated its 15-year anniversary in 2006 with the *Starter Set* DVD and new CDs from Gossip, Immad Wasif, and a CD featuring a collection of artists that included **Sufjan Stevens**, Jeff Hanson, **The Decemberists**' Colin Meloy, and more. KRS began releasing a string of video podcasts around that time.

Slim Moon was lured away from KRS in late 2006 after he was given the opportunity to work as an A&R (Artists and Repertoire) representative for the label Nonesuch Records; bands on the Nonesuch roster include folk singer Joni Mitchell, Wilco, and jazz pianist Brad Mehldau. Moon's wife, however, took the helm at KRS while Moon dove headfirst into this new venture. Moon, of course, came upon the opportunity the way he did every other one in his life—through his musical friends. Moon was recommended for the job by a friend whom he worked with on an album by folk singer Laura Veirs—that friend just happened to be the Vice President of Nonesuch Records, who thought Moon would be the perfect fit for the newly formed A&R department. KRS became a bicoastal company when Moon moved to New York City to work at Nonesuch, but the KRS roster, mission, and staff remained in tact.

In 2007, Kill Rock Stars released a two-disc collection of rare songs by former roster member **Elliott Smith**. The collection, entitled *New Moon,* is a barrage of songs that Smith recorded from 1995 to 1997 while he was signed to the label. Portions of the proceeds of the sales from the collection benefited a social services agency in Portland, Oregon, that assists homeless youths. KRS made the album available on vinyl as well as CD; the producer on the record was Smith's longtime engineer and friend Larry Crane. The case surrounding Smith's untimely death remains open.

The full KRS roster includes the following bands: The Advantage, Amps for Christ, Anna Oxygen, BARR, Bonfire Madigan, C Average, Billy Childish, **The Decemberists**, Deerhoof, Erase Errata, The Everyothers, Exceptor, Godzik Pink,

Gold Chains & Sue Cie, Gossip, Gravy Train!!!!, Jeff Hanson. Har Mar Superstar, Harvey Danger, Hella, Danielle Howle, John Wilkes Booze, The Mae Shi, The Makers, Metalux, Meka Miko, Mike "Sport" Murphy, Nedelle, need new body, The No-Neck Blues Band, Numbers, The Old Haunts, the pAper chAse, The Robot Ate Me, **Sleater-Kinney**, Slumber Party, **Elliott Smith**, Star Pimp, Stereo Total, The Planet The, They Shoot Horses Don't They, The Mary Timony Band, Two Ton Boa, Laura Veirs, Mike Watt's Hoot Page, Wooden Wand, Wrangler Brutes, XBXRX, and Xiu Xiu.

Further Readings: Raha, Maria. *Cinderella's Big Score: Women of the Punk and Indie Underground (Live Girls).* Jackson, TN: Seal Press, 2004; Turner, Cherie. *Everything You Need to Know About the Riot Grrrl Movement: The Feminism of a New Generation.* New York: Rosen Publishing Group, 2001; http://www.buyolympia.com; http://www.killrockstars.com; http://www.lindaperry.net; http://www.riotgrrl.com; http://www.ronniespector.com.

LE TIGRE

This feminist electronic punk/indie rock trio has knocked down more barriers than a highly productive day at the United Nations with its controversial lyrics (it attacked former New York City Mayor Rudy Giuliani in one song while name-dropping the group's feminist icons in another), political mindedness (the group members adorned matching outfits bearing the words "Stop Bush" at an in-store appearance at a Tower Records location in 2004), and by its sheer unabashed pride (the newest addition to the all-female group, JD Samson, dons a full mustache on her face and a tattoo of the word across her chest).

Le Tigre quickly developed a following and became icons to female music fans nationwide for various reasons, be they political, feminist, or strictly musical. Founding members Kathleen Hanna and Jo (Johanna) Fateman met in Portland, Oregon, at a show by the Washington, D.C.–area **Riot Grrrl** band, Bikini Kill (of which Hanna was a founding member) before meeting again at a Halloween party in New York City a few years later.

Following Bikini Kill's amicable split in 1998, Hanna released her solo album, *Julie Ruin,* for which she recruited Fateman's sample skills. While working on a video for the album, Hanna and Fateman began working with their musician friend Sadie Benning, who added visuals to the mix. But instead, the trio ended up with a stack of cassette tapes featuring all-new material, the result of which became the group's highly danceable, sample-heavy, **Lo-fi** self-titled debut album (Mr. Lady Records, 1999). Le Tigre's 2001 EP, *From the Desk of Mr. Lady,* which name-drops the group's label, the now defunct San Francisco–based feminist/punk label, was a poignant, angry collection of a half dozen experimental tracks that meshed politics with dance beats.

Benning amicably departed from the group mid-tour in 2000, with Samson joining the fold after having run the projector for the group during its tours. With the tour already in full swing, Samson, who originally came on board as the group's roadie/technician, seemed like a natural fit for the group with her natural stage presence and charisma. Samson's bold decision to bravely display her homosexuality has made her an icon in her own right, inciting the band's young fans to support gay/lesbian rights, and the group's nonjudgmental openness has inspired many fans to come out of the closet themselves.

Intending to create "a new kind of feminist pop music, something for the community to dance to" (www.Letigreworld.com), Le Tigre has outdone its own expectations, taking risk after risk, and selling countless albums. The group proudly continues the legacy set forth by such groups as Bikini Kill, namely, by waving the **Riot Grrrl** flag and calling for young women to read up on the history and milestones of the feminist movement.

Le Tigre's sophomore album, *Feminist Sweepstakes* (Mr. Lady Records, 2001), was its first full-length album to feature new member Samson, who was now singing backup vocals and supplying samples and beats. *Feminist* showcased the group's talent for lyric writing and its staid path to stardom, proving it was no novelty act. In 2002, the group released a remix album featuring remixes of select tracks from its previous recordings that had been reworked by the likes of **DFA Records**' co-founders James Murphy and Tim Goldsworthy.

In 2003, Le Tigre launched a North American tour with supporting acts **Out Hud** and Lesbians on Ecstasy before the release of its 2004 album, *This Island*, the cover of which featured the trio dressed as a sort of three-tier prom date, with Samson as the leading "man." The group left Mr. Lady behind to sign with major conglomerate Universal Records for *Island*, which featured a track that was produced by Ric Ocasek, the former front man for The Cars. With *Island*, the group achieved a seemingly oxymoronic feat by releasing its most revolutionary album to date on a major label. And despite staunch opposition by a select few fans who cried "sellout," the album received rave reviews and sold moderately well, helping the group to kick off a 2004 tour, which included a slot on that year's **Coachella Valley Music and Arts Festival** and **Lollapalooza** and an appearance at the "Bands Against Bush" event that fall. "TKO," the standout track from *Island*, received heavy radio airplay.

Le Tigre allowed a mod squad group of musicians, performer/one-woman musician Peaches, dance duo Junior Senior, and Morel, to tinker with a collection of its releases for *This Island Remixes Vol 2*, which was released by the Chicks on Speed Records label in 2005. Le Tigre spent the better part of 2005 playing gigs to protest the Bush administration; it was joined by such groups as **Ted Leo and the Pharmacists**, The Coup, Thievery Corporation, and more for a free antiwar concert at the Washington Monument. Le Tigre also toured Europe and performed on the *Late Night with Conan O'Brien Show* in 2005

The attention-garnering Samson headed out on the road with her musical side project, New England Roses, for an East Coast tour in support of their debut album, *Face Time with Son* (Doggpony Records) in 2005. Samson celebrated the released of her own calendar, "JD's Lesbian Utopia," in 2006, while her Le Tigre bandmate Fateman worked on her own side project—the revamping of a New York City–based salon called Seagull Haircutters. Hanna, meanwhile, was featured in the 2006 documentary about the **Riot Grrrl Movement**, *Don't Need You: The Herstory of Riot Grrrl*.

Collectively, Le Tigre contributed to Yoko Ono's 2007 album, *Yes, I'm a Witch*, alongside such musicians/bands as **Cat Power**, Peaches, and **The Polyphonic Spree**, among others. Le Tigre's music received the third round of remixes on a 2007 release by the New York City–based DJ pair/production team A Touch of Class. The group worked through 2007 on collecting footage and material for a forthcoming DVD/live album. JD and Jo announced a DJ tour as their side project MEN in the beginning of 2008. It was the first music-related activity for the band since its much-needed hiatus in 2007, when the bandmates let fans know they needed time "to clean our apartments and watch TV for awhile" (http://www.letigreworld.com/) via a posting on the band's Web site.

Further Readings: Gaar, Gillian G., and Yoko Ono. *She's a Rebel: The History of Women in Rock and Roll.* Berkeley, CA: Seal Press, 2002; Taormino, Tristan, Karen Green, and Ann Magnuson. *Girls Guide to Taking Over the World: Writings From The Girl Zine Revolution.* New York: St. Martin's Griffin, 1997; News section, July 31, 2007. http://www.letigreworld.com.

LILITH FAIR

One of the top-grossing concert series in 1997, with ticket sales totaling upwards of $28 million (www.Lilithfair.com), was an all-female, pro-feminist event that was created by Sarah McLachlan, the Canadian-born singer-songwriter who had just released the smash hit album *Fumbling Towards Ecstasy*.

McLachlan's inspiration for the festival was, in fact, spawned from her frustration with what she saw as a male-dominated (and pro-male) music industry, which included radio programmers who openly refused to play songs by female artists back to back. Further infuriated by a concert promoter's doubt regarding a co-female tour featuring herself and opener singer-songwriter Paula Cole, McLachlan was determined to make the voices of talented Eves like herself heard. Consequently, McLachlan launched a 41-city concert that featured only female acts that she titled Lilith Fair. McLachlan even went so far as to handpick all of the artists for each of the 57 shows on the bill back in 1997. Despite a wave of backlash from sexist DJs, skeptical journalists, many of whom claimed that an all-female concert would not sell any tickets, let alone be a success, and various naysayers (including the Rev. Jerry Falwell, who was quoted as claiming Lilith Fair was nothing more than a "promotion of lesbianism and paganism" [Falwell, 1999]), Lilith Fair was a success.

Empowered by the sheer amount of ticket sales, McLachlan was interviewed copiously in the press, which opened the doors for the faux newspaper the *New York Onion* to poke fun at the organizer, claiming that she said Lilith Fair was a "mass ovulation celebration of our fertility. It's a celebration of our sisterhood" (http://www.theonion.com/content/node/28925). Former *Entertainment Weekly* music critic David Browne claimed that "McLachlan and her Lilith compadres are for Generation X what Joni Mitchell was for baby boomers. Every generation needs its confessional singer-songwriter" (Gordinier, 1998).

The 16 artists that performed on the Main Stage on the 1997 bill included Fiona Apple, Tracy Bonham, Meredith Brooks, The Cardigans, Mary Chapin Carpenter, Tracy Chapman, Paula Cole, Shawn Colvin, Sheryl Crow, Emmylou Harris, the Indigo Girls, Jewel, Lisa Loeb, Sarah McLachlan, Joan Osborne, and Suzanne Vega. Much like **Lollapalooza**, Lilith Fair was an enormous outdoor event that spanned large outdoor arenas and included Second Stage and Village Stage. The Grammy winning concert creator ensured that proceeds from the shows were donated to local such nonprofits as the National Coalition Against Domestic Violence, Amnesty International, and the Breast Cancer Fund. The concerts were so successful, in fact, that donations totaled $700,000.

McLachlan's magical, pro-feminist **DIY (Do-It-Yourself)** concert series made its second trek across the United States and her home country of Canada in the summer of 1998. Word had spread about the positive atmosphere and the sense of community that concertgoers felt while attending the event; attendance at the second annual Lilith Fair had grown to more than 20,000 performers and attendees. The Main Stage bill now listed 25 performers, which included such repeat and new Lilith Fair performers as Erykah Badu, Tracy Bonham, Meredith Brooks, Mary Chapin Carpenter, Paula Cole, Shawn Colvin, Cowboy Junkies, N'Dea Davenport, Des'ree, Missy Elliot, Emmylou Harris, the Indigo Girls, Diana Krall, Chantal Kreviazuk, Queen Latifah, Lisa Loeb, Luscious Jackson, Sarah McLachlan, Natalie Merchant, Meshell Ndegeocello, Sinéad O'Connor, Joan Osbourne, **Liz Phair**, Bonnie Raitt, and Suzanne Vega.

McLachlan, who played every show during the tour, had released a live album, gotten married, and enjoyed several radio hits—all by the time the final Lilith Fair came about. The 1999 tour featured even more acts, stages, and fans, making Lilith Fair one of the most successful all-female concerts in music history and one of the most popular festivals of the 1990s. The event helped to kick-start the careers of various musicians who appeared on the bill, including comedian Sandra Bernhard (who actually sang), Shawn Colvin, Deborah Cox, Sheryl Crow, the Dixie Chicks, the Indigo Girls, Queen Latifah, Lisa Loeb, Luscious Jackson, Martina McBride, Monica, Mýa, Meshell Ndegeocello, **Liz Phair**, The Pretenders, Cibo Matto, Susan Tedeschi, and Suzanne Vega.

In just a few years, Lilith Fair had made a lasting impact on the music business and helped pave the way for women in music across all genres. Several of the festival concerts were made available on live CDs and DVDs, and in 1999 aspiring singer-songwriters could compete for a slot on one of the smaller stages at Lilith Fair. That year, however, would bring the curtain call for Lilith Fair. In an interview with CNN, during which she also informed fans that the 1999 festival would mark the final Lilith Fair, McLachlan revealed her plans to start a family and take a break from constant touring. McLachlan later lamented that, as an oversight, she had not included some major name female acts on the bill such as Tori Amos, Alanis Morissette, Joni Mitchell, Annie Lennox, and TLC.

McLachlan, who maintained that the Fair did not exclude men but "simply celebrates women" (Vowell, 1997), welcomed her final bow with grace. Lilith Fair beat out Ozzfest and **Lollapalooza** in terms of ticket sales and attendance. All told, Lilith Fair, which McLachlan reportedly named after the infamous woman who led Adam into the Garden of Eden (surprisingly, it was not Eve), had served to help McLachlan prove her point—that women can rock just as hard, if not harder, than men.

Further Readings: Childerhose, Buffy. *From Lilith to Lilith Fair: The Authorized Story.* New York: St. Martin's Griffin, 1998; Gaar, Gillian. *She's a Rebel: The History of Women in Rock and Roll.* Berkeley, CA: Seal Press, 1992; http://www.cnn.com/SHOWBIZ/Music/9807/28/ lilith.fair/index.html; http://www.lilithfair.com; http://www.sarahmclachlan.com; http:// www.usaweekend.com/98_issues/980816/980816sarah_mc.html.

LO-FI

One of the more popular, and cost-effective, subgenres of indie rock, Lo-fi rock is a no-frills approach to music recording that does not require, or lend itself to, the overproduced sounds that befall many artists crowding the mainstream airwaves. A major characteristic of this rock subgenre is the sound of the production process, the lost art of home tape recording, which can clearly be heard in the background via echoes of raw "hiss" and "crackling" sound; bands employing this production method typically steer clear of the bells and whistles that accompany expensive studio sessions and "polished" results.

Favored by such bands as American indie bands **Yo La Tengo** and **Guided By Voices**, 1990s indie rock princess **Liz Phair**, **Sub Pop Records** artists **The Shins**, and having been pioneered by rocker **Lou Barlow**, Lo-fi gets its name for the inherent nature of its sound-low fidelity. Such bands as alt rockers Cracker enjoy residing on the thin line between Lo-fi rock and other genres (in its case, country, folk, and traditional rock 'n' roll), while groups such as **The Apples in Stereo** and multi-instrumentalist/recording artist **Beck** are recognized in large part by their stripped-down sound. Other Lo-fi indie acts include indie trio Sebadoh, influential early 1990s indie band **Pavement**, New York City musician Stephin Merritt's band Magnetic Fields, and **Elephant 6 Recording Company** artists The Olivia Tremor Control and Neutral Milk Hotel.

Lo-Fi artists **The White Stripes** have utilized their bare bones aural style as a marketing tool, enticing fans who favor the **DIY (Do-It-Yourself)** movement over those bands that hire showy producers who overembellish tracks and albums with music recording programs like Pro Tools. The Lo-fi sound, which usually comes about under dire financial constraints set under a guise of artistic preference, may have very well been pioneered by garage rock acts and early folk musicians like Bob Dylan, whose initial demos became the legendary *The Basement Tapes*. The raw recording quality of such recordings caught on in the rock scene in the late 1960s, leading to the implementation of the dual mono recording technique in which two microphones are attached to the recording device. Punk acts in the 1970s spearheaded the movement, releasing poor quality recordings that were heralded as works of high art. The Lo-fi sound also incorporates the "accidental" live background sounds that are recorded along with the music.

Pop music's first bootleg recordings were then circulated among music fans, causing further damage to the quality of the initial recording and resulting in an even rawer (and even more dismantled) sound—hence the "hiss" and "crackle" noises most Lo-fi artists strive to attain, which has since been known as distortion. Bands subsequently began recording music in poorly built home studios and soon the electronica acts caught on, making music in damp basements, producing homemade recordings with an intimate quality to them.

Lo-fi rock's roots are deepest in the 1980s, a time when 4-track recorders were readily available to any **DIY (Do-It-Yourself)** musician with a microphone and a penchant for making and distributing his or her demos. Pioneer labels of the sub-genre include the New Zealand indie label Flying Nun Records, the Olympia, Washington–based indie label K Records and the group fronted by its founder, **Beat Happening**, which released the majority of its albums on vinyl (which helped to capture that raw sound even more efficiently).

Lo-fi received wider recognition with such artists as the melancholic American singer-songwriter **Elliott Smith**, **Beck**, Sebadoh, **Pavement**, and others who were able to break beyond the basement studio. Still, Lo-fi connoisseurs prefer to record on worn, old equipment in order to cull the rawest sound possible. Para-doxically, the Lo-fi movement of the 1980s existed side-by-side with the polished, showy tracks being released by more mainstream acts. Modern acts that have maintained their Lo-fi sound include **R.E.M.** and several U.K. **post-punk** bands.

Further Readings: Spencer, Amy. *DIY: The Rise of Lo-Fi Culture.* London: Marion Boyars Publishers, Ltd., 2005; Zummer, Thomas, Michael Sarff, and Carol Stakenas. *Lo-Fi Baroque.* New York: Thread Waxing Space, 1998.

LOLLAPALOOZA

The brainchild of Perry Farrell, the lead singer of the Los Angeles–based rock group Jane's Addiction, Lollapalooza was one of the first traveling music festivals.

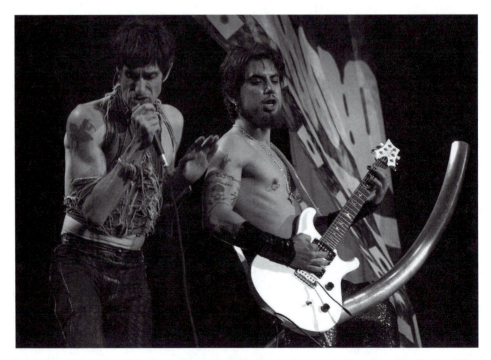

Perry Farrell and Dave Navarro of Jane's Addiction perform at Lollapalooza in Noblesville, Indiana, in 2003. [AP Wide World Photos]

It was originally conceived to be a farewell tour for Jane's Addiction, but the festival became larger than life after the first concert took place in 1991, thanks mostly to the eclectic lineup of performers ranging from rappers, rock bands, dance acts, comedians, and punk, alternative, and indie acts.

The grounds on which the Lollapalooza concerts were staged were filled with political activism booths, performance artists, and off-the-wall sideshows such as the Jim Rose Circus, the members of which became infamous for attaching irons and other heavy objects from chains affixed to their nipples and noses; it was also a marketplace where artists and craftsman from all over the country could sell their wares.

Lollapalooza gained popularity for the simple fact that it brought music to people, instead of requiring them to travel to see the music. The festival, which ran for seven successful years before hitting a speed bump in 1997 when ticket sales flopped, lived up to its name—the word came from a Three Stooges movie; it means "something strange or unusual"—in more ways than one. Bands sharing the main stage included rapper Ice-T and Trent Reznor's electronica band **Nine Inch Nails** (1991), the Red Hot Chili Peppers and Ice Cube (1992), Arrested Development and Rage Against the Machine (1993), the Smashing Pumpkins and A Tribe Called Quest (1994), **Sonic Youth** and Cypress Hill (1995), Metallica and the Wu-Tang Clan (1996), and Snoop Doggy Dogg and Devo (1997).

Aside from crossing the barriers defining musical genres with ease, Lollapalooza also succeeded in blurring cultural lines. Nonmusical acts that performed or appeared at the festival included the Shaolin Monks, virtual reality games, open-microphone or poetry readings, tattooing and piercing took place in booths on the grounds, and nonprofit groups from all over the country set up tables in the areas surrounding the stages. While the main stage featured bigger name acts, Ferrell's idea to feature up-and-coming acts on the side stage was a groundbreaking move in the concert business, paving the way for such modern festivals as **Coachella Valley Music and Arts Festival** and the Warped Tour.

Lollapalooza is widely considered a touchstone of the independent or "indie rock" movement—in both practice and concept; many of the bands that performed on stage at the festival enjoyed widespread commercial success later in their careers. Some of the "indie rock" acts that performed at Lollapalooza include Butthole Surfers, The Flaming Lips, **Guided By Voices**, **Beck**, **Blonde Redhead**, **Built to Spill**, Kings of Leon, Eels, Wolf Eyes, Kasabian, **The Bravery**, **Death Cab for Cutie**, and VHS or Beta, among others.

Lollapalooza also secured its entry into the pages of pop culture and the broader history of "indie" rock; the festival was often mentioned or parodied in the media, for example, on television (*The Simpsons* hosted "Homerpalooza" in a 1996 episode and a character on the Comedy Central show *South Park* participated in a music festival called "Lalapalapaza") and in other musical genres (satirical musician "Weird Al" Yankovic titled his 1993 album *Alapalooza*).

After seven years, the engine behind Lollapalooza seemed to run out of steam. In 1998, as Ferrell turned his focus to his other projects, Lollapalooza failed to secure willing headliners, and the show was canceled due to a drastic drop in ticket sales. However, with the reformation of Jane's Addiction a few years later, there came hope. Ferrell scheduled a 30-city tour in 2003 for Lollapalooza, but high-priced tickets and heavy corporate sponsorship derailed Lollapalooza's big comeback. After similar efforts, the tour was subsequently canceled again in 2004.

Just before all hope was lost, Ferrell consulted with Capital Sports & Entertainment, a company that has successfully sponsored the Austin City Limits Music Festival, to manage the Lollapalooza brand and salvage it from the annals of a used CD store's 99¢ dust bin. Lollapalooza came back to life in 2005 for two days in Grant Park, Chicago, featuring 70 acts on five stages; it attracted 65,000 people. Lollapalooza 2006 was held August 4–6; various indie bands took the stages, including **The Dresden Dolls**, the **Editors**, **My Morning Jacket**, Ween, **Death Cab for Cutie**, **Ryan Adams**, Panic! At the Disco, **Cursive**, The Subways, and more. A large majority of the stages and tents, however, bore the names of various products and drinks, proving that commercialism had seeped into the throes of the very place where indie rock got started—the AT&T stage featured Queens of the Stone Age, the Bud Light stage featured **Sonic Youth**, and the Adidas-Champ stage featured **Sleater-Kinney**. Rumors about the addition of the Smashing Pumpkins to the festival's bill circulated, but the group failed to reunite on stage; instead Panic! At the Disco covered the song and the Red Hot Chili Peppers were the star headliners. **The White Stripes'** front man, Jack White, and his band The Raconteurs, however, paid tribute to the band by playing a cover of that group's song "Tonight, Tonight."

The 2007 installation of the festival took place on August 3–5; it featured headliners Pearl Jam, Daft Punk, Ben Harper & the Innocent Criminals, Muse, **Iggy and The Stooges**, as well as such acts as Kings of Leon, **Snow Patrol**, **Yeah Yeah Yeahs**, **Modest Mouse**, and Regina Spektor, among others. The August scheduled 2008 lineup includes headliners Pearl Jam and Daft Punk, as well as acts such as **Iggy and The Stooges**, Muse, **My Morning Jacket**, Patti Smith, **Snow Patrol**, Kings of Leon, the **Yeah Yeah Yeahs**, Spoon, Regina Spektor, Interpol, **Modest Mouse**, Amy Winehouse, The Roots, The Black Keys, Perry Farrell's new group Satellite Party, and more.

The 2008 festival dates are August 1–3 in Chicago, featuring such headlining acts as Pearl Jam, Daft Punk, and **Iggy and The Stooges**.

Further Readings: Beck. *Online Diaries: The Lollapalooza Tour Journals of Beck, Courtney Love, Stephen Malkmus, Thurston Moore, Lee Ranaldo, and Mike Watt.* New York: Soft Skull Press, 2001; Blackman, Nicole, and Juliette Torrez. *Revival: Spoken Work from Lollapalooza 94.* San Francisco: Manic D Press, 1995; http://www.lollapalooza.com.

M

MANDO DIAO

Though Mando Diao's music sounds as American as **The White Stripes**, The Strokes, and traditional R&B, the five-piece band actually originated in Borlänge, Sweden. On the surface, Mando Diao shares the same Mod sensibility as other Swedish bands like The Hives. But growing up, the group's influences were far more conventional, gravitating more toward Guns N' Roses, The Beatles, and The Who than cherry-picked obscurities from the 1960s. The end result of those influences is even more confounding, merging bratty garage pop with traces of easy listening and country twang.

While many emerging bands have the benefit of a lively underground scene, Borlänge's high crime rate kept the members of Mando Diao inside and listening to their records. In the early 1990s, while only a teenager, guitarist Gustaf Norén heard **Nirvana**, and the deal was sealed—he wanted to play music. Meanwhile, across town, in an attempt to form a band of his own, guitarist Björn Dixgård and keyboardist Daniel Haglund played in a band called Butler. After cycling through a variety of bassists, guitarists, and drummers, Butler eventually evolved into Mando Diao in 1999 with the additions of Norén on guitar, bassist Carl-Johan Fogelklou, and drummer Samuel Giers. The name "Mando Diao," the band claims, is an entirely made-up phrase intended to be unique only to the band.

When Mando Diao formed, no member had even reached his 20s. What happened after that is what happens to many young bands mates that are lucky enough to succeed—they abandoned all hope of succeeding in school and hit the local circuit. Shortly after, Mando Diao landed a record deal with EMI Music Sweden.

In 2002, Mando Diao released its first EP, *Motown Blood,* on EMI Music Sweden. Many bands see a major label on the level of EMI as the ultimate symbol of compromise, but during the recording of "Motown Blood," EMI and the band agreed to maintain an unpolished, rougher sound within the quality of the band's songs. What is more, after a handful of EPs over the year, Mando Diao released its first full-length album, *Bring 'Em In,* on the label in 2003.

On *Bring 'Em In,* Mando Diao owes a debt to the 1960s Mod scene and, more recently, The Strokes. The album, which was well recognized by critics, features songs such as "Paralyzed" (the video for which shows the bandmates sporting muss-cuts and wedged into tight leather pants); the influence of **The Velvet Underground** and The Rolling Stones looms large. On the single "Sheepdog," Mando Diao weaves those 1960s roots with the brattiness of 1990s Britpop acts such as Oasis. The international success of *Bring 'Em In* sent the band on tour with such Swedish pop heavyweights as The Hellacopters and Kent.

While some had pigeonholed Mando Diao as a garage-rock derivative, the band proved its versatility to skeptics. *Hurricane Bar,* Mando Diao's second full-length release, hit the shelves in 2004. Songs off *Hurricane Bar* such as "You Can't Steal My Love" had a harder mid-1990s feel. The band continued to build a large fan base in Germany and Japan. In 2006, Mando Diao released its third full-length album, *Ode to Ochrasy,* which effectively fused the garage-rock, R&B, and even country influences that were present during moments on the band's earlier efforts. *Ode to Ochrasy* sold well and eventually went Gold. On a sad note, the bandmates mourned the loss of their music collaborator/friend Marius B. Larsen, who died on December 19, 2006.

What also emerged from Mando Diao through the band's career was a confidence that could come only from a bunch of kids in their 20s. On the band's Web site, Norén had claimed that the band's music was better than The Who, The Kinks, and The Small Faces. That is always a dangerous debate, despite Mando Diao's global success. In March 2007, Mando Diao launched a mammoth world tour that included a stop at the **South by Southwest (SXSW)** music festival in Austin, Texas, and an appearance at the **Coachella Valley Music and Arts Festival** in Indio, California. EMI released Mando Diao's fourth studio album, *Never Seen the Light of Day* in December 2007.

The band toured Europe in 2008; the band, still reeling from a 2007 show at Sweden's Umeå Folk Music Festival where 30 people were injured when a floor caved in at the show, offered free tickets to fans for its 2008 Umeå show.

Further Readings: http://www.coachella.com; http://www.hellacopters.com; http://www.mandodiao.com; http://2007.sxsw.com.

MATH ROCK

This indie rock subgenre's name may conjure images of lonely, number-obsessed rock wannabes attempting to put together complicated rhythmic combinations and prime number–oriented counts. But in contrast, this subgenre of music (albeit this subgenre can be very technical in nature) is a highly regarded style of indie rock music that has exactly the opposite purpose—to be unpredictable. Taking their cues from jazz legends who possess uncanny abilities to create unpredictable, yet clever and sonically pleasing chords, rhythmic sections, and tempos, math rockers strive to add an extra element to indie rock that makes their music a tad bit more calculated (in a freeform jazz-style, of course).

This experimental subgenre emerged in the 1980s. Bands that are categorized in the genre include **The Blood Brothers**, An Albatross, Slint, **Bellini**, Polvo, Hex Error, Replicator, Shipping News, Volta Do Mar, Thumbnail, The Paper Chase, Drive Like Jehu, Faraquet, **Del Rey**, Brass Knuckels for Tough Guys, The Mercury Program, Plot to Blow Up the Eiffel Tower, Chavez, June of 44, the 1.6 Band, and Rodan. The genre, though it is considered an offshoot of indie rock, is actually a spin-off of technical rock bands, some of which have been categorized as "prog" or "progressive" rock acts, such as Rush, King Crimson, and Helmet. Math rock bands share an integral characteristic with these acts in that they, too, have concocted rhythms derived from mathematical equations.

Math rockers devise clever rhythms that in essence seem arbitrary, for example, a standard 4/4 beat measure, but when that section is mixed with another seemingly innocuous section, the song becomes a mathematical force that was produced from a series of intelligently created sequences that, as a whole, may leave the listener with a chaotic feeling or sense. Math rockers work mostly with atypical or nontypical musical structures, and their fanatical nature sets them apart from other groups for their sheer song building ambition. It may take a math rock band twice as long to create a song or even shirt riff, but the result is usually a catchy yet complex structure that usually results in a love/hate relationship with many fans.

The lyrics in a math rock song are just as unpredictable and groundbreaking (math rockers are always trying to outdo themselves) as the underlying song structures. Layered over asymmetrical time signatures (that is, 13/8 or 7/8), words sung in math rock songs usually have a subconscious or subliminal connection to the song itself. Fans of math rock are intrigued by the band's thought process, and they are often impressed with the creative twists math rockers manage to out on their music. In some ways, math rock fans are curious about the overall creative process and may listen to one song repeatedly in an attempt to understand the thought process behind the composition. Some math rock bands, such as Don Caballero and 65daysofstatic, leave lyrics out of the mix entirely, allowing the music to become the sole entity or their work.

Math rock stems from various musical genres such as rock, progressive or prog rock, punk, and even heavy metal, allowing its creators multiple options in terms of the sound and style of their creations. Math rockers are not averse to the negative connotations that may accompany the label of the math rock subgenre. In fact, since math rockers strive to stand apart from the crowd, they seem to welcome any and all criticism and feedback, as it motivates them to keep making music outside of boundaries and anything predetermined.

Math rock can be traced back to the 1960s and the 1970s with musicians who experimented with various time signatures, such as **Frank Zappa**, Rush, King Crimson, Yes, Jethro Tull, and Captain Beefheart. Many of these bands, which were considered prog rock artists, laid the groundwork for modern math rockers who strive to create even more complex rhythms and mind-bending song structures.

Several of the record labels that support math rock artists include Touch and Go Records and Quarterstick Records. Former **Big Black** and Rapeman band member Steve Albini is an icon in the math rock subgenre. He has worked with several math rock bands to help produce their albums. Math rock bands have settled in such cities as San Diego, Pittsburgh, Washington, D.C., Richmond, and even in Japan. Math rock's semiofficial birthplace is in Chicago, Illinois, where the term reportedly surfaced for the first time. The term was the result of an attempt by the likes of Albini, who attempted to describe the genre, its sound, and structure to curious listeners.

Further Reading: Martin, Bill. *Listening to the Future: The Time of Progressive Rock, 1968–1978.* LaSalle, IL: Open Court Publishing Company, 1997.

MC5

Only three of the original five members of this Detroit, Michigan–based punk band survived the decades of sex, drugs, and rock 'n' roll the band indulged in—guitarist Wayne Kramer, bassist Michael Davis, guitarist Fred "Sonic" Smith, vocalist Rob Tyner, and drummer Dennis Thompson. Formed in 1964, MC5, which stood for the Motor City Five, is widely considered one of the founders of punk rock. Along with its neighborhood counterpart **The Stooges**, MC5's brand of hard-hitting, take-no-prisoners punk rock and overall volatile, antiestablishment attitude laid the groundwork for future generations of punk bands.

Formed in 1967 when the guys were still in high school, the band rose to fame under the guidance of its manager, John Sinclair, a former high-school teacher who later founded the infamous and radical White Panther Party; he was also anointed Motor City's "King of the Hippies." Sinclair, who engaged in more than one altercation with the police, managed to help the group rise up from the dredges of Detroit area nightclubs and dive bars to become one of the most well-known punk acts of the 1960s and the 1970s.

Led by big-haired front man Rob Tyner, MC5 started out when he and his fellow band members—guitarists Fred "Sonic" Smith and Wayne Kramer and bassist Pat Burrows—were still in high school. MC5 started out playing local gigs at their friends' houses, but when word of their riotous live shows spread, the group was soon touring bigger venues across the gritty city. MC5 was, in fact, the epitome of punk rock—the bandmates played loud distortion-fueled songs, wore the American flag on stage, called out for crowds to start revolutions, and exhibited radical behavior wherever they went. Bassist Michael Davis, guitarist Wayne Kramer, guitarist Fred "Sonic" Smith, drummer Dennis Thompson, and lead vocalist Rob Tyner—MC5's full lineup—soon became icons and idols of the youth punk movement.

Not surprisingly, MC5 was offered a record deal after an A&R (Artists and Repertoire) representative caught the group's show at an anti-Democratic Convention, where it was performing as part of the Yippies' Festival of Life concert in Chicago. Elektra Records saw marketing and sales potential in the band and inked a deal with it right away. Indeed, the group's messages and aesthetics resonated with youths, and the band's debut 1969 album, *Kick Out the Jams,* which was recorded at Detroit's Grande Ballroom, hit the national Top 40. Censorship, however, reared its evil head when various record stores refused to carry the album due to the fact that Tyner repeatedly chanted "Kick out the jams, motherf- -ckers!" Elektra infuriated the group when it released a toned-down version of the album with a stripped-down version of the song that did not include the expletive.

Like all fast-moving trains, though, the band was destined to crash and burn. Citing a difficult road ahead (not to mention the dark cloud of legal fees), Elektra dropped the band just before 1969. That same year, Sinclair was jailed for yet another time, this time for possession of marijuana, and the group's future wavered in a sea of uncertainty. Atlantic Records took a chance on MC5, though, and inked a deal with the corrosive fivesome for its next album. *Back in the U.S.A.* (1970) was considered by critics to be one of the "greatest hard-rocking albums of all time," but without Sinclair's extremist views, the album—and the band—had lost all of its political furor.

Atlantic gave the group another chance and kept it on deck, but when its follow-up album, 1971's *High Time* failed to move units or sell well, the label dropped the group. Inner band troubles weighed heavy on the group, and the bandmates ousted a heroin-abusing Davis, who was replaced by bassist Steve Moorhouse, but soon after, Thompson and Tyner reported their desire to stop touring. In 1972, the group members announced their "retirement" as patrons of punk, and they played their final show on New Year's Eve at the Grande Ballroom for a paltry $500. Smith wed outspoken poet/rocker Patti Smith in 1980 and formed Sonic's Rendezvous Band, but throughout the mid-1980s, he was seldom heard from as the hard rocker spent much of his time raising a family with his new wife.

The surviving members of MC5 formed other music bands, but after Tyner's death of a heart attack in 1991, the group reunited to play a benefit concert for his family. The band may have been MIA after that, but record stores stocked reissues of its albums in the mid-1990s. Various labels (Alive Records, Total Energy Records, and Munster Records) put out reissues in 1994: *Power Trip* and *American Ruse,* in 1995: *Thunder Express,* and in 1996: *Teen Age Lust.* Smith passed away from heart failure in 1994, but the next year Kramer came back into the spotlight with his debut solo album, *The Hard Stuff,* which pretty much explained his battles with drug addiction.

Two live albums, *Greatest Hits* and *Motor City Is Burning,* appeared in 1999 and 2000, followed by a series of records that showed the fire that MC5 lit was still burning. The band's influence continues to live on; and records of its material surfaced again in 2000, *The Big Bang! Best of The MC5,* and in 2002, *Human Being Lawnmower: The Baddest & Maddest of The MC5.* The celebratory albums seemed endless; in 2005 Castle Us Records released *The Live Bootleg Anthology: Are You Ready to Testify?* and in 2007, the band's debut live gig saw the light almost 40 years later with *Live at the Grande Ballroom 1968* via Get Back Italy Records.

Over ten years passed before the three remaining members—Kramer, Davis, and Thompson—met up again in 2003 to perform with guest musicians singer Nicke Andersson and singer David Vanian (of the band The Damned). The new band toured during 2004 and 2005 as DKT/MC5. The Rock and Roll Hall of Fame in Cleveland, Ohio, tempted the band and its fans with the hopes of being inducted into The Hall, but the group received only a nomination in 2003, losing out to The Clash, AC/DC, The Police, and Elvis Costello and the Attractions.

Filmmakers paid tribute to MC5 with the 2004 documentary *MC5: A True Testimonial*. The film, which took eight years to make, combines recent and archived interview footage with the band and the band members' friends and performances. A *New York Times* article on the film revealed that the film's inclusion of recorded phone conversations and surveillance footage was the result of an investigation by the government, which felt that the "band's stance was so revolutionary that the F.B.I. kept files and film on its members" (Mitchell, 2004).

In 2006, Davis was injured in a motorcycle accident and the band's gig at a tribute concert, the Joey Ramone Birthday Bash, at Irving Plaza in New York City, was canceled. MC5's name has appeared in the news in various incarnations. Most mentions occurred through influences cited by modern acts such as **The White Stripes** and even Rage Against the Machine, but in one odd twist, the band's name came up when a story about the band's former manager, Danny Fields, filed a lawsuit against the magazine *OUT*, accusing it of portraying him as a pedophile. Smith's widow, Patti Smith, celebrated the memory of her late husband on his birthday during a performance in Brooklyn, New York, in 2007, during which she sang a song that she wrote in his honor called "Dancing Barefoot."

Further Readings: Callwood, Brett. *MC5, Sonically Speaking.* Shropshire, England, United Kingdom: Independent Music Press, 2007; Simmons, Michael, and John Sinclair. *Guitar Army: Rock & Revolution with the MC5 and the White Panther Party.* London: Process, 2007; http://movies.nytimes.com/movie/review?res=9E02E0DC143AF930A15757-C0A9629C8B63.

MEAT PUPPETS

Kurt Cobain's favorite band also happened to be the band that bolstered the lifeline of the reigning underground label in the 1980s, **SST Records**. The Meat Puppets—brothers Curt and Cris Kirkwood and drummer Derrick Bostrom—emerged in the 1980s in Phoenix, Arizona. After quickly changing their name from The Bastions of Immaturity to the Meat Puppets, the name of one of Curt's tracks from their early days, the three-piece punk outfit started out with a hardcore edge and began rehearsing in a run-down old shed that stood behind one of the two houses the bandmates inhabited.

After putting out a self-released EP, *In a Car,* the band's loud, raw sound attracted the founder of **SST Records** and **Black Flag** front man, Greg Ginn, who signed the band for its self-titled 1982 debut. The Meat Puppets, though, quickly tired of punk rock and started incorporating psychedelic, acid rock, hard rock, and even country music sounds into the group's music. Joining such bands as **Sonic Youth**, **Hüsker Dü**, and Dinosaur Jr. on the SST roster, the Meat Puppets's music seemed to possess no sense of direction at all. On the group's sophomore album, *Meat Puppets II,* which contained the songs "I'm a Mindless Idiot" and the instrumental track "Aurora Borealis," named for the Northern Lights, Curt's guitar playing revealed a raw talent that had ripened to its peak. Still possessing jagged edges, the group never hesitated from tearing through a catchy melody with buzz saw–like guitars and what sounded like a drum set crashing down a long set of rusty metal stairs.

The band developed a cult following in the mid-1980s, mostly for its punk attitude and a never-heard-before fusion of punk, classic rock, country-western, and jazz. The band released an album for nearly every year of its existence, puzzling critics with its haphazard sounds and oddball song titles. The group's 1985 album, *Up on the Sun,* showed the band was softening around the edges a bit, but it also proved the band was not just another set of three-chord wannabes. The more straightforward *Sun* opened the door for reviews in such mainstream arenas as *Rolling Stone* and MTV, both of which seemed to be simultaneously mystified and in awe of the group's sonic accomplishments. The Meat Puppets soaked up the psychedelic sound like a tie-dye shirt; and fans seemed to follow both blissfully and blindly.

College radio helped the band reach even more fans, and the group's subsequent albums—the 1986 EP *Out My Way* and the 1987 LPs *Mirage* and *Huevos*—were circulated heavily in the underground scene. *Way* showed no major changes for the band, although if examined closely, it foreshadowed the band's new directions and ambitions. In 1986, *Rolling Stone* critic David Fricke claimed the album was "a decisive step in the Meat Puppets' march away from one-dimensional punk to hearty, heartfelt pan-American rock and roll" (Fricke, 1986). The band continued to tour successfully to packed rooms full of sweaty, angst-filled teens, but the more mainstream angle and the pop sounds of *Mirage* turned some fans sour. *Monsters* (**SST Records**, 1989) was received poorly, and it was considered dead in the water in the band's old fans' eyes.

By the mid-1990s the band had broken up and then gotten back together. Upon the band's return to the limelight, the Meat Puppets inked a deal with major label London Records, which secured it a spot as guests in the pilot for the teen drama *Beverly Hills 90210.* Though the act was considered career suicide in the underground scene, the band managed to stay afloat. It adopted a smoother production style and put out the 1991 album *Forbidden Places,* the title of which could have been interpreted to have been a public acknowledgment of the band's foray into the punk and indie rock musician's version of no man's land—the mainstream.

Still, the Meat Puppets survived, and in much the same way as **Nirvana** did, the group managed to cross over successfully into mainstream rock, although the Meat Puppets would never experience the same altitude of success or name recognition as its flannel-wearing peers. **Nirvana** gave the band a leg up when that group invited the Meat Puppets to tour with it. The Kirkwood brothers also benefited from their cameo appearance during **Nirvana**'s famed 1993 MTV Unplugged performance when they played the guitar parts for **Nirvana**'s cover of three of their songs.

The Meat Puppets rode the wave of success and media attention it garnered from that three-song stint on MTV, coasting on the wave for its first hit album, *Too High to Die* (London, 1994). Ironically enough, the single from the album, "Backwater" did not receive much radio play or attention—until after the death of Kurt Cobain in 1994. Following that sad event, airplay and sales of the song—which were both supported by constant airplay of the MTV Unplugged performance—soared and the Meat Puppets were beginning to become a household name. The sad part about the whole thing was the band's success was based on the loss of a very close friend. The Meat Puppets toured with such groups as Stone Temple Pilots, Blind Melon, and Soul Asylum. It was around this time that Cris allegedly became addicted to heroin.

The dichotomy of "Backwater," which helped *High* go Gold, was evident in the group's follow-up album, *No Joke!* The Meat Puppets toured with Primus in support of the album, but the lukewarm *Joke* caused the band to second-guess its efforts, and the Meat Puppets disbanded for the second time. Curt and Derrick pursued other musical interests, while Cris found himself in and out of jail. Things seemed to sour even more for the band when the Kirkwoods' mother passed away in 1996; those years were further darkened by the loss of Cris's new wife who died of an overdose in 1998.

Meanwhile, Curt formed the Royal Neanderthal Orchestra, later dubbing it the Meat Puppets. This new incarnation of the group did not feature either Cris or Derrick—but they were not officially ousted from the band either. The new Meat Puppets—which included a former member of the band Pariah and a bassist who had played for a while with Bob Mould—released its first album in five years on a subsidiary of Atlantic Records. The band attempted to tour in support of *Golden Lies,* but ticket sales were poor and the band went on an indefinite hiatus.

Curt and Derrick pushed on, forging solo careers. In 2002, Curt joined forces with ex-**Nirvana** bassist Krist Novoselic and former Sublime drummer Bud Gaugh to record music and tour under the name Eyes Adrift. Cris's luck took an unforeseen turn when he was the victim of road rage in 2004. An angry driver shot the musician in the abdomen after he got into a fight over a parking space.

Seven years after the attempt to reincarnate the Meat Puppets, the Kirkwood brothers reunited for the well-received 2007 album *Rise to Your Knees* (released on the Kansas City, Missouri–based indie label Anodyne Records). Minus Derrick, the Kirkwoods played a tour of the East Coast in support of the album, hitting the 2007 **CMJ Music Marathon** in New York City and **South by Southwest (SXSW)** music festival in Austin, Texas.

The band was added to the lineup for the 2008 Tempe Music Festival in Arizona alongside music acts Cowboy Mouth and Fergie.

Further Readings: Anderson, Kyle. *Accidental Revolution: The Story of Grunge.* New York: St. Martin's Griffin, 2007; Fricke, David. "Meat Puppets: Out My Way (Album Review)." *Rolling Stone,* October 23, 1986. http://www.rollingstone.com/artists/meatpuppets/albums/album/97116/review/5941046/out_my_way; http://www.anodynerecords.com; http://www.meatpuppets.com; http://www.themeatpuppets.com.

MELVINS

The Melvins, comprised of vocalist/guitarist Buzz (aka "King Buzzo") Osborne, drummer Dale Crover, and bassist Kevin Rutmanis, is the band that most directly inspired **Nirvana**. The heavy metal/**grunge** trio was formed in 1984 by Osborne and his high school pals Matt Lukin (bass) and Mike Dillard (drums) in the small town of Montesaro, Washington, which is located around 100 miles southwest of Seattle. Influenced by **Black Flag** and Black Sabbath, the Melvins played slow tempo **grunge** music that lacked structure, was denser, and often included nonsensical lyrics that revealed a dark sense of humor (evidenced in the band's name, which was inspired by a handicapped employee who worked at a nearby Thriftway store).

The Melvins contributed to the infamous 1986 C/Z Records compilation *Deep Six* before releasing its debut EP, *Six Songs,* that same year on Ipecac Recordings, which was run by former **Alternative Tentacles Records** manager Greg Werckman; *Six Songs* later became known as *10 Songs.* In December 1986 the Melvins recorded its first full-length album, *Gluey Porch Treatments,* which was released in 1987 on Alchemy Records. *Gluey,* a barrage of pure noise, included some of the band's old garage-made demos. It was followed up by the 1989 album *Ozma* (Boner Records), which featured Lori "Lorax" Black (who is, oddly enough, the daughter of child star Shirley Temple Black), who had replaced Lukin upon his departure.

At first, the Melvins's success never stretched far from the group's small northwestern town—until Kurt Cobain, who was a self-confessed fan of the band (rumors claim he actually tried out for the band in 1980 and worked as the band's roadie), gave the group a leg up. Cobain reportedly met the band after Crover hooked **Nirvana** up with the man who would become that band's drummer, Dave Grohl. Soon the Melvins were gaining the attention the group had long deserved —thanks in most part to the praise and help from its new friend, Kurt Cobain. Cobain, in fact, was instrumental in the band's record deal with Atlantic Records, and he helped produce the Melvins' 1993 album, *Houdini.* Armed with a heavier, though more focused sound, *Houdini* hit the Billboard charts and sold moderately well. Oddly enough, the Melvins released its next two albums—1994's *Stoner Witch* and *Prick*—under the band name SNIVLEM.

The Melvins' future seemed secure, but nothing is what it seems in the music business. The band was dropped from the Atlantic roster in 1997 after just three albums. Left to the bandmates' own devices, the Melvins used their **DIY (Do-It-Yourself)** skills and returned to the indie label Ipecac for what seemed like a nonstop stream of albums from 1998 onward: *Alive at the F*cker Club* (1998), *The Maggot* (1999), *The Bootlicker* (1999), *The Crybaby* (2000), *Electroretard* (2001), *Colossus of Destiny* (2001), *Hostile Ambient Takeover* (2002), collaboration *Pigs of the Roman Empire* (2004), and *Houdini Live: A Live History of Gluttony and Lust* (2006). In 1998, the group received a lot of press for its appearance on the Ozzfest bill. Atlantic, however, released the Best Of album *Melvinmania* in 2003; it featured old rare tracks and Melvins classics.

In 2004, Crover and Osborne hit the road together as a celebration of 20 years as bandmates. The duo also put out a coffee table–style book (with CD), *Neither Here Nor There,* a collection of strange graphic works, collages, and posters. That same year, the band worked on a collaboration with the Dead Kennedys' Jello

Biafra on the album *Never Breathe What You Can't See* (**Alternative Tentacles Records**).

The Melvins' music has influenced bands decades after the height of its career, the most of which included Mudhoney (of which former Melvins' bassist Matt Lukin is a member), the band Mangy, and doom metal act Absolutego.

The Melvins toured in 2006 in support of the album *A Senile Animal,* which was released on Ipecac. The band worked on a 2007 full-length album for which the band has already written the song "Suicide in Progress." That same year, the band made plans for a tour of Europe. Norman Records and Bifocal Media released a book of comic art by artist Brian Walsby that featured the Melvins's illustrated 2006 tour diary and a rare CD recording of eight demos made by the band in 1987 called *Making Love.*

Further Readings: Grossberger, Lewis. *Turn That Down! A Hysterical History of Rock, Roll, Pop, Soul, Punk, Funk, Rap, Grunge, Motown, Metal, Disco, Techno & Other Forms of Musical Aggression Over the Ages.* Cincinnati, OH: Emmis Books, 2005; http://www.ipecac.com.

MISFITS

From their theatrical pancake white face makeup to the locks of jet-black gelled hair they combed to a sharp point that flowed from their foreheads down the tips of their noses (a hairdo that became known as the "Devilock"), the members of the Misfits were unmistakably original. While some were quick to disregard the group as "campy," others forged a cult following of the group that has lasted decades after the group's reign as pioneers and purveyors of the Horrorpunk genre ended. Although much like the band's front man/principal songwriter **Glenn Danzig**'s later project, **Danzig**, the underground group experienced the pinnacle of its success only *after* the band had broken up.

Formed by singer-songwriter **Glenn Danzig** (who would later go on to form the bands **Danzig** and Samhain) and Jerry Only, the Misfits spread their musical terror across the group's native state of New Jersey after forming in 1977. The band's music was an amalgam of metal, rock, and punk—and the group's persona was larger-than-life. With **Danzig**'s dark on-stage persona and the band's jarring sonic wall of pounding drums, buzz saw–like guitars, and lyrics that circulated about all things related to blood, guts, and gore, the Misfits quickly attracted a legion of die-hard fans (known as "fiends"—the nickname was derived from the term used for the group's iconic skull logo, which became known as "the fiend") who mimicked the band's look, sound, and fashion sense. Over the years, the Misfits have influenced bands both sonically and visually; these acts include Marilyn Manson, Slayer, Metallica, Slipknot, Rob Zombie, Pantera, My Chemical Romance, Guns N' Roses, and AFI, among others.

Brandishing its iconic skull logo and B-level horror movie aesthetic, the Misfits began rehearsing and recording music for its 1977 debut single, "Cough/Cool," which the band put out on its own Blank Records. The Misfits, which was named after Marilyn Monroe's last film of the same name, entertained a rotating lineup of musicians. Early incarnations of the group included founding member/vocalist/

songwriter **Glenn Danzig**, founding member/bassist Jerry Caiafa (aka Jerry Only), guitarist Doyle Wolfgang Von Frankenstein (Jerry's younger brother), a drummer who was simply known as Manny, and guitarist Franché Coma; guest members included Marky Ramone of the punk act the **Ramones** and Dez Cadena of **Black Flag**).

Before some of the band members had graduated from high school, the group played its first gig at the infamous CBGB club in New York City in April 1977. The Misfits' Halloween-inspired song titles and theatrical on-stage costumes scared off some labels, but Mercury Records saw an opportunity in the band and offered it some recording time. The Misfits bandmates proved to be savvy businessmen, though; in exchange for the studio time, the label agreed to name one of its sublabels Black Records, on which it released an album by the experimental rock/art punk group **Pere Ubu**.

Suffering from tour-related paranoia, member Franché Coma eventually left the group, leaving **Danzig** with no choice but to place an ad for new bandmates in the newspaper. Crowned with their official stage names, new members Joey Pills and Bobby Steele joined the Misfits at the end of 1978. At a show that year, the group poured grape Kool-Aid on the audience in playful mockery of **The Brian Jonestown Massacre**. That same year, the Misfits recorded one of the group's signature songs—the aggressive, anthemic "Attitude," which was featured on an LP compilation put out by Flipside *Vinyl Magazine*.

The Misfits's long stint at the famed Kansas City, Missouri nightclub Max's Kansas City ended when the band was banned from the club after Steele allegedly hit a fan with a glass. The Misfits bandmates rubbed elbows with celebrity musicians throughout their careers—Blondie's Debbie Harry, **Frank Zappa**, and Iggy Pop all reportedly showed up at their shows. Rumors circulated that Steele once puked on John Lennon's shoes, and he claimed he partied with legendary Sex Pistols' firecracker Sid Vicious. It seemed, however, that the group was far more popular with the police; **Glenn Danzig** and his crew were repeatedly arrested for clashes at their shows—many of which seemed to involve broken glasses and bottles.

Band members left and joined the band faster than the band could change chords. At various live shows, **Black Flag** front man Henry Rollins joined the band on stage. The Misfits continued to tour and play gigs at such clubs as New York City's famed CBGB. In 1978, the band released its debut EP, *Bullet,* on its own Plan 9 Records (which, **Glenn Danzig**, a self-confessed film junkie, named after the 1959 Ed Wood film *Plan 9 from Outer Space*). The controversial album art featured a graphic, cartoon-like image of John F. Kennedy's assassination. In 1979, the band put out two EPs—*Night of the Living Dead,* which was released on Halloween, and *Horror Business.* The Misfits sold copies of the *Night* EP at its live shows, where the band announced plans to launch its fan club, the Fiend Club, which would have its base in **Glenn Danzig**'s apartment in New York City. Meanwhile, the group was touring with the punk band The Damned and the possibility of an opening slot for The Clash came about. **Glenn Danzig**'s temper, however, squashed that opportunity; the Misfits were tossed off the tour with The Damned after **Glenn Danzig** ended up in jail by getting himself entangled in a bar brawl.

In 1982, news surrounding the band covered two very different events—the band released its debut album *Walk Among Us* (Ruby/Slash Records), and the band was arrested for what the authorities claim was grave digging while the group was touring in New Orleans. *Walk* is still considered to be one of the preeminent punk albums; the album's tracks sounded like titles of horror films and the album further solidified **Glenn Danzig**'s prowess as a singer/performer. By this time, he had been crowned the "dark Elvis" of rock. Riots ensued at the band's shows; one of the most violent occurred at a San Francisco gig after someone in the crowd launched an unopened beer can at Doyle's head.

In 1983, the Misfits opened for **Black Flag**, and that same year the group recorded what would be its last album with **Glenn Danzig**. The *Earth A.D./Wolfsblood* (Caroline Records) LP flashed the band's hardcore strengths. The Misfits's tour schedule was full and fans were clamoring to buy its albums, but **Glenn Danzig** had bigger plans. While fans claimed the subsequent events were a result of Danzig's ego, the band's impending breakup could very well have been a product of the group's haphazard and highly unpredictable path. **Glenn Danzig** reportedly confided to his longtime friend Henry Rollins that he wanted to form another band that would allow him to take the form he had dreamed about for so long, that of the dark lord of rock. **Glenn Danzig** publicly announced his plans to form a band called Samhain, and the Misfits were now part of rock history. But before hammering the nails on the coffin that would encase the Misfits, **Glenn Danzig** and company put out a three-song 1984 farewell single, "Die Die My Darling."

A 1985 TV cartoon honored the band by naming a troublesome music group the Misfits; the show helped to introduce a whole new generation of teenagers to the band and its legacy. The New York City—based independent label, which was putting out a lot of Plan 9 records at the time, released a collection of Misfit songs that **Glenn Danzig** had complied; the simply titled *Misfits*, commonly referred to as *Collection I*, was released in 1986. Pop culture paid another homage to the group in 1987 when the popular children's comic *Teenage Mutant Ninja Turtles* featured a story called "Ghouls Night Out" that was dedicated to the band. The music community honored the band when Metallica covered a few Misfits songs for the 1987 EP *Garage Days Re-Visited,* and in 1988 the **Sub Pop Records** band Mudhoney and **Sonic Youth** put out a split 7-inch that featured a sample of the Misfits's "Halloween" song.

Glenn Danzig, meanwhile, continued to release Misfits material after the band had broken up—without the consent of the other band members. The Misfits filed a lawsuit against **Glenn Danzig**, and Jerry Only sought the legal rights to the band's name. Only was successful and he founded a new incarnation of the band now known as the "Newfits" with Doyle, drummer Dr. Chud, and guitarist/new front man Michale Graves. Graves fronted the band from around 1995 to 2000, establishing himself as the iconic front man of the band during its second incarnation. The 1999 album, *Famous Monsters* (Roadrunner Records) helped set this lineup apart from the band's **Danzig** era with a cleaner production style and Graves's vocals, which some felt were cleaner, but less angry, than **Glenn Danzig**'s yawps. Both Graves and Chud walked out on the band mid-show at the House of Blues in Chicago. Upon their departure, Only took on the vocal duties, along with his bass responsibilities. That same year, **Glenn Danzig** attempted to sue Warner Bros., accusing the record company of having owed him and the group unpaid royalties. **Glenn Danzig** did not win the lawsuit, however, and the label was able to reissue *Walk Among Us*.

Doyle and Only formed a band together called Kryst the Conqueror, and they started the label Cyclopean Music Inc. The first posthumous Misfits album, *Static Age* (Caroline Records) surfaced in 1995; it featured two of the band's biggest signature songs, "We Are 138" and "Teenagers From Mars." Tracks from the album were recorded in 1978, but they did not surface until this recording. Still, though released two decades after its creation, *Static* eschewed the early 1970s; the 19-track album also featured "Attitude" and "Hollywood Babylon," a graphic song that depicted the dark side of the city of dreams.

Further lawsuits ensued in the mid-1990s. **Glenn Danzig** was able to put a gag order on a 1993 Misfits tribute album when he sued over the use of the band's likeness. The battles ended, however, the next year when Doyle, Only, and **Glenn Danzig** reached an agreement to equally share licensing rights for the group. The settlement, which was finalized in 1996, allowed Only and his new bandmates sole ownership of the band name whenever they performed, but it granted **Glenn Danzig** an equal share of all earnings related to the sale of Misfits merchandise, including, ironically, a Jerry Only doll that debuted in 1999 and a Misfits shoe collection, which came out shortly afterward.

Rumors circulated in 1994 about a possible Misfits reunion when Only told music journalists about his plans to find a new singer so the group could play again as the Misfits. Plan 9 Records eventually folded, and in 1995 Only and Doyle bravely approached **Glenn Danzig** at his parents' house to invite him to rejoin the Misfits. **Glenn Danzig**, who reportedly never sat down with the two to discuss the invitation, outright refused by having them thrown out.

Glenn Danzig later sold the master tapes to all of the Misfits recordings to Caroline Records, and the label made immediate plans to release reissues. Portions of the reissues were included in the 1996 Misfits box set. However, a difficult and demanding **Glenn Danzig** made waves when he threatened to pull the plug on the deal unless Caroline put out an album called *Collection II* on which he had been working. Strangely enough, Doyle, Only, Coma, Mr. Jim, Steele, and new members Dr. Chud and Graves appeared at a public signing for the box set in New York City. A **Glenn Danzig**–less lineup released the album *American Psycho* on Geffen Records in 1997. The 17-track album was rife with the same coffin and macabre titles from the band's heyday, but fans seemed divided into two camps over the genuineness of the band in the midst of **Glenn Danzig**'s absence.

VH1 ranked the band #91 on its list of "100 Greatest Hard Rock Bands Of All Time" in 2000. And in 2001, a so-called "missing" Misfits album resurfaced.

Caroline Records put out *12 Hits From Hell,* a collection of tracks that were recorded in 1980 but never made it onto a full-length album; a few of the sessions from the album had been used for the group's demo. That same year, **Glenn Danzig** kicked off a three-year-long "Misfits 25th Anniversary Tour," during which he played classic Misfits songs in half-hour-long sets. **Glenn Danzig** was joined by Doyle, who sported the iconic devilock. Rumors of a reunion were quickly squashed by **Glenn Danzig**. Doyle and **Glenn Danzig**, however, continued to play together for the "Blackest of the Black" tour in 2005 and also for select dates on **Glenn Danzig**'s own 2006 tour. The so-called "final" tours preceded **Glenn Danzig**'s work as a producer for Doyle's new project Gorgeous Frankenstein. One of the Misfits's only records to hit the Billboard charts, the 2003 album *Project 1950* (Rykodisc) on which the band covered classic 1950s songs, debuted at #2 on the Heatseekers chart.

But, as the group's living dead fantasies surmise, some things never die. In the mid-2000s the band started writing and recording music for a new studio album. Rumors have circulated that the new record will feature early member Dez Cadena and former **Black Flag** drummer ROBO (who had been a brief member during the band's "classic" days, although he'd left the band following a series of disagreements with **Glenn Danzig**), as well as returning members Graves and Doyle. The band performed at the 2007 Desensitized music festival in the United Kingdom in the fall of 2007. The band's new Web site contained a list of tour dates. In 2007, the Misfits contributed songs to singer/aspiring filmmaker Rob Zombie's feature-length film *Halloween.*

The year 2007 was a big year of celebration for the Misfits as it marked theirthe group's 30th anniversary. Jerry Only hosted a Halloween special on Sirius Satellite Radio's punk channel in 2007. The band kicked off a mammoth world "30th Anniverscary Tour" that October. The anniversary also launched a series of merchandising opportunities for the savvy band. The Misfits song "Spinal Remains" from the group's *Static Age* album was featured in the PlayStation 2 game "Jackass: the Game," and the guys put out a refurbished logo by artist Dave Burke. Misfits Records celebrated the success of the artists on its roster: Balzac, Osaka Popstar, and Juicehead.

Further Readings: Gaines, Donna. *A Misfit's Manifesto: The Spiritual Journey of a Rock-and-Roll Heart.* New York: Villard, 2003; http://www.misfits.com; www.misfitsrecords.com.

MISSION OF BURMA

Boston's best-loved **post-punk** band furthered the legacy of punk with its love of noise, smart yet equally angry lyrics, and all-out punk aesthetic. Formed in 1979, Mission of Burma (named for nothing more than a sign band member Clint Conley had spotted in New York City), held court over the punk scene through to the next decade, but the group never quite got the recognition or notoriety its efforts deserved until after it had disbanded in 1983 (the group eventually reformed in 2002).

Guitarist and front man Roger Miller formed the group with bassist Clint Conley, engineer Bob Weston (who replaced Martin Swope on the decks), and drummer Peter Prescott; Mission of Burma (MOB) created intense music that captured the rebellious spirit of punk while creating the mold for **post-punk** with its rapid rhythm changes, tape loop samples, and oddball time signatures. MOB, whose influences included **Iggy and The Stooges** and **MC5**, released the majority of its records on **Ace of Hearts Records**, a local label that allowed the group complete artistic freedom, but with its limited distribution, kept the band from reaching fans nationwide. Though Weston was not officially a band member, MOB often treated him as such because the loops he created were an integral part of the band's sound; Weston's contribution of using effects and prerecorded sounds allowed the bandmates to stretch beyond what they thought they could do with their instruments.

Their debut album, *Signals, Calls and Marches* (**Ace of Hearts Records**, 1981) contained the hit songs "That's When I Reach for My Revolver" and "Academy Fight Song," explosive tracks that made their way to college radio play lists in the Boston area. MOB's hook-filled tracks, unpredictable subject matter (religion and corruption, the German-born painter Max Ernst, and songs titled "This Is Not a Photograph"), and impressive harmonies blew fans away; the group's simple approach to songwriting forced people to think twice about setting the limits of what bands could do with just a guitar, bass, and drums. MOB utilized the cultural movement known as Dadaism, a World War I movement in which artists celebrated an antiwar stance via their art, as inspiration for its lyrics.

MOB toured, frequently hitting cities where the band was well received—primarily Washington, D.C., and New York City, but MOB's gigs rarely stretched beyond the intimate indie rock circuit. Consequently, MOB's music never reached the millions of listeners who later, most likely following the dot-com boom, became fans. MOB's onstage performances garnered mixed reviews—they were hardly consistent and critics often poked fun at the group's inability to present a regular solid live show.

MOB released the intense album *Vs.* in 1982 (**Ace of Hearts Records**), a work that showcased Prescott's drum machine–like beats and the band's signature call-and-response vocal style. The band was riding high, but its ear-splitting club circuit days came back to haunt the group when Miller was diagnosed with tinnitus, a ringing in the ears that is caused by loud noise and constant periods spent listening to music at high volumes. MOB toured in 1983 before going on an indefinite hiatus.

Over the years, countless bands have cited MOB as an influence—**Nirvana, Superchunk, Sonic Youth, R.E.M., Fugazi**, and more. The group reformed in 2002 for a tour across Europe and the United States. The band released its first album in over 20 years—*ONoffON* in 2004 on Matador Records. The album showed a more mature MOB doing what it did best, and fans welcomed this time capsule trip back to the 1980s with the **post-punk** gods who were more than happy to lead the way with this reunion record.

MOB then started work on its third studio album, the tentatively titles "Aluminum Washcloth," which was released as *The Obliterati* in 2005. Media outlets such as **Pitchfork Media** applauded the album, and it made its way to several "Best Of" lists that year. Rykodisc re-released several early MOB recordings soon after. MOB's members pursued various projects; Miller played keyboards for the Alloy Orchestra. MOB's 2006 album, *The Obliterati* (Matador Records) proved to be the group's most aggressive work to date, proving that MOB still possessed the same raw piss and vinegar that made the band the legend it finally came to be.

In 2007, MOB played local shows in the New England area and was nominated in several categories in the 2007 *Boston Phoenix* Best Music Poll, including Best Local Act and Best Local Album. A documentary about the band's life, career, and music called *Not a Photograph: The Mission of Burma Story,* was released via Element Productions in November 2007. The DVD of the film featured liner notes written by Michael Azerrad, who wrote about the band in his book *Our Band Could Be Your Life: Scenes from the American Indie Underground 1981–1991.*

Matador Records put out reissues of the majority of the band's material in March 2008.

Further Readings: Azerrad, Michael. *Our Band Could Be Your Life: Scenes from the American Indie Underground 1981–1991.* New York: Back Bay Books, 2002; http://www.alloyorchestra.com; http://www.rogermiller.home.mindspring.com; http://www.rykodisc.com; www.matadorrecords.com; www.missionofburma.com.

MODEST MOUSE

Formed in 1993, this Issaquah, Washington–based indie rock group—front man and guitarist Isaac Brock, drummer Jeremiah Green, bassist Eric Judy, and occasional member Tom Peloso (cello, keyboards, and upright bass)—was the cause of a bidding war between major record labels. Its roots, however, remain tightly embedded in the indie scene, having been catapulted into the stratosphere of success by the music the group made in a practice space known as "The Shed," which was located conveniently next to the trailer of one band member's mother.

The name Modest Mouse was inspired by the 1921 story "The Mark on the Wall" by the peculiar British writer Virginia Woolf, which Brock had enjoyed. In the story, Woolf described the working middle class as "modest mouse-colored people" (DuBrowa, 2007). Modest Mouse's earliest recordings were made at K Records's founder Calvin Johnson's Dub Narcotic Studios. The group's self-titled debut came out in 1994 via K Records, which mainly releases music by artists in and around the Olympia, Washington area, and had a minimal take off, but Modest Mouse's success seemed to ascend higher and higher with each release.

The Seattle, Washington–based label Up Records (home to **Built to Spill** and The Black Heart Procession) put out the group's 1996 LP, *This Is a Long Drive for Someone with Nothing to Think About,"* which cemented many a theory that Modest Mouse could be a band for the outcasts due to the fact that the album truly revealed Brock's damaged genius. Up also put out the group's 1996 live EP, *Interstate 8,* before the group headed back to K for its 1997 EP, *The Fruit That Ate Itself,* a work that showcased the group's sonic diversity.

The combination of existential lyrics (with Brock waxing poetic about the likes of God and the 1979 film *Mad Max*), eclectic sounds (a violin mixed in with the group's **post-punk** sound) and the group's uncontainable energy—which peaked with its breakthrough album *The Lonesome Crowded West* (Up Records, 1997)—caught the attention of major record labels, as did the group's online presence and Brock's transparent troubles. A label war consequently ensued and music giant Sony Music won out. *West* has often been considered one of the defining albums of mid-1990s indie rock. Brock, however, experienced a personal low two years later when he was accused of date rape. The media broadcast the story nationwide, but Brock was never formally charged.

Modest Mouse released a collection of rare tracks called *Building Nothing out of Something* in 2000 (Up Records) before the ingredients of a major label and an ambitious, angst-ridden indie group were thoroughly mixed—the result of this pairing, though, proved fruitful, resulting in *The Moon & Antarctica* (2000), an album with the scope (and budget) to match the expanse of its title.

The group suffered a minor slap in the face when a token few media outlets suggested the band had "sold out" by signing with Sony's Epic Records, and amid constant panic that the group was going to be dropped by the label, Brock fell into a pattern of self-destruction and downright bad luck. Fans briefly deserted the band when the group licensed the use of its song "Gravity Rides Everything" in a Nissan commercial in 2003.

Throughout the 2000s the band hit a few lows. Brock's troubles escalated when he was involved in a 2002 drunk-driving accident during which he was not injured, but the passenger in the car suffered a minor injury. As a result Brock was brought up on charges of attempted murder, but they were later dropped. In 2004 two of Brock's friends passed away, and the group's long-time drummer, Jeremiah Green, suffered a nervous breakdown. Amid all of the bad luck surrounding Modest Mouse, Brock put his focus into his side project, a band called Ugly Casanova.

Shortly after, Brock and crew began a new album with Modest Mouse; but the material for the album was consequently scrapped. Guitarist Dann Gallucci joined the group, and Modest Mouse released the cynically insightful EP *Everywhere and His Nasty Parlour Tricks* in 2001. K Records eventually released a "lost" album called *Sad Sappy Sucker* that was rumored to have been Modest Mouse's 1994 debut. Brock refused to answer interviewer's questions about how life differed being on a major label or about "selling out" to big advertising; he instead focused on making records, and headlines. The band's reputation for overindulgence marched on, but its success never waned.

Modest Mouse put out its next full-length album, *Good News for People Who Love Bad News,* in 2004; having sold over 1.5 million copies, the album is the band's most critically acclaimed record to date. *News* also earned the band two Grammy nods in 2005—for Best Alternative Music Album and Best Rock Song for the album's single "Float On." Modest Mouse was added to the bill for that summer's **Lollapalooza** tour, but the two-day festival was canceled due to poor

Members of Modest Mouse, clockwise from upper left, Eric Judy (with beard), Johnny Marr, Joe Plummer, Tom Peloso, Jeremiah Green, and Isaac Brock pose for a photo at the Crystal Ballroom in Portland, Oregon, on March 14, 2007. [AP Wide World Photos/ Don Ryan]

ticket sales. Modest Mouse made a cameo appearance performing at a club in a 2004 episode of Fox TV's hit drama *The O.C.* Much to some indie fans' dismay, the "Float On" single was covered on the best-selling album *Kidz Bop: Vol. 7* (Razor & Tie, 2005), which features popular songs performed by average kids.

Christopher Mills, who has directed videos for other indie acts such as **Broken Social Scene** and Interpol, directed the video for "Float On," which received heavy rotation on MTV, giving the group even more exposure. The computer-generated imagery and stop-animation video garnered even more attention for the group. Modest Mouse played the Austin City Limits Music Festival that same year—the group was back on top.

Drummer Jeremiah Green rejoined the band in 2004 for a full-fledged summer tour, and the group released an unofficial bootleg CD of the shows entitled *Baron Von Bullshit Rides Again.* Modest Mouse also made an appearance on Up Records's 10th anniversary live DVD. Modest Mouse performed in 2004 at mtvU's first annual Woodie Awards, which honors artists who have made an impact on the college music scene over the last year; the group walked away with the "Woodie of the Year" award as well as the "Silent But Deadly Woodie" award for the video for the song "Float On."

American singer-songwriter and Sun Kil Moon front man Mark Kozelek, who is a self-confessed fan of the group, recorded a covers album of select Modest Mouse songs for the 2005 album *Tiny Cities*. Modest Mouse headlined the music and technology festival, the U.S. Download Fest, with **Arcade Fire** that summer while adding a few additional dates to its 2005 tour schedule.

The year 2006 was a busy year for Modest Mouse. The group played the Head Bang! Festival in Miami, Florida, Australia's The Falls Festival, Manchester, Tennessee's four-day camping/music festival Bonnaroo and launched a North American tour with indie act **Camper Van Beethoven**. **The Smiths**' former guitarist, Johnny Marr, who had been collaborating with Brock on songs for the group's new album and playing select dates with Modest Mouse, became an official member of the group that same year. Modest Mouse headed to Sweet Tea Recording Studio, where *Good News* was recorded, for its 2007 album, *We Were Dead Before the Ship Even Sank*. Modest Mouse toured in the spring of 2007 in support of the album. A 37-minute 1997 documentary covering the group's making of the *West* album was discovered in 2006.

St. Martin's Press released an unauthorized Modest Mouse biography in November 2006 entitled *Modest Mouse: A Pretty Good Read,* which features quotes from the band and photographs tracing the group's tumultuous career. "Dashboard," the first single from Modest Mouse's 2007 album, was leaked online before it was officially sent to radio stations across the United States. MySpace.com debuted a special ten-day event exclusive to Modest Mouse, during which the site premiered the band's videos. Modest Mouse kicked off a fall 2007 tour at The Blue Note club in Columbia, Missouri.

Modest Mouse toured the world in 2008, hitting major festivals in Australia.

Further Readings: Goldsher, Alan. *Modest Mouse: A Pretty Good Read.* New York: St. Martin's Griffin, 2006; http://www.modestmousemusic.com; http://www.myspace.com/modestmouse.

MY BLOODY VALENTINE

One of the definitive noise pop acts of the 1980s, My Bloody Valentine was a pioneer of the **shoegazing** subgenre. Formed in Ireland in the mid-1980s, My Blood Valentine, which took its name from a low-budget Canadian horror flick, was comprised of founding members Colm O'Ciosoig (drums), singer/guitarist Kevin Shields (who had been a member of Primal Scream and Dinosaur Jr.), Debbie Googe (bass), and Bilinda Butcher (guitars and vocals).

The young British/Irish foursome released a few EPs on independents, including Lazy Records, Fever Records, Tycoon Records, and Creation Records before signing to **Sire Records** for My Bloody Valentine's genre-defining, history of indie rock–worthy record *Isn't Anything* in 1988. The recording set the mold for dream pop acts to follow, and it defined a generation that favored distortion over polished production and the feel-good rewards of the unpredictable over the thought-out music that would take the group to mainstream victory.

My Bloody Valentine influenced countless bands with its rough-edged, ethereal experimental rock, but the group wanted no part in subscribing to the "rules" of the rock scene nor did it promote the violent tendencies of its punk contemporaries; The group simply favored making music that seemed to follow little direction at all—opened-ended, beautiful compositions that were a little rough around the edges.

The British press attempted to make sense out of the group's stone-like onstage presence, and audiences were captivated by the group's playing chops. The group's 1991 **indie pop** album, *Loveless,* was hailed as a masterpiece by critics and fans alike for capturing the essence of indie rock with 11 perfect tracks of layers of dreamy guitars, sweeping dance rhythms, the sheer melodic synergy of the instruments, and natural free-flowing atmospheric ambience. Many fans compared the group's achievements to timeless albums recorded by **Sonic Youth**, Television and **The Jesus and Mary Chain**. Surprisingly, the album, which was recorded for a cool $500,000, sounds as stripped down as the band's early recordings. Shields wrote all of the songs on *Loveless* save one. The artistic *Loveless* topped the charts and became a timeless keepsake for indie fans worldwide through which they could travel back in time to the beginnings of indie rock—with just the push of the "play" button. Many critics herald it as the greatest album of the 1990s.

However, My Bloody Valentine soon suffered the wrath of such a hefty recording budget; while the album was an artistic success, it did not quite pay back the record company's generous production costs, and the group was subsequently dropped from the label. Shields constructed a home studio in which My Bloody Valentine attempted to recreate the magic of *Loveless,* but to no avail—the one-time trick proved that lightning rarely strikes a band twice.

While the group made valiant efforts with two full-length recordings, Shields and the band decided against releasing their new creations to the public. The reels were tossed aside and the band slowly dissolved, leaving Shields as the last remaining member. Shields made the occasional guest appearance on various albums, among them the soundtrack to the 2003 hit film *Lost in Translation* starring Bill Murray, but for almost two decades My Bloody Valentine was left to hinge within the pages of the history of indie rock like a too-perfect mirage that faded before anyone could get the chance to get too close.

In the fall of 2007, the band did, however, announce its first show since 1992; the band played a few select shows in the United Kingdom. My Bloody Valentine also played 2008's **Coachella Valley Music and Arts Festival**, and the group released plans to put out material that Kevin and Bilinda recorded as a follow-up to the *Loveless* album.

Further Readings: McGonigal, Mike. *My Bloody Valentine's Loveless* (33⅓). New York: Continuum Publishing, 2007; http://www.article/feature/36737/Staff_List_Top_100_Albums_of_the_1990s/page_10; www.mybloodyvalentine.net.

MY MORNING JACKET

These purveyors of epic atmospheric instrumentals and experimental, psychedelic country/rock tunes hail from a most unlikely hotbed of indie rock—Louisville, Kentucky. Formed in 1998 by lead singer/guitarist Jim James and his cousin, guitarist Johnny Quaid, along with bassist Two-Tone Tommy and drummer J. Glenn, My Morning Jacket rehearsed on a farm in Louisville before releasing its debut album, *The Tennessee Fire* in 1999 on Darla Records. James came up with the band name when he discovered a tossed-out coat with the initials MMJ inscribed on the tag.

Fans immediately gravitated toward James's husky voice and the group's cacophony of instruments—steel guitar, harmonica, harpsichord, and more—not to mention the near-perfect harmonies and the songs' reverberating melodies and disproportionate sound. MMJ built a solid following online, and, despite the fact that most people may consider the words "alt-country rock band" to be an instant repellent, stalwart indie fans clamored to buy MMJ's music. MMJ released its sophomore album, *At Dawn* (Darla), in 2001; the album marked the addition of two new members—keyboardist Danny Cash and new drummer KC Guetig.

Dawn saw the band fine-tuning what it did best on *Fire*, but with better production quality and an even broader stage on which James's larger-than-life voice shone like a star in the group's gigantic universe of sound. MMJ toured with **Guided By Voices**, gathering an even bigger fan base until it was scooped up by major label RCA/ATO Records; the group was able to forge a deal with the label that would keep its artistic integrity intact. MMJ's major label debut, *It Still Moves*, was released in 2003; with *Moves*, things seemed to grow to epic proportions for the group—bigger atmospheric sounds, wider pastures for James's yawl, and longer songs—the album runs a total of 70-plus minutes. *Moves*, which has often been cited as one of the group's best recordings, also resulted in even more demand from the public. Taxing tour schedules took their toll on the group, and both Cash and Quaid announced plans to leave the band in 2004.

New members Carl Broemel (guitars) and Bo Koster (keyboards) were added to the mix shortly after, and MMJ picked up where it left off. The group released its fourth full-length album, *Z*, in 2005. The songs got even longer and the atmospheric orb grew even bigger—the ambitious album garnered the group bigger raves from critics and fans, and the record shot to #2 on the Billboard Heatseekers chart.

MMJ was part of a music experiment in Boston when the group joined the Boston Pops on stage in 2006 as part of the "Pops On the Edge" concert series, at which conductor Keith Lockhart merged classical music with the sounds of such popular bands as MMJ. MMJ released the two-disc live album *Okononos* in late 2006 as well as a concert DVD. MMJ opened for Bob Dylan for two nights in the summer of 2007 as part of the 11th Annual KOTO Doo-Dah concert in Colorado. James, meanwhile, slated a few solo shows and prepared for the release of his pre-MMJ band's sophomore album.

MMJ played the 2008 **South by Southwest (SXSW)** music festival in Austin, Texas, Bonnaroo in Manchester, Tennessee, and **Coachella Valley Music and Arts Festival** in Indio, California.

Further Readings: Rudder, Randy, and Roseanne Cash. *Country Music Reader.* Nashville, TN: Music City Book Publishing, 2006; http://www.darla.com; http://www.mymorningjacket.com; http://www.rcarecords.com.

THE NEW PORNOGRAPHERS

This Vancouver, Canada–based outfit formed around the nucleus of musician A. C. Newman, who recruited a half dozen members to make edgy rock splintered with catchy, hook-heavy pop melodies, tongue-in-cheek song titles, and subjective lyrics.

Formed in 1997, The New Pornographers, whose name Newman claims mixes the "new"-style names of 1960s bands while sounding "modern in a false way" (Handler, 2005) is more of a musical collective than a band, with its members contributing equal doses of talent and creativity. The ambitious octet released its debut album, *Mass Romantic,* in 2000 via the New York City–based Matador Records, bringing its "intelligent" rock to the masses, who compared the group to such bands as the 1970s American rock/power pop band Cheap Trick, the mod-style 1960s British rock group The Kinks, and Beatles producer extraordinaire Phil Spector. The album, which received wide critical acclaim, featured the very first song the band recorded together—"Letter from an Occupant," as well as the ironically titled tracks "The Slow Descent into Alcoholism" and "The Fake Headlines."

The New Pornographers—front man/lead vocalist/guitarist (and player of the oboe, harmonica, synthesizer, xylophone, and pump organ) A. C. (Carl) Newman, vocalist/guitarist/melodin player and synthesizer programmer Dan Bejar, guest vocalist Neko Case, vocalist/pianist Kathryn Calder, bassist/guitarist/ebow player/ vocalist and synthesizer programmer John Collins, drummer/percussionist/vocalist Kurt Dahle, guitarist Todd Fancey, and synthesizer programmer Blaine Thurier—enjoyed a quick splash of success following the release of the group's debut. Ray Davies, the lead singer and principal songwriter for The Kinks, joined the Canadian supergroup on stage at its 2001 **South by Southwest (SXSW)** performance in Austin, Texas (each of the other band members also play in a handful of other well-known musical outfits).

After a North American tour, Newman's troupe amicably split to focus on each member's other musical endeavors, with Neko Case touring with the subdued Australian alt rock band Nick Cave and the Bad Seeds in support of her debut solo album, *The Virginian* (Bloodshot Records, 1997), which she recorded under the name Neko Case & Her Boyfriends. Everyone came back to the fold, however, to record and release the band's sophomore album, *Electric Version* (Matador Records, 2003). *Version,* which clearly exhibited the band's influences—new wave, British invasion, and prog rock—and Newman's nonlinear songwriting style were heralded by critics for their "wit," "energy and joy" (www.rollingstone.com). Newman released his debut solo album, *The Slow Wonder,* a collection of 11 tracks that showcased his eccentricity and talents as a singer-songwriter, and yet while some fans were left longing for Neko Case's spunky/twangy vocals, they were hooked on Newman's craft.

Newman turned his focus again to The New Pornographers for the group's third album, the complex rhythm-filled *Twin Cinema* (Matador, 2005), which featured two new vocal additions—The Blacks' vocalist Nora O'Connor and Newman's niece Kathryn Calder, who usually sits quietly behind the piano. Newman reportedly had two of his favorite current bands on the brain, Frog Eyes and **The Fiery Furnaces**, when he recorded the rock-out-loud album; tinges of these influences can be heard throughout the 14 tracks, while he mindfully extracted the band's other influences—The Beatles, Brian Eno, The Moody Blues, Wings, and Tubeway Army—from the fray.

In 2006, the group released the live album *LIVE!,* which featured tracks recorded during its 2005–2006 tour; on tour The New Pornographers were joined by **Belle and Sebastian** on select dates. *LIVE!,* of which only 1,000 copies were pressed, was available only at the band's live shows. The New Pornographers kicked off a fall tour and hit the stage at the 2007 **Coachella Valley Music and Arts Festival** before playing a few select gigs in London, stopping just long enough to hit the stage at the Glastonbury Festival in the United Kingdom in support of the group's fourth full-length studio album, *Challengers.* Newman cited the group's new intention to record epic songs for the album that surpassed the five-minute mark; Benjar penned three tracks on the album, which was released in 2007 on Matador Records.

The New Pornographers were nominated for a Canadian Independent Music Award in 2008; the group kicked off a U.S. spring tour that same year in support if its latest album, *Challengers.*

Further Readings: Marten, Nevelle, and Jeff Hudson. *Kinks.* San Marcos, TX: Bobcat Books, 2007; http://www.matadorrecords.com; http://www.myspace.com/thenewpornographers; http://www.thenewpornographers.com.

NEWSOM, JOANNA

Varying between wide open pop orchestrations and quieter, minimalist songs, California-born Joanna Newsom is a bit of an indie rock chameleon who changes sound and scope whenever she sees fit. The classically trained, Bohemian-looking singer-songwriter also plays harp, harpsichord, and piano; she is a bandmate of Deerhoof's Greg Saunier in the group Noise Cop and a former band member of the group The Pleased.

Newsom's music—a fusion of pop and folk—may be too nichy for most listeners, but her fresh female folk-indie persona resonated with the indie public. And while Newsom's compositions are far more sophisticated than those of her peers, Newsom's soulful, moody songs are par for the course on indie record store shelves. After circulating her CD among friends, Newsom's music found its way into the hands of such musicians as **Cat Power** and Will Oldham, who invited the singer to open for them. Bolstered by this exposure, Newsom made the rounds on the late-night talk show circuit as the featured performer, and Newsom's kitschy act caught on, widening her exposure and filling her tour date schedule. Listeners of Newsom's develop polar reactions to her off-kilter, somewhat shrill—yet sweet—voice, declaring utter devotion or repulsion to it.

Newsom toured briefly in 2004, playing select dates with **Devendra Banhart**, before releasing her debut album, *The Milk-Eyed Mender,"*on Drag City Records (home to over 100 artists including Stereolab, Half Japanese, and the Make-Up). Newsom's sophomore effort, the concept album *Ys,* with its complex, highly orchestrated tracks, is the type of album for diehard devotees of independent music. The cover art features a renaissance-style oil portrait of Newsom by a local artist in California that is said to be reminiscent of the old-fashioned recording process used to make the album.

In 2007, Newsom released the EP *Joanna Newsom and the Ys Street Band,* a work that openly reveals Newsom's Celtic influences and penchant for Appalachian music and may prove a challenge for first-time Newsom listeners. The svelte singer-songwriter, whose fashion sense is often as compelling as her musical creations, toured in support of *Ys* through 2007. Newsome wrapped up a long U.K. tour in the spring of 2008.

Further Readings: Lornell, Kip. *The NPR Curious Listener's Guide to American Folk Music.* New York: Perigee Trade, 2004; http://www.dragcity.com; http://www.joannanewsom.co.uk.

NINE INCH NAILS

The album *Pretty Hate Machine* (TVT Records, 1989) by Nine Inch Nails (NIN) was the first indie album to sell over a million copies. It broke into the mainstream with such a force that it remained on the Billboard charts for two years. The album—and its creator, a brooding musician named Trent Reznor—introduced industrial music to mainstream audiences, and the band's disturbing videos were out into heavy rotation on MTV. The album featured such hits as "Head Like a Hole" and "Terrible Lie," which have remained hits today.

Born Michael Trent Reznor in 1965, in Mercer, Pennsylvania, Reznor studied classical music before getting interested in more aggressive music. Reznor joined the group The Innocent for a short while before working at a record store and dropping out of college (he was studying computers) to venture out on his own as a musician. The multi-instrumentalist/producer/performer experimented with computer programs and made his own demo. Reznor secured a record deal with TVT after a lengthy attempt to make a deal with other labels, and he eventually toured with the band Skinny Puppy and later, **The Jesus and Mary Chain**. Armed with a backup band of various musicians, NIN continued to tour, and although audiences were not yet ready to embrace industrial music, Reznor's songs had a dance club edge to them that gave him the entrance to radio that he needed.

NIN's stint on the 1991 **Lollapalooza** tour, however, opened doors even wider for Reznor. Word of mouth spread about the band, and fans at the festival were intrigued by Reznor's devilish, lone-star-type persona. This type of buzz helped *Pretty Hate Machine* sell even more copies. NIN's creepy music and NIN's quiet, mysterious guise served only to escalate the public's interest. Various rumors abounded about Reznor and the band's name. People believed that Reznor came up with the name because, supposedly, the nails driven into Christ's wrists and feet when he was hung on the cross were "nine inch nails"; but as it turns out, Reznor was just pleased with the way the acronym looked on album covers.

Citing the label's failure at supporting him artistically and financially, Reznor sought to sever his ties with TVT Records and venture out on his own. After a lengthy legal battle, NIN was freed from its contract and signed with Interscope Records. Reznor dabbled in a few side projects, but when the label gave him the opportunity to start his own imprint, he jumped at the chance. Reznor founded the nihilistically titled Nothing Records in 1992 and kept working on more material. NIN's follow-up, the EP *Broken* (Nothing Records, 1992), featured heavier guitars, even more haunting loops, and louder, clanging guitars. It was also, as the liner notes added, recorded, produced, and performed "without the permission of the record label" (www.rollingstone.com).

A true **DIY (Do-It-Yourself)**-er, Reznor's music continued to top the charts; in 1992 and 1995, he won the first of many Grammy Awards (both were for Best Metal Performance). MTV was playing NIN's videos often, but Reznor's rise to success hit a snag when the FBI conducted an investigation abut the video for the song "Down In It" for its violent and real-seeming ending. However, this actually served to pique the public's fascination with Reznor and the band. Reznor's persona grew even more mysterious to his fans, and his music grew even darker and more sinister. Film screens at NIN concerts showcased snippets of semiviolent footage and disturbing images that Reznor had culled together.

Seeking refuge, or perhaps to add even more moroseness to his image, Reznor moved to Los Angeles and took up residence in the mansion where Charles Manson and his followers murdered actress Sharon Tate in 1969. Claiming to have been inspired creatively by his surroundings, Reznor released a whole new album of material. *The Downward Spiral* (1994) was even darker, more layered, and more successful than any of Reznor's other works. The album was certified multi-Platinum, and it debuted at #2 on the Billboard charts. Reznor had successfully built himself a dark empire—and he was crowned the dark lord of industrial music. NIN's remake of the Johnny Cash classic "Hurt" was nominated for a Grammy Award for Best Rock Song in 1996.

Armed with a cult following, NIN (in yet another lineup of musicians), NIN played the 1999 Woodstock Festival, where the crowd was whipped up into a frenzy and the band members smothered themselves in mud before taking the stage. Reznor's image and controversial lyrics made him a sex symbol of the 1990s. Reznor continued to dabble in side work, composing the soundtrack to

Oliver Stone's controversial 1994 film *Natural Born Killers;* yet on the other side of the spectrum, he contributed music to Tori Amos's album *Under the Pink.*

Now at the height of his career in the early 1990s, Reznor took a young musician under his wing. Marilyn Manson became a sort of apprentice to Reznor, but the young musician ended up betraying Reznor's kindness and ventured off on his own, claiming that Reznor was of little help to him. Reznor moved to New Orleans and built a home studio in what was once a funeral home. NIN, meanwhile, was influencing other bands, but Reznor reportedly suffered from writer's block and was not able to produce any new songs.

NIN returned after a five-year hiatus with 1999's *The Fragile,* but sales were not strong enough to lift NIN out of its current slump. NIN laid low for a few years before Reznor resurfaced in 2005 to collaborate with a string of musicians such as Peaches, **TV on the Radio**, and Bauhaus. NIN hit the road and played its big comeback show at the 2005 **Coachella Valley Music and Arts Festival** in Indio, California, where doubtful critics were pleasantly pleased with Reznor's newfound fury. NIN's 2006 EP, *Every Day Is Exactly the Same,* and NIN participated in an experimental music/marketing campaign with the company USB. The campaign included hidden URLs and phone numbers linking fans to what would become NIN's next album. The buzz served as a platform for NIN's sixth studio album, the 2007 concept album *Year Zero.*

In yet another attack on record labels—and the music industry as whole—Reznor encouraged fans to "steal" music by illegally downloading it online. The black-haired singer validated his cry by claiming that labels are simply entities that charge exorbitant prices for CDs. Reznor's fury was reportedly spawned by his discovery that NIN's latest album, "Year Zero" was selling for a far higher price than other albums. A remixed version of the album entitled *Y34RZ3ROR3M1X3D,* featuring the remixing talents of various artists including New Order and Ladytron, was released by Interscope Records in November 2007.

NIN's newest record, *Ghosts I–IV,* a 36-track instrumental collection, was released in 2008. The band followed **Radiohead**'s example by allowing fans to download the album in four different editions: the first nine tracks were downloadable for free, while all 36 tracks could be purchased for $5, and a two-CD set is only $10, while the deluxe limited edition package could be purchased for $75.

Further Readings: Huxley, Martin. *Nine Inch Nails.* New York: St. Martin's Griffin, 1997; Udo, Tommy. *Nine Inch Nails.* San Marcos, TX: Bobcat Books, 2007; http://www. interscope.com; http://www.nothing.nin.net.

NIRVANA

The true story behind the life, mind, and death of Kurt Cobain, the troubled lead singer of the Seattle, Washington–based **grunge** band Nirvana, still remains a mystery. But the legacy the artist and his band left behind helped to pave the way for indie rock musicians, after the group crossed over into the mainstream like no other band in history.

Nirvana (in Sanskrit, the band name literally means "to cease blowing," as in a candle that is blown out) formed in 1991. Their noisy, fuzzy guitar playing, combined with Cobain's strained vocals, songs about teen angst, drugs, suicide, and other dark topics, was an instant magnet for disaffected teens of that decade. The group's revolutionary sound and approach to songwriting (people called it "incoherent") served only to intrigue fans and the media more, but the constant spotlight and attention seemed to haunt the shy Cobain, who suffered from depression and battled chronic bronchitis.

Nirvana's increasing success served to popularize indie rock and bring it to mainstream audiences that had before entertained only overproduced pop and label-manufactured songs. But even though they were swiftly becoming the faces of a generation, Nirvana's bandmates stayed true to their humble roots—touting their favorite bands, dressing in sloppy flannel shirts, and donning messy unkempt haircuts.

Though their melodies were based strictly in pop, Nirvana's music was raw, abrasive, and sometimes haphazard in its methodology. The group members never catered to the public, who looked upon them as gods; they simply played music they liked—their way. Even Cobain's singing style was unorthodox; he often wailed so much that his words were indecipherable and he frequently sang off-pitch, putting forth a ragged vocal style that inadvertently became the group's staple sound, which helped to create and define the "**grunge**" subgenre.

Cobain and bassist Krist Novoselic met and developed a mutual love of The Beatles and the Olympia, Washington–based punk act the **Melvins**. Their first band together, The Stiff Woodies, featured Cobain on drums. Cobain took over guitar duties, and the group renamed itself Skid Row before changing lineups again and taking on the name Nirvana. Nirvana, like **R.E.M.**, started out playing local parties; a demo the group had recorded made its way into the hands of a founder of the local label **Sub Pop Records**. Like many indie rock bands, however, the label took means to market the band based on the bandmates' drab dress and "locals" look; Cobain was infuriated and felt betrayed. It was the first in a long line of disappointments the singer would experience in the music industry.

Nirvana's debut single, "Love Buzz" (**Sub Pop Records**, 1988), created a stir about the band, and its 1989 debut full-length album, *Bleach* (**Sub Pop Records**), did even more for the group's career. The album art featured a photographic negative of the bandmates whipping their hair in mid-head bangs, their faces shrouded by their locks. One of the first "**grunge**" rock records of the era, *Bleach,* which was produced for a mere $600, was a dichotomy of playful, angry songs like "About a Girl" and "Negative Creep." Nirvana toured and its songs received adequate play on college radio stations.

Before long, a sort of cult had formed around the band and especially Cobain, who many perceived to be a genius plagued by personal demons. Thanks to great sales numbers, the group was awarded a bigger budget; for its next album, the band recruited producer Butch Vig, who helped the group record a demo, which the bandmates shopped around to major labels. Nirvana recruited ex-Scream member Dave Grohl as its drummer, and the group saw a hefty paycheck of $287,000 from new label DGC with which to work on its next album, *Nevermind*. Few people clearly understood the scope of the band's potential; following Nirvana's tour with noise rocker **Sonic Youth**, the 50,000 copies of the album that had been pressed sold out within what seemed like minutes.

Containing the group's seminal, career-making hit song "Smells Like Teen Spirit," the title of which Cobain culled from an antiperspirant with a similar name, *Nevermind* knocked Michael Jackson's new album off the chart and went on to sell well over 10 million copies. Startled by their newfound success, Nirvana bandmates did what any indie band members that dreamt of success but never quite expected it would do—they panicked. Shortly thereafter, Cobain began dating Hole guitarist/singer Courtney Love; the relationship would prove to be a tumultuous one. People close to Cobain, in fact, questioned the purity of Love's intentions with the singer, and Cobain's bandmates developed a disdain for the bleached-blonde singer. A 1998 documentary called *Kurt & Courtney* even went so far as to allege that the dramatic Love had a role in Cobain's death.

The group's success soon became unstoppable, moving like a freight train out of control. Rumors about Cobain's heroin addiction surfaced amid his marriage to Love, and the couple each fought for custody of their daughter, Francis Bean. Meanwhile, the pressure to record a stellar follow-up to the seemingly flawless *Nevermind* was weighing down on the group. And while *In Utero* (DGC, 1993) was considered a success, Cobain, who battled with his newfound fame, locked himself in the bathroom and threatened suicide.

Still, the band soldiered on, touring the United States and then Europe. The band performed a popular acoustic show on an episode of MTV's *Unplugged,* but tragedy struck when Cobain, who had decided to stay in Europe with Love in March of 1994, was found unconscious in their hotel room. Love revived the singer with an illegal drug, and the band was awestruck when a suicide note was reportedly found. Cobain returned home to the States, only to enter and escape from a rehab center. Cobain's mother filed a missing persons report; his body was found days later on April 8, 1994, in his Seattle, Washington home. He had died of one gunshot wound to the head; authorities ruled it a suicide.

A dramatic and heated battle ensued between Love and the remaining members (Grohl and Novoselic) of Nirvana following Cobain's death. The debate, which circled around who would own and control the masters of Nirvana's recordings, dragged on for months. The three decided to form the Nirvana L.L.C. partnership, but when a decision among the three could not be reached, the matter remained in court all the way until 2001; the unsettled matter weighed so heavily on Grohl and Novoselic that they felt the need to draft an open letter to Nirvana fans to reassure them that "the music of Nirvana will be immortal and, with fans like you, we are confident our hopes will be realized" (www.novoselic.com). Love argued that the L.L.C. should be dissolved, and the three waged war in court in 2002. Love did give in slightly when she allowed the use of the band's final studio recording

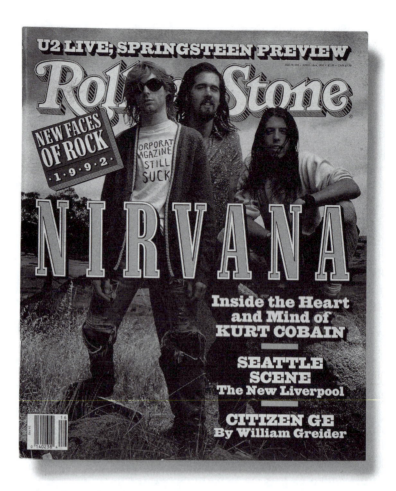

Nirvana's Kurt Cobain bites the hand that tries to feed him on an April 1992 cover of *Rolling Stone* magazine. [Photo by Mark Selinger *Rolling Stone*, April 16, 1992. Copyright Rolling Stone LLC 1992. All rights reserved. Reprinted by permission.]

together (in the form of one song), and the resulting 2002 compilation album *Nirvana* and the 2004 box set *With the Lights Out* were released.

The set featured live performances, radio performances, rare tracks, and hit songs. In 2005, word spread of a documentary that would allow Kurt to tell things in his own words (he served as the narrator through snippets of interviews conducted by author Michael Azerrad). The project was culled from 25 hours of live footage, including interviews with Cobain himself. The result, a documentary entitled *Kurt Cobain: About a Son,* debuted in the fall of 2007 via Sidetrack Films. A DVD of the band's legendary MTV *Unplugged* performance emerged in 2007.

The second album to be released after Cobain's death was 1996's *From the Muddy Banks of the Wishkah,* a collection of B-sides and the band's favorites, which was put together by Novoselic and Grohl; it sold over 1 million copies. By December 2001, *Bleach* had sold well over 1.5 million copies (Basham, 2001); *Nevermind* had sold over 7 million copies, and *In Utero* had sold over 18 million copies (www.amazon.com.uk).

The recording of the MTV *Unplugged* session became a must-have for Nirvana fans; the album, which was released after Cobain's death, sold over 4 million copies and won a Grammy for Best Alternative Music Performance. Cobain's personal journals were released posthumously after Love passed them on to her manager and, while the band mourned the loss of a friend and the Seattle community was pained by the death of a local legend, countless biographies, online museums, and personal tributes popped up about the singer. Memorials were set up to honor the fallen singer, and an unofficial site was set up in his honor.

Novoselic became a political pundit; he wrote a book arguing for the restructuring of voting zone laws, and he even thought about running for lieutenant governor of his home state of Washington. Grohl formed the indie act Foo Fighters and played drums for various bands such as Tenacious D, **Nine Inch Nails**, and Queens of the Stone Age, as well as forming a side project group called Probot.

A London newspaper reported that Cobain's identity was stolen in 2008, and thieves plundered about 40 million pounds' worth of his estate by using his social security number.

Further Readings: Azerrad, Michael. *Come As You Are.* London: Virgin Publishing, 1994; Cobain, Kurt. *Journals.* Reissue edition. New York: Riverhead Trade; 2003; Cross, Charles R. *Heavier than Heaven: A Biography of Kurt Cobain.* New York: Hyperion, 2002; Novoselic, Krist. *Of Grunge and Government: Let's Fix This Broken Democracy.* New York: Rdv Books, 2004; http://www.cobain.com; http://www.geffen.com/nirvana; http://www.interscope.com/nirvana; http://www.kurtcobainmemorial.org.

NME (*NEW MUSICAL EXPRESS*)

NME (*New Musical Express*) is a weekly U.K.–based music publication that was launched in the early 1950s. The paper gained notoriety—and flack from the media and its fans, on occasion—for its bold editorial stances, which were sometimes considered flowery, in support of up-and-coming bands and artists. *NME* has managed to stay afloat in the increasingly overcrowded publishing marketplace mainly because of its focus on guitar-based indie bands and artists, whereas its competition has followed the pack by covering bigger and better-known mainstream acts.

Leaving behind its origins as a jazz and standards-focused magazine, *NME* launched headfirst in its quest to cover the more thrilling, fast-paced genres of rock and pop. Capturing the hearts and minds of teenagers for over 50 years, with cover photos of on-the-edge-of-stardom bands and bubble-gum popping taglines capped with exclamation points touting each featured artist as the "next big thing," *NME* was the biggest selling weekly music magazine in Britain in the 1960s and the 1970s, an accomplishment that the paper has mostly maintained for over 50 years.

The "new" in *New Musical Express* was added by the paper's second owner, London music promoter Maurice Kinn, who purchased the publication in 1952 for

£1000—the equivalent of almost US$2,000. *New Musical Express* outlived its competitors, including publications such as *Melody Maker, Sounds,* and *Record Mirror,* all of which folded years later after decades of success and despite their strong circulation figures; *NME* currently reaches 70,000 people each week, maintaining its position in the upper echelons of rock rags; its peak subscription base reached 230,000 in the 1960s (BBC News online, 2002).

Emerging on the eve of the birth of rock 'n' roll, which was so named by Cleveland's own, DJ Alan Freed, *NME* catered to music aficionados with profiles and interviews of jazz legends, big band leaders, and the pop singers of the late 1950s. But *NME,* forever brazen, made its big entrance on the music mag circuit when it did something no other magazine had done before. Taking its cue from *Billboard* magazine, *NME* published a back page singles chart that was based on album sales, instead of charting albums based on the number of copies of sheet music sold, which was the standard practice of nearly every other music publication available on newsstands.

NME's Beatlemania coverage in the 1960s, along with a completely new design and fresh journalistic approach, solidified the magazine's success, and *NME*'s reputation was forever cemented in the eyes—and hearts—of Britain's unruly youth culture. *NME* featured in-depth interviews with the likes of Liverpool's beloved foursome and The Rolling Stones—and sales soared; what had started as a matte newspaper print tabloid had suddenly morphed into a loud, glossy, oversized magazine that touted hot-off-the-press news and interviews with the hippest new bands and emerging musical acts.

Fresh-faced with its new format, *NME* hosted its first annual *NME* Poll Winners Concert in 1953 at Royal Albert Hall of Arts and Sciences. Tin Pan Alley and the British rock 'n' roll scene considered the concert as one as important and prestigious as the Academy Awards ceremony is to Hollywood. The popular show became an important event in the music world, featuring bands voted most popular by the magazine's readers. Artists and bands on bills in the 1960s included The Rolling Stones, The Beatles, Dusty Springfield, The Animals, and The Moody Blues. *NME* ran a headline calling the Poll Winners Concert the "Greatest Pop Talent Parade the World Has Ever Known" (http://www.nme.com/awardshistory). These concerts, which were subsequently aired on ABC TV a few weeks after the live shows were held, have remained highly attended events, and they have been a mainstay of the magazine ever since. DVDs of the earlier concerts are still available. The concerts, however, experienced a speed bump in the late 1960s when rock fans deemed such events as passé.

After cruising its way through the 1960s, *NME* faced troubled waters in the 1970s when the likes of *Melody Maker* emerged on the scene. Threatening to wean *NME*'s readership off of its weekly rations of rock news, profiles, and album reviews, *Melody Maker*—which left *NME* in the dust in terms of prog rock and psychedelica coverage—and other similar competitive magazines nearly flatlined the magazine. Still, *NME* stayed afloat, due in large part to the advent of editor Alan Smith, who took the editorial helm in the early 1970s.

That same decade, talented young writers such as Lester Bangs, the famed rock critic who was fired from *Rolling Stone* and who is often credited with coining the term "punk music," and Tom Wolfe, novelist and author of *The Bonfire of the Vanities,* flocked to the paper, writing hip, smart copy and adding an edge that helped *NME* surge to the front row of the magazine racks again. Even the paper's in-house staff received a star-studded boost with the likes of stars-in-the-making as employees: Bob Geldof, the Irish singer/songwriter/activist who played in the band The Boomtown Rats and experienced great success with the well-known song "I Don't Like Mondays," and Chrissie Hynde, the lead vocalist/front woman for the famed American rock group The Pretenders. *NME* continued to add stars to its masthead, with bylines by Nick Kent and Charles Shaar Murray, to name a few.

Nick Logan assumed editorship in 1973 while the paper floundered (and glam rock outshined anything in its path). In an ironic turn, the Sex Pistols, whose band members guffawed at what they viewed as *NME*'s "poseur" position, was featured on the paper's cover in 1997. The riotous English rock group sang of the members' disdain in their signature song "Anarchy in the U.K.," in which lead singer John Lydon (aka Johnny Rotten) quipped, "I use the enemy, I use anarchy." The line is allegedly a play on words in which Lydon uses the word "enemy" in place of "NME" to express the group's dissatisfaction with publications such as *NME* that placed the group on the covers of their magazines in order to engage the "punk" aesthetic.

Ironically, the paper featured the riotous crew on a 1977 cover at a time when the paper reclaimed its street cred, thanks in most part to the addition of writers Tony Parsons, who became a British journalist and best-selling author, and Julie Burchill, who started at the magazine at the age of 17 and has since become one of the most outspoken journalists in Britain. Punk was back on *NME*'s good side, and the threat of closure by the paper's parent company, IPC Media, after *NME* failed to grasp onto the kaleidoscope of action that coincided with the rise of prog rock and psychedelica, now just all seemed like a bad dream.

With bands that had scoffed at *NME* just months before begging to grace its covers, the magazine was back on track. A redesign and the addition of yet another editor, Neil Spencer, around 1977–1978 pushed *NME* closer to the hearts of youths, with covers featuring such bands as Gang of Four and Joy Division.

NME jumped on the political bandwagon around that time and took a more political stance around 1978, joining efforts to rally against parties like the National Front, an extreme right-ring political party whose leaders donned Nazi-like attire. Things seemed out of tune again for the paper in the 1980s as the punk scene deflated a bit and the paper struggled to stay on track with the emerging new sounds of rap and hip-hop. Still struggling with its identity in the wake of the new musical era, *NME* was saved by the grace of mod crooner Morrissey, whose band **The Smiths** became the focal point of the paper, giving it direction and focus and thus earning *NME* the enigmatic nickname "The New Morrissey Express." Unfortunately, the pale-skinned Irishman's jet-black pompadour was not enough to save the paper, and *NME* faced the prospect of closure yet again. With sales dwindling and readership loyalty on rocky ground, new editor Ian Pye stepped in 1985 during an exceedingly difficult time for the paper, which alternated between hip-hop covers and rock's mainstays—neither of which seemed to please fans enough to salvage the paper's now dimly lit future.

NME made a last ditch effort to gain fans' respect (and perhaps to have a memorable goodbye statement) by including a poster of the Dead Kennedys' 1985 album, *Frankenchrist,* on its front page. The salacious poster by H. R. Giger, which would eventually land the band in court on indecency charges because the image depicted several graphic sex acts, was titled "Penis Landscape." But what seemed like a fitting middle-finger finale had blossomed into the paper's third rebirth. Alan Lewis stepped in as editor, restaffing and reorganization took place, and the paper began its steep ascent back to the upper echelons of rock journalism by embracing new musical trends with wit and a brazen attitude that was a fitting complement to the rock 'n' roll icons it covered.

NME continued to break new ground with innovative off-the-page endeavors such as the C81 cassette in 1981, which was released by **Rough Trade Records** and featured tracks by such top indie bands as **Orange Juice**, Linx, and **Aztec Camera**; the cassette was available to readers by mailing in the coupon found in the magazine. A follow-up was released five years later.

Poised to reign supreme in the 1990s, *NME* turned to the new British musical elite—and a genre known as **shoegazing**—before looking eastward across the pond to Seattle, Washington, in the United States, where **grunge** bands such as **Nirvana** and Pearl Jam were lighting a fire under music critics and fans (and threatening to burn up the mainstream) everywhere. Pearl Jam managed to sweep up nearly almost all of the *NME* Awards in the 1980s, and the paper continued to cover Eddie Vedder and crew at every opportunity.

Yet while *NME* was being toted in torn-up, patch- and pin-covered backpacks by music fans everywhere, the magazine's former ally, Morrissey, was at ends with the paper in 1992, claiming that *NME* had accused the singer of allegedly using racist imagery and writing racist lyrics in his songs. After that much-publicized debate lost the wind in its sails, *NME* focused on the music again, and soon the paper was making stars simply by putting bands on its cover. *NME* took jabs at the British Phonographic Industry's BRIT Awards, which the magazine called "a back-slapping farce notable for keeping an eye on the sales figures rather than artistic achievements" (http://www.nme.com/awardshistory).

NME became the first publication ever to put Oasis on a cover in 1995, catapulting the Gallagher brothers to superstardom. *NME,* now being guided by new editor Steve Sutherland (a former assistant editor at the paper's nemesis, *Melody Maker*), suffered a flood of departures by staffers as a result of Sutherland and his editorial decisions. One of music's saddest moments hit the paper in 1994 with the death of Kurt Cobain, but *NME* trudged onward, plastering the likes of Blur on its cover and establishing an *NME* Stage at the Glastonbury Festival in 1995. Britpop soon diffused and *NME* was in hock again after a failed attempt to cover DJ culture. Steve Sutherland led the charge when *NME* launched its Web site in

1996; Anthony Thornton subsequently replaced him and gave the site an over-haul. *NME* instituted its Britbus Tour in 1996, featuring The Bluetones, The Cardigans, Heavy Stereo, and Fluffy.

In an ironic twist, *NME*'s parent company, IPC Media, merged the magazine with its biggest rival, *Melody Maker,* which folded in 2000 after 75 years due to poor circulation numbers. *NME* also acquired the rival magazine's online sub-scription base and content. *Melody Maker* had been branded as one of the world's longest-running music weeklies on IPC Media's home page. The twenty-first cen-tury proved to be fruitful for *NME,* now armed with a strong online presence and touting itself as "The World's Fastest New Music Service" (www.nme.com). Editor Conor McNichols joined the staff in 2002 as head editor, and the magazine was instrumental in launching the careers of such bands as The Strokes and **The White Stripes**. Two *NME* concerts took center stage in the early 2000s—2000 saw the return of the *NME* Awards (which had taken a brief hiatus) at the Mermaid Theatre in London, and in 2001, the controversial, over-the-top *NME* Carling Awards were held, celebrating the likes of Marilyn Manson, Coldplay, Primal Scream, and U2.

With McNichols's arrival came the advent of *NME Originals,* collections of articles and photographs from previous issues. *NME* suffered a bit of flack for its new habit of overhyping bands, and the paper faced criticism after claims that it fudged the winners of the annual Album of the Year poll in 2005 to boost the chart positions for more high-profile bands. The paper denied the claims and the charge was dropped; to this day, the magazine's presence remains strong. *NME*'s Carling Awards touted The Strokes, New Order, Kings of Leon, and the Kaiser Chiefs in 2004 and 2005.

An Irish edition launched in the latter part of 2006. *NME*'s string of concerts and awards shows—The NME New Music Tour, the NME Awards, and the NME New Rave Revolution Tour and the O2/NME Rock 'n' Roll Riot Tour, both of which started in 2006—continue to sell out venues. *NME* regularly includes compilation albums with copies of the magazines that go to subscribers, and the magazine also opened its own club, Club NME, a music venue that occurs in the United States, Ireland, and the United Kingdom. In 2006, Universal UK released the two-disc compilation "NME Presents the Essential Bands 2006," featuring such Britpop acts as the Kaiser Chiefs, **Arctic Monkeys**, and Razorlight.

Primal Scream was given the "Godlike Genius Award" at the 2007 Shockwaves NME Awards Show at the Hammersmith Palais in London. Bands that performed for the 2007 Shockwaves NME Awards Indie Rock Tour included Russian-born singer-songwriter Regina Spektor, **Babyshambles**, !!! **(Chk Chk Chk)**, **The Shins**, Kings of Leon, The Young Knives, We Are Scientists, **The Rapture**, Kaiser Chiefs, Lostprophets, Amy Winehouse, the Long Blondes, and Kasabian.

NME praised Beth Ditto, a self-described "fat, feminist lesbian" (http://www.cnn.com/2006/SHOWBIZ/Music/11/24/tbr.ditto/index.html) singer from the state of Arkansas who fronts the band The Gossip, as the "coolest person in rock" (http://www.nme.com/news/the-gossip/34307) in 2006; Ditto, though was less than pleased when the magazine almost decided against featuring a photo-graph of her posing nude on its cover, calling the publication "chickens- -t" (Paine, 2007).

The Los Angeles, California–based venue Spaceland, where the Club NME Los Angeles has its home base, formed the independent label, Spaceland Recordings, in the spring of 2007. The label will also host live events and special concerts. The first recordings that were made available by Spaceland were by bands Irving, Asobi Seksu, The Drones, and Darker My Love.

The 2008 NME Awards were held on February 28; the **Arctic Monkeys** won the award for Best Band.

Further Readings: Derogatis, Jim. *Let It Blurt: The Life and Times of Lester Bangs, America's Greatest Rock Critic.* New York: Broadway, 2000; Johnstone, Nick. *Melody Maker History of 20th Century Popular Music.* Chicago: Trafalgar Square Publishing, 1999; Morthland, John, and Lester Bangs. *Main Lines, Blood Feasts, and Bad Taste: A Lester Bangs Reader.* New York: Anchor, 2003; Osborne, Roger. *30 Years of NME Album Charts.* London: Pan Macmillan, 1993; Roach, Martin, and New Musical Express. *"NME" Top 100 Singles.* New York: Chrysalis, 2002; Tobler, John. *"NME" Rock 'n' Roll Years.* London: Hamlyn, 1992; http://www.nme.com.

O

ORANGE JUICE

Orange Juice is the Scottish pop band that helped set the bar for the indie/pop rock sound—melodic guitars, self-effacing lyrics, and funky rhythms—in the United Kingdom. The ever-stylish quartet, which stood up against misogyny in songs and in the music business, emerged in 1976. Tagged as a pop/**post-punk** act, Orange Juice, consisting of lead singer/songwriter/guitarist Edwyn Collins, drummer Steven Daly, bassist David McClymont, and guitarist James Kirk, was considered the "darling" of the music press, as critic after critic lauded its records with songs of praise.

Fans can travel back in time with the group's 2005 album, *The Glasgow School* (Domino Records), a retrospective of Orange Juice's early hit singles, which were released on the Glasgow-based independent label Postcard Records. Music critic Simon Reynolds, who has penned articles and music reviews for the *New York Times, SPIN* magazine, *Melody Maker,* and more, touted the group as "literate, playful, witty, camp" (Reynolds, 2006), and a group that helped the music community recover from the untimely suicide of Joy Division's Ian Curtis. Reynolds went so far as to say Orange Juice, which was inspired by punk, "walked and acted in ways that broke with both rock's rebel swagger and **post-punk**'s militant solemnity," forever marking the group as a leader in the **post-punk** movement.

Orange Juice's 1982 album, *You Can't Hide Your Love Forever* (Polydor Records, 1998) showed listeners what music writers were all aflutter about. The buzz of the group's guitars, the upbeat feel of the songs, and the group's up-front defiance of punk's "nihilism" during Orange Juice's heyday were focal points of *Love,* a work that showed influences by **The Smiths**, Television, and **Talking Heads**.

Topping the U.K. charts album after album, Orange Juice released its 1982 album, *Rip It Up,* which featured the Top 10 hit "I Can't Help Myself." For "Myself," Orange Juice attempted to produce a more funk-driven sound. Orange Juice's lineup changed throughout the course of its career. Drummer/songwriter Stephen Skinner and guitarists/songwriters Zeke Manyika and Malcolm Ross became later members of the group, contributing to its more recent recordings.

Following the exit of everyone save Collins and Manyika, Orange Juice was diluted to a duo. The pair worked on the group's next two albums—*Texas Fever* and a self-titled effort (1984)—both of which contained hit songs; these hits helped the group to make its debut in the *Guinness Book of British Hit Singles.* Orange Juice's star faded briefly until 1995 when the single "A Girl Like You" earned Collins some commercial credit and attention. Two greatest hits collections surfaced in the mid-2000s.

Further Readings: Reynolds, Simon. *Rip It Up and Start Again: Postpunk 1978–1984.* London: Penguin, 2006; http://www.twee.net/labels/postcard.html.

OUT HUD

Sharing band members with bands from both coasts—California's **!!! (Chk Chk Chk)** and New York City's **LCD Soundsystem**—this New York City via Sacramento, California group combines dub, disco, and **post-punk** to create punk/rock music that attracts fans of all ages. Members of the band had been in other groups together when they were teenagers. The name of the band has yet to be officially explained, but band members have suggested in interviews that the name Out Hud was inspired by a photograph they took of a HUD (Housing and Urban Development) building in Washington, D.C.

Out Hud benefited from the power of word of mouth that was generated by the high energy and the danceability factor at the band's live shows—word spread throughout the Internet and followed the bandmates all the way from the West Coast to Brooklyn, where they relocated in 2001. The quintet consists of a unique musical lineup for a "rock" band—cello (Molly Schnick), bass (Nic Offer), guitar (Tyler Pope), their beloved drum machine "Phyllis" (Phyllis Forbes), and mixing board master Justin van der Volgen.

Initially the band, which formed in 1996, strove to secure deals with the diverse Chicago label Thrill Jockey Records by submitting demos, but Out Hud did not strike indie gold until Red Alert, an intimate **DIY (Do-It-Yourself)** California indie label, signed the group and released its first 7-inch record. Eventually, the band signed to Colorado's Gold Standard Laboratories (or GSL) (which, the band claims, gave it complete creative freedom). The band then moved to Dead Turtle Records before settling with the Southern Records imprint Kranky Records.

Out Hud dedicated its 2003 record, *S.T.R.E.E.T. D.A.D.* (Kranky), to the cellist's father, who was patient while the band recorded the album in his house—it took six years. The self-proclaimed perfectionists in the group, though, hit a low note that year when the band was dropped from a tour with the English electropop quartet Ladytron—the day before the band was supposed to go on the road for the tour. Although the cancellation was never fully explained, the band did not suspect foul play on Ladytron's part.

Out Hud released a split EP with **!!! (Chk Chk Chk)** in 2004 for Gold Standard Laboratories' *Lab Remix Series, Vol. 2,* followed by two subsequent singles on Kranky in 2005: "One Life to Leave" and "It's for You." Out Hud's second album, *Let Us Never Speak Of It Again,* which (Kranky, 2005) was recorded at National Recording Studios in Maryland, sparked select tour dates, including a stint at a well-known trendy art/music party at the Roxy nightclub in New York City. Out Hud's female band members Phyllis Forbes and cellist Molly Schnick added a significantly increased amount of vocals to *Let Us Never Speak Of It Again* than on the band's previous releases.

Adhering to the **DIY (Do-It-Yourself)** movement, Out Hud designed all of its own album cover art, and the male members of the band all lived together in a warehouse where the group held band practices. Out Hud promised a more experimental and energetic follow-up to *Let Us Never Speak Of It Again,* which it claimed would bring the band "back to their GSL roots" (Schreiber and Carr, 2003), but amid rumors of a possible split, Out Hud disbanded in 2006 so that each member could pursue his or her own solo projects.

Further Readings: George-Warren, Holly, Patricia Romanowski, and Jon Pareles. *The Rolling Stone Encyclopedia of Rock & Roll (Revised and Updated for the 21st Century).* Forest City, NC: Fireside, 2001; http://www.brainwashed.com/outhud; http://www.goldstandardlabs.com; http://www.thrilljockey.com.

P

PAVEMENT

Rivaling Sebadoh as one of the most influential bands of the 1990s, Pavement made an indelible mark on indie rock with its raw **Lo-fi** sound, intelligent yet cryptic lyrics, and prolific front man Stephen Malkmus's unique, near moaning vocal style (the scraggly haired singer-songwriter has told interviewers on more than one occasion that he is not too fond of his voice).

Formed in the summer of 1989 in Stockton, California, after Malkmus graduated with a music degree from the University of Virginia, Pavement fused clever lyrics with noisy rock and **DIY (Do-It-Yourself)** mentality, helping the band to capture the hearts of indie rock fans hungry for music that reflected musicians' honest—and even flawed—selves, which suited Malkmus's let-it-all-hang-out style. The underground band started out as a studio project between Malkmus and his guitarist/vocalist friend Scott Kannberg, but it soon started to take on the structure of a full-fledged group when drummer Gary Young joined the fold for its debut 7-inch, "Slay Tracks," which cost roughly $800.00 to make and quickly made its way around the underground scene.

A series of well received 7-inches released on the band's own label Treble Kicker preceded Pavement's addition to the Drag City Records' roster and the recruitment of a second drummer to the mix, Bob Nastanovich, and bassist Mark Ibold. Word of mouth spread like wildfire about the band's music, bolstering Pavement's platform outside the tightly knit inner circle of music critics and die-hard indie fans. With the new lineup intact, Pavement geared up for the release of its 1992 LP, *Slanted and Enchanted* (Matador Records), a collection of do-it-our-way melodic songs filled with Malkmus's ingenious lyrics. The album sold an impressive 150,000 copies, helping the band to launch a tour in support of the album; Young's on-stage high jinks soon outshone the music, though, forcing the band and Young to part ways in 1993.

Young was replaced by Steve West for the band's EP *Watery, Domestic* (Matador, 1992), a release that showcased a cleaner, less frazzled band. Critics predicted Pavement would break into the mainstream with its 1994 record, *Crooked Rain, Crooked Rain,* but Malkmus's oddball, literate lyrics and the group's impulsive sound were too unpredictable for fans who purchased albums only by artists they heard on the radio. Nonplussed by the rejection, Pavement gladly returned its focus to the underground where indie fans welcomed the group with open arms. Still, *Crooked* debuted at #121 on the Modern Rock charts and the smirky track, "Cut Your Hair," went into heavy rotation on MTV. Instead of breaking into the mainstream, Pavement had simply burst beyond the cult status bubble that had formed around it.

In 1994, Malkmus and Nastanovich collaborated with their college pal David Berman for the debut album by their new project, Silver Jews. Pavement's third album, *Wowee Zowee* (Matador, 1995), the most eccentric to date, received mixed reviews, but the band was back in full force as indie's reigning king. Pavement appeared at **Lollapalooza** in Chicago that year before recruiting hit producer Nigel Godrich (who has worked with artists such as **Beck** and **Radiohead**) for 1999's *Terror Twilight* (Matador), which was well received. Still, the high point of *Terror* was unable to trump rumors of a split, resulting from Malkmus's growing number of solo gigs.

Malkmus announced Pavement's breakup in the fall of 1999 at a live show, but its label, Matador Records, remained hush on the news despite the fact that Malkmus and Kannberg were already hard at work on their debut albums with their respective groups, the Jicks and the Preston School of Industry. Malkmus made the breakup official in a 2000 interview with *SPIN* magazine.

Matador released an expanded version of *Slanted & Enchanted* in 2002, featuring B-sides and over 30 bonus tracks. A retrospective DVD soon followed. Matador Records has reissued a series of the band's albums—*Slanted & Enchanted: Luxe and Reduxe* in 2002, *Crooked Rain Crooked Rain: L.A.'s Desert Origins* in 2004, and *Wowee Zowee: Sordid Sentinels Edition* emerged in 2006.

Further Readings: Javanovic, Rob. *Perfect Sound Forever: The Story of Pavement.* Boston: Charles Justin and Co., 2004; http://www.matadorrecords.com/pavement; http://www.myspace.com/pavementrock; http://www.stephenmalkmus.com.

PEDRO THE LION

Pedro the Lion is the musical alter ego of Seattle native and Christian David Bazan (though Bazan would be loathe to be called a "Christian" rocker). Pedro the Lion, which was formed in 1995, became a one-man melodic pop outfit after several failed attempts to form a full band. Bazan, who is also a member of the instrumental rock group Unwed Sailor, played in several hardcore groups before branching out on his own and has toured and recorded relentlessly as Pedro the Lion, releasing approximately an album or EP every year since Pedro's inception.

Bazan's first EP, the six-track *Whole* via the independent Seattle alt rock label Tooth & Nail Records (1996), shed some light on the breadth of talent this man-behind-the-beast musical maven possesses. It was also a conceptual album that served as a vehicle for Bazan's explorations of faith and religion. The existential album won fans over instantly with its seamless blend of **emo** and **punk**—and Bazan's heartstring-tearing vocals.

Pedro the Lion's debut full-length album, *It's Hard to Find a Friend* (Made in Mexico, 1998) won critics over with a collection of songs about close-to-the-heart topics such as Trans Ams and draft dodgers that also exhibited Bazan's songwriting talents. The intimate album added another spot to the connect-the-dots array of **emo**-indie albums by Bazan. *The Only Reason I Feel Secure* (Made in

Mexico, 1999) and *Winners Never Quit* (**Jade Tree Records**, 2000) followed next, proving that Bazan's darker side had depth. Considered a "concept" album, *Winners* teeters on the delicate balance of brood and gloom and hope and serenity, via the almost quiet pace of Bazan's voice and jangling electric guitars.

Seattle indie label Suicide Squeeze put out Pedro the Lion's 2000 EP, *Progress,* and Pedro the Lion continued with an assembly line of EPs released on **Jade Tree Records**—the remixed, remastered, and repackaged versions of *The Only Reason I Feel Secure* and *It's Hard to Find a Friend.* Bazan's third full-length album, *Control* (**Jade Tree Records**, 2002) came in the form of another concept album—this time circling the topic of the end of a "hyper-modern marriage." However, critics felt that Bazan indulged in his incredible storytelling abilities so much so that it diluted the album's focus.

Pedro the Lion toured extensively in 2004 after the release of *Achilles Heel* (**Jade Tree Records**), which is widely considered Pedro the Lion's most "emotionally complex" and "expansive" album. *Tour EP '04* (2005) featured on-the-road recordings by the Pedro the Lion as well as in-studio tracks and covers of songs by **Radiohead**, American singer-songwriter Randy Newman, and **Cat Power**. The album was also made available online via iTunes.

Pedro the Lion's religious commentaries and Christian overtones (both negative and reactionary) did not turn off fans who may have otherwise never listened to a record that mentioned Jesus without some sort of ironic context. The party ended in 2006, though, when Pedro the Lion's backing musicians departed to make their own solo albums—and Bazan removed his lion's mask to create music with the newly formed group Headphones, which features musicians Frank Lenz and Nick Peterson (founding member T. W. Walsh later left the group). A full-length from Headphones was slated for release on **Jade Tree Records** in 2007, but it never came to fruition. Headphones performed at the 2007 Sasquatch! Music Festival at the Gorge Ampitheatre in George, Washington, and Suicide Squeeze's tenth anniversary show in Seattle.

Bazan recorded his debut solo EP, *Fewer Moving Parts* (Eat My Flesh, Drink My Blood, 2006) in his home studio. *Parts* features two versions of five new songs (including acoustic and instrumental versions of the same song); graphic novelist Zak Sally created the album's cover art. Bazan toured for a few select dates with musician friends Vic Chesnutt, Will Johnson, Scott Danbom, and Mark Eitzel as the Undertow Orchestra in the late spring of 2007.

Further Readings: http://www.pedrothelion.com; http://www.toothandnail.com; http://www.unwedsailor.net.

PERE UBU

From the group's name to its diva-esque specific stage lighting requests, almost everything about Pere Ubu was odd, or as fans would describe it, "abstract." Still, the Cleveland, Ohio–based band was celebrated for its artful ambitions, and its brand of self-described "avante garage" made a lasting impression on critics and diehard indie fans. Despite the fact that the group never broke into the mainstream or experienced wide success, it has become one of the most highly regarded underground American acts of the last few decades.

Forged from the ashes of the proto punk group Rocket From the Tombs in Cleveland, Ohio, in 1975, the inventive quintet was named after the main character in a French play. Pere Ubu's music has been described in many ways—art punk, **post-punk**, alt rock, experimental, and even proto-punk. At Pere Ubu's core, however, was a sense that music was a higher art, but the bandmates were not too highbrow to have fun.

Front man David Thomas, who was also known as Crocus Behemoth, had such a peculiar shriek-like voice that was as distinctive as the band's music. And his vocals, backed by the angst-fueled music made by guitarist Peter Laughner, guitarist Tom Herman, bassist Tim Wright, keyboardist Allen Ravenstine, and drummer Scott Krauss, resonated with fans throughout the band's 30-year-long career (the band took a five-year hiatus from 1982 to 1987).

Pere Ubu's sound was like a canvas splattered haphazardly with splashes of garage rock, blues, and experimental music. The group released its debut single, "30 Seconds Over Tokyo," in 1975 on Thomas's label, Hearthan Records. The title of the song revealed the group's intelligence and what would become a long string of literary and historical references to fans who recognized that the song title was borrowed from a book of the same name that told the story of a World War II lieutenant who witnessed firsthand the Doolittle Raid, the first air raid by the United States to strike the Japanese home islands during World War II (also the subject of a 1944 movie starring Spencer Tracy).

In 1976, the group put out a follow-up single, "Final Solution," on the same label. By this time, the group's singles became known as Hearpen singles (which are essentially a box set of the first four singles) because of mysterious legal disputes that have not been clarified. Growing in popularity, Pere Ubu played a stint at New York City's famous club, Max's Kansas City. A third single, "Street Waves," followed in 1976, and, after having gained a sort of cult following, Mercury Records's imprint Blank Records showed interest in and signed a deal with the group. Meanwhile, the fruits and consequences of success (i.e., Laughner's long-standing battles with drugs and alcohol)—as well as the fact that the band members had very strong creative differences—had taken their toll on the group. Laughner, though, departed Pere Ubu after the release of "Streets" so that he could focus on music that the band considered too "Dylan-esque" for its tastes. Soon after his departure, however, he lost a long battle with drug addiction and passed away in 1977. Wright, who was originally the group's soundman before he learned to play bass, also left the group to join the New York City–based "no wave" group DNA.

New band member Tony Maimone came on board for the group's debut 1978 album, *The Modern Dance* (Blank Records). Sales of the breakthrough album were less than impressive, but the cultural impacts of the album are infinite—punk acts have for years cited the work as an influence. The album art featured a working class man wearing ballet shoes in what appears to be the middle of a celebratory dance. *Dance* featured smart lyrics, but the jokes on the album proved that Pere Ubu bandmates were not ones to take themselves too seriously. Band member Ravenstine's synthesizer work is an especially prominent component of this record. Pere Ubu's next album, 1979's *Dub Housing*, showcased the band's experimental talents. With *Housing*, Ubu's fan base grew. The album is still considered an important album that is relevant almost 30 years after its initial release.

But by the time of Pere Ubu's 1979 album *New Picnic Time* (the album was originally—and ironically—titled "Goodbye"), the band's internal structure was beyond repair, and, citing creative roadblocks, the band broke up. Pere Ubu, however, managed to pick up the pieces a few months later, but bandmate Herman decided not to return. He was replaced Mayo Thompson, who had played with the Texas-based psychedelic rock band Red Krayola. Pere Ubu pursued a pop focus for its next album, 1980's *The Art of Walking*, which led to a tour of Europe, but this newfound well of creativity was not enough to sustain the band for long. Soon, a new drummer, Anton Fier, was brought in when Krauss left the band. And shortly after Pere Ubu's 1982 album, *Song of the Bailing Man*, was released, the band broke up yet again.

This time, though, Pere Ubu remained in fragment until Thomas recruited Ubu members for a side project of his in 1987. Five years after the band had disbanded and fresh from a much-needed break, Pere Ubu was inadvertently brought together again. The group's second coming produced what is widely considered a highly successful comeback album, 1988's *The Tenement Year*. The album, which many consider to be more commercial than the group's previous works, proved fruitful—both creatively and financially—for the group. A more accessible sound—clever yet personal lyrics and more straightforward rock sounds—plus the addition of new members percussionist Chris Cutler and guitarist Jim Jones (Thomas, synthesizer player and saxophonist Allen Ravenstine, bassist Tony Maimone, and drummer Scott Krauss were still in the fold) were evidence of a more solidified and focused Pere Ubu.

"Cloudland" (Polygram Records) appeared in 1989 and the band experienced its first-ever MTV single. "Waiting for Mary" received heavy rotation on the music channel, the album earned the band comparisons to the **Talking Heads**, and the band's star seemed to be rising higher. During the ascension, though, Ubu founding member Ravenstine left music behind altogether and began flying planes, and new addition Cutler exited the band. The dual exodus made room for Eric Drew Feldman, once a part of the Captain Beefheart lineup, to join the lineup for Pere Ubu's next effort, 1991's *Worlds in Collision*. Feldman, too, however, was drawn like a magnet to outside musical forces, and he joined **Frank Black**'s band. Pere Ubu seemed to be cursed by bandmates who came and went so quickly it seemed as though the band could not keep anyone for longer than one album. *Story of My Life*, another appropriately autobiographically titled album, appeared in 1993, and the four remaining members were soon left with three.

The 1996 five-disc box set, *Datapanik in the Year Zero*, celebrated Pere Ubu's contributions to the history of experimental music. It also served to lure Ubu alum

Thomas back into the fold, and Ubu's "weirdness" proved to be a power very few could resist. A string of side projects, pink slips, and miniature reunions ensued through the 2000s. Pere Ubu released the conversation-starting album *Why I Hate Women* on Morphius Records in 2006. *Women* was a magnified version of all things Ubu—Thomas's off-kilter vocal techniques, the band's envelope-pushing experimentalism, avante-punk sounds, and a weird mix of pop blueprints, shrieking synthesizers, and a general sense of weirdness that made Pere Ubu's music simultaneously time capsule–worthy and modern at the same time.

Further Readings: Rolling Stone Magazine. *The Rolling Stone Illustrated History of Rock and Roll: The Definitive History of the Most Important Artists and Their Music.* 3rd ed. New York: Random House, 1992; http://www.unwedsailor.net/.

PERFORMING SONGWRITER MAGAZINE

Few magazines these days cater to anyone but mainstream acts that are constantly heard on the radio—save for *Performing Songwriter* magazine, an independently owned and operated publication that aims to cover indie artists who are going it alone. The Nashville, Tennessee–based magazine, which was founded in 1993 by Lydia Hutchinson (in her guest bedroom, no less) features such artists as Ben Harper and **Liz Phair**.

The monthly publication, which Hutchinson claims to have created without any official or substantial start-up revenue, focuses on just what it states on the cover—performing songwriters. Cover subjects have included more well-known acts such as Bonnie Raitt, Keith Urban, and James Taylor, but the editorial goals of *Performing Songwriter,* which has a circulation of 55,000 and a readership of 130,000, are aimed at informing its readers about up-and-coming acts as well as veteran stage acts that have long paid their open mic dues.

Based in the heart of Nashville, a hotbed of hopeful singer-songwriters, *Performing Songwriter* has played a major role in the ever-growing **DIY (Do-It-Yourself)** movement that helps pump the lifeblood of indie rock—it is considered an indie "bible" of sorts to some. Having survived the highs and lows of the music business (folding labels, canceled recording contracts, censorship and even copyright issues), the magazine thrives on the fact that there is always a new crop of musicians and bands—even in the wake of the ever-changing music business landscape; it continues to be run by its founder, who also serves as the magazine's editor and publisher. The staff consists of less than a dozen music fans who help to produce the magazine's various sections—interviews, CD reviews, equipment and gear discussions, music charts, Music City profiles, and essays written by such guest writers as Roseanne Cash and Carly Simon.

Further Readings: Gaitskill, Mary, and Daphne Carr. *Da Capo Best Music Writing 2006.* Cambridge, MA: Da Capo Press, 2006; http://www.performingsongwriter.com.

PHAIR, LIZ

Widely considered one of the pioneering women in indie rock, Liz Phair made even bigger headlines a decade after the release of her debut album when Meghan

O'Rourke, a writer for Slate.com, claimed that the thin, blonde-haired, blue-eyed singer-songwriter "committed an embarrassing form of career suicide" by means of her self-titled fourth album when she chose to work with a blatantly commercial record production group known as The Matrix, which had worked on albums by pop punk princess Avril Lavigne. This partnership, for Phair, however, had all but wilted and destroyed her **DIY (Do-It-Yourself)** status as an indie rocker.

Media controversy aside, Phair built a reputation for herself and created quite a buzz in the early 1990s with her unique blend of **Lo-fi** music, sexually explicit lyrics, feminist attitude, and feisty in-your-face indie rock mentality. Born Elizabeth Clark Phair, Liz Phair was born on April 17, 1967, in New Haven, Connecticut, and was raised by her adoptive parents in Winnetka, Chicago. After studying art at Oberlin College in Ohio, Phair followed a pair of musician friends to San Francisco, where she struggled to make it as an artist selling charcoal drawings, so she attempted to kick-start her career with some homemade tapes that she made under the name Girlysound. Following her move back to Chicago, Phair met and befriended Brad Wood, who was then the drummer for the Chicago-based alternative rock band Urge Overkill, as well as record label head John Henderson, who ran the Chicago-based indie rock label Feel Good All Over.

True to form with the music industry, Phair's relationships within the music world helped her songs get into the hands of the head of Matador Records, Gerard Cosley. Cosley signed Phair in the summer of 1992, and she released her debut album, *Exile in Guyville* (1993), the title of which Phair adapted from an Urge Overkill song. The album garnered rave reviews from critics, but despite the support of media outlets like MTV, the album only sold just over 200,000 copies. Consequently, Phair struggled to enter the mainstream; but the singer, who plays guitar and piano, did not give up. Several fans and music insiders have reportedly said that the album would have had more success if it had been released in the heyday of the "women in rock" phase of 1996–1997. Still, *Exile* is considered one of the quintessential indie rock albums—in part because of her impressive guitar abilities on such songs as "Mesmerizing" and the feisty, catchy lyrics of the salaciously titled track "F- - - and Run." That album, due in large part to the fact that MTV aired the video for the song "Never Said" in heavy rotation, was a huge success and appeared on the Billboard charts, debuting at #27 and breaking records for an independent release.

Phair released her sophomore album, *Whip-Smart,* a year later and caught the attention of millions by appearing on the cover of *Rolling Stone* magazine in October 1994 wearing a barely there negligee. That same year, Phair launched her first tour, but the singer suffered from stage fright and experienced difficulties on stage. Despite the album's apparent success on paper (it contained "Supernova," which is still considered one of her signature songs and the first to make the Hot 100 at #78), the reviews were lukewarm and Phair never toured in support of the album.

In 1995, Phair married Chicago-based film editor Jim Staskausas, who had worked on some of her music videos. Ever the feminist, Phair retained her maiden name. In December 21, 1996, Phair gave birth to her first child, James Nicholas

Singer-songwriter Liz Phair performs at the Avalon Rock Club in Boston on October 14, 2005. [AP Wide World Photos/Robert E. Klein]

Staskausas. Phair reentered the music world with her third album in 1998, the more personal and somewhat autobiographical (and oddly titled) *Whitechocolatespaceegg*. The album, which critics claimed might have been too mature for her audience to grasp, maintained Phair's feisty persona; it debuted at #35 on Billboard's Top 200 albums chart. In 1998, Liz Phair appeared on the bill for three dates of the **Lilith Fair** as a substitute for Sheryl Crow.

Newly divorced and caring for her son as a single mom in Manhattan, Phair took a brief hiatus until 2003, when she signed to major label Capitol Records and, for her fourth studio album, the svelte singer sought the help of The Matrix, the "it" production team of the moment that helped Avril Lavigne cement her stardom. Phair collaborated with singer-songwriter Michael Penn (who produced several songs), Jimmy Chamberlin and Wendy Melvoin (both of whom were featured guests), and Pete Yorn (who collaborated with Phair on four of the album's songs) for the album. Little did the indie rock queen realize the price she would pay for enlisting The Matrix and turning down a road few indie rock artists have gone before. The slicker album, *Liz Phair* (Capitol Records, 2003), earned Phair a wash of criticism and backhanded remarks from fans and critics alike, who bashed the album and branded her a "sellout." But Phair, ever the tough-as-nails rocker, faced her attackers head-on by fighting back—her "no apologies" letter to the editor appeared in a 2003 edition of the *New York Times*.

Despite the smear campaign that it fueled, the self-titled album was considered a commercial success. The album's single "Why Can't I" peaked at #27 on the Billboard 200, and several of the album's songs appeared in soundtracks to various movies and television series, including the 2003 comedy starring Jennifer Garner, *13 Going on 30* and *The O.C.* Phair performed at the 2005 **Lollapalooza** music festival in her home base of Chicago. Addressing her critics, the single mom told MTV in a 2003 interview, "Way back in indie-ville, everyone was plotting about how huge they could be and all this crap, but nobody wanted to sober up enough to get up in the morning and actually find out what business is all about. My feeling is, your album will be sold through a distribution mechanism, whether you participate or not, and I think it's more revolutionary to be part of that" (Moss, 2003).

Phair shied away from the spotlight after the much-publicized criticism over her 2003 album, appearing sparingly in the media and keeping her involvement with the indie music scene light. She contributed backing vocals to the 2004 album by rock group Jimmy Eat World, and she made a cameo appearance on an episode of the NBC drama *American Dream* in which she portrayed 1960s singer Jackie DeShannon. Though not yet having completely rebounded from the media melee surrounding the release of her 2003 album, Phair released *Somebody's Miracle* (Capitol) in the fall of 2005.

Phair spoke out about the emotional impacts of adoption in an interview with *Women's Health* magazine in 2006. Phair joined the likes of indie rock singersongwriter/actress Minnie Driver as a collaborator on her 2007 sophomore album. Phair continued to post podcasts on her Web site through 2007.

In 2008, just about 15 years after the release of her seminal album, *Exile in Guyville,* Phair was listed among the greatest female guitarists by the female-centric music/arts/fashion magazine *VENUS*. Phair is marking the 15th anniversary of *Exile in Guyville* with the reissue of the disc, which will be released in the fall of 2008 by her new home, the independent label ATO Records. The reissue—which features four never-before-released songs from her original recording sessions—precedes Phair's newest studio album. Dave Matthews (the founder and co-owner of ATO) makes a special cameo appearance on the co-released DVD *Guyville Redux,* a 60-minute DVD that accompanies the reissued album.

Further Readings: Freedman, Estelle. *No Turning Back: The History of Feminism and the Future of Women.* New York: Ballantine Books, 2003; Joy, Camden. *The Last Rock Star Book: Or Liz Phair, a Rant.* Portland, OR: Verse Chorus Press, 1998; http://www. capitolrecords.com; http://www.lizphair.com; http://www.matadorrecords.com/liz_phair.

PITCHFORK MEDIA

It is becoming more and more important for bands nowadays to develop a strong online presence. The Chicago-based music review site, or "music webzine," as it has been called, Pitchfork Media, is among the top online sites that can give a band gold-star status (the others being MySpace and YouTube). The "tastemaker" site, which generates revenue through advertisements, receives a reported 1.3 million unique visitors per month.

Touting itself as "a web site dedicated to music and the discussion thereof," Pitchfork Media's erudite staff's addition, "And we rule" (www.aboutus.org/Pitchforkmedia), to that previous statement sheds some light on Pitchfork Media's reputation for brutal honesty, extraneously opinionated reviews, and harsh criticism. But, along with that cache, the site has been known to help make the careers of new and relatively unknown bands—just by publishing (the rarely seen) glowing review. For instance, then unknown Detroit rock duo **The White Stripes**' popularity soared after Pitchfork Media posted a 8.9 (out of 9) review of the group's 2002 album, *De Stijl*. New York City golden boys The Strokes reaped similar benefits when the site showered the band with such raves, and the manager of the indie band Tapes 'n Tapes credits its success with a positive review from the site.

However, Pitchfork Media has not always been that easy to please. The site's reputation is often preceded by the staff writers' finicky tastes and their affinity to shower bands whose work they consider to be less worthy with what can be construed as "snide" comments and overly editorialized or opinionated remarks. Since its inception in 1995 by creator Ryan Schrieber, then a high school graduate who had a lot of experience reading and collecting music zines, but little to no previous writing experience or journalism training, Pitchfork Media has risen to the upper echelons of rock's social scene and has become a centrifugal force of the indie rock genre. The Chicago-based site reviews music mainly in the independent rock vein; but it also posts news, reviews, and columns about bands within other genres such as jazz, pop, dance, electronic, hip-hop, and folk.

Pitchfork Media, which was briefly known as Turntable, posts breaking news, album and track reviews (as well as reissues and boxed sets), interviews, regular columns, free music downloads, and highly anticipated top albums and singles lists. The site also has its own music festival, and it has reached beyond the circle of those "in the know" to gaining a strong online (and even mainstream) presence for anyone perusing the Internet for the latest in music. Schreiber reportedly named the site for Al Pacino's character's tattoo in the 1983 film *Scarface*.

Yet despite the site's infamous reputation for running highly opinionated, often elitist reviews by its writers, Pitchfork Media's success has never waned. Instead it has increased in popularity, presence, and prestige; and with that also come parodies and criticism. Most memorable, perhaps, was a comment by comedian David Cross, star of the HBO comedy series *Mr. Show,* who took a jab at the site with his 2005 list of favorite CDs. Cross, who was invited by the site to compile the list, titled it "Top Ten CDs That I Just Made Up (and accompanying made-up review excerpts) to listen to while skimming through some of the overwrought reviews on Pitchforkmedia.com" (http://www.pitchforkmedia.com/article/feature/10279-guest-list-david-cross-albums-to-listen-to-while-reading-overwrought-pitchfork-reviews) in a an effort to retaliate against a critical review that one of the site's writers had recently posted about his 2004 comedy album, "It's Not Funny" (**Sub Pop Records**). The staff at Pitchfork Media, however, was able to resist the urge to take itself too seriously and posted the list. A drinking game based on PitchforkMedia's content (such as album ratings) has been circulated on the Internet by a blog associated with the comedy magazine *Cracked*.

Pitchfork Media's reviews of albums by such indie acts as **Arcade Fire**, **Sufjan Stevens**, **Broken Social Scene**, **Clap Your Hands Say Yeah**, and other indie rock bands certainly helped to boost their careers. Record labels have even claimed that they have run out of print runs of their band's records after receiving a positive review on the site. While it may seem that a scathing review would hurt a band's success, such negative reviews actually seem to have a "sticks and stones" effect, since none of them have decidedly destroyed a band's career. The site has, however, posted lists that boldly showcase the site's cynical attitude toward the music industry—such as Schreiber's own "The 15 Worst Releases of 2005," in which he stated, "When I look back at all the absolute garbage releases this year, it makes me wonder how we can remain so consistently optimistic about the state of music" (http://www.pitchforkmedia.com/article/feature/10352-staff-list-2005-comments-lists-the-15-worst-releases-of-2005).

Only a handful of albums have received the site's top honors—a perfect 10.0 out of 10.0 rating. They include Wilco's 2002 album, *Yankee Hotel Foxtrot,* and full-lengths by Miles Davis, **Radiohead**, . . . **And You Will Know Us By the Trail of Dead**, and **The Flaming Lips**. Countless others (such as indie rock icons **Sonic Youth**'s 2000 album, *NYC Ghosts & Flowers,* and full-length albums by KISS, **Liz Phair**, and **The Flaming Lips**) have garnered 0.0 ratings. The Web site itself has been written up by prominent news sources like the Associated Press and the *New York Times,* which, in a 2005 article, said, "Pitchfork has emerged as one of the more important indie taste-makers in any medium" (Carr, 2005). In a 2006 *Washington Post* article, for which one of its reporters shadowed the site's Editor-in-Chief at **South by Southwest (SXSW)** in Austin, Texas, a staff member for London's Reckless Records claimed he follows content on the site "the way a stockbroker might monitor CNBC" (Freedom du Lac, 2006).

Pitchfork Media has inspired similar Web sites, and it outranks *Rolling Stone* on Amazon.com's top music sites list, which put the site before the 30-plus-year-old music magazine, citing Pitchfork Media reviews alongside its own online "Best Of" CD lists. The *Washington Post* ran an article about Pitchfork Media in April 2006, entitled "Giving Indie Acts A Plug, or Pulling It," discussing the impact its reviews have on the future of (and sales of albums by) featured bands. According to the *Post,* "Pitchfork has achieved a sort of mythical status, like an indie-rock yogi: Readers climb the digital mountaintop to see what wisdom its team of freelance writers might dispense about this off-the-radar band or that one, and then they act accordingly—as happened two years ago, when Pitchfork published its now-famous 9.7-point review of 'Funeral,' by the relatively unknown Canadian band Arcade Fire. 'Funeral' became the fastest-selling title in the history of Merge Records" (Freedom du Lac, 2006). The *Post* also suggested that the site could possibly be poised to become "the new *Rolling Stone*" (Freedom du Lac, 2006).

Schrieber still tops the masthead as Editor-in-Chief, employing countless unfiltered and brutally honest writers and reviewers and a staff of over 20 editors, photographers, and interns. The site reportedly receives approximately 150,000–160,000 readers a day and 1.2 million unique hits each month. Pitchfork Media launched several music festivals, including the Intonation Music Festival, which was held in Chicago's Union Park in July 2005, featuring **The Decemberists** and **Broken Social Scene**. The Pitchfork Music Festival, which occurred at the very same park in the same month of 2006, featured bands The Wrens and **Out Hud**. The 2006 Pitchfork Music Festival sold out quickly at 15,000 tickets per day—the park's capacity is 30,000 people, but Schreiber was concerned about overcrowding. Approximately 36,000 fans attended the 2006 festival to see the 41-odd bands on that year's lineup—**Mission of Burma**, **Ted Leo and the Pharmacists**, Hot Machines, The National, and more.

Over 100 tickets were sold to the 2007 concert within the first minute; one-day passes cost $25 and two-day passes cost $35. Pitchfork announced the debut of its 2007 **South by Southwest (SXSW)** music festival party, a sort of miniature indoor version of the Pitchfork Music Festival, at which the 2007 lineup was announced. Bands that performed at the party included all-girl British pop group The Pipettes, Crystal Castles (the Canadian band that shares the name of the 1980s Atari video arcade game), and the punk/psychedelic act Deerhunter, among others.

A 2006 feature article posted on the Web site for California-based technology magazine *Wired* discussed Pitchfork Media's impact on the career of the indie group **Broken Social Scene**, stating that after the site's Editor-in-Chief posted a 9.2 out of 10 rating, the group's fate was sealed—and destined for success. The same article credited the site for stealing the fanfare—and readership—of established music magazines such as *SPIN* (Itzkoff, 2006). Self-proclaimed "music nerds" flock to the site daily for the latest news, gossip, and reviews (and even podcasts)—the site even has an RSS (really simple syndication) feed that automatically updates subscribers on daily content. Naysayers who are turned off by the site's "snobby" reviews choose to get their music information from competitive sites like Popmatters.com and Metacritic.com.

Further Readings: Pruett, Jon, and Mike McGuirk. *The Music Festival Guide: For Music Lovers and Musicians.* Chicago: Chicago Review Press, 2004; http://www.myspace.com; http://www.pitchforkmusicfestival.com.

PIXIES

Widely considered the seminal indie (or alternative) rock band of the 1990s for many reasons, the Pixies not only developed a huge college student and indie fan cult following for its musical ingenuity, but the group also created a spot for itself in the pages of music history for the development of a new blend of rock, pop, and indie music. The Pixies' sound, persona, and attitude influenced countless bands, and its unique songwriting style made the group a legend in the eyes of its peers. The Pixies were also highly prolific, and its original, emotive, and catchy music has made the group an icon in the world of indie rock.

The Boston-based band's road to stardom, however, was not as smooth and golden as its melodic pop effects may have led some to believe—front man **Frank Black** and the band's bassist, Kim Deal, who feuded over Deal's push to incorporate her songwriting into the band's canon of music, fueled tensions within the band that contributed to its breakup in 1993.

Early on, MTV was hard-pressed to air the group's videos, and radio found no reason to play its songs. The group's enigmatic lyrics added to the group's mysterious underbelly, and the band's front man, **Frank Black**, struggled with personal demons during his solo career after the band called it quits. Still, struggle being the epitome of rites of passage for bands across the indie genre, the band rose above it all with its music—and the unforgettable hooks in the group's shiny pop-infused singles—emerging as the undisputed champions of indie rock that, like another fledgling band called **Nirvana**, helped break indie rock into the mainstream.

The Pixies, whose noisy, surf, and punk rock–influenced sound left behind a legacy few bands have been able to replicate, were formed in the mid-1980s by University of Massachusetts college students guitarist Joey Santiago and drummer Charles Thompson. Bassist Kim Deal joined the band after answering a newspaper ad in which the band sought out a musician who liked the music of **Hüsker Dü**. Thompson adopted his signature stage names **Frank Black** and Black Francis, and the bandmates settled on the band name the Pixies when Santiago found the word in the dictionary one lazy Massachusetts afternoon.

The Pixies scored an opening slot for the alt rock band Throwing Muses, the first act signed by 4AD Records; while on tour, producer/manager Gary Smith heard the band's music and was instantly convinced the group was headed for stardom. Smith recorded the foursome's demo, "The Purple Tape," which the group circulated around the Boston area. The tape, which made instant cult heroes out of the group for local Beantowners, made its way into the hands of 4AD record head Ivo Watts-Russell, who signed the band in 1987. 4AD re-released the demo as the LP *Come On Pilgrim* before the group headed into the studio with producer Steve Albini for its debut full-length album, *Surfer Rosa*. The combination of Black's deep-throated warble, Deal's showy bass lines, and the rest of the band's raw rock/pop prowess convinced fans that Watts was correct in his assessment—Boston had a new team of hometown heroes.

Still, despite the group's success, the Pixies enjoyed bigger success across the pond in Britain, where fans gobbled up the group's sweet yet tangy music as fast as the group could create it. Riding high on its successes, the Pixies signed to Elektra Records for the release of its sophomore album, *Doolittle* (1989), a dynamic album that featured two of the group's—and indie rock's—biggest songs: "Here Comes Your Man" and "Monkey Gone to Heaven." A substantial tour followed in support of *Doolittle*, but increasing strain resulting from interpersonal disputes forced the band apart. The Pixies took a brief hiatus in 1990, after which Black pursued a solo career, and Deal formed the alt rock group The Breeders.

The band regrouped in late 1990 for *Bossanova,* a more fragmented, arty record that fans claimed was the odd-man-out in the group's catalog. A tour in support of *Bossanova* was canceled due to bandwide "exhaustion," but fans knew the end was drawing near for the versatile quartet. Black's solo career flourished and waned, The Breeders hit Gold with the 1993 single "Cannonball," and Elektra/4AD attempted to relight the fire that fueled the band's fan base with the release of the archive collection *Death to the Pixies: 1987–1991,* as well as a recording the band made at the BBC and B-sides albums, but the bandmates remained apart.

Black, who had invited Santiago to join him on stage during the dark sunglasses–favoring ex-Pixies front man's concerts during the time he was promoting his 2001 album, *Dog in the Sand,* announced to the press that he was entertaining the idea of patching things up with Deal and getting the band back together in 2004. The dream came true for dedicated Pixies' fans when the Boston quartet kicked off its official reunion tour that same year, hitting cities across North America and Europe. One thousand limited edition copies of the band's 15 reunion gigs were released soon after. 4AD released the live DVD retrospective *Wave of Mutilation: The Best of the Pixies* in 2004, right after the group's highly publicized performance at that year's **Coachella Valley Music and Arts Festival** in Indio, California. But the magic did not last long—the band that was the Pixies did not forge on into the new decade; its members soldiered on to pursue their own musical endeavors, leaving behind a legacy no other indie band has since been able to rival.

The Pixies band members, though, continue to sprinkle the news— in 2008 former Pixies guitarist Joey Santiago provided music for a Nike-sponsored soccer documentary, while Black Francis caused a ruckus in February when he played a free show before his gig in Dublin. Francis's newest solo album, *Fast Man/Raider Man,* was released in June; it was recorded over two years in Los Angeles and Nashville. The Pixies planned to release DVDs of the band's reunion tour, while rumors circulated that the bandmates would record their first studio album together since 1991's *Trompe Le Monde.*

Further Readings: Frank, Josh. *Fool the World: The Oral History of a Band Called Pixies.* Chicago: St. Martin's Griffin, 2006; http://www.4ad.com/pixies; http://www.4ad.com/throwingmuses.

THE POLYPHONIC SPREE

With their flowing, multicolored floor-length robes and ballroom-filling parade of band members, this Dallas, Texas–based group more closely resembles a church choir or a band of devout missionaries than a group of performers whose mission it is to help you let the group's unadulterated **indie pop** music into your heart. Despite the bandmates' monk-like attire, The Polyphonic Spree is not a religious group nor does it adhere to any denominational decrees. Formed by Tim DeLaughter, the band—which at times surges on stage at 20-plus members—

Vocalist Tim Delaughter (center) of The Polyphonic Spree performs with bandmates as the opening band for David Bowie at the Fleet Center in Boston on March 30, 2004. [AP Wide World Photos/Robert E. Klein]

was formed after the Texas-born musician's former band, Tripping Daisy, fell apart following the sad death of his bandmate, Wes Berggren.

The aesthetic and structure of the group were designed in the same vein as 1960s pop groups that sounded as though they had invited hordes of people on stage to sing their sunny choruses. The band created a demo, "The Beginning Stages of . . ." and circulated it to friends and family. The demo made its way into the hands of the people at Good Records, a Texas-based independent label that released the album in 2002. The lush harmonies and choir-style backing vocals served as a sunny backdrop to DeLaughter's Beatles-like arrangements and the full sounds of the group's 13-member band that resembled the lineup of instruments more commonly found at an elementary school recital than on stages at indie rock venues—a trombone, violin, theremin, flute, French horn, and more. The upbeat *Stages* was a venerable "upper" record that, despite its kitsch factor, lent a certain amount of cache to the group's gimmicky persona.

With DeLaughter at the helm as musical director and lead vocalist, The Polyphonic Spree, which tours in a parade of colorful vans, composed a song for a Volkswagen commercial in 2003. Unlike other bands that have suffered criticism for selling their songs to harp products in order to further capitalist gain, The Polyphonic Spree's out-there antics seemed a proper fit for the avant-garde commercial. The group toured aggressively, including opening for David Bowie on a few dates of his sold-out 2004 tour, and released its first official full-length album, *Together We're Heavy* (Hollywood Records) that same year. The two-disc album, broken up into "sections," was more of a concept album than a standard release that served as a sequel to the group's first album instead of a stand-alone record. "*Heavy*" combined sounds of the 1960s, the 1970s, and the 1990s in a more polished effort that showed that DeLaughter had bigger plans up that oversized sleeve of his.

The Polyphonic Spree joined the late **Elliott Smith** to contribute songs to the soundtrack for the independent film *Thumbsucker* in 2005. The Polyphonic Spree's 2007 EP, *Wait,* took a surprisingly dark turn, but the sun shone again with the group's 2007 full-length, *The Fragile Army* (TVT Records). *Army,* for which the bandmates swapped their rainbow-colored robes for dark, military-style outfits on stage, continued where *Heavy* left off, adding sections 21–32. The record was such a hit that even glam rocker David Bowie told the press at one of the group's shows at New York City's Grand Ballroom that it was the group's "best and deepest album yet" (www.aquariusrecords.com). The Polyphonic Spree took its whirlwind musical army on tour in support of *Army* in the summer of 2007; the bandmates kicked off the tour with a show in their hometown of Dallas, Texas. The band was showcased in the Bigger Picture Concert Series, a collection of films shot at the **South by Southwest (SXSW)** music festival in Austin, Texas.

Further Readings: Brunning, Bob. *1960s Pop.* New York: Peter Bedrick Books, 2001; http://www.goodrecords.com; http://www.hollywoodrecords.go.com; http://www.thebiggerpicture.us/sxsw.html; http://www.thepolyphonicspree.com.

POP PUNK

The term pop punk was first coined in the 1970s back when such bands as the Buzzcocks, the **Ramones**, The Undertones, and The Jams experimented with the two dichotomous sounds (and the alter egos that accompanied them) in a playful manner. The result of this mix was fast-paced, yet catchy chord progressions and emotive, yet rhythmic choruses.

In the 1980s, pop punk music was headed in the direction toward ear-pleasing pop music of the day and away from the harsher, edgier punk sounds. The California-based record label Lookout! Records signed several pop punk artists during this time, helping the subgenre to gain roots and grow in popularity. **Green Day** spearheaded the pop punk movement during this era, with its playful lyrics, yet thunderous drum beats, edgy guitars, and feisty punk-like persona. Still, **Green Day**'s music swayed toward the pop side of the music spectrum, and its songs were in heavy rotation on mainstream radio. **Green Day**'s history, sound, look, and music are a great example of the thin line that pop punk teeters on between indie and mainstream.

Green Day and its record label, Reprise Records, were involved in a mini scandal that was a foreshadow of things to come. When **Green Day** released its 1994 album, *Dookie,* fans started whispering the word "sellout." But soon, the whisper turned into a shout, and there was an all-out on-paper-and-blog war over the issue. **Green Day**, which had for years been signed to smaller indie labels, took hold of that music business Holy Grail, the major label recording contract, when it signed to Reprise. Reprise paid for the recording and production of *Dookie,* a hugely successful album that gave the band exactly what it had been hoping for—exposure to a bigger audience, namely the mainstream masses. The immense success of *Dookie* was a defining moment in the band's history—it quickly sold over 7 million copies (http://top40.about.com/od/artistsdk/gr/greendaydookie.htm). Loyal fans considered the band and the album "sellouts" in that the album was liked and enjoyed (and bought) by so many Top 40–loving fans. Pop punk took a turn from being a sonically experimental, tongue-in-cheek subgenre to what some saw as being a commercialized, bought-and-sold commodity.

Blink-182 was an even louder, more rambunctious manifestation of the direction pop punk was headed in the 1980s to the early 1990s. The group's playful, irresponsible teenager persona, mixed with punk-inspired riffs and off-kilter sense of humor put it right smack dab on the line between pop and punk, making the seminal pop punk band of the next decade. This splintering off of pop punk sound and attitude soon thinned the subgenre out even more, and bands that veered even closer to the pop side started popping up all over the world. Canadian rockers Sum 41, on the other hand, with their MTV-affected hair styles and Hot Topic wardrobe, helped to usher in the next phase of pop punk history. Bands such as Good Charlotte, Simple Plan, and Bowling for Soup, each of which has its own regard for the punk legends of yesteryear, are pop punk bands that are considered by some to rest on the bubblegum pop side of the spectrum. Other pop punk bands that have popped up in the subgenre include The Offspring, Taking Back Sunday, Saves the Day, and Weezer, a band that has become phenomenally successful on both the indie and mainstream sides of the record store.

Today, however, 30 years after the original pop punk bands played mad scientists with this oxymoronic mix, the term pop punk has absorbed some negative undertones and has been associated with bands that some punk fans may refer to as "poseurs." More clearly, the term pop punk has been used to describe musical acts such as Avril Lavigne, The All-American Rejects, and other acts that have appeared on the Top 40 musical charts. In the eyes of some punk fans, these bands are more bubblegum pop than their pop punk predecessors. Therefore, the punk affects and aesthetic that these acts have absorbed into their images are mere theater parlor tricks than true punk rock acts. The result has been that the term is being used as a derogatory phrase associated with acts that have more in common with Britney Spears than Blondie. Modern pop punk bands, however, have proven that they know the marketplace; several pop punk acts, such as Fall Out Boy, have consistently and continually topped the billboard charts with their music.

Further Reading: Diehl, Matt. *My So-Called Punk: Green Day, Fall Out Boy, The Distillers, Bad Religion—How Neo-Punk Stage-Dived into the Mainstream.* New York: St. Martin's Griffin, 2007; http://top40.about.com/od/artistsdk/gr/greendaydookie.htm.

POST-PUNK

Post-punk is a genre of music that got its start at the beginning of the 1980s when bands that were influenced by the 1960's and the 1970's forefathers of punk decided to carry on the torch. The term "post" was attached to the subgenre when, with the turn of the century, music was heading in the direction of alternative rock. This revivalist punk movement was spearheaded by bands such as Gang of Four, **Talking Heads**, The Fall, The Human League, Adam & the Ants, **Aztec Camera**, Cabaret Voltaire, Wire, Contortions, Joy Division, The Raincoats, **Big Black**, Killing Joke, **Mission of Burma**, and **Orange Juice**, all of which have in some way continued the punk tradition in the spirit of their music and shared the punk aesthetic of their idols.

A post-punk revival occurred again in the 2000s when bands that honored punk bands started making music akin to that of acts such as the **Ramones**, The Clash, and the Sex Pistols. Post-punk artists, however, were more adept at (and forgiving of) creating radio-friendly tracks than their forefathers who may have considered such an act as crossing the line of "selling out." Post-punk acts, on the other hand, released music they simply felt was more accessible to fans that respected the work of groundbreaking punk bands.

The entire post-punk stream of history, starting with early post-punk bands in the 1980s—groups such as Big Flame, Wire, Gang of Four, and Joy Division—was simply the first wave of punk admirers to play their own hybrid of punk music. Bands in the 2000s (such as **The Rapture**, The Strokes, and **Franz Ferdinand**) honored the punk pioneers while adding a twist of new wave music.

Post-punk groups really took liberty with their sounds. While their inherent sound or framework was rooted in punk, their music was creatively their own. Such experimentalism set the stage for the future of underground music, creating a perception of unlimited sonic possibility. Post-punk rockers strove to maintain the common thread of punk music—that of fast-paced songs created or built around a few simple chords and basic song structures.

Recognizing a growing trend, record labels such as **Rough Trade Records**, 4AD, Mute Records, and Factory Records signed post-punk artists and fostered their efforts to pay tribute to the past while making waves for the future. Consequently, with so many post-punk artists creating so many diverse sounds and albums, the meaning of the term "post-punk" began to thin out. Post-punk, however, retained its respectability within the underground scene. Still, post-punk helped with the birth of newer hybrids and offshoots of subgenres such as new wave, goth rock, no wave, and alternative rock.

Further Reading: Reynolds, Simon. *Rip It Up and Start Again: Postpunk 1978–1984.* New York: Penguin, Feb. 2006; Sabin, Roger. *Punk Rock: So What? The Cultural Legacy of Punk.* New York: Routledge, July 1999; http://www.post-punk.com.

POST-ROCK

Post-rock is a highly experimental form of indie rock whose description sounds more like a jigsaw puzzle than a subgenre of music. Post-rockers take traditional rock sounds and foundations—guitar, bass, and drums—and mix them up in new creative ways to make groundbreaking new sounds. This so-called rock "instrumentation" means that post-rockers use all of the ingredients of traditional rock bands, but they create full, sweeping chord progressions, rhythms, melodies, and harmonies.

In other words, post-rockers are minimalists that create mostly instrumental pieces employing less commonly used instruments such as oboes, cellos, the piano, synthesizers, and such in their rock compositions. Post-rockers' music is actually not typically similar in sound to indie rock, but it is categorized as such for its experimental and **DIY (Do-It-Yourself)** nature. Post-rock music is also usually ambient and can also include acts from other subgenres such as **shoegazing**, space rock, art rock, and progressive rock movements. Post-rockers were also among the first acts to combine electronically generated and digitally made music with traditional rock instruments.

The term "post-rock" was reportedly coined by music journalist Simon Reynolds in the mid-1990s who said that they were "using rock instrumentation for non-rock purposes" (http://music.download.com/2001-8606_32-0.html). Notable post-rock acts include Slint, Talk Talk, Flying Saucer Attack, Mogwai, Stereolab, Godspeed You Black Emperor, Cul de Sac, Tortoise, the beautiful, ethereal arrangements of the **Rachel's**, and Sigur Rós. Post-rock rose to popularity in the late 1980s and the early 1990s as indie fans were slowly introduced to rock music that was full of sweeping orchestral arrangements, out-of-this-world string sections, heavenly chord progressions, and lyric-less songs that seem to speak louder than other rock songs with screaming singers.

Chicago, Illinois, became a hub for post-rock when the group Tortoise formed in 1990. The minimalist, jazz- and electronica-influenced act was also considered a pioneer of the post-rock sound for its clever instrumentation, blend of genres, and unique combination of instruments. Tortoise member John McEntire and his musician friend Jim O'Rourke became known as important post-rock producers. Post-rock music has often been compared to the musical works of big-name producers Brian Eno and the classical composer Phillip Glass. The rich, textured sound of post-rock has become attractive to bands in other genres such as metal acts that have been experimenting with yet another subgenre that has been coined "post-metal."

Further Reading: Berger, Harris M. *Metal, Rock, and Jazz: Perception and the Phenomenology of Musical Experience (Music Culture)*. Middletown, CT: Wesleyan University Press, 1999; http://music.download.com/2001-8606_32-0.html.

Q

Q AND NOT U

D.C., **DIY (Do It Yourself)**, Dischord (Records), democracy, and **dance punk**—these are the five D's that might have summed up the career of Q and Not U. While Q and Not U grew up amid the punk scene in Washington, D.C., the band often defied strict categorization. Its sound initially contained elements of what would eventually be defined as **dance punk**: needly guitars, vocals that shifted from pouty to desperate to screamo, punched-up disco drum passages, and synthesizer parts that turned on a dime from 1970s funk to Casio-sample Latin. As the quartet grew, Q and Not U accumulated a variety of different styles without being bogged down by its versatility—a quality that became the band's central strength.

Though Q and Not U broke up in 2005, its origins characterized the lively grassroots indie music scene of Washington, D.C., during the late 1990s. Vocalists/guitarists Christopher Richards and Harris Klahr, bassist Matt Borlik, and drummer John Davis converged not in finished suburban basements but amid the distorted noise of such venues as the Black Cat, which also was a springboard for the careers of such bands as Dead Meadow and **Ted Leo and the Pharmacists**.

At a time when every D.C. suburbanite with body piercings and patch-covered jean jackets seemed to have been playing together in a band since his or her pre-teens, Q and Not U stumbled together in 1998 after each one left his previous groups. Richards originally played in a band with Borlik's younger brother, Borlik played in a band of his own, and the three often played shows together in Maryland and D.C. Davis drummed for the prog-tinged outfit Corm, which disbanded in 1997, while Klahr played guitar for the Glenmont Sound System, which broke up shortly before the formation of Q and Not U.

Q and Not U quickly signed to the punk label Dischord Records after Ian MacKaye, the label's co-owner (and **Fugazi** and Minor Threat front man), attended one of the band's shows. The band's first single, "Hot and Informed," was released in 1999, and in 2000, Q and Not U's first full-length album, *No Kill No Beep Beep,* hit record stores. The album was lauded by critics and attracted a small group of loyal listeners. In keeping with Dischord Records' **DIY (Do-It-Yourself)** traditions, Q and Not U managed its own tour schedule and handled its own marketing. And like many Dischord bands, Q and Not U also wrote progressive, politically charged lyrics, but the band's lyrics were broad enough to avoid the anger and preachiness that often pigeonholed other bands on the label.

Due to creative differences, Borlik left Q and Not U in 2001. Rather than audition for a full-time bassist, Richards, Klahr, and Davis spent the rest of the band's duration exploring the possibilities of a three-piece band. The offerings on Q and Not U's 2002 release, *Different Damage,* were wirier, scrappier, and ultimately more ambitious. The band seemed to lock in as a three-piece on 2004's *Power.* The drums served the songs more, the twitchy guitars settled into a jangle, and the band's pop core was ultimately solidified. The tracks "Wonderful People" and "Book of Flags" most strongly emphasized this development.

Q and Not U's 2005 breakup was largely drama-free. Richards, Klahr, and David simply agreed that it was time to discontinue the band. However, several spin-offs grew from Q and Not U's breakup. In 2005, Richards began performing under the name Ris Paul Ric. In 2006, Richards also formed Rubber Bullets with Baltimore's DJ Dave Nada. Davis collaborated with vocalist Laura Burhenn to form Georgie James, a poppy, ballad-prone duo whose debut single, "Need Your Needs," was released in January 2007. Richards accepted the job of editor of the New York–based music magazine *FADER* in 2008.

Further Readings: MacKaye, Ian, Susie Horgan, and Henry Rollins. *Punk Love.* New York: Universe, 2007; http://www.dischord.com; http://www.myspace.com/cormdc; http://www.myspace.com/georgiejames; http://www.myspace.com/rispaulric; http://www.tweedmag.com.

RACHEL'S

You might not think classical orchestration has any place in the indie rock genre, but this Louisville, Kentucky trio has proven that indie rock can be stunning, lyric-less, and **DIY (Do-It-Yourself)** all at the same time. Typically described as a classical **post-rock** group, the Rachel's—violist Christian Frederickson, pianist Rachel Grimes, and guitarist Jason Noble—was originally a solo effort started by Noble, but once the trio started working together, the fit seemed natural.

Influenced by the work of English composer Michael Nyman, the Rachel's draw on their classical roots to create sweeping arrangements that are more emotive than many indie albums filled with heart-spilling lyrics. The Rachel's tour regularly—but the group does not perform in the traditional indie rock venues; the group instead chooses to perform at settings more befitting its haunting compositions—libraries, bowling alleys, churches, and even the occasional movie theater or ballroom.

The Rachel's debut album, *Handwriting* (Touch and Go's Quarter Stick Records, 1995) proved wrong the skeptics who thought the pairing of an indie rocker with two classical musicians would result in a bunch of off-center clamoring and nonsensical noise. *Handwriting* helped the Rachel's kick off a career of creating beautiful music that could possess the poignancy of indie rock while following the rhyme and reason of classical music.

The sophomore effort *Music for Egon Schiele* (Quarter Stick Records, 1996) is the Rachel's most striking recording to date. Filled with a dozen tracks, the album was a companion to a production to a theater-dance performance about the painter of the same name; the tracks flow in an uneven ebb and swell that takes the listener on an emotional journey that only a select few of the artists within the indie rock genre have been able to do. All of the tracks on the album, which were written by Grimes, seem to be woven together as though they were part of a soundtrack to a silent movie.

For the group's follow-up album, *The Sea and the Bells* (Quarter Stick, 1996), the Rachel's contracted a dozen or more musicians to bring its original compositions to life. No less stunning than the group's previous two efforts, *Sea* continues to blur the line between worlds dominated by **Pavement** and Sergei Prokofiev. the Rachel's have also contributed and composed music for films and live theatrical performances; its music has appeared in such works as Oliver Stone's 1999 film, *Any Given Sunday*.

By the release of the group's 1999 album, *Selenography* (Quarter Stick) the Rachel's had added additional members and swelled to a total of ten members. *Selenography* gave life to the group's more complex ambitions in a more imaginary realm. The Rachel's released a split CD in 2000 with label mates Matmos before releasing the results of years of crafting new material with the groups' 2003 effort, *Systems/Layers* (Quarter Stick). Considered an essential for indie rock lovers with a penchant for the unusual, *Systems/Layers* further supported the theory that the Rachel's hybrid music was more than a gimmicky effort to move albums; it was truly another feat in a catalog of records created by a group with the ambition to go where no other indie act had gone before.

The Rachel's continued to tour through 2005 in support of *Systems/Layers,* but not much was heard from the Rachel's camp in the years following its release. Rumors circulated about a follow-up album, but after a record failed to surface in 2007, fans resorted to holding their breaths again (although the group did contribute songs in 2007 to a new horror film based on the works of the author H. P. Lovecraft). The band announced its continued hiatus in 2008 as its members focused on various side projects.

Further Readings: Jones, Michael. *Second-Hand Stories: 15 Portraits of Louisville.* Lulu. com, 2006; http://www.prokofiev.org; http://www.rachelsband.com; http://www. touchandgorecords.com.

RADIOHEAD

Often considered one of the most important and influential rock bands of all time, Radiohead formed in 1988 in England. These purveyors of experimental electronic music blend rock, bits of jazz, classical, computer-generated sound effects, and angst-filled lyrics that many consider to have been influenced by the sounds of such bands as **R.E.M.**, **My Bloody Valentine**, and even Pink Floyd.

Radiohead—Oxford University students front man/guitarist Thom Yorke, guitarist Jonny Greenwood, guitarist/vocalist Ed O'Brien, bassist Colin Greenwood, and drummer Phil Selway—seemingly came out of nowhere, mesmerizing American fans with the hit single "Creep" from the group's 1993 debut album, *Pablo Honey* (Capitol Records). With some help from college radio, the band's music became increasingly popular, and the band put out its follow-up album, 1995's *The Bends* (Capitol). Radiohead's swirling Brit pop sound, computerized sound effects, haunting guitar riffs, and Yorke's sweeping, yet phantasmic vocal style proved the band was more than a one-hit wonder, and the music industry realized the band had unlimited experimental ability and potential.

Radiohead had what seemed like overnight commercial success, but with each album the group put out it seemed to be trying to step back from that arena to keep making accessible yet thought-provoking music. Radiohead's videos went into heavy airplay on MTV and mainstream radio, but its approach to music remained independent in nature. "Creep" went straight to the top of the charts, and the band toured as the opening act for such groups as Tears for Fears. With Radiohead's futuristic sound and space-man-like computer programmed effects,

Radiohead was poised to usher in a new genre of electronic music that both mainstream and underground fans enjoy. The success of the surreal single "Fake Plastic Trees" from *The Bends* helped the album reach Gold status.

The band's next album, 1997's *OK Computer,* did not quite reach Gold status, but it is considered one of the group's seminal works. The eerie sound of Yorke's voice and the catchy rack "Karma Police" helped the album to hit #21 on the Billboard charts ("Karma" peaked on the Modern Rock charts), and the album earned the group its first Grammy nod (and award) in 1998 for Album of the Year.

Years of touring had ceased for the band as it worked on its follow-up albums, the highly anticipated *Kid A* (Capitol, 2000) and *Amnesiac* (Capitol, 2001), two albums that sent the band's success into the stratosphere. The albums were essentially two pieces of a 20-plus song recording session that the band had done; the result was two separate albums that complemented each other well while being able to stand alone, and it seemed like yet another simple feat for the English rockers. The first album, *Kid A,* surprised fans in that it was a radical change in musical direction for the band. Though the band lineup was intact, the group left behind all of its previous musical ideas and blueprints and forged forward with a completely guitar-free atmospheric landscape that instead included synthesizers, loops. and computerized sound effects. *Kid A* earned the group a 2001 Grammy for Best Alternative Album and sold 55,000 copies on its first day in stores (http://news.bbc.co.uk/2/hi/entertainment/955767.stm). *Amnesiac* received a 10.0 rating from the critics at **Pitchfork Media**, in which the reviewer called Radiohead the "greatest band alive" (DiCrescenzo, n.d.). *Amnesiac* hit #1 in the United States and #2 in the United Kingdom. Radiohead kicked off a massive world tour soon after.

Radiohead took a well-deserved hiatus between 2002 and 2004 before resurfacing with its controversially titled 2003 album, *Hail to the Thief* (Capitol), which many claimed was an indirect attack at the president of the United States (whom the title alleges "stole" the 2000 presidential election). The album went to the top of the charts at #1 and produced several hit singles. The album's producer Nigel Godrich earned recognition and a Grammy for his work on the album. Radiohead headed off on tour yet again (hitting what seemed to be all four corners of the earth on this international tour) and, having fulfilled its six-album contract with its label, Capitol Records, Radiohead was without a record deal for the first time in its career.

Radiohead's bandmates spent some time off from the band with their families while Yorke worked on and released his debut solo album, *The Eraser,* in 2006 on XL Recordings. Radiohead took a true **DIY (Do-It-Yourself)** turn for its seventh studio album, 2007's *In Rainbows*. Instead of seeking a new record label contract or forming its own record label, the band decided to forego the whole "CD sales" route and instead allowed fans to decide the price they felt was fair to pay for it (plus a small handling fee, of course). The album, along with two vinyl albums, photographs, artwork, extra songs, and lyrics could be purchased online for as low as a penny (and for the value-added version, some paid as high as $80).

Radiohead was slated to headline the 2008 **Lollapalooza** music festival alongside **Nine Inch Nails**. The band was honored by a music festival in Spain, which paid tribute to the band by building a lineup of bands that had been influenced by the innovative British group. Radiohead announced a worldwide tour in support of *In Rainbows* in the spring of 2008.

Further Readings: Donwood, Stanley, and Dr. Tchock. *Dead Children Playing: A Picture Book (Radiohead).* London: Verso Books, 2007; Hale, Jonathan. *Radiohead: From a Great Height.* Toronto, ON, Canada: ECW Press, 1999; Paytress, Mark. *Radiohead: The Complete Guide to Their Music.* London: Omnibus Press, 2005; Tate, Joseph. *Music and Art of Radiohead.* London: Ashgate Pub. Ltd., 2005; http://www./article/record_review/21226-kid-a?artist_title=21226-kid-a; http://www.inrainbows.com; http://news.bbc.co.uk/2/hi/entertainment/955767.stm; http://www.radiohead.com/.

RAMONES

The seminal punk band of all time, the Ramones was composed of a bunch of fun-loving, hard-rocking, tall, skinny, Queens, New York natives who wore their hair long, their pants tight, their black leather jackets short, and sang speedball lyrics like "Gabba Gabba Hey" and "I Wanna Be Sedated."

Formed in 1974, the Ramones—Joey, Johnny, Dee Dee, Marky, C. J., Tommy, Richie, and Elvis (all of whom took on the same stage surname)—are considered "the first punk rock group." The band's founding members—Johnny, Dee Dee, Tommy (the manager), and Joey—played a record 2,263 (http://www.ramones.com/index_main.html) shows from the group's inception right up until its end in 1996. The group was defined by its characteristic look and the head-pumping drum beats, lightening-quick guitar riffs, simple yet playful lyrics, and singer Joey's talk-sing vocal style that seemed to call punk rockers to arms, asking them to join in for a "Blitzkrieg Bop" and lament over the fact that "The KKK Took My Baby Away."

A light-hearted bunch, the Ramones released over 20 studio albums during the group's 20-plus-year-long career. The Ramones were, according to the group's official biography, "the first band of the mid-1970's New York punk rock uprising to get a major-label contract and put an album out," "the first to teach the British how noise annoys," and "the first new American group of the decade to kick the smug, yellow-bellied sh-t out of a '60s superstar aristocracy running on cocaine-and-caviar autopilot" (*Hey! Ho! Let's Go: The Anthology,* Rhino/Wea, 1999). The band's **DIY (Do-It-Yourself)** mentality showed through in its lyrics and song titles; the group's do-it-my-way oaths were evident in its three chord, 2½-minute-long songs, and its name was inspired by none other than Paul McCartney, who had once dubbed himself Paul Ramon.

In short, the Ramones is one of the most original acts of the last three decades—and its influence and impact has lasted long after the band's biggest highs (its 1977 song "Sheena Is a Punk Rocker" charted in the United States and the United Kingdom) and lowest lows (several members have since passed away). The Ramones started playing at the underground punk club CBGB in New York City, and soon it was a staple act there. The band released its eponymously titled debut album in 1976, and the band kicked off what seemed like a 20-plus-year-long tour. The heavier and yet appropriately titled album *Leave Home* (**Sire Records**) appeared in 1977 on the eve of the band's departure for Britain where the group started a punk revolution in the music scene and pretty much laid the groundwork for bands such as The Clash and the Sex Pistols.

Tommy Ramone stepped out of the limelight and gave his leather jacket and moptop haircut, figuratively, to new member Marky, who joined the group in 1978. The group's next album, *Road to Ruin* (**Sire Records**, 1978), failed to bring the band's platform or popularity beyond the local or underground scene. The Ramones tried acting for short while with the 1979 film *Rock 'n' Roll High School*. The movie received mixed reviews; critics considered it "campy," while others who had a soft spot for the band considered sitting through the film to be a surreal experience.

Seeking a wider audience, the Ramones sought the help of Beatles producer Phil Spector for the group's 1980 album, *End of the Century* (Rhino Records), and the group worked with Dave Stewart of Eurythmics for the single "Howling at the Moon." Amid this minor identity crisis, Marky left the group; he was replaced by Richie Ramone who had played drums for the band The Velveteens. The Ramones got the national exposure the group had been seeking when it created the score for the film of horror author Stephen King's novel *Pet Sematary* in 1989. But the constant skewing of the band's focus and identity had its consequences. Dee Dee left the group to pursue of all things a rap album; with his new persona he was known as Dee Dee King. Marky and Dee Dee teamed up to play together as The Ramainz, and the Ramones recruited newbie C. J. Ramone.

Meanwhile, each member of the Ramones was involved in battles with drug abuse and addiction—Dee Dee was using heroin and Joey had become an alcoholic. The band hired some outside help for its 1992 album, *Mondo Bizarro,* which featured Living Colour band member Vernon Reid. *Mondo* featured the song "Censorshit," through which the band voiced its opinions about the censorship campaign that Tipper Gore had recently launched. The band put out the live version of its 1995 album *It's Alive* in 1997; *Alive* featured Ramones's classics such as "Teenage Lobotomy" and "Rockaway Beach." The DVD *It's Alive: 1974–1996* was a collection of rare and public live performances by the band around the world.

The band continued to slowly fall apart through the early to mid-1990s. while many of the band members were undergoing recovery from various addictions, Marky started his own band called Marky Ramone and The Intruders and Joey left to manage a band called The Independents. The band played its final show in August 1996 at The Palace in Los Angeles.

The music world suffered a great loss five years later when Joey passed away on April 15, 2001; he had announced earlier in 2001 that he had been diagnosed with lymphoma and had been in treatment for at least six years by that point. The band's impact and influence may have been ambiguous up until that point, but Joey's obituaries across the world heralded him. The *New York Times* said, "As a front man, Mr. Ramone was a revelation" (Powers, 2001).

Just two months later, before the music world could recover, Dee Dee died from a heroin overdose on June 5 of that same year. Just three years later, a third Ramone passed away: Johnny Ramone was pronounced dead on September 16,

2004 of prostate cancer, leaving Tommy as the only living original member. The title of the 2004 documentary *End of the Century* spoke volumes about the loss of the three Ramones. The film features live and studio footage, interviews, and the personal stories of these young men who helped bring punk into the hearts and souls of so many millions of music fans around the world. The Ramones were inducted into the Rock and Roll Hall of Fame in 2002. Tommy's band, Uncle Monk, released its debut album in 2005. In 2005, Rhino Records released the box set *Weird Tales of the Ramones,* a collection of CDs, videos, and graphic art of the band from over the years.

Fans, musicians, and music scenesters celebrated what would have been Joey Ramone's 52nd birthday on May 19, 2003, at The Fillmore New York at Irving Plaza. In 2004, the music world came together to join Johnny Ramone in a 30th anniversary celebration of the band at the Avalon nightclub in Hollywood. The event, which featured the Red Hot Chili Peppers, The Dickies, C. J. and Marky Ramone, and Eddie Vedder, was an effort to raise money for prostate cancer research.

The Ramones' celebrations continued in 2006 when the film *Too Tough to Die: A Tribute to Joey Ramone* (*Too Tough To Die* was the name of the band's eighth studio album) premiered at the Tribeca Film Festival in New York. In 2007, the Converse sneaker company paid tribute to the Ramones by issuing a new line of "Chuck's" that features the Ramones emblem as part of the Project (RED) charity. The Ramones' self-titled debut album was honored in 2007 when it was added to the impressive collection at the Recording Academy's Grammy Hall of Fame.

Another revealing book, the authorized biography "*I Slept with Joey Ramone,*" which was written by the late singer's brother, was published in 2007. The film version of the film has yet to be released. That same year, Richie Ramone was involved in a $1 million copyright lawsuit with Wal-Mart and Apple, with regards to illegally downloaded copies of the band's songs.

The Ramones caused waves in the news yet again in 2008 when Marky Ramone launched a condom kit for the sex education company Ready two Go, in an effort to promote safe sex.

Further Readings: Powers, Ann. "Joey Ramone, Punk's Influential Yelper, Dies at 49," September 16, 2001. http://query.nytimes.com/gst/fullpage.html?res=9405EFDC1E31-F935A25757C0A9679C8B63&n=Top%2fReference%2fTimes%20Topics%2fPeople%2fR%2fRamone%2c%20Joey; Ramone, Dee Dee. *Chelsea Horror Hotel: A Novel by Dee Dee Ramone.* New York: Thunder's Mouth Press, 2001; Ramone, Dee Dee, Veronica Kofman, and Legs McNeil. *Lobotomy: Surviving the Ramones.* 2nd ed. New York: Thunder's Mouth Press, 2000; True, Everett. *Hey Ho Let's Go: The Story of the Ramones.* London: Omnibus Press, 2005; http://www.ramones.com/index_main.html; http://query.nytimes.com/gst/fullpage.html?res=9405EFDC1E31F935A25757C0A9679C8B63&n=Top%2fReference%2fTimes%20Topics%2fPeople%2fR%2fRamone%2c%20Joey.

THE RAPTURE

This four-piece, New York City–based dance/**post-punk** disco group exploded on the scene after James Murphy, the mastermind behind the dance-rock outfit **LCD Soundsystem**, and Tim Goldsworthy, engineer at **DFA Records**, remixed The

Rapture's song "House of Jealous Lovers" in 2003. Before that, the quartet, which formed back in 1998 in San Diego, California, had been gaining steady momentum in the indie rock world, but it was not until the group teamed up with Murphy and his label, **DFA Records** (a subsidiary Mercury Records), that The Rapture's career really started to take off.

Incidentally, prior to teaming up with **DFA Records**, The Rapture, whose name is synonymous with high-octane dance riffs and get-off-your-feet rhythms (the Rapture also happens to be the term for the Christian doctrine that teaches that Christ will return for His saints, although there is no evidence that the band derived its name from this event), had experienced successes with its first two recordings: an eight-song LP called *Mirror* that was released by the San Diego–based art punk label Gravity Records, and a single that contained a cover of the English **post-punk** group Psychedelic Furs' song "Dumb Waiters," which came out on Sonny Kaye's Gold Standard Laboratories.

Riding the wave of success from those recordings, The Rapture, comprised of Vito Roccoforte (percussion), Luke Jenner (guitar and vocals), and Matt Safer (bass and vocals), toured with bands such as Nuzzle, Gogogo Airheart, and **emo** groundbreakers **Sunny Day Real Estate** before moving to New York City and teaming up with Murphy, Goldsworthy, and **DFA Records**.

Catapulted onto the indie rock map by critical raves and heavy rotation of the "House of Jealous Lovers" single, The Rapture logged odometer-breaking miles on the road in 2000, touring with bands Love Life, Black Dice, and Delta 72. The Rapture released the DFA-produced single "Out of the Races and Onto the Tracks" in 2001, which became an instant club hit and lifted the group's success even higher. The Rapture appeared on the 2002 compilation *DJ-Kicks: Playgroup* and was a featured band on the *Yes New York* compilation in 2003 alongside fellow New York City (NYC) indie groups **Le Tigre** and The Strokes.

The Rapture's 2003 full-length, *Echoes,* proved that the group's blend of electronica, **post-rock**, dance-punk acid house, and a bit of disco was a few notches above plain-stated comparisons to contemporaries such as !!! (**Chk Chk Chk**) and the Happy Mondays, with whom critics claimed the group shared too many similarities. It also catapulted The Rapture's Energizer Bunny–like live antics to the stage for the **NME (New Musical Express)** Awards Tour in 2004 with other bands who were on the rise (**Franz Ferdinand** and The Von Bondies). The Rapture bandmates shared the bill with their idols, the 1980 English pop group The Cure at the Curiosa concert in 2004 in New York City, which was organized by The Cure's Robert Smith.

The Rapture organized a benefit gig in 2006 at the downtown NYC venue Crash Mansion to raise money for their friend Chris Schorb's medical treatments; Schorb had been diagnosed with brain cancer. The Rapture was asked to appear on the 2004 compilation album *DJ-Kicks: Erlend Øye,* and **DFA Records** recruited the band for two songs for the three-disc album *DFA Compilation #2* in 2004.

Taking time off from touring, The Rapture headed into the recording studio and emerged with the single "Get Myself into It," a song that was featured on the soundtrack of the 2002 film *The Rules of Attraction*. The group then launched its first North American tour since 2004 in support of its third full-length album, *Pieces of the People We Love* (Motown/Universal, 2006). Produced by British indie rock producer Paul Epworth (who has worked with **Bloc Party** and rapper The Streets) and Ewan Pearson (whose credits include albums by Depeche Mode), *Pieces* featured tracks with producer/mixer Danger Mouse (the creator of the underground mash-up hit *The Grey Album,* which blended songs from The Beatles' *The White Album* and rapper Jay-Z's *The Black Album*).

The Rapture expanded its creative talents by mixing the track "Me Plus One" by Norwegian singer/DJ Annie in 2005. The Rapture also contributed a song to the third compilation in the "Give. Listen. Help" series, which is available through Urban Outfitters and Filer, to raise money for the Susan G. Komen Breast Cancer Foundation.

The Rapture's Luke Jenner maintains the "Record Nerd" column on the group's Web site, updating and informing fans about the band's favorite music. The group headlined the after-party for MTV's Video Music Awards in 2006 and appeared at an in-store signing at HMV Records in Manhattan. In November 2006, the group played a sold-out homecoming show at NYC's Bowery Ballroom as part of the **CMJ Music Marathon**. *People* was ranked among **NME** (**New Musical Express**)'s Top 50 albums of 2006, and The Rapture's 2006 track "Get Myself into It" broke the magazine's list of the Top 50 tracks of 2006.

On the heels of a North American tour (for which the group took along the Los Angeles pop-funk quartet Under the Influence of Giants), The Rapture secured a series of 2007 tour dates in the United Kingdom, including a spot on the bill for the **NME** (**New Musical Express**) Awards show and a stint at the V Festival in Australia. The Rapture kicked off a selection of tour dates with **The Killers** in the fall of 2007, at which time the group also released the new single " W.A.Y.U.H. (Whoo! Alright-Yeah ... Uh Huh)." In conjunction with efforts to release 12-inches of all of its singles, the group formed its own record label, Throne of Blood Records. Throne of Blood will feature remixes by prominent dance producers.

Pop star Justin Timberlake proved that even mainstream artists have a taste for underground sound when he told that he wanted his next album to sound like a work by The Rapture (Collis, 2007). The Rapture continued touring right through 2008.

Further Readings: http://www.dfarecords.com; http://www.lcdsoundsystem.com; http://www.therapturemusic.com.

R.E.M.

Once upon a time, the letters R.E.M. resonated more with scientists than music fans, and Michael Stipe was just another college kid who had dreams of stardom. R.E.M. started playing shows anywhere it could get gigs—dingy basements on college campuses and small clubs and cramped stages in old churches. The group's first-ever live show was at the 11:11 club in the bandmates' hometown of Athens, Georgia, in April 1980; police raided the event during the band's set and closed the venue's doors forever.

Armed with engaging guitar pop, R.E.M. attracted listeners who were tired of the punk and hardcore acts that were blowing out speakers and packing clubs in the 1980s. As innovators of guitar pop, R.E.M. made an indelible mark on music history with its debut song, "Radio Free Europe." The group's **DIY (Do-It-Yourself)** attitude and fresh approach to music made instant fans of the bandmates' college peers, as did their debut album, *Chronic Town* (A&M, 1982), which solidified the band's signature sound.

Album sales soared, and the band's 1987 work, *Document,* was the second brick in a lengthy yellow-brick-road-like path that R.E.M.'s career would follow for the next two decades. One of the standout tracks on *Document,* the fast-paced apocalyptic "It's the End of the World As We Know It (And I Feel Fine)" remains one of the band's signature and most popular songs to date.

With 1988's *Green* (Warner Bros.) R.E.M.—composed of college dropouts front man/vocalist Michael Stipe, drummer Bill Berry, guitarist Peter Buck, and bassist Mike Mills—almost instantly became a worldwide success, and the group's tour schedule showed the odometer-breaking fruits of its labor. The gig lineup was so intense, in fact, that it forced the group to take a six-year-long hiatus from the road. The fact that *Green* was released on a major label ruffled a few fans' feathers, but others stuck with the band, arguing that years of roughing it—and Stipe's social and political activism—meant the band deserved a break.

R.E.M. returned to the studio in the early 1990s and emerged with *Out of Time* (Warner Bros., 1991) and one of their seminal records, *Automatic for the People* (Warner Bros., 1992), featuring signature songs like the emotive ballad "Everybody Hurts," the hit song "Man on the Moon," and the striking "Nightswimming," which showcased Stipe's vocal potentials. R.E.M.'s 1994 album, the noisy *Monster* (Warner Bros.), featured a tribute to the late Kurt Cobain, and it even featured a track on which **Sonic Youth**'s Thurston Moore contributed vocals. The track "What's the Frequency, Kenneth?" (the title of which was inspired by a strange experience CBS news anchor Dan Rather once had after he was assaulted in NYC) became a timeless hit that would remain popular into the next decade.

In 1992, R.E.M. made headlines by receiving a whopping seven Grammy nominations; the group walked away with three awards, including "Best Pop Performance by a Group." R.E.M. kicked off its famous "Monster" tour in 1995—a venture that seemed to personify the group's larger-than-life status. But gargantuan ticket sales did little to outweigh a tragic mid-tour event when Berry suffered a brain aneurysm and had to have surgery. The operation was a success, but Berry experienced further medical problems throughout the tour. Stipe also experienced some medical challenges of his own when he had to have hernia surgery.

The foursome was not out of the weeds yet—in 1996 the bandmates filed a sexual harassment suit against their long-time manager, Jefferson Holt—but their luck certainly took a 180-degree turn when they inked a new deal with Warner Bros. Records for a reported $80 million. The lackluster success of R.E.M.'s

R.E.M. singer Michael Stipe (far left) and bandmates in 1996. [AP Wide World Photos]

1996 album, *New Adventures in Hi-Fi* (even though it debuted at #2 on the charts), allowed the group's members to focus their energy on their respective side projects —Stipe joined his special pal musician Patti Smith on the road and also turned to writing by documenting his experiences in the memoir *Two Times Intro: On the Road with Patti Smith*, Buck collaborated with other musicians, and Mills played with various bands and musicians including Hootie & the Blowfish.

With R.E.M.'s remarkable worldwide success also came a microscopic examination of the bandmates' personal lives. Rumors circulated about the possibility that Stipe was gay, and the chatter escalated to a higher level when the tabloid press reported that the svelte singer was HIV-positive. Stipe responded to the accusations, "I felt like I was being looked on as a coward for *not* talking about it, and I abhor that" (VH1's *Behind the Music: R.E.M.*, 1998). Stipe did not publicly address his homosexuality until 2001 in an interview with *TIME* magazine.

Fans were saddened by the news of Berry's departure in 1997 (the split was amicable; he chose to retire on his farm perhaps to rest after having a ruptured brain aneurysm back in 1995), but the band soldiered on as a three-piece. R.E.M. hired a drum machine to take over Berry's responsibilities and released the experimental album *Up* in 1998. R.E.M. hired a fill-in tour drummer for its 2001 album, *Reveal*. The prolific band released an album nearly every year afterward and continued to top the charts. Stipe's political and social causes continued to make headlines. R.E.M. joined such bands as Pearl Jam and **Bright Eyes** on the 2004 Vote for Change tour in support of then presidential candidate John Kerry. R.E.M.'s 2004 album, *Around the Sun,* showed signs of the R.E.M. from its early years. A singles collection followed that same year.

One of the preeminent bands to raise the indie flag, R.E.M. has sold over 70 million albums. But the band has not forsaken its roots—the band members continue to remain active in politics in their home city, and the group used a popular phrase coined by the owner of a local eatery ("Automatic for the People") for one of its best-known recordings. It is rumored, too, that several members of R.E.M. have open bar tabs at a local drinkery in Athens, Georgia.

In 2007, the group was inducted into the Rock and Roll Hall of Fame in Cleveland, Ohio. The band continued to tour through 2007, recording songs for various political and social causes, including a cover of John Lennon's "#9 Dream" for a double album to benefit Amnesty International. Warner Bros. Records released the band's first-ever live album, the CD/DVD combination package "R.E.M. Live," in October 2007.

R.E.M.'s hometown of Athens, Georgia, celebrated the band by honoring it with the Athens Historical Society's presentation of "R.E.M. in Perspective: An Athens History," a collection of vintage performance footage, followed by a panel discussion. Meanwhile, Stipe continued to pontificate as he appeared on media outlets such as CNN and was featured in countless magazine interviews, while Peter Buck collaborated with R.E.M. instrumentalist Scott McCaughey on his project, The Minus 5.

R.E.M. was the headlining act for the 2008 Sasquatch! Music Festival at The Gorge Amphitheatre in Washington state. The group also celebrated the release of its 14th studio album *Accelerate* (Warner Bros., 2008).

Further Readings: Black, Johnny. *Reveal: The Story of R.E.M.* San Francisco: Backbeat Books, 2004; Brown, Rodger Lyle. *Party out of Bounds: The B-52's, R.E.M., and the Kids Who Rocked Athens, Georgia.* Atlanta, GA: Everthemore Books, 2003; Janovic, Rob. *Michael Stipe: The Biography.* Atlanta, GA: Portrait, 2006; VH1's "Behind the Music: R.E.M.," 1998; http://www.minus5.com; http://www.remhq.com.

RIGHTEOUS BABE RECORDS

The logo image for this record label speaks to its founder's beliefs, morals, and spunk—a strong, buff-looking female wearing a nontraditional dress showing off her biceps. Founded by "make my own rules" folk singer-songwriter **Ani DiFranco** in 1990, the Buffalo, New York–based label was first formed as a vehicle through which **Ani DiFranco** could release her own music. The **DIY (Do-It-Yourself)** pioneer, who was never one to give up or be held down, founded the label in an effort to stave off the creative control and artistic restrictions that labels she had previously worked with tried to impose on her.

The dreadlock-wearing singer/activist/feminist/indie icon initially called the label Righteous Records (perhaps in an effort to express her exuberance over her entrepreneurial success), but after DiFranco discovered a label with the same name, she added the "Babe." With its home in DiFranco's hometown of Buffalo, New York, Righteous Babe Records's roster includes 15 burgeoning and diverse artists including Andrew Bird, Michael Meldrum, Anaïs Mitchell, Bitch and Animal, Drums & Tuba, Hamell on Trial, Toshi Reagon, Arto Lindsay, Utah Phillips, That 1 Guy, Sekou Sundiata, Sara Lee, and Kurt Swinghammer.

In full DiFranco style, the label attempts to build relationships with local business owners and vendors by attempting to employ only local photographers for gigs, graphic artists for album art, and distributing music and merchandise through local stores. Recently, DiFranco, with the help of her manager, Scot Fisher, moved the label to a local dilapidated and neglected church, The Asbury Delaware Methodist Church. DiFranco utilized her **DIY (Do-It-Yourself)** spirit and entrepreneurial insight for the rehabilitation of the church—not to mention $1 million in cash equity from the Righteous Babe Records bank accounts.

After partnering with the Buffalo Economic Renaissance Corporation and the city's governing officials, DiFranco's new project became one of the first times that tax credits from the state and a historic preservation group were combined for a single local project. DiFranco's dream of creating "a dynamic place that will have a momentum of its own once all the creative people are in there, and there is music happening at night, and art hanging on the walls and crazy cinema in the basement" (Takemoto, 2007) came to fruition when the label moved its headquarters there in 2006. The Church, as it is affectionately known, is now a fully operational music/performance space, arts center, and forum for local events.

Ani DiFranco has released almost 20 of her own albums on Righteous Babe Records, including her career retrospective, the two-disc *Canon,* which was released in September 2007. On September 11, 2007, at the St. James Episcopal Church in Austin, Texas, the label and its artists paid tribute to Righteous Babe Records recording artist Sekou Sundiata who passed away due to heart failure. Less than a half dozen people are employed at the label, including Ani's mother, who works as the bookkeeper. The indie artist also releases copies of her taped live performances that are known as the Official Bootleg Series.

Further Readings: Kalmar, Veronika. *Label Launch: A Guide to Independent Record Recordings, Promotion and Distribution.* New York: St. Martin's Griffin, 2002; http://www.righteousbabe.com.

RIOT GRRRL MOVEMENT

The punk movement inspired youths in the late 1970s–1980s to forge their own way in life and music. To most of the public and mainstream listeners, punks were perceived to be violent and even dangerous individuals with little regard for morals or the law. While these misconceptions served to stain the reputation of punks, the positive effects of the punk movement often went unnoticed by the general public.

One of the biggest outcomes of this time period, though, was the Riot Grrrl Movement, which followed two decades later, reaching its peak in the 1990s. During this time young women in the punk scene made a collective underground shift toward social and political awareness. Riot Grrrls (and even some boys) adhered to a basic ideology that strove to uphold equal rights and they opposed sexism, which was, for some who were part of the original punk movement, an unconscious yet outspoken negative stereotype of the scene.

Led by all-female acts such as the Olympia, Washington–based bands Bikini Kill and Bratmobile, the Riot Grrrl's mantra was "Revolution Girl Style Now." Riot Grrrls were intensely loyal to indie record labels, and they played a major part in the development of the **DIY (Do-It-Yourself)** aesthetic, which involved self-promotion and an overall anticorporate stance. Local, homemade fanzines helped to spread the word about the Riot Grrrl Movement; soon, teen glossy magazines were picking up on what they perceived to be a rising trend. But the Riot Grrrls were not interested in creating a fad—they wanted equality in the music business and a fair deal on all fronts.

This **DIY (Do-It-Yourself)** activism spread quickly across the States, inspiring young female musicians to rise up (and speak out) against their detractors—male musicians who claimed women could not play as well as them, club promoters who favored all-male acts, and a general consensus that "punk" meant young skinny boys playing angry music. Online and print zines such as Guerrilla Girls, Riot Grrrl, Ink., CyberGrrrl, Blue Stockings, and Geek Girls took the movement to another level by sharing stories and experiences of young female Riot Grrrls and educating young women about the movement's plans, pioneers, and purpose.

Certain bands and artists wore the Riot Grrrl badge more loudly and proudly than others. Acts such as Bikini Kill, the members of which pretty much designed the effort out of a need to strip punk music of its "for boys by boys" mentality and outlook, worked to incite other female acts to join its league. The group Bratmobile was also extremely instrumental in getting the Riot Grrrl Movement off the ground. Its efforts culminated in the K Records–sponsored indie music festival International Pop Underground Convention (IPU), which was held in August 1991. Decrying the corporate entities that these bands felt were trying to prostitute their music and style, the bands on the roster celebrated their independence with two days of hard-rocking music and social and political commentary. Bands on the all-female roster included acts such as 7 year Bitch, Bratmobile, Heavens to Betsy, and Lois Maffeo. Concerts featured just after the events included bands who supported the movement, such as the **Melvins**, Nation of Ulysses, Thee Headcoats, Girl Trouble, The Fastbacks, L7, and The Pastels, among others.

By the early 1990s, the Riot Grrrl Movement had become as much a genre of music as it had a political wave. Riot Grrrl acts started sprouting up all over the country, with female band members and musicians wearing pins, T-shirts, and other paraphernalia supporting the cause. The feminist angle of the Riot Grrrl Movement eventually spawned several gay and lesbian activist groups. Band members, such as those of **Le Tigre**, began to proudly wear their lesbianism as proudly as they did their profession as musicians.

Women in the movement were savvy about being heard. Their response to the right-wing Christian Coalition's Right to Life's petition against abortion could be heard through such events as the band L7's 1991 Rock for Choice, which was formed to "mobilize the music community to protect abortion rights and women's health clinics" (http://feminist.org/rock4c/index.html). Similar vocalizations could be heard in the background of the hearings of Supreme Court Justice Clarence Thomas, who was accused of sexual harassment.

The first Rock for Choice concert was held in October 1991 in conjunction with the Feminist Majority Foundation. Bands such as Hole, Sister Double Happiness, and **Nirvana** played at the historic event. Today, Rock for Choice lives on through concerts across the United States, which have featured big name acts such as No Doubt, **Liz Phair**, Stone Temple Pilots, Paula Cole, Joan Jett, the Bangles, Pearl Jam, Joan Osborne, the Red Hot Chili Peppers, Rage Against the Machine, and even one of the key the bands who helped start the ball rolling in the first place, Bikini Kill, among others.

Bands in the **grunge** genre associated closely with the Riot Grrrl Movement. Similarly, a scraggly looking, multi-hair-colored punk band from Los Angeles called L7 was a bold supporter that eventually became an icon that symbolized **grunge**/Riot Grrrl synergy. Various Riot Grrrl chapters were founded in all corners of the country, each helping to further the message and cause.

The Riot Grrrl Movement thrives today, although the intensity has been diluted since its heyday, due in part to the leveling off of the equality in music that was the result of the efforts of bands involved in it. Musicians such as **Ani DiFranco**, Peaches, and the girls of the group **Sleater-Kinney**, however, still wear their Riot Grrrl pride loudly on their sleeves, singing about the frustrations and stereotypes that stem from being female in a male-dominated music business and keeping the **DIY (Do-It-Yourself)** spirit alive by founding their own record labels.

Pop culture, however, in its usual profit- and dollar-seeing habits, has attempted to assume close ties with the Riot Grrrl Movement. As a result, irresponsible media have at times attached the Riot Grrrl label to anything mainstream that has a tinge of anything feminist (an example of this is the 2007 teen flick *Nancy Drew*, which some reviewers confused as "Riot Grrrl"-esque simply because its protagonist was a young female who has a take-charge attitude). But the true, undiluted Riot Grrrl spirit lives on in female artists and musicians who seek equality and equanimity across all professions (not just the music industry, although that is a good place to start) for themselves and their peers.

Jennifer Miro, a long-time band member of the San Francisco–based punk rock/new wave band The Nuns, said of the movement's beginnings, "There were a lot of women in the beginning. It (the Punk Movement) was women doing things. Then it became this whole macho, anti-women thing. Then women didn't go to see punk bands anymore because they were afraid of getting killed. I didn't even go because it was so violent and so macho that it was repulsive. Women just got squeezed out" (Leblanc, 1999).

Further Readings: Wrekk, Alex. *Stolen Sharpie Revolution: A DIY Zine Resource.* Bloomington, IN: Microcosm, 2003; http://www.feminist.org/rock4c/index.html; http://guerrillagirls.

com; http://www.riotgrrrlink.com; http://www.bluestockings.com; http://www.geekgirls.com.

RITES OF SPRING

As a band, Rites of Spring did not last long. However, its life span from 1984 to 1986 offered a snapshot of the expanding Washington, D.C., punk rock community during that decade and the frantic work ethic and proneness to distraction of the bands involved. Everyone in the group had side project upon side project and was either playing a show or watching one. Rites of Spring recorded only one album as a group, amassed 17 total songs, played roughly 15 total shows, and broke up as quickly as the band formed. But the story of more influential D.C. bands such as **Fugazi**, and of **post-punk** and **emo**, begins largely with Rites of Spring.

Rites of Spring was born in 1984 with Guy Picciotto on vocals and guitar, bassist Mike Fellows, guitarist Eddie Janney, and drummer Brendan Canty. With Picciotto and Canty only in their teens, the band would become known for focusing less on the expected political furor and more on its members' own personal and emotional conflicts, which resonated more immediately with their listeners.

It seems everyone in a D.C. punk band was only a handful of degrees from **Fugazi** and Minor Threat front man Ian MacKaye (Janney and MacKaye played in a handful of bands together prior to Janney's involvement with Rites of Spring); including Rites of Spring, which released its first album in 1985 via Dischord Records, MacKaye's legendary uber-punk label.

Rites of Spring, however, would play a large role in galvanizing an entire genre. While the term "**emo**" has been remolded by fey acoustic acts and shows like *The O.C.* to mean meek, introverted, and ambivalent, Rites of Spring hardly matched that description. The group's debut songs were violent, heart-shredding affairs that were not afraid to miss notes or make mistakes. However, if critics had even been paying attention at the time, they would likely have noticed the band's attempts at an uncharted territory in punk rock: precision. Unlike its three-chord, amphetamine-paced predecessors, Rights of Spring's first and only full-length contained rough but mathematical guitar lines and brash but intelligent drumming.

In the term's early phases, **emo** simply characterized emotional intensity, rather than any windswept opining. Rites of Spring certainly had enough of the former. Front man Guy Picciotto, all flailing curly hair during the band's live shows, belted out larynx-gouging passages about angst, loss, nostalgia, and loneliness. While most bands gig aggressively to gain attention, each of Rites of Spring's limited public shows became highly anticipated spectacles in and of themselves. On nearly every occasion, the band's shows ended with equipment destroyed and the band sweat-drenched and thoroughly exhausted.

After recording a four-song EP, *All Through a Life* in 1986, Rites of Spring broke up. That breakup, however, was only the beginning. All four members went on to bigger and better opportunities. Janney joined the **emo** band **Girls Against Boys**. Fellows went on to work with Government Issue and the Royal Trux. And, in what many consider the most important result of the breakup, Picciotto and Canty teamed up with Ian MacKaye to form **Fugazi** in 1987. In 1991, Dischord Records released *End on End,* which compiled all the songs Rites of Spring had written in its short but influential career.

Further Readings: Robbins, Ira A. *The Trouser Press Guide to 90's Rock.* 5th ed. Palmer, AK: Fireside, 1997; http://www.dischord.com; http://www.dischord.com/band/ritesofspring; www.dragcity.com/bands/rtx.html; http://www.gvsb.com; http://www.southern.net/southern/band/RITES.

ROGUE WAVE

The Oakland-based band Rogue Wave was born, in some sense, out of the dot-com crash in the early 2000's. Rogue Wave front man Zach Rogue was working as a Web developer in San Francisco, clocking in between 70 and 80 hours a week. Then, as with many Internet startups in the early 2000s, layoffs loomed, and Rogue lost his job in 2002. The layoff came as a revelation to him—he hated his job, despised the corporate world, and wanted to pursue music. Soon after, Rogue left his old band, the Desoto Reds, with which he was frustrated creatively. He moved to New York in 2002 bringing with him a demo tape of song ideas. Jobless, and with no specific employment or musical plans, Rogue eventually formed what would become Rogue Wave.

When Rogue arrived in New York, he hooked up with friend and producer Bill Racine at Racine's house in Woodstock, New York, where they reworked many of the songs on Rogue's demo tape. Within a year of losing his job, Rogue's songs were formed into Rogue Wave's first album, *Out of the Shadow,* which, at that time, had yet to be released on a record label.

Out of the Shadow saw Rogue taking up most of the instrumental duties, with the occasional friend filling in on drums. For touring purposes, Rogue began to recruit a full-time band, for which Rogue solicited band members by posting an ad on craigslist.org, asking anyone who was interested in Rogue's biggest influences— The Who, **Yo La Tengo**, the **Pixies**, among others—to respond. The band that resulted consisted of Rogue on guitar and vocals, drummer Pat Spurgeon, bassist Sonya Westcott, and keyboardist/guitarist Gram LeBron.

In scientific terms, a rogue wave is an abnormally large ocean wave that forms inexplicably and without pattern. Rogue took the phrase for his band's name because he felt the phrase represented the unpredictability of human experience. *Out of the Shadow* combined ragged, bare-bones acoustics with the mellowness of 1970's California pop, a sound that eventually won over some A&R (Artists and Repertoire) representatives from **Sub Pop Records**. The album was officially released on **Sub Pop Records** in 2004.

Out of the Shadow was generally well regarded by critics. The song "Every Moment" was featured on the soundtrack for the hit 2004 movie *Napoleon Dynamite,* and the band began touring with the likes of **The Shins**, **TV on the Radio**, and Mates of State. In late 2004, Westcott left the band and was replaced by Evan Farrell.

On the heels of *Out of the Shadow* came Rogue Wave's second full-length album, *Descended Like Vultures* (**Sub Pop Records**, 2005). The album earned Rogue Wave further comparisons to bands like **The Shins** and **Death Cab for Cutie**. The band followed the album by touring with psychedelic pop band Mazarin in 2005, and such groups as The Stills, Guster, and singer-songwriter and **Broken Social Scene** guitarist Jason Collett in 2006.

In 2006, Spurgeon suffered kidney failure. In September of that year, Rogue Wave held a benefit show featuring Ben Gibbard of **Death Cab for Cutie**, along with members of Nada Surf and Guster to help pay for Spurgeon's kidney transplant. In January 2007, Spurgeon successfully underwent kidney transplant surgery. While Spurgeon recuperated, Rogue Wave became one of many indie rock bands to plug their music on high-school TV dramas, much to the angst of many indie purists. In February 2007, Rogue Wave's cover of the **Pixies**' "Debaser" was used on an episode of FOX's *The O.C.,* and "Eyes" was heard on the NBC show *Friday Night Lights*.

The band announced its 2008 tour dates, which included summer dates as the opener for surf rocker Jack Johnson. The bandmates also let fans know of some sadder news—the passing of their friend and former bassist Evan Farrell who was killed in an accidental house fire. Rogue Wave bandmates—Zach Rogue, Pat Spurgeon, Gram Lebron, and Patrick Abernethy—continued to tour in support of their September 2007 album, *Asleep at Heaven's Gate,* which was released by Brushfire Records.

Further Readings: Jay, Richard, *How To Get Your Music in Film and TV.* New York: Schirmer Books, 2005; http://www.roguewavemusic.com.

ROUGH TRADE RECORDS

This London-based independent record label has a rich 25-year history that spans two decades of music, stemming from its beginnings during a punk/reggae boom when recent college graduate Geoff Travis founded the label in 1978. Rough Trade began as the Rough Trade record shop located on Kensington Park Road in the West End, growing in size and scope when Travis decided to release albums by local bands he knew and befriended. Travis had adopted the name after seeing a band of the same name; the term is slang for money offered by straight men to other males in exchange for sex.

Rough Trade's first release was a single by one of the first French punk groups to emerge, Metal Urbain, which garnered the label local attention. Rough Trade went global, however, when Travis "discovered" a local new wave band called **The Smiths**, which he signed in the mid-1980s. Catapulted by the success of the group, Rough Trade experienced widespread success and ultimately expanded its distribution division. With the signing of **The Smiths**, Rough Trade had transformed from cult status to a mainstream presence that exceeded everyone's expectations.

The Smiths enjoyed worldwide success, eventually becoming the definitive Britpop group of the 1980s. The band and the label butted heads, however, over the band's 1986 signature album, *The Queen Is Dead,* over questionable lyrics in the song "Frankly, Mr. Shankly," which many people suspected was a dig at Travis himself. The album was halted for approximately seven months until Rough Trade finally released it; *Queen* has often been ranked one of the greatest albums of all time. Rough Trade flourished in the 1980s, releasing albums by bands-on-the-make such as **Camper Van Beethoven**, **Beat Happening**, and **Galaxie 500**.

Rough Trade, on the other hand, experienced its own snag when the label—due in most part to poor management—went bankrupt and **The Smiths** eventually signed to EMI Records. As a result of the bankruptcy, the entire Rough Trade ship went down around 1989, with Travis attempting to resurrect the label via its various incarnations—Rough Trade Recordings and Trade 2. With the label's bankruptcy came consequences, and Travis was forced to sell certain assets—namely **The Smiths**' catalog, which he sold to Warner Music, but the sale allowed Travis to pay off his debts and stay in business.

Rough Trade was sold to One Little Indian Records (also based in the United Kingdom), which releases albums by the likes of Björk. Travis briefly worked with Indian before parting ways due to irreconcilable differences, until the mid-1990s when he was finally able to pay off his debts and legally secure the Rough Trade name. The Rough Trade label rose from the ashes to become one of the most significant and groundbreaking independent labels, signing such modern bands as **The Whites Stripes**, **Belle and Sebastian**, the Brakes, **The Fiery Furnaces**, and The Libertines to its lengthy roster.

One of the first bands Travis signed under Rough Trade's new incarnation was the New York City–based garage rock group The Strokes, which has gone on to become one of the most popular and commercially successful indie rock acts of the twentieth century. Travis jumped on the Canadian music bandwagon in 1997, signing artists such as singer-songwriter like Beth Orton to the company's management department (Orton claims to have been a regular at the record shop back when it was first open), but the first Canadian band signed to the Rough Trade roster was the **indie pop** outfit **The Hidden Cameras**. Rough Trade later added the Canadian quintet Royal City and the widely popular octet **Arcade Fire**, whose success story is an inspiration of its own.

Rough Trade signed the English underground **post-punk** band The Fall, which helped the label gain momentum in the music industry. An English **post-punk** band that had been going strong since its inception in the 1970s, The Fall released its debut album, *Grotesque (After the Gramme),* in 1980. Tagged as the group's "first great album," The Fall has enjoyed a lengthy and prolific career—replete with hit singles—that continues today.

In 1993, Rough Trade released the soundtrack to music journalist/author Greil Marcus's book *Lipstick Traces,* in which Greil accounts the rock history of the twentieth century. The label's **DIY (Do-It-Yourself)** roots (Travis claims to have been inspired by local fanzines like one called *Sniffing Glue*) are chronicled in the book *Rough Trade: Labels Unlimited* by music journalist/author Rob Young (Black Dog Publishing, 2006), which details Rough Trade's beginnings as a young label that supported burgeoning punk bands and released albums by such groups as The Raincoats, Cabaret Voltaire, Scritty Politty, The Fall, Linton Kwesi Johnson, Metal Urbain, Stiff Little Fingers, and Robert Wyatt. The book—which also features a Q&A exchange between Travis and the label's co-owner Jeanette Lee—rides the wave of the label's crumble in the early 1990s to its resurrection later on in that same decade with the signing of several up-and-coming acts such as **Babyshambles**, **Arcade Fire**, Antony and the Johnsons, and Pulp. The book contains interesting tidbits of information about the label and its founder, who, in all of his early wisdom, had attempted to secure releases by Run-D.M.C. and De La Soul.

Rough Trade Publishing (RTP), an off shoot of Rough Trade, was formed in 1991 amid the crumbling of the label by former Rough Trade employees Cathi Gibson and Peter Walmsley. RTP releases albums by such bands as The Jon Spencer Blues Explosion, Trans Am, Rocket from the Crypt, The Sea and Cake, The Black Heart Procession, and more. Rough Trade's stateside office located in San Francisco, California, made waves of its own when it released the groundbreaking—and still notable—1981 compilation *Wanna Buy a Bridge?* which featured tracks by artists from the 1970s and the 1980s such as Delta 5, Cabaret Voltaire, Young Marble Giants, The Slits, and more. That satellite office scored big in the 1990s when it pioneered albums by bands such as Lucinda Williams, Straightjacket Fits, and Two Nice Girls, among others.

Several CD compilations have captured the essence of the label and its history —2001's *Rough Trade Shops: 25 Years* (Mute Records) featured four CDs of music that best represents the most popular albums the Rough Trade record shop sold —The Sugarcubes, Boards of Canada and The Birthday Party, and Lee "Scratch" Perry, and Dub Syndicate, among others. Countless other compilations and albums celebrated the label's successes; among them, 2006's *Rough Trade Shops: Counter Culture, Vol. 2* which marked the label's 30th anniversary, featured 30 songs by acts such as **LCD Soundsystem**, the **Pixies**, Björk, and more. The tracks on *Rough Trade Shops* were handpicked by selected "curators"—**LCD Soundsystem**'s James Murphy, **Sonic Youth**'s Thurston Moore, **Sire Records**' co-founder Seymour Stein, and English musician and former Pulp front man Jarvis Cocker —among others; each curator contributed his or her own set of liner notes for the album.

The Scottish indie/**Twee pop** group **Belle and Sebastian** released its first album on Rough Trade in the fall of 2003—*Dear Catastrophe Waitress,* the group's first official studio album, was a critical and commercial success for the group, helping to secure the group's position as one of the most highly influential bands in the indie rock scene. The label celebrated its 25th anniversary at the V&A Museum in the United Kingdom with over 20 shows in just 10 days; bands spotlighted on stage included The Raincoats, Beth Orton, and the Tindersticks.

Amid tabloid controversy surrounding front man Pete Doherty's alleged drub abuse, Rough Trade dropped **Babyshambles** from its roster in 2006. The band's January 2006 full-length album, *Down in Albion* (Rough Trade), however, had sold over 100,000 copies in just a few months after its release—with very little publicity.

Travis also runs the Warner division label Blanco Y Negro, which has distributed albums by the likes of group **The Jesus and Mary Chain** (the group disbanded in 1999, although the members reunited on stage for the 2007 **Coachella Valley Music and Arts Festival** in Indio, California) and the American alt rock band Dinosaur Jr., both of which helped make Rough Trade one of the biggest-selling labels in the industry.

Rough Trade hit a significant snag in 2007 when Sanctuary Records, which held a 49-percent stake in the company, posted a loss upwards of $111 million, which forced the shareholders to consider selling their stakes in Rough Trade. The sale, however, never went through and Rough Trade remains a large part of the Sanctuary Records Group.

Bands signed to the Rough Trade roster include the following:

1990s	Dr. Dog	Phantom Buffalo
Aberfeldy	Cara Dillon	Queen Adreena
Antony & The Johnsons	Baxter Dury	Eddi Reader
Arcade Fire	Eastern Lane	Relaxed Muscle
A.R.E. Weapons	Equation	Alasdair Roberts
Virginia Astley	**The Fiery Furnaces**	Royal City
Babyshambles	Adam Green	Hope Sandoval & The Warm Inventions
Beachwood Sparks	Hal	Scissors for Lefty
Bell Orchestré	**The Hidden Cameras**	Scritti Politti
Belle and Sebastian	Lavender Diamond	The Strokes
Brakes	Jeffrey Lewis	**Sufjan Stevens**
British Sea Power	Jenny Lewis	Sun Kil Moon
Basia Bulat	The Libertines	Super Furry Animals
Jarvis Cocker	The Long Blondes	Emiliana Torrini
Cornershop	Low	The Tyde
The Decemberists	The Mescalitas	**The Unicorns**
Delays	The Moldy Peaches	The Veils
Detroit Cobras	Oneida	

Further Readings: Young, Rob. *Rough Trade: Labels Unlimited.* London: Black Dog Publishing, 2006; Young, Rob. *Warp (Labels Unlimited).* London: Black Dog Publishing, 2005; http://www.myspace.com/roughtraderecords; http://www.roughtraderecords.com.

SAY HI TO YOUR MOM

This indie group has been heralded for recreating a "futuristic feeling of Ziggy Stardust–era Bowie" by *SPIN* magazine (Grose, 2005). Both "pretentious indie rock" and "Paul McCartney" are listed as the first two influences on Say Hi to Your Mom's MySpace page (http://www.myspace.com/sayhitoyourmom). Joking or not, the Brooklyn, New York–based four-piece band grafts together all the ironic role-playing references, chunky guitars, and Atari-game synthesizers of the former with the pop precision of the latter.

Say Hi to Your Mom formed, largely, within the confines of Los Angeles (LA) native Eric Elbogen's computer, bedroom, and imagination. Despite the kookiness and neurosis suffusing of most of Say Hi to Your Mom's lyrical content, the bands that Elbogen listened to at an early age during the 1980s and the 1990s, such as **The Velvet Underground** and The Rolling Stones, were fairly conventional. He began writing songs and playing in bands, mostly in the LA area, but Elbogen moved to New York in 2002 and began crafting songs under the name Say Hi to Your Mom—which then consisted only of Elbogen, a guitar, computer, and a drum machine.

Elbogen has often been coy regarding the origin of the band's name. In one interview, Elbogen claimed the phrase "Say Hi to Your Mom" was actually his legal name. In another interview, he claimed the phrase was said to him by an alien who had abducted him and, before him, his mother. That aloofness, combined with Elbogen's moodiness, fixations on pop-culture minutiae, and talents for self-criticism, would shape the personality of the band.

Elgoben released Say Hi to Your Mom's first full-length album, *Discosadness,* in 2002 on his own label, Euphobia Music. Long song titles like "They Write Books about This Sort of Thing" and "Unless the Laker Game Was On" belied the album's vulnerability and artfully stripped-down sound. *Discosadness* also marked the beginning of what would become a motif in the band's album art. Each album cover displayed a sketch of the same dejected-looking, cylinder-headed robot against a minimal, monotone background.

Still with only a guitar and a drum machine, Say Hi to Your Mom's second, more upbeat full-length album, *Numbers & Mumbles* followed in 2004, again off Euphobia. Spaceships, corduroy, the movie *Ghostbusters,* and video games all found a way to be subject matter in Elbogen's songs.

While on tour, Elbogen recruited a backup band to accommodate most of his PC-made music. That backup band—drummer Chris Egan and keyboardist Jeff

Sheinkopf—became his permanent bandmates during the recording of 2005's *Ferocious Mopes*. *Ferocious Mopes* had the same tendencies toward self-consciously long, unsleek song titles such as "The Forest Scares the Hell Out of Me" and "Yeah, I'm in Love with an Android." However, having a fuller rhythm section allowed the band to more fully hone its pop instincts and explore its more aggressive side

In 2006, Say Hi to Your Mom released *Impeccable Blahs*, which was Elbogen's final album with Egan and Sheinkopf. The songs on the album, which all seem in some way to be about vampires, were the punchiest, most pop oriented the band had produced. The vampire theme seemed to be arbitrary, a way for Elbogen to have fun and nothing more. The song "Angels and Darlas," for instance, was named for those characters in the show *Buffy the Vampire Slayer*, of which Elbogen is an ardent fan.

After *Impeccable Blahs*, however, Elbogen, Egan, and Sheinkopf agreed not to tour together. This decision came largely due to Elbogen's conflicts with his own life. In October 2006, on the band's Web site, Elbogen posted a news entry saying that, upon turning 30, he had grown tired of the life he led as a 20-something in New York—living with six roommates, as well as the planned demolition of his apartment. Elbogen moved to Seattle near the end of 2006.

Near the beginning of 2007, Elbogen recruited a new band and planned a nationwide tour. Say Hi To Your Mom's fifth album, *The Wishes and the Glitch*, came out in the spring of 2008. The band has recently also become known simply as Say Hi.

Further Readings: Kirschling, Gregory. "Natalie Portman Sounds Off." *Entertainment Weekly*, No. 962, October 24, 2007; http://www.sayhitoyourmom.com.

SERENA-MANEESH

Through his teens, Oslo, Sweden native/indie renaissance man Emil Nikolaisen approached his career like a speed dater, stinting in many bands before settling down to front his current group, Serena-Maneesh.

In 1995, Nikolaisen clocked in briefly as a guitarist for the Christian math-metal band Extol. In 1997, he played drums for the Franco-funk band The Loch Ness Mouse. After leaving The Loch Ness Mouse, Nikolaisen performed under the name Krazy Katzy as the drummer, songwriter, and producer for the Norwegian punk band Silver. Working with his younger brother, who performed by the name Blanco Summer, Silver recorded the album *White Diary*, which saw a 2004 release well after Serena-Maneesh had gained traction.

In Silver, Nikolaisen found the release of a first single "Angels Calling," but Nikolaisen sought riskier, unexplored musical territory. Just before the release of Silver's *White Diary*, Nikolaisen left the band, hoping to form a band that would allow him greater creative control and responsibility in his music. In the early 2000s, the band that formed around Nikolaisen, as he moved away from Silver, became Serena-Maneesh.

Currently, Serena-Maneesh's sensibility is as gargantuan, daunting, and diverse as Nikolaisen's background. Along with Emil Nikolaisen, the band consists of Nikolaisen's sister, bassist Hilma Nikolaisen, drummers Einar Lukerstuen and Tommy Akerholdt, guitarist Øystein Sandsdalen, viola player Eivind Schou, and frequent guests complementing the rhythm section. Translated loosely, "serena" can mean both "serene" and "veil"; "maneesh" is a modification of the Norwegian word for the spectator area that surrounds a stage.

The band's sound is equally broad, rangy, yet evasive: it possesses the alternating female/male lyrical deadpanning of **Sonic Youth**, guitars and vocals reminiscent of **My Bloody Valentine**, and vocals that drift in like weather patterns, and the slap-bang drumming of **Iggy and The Stooges**. Songs develop slowly and organically before abruptly switching gears. For Serena-Maneesh, singing is not for content so much as it is for atmosphere.

In 2002, Serena-Maneesh released its first EP, *Fixxations,* which garnered short-lived attention from listeners. *Zurück,* a follow-up EP compiling four years of previous work, received an equally lukewarm response. It was not until 2005, with the release of the Serena-Maneesh's self-titled debut on Honeymilk Records, though, that the band solidified professionally. Like the band's array of influences, its full-length debut came together, seemingly, from many disparate locales and sources of inspiration. *Serena-Maneesh* was recorded in Chicago, in production mogul Steve Albini's Electric Audio studio, in Brooklyn, in Oslo, and in Stockholm. Michigan-native singer-songwriter **Sufjan Stevens** played the flute and marimba on the album, and Daniel Smith of the New Jersey–based eccentric **indie pop** group the Danielson Famile added his own sensibilities to the album.

Songs off the debut, for example, "Sapphire Eyes" and "Drain Cosmetics," were quickly made into videos. Later that year, the album was distributed (with two extra tracks) on record labels in France and Germany. Soon after, Serena-Maneesh toured with Oregon-based **indie pop** group **The Dandy Warhols**, and, in 2006, the band toured with the English rock act Oasis. Also in 2006, the band was awarded a Spellemannsprisen award, Norway's equivalent to a Grammy. In the spring of 2007, Serena-Maneesh opened for **Nine Inch Nails** for select dates in Australia and Japan.

The band continued work on its new double album for the Smalltown Supersound label.

Further Readings: http://www.honeymilk.no/serena_index.html; http://www.serena-maneesh.com.

THE SHINS

This Portland, Oregon–based (via Albuquerque, New Mexico, where the group was formed) pop band was catapulted into cult status when actress Natalie Portman name-dropped the group in the 2004 offbeat hit drama film *Garden State* when she claimed, "The Shins will change your life" (Kirschling, 2007). The group, which formed in the late 1990s, already had a leg up though, when

McDonald's featured its song "New Slang" in a French fry ad and a TV commercial for Gap, Inc. featured some of James Mercer's guitar jangling. The Shins, however, have not gone completely mainstream, nor has the group been stripped of its indie rock credibility. Instead, the group has sold millions of albums and topped countless Billboard charts—and stayed in the hearts of loyal fans.

Despite the group's movie and TV credits, The Shins—front man/singer-songwriter/guitarist James Mercer, keyboardist/guitarist Marty Crandall, bassist Dave Hernandez, and drummer Jesse Sandoval—are most known for their music: pop melodies, pretty acoustic guitars, and soothing keyboard sounds that provide the backdrop for narrative lyrics and Mercer's laid-back vocal style.

The Shins released a string of 7-inches on Omnibus Records under the name Flake Music and toured in 2000 with the indie rock group **Modest Mouse** before signing to the prolific Seattle indie label, **Sub Pop Records**, which put out the group's **Lo-fi** debut full-length album, *Oh, Inverted World,* in 2001. *Inverted* earned the group comparisons to fellow indie rockers **Echo & the Bunnymen, Belle and Sebastian**, and Neutral Milk Hotel, but the group's well-crafted lyrics and the subtle, yet poignant emotions captured by acoustic guitar and rolling harmonies, set it apart. A track from "Inverted" called "One By One All Day" was The Shins's first piece of music to be used in a film—it was featured in the 2003 movie *A Guy Thing*.

The pop masters released their sophomore album, *Chutes Too Narrow*, in 2003 on **Sub Pop Records**. The album, which many critics claimed was a "daring" venture for the group, is the biggest selling album in **Sub Pop Records** history, having quickly sold 500,000 copies at the time, beating out the number of copies sold by the last album to hold that title, **Nirvana**'s 1989 album, *Bleach*. Songs from *Chutes* were featured in two feature films: 2004's *In Good Company* and 2005's *Winter Passing*. *Chutes* and *Inverted* have sold a combined 1 million copies.

Actor/director Zach Braff of the NBC TV drama *Scrubs*, who was a big fan of the band, decided to use The Shins' music for the soundtrack to his directorial debut, the film *Garden State*—and the pairing was perfect. The soundtrack (Sony music), which featured music by the bands Frou Frou, Coldplay, Zero 7, Iron & Wine, and Nick Drake, won a Grammy Award for "Best Compilation Soundtrack Album for a Motion Picture, Television or Media" in 2005. Critics almost unanimously agreed, though, that The Shins' songs were the shining moments in the film and the reason the soundtrack became a "must-have" for indie fans everywhere. The success of the film, which grossed a cool $26 million, caused sales of *Inverted* to skyrocket.

The Shins released its third full-length album, *Wincing the Night Away*, in 2007 (**Sub Pop Records**), proving the group was more than Zach Braff's favorite iPod selection. Featuring huge melodic arcs and assuring fans that Mercer and company can fill stadium arenas with their sound, *Wincing* included hip-hop influences, psychedelic leanings, and even synthesizer samples. The first single from the album, "Phantom Limb," garnered a lot of press (it is about a lesbian couple),

Lead singer James Russell Mercer of the Oregon-based indie rock band The Shins performs at the Orpheum Theater in Boston on March 15, 2007, in support of the group's album *Wincing the Night Away*. [AP Wide World Photos/Robert E. Klein]

but the media did not harp on the subject matter too long that it detracted from the musical quality.

Mercer, long known for slipping poetic one-liners in The Shins' songs, recorded a great deal of *Wincing* on his own before presenting it to the label. Mercer did so in his studio in his home in Portland, Oregon—the very same house where soft-hearted indie crooner **Elliott Smith** had lived and recorded his music. Within the first week of its release, the album sold over 110,000 copies and hit #2 on the Billboard charts. *Wincing* beat the record previously held by another **Sub Pop Records** band, **The Afghan Whigs**, for the highest placing LP, whose 1996 album had hit #79.

Mercer and company hit the road in 2006, appearing on the bill for the Sasquatch! Music Festival at the Gorge Ampitheatre in George, Washington, and the Siren Music Festival on Coney Island in Brooklyn, New York. The group played a show with fellow indie rockers **Belle and Sebastian** at the Hollywood Bowl in California in 2006. The Shins added a new member to the fray in early 2007—multi-instrumentalist Eric Johnson of the experimental folk-rock group the Fruit Bats. Mercer added a few new additions to his own family that year as well when he eloped in 2007 (the couple had a child together that spring).

The group also launched a massive, multilegged tour in support of the album, playing with rockers Vive Voce at the Paramount Theatre in Austin, Texas, that spring before hitting the road with the Warped Tour 2007, performing on CBS's *Late Show with David Letterman,* appearing live on NBC's *Saturday Night Live,* and gigging at the Shockwaves NME Awards 2007 Show. London-born singer-songwriter Lily Allen and California's Cold War Kids were the openers for The Shins' 2007 North American tour.

Mercer provided backing vocals for two tracks on **Modest Mouse**'s 2007 album, *We Were Dead Before the Ship Even Sank.* The Shins got on board to help raise money for Los Angeles, California's KCRW radio station as part of "A Sounds Eclectic Evening" event. In a showcase of generosity and the spirit of giving back, The Shins recorded songs for the 2007 Waxploitation compilation to benefit the people of Darfur. Other bands that contributed songs to the album include The Black Keys, **Bloc Party**, **Bright Eyes**, The Cure, and Animal Collective, among others.

The band announced that two of its albums, *Wincing the Night Away* and *Oh, Inverted World,* were certified Gold in 2008. The group was also nominated for three Grammys that year, including Best Alternative Music Album, a category in which the band lost out to **The White Stripes**.

Further Readings: Robbins, Ira. *The Trouser Press Guide to 90's Rock (Trouser Press Record Guide).* 5th ed. Palmer, AK: Fireside, 1997; http://www.myspace.com/theshins; http://www.subpop.com; http://www.theshins.com; http://www.waxploitation.com.

SHOEGAZING

Taking its name from the stance singer-songwriters took while performing it, this subgenre of indie rock emerged in England in the early 1990s. One album, however, is credited with capturing the essence of the signature "shoegaze" sound—1991's *Loveless* by the Irish/British rock quartet group **My Bloody Valentine**. Other bands that are often categorized under the shoegazing umbrella include Ride, Curve, Lush, and **The Jesus and Mary Chain**.

The shoegazing sound incorporates a generous heaping of distortion, clouded by noisy guitars, detailed drum fills, and vocals and melody that were seamlessly mixed into this overwhelming wall of sound in which it was difficult to distinguish one sound or instrument from another. The British music magazine **NME (New Musical Express)** is often credited with developing the term, while the term itself single-handedly explains the subgenre's signature qualities—subdued or passive-sounding vocals, introspective lyrics, and fuzzy guitars. **NME (New Musical Express)**'s rival publication, *Melody Maker,* had its own way of describing the shoegazing movement. Resident journalist Steve Sutherland took a negative stance on it, coining the phrase "The Scene That Celebrates Itself," claiming the pop was "dreamy" and lyrics "simpleminded" (http://www.last.fm/group/Shoegaze/forum/4445/_/76149). Rumors also abounded that the term was taken from subversive author William S. Burroughs's 1959 novel *Naked Lunch.*

Shoegazing is hardly ever discussed without the inclusion of English producer Alan Moulder, who worked with a majority of these bands. Moulder produced music by U2, Depeche Mode, **My Bloody Valentine**, the Smashing Pumpkins, and **The Jesus and Mary Chain**, among others. Moulder helped to shape the shoegazing sound with his production vision and an ability to layer multiple sounds that neither seemed forced or disjointed.

Alan McGee, the founder of the independent British record label Creation Records (home to several pioneering shoegazing bands), also played a big part in the history of the shoegazing subgenre. McGee, who formed the label back in 1983, signed the Scottish alternative rock group **The Jesus and Mary Chain** a year later, releasing its debut album, *Psychocandy,* which helped to shape the future of shoegazing. That album, which is considered one of the touchstones of indie rock, also influenced future bands such as **My Bloody Valentine**, Butthole Surfers, and The Stone Roses, which would carry the shoegazing torch into the next decade. *Psychocandy* captured the fuzzy distortion of the 1960s rock group **The Velvet Underground**, mixing with it the pop sensibilities of The Beach Boys and an overdose of feedback, an effect by which a piercing noise is produced by the return of sound from an audio output (such as an amp or a speaker) to an input (such as a microphone). In an ironic twist though, **The Jesus and Mary Chain** opted for an inexplicable position during the band's live performances—to the dismay of ticket holders, the bandmates often played with their backs to the audience.

The group to help define the signature look of the shoegazing subgenre (namely looking down at one's shoes during a live performance) was **My Bloody Valentine**, which signed to Creation Records in 1988. The bandmates' shoegazing tendencies, however, derived from the need to look down at their feet in order to adjust the guitar pedals while they played. The group's 1988 debut full-length album, *Isn't Anything,* helped put the subgenre—and the band—on the indie rock map, and in turn, kick-started the shoegazing movement. The seamless distortion and faded vocals influenced countless shoegazing bands to come.

My Bloody Valentine's 1991 EP, *Loveless* (another of Moulder's production successes), however, has become the band's best-known release to date. It is also the recording that critics claim best captured the shoegazing sound (this album also nearly caused Creation to go bankrupt after the label bankrolled the estimated $500,000 production costs to make the album); it is considered the climax of the shoegazing genre and still ranks among the top indie albums of all time.

One of the most prominent shoegazing bands of the 1990s, the British band Lush honed its pop skills as time waned on, but its longevity kept the shoegazing subgenre alive and well from its formation in 1988 well into the next two decades. The English quartet released a trio of full-lengths that eschewed the shoegazing sound after its debut EP cemented the group's status as one of the best-selling British bands of the early 1990s. The Cocteau Twins' Robin Guthrie produced Lush's second EP, *Mad Love* (1989). Lush toured as part of the second annual **Lollapalooza** festival with the likes of **The Jesus and Mary Chain**, Pearl Jam, and the Red Hot Chili Peppers.

Lush's label, 4AD Records, was home to several other shoegazing bands such as the English **indie pop** trio Pale Saints, which captured the shoegazing sound with clever production. The Pale Saints' 1990 album, *The Comforts of Madness,* ranks among the top shoegazing albums of all time; the **indie pop** trio mastered the mix of feedback and noise with clever pop. The prolific Scottish indie rock trio the Cocteau Twins was also among the most influential shoegazing bands of that era, signed to 4AD in the early 1990s. While their earlier albums did not represent the group's shoegazing talents, the dream pop (dream pop is a fusion of pop and **post-punk** music) group's 1990 LP, *Heaven or Las Vegas,* became the group's signature album in the vast history of the subgenre. The Cocteau Twins' foray into the subgenre came about only after the group decided against hiring a bass player to replace a departing bandmate. Instead, the group members doubled up on guitars and focused on building a layered sound that, through *Heaven* and other releases such as its 1984 LP, *Treasure,* would evolve shoegazing even further, changing the direction toward an even bigger, more convoluted sound than ever before.

The English alt/space/psychedelic rock trip Spacemen 3 contributed to the shoegazing legacy by adding unintelligible vocals to a thick wall of sound and droning guitars. This group's shoegazing tendencies, however, are rumored to have been the effect of years of heroin abuse. Spacemen 3's distinct shoegazing album was its 1989 album, *Playing with Fire,* a recording that was drenched in reverb and distortion.

The British shoegazing quartet Ride (of which Oasis bassist Andy Bell was a member) received critical acclaim, but the group did not experience the commercial success that its shoegazing contemporaries did. Ride's most notable shoegazing releases—1990's trippy LP *Nowhere* and 1992's *Going Blank Again* (replete with an eight-plus-minute instrumental)—became signature albums in the shoegazing movement. Ride was heavily influenced by **My Bloody Valentine**.

Britain's Chapterhouse, which had been performing gigs with Spaceman 3, was another notable shoegazing band. It was the band's noisy live shows and insular lyrics that earned it the shoegazing tag. Chapterhouse's 1991 LP, *Whirlpool,* is often listed among the top shoegazing albums of all time. The band, however, received some flack for playing riffs that sounded too similar to those made popular by **My Bloody Valentine**. Chapterhouse was also responsible for introducing drum samples to the shoegazing subgenre—for years, shoegazing bands had prided themselves on playing intricate, layered drum kit fills.

Heavily influenced by the Cocteau Twins and **My Bloody Valentine**, the English dream pop quintet Slowdive signed to Creation Records in the early 1990s. Slowdive's early EPs received praise from the British musical press, but its 1991 debut full-length album, *Just for a Day,* was considered a disappointment. Slowdive's second album, 1993's *Souvlaki,* became a legendary shoegazing release for the layered guitar tracks and full wash of sound. *Day,* however, seemed to have been a victim of bad timing, having been released right around the time that **grunge** music made by such bands as **Nirvana** were wooing everyone in the music industry. Consequently, shoegazing bore the brunt of the backlash, and Slowdive's subsequent releases did not sell well.

The early 1990s English alt rock quartet Catherine Wheel possessed certain shoegazing characteristics with its noisy rock and penchant for overusing guitar pedals onstage. The group shed its shoegazing tag like an old skin with its sophomore album, *Chrome* (Fontana Island, 1993), leaning toward a fuller rock sound. The English group Swervedriver, which was also signed to Creation Records, cleverly melded shoegaze with hard rock. Swervedriver, which formed in 1989, disbanded in 1999 after experiencing label trouble.

The English musical collaboration Curve arrived late to the shoegazing scene, but the band managed to stay a float well into the mid-2000s. The group's dark lyrics caused some critics to claim that the entrance of Curve was the exact moment where shoegazer met goth. Modern groups that bear heavy shoegazing influences include the Black Rebel Motorcycle Club, M83, Bethany Curve, Scarling, and Televise, which was formed by former Slowdive drummer Simon Scott.

Several spin-offs of shoegazing have emerged within the indie rock spectrum—among them electrogazing (created by groups like Shockwave), emogazing (made popular by groups like Garbage) and even Viking Death Metal Shoegazing (which was reportedly created by ex-Cocteau Twin Elizabeth Frazer).

Further Readings: Azerrad, Michael. *Our Band Could Be Your Life: Scenes from the American Indie Underground 1981–1991.* City, State: Back Bay Books, 2002; http://www.cocteautwins.com; http://www.creation-records.com; http://www.4ad.com; http://www.mybloodyvalentine.net; http://www.spacemen3.co.uk; http://www.subpop.com/bands/JAMC/website; "What Is Shoegaze?" http://www.last.fm/group/Shoegaze/forum/4445/_/76149.

SIRE RECORDS

Long before it was an imprint of major label Warner Bros. Records, Sire Records was at the center of indie music. Founded by near-poor former *Billboard* magazine clerk/entrepreneur/Brooklyn native Seymour Stein and producer Richard Gottehrer in 1966, Sire Records aimed to sign talented artists they truly believed in. Stein, who built the label with Gottehrer from the ground up, became well known for his musical instincts, penchant for risk-taking, and ear for talent. When Stein saw the **Ramones** perform in the late 1960s, he said he had a desire to "sign them on the spot" (Devenish, 2005). The **Ramones** recorded its first album for Sire, which was released in 1967 and recorded for as little as around $7,000. Later, Stein would sign such acts as The Dead Boys and **Talking Heads**. Such deals helped build Sire's reputation and foundation as one of the rising star labels of the era. The visionary record label founder and his partner often found themselves competing head-to-head with major labels like Columbia to sign hot up-and-coming acts, but Stein often won out due in large part to his seemingly crystal-ball-like ability to recognize trends before they were popular.

Even one of the first acts that Stein signed—a Dutch group called Focus—experienced success with its 1973 single "Hocus Pocus." Stein saw promise in a young band from New York City called **Talking Heads** and a rising star in a young David Byrne, who would go on to become a Grammy winner and an icon. Stein, who heard about **Talking Heads** from the **Ramones**, first saw the group perform at New York City's CBGB nightclub (where, he claimed in a *Rolling Stone* interview, he often slept).

Word of Stein's groundbreaking efforts spread throughout the music industry, and he earned a reputation for standing up for artistic integrity and nurturing his artists' wants. The music industry quickly recognized Stein's synergy with the artists on the Sire roster and their music—he was a stalwart supporter of each and every band he signed. In that sense, he was a throwback to the label founders of yesteryear mostly in part to the fact that he was a true fan who simply wanted to help talented musicians put out good music. Stein's reputation preceded him and Sire Records' success and reach grew exponentially.

In the 1980s, Stein focused on new wave acts, signing bands such as **The Smiths**, The Cure, Soft Cell, Depeche Mode, Tom Tom Club, and even Madonna. Stein reportedly liked the young star's demo tape so much he asked his staff to bring her to the hospital where he was recovering from a heart attack so he could meet her and sign her to his label. Stein was also intelligent enough to realize that a partnership with a major label like Warner Bros. (WB) could have more of a positive impact on his bands than a negative one. The distribution deal the label signed with WB helped give his acts a larger platform and broader reach in the marketplace. But Stein maintained all creative control and he protected his artists from outside legal woes or restrictions from lawsuit- or controversy-fearing label executives.

The Pretenders' front woman Chrissie Hynde attributes her personal success to Stein. After signing the band in the early 1980s, The Pretenders stayed with the label for nearly two decades. Even Madonna, who has since risen to pop culture's highest heights, was humbled by Stein's passion for the music and his drive to help bands that he believed in. (Believe it or not, Madonna was a risk for Sire, and the long shot, as Stein's instincts always did, proved fruitful.)

In the 1990s, Sire was still signing cutting edge acts. Bands such as K. D. Lang and Seal were added to the roster. And in the 2000s, Sire continued to sign such burgeoning acts as The Von Bondies. But even Sire had its share of bumps; Sire soon parted ways with folk/pop singer Mandy Moore after inking a deal with her in the mid-1990s; the two cited "creative differences" as the reason for the split. In 2005, almost 40 years after he founded Sire, Stein was inducted into the Rock and Roll Hall of Fame in Cleveland, Ohio, and was awarded the Lifetime Achievement Award; past recipients include John Lennon, *Rolling Stone* magazine founder (and Rock and Roll Hall of Fame founder) Jann Wenner, and talent scout/producer John Hammond.

Sire celebrated almost 40 years of groundbreaking history with the 2005 box set *Just Say Sire: The Sire Records,* a collection of 60-plus songs, 20 videos, a

DVD, and a massive booklet containing tributes from the various Sire artists whose careers Stein cultivated and who have become his long-time friends. Bands that contributed songs to the collection include Madonna, Wilco, **My Bloody Valentine**, **The Smiths**, Lou Reed, The Replacements, The Cure, and The Pretenders, among others.

Sire Records kicked of its first **South by Southwest (SXSW)** showcase in 2007. The event featured performances by acts such as Armor for Sleep, The Shys, The Spill Canvas, and Against Me!, among others.

Further Readings: Devenish, Colin. "Sire Boxes Madonna, Heads," August 5, 2005. http://www.rollingstone.com/news/story/7524661/sire_boxes_madonna_heads; Southall, Brian. *The A–Z of Record Labels.* Tampa, FL: Sanctuary Publishing, Ltd., 2000.

SLEATER-KINNEY

These indie punk feminists emerged as part of the **Riot Grrrl Movement** that spawned from the underground music scene in the early 1990s. Armed with politically charged lyrics, a **DIY (Do-It-Yourself)** work ethic, and unabashed opinions on sexuality, sexism, and the male-dominated structure of the music business, Sleater-Kinney—Carrie Brownstein, Corin Tucker, and Janet Weiss (who joined the group in 1997, replacing early member Lora MacFarlane)—formed in the mid-1990s in Olympia, Washington.

Turning in bobby pins for hardcore bass lines and bold political banter, Sleater-Kinney has inspired young women with its drive and determination. Tucker, who had been playing in the group Heavens to Betsy, and Brownstein, who played in the "queercore" band Excuse 17, formed Sleater-Kinney after meeting at their respective gigs; they connected via their musical adoration of a local act known as Bikini Kill, which had been proclamating its radical feminist views and spouting hardcore punk music that proved its members could hang with the boys.

Tucker and Brownstein left their prospective groups behind and recorded Sleater-Kinney's self-titled debut album (Chainsaw Records, 1995), a supercharged punk record that called to arms girls who were fed up with the "boy's club" mentality of the indie scene. *Sleater-Kinney* proved the fervent feminist trio was a musical force to be reckoned with, but not everyone believed that the girls had much staying power. The media did little to help squash notions that the band was nothing more than a novelty act—three angry young women packing Hello Kitty purses with a few gripes about boys who had done them wrong. But as the group soldiered on, its message grew stronger and soon fanzines were getting behind the group, helping to spread its message—and attracting fans outside the **Riot Grrrl** realm.

For Sleater-Kinney's sophomore LP, *Call the Doctor* (Chainsaw Records, 1996), lead vocalist Tucker adopted a fierce yawl, proclaiming, "I'm the queen of rock 'n' roll" on the track "I Wanna Be Your Joey Ramone." Similarly, such bold statements revealed a trifecta of women who were not ones to take themselves too seriously, but it also drove home the fact that they were also a trio of women who were ready to stand up and fight anyone who did not take their messages or ideas seriously. In

1998, *Rolling Stone* claimed the album would help the group to become "the first female band to rule the world" (http://www.rollingstone.com/artists/sleaterkinney/albums/album/213012/review/5945176/call_the_doctor), but Sleater-Kinney was not the type of band to treat the crown so lightly. In a 2002 *New Yorker* article, music writer Ben Greenman served as the megaphone for what would have likely been the group's response, stating that it would be "insulting to call Sleater-Kinney the best female rock band in the world when they're one of the best rock bands, period" (http://www.newyorker.com/archive/2002/08/12/020812gore_GOAT_recordings).

Sleater-Kinney went on the road, performing its anthemic punk music for hordes of enthused young women who were starting to push their way through mosh pit–loving males to the front row. Standing behind its pro-choice stance and inciting women to stand up for equal rights, Sleater-Kinney was quickly garnering critical acclaim, but the fact that the group had not sold millions of records was not a topic of concern. Instead, the bandmates felt that the simple feat of communicating their message or creating a discourse about their songs' subject matter—gay rights, women's rights, and the government—was more rewarding than big royalty paychecks. The often-surprising group even went so far as to politely turn down an invitation to play **Lilith Fair** because the bandmates did not want to play a festival their fans could not afford (tickets ran about $35 for the show).

Sleater-Kinney quickly became icons and idols for female music fans nationwide (Tucker's idols growing up were **Sonic Youth**'s Kim Gordon and poet/singer-songwriter Patti Smith), while Brownstein, who was not shy about revealing the fact that she is gay, inadvertently became a sort of poster child for gay rights. Meanwhile, Weiss, who also plays for the indie rock group Quasi, made her official appearance on Sleater-Kinney's 1997 album, *Dig Me Out,* the group's first recording with the **Kill Rock Stars** label. Critics claim this was the point that the bandmates were finally able to shed their Grrrl image and be recognized as the talented musicians they were—without all of the political and social commentary that had been forever linked to them like a dragging tailpipe. The two-guitar attack and synergy of their playing was a powerful force, and critics lauded the album with high praise.

The Hot Rock (**Kill Rock Stars**, 1999) gathered even bigger praise, and the loud ladies were heralded for taking punk rock to the next level and making it their own. *One Beat* (**Kill Rock Stars**, 2002) was considered equally great, pushing the group's exposure to the realm of mainstream listeners. Pearl Jam invited Sleater-Kinney to tour as its opening act in 2003, and the experience served as inspiration for Sleater-Kinney's highly acclaimed seventh studio album, *The Woods* (**Sub Pop Records**, 2005). The esteemed album, which was produced by David Fridmann (who has worked with The Flaming Lips and Weezer), reportedly worked with Sleater-Kinney to tamper with the framework of the group's sound and venture further than it ever had before; the result was a work that many considered Sleater-Kinney's best yet. It sold upwards of 70,000 copies and topped the Billboard Top Independent charts.

After *Woods,* however, the group spilled the bad news that it would be going on an indefinite hiatus, citing that the efforts put into recording the album nearly tore the group apart. Sleater-Kinney's final concert was fittingly performed at the famed 9:30 Club in Washington, D.C. in August 2006. The group reached out to fans on its Web site, asking for retrospective photos or footage of the band to include in a DVD. Sleater-Kinney has not recorded or released any new material since the bandmates began that period of much-needed time off. During the group's indefinite hiatus, Tucker continued her work on the board for the non-profit Rock 'n' Roll Camp for Girls in Portland, Oregon. Brownstein continued to work as a music blogger for National Public Radio through 2008.

Further Readings: Turner, Cherie. *Everything You Need to Know About the Riot Grrrl Movement: The Feminism of a New Generation.* New York: Rosen Publishing Group, 2001; http://www.chainsaw.com; http://www.choiceusa.org; http://www.girlsrockcamp.org; http://www.killrockstars.com; http://www.sleater-kinney.com.

SMITH, ELLIOTT

Folk-punk singer Elliott Smith left behind a repertoire of moody, introspective songs and a legacy as one of the most talented (and tormented) singer-songwriters of the twentieth century when he passed away on October 21, 2003, at the age of 34. Police ruled Smith's death a suicide (his wounds appeared "self-inflicted" according to the Los Angeles County Coroner's office), but the case is still technically considered "open."

Smith, who rose to fame in the early 1990s, battled a lifetime of alcoholism and depression. After leaving the band Heatmiser, Smith forged on alone, releasing his debut solo effort, *Roman Candle* (Cavity Search Records, 1994), a record of culled together **Lo-fi** home recordings that earned the troubled troubadour comparisons to such soft-spoken singer-songwriters as Jackson Browne, Bob Dylan, and Nick Drake. But Smith had more in common with these legends than it appeared on the surface—he, too, had something personal to reveal, something deep to say, about the world, its trappings, and our fateful positions in it.

For his 1995 eponymous album (**Kill Rock Stars**), Smith continued to pluck his guitar, composing sad, emotive songs about drugs, addiction, love, and nightmares. Born in Omaha, Nebraska, Smith spent the majority of his life making music and playing in Portland, Oregon; the accomplished guitar player was also adept at playing drums, bass, harmonica, clarinet, and piano. Smith became a local star in his hometown, but his star rose even higher when Smith was approached by his friend, director Gus Van Sant, to write a song for his 1997 film *Good Will Hunting;* the song, "Miss Misery," was nominated for an Oscar for Best Original Song.

DreamWorks Records signed Smith for his next album, 1998's *XO,* which showcased more of the singer's pop sensibilities and his maturation—and development—as a songwriter. The melodic flow of Smith's songs and the smooth harmonies sounded much like The Beach Boys on Prozac—but Smith's lonely tracks did not deter listeners for their dark point of view. Instead, fans seemed intrigued (and even touched) by his honest efforts. *XO* was Smith's best-selling album; this effort and his 2000 record, *Figure 8* (DreamWorks) featured fuller productions and songs that seemed to shed light on the shy performer's inner thoughts. Tracks such as "Everything Means Nothing to Me," "Wouldn't Mama Be Proud," and "Somebody That I Used to Know" could have possibly been autobiographical statements, but even though Smith did not shy away from discussing his personal demons, he never directly referenced the depth of his sadness or the inner conflict he faced day to day.

Smith began work on what was to be his sixth studio album, *From a Basement on the Hill* (Anti Records, 2004), but he did not live to see its release. The album, which oddly included the song "A Fond Farewell," was released exactly two days before the one-year anniversary of his death. Smith had made plans to release a two-disc album, but his friends in the music industry were forced to choose the track listing for him when he passed. *Hill* peaked at #19 on the Billboard charts; one track he had written, "Suicide Machine," was barred from the album by Smith's remaining family members.

Smith's records have sold over half a million copies since his death. In 2005, 22 unreleased tracks were leaked online, and fans suspected a forthcoming post-humous record. *To: Elliot From: Portland* (Expunged Records), a collection of covers of Smith's songs by his musician friends, was released in the spring of 2006; the album cover art features a sketch of the artist, walking alone down the street with his hands in his pockets. Portions of the proceeds from the album were donated to Smith's memorial foundation for the charity Free Arts for Abused Children. The album was mixed and produced by his ex-girlfriend at a music studio that Smith had helped a friend start. Another posthumous album, *New Moon* (**Kill Rock Stars**) surfaced in 2007; Smith's friend and former producer Larry Crane chose the tracks for the two-disc collection. Rock photographer Autumn de Wilde put out a book of over 200 photos of Smith entitled *Elliott Smith;* the 2007 tribute features forewords by Beck and by **Death Cab for Cutie**'s Chris Walla.

Often tagged "the patron saint of indie music," Smith's passing left an indelible hole in (and mark on) the world of indie rock. Tributes to Smith continued to pop up all over—a 2008 tribute to the musician was held in March at Emo's Lounge in Austin, Texas, featuring members of the bands Zykos, Lions, Lalaland, and Rite Flyers, among others.

Further Reading: Nugent, Benjamin. *Elliott Smith and the Big Nothing.* Cambridge, MA: Da Capo Press, 2005; de Wilde, Autumn. *Elliott Smith.* San Francisco: Chronicle Books, 2007; http://www.anti.com; http://www.elliottsmithbsides.com; http://www.freearts.org; http://www.interscope.com; http://www.sweetadeline.net.

THE SMITHS

Of all the indie bands to emerge in the 1980s, the British rock group The Smiths made one of the most lasting impressions in rock history. Entrenched in the **DIY (Do-It-Yourself)** mentality and fueled with a love for pop music, The Smiths were formed in 1982 in Manchester, England, by the most dichotomous of duos—the edgy, rock 'n' roll purist, guitarist Johnny Marr and the group's front man Morrissey, who often played the part of a melancholic, self-absorbed, troubled poet (he also often wore a fake hearing aid on stage and made public declarations of his own celibacy). The pair met through a mutual friend who knew Marr was looking for a lyricist.

Morrissey, though he had briefly been in a band called the Nosebleeds, was primarily a struggling writer; he had written two books: one about deceased actor James Dean and the other about the raucous New York City band the New York Dolls. Marr, on the other hand, was already an accomplished musician (he plays guitar, harmonica, keyboard, and he sings). The pair—who had for years suffered from a severe personality conflict that kept them on the borderline of being "on the outs" with one another—teamed up to make the best of their skills; Morrissey was a great lyricist and attention-grabbing front man, and Marr was a brainiacish guitar player who wrote solid pop melodies.

The Smiths—of which the additional founding members included bassist Andy Rourke and drummer Mike Joyce—was signed to the independent label **Rough Trade Records** just a year after the band's formation; the band soon released its debut single, "Hand in Glove." The single was just the first in a long line of controversial song titles (and misinterpreted lyrics) that would both haunt and earn the band publicity-worthy headlines for the remainder of its career. Heralded by legendary DJ John Peel, buzz around the single and the group started to grow, and the band slowly became a staple of the underground music scene in the United Kingdom. Soon, though, Morrissey's dramatic persona and the band's catchy, synthesizer-powered indie/alternative pop/rock music made them cult heroes.

The upbeat, danceable tempo of the group's songs and Morrissey's swaggering vocal style caught on like wildfire after the release of the follow-up single "This Charming Man," which helped the band gain an even bigger following. The single went to #25 on the Billboard charts, and the band's next single, "What Difference Does It Make," peaked even higher, hitting #12. The British press started covering the band like paparazzi on Hollywood celebrities, and with the help of college radio, soon fans in the United States caught wind of the Brit act. The Smiths released its eponymous debut album in 1984. The raw-sounding album featured the track "Suffer Little Children," which was surrounded by a heap of debate because the topic of the song was a series of graphic real-life murders that occurred in Britain in the 1960s. The band also stuck out for its attention to the arts; the group's album cover art stood out among the pop-inspired albums on the shelves—in fact, the cover of the group's debut album was a film still from the 1968 film *Flesh,* and snippets of the group's lyrics and titles of songs have been borrowed from literature ("Pretty Girls Make Graves" is a line from a Jack Kerouac novel; it is also the name of a popular modern indie rock band).

In the early 1980s, The Smiths performed on the popular British music TV show *Top of the Pops*— the bandmates performed barefoot. In 1984, The Smiths released what would become the group's first top ten single, "Heaven Knows I'm

Miserable Now." The next year, though, Morrissey turned up the volume on his press- and publicity-related antics. The pompadour-haired singer pushed the title of the band's 1985 sophomore album, *Meat Is Murder,* to nearly unreasonable lengths when he insisted that none of the band members be photographed eating meat. He even went so far as to declare that he was a vegetarian. *Meat* debuted at #1 on the charts, and there was no turning back. Armed with new member guitarist Craig Gannon (a former member of the band **Aztec Camera**, who replaced Rourke during a temporary eviction from the band based on the fact that he was struggling with a heroin addiction), The Smiths released its third studio album, *The Queen Is Dead,* in 1986. The title was inspired by Morrissey's own criticism of the British government (he had been outspoken about his disenchantment with Prime Minister Margaret Thatcher on more than one occasion), and the album topped critic's charts all over the world. **NME (New Musical Express)** ranked *The Queen* second on its list of the Best Albums of All Time and *Spin* magazine added the album to the top of its 2005 list of the" 100 Greatest Albums from 1985 to 2005." Considered one of the best rock albums for its pop sensibility and clever lyrics, *The Queen,* however, did not sell as well as expected in the United States.

Later in 1986, Gannon was fired and Rourke came back on board, but the band's plans for a new album were put on hold when Johnny Marr was involved in a car crash. The guitarist did not sustain any major injuries, but the band canceled a few shows to give him time to heal. The Smiths' next series of singles were successful, especially the hit "Panic," in which Morrissey sang over and over, "hang the DJ." The band's follow-up single, "Shoplifters of the World Unite," was a big hit in the United States. It has gone on to become one of the band's signature songs, peaking at #12 on the charts.

The transition from 1986 to 1987 was a tough one for The Smiths. Inner band strife was coming to a boiling point over the band's new musical direction—Morrissey was forever devoted to the sound of 1960s pop while the frustrated Marr wanted to move toward the decade they were in. A lack of compromise resulted in the band's breakup in 1987. **NME (New Musical Express)** announced the bad news with the bold headline "Smiths to Split," and fans around the world mourned the loss of what is considered one of the greatest **post-punk** bands of all time. Two "posthumous" albums were released later that year: *Strangeways, Here We Come* and the live album *Rank.*

Ever the idealist dreamer, Morrissey embarked on a solo career. Since the band's split in 1987 he has released more than eight studio albums and built a solid foundation as a rock 'n' roll icon. Marr, in the meantime, played sessions and became members of various bands such as **Talking Heads**, Sinéad O'Connor, the Pet Shop Boys, Billy Bragg, The Pretenders, The The, and Electronic before he found his permanent home in 2006 as an official band member of the popular indie band **Modest Mouse**. Rourke joined the Buzzcocks when that group reunited in 1991. Morrissey continues to record albums and tour as a solo artist.

A reunion tour is highly unlikely; in fact, the media reported that Morrissey rejected a $75 million offer to reunite and tour with the original lineup (Cohen, 2007). Both Rourke and Joyce sued Morrissey and Marr in 1996 claiming that the pair owed them money from the band's heyday. The legal matter was settled outside of court (although two years later a judge did rule in favor of Joyce), but the rift still remains in tact.

NME (*New Musical Express*) magazine ranked the controversial song "This Charming Man" #11 on its list of the "50 Greatest Indie Anthems Ever" in 2007, almost 25 years after its original release. Rourke and Joyce contributed to the 2007 documentary *Inside The Smiths,* telling the story of the band from their point of view. Only one other documentary captured what it was like to have been in the middle of this Manchester maelstrom—the 2006 unauthorized documentary *The Smiths: Under Review,* a collection of live footage, videos, interviews, TV appearances, and rare footage. Morrissey continued to tour in 2007, and he announced plans to release two new albums on a new record label in 2008.

Several Smiths albums have been reissued over the years (mostly through Warner Bros. Records), and compilations have emerged as well; *"Singles"* debuted in 1990 and *The Very Best of The Smiths* (featuring a black and white photo of the English actor Charles Hawtrey on the cover) was released in 2001. The Smiths have influenced countless bands over the years—including Oasis, The Verve, Suede, The Stone Roses, and The Libertines, among others.

Further Readings: Cohen, Jonathan. "Morrissey Rewards Diehards, Quashes Smiths Reunion," August 23, 2007, http://www.billboard.com/bbcom/news/article_display.jsp?vnu_content_id=1003630174; Goddard, Simon. *The Smiths: Songs That Saved Your Life.* 3rd ed. Kew Gardens, Richmond, Surrey, England, United Kingdom: Reynolds & Hearn, 2006; Woods, Paul A. *Morrissey in Conversation: The Essential Interviews* Medford, NJ: Plexus Publishing, 2007; http://www.askmeaskmeaskme.com; http://www.morrisseymusic.com.

SNOW PATROL

Rivaling English rockers **Radiohead** for the top slot among the best indie acts of all time, Snow Patrol has been called one of "the most exciting guitar bands in the UK" (http://www.nme.com/news/snow-patrol/24607). This four-piece whimsical indie rock group from Northern Ireland was waiting in the wings for years until its 2003 single "Run" caught the attention of radio deejays, who spun the track until it ended up on the charts.

Initially formed in Scotland in the mid-1990s, Snow Patrol—lead vocalist/guitarist/songwriter Gary Lightbody, guitarist/backing vocalist Nathan Connolly, bassist Paul Wilson, sample master/keyboardist Tom Simpson, and drummer Jonny Quinn (founding member Mark McClelland has since left the group)—enjoyed more than a few past identities, having been known as "Shrug" and "Polar Bear" before settling on Snow Patrol after losing a lawsuit filed by an American band that was already known as Polar Bear.

Snow Patrol's first gigs and recordings remained under the radar for several years; the band played gigs in local pubs and at Dundee University, where many of the band members studied, but the pedigree of musicians the band worked with has never been a topic of contention. **Belle and Sebastian**'s drummer Richard Colburn and front man Stuart Murdoch added their talents to the group's first EP, *Starfighter Pilot,* which was released on the U.K. indie label, Electric Honey Records in 1997.

Jeepster Records (**Belle and Sebastian** was the first band on its roster) took the reins to put out Snow Patrol's follow-up EP, *Little Hide,* a few years later, and the group experienced minor success with a single from that album. The group's appearance in a documentary about Jeepster Records and an interview on MTV in the late 1990s bolstered its platform, and the group finally earned a spot on the indie rock map.

Snow Patrol's first full-length album, *Songs for Polarbears,* featuring 19 tracks, was released by Jeepster in 1998 (the 2006 re-release features 23 tracks). Featured on the album are nine B-side tracks that were originally recorded as promotional material, many of which have since become rare tracks. Members of Snow Patrol joined the Scottish supergroup The Reindeer Section, which features members of **Belle and Sebastian**, **Arab Strap**, and Mogwai. Despite the artistic success of Snow Patrol's recent releases, poor album sales prompted Jeepster Records, however, to let Snow Patrol go from its roster. Island Records imprint A&M Records picked the group up in the early 2000s for its third release, *Final Straw,* and despite general pessimistic predictions about the album's sales, the appropriately titled album demonstrated the group's ability to make quality, anthemic rock that was suitable for digestion by the masses. Tracks on the record showed Lightbody and company dipping their amps into various genres—from **shoegazing** to electronic affects, showcasing the texture of their instrumental capabilities and the depth of Lightbody's vocal prowess. Snow Patrol's first single, "Ask Me How I Am" off its 2001 sophomore release, *When It's All Over We Still Have to Clear Up,* garnered the group even more exposure, perhaps, through online downloads by fans.

The album's success skyrocketed, topping charts and selling over 2 million copies in the United States and achieving the feat of becoming the 26th most popular album that year in Britain. Excessive touring, however, took its toll on the group, resulting in McClelland's departure. Snow Patrol brought its longtime touring keyboardist, Tom Simpson, on board to round things out again. Universal Records released a live DVD of the group's performance at London's Somerset House in 2004. Snow Patrol released the album *Live and Acoustic at Park Ave.* in 2005.

In 2005, Snow Patrol orchestrated *The Trip,* a compilation featuring some of the group's favorite bands and influences—**TV on the Radio**, Rilo Kiley, Four Tet, Mylo, Jack Knife Lee, and more. A venerable mix tape, *The Trip* cleverly blends the **indie pop**, rock, electronic, and hip-hop genres together seamlessly. The Los Angeles, California–based label Vitamin Records released a tribute album to the band, *The String Quartet Tribute to Snow Patrol,* in 2005. Snow Patrol earned the opening slot on Irish supergroup U2's "Vertigo" tour in the summer of 2005.

The group's fourth full-length album, *Eyes Open,* followed in 2006, with melancholic pop songs that earned it quick comparisons to London's mega rock band Coldplay. The standout single from that album, "Chasing Cars," received extensive radio play, helping the album to top critics' "Best Of" lists that year. *Eyes Open,* which features the vocals of several Celtic choir stars, garnered the group almost instant success, charting in its homeland and in the United Kingdom and even reaching number one on Ireland's album charts—the group's first feat of that kind. Subsequent singles from *Eyes*—"Hands Open" and "You're All I Have"— added to the album's accolades, helping the band to sell out shows all over the globe (tickets for various shows sold out in a matter of hours).

Eyes was certified Gold (and then it spiraled to multi-Platinum status), and Snow Patrol became the first U.K. rock act in 13 years to appear on the Billboard Hot 100 Singles Chart. The group launched an extensive North American tour in support of *Eyes* shortly after its release, but the lineup was cut short when Lightbody came down with a case of throat polyps. Lightbody healed quickly, though, and the group resumed its tour schedule, adding dates at festivals in Europe, Australia, and Asia before heading stateside.

Snow Patrol donated proceeds from the sales of a collection of songs it contributed to called "The Cake Sale" to the charity organization Oxfam International's "Make Trade Fair" program in 2006. The group's "give-back" campaign continued: a portion of the proceeds from sales of yet another single from *Eyes* benefited the Save the Children foundation and a cover of John Lennon's song "Isolation" for a video campaign to support Amnesty International's efforts to secure justice against war criminals in Sudan.

In 2006, *Eyes Open* received a nomination for the top Album of the Year prize at the Choice Music Prize, which honors the album "that best sums up the year in Irish music" (http://www.nimusic.com/shownews.asp?id=376). iTunes named *Eyes* the Best Alternative Album of 2006. The apex of success for "Chasing Cars" (which hit #5 on the Billboard Hot 100 Chart) came when it was nominated for Best Rock Song at the 2006 Grammys; however, fellow Irish rockers U2 walked away with the prize. *Q* magazine nominated the track for Best Track and *Eyes* for Best Album that same year. Snow Patrol topped its 2006 successes off with a performance at the 2006 American Music Awards in Los Angeles.

The year 2006 was a busy year for Snow Patrol. The band performed at the **South by Southwest (SXSW)** music festival in Austin, Texas, appeared on NBC's *Tonight Show with Jay Leno,* its single "Chocolate" (Polydor Records) was featured on the soundtrack to the dramatic 2006 film *The Last Kiss,* and "Chasing Cars" was featured on the finale for ABC's hit TV drama *Grey's Anatomy* and entered the U.K. charts at #15. The group hit a minor snag, though, when it was forced to cancel the remainder of its tour dates in France and Germany in the fall of 2006 when Band member Paul Wilson injured his arm and shoulder.

In 2007, Snow Patrol was nominated for Best British Group, Best Album (for *Eyes Open*), and "Chasing Cars" was nominated for Best Single at the annual BRIT Awards. The group performed alongside indie groups **The Killers** and California alt rock/funk band Red Hot Chili Peppers at the awards ceremony. The group received three nominations for the 2007 Meteor Ireland Music Awards—Best Irish Band, Best Irish Album, and Best Live Performance.

Snow Patrol shared the main stage with the Foo Fighters at the 2007 V Festival in England after heading out on tour with the bands OK Go and Silversun Pickups and appeared on the bill for that summer's two-day Oxegen music festival in Ireland and playing Scotland's "T in the Park" festival with the **Arctic Monkeys**, Kings of Leon, **The Killers**, Razorlight, and **Arcade Fire**, among others. The band finished up some 2007 tour dates before taking a brief break.

Further Readings: "Choice Music Prize Irish Album of the Year," November 1, 2007, http://www.nimusic.com/shownews.asp?id=376; "Snow Patrol Score Major US Chart Hit," http://www.nme.com/news/snow-patrol/24607; http://www.snowpatrol.com; http://www.vitaminrecords.com.

SONIC YOUTH

The band that defined for generations what it means to be "indie," Sonic Youth—which is still comprised of its original core members—has been the iconic underground rock/punk act of indie rock. The noise rock group's history is so rich and varied and its songs so innovative and rule breaking, few have been able to put their finger on the secrets to how the group has put out almost 20 successful albums throughout its career. Formed in 1981, amid the heyday of punk and pomp in New York City (NYC), Sonic Youth (who were briefly known as the Arcadians) unleashed a storm of distortion, feedback, and jarring guitars on the masses in the group's home city, meshing its **DIY (Do-It-Yourself)** ideals with the art scene and punk aesthetic of the 1980s.

Inspired by the sounds of **post-punk**, hardcore punk, and no wave music and moved by the wild lyrics of poet/musician Patti Smith and the unpredictable, supercharged energy of the NYC punk act **Iggy and The Stooges**, Sonic Youth forged its own niche, playing its first official live show at a ten-day musical festival that band member Thurston Moore organized. Front man/guitarist/vocalist Moore, bassist/guitarist/vocalist Kim Gordon, and the band's first drummer Lee Ranaldo started out performing with gigging drummer Richard Edson and composer Glenn Branca, who signed the group to his own label, Neutral Records. Sonic Youth released a self-titled EP, recorded at Radio City Music Hall, which garnered rave reviews from the press, but got little exposure or distribution.

Bob Bert stepped in to replace Edson, but he was quickly replaced by Jim Sclavunos, who eventually gave way to Steve Shelley, who became the group's first permanent drummer. Sonic Youth toured Europe to solid reviews, but the press in the group's home city was not too kind to it. Popular music critic Robert Christgau started a feud with Moore when he pigeonholed the group in with a larger caste of bands that simply played noise loudly—and badly—through their amps. Moore, who was infuriated by the comment, retitled a few of the group's songs in an effort of retaliation. Moore's ill temper proved fruitful, however. When the group returned after a few stints of bad luck in Europe, where Moore had

Sonic Youth (left to right): Lee Ranaldo, Kim Gordon, Steve Shelley, and Thurston Moore. [AP Wide World Photos]

destroyed stage equipment, it was received with open arms by fans in New York City who were anxious to see this raucous, precarious band up close.

Sonic Youth's debut album, *Confusion Is Sex* (**SST Records**, 1983), a raw, moody effort, seemed to convince listeners that the band's only ambition was to destroy the institution of making music with a wall of destructive sound. Sonic Youth secured a distribution deal with **Rough Trade Records** and released its third full-length studio album, *Bad Mood Rising* (1985), which revealed the group's ultimate plan—to make art of out experimentation. Sonic Youth's music became the definitive sound of NYC's Lower East Side—a grungy, unpredictable array of sounds that, while they did not seem to have any business being together, seemed held together by some invisible glue. In 1986, Sonic Youth released the dark "*EVOL*, and with the group's 1987 "all rock" album *Sister,* the group had finally stuck it to Christgau when it was voted among the top albums on the "Pazz & Jop" Best Of list published annually by *The Village Voice*, the paper where he worked.

Sonic Youth venerably stopped time in the indie world with its 1988 double album, *Daydream Nation,* a work that proved the group had finally found its voice. *Nation* was a noisy, nonstop rock album that the music community declared a tour de force. The album, which quickly sold out of record stores, featured the hit single "Teen Age Riot," which became a regular feature on college radio stations. With *Nation,* Sonic Youth walked the thin line between mainstream media and its indie roots, but the group somehow always managed to teeter on the tightrope, never wavering too close to the "dark" side on popular culture; *Rolling Stone* called the album one of the best releases of the decade.

Sonic Youth continued to tour around NYC, and several labels attempted to court the band, until Sonic Youth eventually signed to Geffen Records for 1990's *Goo*. Sonic Youth's impact on indie music was captured in the 1992 documentary *1991: The Year Punk Broke*, which captured the group touring with a then-unknown band called **Nirvana**. Sonic Youth also toured in 1991 as an opening act for Neil Young, which gave the group its first taste of playing arena shows for thousands of fans.

Producer Butch Vig (who produced **Nirvana**'s *Nevermind* album) worked with the scraggly four-piece band on its next album, *Dirty* (Geffen, 1992). The famous and iconic album cover art—a ragged looking orange doll made of yarn—became an icon that has long been associated with the group. By this time, Sonic Youth was on par with the **Pixies** as one of the most influential acts of the 1990s, and *Dirty* showed that the band might actually give **Frank Black** and his crew a run for the trophy for the coolest indie rock band. Sonic Youth seemed to mature, taking the best parts of its previous albums—well-crafted melodic pop, unyielding noise, uncontrollable intensity, and pure rock—with *Dirty*. The album went Gold, making its way into the hands of mainstream listeners, and producing hits like "Sugar Kane" and "Youth Against Fascism."

Sonic Youth's hard-rocking, highly atmospheric albums began to top each other on the music charts, and the group played packed shows weekly. Amid the mayhem of success, Moore and Gordon were married; they had a daughter in 1994 and moved to the quiet, woodsy town of Amherst in western Massachusetts. The band stayed together despite geographical obstacles, and Sonic Youth released its highest charting album yet, *Experimental Jet Set, Trash and No Star* (1994), an unconventional effort that showcased a more thought-out (though not too polished) production quality.

In the mid-1990s, Sonic Youth (SY) achieved two rites of passage among the popular culture set—the band headlined 1995's **Lollapalooza** music festival, and it made a cameo appearance on an episode of *The Simpsons*. The group built a home recording studio, where it worked on its next release, *Washing Machine* (Geffen, 1995). The Breeders' Kim Deal contributed backing vocals to *Machine*, which contained poetic lyrics and cleverly layered arrangements. Moore and company also founded their own Sonic Youth Recordings, on which they put out several EPs before returning to their label for their next full-length album, *A Thousand Leaves*, in 1998, proving the then 30- and 40-something-year-old Moore and company still had the spunk that got them started.

Musician/producer/guitarist (and sometimes bassist and synthesizer player) Jim O'Rourke became an official SY member with 2000's *NYC Ghost & Flowers* and 2002's *Murray Street* (Geffen). The second in a trilogy of albums about the storied tales of NYC's Lower East Side, *Murray* marked the band's 16th album; it was named for the street that was home to the band's NYC recording studio. Now filling out stages as a quintet, Sonic Youth released 2004's *Sonic Nurse*, an album that featured more pop culture references than an episode of *Seinfeld*. When O'Rourke announced his departure, former **Pavement** member Mark Ibold filled in for him on tour.

An accomplished poet, Moore released his fifth book, *Mix Tape* (Universe Publishing, 2005), a retrospect about the cassette tape in which the scraggly singer/guitarist discussed the musical play lists of the artistic glitterati—actors, directors, talk show hosts, and more. In 2006, Sonic Youth released *Rather Ripped* (Geffen), an accessible album on which a 50-ish Gordon wailed as if it was 1981. The Library of Congress honored the group's genre-defining sound by admitting *Daydream Nation* into its National Recording Registry.

Moore released his second solo album, *Trees Outside the Academy* (Ecstatic Peace Records) in 2007. That same year, in what seemed like an oxymoronic turn of events, Sonic Youth partnered with Starbucks to release a hits album, which will be sold in the chain stories throughout the United States. Kim Gordon rationalized the deal by saying that the coffee mega chain is "less evil than Universal Music" (Maher, 2007), the band's current label. Sonic Youth has remained active in the music scene, dabbling in various projects. In 2007, the band recorded a version of the Bob Dylan track "I'm Not There," which was featured in the Todd Haynes–directed film of the same name. The band's song "Kool Thing" was featured in the PlayStation 2 game "Guitar Hero III."

The bandmates continued to marvel the public by dabbling in anything and everything they could. The group announced plans to produce a traveling art show featuring the work of artists who have worked on veteran rockers' album covers. Moore and company toured through 2008. At a concert at the Bruce Manson Castle in New Zealand in February that same year the group performed its entire 1998 album *Daydream Nation*. Still, Sonic Youth managed to squeeze in time to work on a new album scheduled for release in 2009.

Further Readings: Foege, Alec. *Confusion Is Next: The Sonic Youth Story.* New York: St. Martin's Griffin, 1994; Maher, Dave. "Kim Gordon: Starbucks 'Less Evil Than Universal.' " http://www.pitchforkmedia.com/article/news/45890-kim-gordon-starbucks-less-evil-than-universal; Moore, Thurston. *Alabama Wildman.* Sudbury, MA: Water Row Press, 2000; Moore, Thurston. *Mix Tape.* Riverside, NJ: Universe Publishing, 2005; http://www.ecstaticpeace.com; http://www.geffen.com; http://www.robertchristgau.com; http://www.sonicyouth.com; http://www.sonicyouth.com/dotsonics/thurston.

SOUTH BY SOUTHWEST (SXSW)

Much like the word "hipster" (a term that has often been associated with svelte, trendy inner city twenty-somethings), South by Southwest (SXSW) had a long history before it became a household name. The popular music conference and festival began rocking Austin, Texas, for its first show in 1987, almost 20 years before the southern city was a preeminent destination on the music map. Music business veterans and Austin natives Nick Barbaro, Roland Swenson, and Louis Black co-founded the festival after attending the successful New Music Seminar in New York City in the mid-1980s.

SXSW has expanded profoundly in proportion and scope and now includes a film festival. The 2007 festival showcased over 1,500 acts on over 70 stages and attracted 123,000 fans, music journalists, and band members, of which over 11,000 participated in the music conference. At the 2007 Film Conference and

Festival, 240 films were screened, attracting over 5,000 attendees. Over 4,000 people participated in the 2007 SXSW Interactive Festival, which brings together "the world's most creative web developers, designers, bloggers, wireless innovators and new media entrepreneurs" (http://2006.sxsw.com/interactive/).

Much like the popular 1980s shows *Solid Gold* and *Star Search,* SXSW is *the* showcase arena for up-and-coming breakthrough artists looking to score big (albeit on the indie circuit). Bands and musicians hobnob with music journalists, publicists, managers, and label heads at local bars, gigs, and daily discussion panels (covering everything from record deals, legal and copyright issues, marketing, promotion, and technology) at SXSW's band camp–style atmosphere.

The idea for SXSW was borne from—and inspired by—the very (isolated) location that has since made it famous. Positioned almost equal distance between the East and West coasts, which have long dominated the music scene, Austin, Texas, seemed like the perfect place for a music festival, which would bring the two coasts together. International bands were drawn to the festival by SXSW satellite offices, which were set up in places such as Europe—and the 700 attendees who flocked to the 1987 event have since grown more than tenfold.

Combining the Internet with creative forces and individuals who are passionate about music, SXSW is a breeding ground for the very aesthetics and values that have been intrinsic to the indie genre. Held over what is usually a span of four days, the music portion of SXSW has featured keynote conversations with the likes of Neil Young and featured live audience interviews with the Beastie Boys. Past keynote speakers have included Bob Mould (1995), **Nirvana**'s Krist Novoselic (1996), and Lucinda Williams (1999). Rare appearances have been a proud highlight of the festival. In 2007, *Rolling Stone* editor David Fricke conducted a live interview with **The Smiths**' Morrissey before the English singer performed at the Austin Music Hall.

SXSW features music of an array of genres—pop, country, jazz, reggae, blues, electronica, indie, and hip-hop; venues, which are within walking distance of one another, run the gamut from dive bar to polished concert hall. Badges cost upwards of $350, the majority of which are purchased by either college students or employees of the music business, who are able to expense their whole trip— including airfare, dinners with bands, and, pending approval from their company's finance department, the occasional backstage massage.

The 2007 SXSW roster included such acts as **The Apples in Stereo**, **Bloc Party**, Cold War Kids, comedian David Cross, Lily Allen, Interpol, Les Savvy Fav, Mates of State, **Meat Puppets**, Ozomatli, Pete Townshend, **Say Hi to Your Mom**, The Pipettes, **The Walkmen**, Thurston Moore, Wooden Wand, and Zach Galifianakis, among others.

The South by Southwest, Inc. company launched its Canadian counterpart, North by Northeast (NXNE), in the mid 1990s, which is held annually in Toronto, Canada, in late spring. The event is held in conjunction with the Toronto, Canada–based alternative weekly newspaper, *NOW*.

The 2008 SXSW conference (the 22nd annual event) was held from March 7–16 in Austin, Texas. Bands on the bill included Corn Mo and the .357

Lover, Faux Fox, Kaki King, Martha Wainwright, and The Slits, among hordes of others.

Further Readings: Pruett, Jon, and Mike McGuirk. *The Music Festival Guide: For Music Lovers and Musicians.* Chicago: Chicago Review Press, 2004; http://sxsw.com.

SST RECORDS

In true **DIY (Do-It-Yourself)** style, **Black Flag** guitarist/founder Greg Ginn formed this record label as an outlet for his band's music in 1978 in Long Beach, California. Like many musicians, Ginn felt that giving away the creative rights to his music was the equivalent to waiving the white flag. In its early days, SST (which Ginn named after the electronics company Solid State Transformers) was simply an outlet for **Black Flag**'s music; SST's first release was **Black Flag**'s LP *The Damaged,* which is considered one of the best punk albums of all time. As the band and Ginn became more well known, the label began to release other bands' music. Heralded for his hardworking, steadfast **DIY (Do-It-Yourself)** attitude and resourcefulness, Ginn's label grew in size and scope—and influence.

Employing only local guys in the underground scene—Steve "Mugger" Corbin, Chuck Dukowski, and Joe Carducci (all of whom were also part owners of the label)—SST was soon prosperous enough that Ginn and company could share the wealth. SST soon signed local bands in the Los Angeles area such as the Minutemen, The Stains, and the Descendents, all of which also happened to be friends of **Black Flag**. The success of albums by those bands allowed SST to branch out beyond the Golden State. In the late 1980s, SST Records hit its pinnacle when Ginn added such bands as **Hüsker Dü**, Dinosaur Jr., Screaming Trees, **Bad Brains**, **Sonic Youth**, and Soundgarden to the roster. Ginn's business savvy proved profitable when he branched out and formed a few subset labels.

But SST's high note hit a standstill when artists on the roster claimed, in an odd turn of indie rock irony, that the label had not paid them long overdue royalties. Legal battles ensued, and the label eventually lost the legal rights to its back catalog. Meanwhile, **Black Flag**'s record sales were down, and one of its albums was actually considered a "flop." The bandmates stopped talking to each other for a while, and SST struggled to buy back the rights to the catalog. In the wake of all that legal trouble, **Sonic Youth** bought the rights to its master tapes and signed to Geffen Records. SST, which had also started releasing and working on jazz material, eventually went into hibernation during the 1990s, a time that was considered the label's darkest days.

Ginn strove to revive the label in the 2000s, but his hopes led only to empty promises. The catalog for such bands as **Bad Brains**, the Minutemen, **Black Flag**, **Hüsker Dü**, and the Descendents remain intact on the label.

Further Readings: http://www.sstsuperstore.com.

STEVENS, SUFJAN

Indie folk singer Sufjan Stevens was born in the rough-and-tumble city of Detroit, Michigan, but his songs are light and airy, covering close-to-home topics such as family, friends, and faith; the multi-instrumentalist musician has even been known to wear elaborate wings on stage during live performances.

Following his departure from the band Marzuki, Stevens left his home state and set out on his own, reaching New York City in 2000. Stevens, who has become part of the folk music revival of the twentieth century, made an ambitious announcement of his plans to record 50 concept albums—each covering one of the states of the United States. The first of such efforts, *Greetings From Michigan: The Great Lake State* (Asthmatic Kitty, 2003) featured songs with lengthy titles and melancholic, nostalgic tones about regular people living regular lives. Each work will no doubt suffer in comparisons to the cache of state-ly recordings, but "Illinois" (or *Come on Feel the Illinoise*, as the title reads) (Asthmatic Kitty, 2005), which included touching songs with even lengthier titles, earned Stevens praise, with its on-target, poetic descriptions of Midwestern life told through the eyes of an über sensitive folk singer. *Rolling Stone,* the *New York Times, The Onion,* and **Pitchfork Media** commended "Illinois," which sold upwards of 500,000 copies, with glowing reviews.

Stevens, who helps run the Asthmatic Kitty Records label through which his records are released, adheres to the **DIY (Do-It-Yourself)** ethic: writing, recording, and producing his own songs on what many artists would consider a shoestring budget. Word of mouth spread about his debut album, *A Sun Came!,* a 21-track collection of skillful orchestral arrangements and songs that varied so drastically in sound, many fans offered that the singer-songwriter was merely using artistic license to explore genres until he found the right combination.

Often playing upwards of 20 instruments on an album, the prolific Stevens released the box set in 2006 titled *Songs for Christmas,* a five-disc collection of dusty old EPs the Michigan native had recorded early in his career. The box set also included a lengthy booklet with an essay by novelist Rick Moody, who wrote the book *The Ice Storm.* Stevens wrote so much material for the second installation of his state-by-state endeavor that he culled the remaining tracks into the 2006 work *The Avalanche: Outtakes and Extras from the Illinois Album!.*

Throughout his career, Stevens's fan base has grown. The old-world feel of his songs and the raw honesty of his lyrics have helped to increase exposure for the new folk movement he has been a part of since his start. By giving a modern twist—twinkling guitars, electronic effects, and sweet sounding harmonies—to old-fashioned topics, Stevens has revitalized the indie folk genre. In 2005 he was awarded the New Pantheon Music Prize, which has replaced the Shortlist Music Prize of late. Stevens released the album *Swan Songs* in 2007. The band performed on the bill for the 2008 Tibet House benefit in New York City.

Further Readings: Weissman, Dick. *Which Side Are You On? An Inside History of the Folk Music Revival in America.* London: Continuum International Publishing Group, 2006; http://asthmatickitty.com; http://www.sufjan.com.

SUB POP RECORDS

Sub Pop Records grew from a fanzine called *Subterranean Pop* that college student Bruce Pavitt had founded. Back in the late 1970s when everyone was raging about

U.K. bands, Pavitt was supporting the homemade sounds of local bands. After moving from Olympia, Washington, to the bustling city of Seattle in 1986, Pavitt circulated cassette-only recordings of local acts, which he peddled at gigs and at Fallout, a record/skateboard store that he owned with his friend Russ Battaglia.

Sub Pop soon became the glue that held the Seattle scene together as Pavitt and company started putting out music by such bands as **Nirvana**, Mudhoney, Tad, and Soundgarden. The media outlets created a frenzy around the burgeoning label, generating buzz and introducing the underground scene to the mainstream. But long before the label's apex of success, it was putting out music that would go down in the annals of music history. Pavitt released a compilation called *Sub Pop 100*, and in 1987, the label released the debut EP *Dry as a Bone* by the first-ever **grunge** act, **Green River**.

Oddly enough, too, Pavitt's relationship with the band Soundgarden was formed after he met the man who would become Sub Pop's co-founder, Jonathan Poneman. Poneman and Pavitt were soon a seamless team, who, together, started signing local acts they knew from the neighborhood and music scene. Sub Pop released the debut EP *Screaming Life* by the up-and-coming act Soundgarden in 1987. Pavitt befriended other local musicians from the bands Tad and Mudhoney through odd jobs he held as a DJ and an employee at a store that supplied elevator music.

Sub Pop's fate was sealed in 1988, however, when Pavitt signed an up-and-coming act called **Nirvana**. Clad in flannel shirts and scraggly beards, **Nirvana** seemed like just another aspiring rock band. But the label's instincts proved fruitful when it spent what may have seemed like the rest of its money on a band with messy hair and sloppy vocals that hardly anyone had heard of. Sub Pop financed **Nirvana**'s debut single, "Love Buzz," before sending the group to tour in Europe and then flew the trio back to the United States to record its debut album, *Bleach*. The album, which was recorded for a reported sum of approximately $600, sold only 35,000 copies in its first two years. But by 2001, sales of *Bleach* were tallied at over 10 million copies. Near broke and teetering on bankruptcy, Sub Pop's luck took a 180-degree turn when major labels suddenly came calling to buy out the two acts it had spent almost all of its money on—Soundgarden and **Nirvana**, which were bought by Geffen. Pavitt and Poneman were suddenly freed of their financial woes—and the two were both made instant stars in the music business.

Free to surf the waters of the music business without a financial care in the world, Sub Pop expanded its scope to sign bands on the East Coast, such as **The Afghan Whigs** (which hailed from Chicago). But to this day, the label prides itself on primarily signing and promoting local acts from the Northwest. Ever the pioneer, Pavitt started a newsletter that would become a big hit on the underground music scene, and the label was heralded for its **DIY (Do-It-Yourself)** ethic and aesthetic. Pavitt is still involved in the label, but he leaves the daily responsibilities to Poneman. There are over 40 active bands signed to the Sub Pop roster. Bands on the roster include The Postal Service, Kinski, Go! Team, Iron and Wine, **The Shins**, The Helio Sequence, Mudhoney, The Catheters, **Comets on Fire**, Fruit

Bats, The Thermals, **The Album Leaf**, and Wolf Parade. The label has even signed some comedians to its roster, such as David Cross of TV's *Arrested Development* fame. Even to this day, Poneman and Pavitt's instincts seem to be on the money—literally. The Postal Service's 2003 album, *Give Up* is one of Sub Pop's best-selling albums, having sold over 800,000 copies (**Nirvana**'s *Bleach* is reportedly the only Sub Pop album that has sold better than that). The Top 5 selling album by a Sup Pop recording artist is the 2003 album by **The Shins**, *Chutes Too Narrow,* which moved 175,000 copies.

In 2007, Poneman started the label Hardly Art, which operates out of the same Seattle offices where Sub Pop Records is based. Pavitt, who is reveled as a pioneer and supporter of the **grunge** movement, has since retired from the music business.

Further Readings: Rudsenske, J. S., and J. P. Denk. *Music Business Made Simple: Start An Independent Record Label (Music Business Made Simple).* New York: Schirmer Books, 2005; http://chronicle.com/subscribe/login?url=/weekly/v48/i03/03b01801.htm; http://www.subpop.com.

SUNNY DAY REAL ESTATE

Sunny Day Real Estate's live shows veered between frenzied rock fests and mellowed out, **shoegazing**-like slow jams, but even more memorable than Sunny Day Real Estate's front man Jeremy Enigk's seemingly bipolar performances was his haunting voice.

Formed in 1992 during Seattle's emergence as a hotbed for indie rock, Sunny Day Real Estate (SDRE) experienced an intense, though short-lived career that was accented by various time-capsule-worthy events—such as the time Enigk, in a letter to his band following its breakup, addressed the fact that God played a major role in his decision to end the band, a plan that had its roots in the days when he became a born-again Christian.

Throughout its career, though, SDRE—William Goldsmith, Dan Hoerner, Nate Mendel, and Enigk—released albums with guitars so loud they rivaled the sonic boom of punk acts that strove to destroy amps and ear drums, while Enigk's high-pitched howl of a voice tore through crowds to the point that the band could almost be categorized as an **emo** act. SDRE released its debut album, *Diary*, in the spring of 1994 on **Sub Pop Records**. *Diary* was a standout debut for its clever lyrics and the undeniable emotive prowess of Enigk's voice.

SDRE's antipress antics proved puzzling to most—the band released one official band photo and granted only one interview. Relying mostly on the Internet to gain fans and promote its music, SDRE released its second album, the 1995 self-titled LP (aka *The Pink Album*), which boldly presented an album cover painted completely pink.

The band subsequently—and mysteriously—disbanded, and Enigk released his solo effort, *Return of the Frog Queen* in 1996 on the band's label, **Sub Pop Records**. SDRE reformed in 1997, but Mendel, who had left to join Foo Fighters with Dave Grohl, was not among the group's reincarnated lineup. The new lineup put out the 1998 album, *How It Feels to Be Something On,* which, despite the band member changes, kept in line with SDRE's strong points. SDRE performed on *The*

Jon Stewart Show in the early 1990s before the comedian became a cult hit. The band released a live album, *Live,* in 1999.

Several myths surrounded the band, its breakup, and even lyrics about God that Enigk reportedly snuck into his live performances. One rumor, though, proved to be a well-thought-out plan devised by the band that took advantage of the clothing store Nordstrom, which had asked the band to appear in one of its print ads. The band created a fake band name and hired a stand-in lead singer, but the store was wise to the false moniker and the ad came out with the correct band name. Still, the bandmates felt they were in effect sticking it to the man with the stunt, and they were proud of their valiant efforts.

Their seminal work, 2000's *The Rising Tide* (Time Bomb Recordings) divided fans who felt the group was not the same since Mendel's departure, while others lauded it for the album's experimental prog-rock fusion; the album art features a striking photo of a statue of a fallen soldier being lifted up by an angel.

SDRE officially disbanded in early 2002; Enigk, Mendel, and Goldsmith reunited to form the group The Fire Theft and put out its debut self-titled album in 2003 on the Rykodisc label. Enigk continued his solo career, releasing the album *World Waits* in 2006 on the Reincarnate Music label, and Hoerner worked with **emo** star Chris Carraba on some music for his band Dashboard Confessional.

Further Readings: Van Pelt, Doug. *Rock Stars on God: 20 Artists Speak Their Minds About Faith.* Orlando, FL: Relevant Books, 2004; http://www.subpop.com; http://www.sunnydayrealestate.net; http://www.timebombrecordings.com.

SUPERCHUNK

No other band represented the sound, actions, and attitude of indie rock like this Chapel Hill, North Carolina band. Also known as Chunk or Superchunk—singer/guitarist Mac McCaughan, bassist Laura Ballance, drummer Jon Wurster, and guitarist Jim Wilbur (Jack McCook was the group's first, though short-lived guitarist)—played by no one's rules but its own.

Superchunk stayed loyal to its label (which McCaughan founded with Ballance) —local independent Merge Records—despite the onslaught of offers made by various major labels that tried to woo the guitar-heavy act from its home base. The group's greatest legacy was the very thing that kept the band from breaking big—its reluctance to join the music business bandwagon and its tried-and-true **DIY (Do-It-Yourself)** ethic that seemed to both shock (and at times offend) the listening public. A good example of the group's stalwart stubbornness is evident in its 1990 debut single, "Slack Motherf- -er" and its debut self-titled full-length album on which the group managed to upstage the group's sloppiness with full-out indie rock and teen angst. "Slack" was reportedly McCaughan's aural response to the laziness of his co-workers at his part-time job.

Superchunk's punk-like sophomore album, *No Pocky for Kitty* (Merge Records, 1991), made the college radio circuit, and Superchunk became a staple in dorm rooms across the nation. The group's aversion to all things mainstream made the bandmates inadvertent heroes of the underground scene. With songs that sounded as though they were recorded in the early 1990s during the apex of indie rock, Superchunk helped put its home city on the musical map, and the band became a "band to watch" amid the music press.

But Superchunk had little care for the press and their finicky tastes. The prolific group released its third album, *On the Mouth,* on Matador Records in 1993, a work that featured its popular female bassist, Laura Ballance, and the album inspired Ballance and McCaughan to form their own record label, Merge Records. Superchunk collected lost songs, B-sides, and singles for the album *Tossing Seeds: Singles 89–91* before scoring a hit with the single "Hyper Enough" off the group's next album, *Here's Where the Strings Come In.*

The group abandoned its staunch our-way-or-the-highway attitude and created a more accessible album (on which they incorporated new instruments such as piano and organ), *Indoor Living* in 1997. A handful of albums later, Superchunk released the 2001 album, *Here's to Shutting Up,* a more mature work that showcased the elements that made them indie rock heroes almost ten years before—a sense of humor ("Phone Sex"), teen angst ("What Do You Look Forward To?"), experimentalism ("Late-Century Dream"), and the fact that the group employed a hardcore female bassist ("Art Class").

Playing up its habit for humor, Superchunk contributed a cover of Destiny Child's hit single "Say My Name" for the 2007 compilation *Guilt by Association.* In 2007, Superchunk recorded the short track "Misfits and Mistakes," which was slated for the soundtrack of the movie for the animated TV series "*Aqua Teen Hunger Force.*" The band played a free show in May 2007 at the refurbished McCarren Park Pool in Brooklyn, New Your, and in 2008, the group announced the digital reissue release of its 2002 effort *Clambakes* live series via Merge Records' Digital Music Store online.

Further Readings: Schwartz, Daylle Deanna. *I Don't Need a Record Deal! Your Survival Guide for the Indie Music Revolution.* New York: Billboard Books, 2005; http://www.matadorrecords.com; http://www.superchunk.com.

T

TALKING HEADS

One of the first bands to be labeled "new wave," Talking Heads has become one of the most influential rock bands of the last 50 years. Its experimental, yet polished sound and danceable pop melodies helped earn the foursome the description—new wave was an offshoot of punk rock that was still rebellious in nature, but it possessed a more defined sound and streamlined structure. Formed in 1974 in Providence, Rhode Island, by students at the Rhode Island School of Design, Talking Heads was so named by the students as a result of what they saw on TV—mere messengers of empty messages, hence the "talking heads." The band, consisting of front man/lead vocalist/guitarist David Byrne, bassist/guitarist Tina Weymouth, and drummer/percussionist Chris Frantz, moved to New York City where it became an integral part of the underground music scene.

Sire Records signed the band, which by then included new member keyboardist/vocalist/guitarist Jerry Harrison, soon after an Artists and Repertoire representative spotted it opening for punk rockers the **Ramones** at the CBGB music club in New York City. The sharply dressed and sometimes "nerdy" group's combination of artsy funk, danceable rhythms, rock riffs, and hints of punk has sustained its reputation and importance 30 years after its inception. Talking Heads—and especially its innovative front man, who is easy to spot with his signature white hair—has become an icon in the pages of the history of rock, influencing tons of bands years after it formed.

Talking Heads toured with fellow New York City rockers the **Ramones** before putting out the group's debut album, *Talking Heads: 77*, on **Sire Records**. The album contained several songs that would be listed among the group's seminal tracks that would make it one of the most often chart-topping pop hit makers of the 1980s, including the catchy art punk dance hit "Psycho Killer." Then the group teamed up with experimental producer Brain Eno, who has also made hit albums with U2 and Paul Simon, for its sophomore album, *More Songs About Buildings and Food*. The group's smart lyrics, paired with front man Byrne's uniquely affected, lyrical vocal style, and its bare bones rock sound made it a cult hit among indie fans.

Eno's work with the band resulted in the critically acclaimed 1980 album *Remain in Light*. The cover art featured an Andy Warhol–esque lithograph print of the band members; it was the first of the group's albums to reach the Billboard Top 20 charts. *Light* featured the band's well-known single "Once in a Lifetime." "Lifetime" was a truly experimental track filled with Byrne's spoken word and the call-and-response chorus; it also showcased the band's new direction toward African music and layered horn sections. Talking Heads' 1983 album, *Speaking in Tongues* featured two of the group's timeless hits—the art punk inflected, dance-inspiring, Top 20 chart-topping, and MTV hit "Burning Down the House," and the band's first "love" song, "Naive Melody." The band headed out on tour and eventually parted ways with Eno. Director Jonathan Demme captured the essence of the group in his 1984 documentary, *Stop Making Sense*. The film, ironically, captured what would be the group's last big tour; the soundtrack to the film was widely successful.

The exhausting tour and desires by each bandmate to pursue other musical projects led the Talking Heads to release one last album—1985's *Little Creatures* —before taking a much-needed hiatus for a few years. Byrne directed the film *True Stories* in 1988, and the band resurfaced with *Naked* (Warner Brothers, 1988). The album proved that despite the band's deal with a major label, the band's artistic value made it profitable for the label and thus allowed the band to maintain creative control over its music. Although the album was considered more accessible and pop driven, it contained world beat influences and rhythms.

As happens with most bands, the front man wanted to try a solo career. In 1991, the band officially announced its breakup, and Byrne set off on his own. Byrne's success as a solo artist was unprecedented; he has gone on to win both a Grammy Award and as Academy Award as well as a Golden Globe in 1987 for Best Film Score for the film *The Last Emperor*. The remaining members of Talking Heads pursued solo endeavors, and Weymouth and Frantz formed the band the Tom Tom Club. In 1996, Talking Heads (minus Byrne) released an album as The Heads entitled *No Talking Just Head*. The Heads released a collection of live performances by the eight-member reincarnation of the band.

A 15-year anniversary of *Stop Making Sense* brought the band together briefly. In 2002, Talking Heads reunited on stage for one night during the group's induction at the Rock and Roll Hall of Fame in Cleveland, Ohio. A reunion is not likely; Byrne and his former bandmates are reportedly not on the best terms. The feud could possibly stem from a 1996 lawsuit by Byrne over the release of The Heads' album, in which he did not take part. Byrne attempted to stop the album from being released, and he even took legal action against Talking Heads' former manager. Byrne reportedly went so far as to say that the other reason that he and the remaining Heads' band members would likely never reunite was that, besides believing that they would simply just be rehashing the past, "musically we're just miles apart" (http://www.theage.com.au/news/Music/Byrning-down-the-house/ 2005/02/04/1107476787488.html).

Further Readings: Domini, John. *Talking Heads:* 77. Granada Hills, CA: Red Hen Press, 2003; http://www.davidbyrne.com; http://www.talking-heads.net; http://www.theage. com.au/news/Music/Byrning-down-the-house/2005/02/04/1107476787488.html.

TED LEO AND THE PHARMACISTS

Washington, D.C. musician/vegan Ted Leo (it is his real name) founded the "intelligent punk" outfit Ted Leo and the Pharmacists after Chisel, the band he was previously playing with, disbanded in 1997. The politically minded singer briefly formed the group Sin Eaters with his brother Danny and musician Sean Green of the group The Van Pelt before taking a stab at a solo career; his debut solo album, *tej leo(?), Rx/pharmacists,* was released on Gern Blandsten Records. He finally decided to add living, breathing Pharmacists—bassist Dave Lerner and drummer Chris Wilson—to his act in 1999. Former Pharmacists include James Canty, of the glam rock act The Make-Up; Jody Buonanno, of the band Secret Stars; and Amy Farina of the Warmers.

Leo and his new punk outfit released a five-song EP, *Treble in Trouble,* in 2000 on Manhattan's Ace Fu Records (home to such acts as Pinback and Ex Models). With *Treble,* though, Leo was still waving his hell-raising political critic flag. Ted Leo and the Pharmacists put out the group's first full-length album, *The Tyranny of Distance,* in 2001 on the Berkeley, California label, Lookout! Records (to which the bands The Donnas and **Green Day** are signed). *Tyranny* featured members of the groups Tsunami, Golden, Telegraph Melts, and Trans Am, and the group added a new member, keyboardist Dorien Garry.

Leo garnered attention when he paid tribute to his idol, The Clash's Joe Strummer, when he contributed a song to the documentary *Let Fury Have the Hour: The Punk Rock Politics of Joe Strummer,* in 2003. Canty departed the group before the punk rock outfit recorded the acclaimed album *Hearts of Oak* (Lookout!, 2003), which earned the group high praises and comparisons to the highly influential American rock group **Pavement**. *Hearts* was a top pick of the critics that year, receiving rave reviews from *Rolling Stone, SPIN, The New Yorker,* and *Entertainment Weekly* magazines. The album also received heavy play on college radio, placing on the top of the *CMJ (College Music Journal)* charts, which led to several TV opportunities for the group—including a hosting gig for Leo on MTV's *Subterranean* show and a performance on *Late Night with Conan O'Brien.* Leo logged extensive miles on the road in support of this album, trekking across the United States for five separate tours and gigging in the United Kingdom and Japan.

The group released the 2004 concert film *Dirty Old Town: Live at Coney Island* and their 2003 EP, *Tell Balgeary, Balgury Is Dead,* on Lookout! Records. The punk outfit performed at 2005's Bumbershoot music and arts festival in Seattle, Washington, and the **DIY (Do-It-Yourself)** artists released three iTunes only tracks that same year before kicking off a world tour. Never one to turn down an opportunity to speak out against the political powers that be, Leo participated in an antiwar protest in Washington, D.C., in 2005 alongside such bands as The Coup and **Le Tigre**. Leo also packed up the group to play a benefit show to assist **Blonde Redhead**'s singer Kazu Makino, who had been injured in a horse-riding accident.

Garry left the band prior to the release of the group's 2004 album, *Shake the Sheets,* which was produced by Smashing Pumpkins' member James Iha's Stratosphere Sound studios in New York City by Chris Shaw, who has worked on albums by such bands as Dashboard Confessional, Bob Dylan, and Public Enemy. *Sheets* debuted at #26 on the Billboard charts. In 2006, Leo sustained a head injury while on a farm in Massachusetts to record music for the group's new album. A newly healed Ted Leo and the Pharmacists supported indie rockers **Death Cab for Cutie** on that group's North American tour. Leo kept busy in 2006 by writing songs for none other than a musical in Seattle, Washington, entitled "Red Bananas." Leo and his troupe performed at Touch and Go's 25th Anniversary Celebration/10th Annual Hideout Block Party in September 2006 in Chicago, Illinois, as part of a long lineup that included 25 bands such as **Girls Against Boys**, **Calexico**, and The Black Heart Procession, among others.

Ted Leo and the Pharmacists released the group's fifth full-length album, *Living with the Living*, in 2007 on Touch and Go Records. *Living*, the group's first release for that label, earned the band rave tags like "thinking man's punk" (http://www.kwur.com/blog/2007/02/ted-leo-and-pharmacists-living-with.html). *Living*, which was produced by **Fugazi** member Brendan Canty, continued Leo's strain of politically charged albums. Coming off its 2007 North American tour with Leo's brother's group, Vague Angels, the group prepped for an appearance at Noise Pop 2007 in San Francisco, **Coachella Valley Music and Arts Festival** in Indio, California, Spain's Estrella Primavera Sound Festival, and a tour in support of *Living*. Leo played a solo gig at the Northsix music club in Brooklyn, New York, in early 2007 to help raise money for the son of musicians J. Robbins (of the bands **Jawbox**, Channels, and Burning Airlines) and Janet Morgan (who is also in the group Channels), who suffers from spinal muscular atrophy.

The band toured the United Kingdom in 2008, and the bandmates continued to post their political opinions on the band's Web site.

Further Readings: KWUR 90.3 FM Blog, "Ted Leo and the Pharmacists—Living with the Living." February 28, 2007. http://www.kwur.com/blog/2007/02/ted-leo-and-pharmacists-living-with.html; Sabin, Roger. *Punk Rock: So What? The Cultural Legacy of Punk*. New York: Routledge, 1999; http://myspace.com/tedleo; http://www.lookoutrecords.com; http://www.tedleo.com.

10,000 MANIACS

One of the most popular and successful alt rock/college rock/indie bands of the 1980s and the 1990s, this Jonestown, New York–based sextet released eight albums together before the group's iconic singer, Natalie Merchant, who was just 17 when she started contributing vocals, departed the group to pursue a solo career. Named for a 1964 low-budget horror movie called *Two Thousand Maniacs!*, 10,000 Maniacs, also known as Ten Thousand Maniacs, owed a significant amount of its success to the group's front woman, who, with her reputation for dancing barefoot on stage and her rich, vibrant voice, became a symbol of the heart and soul of indie music in the 1990s for the collegiate co-eds who idolized her.

Formed in 1981, 10,000 Maniacs (who went through several name changes—the group was originally known as Still Life before switching its name to Burn Victims and settling on 10,000 Maniacs) was comprised of lead singer/pianist Merchant, guitarists John Lombardo and Robert Buck, drummer Tim Edborg and Jerry Augustyniak, who replaced Edborg in 1983, keyboardist Dennis Drew, and bassist Steven Gustafson. 10,000 Maniacs' folk-influenced pop sensibilities

10,000 Maniacs's Natalie Merchant, circa 1990. [Photofest]

appealed to fans of all ages, with catchy hooks and choruses that showcased Merchant's mesmerizing, and at times haunting, vocals. 10,000 Maniacs influenced countless female-fronted bands in the decades that followed, many of whom were inspired by the band's 60's pop-inflected, 70's punk-infused sound, which showcased Lombardo's acoustic prowess and Buck's trademark guitar licks. Well-crafted melodies melded easily into radio-friendly songs that simultaneously put forth raw rock energy and intimate lyrics that kept fans wanting more. Max Weinberg, the bandleader for the house band, The Max Weinberg 7, on CBS's *Late Night with Conan O'Brien* (he was the drummer for Bruce Springsteen's E Street Band in the 1970s), toured briefly with the band for select dates in the 1980s.

10,000 Maniacs played locally, distributing its self-released LP *Secrets of the I Ching* in 1983 before the group's manager, Peter Leak (who has also managed singer-songwriter Dido and punk/pop princess Avril Lavigne), helped the band get signed to the Elektra Records division of the Warner Music Group conglomerate and released the group's 1985 major-label debut album, *The Wishing Chair,* a collection of songs that seemed more like poetry set to music than pop tracks. The album, which *Rolling Stone* gave 4½ out of 5 stars, introduced fans to the group's highly danceable pop sound, and, consequently, the group's shows looked like an outdoor free-for-all folk dance. Fuming because of the pressure Elektra put on the band to seek a more "commercial" route, founding member Lombardo departed the band the next year on the eve of the group's sophomore album, *In My Tribe* (Elektra, 1987). *Tribe* proved to be a lucrative album for the group, peaking at #37 on the Billboard charts, where it stayed (fluctuating a bit in terms of rank) for 77 weeks.

Tribe featured four standout hit singles—"Hey Jack Kerouac," "Don't Talk," "What's the Matter Here?" and "Like the Weather." *Tribe,* which was produced by Peter Asher, who has worked with such big-name artists as Bonnie Raitt and Cher, made a star out of Merchant, who once had dreams of becoming a school-teacher. The highly collectible album also featured vocals by **R.E.M.**'s Michael Stipe (with whom Merchant had developed a close friendship) on the track "A Campfire Song" and a cover of the English singer-songwriter/musician/educator/ Islam convert Cat Stevens's "Peace Train." "Peace Train," however, proved unable to live up to its name when Stevens declared his support for the leader of Iran's call for the execution of the author Salman Rushdie; upset by the news, the band re-released *Tribe* without the track.

As a quintet, 10,000 Maniacs put out the politically charged *Blind Man's Zoo* in 1989 (Elektra). *Zoo,* which highlighted Merchant's folk roots, charted at #13 and was eventually certified Gold, selling over 500,000 copies. In 1990, the group released a collection of recordings from its pre-Elektra days. *Hope Chest: The Fredonia Recordings 1982–1983* featured new wave, neo-reggae, and **post-punk** tracks that exhibited the group's broad, genre-crossing abilities and sensibilities. *Our Time in Eden* followed in 1992 (Elektra), containing the hit single "Candy Everybody Wants" and the group's most well-known and signature song "These Are Days," which President Bill Clinton used as his campaign song (10,000 Maniacs later performed at the *MTV Inaugural Ball* for President Clinton in 1993). 10,000 Maniacs's 1993 single "Candy Everybody Wants" featured the group's popular cover of the English crooner (and **The Smiths**' front man) Morrissey's song, "Every Day Is Like Sunday."

At the apex of 10,000 Maniacs' career (following the chart success of the group's 1992 album, *Our Time in Eden*), Merchant decided to leave the group to pursue a solo career. The group's most successful release with Merchant, the live CD recording of its MTV Unplugged performance, however, was released a few months after her departure. The album, which captured what many critics and fans consider to be the hallmark MTV Unplugged concert, went on to sell approximately 3 million copies. *MTV Unplugged* (Elektra, 1993) featured the group's cover of famed New Jersey rock singer-songwriter/musician Bruce Springsteen's song "Because the Night."

10,000 Maniacs pressed on without its raven-haired front woman, adding two new members to the fold. Folk/rock duo John & Mary, comprised of founding member John Lombardo and Mary Ramsey (vocals and violin), joined with the remaining band members to record the group's aptly titled 1997 album, *Love Among Ruins* (Geffen Records). Despite Merchant's absence, *Love* was the group's highest-ever charting album, hitting #24 on the Billboard charts; it featured the group's cover of the 1970's English art rock group Roxy Music's song "More Than This." Throughout this major lineup change, the band adopted the temporary name John & Mary, Rob, Steve, Dennis & Jerry—until it legally regained the rights to write, record, and perform again as 10,000 Maniacs.

Merchant, meanwhile, released her solo album, *Tigerlily,* on her former group's label, Elektra Records, in 1995. Merchant's fans remained loyal to the ambitious singer and the album sold 5 million copies. *Tigerlily* included songs that were reminiscent of 10,000 Maniacs's sound, but Merchant managed to record some standout songs that established her as a solo artist. *Tigerlily* included the song "River," Merchant's homage to her friend, actor River Phoenix, who had recently passed away, as well as an 8-minute long track called "I May Know the Word." Merchant's sophomore solo release in 1998, *Ophelia,* solidified the public's respect for her as a solo artist, resulting in an invitation for Merchant to perform as part of the highly successful all-female music event, **Lilith Fair**. The album reached the Top 10 on the Billboard charts, and Merchant put out the 1999 album *Live in Concert,* a work that led to a solo tour in 2000.

Merchant became increasingly involved with political activist groups, joining antiviolence and animal rights campaigns, performing to raise money for AIDS research, and playing at the annual Tibet House Benefit Concert alongside such acts as rocker Patti Smith, Michael Stipe, Philip Glass, and Phish's Trey Anastasio in 1998. She concluded her 2001 tour with the album *Motherland* (Elektra), topping off a career during which Merchant's collective albums sold over 6 million copies. She also worked as a volunteer for children's and women's issues, nonprofit organizations, got married, and took a brief hiatus to start a family.

10,000 Maniacs moved to Bar/None Records for its next album, *The Earth Pressed Flat,* which sold moderately well for the new lineup. Sadly though, founding member and one of the group's principal songwriters (along with Merchant), Robert Buck, who authored the group's classic songs "These Are Days," "What's the Matter Here?" and "Hey Jack Kerouac," passed away in 2000 of liver failure. The group went on a brief hiatus from 2001 to 2002, returning with the two-disc retrospective *Campfire Songs: The Popular, Obscure & Unknown Recordings* in 2004. Replete with the group's best-loved songs, *Campfire* became a collector's item for fans; it featured a duet song with **R.E.M.**'s Michael Stipe and Merchant singing the song "To Sir with Love" and a cover of the David Bowie track "Starman."

2004 also saw the release of the compilation album *10,000 Maniacs—Time Capsule (1982–1993) by Ten Thousand Maniacs and Natalie Merchant* on Warner Music. This album, however, served the group's career in a more focused manner, featuring original recordings of its signature songs and its MTV Unplugged performance of "Because the Night." 10,000 Maniacs continued to bank on its past successes by releasing the three-album collection (featuring 36 tracks) *Trilogy* on Warner Music in 2006. Merchant stayed busy with her family and artistic endeavors; she was involved with a collaboration between the Royal Shakespeare Company and Opera North in Europe as a sonnet reader in 2007.

Famed rock 'n' roll singer/poet/musician Patti Smith, who was admitted into the Rock and Roll Hall of Fame in 2007, boldly stated that though she preferred her band's version of the song "Because the Night" (she co-wrote the track back in the 1970s with Bruce Springsteen) to the one recorded by 10,000 Maniacs, she did concur that Merchant "is a better singer" (Cohen, 2007).

Further Reading: Cohen, Jonathan. "Backstage at the Rock and Roll Hall of Fame." March 13, 2007. http://www.billboard.com/bbcom/news/article_display.jsp?vnu_content_id=1003722983; McAleer, Dave. *The Book of Hit Singles 4 Ed: Top 20 Charts from 1954 to the Present Day.* Milwaukee, WI: Backbeat Books, 2001; McClachlan, Sarah, and Buffy Childerhose. *From Lilith to Lilith Fair: The Authorized Story.* New York: St. Martin's Griffin, 1998; http://www.maniacs.com/; http://www.nataliemerchant.com/.

TV ON THE RADIO

This Brooklyn, N.Y.–based quintet brought something completely new to the indie rock scene with its experimental blend of atmospheric **post-punk**, electronic, free jazz, trip hop, and **post-rock**. Part of the indie rock resurgence of the 2000s in the "hipster central" neighborhood known as Williamsburg, TV on the Radio (TOTR) is comprised of founding members Tunde Adebimpe (vocals) and David Andrew Sitek (production and keyboards), as well as Kyp Malone (vocals and guitars), Gerard Smith (bass), and drummer Jaleel Bunton; Sitek's brother Jason has sat in on drums for a few recordings.

TOTR has also added the occasional celebrity guest member to its lineup from time to time—guitarist Nick Zinner of the **Yeah Yeah Yeahs**, vocalist Katrina Ford of Celebration, and saxophonist/flutist Martín Perna of the Antibalas Afrobeat Orchestra. The band's members, who can be found sipping coffee at any one of Williamsburg's coffee shops or browsing vinyl at local record stores, are easily recognizable—thanks to Malone's signature jet black Afro, beard, and mustache. Sitek and Adebimpe, who formed the group in 2001, also dabble in many side projects. Adebimpe, who attended New York University's film school, created the video for the **Yeah Yeah Yeahs**' single "Pin," and Sitek, who is also a painter, built his own recording studio and has produced a full-length album for that very same band.

The quintet, which was deemed one of Brooklyn's best bands by several music blogs and Web sites, began handing out copies of its self-produced (with the help of local imprint Brooklyn Milk), self-titled 24-track demo *OK Calculator* (the title of which is a reference to **Radiohead**'s seminal album, *OK Computer*) in its neighborhood, until it caught the attention of the Chicago indie label Touch and Go Records. TOTR released the *Young Liars* EP in 2003, proving the group possessed more soul than the majority of the New York City bands that were making music at that time. TOTR opened for the English punk group The Fall that same year before regrouping in the studio to record its debut full-length album, *Desperate Youth, Blood Thirsty Babes* in 2004. The fruits of that labor included the group's first national tour and stints with the Nebraska indie synthesizer band **The Faint** and Boston alt rock legends the **Pixies**.

Lead guitarist Kyp Malone (left) and lead singer Tunde Adebimpe of the band TV on the Radio perform during the "mtvU Woodie Awards" at Roseland Ballroom on October 25, 2006, in New York City. [AP Wide World Photos/Jason Decrow]

Two releases followed that same year—the single "Staring at the Sun" (via London-based indie label 4AD) and the *New Health Rock* EP (Touch and Go)—as did a tour with the eccentric American musical duet CocoRosie, which was also signed to Touch and Go. After TOTR played the **South by Southwest (SXSW)** music festival, there was no way of slowing things down. The unstoppable TOTR knocked one out of the park when it was awarded the Shortlist Music Prize in 2004 for *Desperate Youth, Blood Thirsty Babes,* which the award committee considered "the most adventurous and creative albums of the year across all genres of music" (Moss, 2004). Other nominees for the prize included fellow up-and-comers **The Killers** and **Franz Ferdinand** and veteran indie darlings Wilco.

Stories about TOTR's intense live shows increased the buzz surrounding the mostly black indie band. Instead of resting on its laurels, the five-piece band headed back to Sitek's home studio Stay Gold, the results of which was the band's response to the Katrina tragedy, a free MP3 "Dry Drunk Emperor," which was named in honor of its subject, President George W. Bush. TOTR, however, canceled a string of live dates, including a performance at 4AD's 25th anniversary concert, after the death of Adebimpe's father in 2005.

Things picked up again with the release of the band's sophomore album, *Return to Cookie Mountain,* in 2006. 4AD released the album in the United Kingdom, but for U.S. distribution, TOTR reached out to music conglomerate Interscope Records (home to a mixed bag of acts such as Eminem, rapper Will Smith, Queens of the Stone Age, U2, and its Brooklyn pals **Yeah Yeah Yeahs**).

Making the move to sign with a major label was a known risk for the band; TV on the Radio acknowledged that the label, which would likely grant the band creative freedom based on the "if it ain't broke, don't fix it" mentality, could very well also begin making artistic demands. In a 2006 interview with **Pitchfork Media**, Sitek said, "A lot of good things could come from it, and a lot of bad things could come from it. I'm sure there's gonna be instances where it's like, 'Hey, why don't you guys cut all your music in half and make two-minute songs about orange juice?' I'm sure that that day's coming. But I'm also sure they're going to be like, 'Hey, that's the coolest thing, let's get it out for free' " (Dahlen, 2006).

The 1970s musician and glam rock icon David Bowie, who met the group back when he purchased a painting from Sitek, sings backing vocals on *Cookie Mountain*. The success of the record catapulted the band into the spotlight, and TOTR was featured in several prominent newspapers and music magazines. *Rolling Stone* said, "The disc might be the most oddly beautiful, psychedelic and ambitious of the year . . . Consider your mind blown" (Ringen, 2006), and the bluntly honest critics at **Pitchfork Media** were even impressed, saying, "This album has such an incredible pull: It doesn't make an atmosphere so much as a space to spend time in, and Adebimpe doesn't become a narrator so much as a witness" (Ringen, 2006). The music review Web site Metacritic.com lauded the album as "one of the ten best records of 2006" (http://www.metacritic.com/music/bests/2006.shtml). The *New York Times* gave the album four stars, and the track "Wolf Like Me" from the album received extensive airplay on several prime-time television shows on such networks as the WB, NBC, and ABC.

TOTR performed the single on *The Late Show with David Letterman,* and the band was featured on the Los Angeles–based radio program *Morning Becomes Eclectic* on KCRW, which has become a launching pad for several indie rock bands. mtvU featured a live interview with the band backstage at the Austin City Limits. TOTR was one of the 20 featured bands to play at MySpace.com's "Rock for Darfur" benefit concert in 2006 to raise money in support of relief efforts by Oxfam International.

In June 2006, TOTR performed as part of The Celebrate Brooklyn Performing Arts Festival, one of New York City's longest-running free outdoor performing arts festivals before kicking off a tour of North America, Japan, Australia, Europe, and South America in support of *Cookie Mountain* in late 2006/early 2007. TOTR was featured on the cover of *SPIN* magazine's "Best of 2006" issue; the magazine listed *Cookie Mountain* Album of the Year in that same issue. The TOTR song "Staring at the Sun" was featured in a 2006 episode of the popular HBO drama "*Entourage.*" TOTR's Adibempe and Bunton made cameo appearances on rapper High Priest's 2006 MP3 single, "Keep Time."

TOTR's video for the song "Province" was nominated for an mtvU Woodie in 2007. The band released a live recording of rits performance at the record store Amoeba Music in Hollywood, California, via its 2007 *Live at Amoeba EP* before continuing its tour with the bands Subtle and the Noisettes.

Further Readings: Dahlen, Chris. "Interview: TV on the Radio." October 2, 2006. http://www.pitchforkmedia.com/article/feature/38737-interview-tv-on-the-radio; Moss, Corey. "TV on the Radio Wins Shortlist Prize, Topping Franz, Killers, Wilco."

November 16, 2004. http://www.mtv.com/news/articles/1493759/20041116/tv_on_the_radio.jhtml; Ringen, Jonathan. "Return to Cookie Mountain" (Review). September 7, 2006. http://www.rollingstone.com/reviews/album/11451605/review/11544925/returntocookiemountain; http://www.amoeba.com; http://www.4ad.com/tvontheradio; http://www.tvontheradio.com.

TWEE POP

Twee pop is to indie rock and pop as PG-13 is to an R rating. They both possess the same power and pomp, but one is just a bit toned down, simpler, and even innocent. Sugary sounding with simpler chord structures but with the same fiery independent streak and with just as important a statement, Twee pop is a sub-genre of indie rock that categorizes bands whose music sways a bit more to pop than rock.

The term was most likely coined after the release of the infamous C86 cassette tape that **NME (*New Musical Express*)** put out in 1986. The bands on this compilation (such as Primal Scream and The Wedding Present), whose chords and progressions were considered more catchy and "poppier" than those of their indie rock peers, soon simply became known as "C86" groups. "Twee" or "Cutie" rock, as it was called, was a term that was collectively coined by such critics as well-known radio DJ John Peel, who considered twee pop music to be more childlike than the rest of the indie rock being played on college radio stations.

Twee pop emerged in the 1980s in the United Kingdom with such bands as The Pastels and The Shop Assistants. Twee pop, in fact, has its roots in the **post-punk** music that leaned closer toward the pop spectrum of the radio dial. **Rough Trade Records** and Postcard Records in Europe curated these types of acts, and, in turn, the media ran full speed ahead with the story. As a result, publications such as **NME (*New Musical Express*)** recognized this new turn in musical history and, hence, the C86 tape was born; the first tape of this kind was C81, which came out five years earlier, but the C86 tape is considered the defining recording at the time.

Back in the United States, such groups as **Beat Happening** sprouted up and such labels as K Records and a handful of even smaller indie labels supported these growing underground pop acts. With this musical wave came the ironic T-shirts: "Twee f- - -er" and "Twee as f- - -." Later incarnations of twee pop arose in such bands as **Belle and Sebastian**, whose soft sounds and whimsical lyrics conjure the sounds of the "dainty" twee poppers who played before them.

Twee pop attracted indie fans that wanted music with a softer edge than punk rock, a more introspective feel than post-punkers, and less of a dance club feel than new wave acts. Twee pop spread throughout the United States and the United Kingdom in the mid-to-late 1980s, and Web sites such as Twee.net sprouted in support of these bands.

A ceremonial concert celebrating the 20-odd-year anniversary of twee pop was held at a two-day festival/concert in 2006 at London's ICA club. Bands on the bill were among those included on the first C86 tape. Other acts on the lineup were those whose music is directly influenced by the C86ers. The *NME*-sponsored lineup included The Magic Numbers, Go Kart Mozart, Vic Godard & The Subway Sect, The Pastels (who appeared as guest DJs), The Wolfhounds, and members of **Aztec Camera**.

Further Reading: Melendez, Benjamin, Daphne Carr, Drew Daniel, and Franklin Duke Burno. *Listen Again: A Momentary History of Pop Music (Experience Music Project).* Durham, NC: Duke University Press, 2007; http://www.twee.net/.

22-20S

Even though the band 22-20s considered itself foremost a blues band, for example, one of its favorite records was Buddy Guy's "Live at the Checkerboard Lounge," its youthful fusion of traditional blues and rock and folk and country elements engaged the rock audiences much more than the bluesmen the group idolized. Formed in Lincolnshire, England, by two teenaged friends, vocalist/guitarist Martin Trimble and bassist Glen Bartup, who had already been playing together for years on the local blues scene. Naming themselves after Delta bluesman Skip James's "22-20 Blues," the pair began gigging in local pubs under the new moniker following the permanent addition of drummer James Irving in August 2002. Keyboardist Charly Coombes eventually came on board permanently to solidify the 22-20s's lineup.

As it was, the 22-20s's initial gigs immediately launched a healthy buzz for the band, and it was quickly fielding interest from various record labels. The 22-20s ultimately settled on Heavenly Records (distributed by EMI) in late 2002, releasing its first single, "Such a Fool," in early 2003 as a limited edition 7-inch. The single later served as fodder for the U.K. press and blogosphere to carry on the hype surrounding the young band.

Things continued to happen quickly for the 22-20s, as the group made its first U.S. appearance at the 2003 **Coachella Valley Music and Arts Festival** held that April in Indio, California. Serving as a preview of songs from its upcoming proper debut, the live six-song EP *05/03,*, which was recorded during the band's 2003 U.K. tour, saw a limited release at home that September (and soon after in the United States). The 22-20s's busy tour schedule saw no rest. On select dates, the group opened for the Australian garage rockers Jet and indie rock quartet Kings of Leon back in the States and made appearances at the Glastonbury Festival in England and Germany's Southside and Hurricane festivals. The 22-20s also packed in multiple shows back home, which coincided with the release of its 2004 single "22 Days."

Amid all the gigging, the 22-20s somehow managed to escape to a North London studio with producer Brendan Lynch, who had worked with such groups as Primal Scream and English singer-songwriter Paul Weller, to complete the band's debut self-titled full-length album. But before the eponymous record was released in the United Kingdom in September 2004, the quartet spent the year on the road, playing slots at such festivals as England's Reading Festival, Scotland's T in the Park, and Japan's Fuji Rock Festival. The singles "Why Don't You Do It for Me?"

and "Shoot Your Gun" kept the 22-20s's name in the press and its music on the radio.

Astralwerks finally released the album stateside in early 2005, and the guys kept chugging forward, supporting such acts on the road as former Blur member Graham Coxon, English alt rockers Supergrass, and the British rock group Oasis. Because of the hectic tour schedule, the writing process for the 22-20s's follow-up album was difficult and tediously long.

Eventually, all of the hype, album delays, and relentless time spent trekking from show to show had taken its toll on the band. The 22-20s became dissatisfied with its music and the direction it was going. Unable to resolve these qualms or ever complete its second album, the band announced an amicable split in January 2006.

Further Reading: Wimble, David. *The Indie Bible 7th Edition (Indie Bible),* 7th ed. Ottawa, ON, Canada: Big Meteor Publications; 2005; http://www.astralwerks.com; http://www.grahamcoxon.co.uk; http://www.heavenly100.com/; http://www.jettheband.com; http://www.kingsofleon.com; http://www.oasisinet.com; http://www.paulweller.com; http://www.supergrass.com; http://www.the22-20s.com/.

U

THE UNICORNS

Before breaking up in 2005, the Montreal-based band The Unicorns was known for its **Lo-fi** pop sensibilities and absurd sense of humor. Multi-instrumentalists Nick Thorburn and Alden Penner met in high school and formed The Unicorns near the end of 2000. Thorburn adopted the stage name Nicolas "Neil" Diamonds, and Penner took on the stage name Alden Ginger—a play on Ginger Alden, Elvis Presley's former fiancée. Drummer Jaime Thompson has since joined the band. As a band, The Unicorns rarely told the truth about anything in interviews. The group wrote songs about a variety of unexpected topics, such as ghosts, unicorns, and video games. The band's playful personality resonated with fans, who were often treated to live shows that featured roadies with Unicorn masks and the occasional fan in a gorilla suit.

On The Unicorns' first release, 2003's *Unicorns Are People Too* off the band's own Caterpillars of the Community label, many songs struck a balance between a sonic efficiency and the band's desire to be jaunty and humorous. The album proved to be an unlikely combination of sounds: sinewy guitar-bass-drums set to **Lo-fi** production, the occasional recorder or glockenspiel, and low-end 70's keyboards. The album had a run of only 500 copies and went largely unheard. However, *Unicorns Are People Too* had all the ingredients of a strong pop record. Such songs as "I Was Born (A Unicorn)" and "William, Clap Your Hands" combined sparse lyrics and gothic humor with caramelized guitar melodies that would define the group's future efforts.

For the recording of its next album, 2003's *Who Will Cut Our Hair When We're Gone?* off Alien8 Recordings, The Unicorns recruited full-time drummer Jaime Thompson. Thompson followed suit with the rest of the band in adopting a stage name, J'aime Tambeur. *Who Will Cut Our Hair* contained some of the same tracks as *Unicorns Are People Too,* but such songs as "Tuff Ghost," and the Casio-fuzzed "Jellybones" earned the band critical acclaim and comparisons to **The Shins**, The Flaming Lips, and the Magnetic Fields.

However, tension and exhaustion set in when the band went on an aggressive tour through the United States, Europe, and Australia. Through the Australian leg of the tour, Penner and Thorburn were barely on speaking terms. Differences also began to develop over how to promote the band—Thorburn and Thompson wanted to hire a manager, while Penner wanted that authority to remain within the band.

In 2005, The Unicorns broke up. Shortly after, Thorburn and Thompson formed the Islands, which released its first full-length album *Return to the Sea* in 2006. Shortly after, differences over the band's work ethic emerged again. Thompson lost interest and announced he would be leaving the Islands while the band was in the middle of a tour. Thorburn quickly recruited a few music students to fill in, and, in 2007, he announced plans to record a second album. Penner went on to write the accompanying music for the film *The Hamster Cage,* which was featured in the Montreal World Film Festival and the Vancouver International Film Festival.

Further Readings: http://www.alien8recordings.com/artists/22/The-unicorns; http://www.islandsareforever.com; http://www.myspace.com/theunicornsband.

THE VELVET UNDERGROUND

Many people place the beginning of the history of indie rock at the first guitar chord played by the New York City–based 1960s trendsetting and influential American rock band The Velvet Underground. Front man/songwriter Lou Reed, who has gone on to publish various books and showcase exhibitions of his photography, had played with various garage rock acts before teaming up with Welsh-born multi-instrumentalist John Cale. They named the band after a book about the underground sex scene that Reed had found the book in his New York City apartment. The band's first songs were considered "laid back" compared to its later tunes, but the members' artiste personas and links to various celebrities (the band's demo tape reportedly made its way into the hands of Mick Jagger) helped the group to gain exposure to the top artists and musicians of that era.

Many biographers of The Velvet Underground herald the band's longevity—especially since it never broke any album sales records—as well as its influence on such important bands and artists as David Bowie, Patti Smith, **The Jesus and Mary Chain**, **R.E.M.**, and **Sonic Youth**, among others. Cale and Reed, who were both classically trained musicians, joined forces with musicians Angus MacLise and guitarist Sterling Morrison to form such various bands as The Warlocks, The Primitives, and The Falling Spikes and began playing at art galleries and poetry readings. MacLise, however, exited the band when he felt the group had "sold out" to play for money. His replacement, drummer Maureen "Moe" Tucker, stuck with the group after joining in 1963 (although she took a brief hiatus when she became pregnant); she sang co-lead vocals on various Velvet Underground songs.

The band signed on for a residency in 1965 at New York City's Greenwich Village haunt, the Cafe Bizarre. There, the band met the famous and eccentric 1960s pop artist Andy Warhol, who became a close friend to the group, as well as its producer. Warhol showcased the band at his film screenings, and he introduced the band to one of its most iconic members, a female singer named Nico, who has become a fixture in the history of rock 'n' roll for her personal style and influence on the 1960s art scene. One of Warhol's most famous paintings, an illustration of a peeled banana, was the cover of the band's 1967 self-titled debut album, "The Velvet Underground & Nico." The record featured the controversial, yet popular, recordings "Heroin" and "Venus in Furs."

The band experienced a very public decline, however, when it performed without Nico when she showed up late to a gig. Without Warhol's backing and the publicity associated with his presence, the band suffered from lack of exposure and internal band strife started to sprout. The band's sophomore album, *White Light/White Heat* (Polydor, 1967), featured the band's poppier side, a bare bones production style, and it was stripped of Nico's vocals. Soon after, Cale quit the group and the band was dropped from its label, MGM/Verve Records. Atlantic Records snapped the band up, though, and it returned to New York City for a second try at rock 'n' roll glory. The band played a stint as the featured band at the famed club Max's Kansas City, but the members of The Velvet Underground could not find mutual harmony. The result was the 1970 album *Loaded,* which featured only two remaining original lineup members (Reed and Morrison) performing the hits "Sweet Jane" and "Rock & Roll."

Soon after, Reed left the group to pursue a solo career that has been both successful and fruitful. The band experienced a shift as it added new members bassist Walter Powers and guitarist Doug Yule. Morrison left the band for good in 1971, and Tucker briefly departed to start a family. Yule continued to play and record with other musicians as The Velvet Underground, releasing music until 1973 when he released the record *Squeeze.* While Reed's career soared, The Velvet Underground, as diehard fans had come to know and love it, was now defunct, although a few live albums surfaced around 1972.

Oddly enough, the band's popularity soared to its highest peak years after its heyday. The Velvet Underground's music was at an apex in the 1980s when fans realized the group's ingenuity and artistic value. Though there is no clear indication or explanation as to why it took so long for the group's music to catch on, the boom of popularity surrounding its music in the 1980s could be attributed to the horde of reissued albums that surfaced in those years.

Ironically, the deaths of Nico, who passed away after an accident in 1988, and Andy Warhol in 1989 (he was shot by a performer who had starred in one of his films), brought the group back together for a song that Cale and Reed had written in honor of the painter/celebrated artist. The original lineup played a reunion show near Paris in tribute to Warhol, and it banded together to play a lengthened version of the song "Heroin." The band toured together for the first time in 25 years in 1993 (U2's Bono joined the group on stage for the song "Satellite of Love"). In 1994, the group put out the double-disc documentary *Live MCMXCIII.* Fans caught wind of an upcoming 1995 studio album, but that rumor pittered out and never came to fruition. The group did release a five-disc box set called *Peel Slowly & See,* a collection of The Velvet Underground's first four albums and some rare tracks.

When The Velvet Underground was inducted into the Rock and Roll Hall of Fame in 1996, the band performed its new song "Last Night I Said Goodbye to My Friend." The track was a tribute to Morrison, who had passed away after a battle with lymphoma in 1995. Patti Smith presented the award to the band.

In 2008, over 20 years since the end of the band, a rare track was unearthed. The media reported that the song titled "I'm Not a Young Man Anymore" is a long-lost track from one of the group's bootlegged performances back in 1967.

The track was released on the auction Web site eBay, and only 100 copies of the green-colored vinyl recording were sold.

Further Reading: Bockris, Victor. *Up-Tight: The Velvet Underground Story.* New York: Cooper Square Press, 2003; Witts, Richard. *The Velvet Underground (Icons of Pop Music).* Bloomington: Indiana University Press, 2006.

THE VILLAGE VOICE

Founded in 1955, *The Village Voice* is a free weekly newspaper that covers art, film, entertainment, politics, and news. The paper's skew is liberal, and the content is often controversial, thought-provoking, and even risqué. The paper's music section is vast and varied, although its main focus tends to be on indie and rock acts.

Famed critic Robert Christgau, who started working there in the early 1970s, was a major player in the development and success of the paper's music section. Christgau helped to start the paper's influential annual "Pazz & Jop" poll, which ranks the best music each year as voted by local music writers and critics. The equivalent to the *Boston Phoenix,* this alternative arts weekly is available to subscribers living outside the New York City (NYC) area for a nominal fee. The opinionated paper, which can be found in bright red kiosks all over NYC, has maintained its ambitions to publish "free-form, high-spirited and passionate discourse into the public discourse" (http://www.villagevoice.com/aboutus/).

The Pulitzer Prize winning paper's founders—Dan Wolf, Ed Fancher and playwright/novelist Norman Mailer—started the paper in an apartment in the East Village. Mailer, who wrote a weekly column, published the controversial essay "The White Negro: Superficial Reflections on the Hipster" in 1956. In it, Mailer announced and celebrated what has now become a popular term in NYC—the "hipster"—a rebel individualist who sets trends and lives outside of society's rules. Mailer, a rule breaker in his own right, often penned columns that celebrated sex, drugs, and other shock-worthy topics. Wolf and Fancher, who were also members of the city's counterculture, served, respectively, as editor-in-chief and publisher of the underground publication.

Since its inception, the paper has moved its offices to a building in nearby Cooper Square. Many famous writers have been published in *The Village Voice;* these scribes include poet Ezra Pound, playwright Tom Stoppard, poet Allen Ginsberg, and novelist Henry Miller, to name a few. Infamous editors have included sex columnist Rachel Kramer Bussel and renowned music editor Chuck Eddy. In 2001, the paper launched its own music festival, the free Siren Music Festival, which features indie acts performing on various stages at the fairgrounds on Coney Island. The paper is also infamous for its racy "Adult" section, which includes personal ads, advertisements, and the sex/love advice column "Savage Love" by well-known columnist Dan Savage.

The Village Voice has earned several Pulitzer Prizes for its reporting and feature stories. By focusing mostly on local news and happenings, *The Village Voice* has managed to stay alive amid the swelling piles of newspapers and magazines that are constantly sprouting up at newsstands across the United States. However, when The New York Times Company purchased the paper, it changed and developed a mainstream focus. This was done in part to help boost distribution, but the attempt to switch the paper's voice had a negative affect that the new investors and owners never expected. Fans of the paper and its Bohemian roots cried foul when the paper was sold to the right-wing, corporate entity.

The paper's no-holds-barred reporting style and eclectic coverage suffered greatly under the new regime, but *The Village Voice*'s reputation and history have helped keep it afloat. The paper's music coverage includes gig listings, band interviews, news, album reviews, and gossip. In a city that never sleeps, *The Village Voice* is right there, always with one eye open, keeping its pages glued to the pulse of the city—one band and aspiring artist at a time.

In the late 2000s, *The Village Voice* expanded its online presence to include blogs and podcasts of its content, and it launched Village Voice Radio, a streaming online radio program that can be heard on StreamAudio. Village Voice Radio's programs have included a weekly music show hosted by Robert Christgau, a show hosted by the Voice's resident gossip hound, Michael Musto, and a weekly concert series broadcast from performances at the hundreds of music venues all over the city.

The paper celebrated its 50th year anniversary in 2005 by publishing "a retrospective of some of the most memorable 'Voice' covers" (http://www.villagevoice.com/specials/?page=50th) and feature stories on its Web site. Voice writer Allen Barra published a piece entitled "50 Years of Pissing People Off" in honor of the milestone (Barra, 2008).

Further Readings: Barra, Allen. "50 Year of Pissing People Off." January 1, 2008. http://www.villagevoice.com/news/0802,barra,78810,6.html; Lim, Dennis. *The Village Voice Film Guide: 50 Years of Movies from Classics to Cult Hits.* Malden, MA: Wiley, 2006; McAuliffe, Kevin Michael. *The Great American Newspaper: The Rise and Fall of the Village Voice.* New York: Charles Scribner's Sons, 1978; "Our History." http://www.villagevoice.com/aboutus/; http://www.radio.villagevoice.com; http://www.villagevoice.com.

W

THE WALKMEN

This New York City indie rock act turned the coin—literally—on a terminated record deal when it invested the remaining funds from its defunct deal with DreamWorks Records after its first group, Jonathan Fire*Eater, broke up. The group's investment, a recording studio and rehearsal space called Marcata Studios, where it housed an array of vintage music equipment, proved to be fruitful.

Growing up together in Washington, D.C., The Walkmen band members have played in bands together since they were in elementary school. The quintet has an experimental approach to music—its 2001 self-titled debut EP is full of noise rock, complex rhythms, and eerie vocals, which has helped put the group in categories with **The Velvet Underground** and the **Pixies**. The Walkmen signed to the Brooklyn indie label StarTime International Records in the early 2000s; the group began playing gigs around its home city and gained a solid fan base.

Critics lauded the group's 2002 work *Everyone Who Pretended to Like Me Is Gone,* an effort that reviews claimed was worthy of fans who enjoy the music of U2. A track from the album was featured in a car commercial, and the band received the official stamp of pop culture approval when one of the tracks from the album was featured on an episode of Fox's *The O.C.*

The Walkmen's continuous publicity efforts paid off; countless TV appearances, interviews, and radio presence helped support the fresh *Bows + Arrows* (Record Collection, 2004), and reviewers touted the follow-up album, *A Hundred Miles Off* (Record Collection, 2006), for its guitar-focused frills and rich textures. The group toured through 2005 and began working on a novel together. Later in 2006, The Walkmen recorded an exact replica cover album of 1960s/1970s singer-songwriter/pianist/guitarist Harry Nilsson's (John Lennon had produced the work) 1974 album, *Pussy Cats*. The Walkmen continued to work on its next album at the group's homemade studio through the fall of 2007. The group toured through 2008.

Further Readings: Rappaport, Doreen. *John's Secret Dreams: The Life of John Lennon.* New York: Hyperion, 2004; http://www.marcata.net/walkmen; http://www.startimerecords.com/walkmen.html.

THE WHITE STRIPES

When this Detroit duo exploded on the indie rock scene with its minimalist, bare bones garage rock, no one suspected that this "brother-sister" team was actually formerly man and wife (the duo reportedly wed in 1996 and divorced in 2000).

Jack White (guitars, vocals, and songwriter) and Meg White (drums) formed the group in 1997, plastering their debut singles and albums with their signature triumvirate colors—red, white, and black—and art deco–style cover concepts. After performing its blend of rock, blues, punk, and soul music at venues in the Detroit club circuit, The White Stripes released its self-titled debut 17-track LP in June 1999 on Virgin Music Group's imprint V2 Records, which landed it opening spots for tours by all-female Olympia, Washington punk rock trio **Sleater-Kinney**, and the California indie band **Pavement**.

It was the group's sophomore LP, *De Stijl* (V2, 2000) (Stijl is the Dutch word for "Style") that launched its career, sending the group off to tour in Japan and Australia. The buzz surrounding Jack, a former upholsterer and the drummer for country band Goober & the Peas, and Meg, a former bartender, increased, and the group's success hit a high note with the release of its third full-length album, *White Blood Cells,* in 2001. The album, which was initially released by the Long Beach, California–based garage and indie rock label Sympathy for the Record Industry before being re-released on V2 Records, topped critics' "Best Of" lists across the country, and, despite debate concerning Meg's questionable timing on the drums, the album cemented general suspicion that this Detroit duo was "the next big thing." The London-based label XL Recordings handles all of the distribution of the band's albums in the United Kingdom.

The cover of the *White Blood Cells* album featured Jack and Meg, dressed in red and white, trapped against a red wall by a group of menacing-looking men, dressed head to toe in black clothing. The album soon became a benchmark in music history, and it exhibited Jack's songwriting talents via a few standout singles from the album—the edgy "Fell in Love with a Girl" and the catchy rock-country track "Hotel Yorba." The White Stripes, which never contracted pricey studio musicians, continued making its brand of stripped-down rock—even with producer Doug Easley (the man behind several records by indie rock singer-songwriter **Cat Power**) manning the controls for *Blood Cells*.

The White Stripes rode the wave of the indie rock resurgence along with such bands as The Strokes—and reaped the rewards. The pressure to create another stellar album did not deter the duo from writing and recording a series of hits that appeared on its 2003 album, *Elephant*. The record was co-released by V2 Records and Jack's own label, Third Man Records, on which he also puts out records by the three-piece Grand Rapids, Michigan band, Whirlwind Heat.

Amid all the hubbub that surrounded the disclosure of Jack and Meg's "secret" marriage (Jack and Meg told the press they shared the same last name because they were siblings, but word of their five-year marriage was eventually leaked), the group's success never waned. *Elephant,* which was recorded in a few weeks in London, has been called the group's "British album" for the its Queen-like harmonies and English references. The catchy, beat-heavy track "Seven Nation Army" and the power-charged "The Hardest Button to Button" have become some of the group's signature songs. The album went on to sell half a million copies.

The year 2003 was a memorable year for The White Stripes. *Rolling Stone* magazine named Jack White the 17th on The 100 Greatest Guitarists of All Time in its special "Guitar Gods" issue. Jack appeared in the 2003 film *Cold Mountain* and wrote and recorded a number of tracks for the film's soundtrack. When Jack and Meg made their mainstream debut on CBS's *Late Show with David Letterman,* their popularity soared. Now that fans who were not "in the know" knew about the band, there was no stopping The White Stripes.

The White Stripes received coverage in *Time* magazine, *The New Yorker,* and *Entertainment Weekly,* and the group performed at the 2002 MTV Movie Awards. "Fell in Love with a Girl" received regular play on MTV, and it was nominated for four MTV Video Awards including Best Video of the Year, Breakthrough Video, Best Special Effects in a Video, and Best Editing in a Video. The video for the song, which was directed by the eccentric yet innovative film director Michel Gondry was an animated short that was done using only Legos.

Things hit a sour note in 2003, though, when Jack was arrested following a physical altercation with fellow Detroit musician Jason Stollsteimer, the singer of the indie quintet The Von Bondies. Jack was later forced to take anger management classes.

Now that Jack and Meg were now celebrities in their own right, Jack had a short-lived relationship with actress Renée Zellweger (they dated from 2003 to 2004) before he teamed up musically with another famous leading lady, Loretta Lynn, for her 2004 album, *Van Lear Rose.* White served as producer for the album, writing and performing with the singer on several tracks. *Rose* received five Grammy nods, winning for Best Country Album, and their duet was awarded Best Country Collaboration with Vocals. Later in 2003 Jack and Meg appeared in the film *Coffee and Cigarettes* by independent film director Jim Jarmusch. The duo went head-to-head with filmmaker George Roca, who had made plans to film The White Stripes for a documentary; the duo claimed he altered his artistic vision too drastically from the initial agreement.

In 2004, the duo was awarded a Grammy for *Elephant* for the Best Alternative Music Album. The group's fifth full-length album, *Get Behind Me Satan* (V2, 2005), though, brought the band to a new level, proving that it could stay true to its sound while experimenting and taking its music to the next level. Highlights from the album included the single "Blue Orchid," the video for which ironically featured model Karen Elson, whom Jack later married in June 2005. Jack performed with Bob Dylan in Detroit that same year, joining the legendary 1960s folk singer on The White Stripes' song "Ball and Biscuit."

Jack and Meg appeared on Comedy Central's hit political comedy show *The Daily Show with Jon Stewart* in 2005. That same year, *Satan* entered #3 on the Billboard charts, sold 75,000 copies in its second week, and received two nominations for the 48th Annual Grammy Awards for Best Alternative Music Album. The White Stripes was nominated for Best Pop Collaboration By a Duo or Group with Vocal for the song "My Doorbell." *Satan* has been called the group's most "diverse" album to date; it has also been accused of having a lack of focus—however, that characterization has never seemed to hinder the band's credentials or success.

The White Stripes toured extensively in support of *Satan* and, as a result, released a five-track EP (V2), which included live recordings and a cover of the song "Walking with a Ghost," which was written by and originally performed by the Canadian **indie pop** duo Tegan and Sara. Jack experienced an identity crisis in 2005 (a la the singer Prince and rapper P. Diddy who have undergone numerous name changes) when he briefly changed his name to Three Quid.

Harsh criticism befell Jack and his minimalist "antisellout" principles in 2005 when he was asked to write a song for a Coca-Cola commercial. To White's surprise, the media published old quotes of the singer boasting his refusal to write a song for a Gap commercial, stating that such an act would be a "sellout," so when White agreed to do business with The Coca-Cola Company, he came under great scrutiny, apparently forgetting his "principles." To the surprise of fans everywhere, White not only proceeded to write the song, he made statements claiming the effort had a deeper meaning and that he had written a jingle for a soft drink that he felt was "love in a worldwide form" that would be "something globally positive" (Harris, 2005).

In 2006, The White Stripes officially entered the hall of fame of popular culture after making a cameo appearance on *The Simpsons*. Several tribute albums to The White Stripes have emerged over the years: *The String Quartet Tribute to The White Stripes* (Vitamin Records, 2003); *A Tribute to The White Stripes* by Diff'rent Stripes (Piccadilly Records, 2003); *A Tribute to the White Stripes* (Big Eye Music, 2004); *Electrostripes: An Electro Tribute to The White Stripes* (Anagram, 2005); *Pickin' on The White Stripes: A Bluegrass Tribute* (Cmh Records, 2005); and *Indie Translations of The White Stripes* (Secret Life Records, 2006). The duo was also covered by Richard Russell, the founder of XL Recordings, who organized an orchestral interpretation of many of The White Stripes' songs for a 2006 album he called *Aluminum*.

Locomotive Music released The White Stripes DVD *Rhinoceros* in 2006, featuring an extensive discography, early footage, and interviews with people who worked with and knew Jack and Meg before The White Stripes was a household name. Fully enjoying celebrity status, Jack White sold his Detroit home for close to $1 million. Inside, the abode is reportedly still home to White's master bedroom (which he hand-painted), a red-and-white-striped laundry room, a secret garden, and its most valuable asset, the former location of The White Stripes' home recording studio for Third Man Records.

Jack White and his wife, Karen, announced the arrival of their second child into the world in mid-2007. The White Stripes signed a one-album deal with Warner Brothers Music that same year, in the wake of the collapse of V2 Records. The duo reteamed after a brief musical break to play at that year's Bonnaroo Music Festival in Manchester, Tennessee, along with such acts as The Police and Tool.

The White Stripes released its sixth studio album, *Icky Thump,* in 2007. In an interview with *Blender* magazine in July 2007, Jack contended that he is often

Jack (left) and Meg White of The White Stripes pose for pho-
tographers as they arrive at the MTV Movie Awards in Los
Angeles on June 1, 2002. [AP Wide World Photos/Mark J.
Terrill]

disliked for his unabashedly honest opinions. The messy-haired singer admitted
the album (reportedly no laptops were used during the recording of it) is about
"feeling positive and being alive" (Dolan, 2007). White's other band, The Raconteurs, which he formed with his musician friend Brendan Benson, released a
new album soon after.

The White Stripes canceled the remainder of its fall 2007 U.S. and U.K. tour
dates when Meg White reportedly suffered from acute anxiety that prevented her
from traveling. The media speculated that Meg was suffering from nerves related
to the release of a sex tape in which she allegedly appeared. After the possible
scandal diffused, Meg recuperated and The White Stripes paired up with co-
producer **Beck** to work on B-sides for the duo's 2007 single "Conquest." The sty-
listic duo released the single in three different colored 7-inches—red, white, and
black.

News surrounding this duo could fill an entire book. The band released both
Spanish and English versions of its 2008 single "Conquest" ("Conquista"). Earlier
in 2008, though, the group was sued for $70,000 for allegedly sampling a

Canadian radio host in a song on the group's 2000 album, *De Stijl*. Bob Dylan contacted Jack White as a possible collaborator for a project involving unfinished songs by Hank Williams from 1953.

Further Readings: Dolan, Jon. "The White Stripes: Jack White." *BLENDER* magazine, July 2007; Graham, Ben. *Maximum White Stripes: The Unauthorised Biography of The White Stripes (Maximum series)*. Abridged edition. New York: Chrome Dreams; 2003; Handyside, Chris. *Fell in Love with a Band: The Story of The White Stripes*. New York: St. Martin's Griffin, 2004; Hannaford, Alex. *The White Stripes*. London: Artnik, 2005; Harris, John. "I'd Like Coke to Buy Me the World . . . ." November 4, 2005. http://arts.guardian.co.uk/filmand-music/story/0,,1607619,00.html; Porter, Dick. *The White Stripes: 21st Century Blues*. Berkeley, CA: Plexus Publishing, 2004; Roach, Martin. *Morphing the Blues: The White Stripes and the Strange Relevance of Detroit*. London: Chrome Dreams, 2004; Sullivan, Denise. *The White Stripes: Sweethearts of the Blues*. Milwaukee, WI: Backbeat Books, 2004; True, Everett. *The White Stripes and the Sound of Mutant Blues*. London: Omnibus Press, 2004; http://us.v2music.com/site/act.asp?ID=82; http://www.sympathyrecords.com; http://www.whitestripes.com; http://www.xlrecordings.com/thewhitestripes.

Y

YEAH YEAH YEAHS

This art-punk/garage rock trio is a regular staple of the indie rock scene in New York City. Yeah Yeah Yeahs, which was originally known as Unitard, is composed of front woman Karen O, guitarist Nick Zinner (the two met at Oberlin College in Ohio), and drummer Brain Chase (whom the duo met at New York University), who was added to the group shortly after its original drummer left the group. Yeah Yeah Yeahs, which was officially formed in 2000 by Zinner and O, began making frenetic indie rock that lends itself to funk, punk, garage music, and indie music.

After landing opening gigs for "it" indie bands **The White Stripes** and The Strokes, Yeah Yeah Yeahs (YYYs) released its self-titled debut on its own label, Shifty Records. Shortly after, YYYs made its rite of passage debut at the **South by Southwest (SXSW)** music festival to rave reviews. Buzz surrounding the band reached white-hot status in its home base of New York City, and soon the group was touring nationwide with such acts as the antirock/blues trio The Jon Spencer Blues Explosion and the New York City noise rock group **Girls Against Boys**.

Known for her unpredictable stage antics and wild-child clothing, which she often makes herself, Karen O became the figurehead for the group, helping to spread news of the band via word of mouth. It did not take long for music fans across the pond to get wind of the group either—in 2002, the group headed over to the United Kingdom to tour with The Jon Spencer Blues Explosion, and its *Yeah Yeah Yeahs* EP received even greater distribution via Touch and Go Records and London's Wichita Recordings.

YYYs added additional touring dates with fellow New Yorkers, the punk fun group the Liars and Washington state's all-female punk rock trio **Sleater-Kinney**. Meanwhile, YYYs was busy at work writing and recording material for its debut full-length album, *Fever to Tell,* which hit stores in 2003. But, despite the fact that the band had signed with major label Interscope Records, which is home to such acts as rapper Eminem, YYYs has retained its edge—and indie credibility. *Fever* sold approximately 750,000 copies worldwide.

The Brooklyn, New York–based trio, which resides in the up-and-coming artistic neighborhood known as Williamsburg, supplied its songwriting talents for a track on the 2002 **Kill Rock Stars** compilation, and the trio put out the EP *Machine,* which features some of its earlier studio recordings (Touch and Go Records). For a while, it seemed as though Yeah Yeah Yeahs's faces were plastered all over the media—the group's members were interviewed in and praised by such publications as *Rolling Stone, Spin,* **The Village Voice**, the *New York Times,* and even *GQ* and *Fortune* magazines.

Karen O has become a star in her own right—most notably because of her fashion statements. **NME (New Musical Express)** magazine and the hip London arts and music magazine *The Face* deemed O a "fashion success" (Rocca, 2003). Her unique urban Bohemian style has caused a tidal wave of fashion trends in Williamsburg, Brooklyn, and the choppy-haired singer even has her clothes made by her own designer, Christian Joy. O modeled clothes she herself designed, and which Joy made, in the group's video for the song "Gold Lion," which was the first single off the *Show Your Bones* album. O confessed her infatuation with—and obsession for—the fashion designer reality show *Project Runway*, which aired on the Bravo channel.

YYY member Chase toured for a brief time with his side project, The Seconds, in 2003. In 2004, the first single off *Fever,* "Maps," became a huge radio hit and received heavy rotation on MTV, helping the album to reach gold status. That same year, Karen O moved to Los Angeles, California, in order to "get plugged back into [her] normal life," as she told a reporter for the U.K. newspaper *The Guardian* (Hanley, 2006); despite the fact that YYYs was now a bicoastal group, the band—and the lineup—stayed intact.

Yeah Yeah Yeahs contributed a song to the 2004 compilation *Future Soundtrack for America* (Barsuk Records, in association with the political awareness organization MoveOn.org and the hip literary magazine *McSweeney's*), which was put together by John Flansburgh of the experimental alt rock duo They Might Be Giants. That same year, such bands as Nico, the New York No Stars, and Super Heroines recorded *A Tribute to Yeah Yeah Yeahs* (Big Eye Music). The band's 2004 DVD, *Tell Me What Rockers to Swallow,* features live footage, an audience interview documentary, videos, a Japanese tour documentary, and the group's live performance at the MTV Movie Awards.

YYYs toured with singer-songwriter **Cat Power** and the indie blues act Entrance, aka the one-man show Guy Blakeslee, in early February 2004. That same year, the group was interviewed as part of the film *Kill Your Idols,* a documentary about 30 years of alternative rock alongside such acts as **Sonic Youth**, the Liars, and A.R.E. Weapons.

In 2005, YYYs went on a brief hiatus so each of the members could pursue his or her own solo projects—O collaborated with Los Angeles producer Squeak E. Clean for a song for a Nike commercial, while Zinner released a book of photography, moonlighted as a guest blogger for *JANE* magazine, produced albums by such groups as the London quintet The Horrors, remixed a song off **TV on the Radio**'s 2005 album, and played with a group called Head Wound City. Clean produced the experimental trio's sophomore album, *Show Your Bones,* which came out in 2006 on Interscope Records. *Bones,* which features an acoustic song, "Warrior," peaked at #11 on the Billboard charts, selling over 50,000 copies in its first week. The group invited fans to design the art for its album in 2005, inviting them to create a flag that, according to NME.com, "(embodies) the symbolic essence that you have vibed off of us totally to the max" (http://www.nme.com/news/yeah-yeah-yeahs/21645). The in-your-face one-woman electronica act Peaches remixed the third single from the *Bones* album, "Cheated Hearts."

Demos recorded by Karen O in 2006 were leaked onto the Internet after some-one found them in an apartment that was once the residence of **TV on the Radio**'s Dave Sitek; O had given them to Sitek as a gift before he moved out, but he apparently left them behind. Sitek, however, managed to contact the person who posted them, and the tracks were taken off-line. Self-proclaimed **Sonic Youth** fans, YYYs recorded an acoustic cover of the indie gods' track "The Diamond Sea" for an iTunes-only release.

YYYs toured extensively in support of *Bones* through the summer and fall of 2006 (a smaller tour in the spring had since sold out), hitting the three-day U.K. rock/alternative/metal Download Festival, the Indian Summer Festival in Glasgow, the **Coachella Valley Music and Arts Festival** in Indio, California, the 2006 Reading Festival (the United Kingdom's oldest music festival), the Leeds Festival, and the San Diego Street Scene music festival in California. Guitarist Imaad Wasif, a member of **Kill Rock Stars**, recordings artists The New Folk Implosion, and the group Lowercase, became a temporary member of the group when he joined it for a string of YYYs's early tour dates. The group played a secret show in October 2006 in Florida in conjunction with the social network Web site MySpace.com.

The band, which had been heralded for the playful tone of its songs, let its sense of humor whine when the group invited fans to submit their best YYYs impressions via video in 2006. The winner was featured in the video for the song "Cheated Hearts." Karen O's even wilder side was revealed when the fashion-centric singer recorded a song with Johnny Knoxville, MTV's own "don't try this at home" host of the hit show *Jackass*. In-your-face electronica singer Peaches joined Karen O and Knoxville for the song "Backass," which was featured in the soundtrack of the movie *Jackass Number Two*.

In August 2006 YYYs joined **Sonic Youth** and additional bands Blood on the Wall and Awesome Color for a few dates at McCarren Park Pool, a former public pool that has been renovated as a music and arts venue in Williamsburg, Brook-lyn. In 2007, Yeah Yeah Yeahs jumped on the commercial media bandwagon along with the likes of such groups as Wolfmother, Gomez, and **Cat Power** in the Edge Music Videocast, a podcast campaign sponsored by Ford cars and trucks, which offered free music videos on iTunes.

YYYs was nominated for Best Alternative Music Album for *Show Your Bones* for the 49th Annual Grammy Awards, which were held at the Staples Center in Los Angeles, California, in February 2007. Other bands nominated in that category were **Radiohead**'s Thom Yorke, The Flaming Lips, the **Arctic Monkeys**, and Gnarls Barkley. Nick Zinner played guitar on former Ronettes singer (and Rock and Roll Hall of Fame inductee) Ronnie Spector's 2007 album, *The Last of the Rock Stars*.

Chase released a jazz CD, *Brian Chase & Seth Misterka Duo,* in 2007. YYYs played the Modern Sky Festival in China that same year. The group's 2007 EP, *Is*

Karen O, lead singer of Yeah Yeah Yeahs, performs at the 2006 Coachella Valley Music and Arts Festival in Indio, California, on April 30, 2006. [AP Wide World Photos/Matt Sayles]

Is, is a collection of five tracks that the band wrote during the 2004 *Fever to Tell* tour. The band worked on material for a new album from the end of 2007 to the start of 2008.

Further Readings: "Design the Yeah Yeah Yeahs Album Cover." November 20, 2005. http://www.nme.com/news/yeah-yeah-yeahs/21645; Hanley, Lynsey. "New York Punk Hipsters Yeah Yeah Yeahs Are Back and Their New Album Might Just Be a Pop Classic." February 26, 2006. http://arts.guardian.co.uk/features/story/0,,1717923,00.html; Rocca, Jane. "O Yeah—I Want to Be Like Karen." August 14, 2003. http://www.theage.com.au/articles/2003/08/14/1060588522984.html; Zinner, Nick. *I Hope You Are All Happy Now* (book of photography). New York: St. Martin's Griffin, 2005; http://www.mcsweeneys.net; http://www.myspace.com/yeahyeahyeahs; http://www.yeahyeahyeahs.com.

YO LA TENGO

Critics' darling Yo La Tengo (Spanish for "I Have It") has managed to stretch the fabrics of creativity for 20 years with 15 releases and an impressive set of mainstream successes under its belt. The trio—which is about to enter the first quarter of a century together as a group—is still considered an "it" band, even as the band members approach their pre-over-the-hill days at an average age of 40.

Formed in Hoboken, New Jersey, in 1984, the ambitious trio—bassist/singer James McNew and husband and wife duo, guitarist/singer Ira Kaplan and drummer/singer Georgie Hubley—released its debut EP in 1986 before its full-length album, *Ride the Tiger* (Matador Records), was dropped. A few other musicians have entered the fold through the years, but these three stalwarts have remained. The group wooed critics with its 1987 album, *New Wave Hot Dogs,* and the follow-up, *President Yo La Tengo* (the two discs were released together in 1996), a garage rock-fueled effort that contained some folk rock tracks and clever lyrics and dextrous songwriting that somehow gets better with each release. Yo La Tengo is also known for its surprising live shows, during which the band members have been known to switch instruments abruptly on stage.

Yo La Tengo (YLT), which has often been compared to the 1970s rock act **The Velvet Underground**, had the opportunity to play dress-up when it was asked to portray the group in the 1996 film *I Shot Andy Warhol.* On the mostly acoustic album *Fakebook* YLT covered Cat Stevens, The Kinks, and blues legend Daniel Johnston. Yo La Tengo released an album just about every year after that, but for 1997's *I Can Hear the Heart Beating As One,* the group tied on some electronica sounds and played around with **shoegazing** and punk rock.

Yo La Tengo's indie rock credentials were cemented with each recording, showing the group was worthy of several citations in the annals of indie rock. YLT is probably also one of the only bands whose covers are celebrated rather than feared; a culmination of their covers was collected on the album *Yo La Tengo Is Murdering the Classics.*

Self-confessed fans of the animated series *The Simpsons,* Yo La Tengo contributed a track for a special psychedelic episode of the show. YLT expanded its TV resume by making a cameo appearance on the TV drama *The Gilmore Girls* for the season finale; such bands as **Sonic Youth** joined the trio. Yo La Tengo released the popular album *And Then Nothing Turned Itself Inside-Out* in 2000 before hitting the road as the backing band for The Kinks' former front man, Ray Davies.

The group's limitless artistic scope grew with an appearance at the well-attended Hoboken music festival Hanukkahpalooza, an eight-night-long festival of music (and lights). In 2003, the group contributed songs to the soundtrack for a series of documentaries about the sea, and that same year Hubley performed as part of a rock opera by singer David Thomas of the experimental rock/art punk group **Pere Ubu**.

Matador Records (2004) celebrated YLT's lengthy career (20 years and going strong) with the compilation *Prisoners of Love: A Smattering of Scintillating Senescent*

Songs 1985–2003, along with an album of rare tracks. YLT came out with its guns blazing for its 2006 album, *I Am Not Afraid of You and I Will Beat Your A- -.* The band also released the 2007 DVD *Science is Fiction: The Sounds of Science,* a combination of the band's live performance and a selection of underwater films by the French filmmaker Jean Painlevé. YLT continued to dabble in various arts; the group scored the soundtrack to the 2008 indie film *The Toe Tactic,* which was screened at that year's **South by Southwest (SXSW)** music festival in Austin, Texas.

Further Readings: Kauffman, Ronen. *New Brunswick, New Jersey, Goodbye: Bands, Dirty Basements, and the Search for Self.* Van Nuys, CA: Hopeless Records, 2007; http://www.matadorrecords.com/yo_la_tengo; http://www.raydavies.com; http://www.ubuprojex.net; http://www.yolatengo.com.

Z

ZAPPA, FRANK

He was considered a musical marvel by many, treasured as a mad-man-esque, mysterious mustached genius by all, and praised as a pioneer in just about every one of his musical, artistic (he even dabbled in film), and oddball pursuits. Frank Zappa is the artist who helped create the mold from which all indie rock values, aesthetics, and mantras have been born.

The wild and crazy Baltimore, Maryland–born composer/musician/producer and conductor played an impressive array of instruments—guitar, bass, drums, vibes, and keyboards. Throughout his half-decade-long career, Zappa did nothing but do things his way. The dark-haired Rock and Roll Hall of Fame inductee was the personification of every indie rock ideal—from playing his own instruments, to writing his own songs, to forming his own bands, and even promoting his political and social opinions and ambitions through his music.

A venerable independent artist, Zappa abhorred authority, and he was often jailed for taking artistic risks that crossed the lines of "moral" society. After joining a local band called the Soul Giants, the larger-than-life musician took the helm of the group and renamed it The Mothers. Zappa and his absurdist ideas and out-there musical ambitions garnered a lot of attention in Los Angeles, where the group performed.

Zappa and his cohorts The Mothers released the ironically titled album *We're Only In It for the Money* in 1968; the band caught a sufficient amount of flack for the album, which poked fun at hippies. But Zappa, who reveled in the spotlight, did not seem to mind whether the attention the group garnered was positive or negative. A finicky Zappa created variant music with The Mothers—starting out with doo-wop before switching to jazz-rock and eventually disbanding the group before reincarnating it years later as an X-rated outfit that dealt jokes at anyone and anything.

In 1971, a fan pushed Zappa from the stage during a performance in London; the startling event put Zappa out of commission for a short while, but the seemingly indestructible guitarist resurfaced to reform The Mothers of Invention as a pop/rock group. Zappa was a stunning soloist and became a guitar god in the rock world, inspiring countless musicians and inspiring young amateurs to up their game.

Ever the entrepreneur, Zappa formed DiscReet Records in 1973, a subset of the Warner Brothers label, on which he began releasing his own material. Sticking to the **DIY (Do-It-Yourself)** mantra, the prolific Zappa released over 50 albums

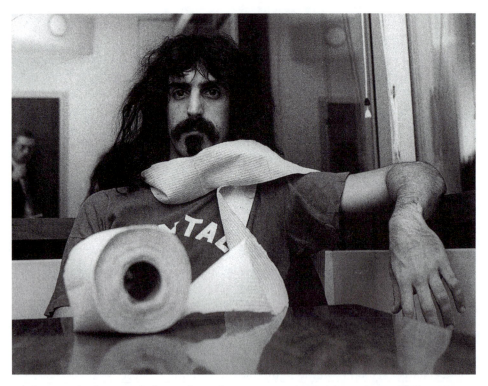

Frank Zappa, lead singer of The Mothers of Invention, in 1968. [AP Wide World Photos]

throughout his career (he released 4 albums in just a few months in 1984, and 20 albums have been released posthumously), many of which he produced himself. Zappa's albums, though they appealed to an eclectic crowd, topped the charts, proving that his chops as a musician certainly outshone his zany ideas and surreal and, at times, seemingly nonsensical lyrics. Zappa's best-known albums include 1966's *Freak Out!,* 1974's *Apostrophe (')*, 1969's *Hot Rats,* 1968's *We're Only In It for the Money*, and 1967's *Absolutely Free*.

A coiffed Zappa, dressed in a suit and tie, testified before the U.S. Senate in 1985 in an effort to disarm Tipper Gore's censorship committee, the Parents Music Resource Center. Snippets from the hearing appeared on Zappa's 1985 record, *Frank Zappa Meets the Mothers of Prevention*. Throughout his career, Zappa recorded and released an impressive amount of material. He earned a Grammy in 1988 for Best Rock Instrumental Performance. Even though there are no accounts of Zappa decrying the music industry as a whole, his do-it-my-way, **DIY (Do-It-Yourself)** lifestyle and approach to his art showed a man who was willing to share the field with the enemy, but he was not too concerned with fitting in or ever becoming one of "them."

Zappa worked to inspire young people to vote in the mid-1980s, using his platform as a musician and an icon to sway political power back into the hands of the people. During the re-release of several of his old master recordings, Zappa was insistent on being a part of the process; in fact, he went even so far as to oversee the process himself.

Zappa's political ambitions came to a brief standstill in the early 1990s when he was diagnosed with prostate cancer. Prior to his death on December 4, 1993, he collaborated with a German symphony and released a long-time project of his, on which he played a digital synthesizer and sampler called a synclavier. In 1995, Zappa was posthumously inducted into the Rock and Roll Hall of Fame by Lou Reed.

In 2007, the rock world commemorated Zappa by naming a street in Germany after him. It was the first street in the European country to be named for a rock 'n' roll star. The St. Louis Symphony Orchestra honored Zappa by including some of his music in its 2007–2008 repertoire. Zappa's production company, Intercontinental Absurdities, is still located in California. August 9, 2007, was declared "Frank Zappa Day" by the mayor of Baltimore, Maryland. The 1979 film *Baby Snakes,* which captures Zappa hosting a concert in New York City, is still a much-talked-about and celebrated film.

Further Readings: Slaven, Neil. *Electric Don Quixote: The Story of Frank Zappa.* 2nd ed. London: Omnibus Press, 2003; Zappa, Frank. *Real Frank Zappa Book.* New York: Simon & Schuster, 1990; http://www.zappa.com.

ZWAN

Billy Corgan formed this indie supergroup after his much loved, generation-defining band Smashing Pumpkins broke up in 2000. Zwan is comprised of an astounding lineup of Corgan's musician friends—guitarist/vocalist Matt Sweeney, who has played with groups as vast and varied as Chavez, Skunk, **Guided By Voices**, **Cat Power**, and Will Oldham; bassist/vocalist Paz Lenchantin, formerly of Papa M and The Silver Jews, she went on to join the highly successful alt rock group A Perfect Circle; drummer Jimmy Chamberlin, a founding member of Smashing Pumpkins; and bassist-turned-guitarist David Pajo, who had played in such bands as Papa M, Slint, Tortoise, Stereolab, Will Oldham, and Royal Trux.

Corgan took over lead vocal and guitar duties for this short-lived supergroup as it toured the local San Diego/Los Angeles area, bringing its work-in-progress sound and repertoire to small club gigs. Zwan's first incarnation—a three-guitar attack featuring Corgan, Sweeney, Lenchantin, and Chamberlin—was known as the Poets of Zwan. This mini tour eventually stretched across the Midwest, where Lenchantin was added to the lineup, becoming the most recently added member to what was originally a quartet. The now-expanded group played a stint of shows in Corgan's hometown of Chicago, Illinois, honing its material even more, growing its catalog to upwards of 60 songs.

Zwan, which had by now morphed into its second incarnation, Djali Zwan, a more "folk"-driven band, as Corgan described it, signed a record deal with the Warner Brothers affiliate label Reprise Records in 2002, releasing its debut single, "Honestly," in 2002, a three-song effort that featured a cover of hard rock/metal group Iron Maiden's classic "Number of the Beast," on which Sweeney handled the vocals. The group's debut full-length release—which would remain its only album together—*Mary Star of the Sea* followed in 2003, resulting in a sold-out five-night stint at the very place where the Smashing Pumpkins played its last gig—Chicago's Metro nightclub.

Mary mirrored the Pumpkins' balance of loud rock songs and intimate balance; however, critics balked, claiming the songs lacked hooks and fans were stunned at Corgan's involvement in such a "happy"-sounding project. Still, it seemed that the jury remained indefinitely "out" on the band's success, as fans both celebrated and complained about Zwan's distinctly non-Pumpkins sound. The album, however, debuted at #3 on the U.S. Billboard charts, and whether out of curiosity, loyalty, or sheer musical adoration, fans clamored to buy the album, helping it sell 267,000 copies.

Corgan released an official announcement of the band's end in the fall of 2003, breaking it gently to his bandmates—and announcing to the world—that his "heart was in Smashing Pumpkins" (Vineyard, 2003). The band consequently canceled its European tour and in 2005, due to "family matters" (Cohen, 2003), according to the press release, Corgan opened up to the press about the group's demise, citing his doubts as to whether the band would "reach its full capacity spiritually and musically" (http://www.mtv.com/news/articles/1478250/20030916/zwan.jhtml); in other accounts, he reportedly felt the band members' antics were to blame for the end of the group.

After the breakup, Pajo focused his efforts on his solo project, Papa M, taking Lechantin with him, while Sweeney stayed busy, producing albums and playing guitar on various LPs and records by such artists as Johnny Cash, rapper El-P, and Dax Riggs. Corgan, on the other hand, lived up to his promise to work with Chamberlin again. The duo teamed up again in 2004 to lay the framework for a Pumpkins' reunion. The Pumpkins' reunion album, *Zeitgeist,* was released in 2007, with founding members Corgan and Chamberlin joined by a new lineup, which does not include former Pumpkins' guitarist James Iha, who has not spoken to Corgan since the Pumpkins' demise.

Further Reading: Cohen, Jonathan. "Corgan Pulls Plug on Zwan." September 15, 2003. http://www.billboard.com/bbcom/news/article_display.jsp?vnu_content_id=1979705; Corgan, Billy. *Blinking with Fists: Poems.* London: Faber & Faber, 2006; Hanson, Amy. *Smashing Pumpkins: Tales of a Scorched Earth.* London: Helter Skelter Publishing, 2004; Vineyard, Jennifer. "Zwan Gone: Billy Corgan Opts for Solo Career." September 16, 2003. http://www.mtv.com/news/articles/1478250/20030916/zwan.jhtml; http://www.aperfectcircle.com.

Appendix A: Top 10 Influential Indie Rock Artists *(in no particular order)*

Sonic Youth
Built to Spill
Pavement
Frank Zappa
The Shins

Death Cab for Cutie
Ani DiFranco
The Dismemberment Plan
Liz Phair
Radiohead

Appendix B: Most Significant Indie Rock Albums *(listed by band)*

The Afghan Whigs
1965 (Sony Records)
October 27, 1998

Air
Pocket Symphony (Astralwerks)
March 6, 2007

Arcade Fire
Funeral (Merge Records)
September 14, 2004

Archers of Loaf
Icky Mettle (Alias Records)
September 7, 1993

Arctic Monkeys
Favourite Worst Nightmare (Domino Records)
April 24, 2007

Beck
Odelay (Geffen Records)
June 18, 1996

Belle and Sebastian
The Life Pursuit (Matador Records)
February 7, 2006

Belle and Sebastian
If You're Feeling Sinister (Matador Records)
November 18, 1996

Big Black
The Rich Man's Eight-Track Tape (Touch and Go Records)
1987

Black Flag
My War (**SST Records**)
1984

Bloc Party
Silent Alarm (Vice Records)
March 22, 2005

Blonde Redhead
23 (4AD Records)
April 10, 2007

Bright Eyes
Cassadaga (**Saddle Creek Records**)
April 10, 2007

Built to Spill
You In Reverse (Warner Bros. Records)
April 11, 2006

Cat Power
You Are Free (Matador Records)
February 18, 2003

Comets on Fire
Blue Cathedral (**Sub Pop Records**)
July 27, 2004

The Decemberists
The Crane Wife (Capitol Records)
October 3, 2006

Ani DiFranco
Living in Clip—Live (**Righteous Babe Records**)
April 22, 1997

Dinosaur Jr.
You're Living All Over Me (Merge Records)
March 22, 2005

Dirty on Purpose
Hallelujah Sirens (North Street Records)
May 2006

Echo & the Bunnymen
Ocean Rain (Rhino Records)
May 4, 1984

The Flaming Lips
The Soft Bulletin (Warner Bros. Records)
June 22, 1999

Franz Ferdinand
Franz Ferdinand (Sony Records)
March 9, 2004

Fugazi
Repeater + 3 Songs (Dischord Records)
April 1990

Green Day
American Idiot (Reprise/Warner Bros.
Records)
September 21, 2004

Guided By Voices
Bee Thousand (Scat Records)
June 21, 1994

PJ Harvey
To Bring You My Love (Island Records)
February 28, 1995

The Juliana Hatfield Three
Become What You Are (Mammoth/PGD
Records)
August 3, 1993

Hüsker Dü
New Day Rising (**SST Records**)
1985

Iggy and The Stooges
Raw Power (Sony Records)
1973

The Jesus and Mary Chain
Psychocandy—Dual Disc (Rhino
Records)
1999

Kaiser Chiefs
Yours Truly, Angry Mob—CD/DVD
combo (Umvd labels)
February 5, 2007

The Killers
Hot Fuss (Island Records)
June 15, 2004

The Magnetic Fields
Holiday (Merge Records)
1994

MC5
Kick Out the Jams—Live (Elektra
Records)
1969

Meat Puppets
Meat Puppets II—Original Recording
Remastered (Rykodisc Records)
1984

Melvins
Houdini (Atlantic Records)
1993

Misfits
Walk Among Us (Rhino Records)
1982

Mission of Burma
Signals, Calls & Marches—Original
Recording Remastered (Rykodisc
Records)
August 1981

Modest Mouse
We Were Dead Before the Ship Even Sank
(Sony Records)
March 20, 2007

My Bloody Valentine
Loveless (**Sire Records**)
November 5, 1991

My Morning Jacket
Z (ATO Records)
October 4, 2005

Neutral Milk Hotel
In the Aeroplane Over the Sea (Merge
Records)
February 10, 1998

Nine Inch Nails
Pretty Hate Machine (Umvd Imports)
November, 1989

Nirvana
Nevermind (Geffen Records)
September 24, 1991

Orange Juice
The Glasgow School (Domino Records)
August 9, 2005

Pavement
Slanted and Enchanted: Luxe & Reduxe—
Original Recording Remastered
(Matador Records)
April 30, 1992

Pere Ubu
The Modern Dance—Original Recording
Remastered (Fontana Geffen Original
Recording Remastered
1978

Liz Phair
Exile in Guyville (Capitol Records)
June 22, 1993

Pixies
Doolittle (4AD)
April 18, 1989

The Polyphonic Spree
Together We're Happy (Hollywood
Records)
July 13, 2004

The Postal Service
Give Up (**Sub Pop Records**)
February 18, 2003

Rachel's
Music for Egon Schiele (Quarter Stick
Records)
February 20, 1996

Radiohead
OK Computer (Capitol Records)
1997

Ramones
Ramones—Original Recording
Remastered (Rhino Records)
1977

R.E.M.
Murmur (A&M Records)
1983

Rites of Spring
End on End (Dischord Records)
1991

Sebadoh
III (Domino Records)
September 1991

The Shins
Wincing the Night Away (**Sub Pop
Records**)
January 23, 2007

Sleater-Kinney
Call the Doctor (Chainsaw Records)
April 29, 1996

The Smashing Pumpkins
Siamese Dream (Virgin Records)
July 27, 1993

Elliott Smith
Figure 8 (Dreamworks Records)
April 18, 2000

The Smiths
The Queen Is Dead (Warner Bros.
Records)
1986

Sonic Youth
Daydream Nation—Deluxe Edition/
Original Recording Remastered (Geffen
Records)
1988

Regina Spektor
Soviet Kitsch (**Sire Records**)
August 17, 2004

Sufjan Stevens
Illinoise (Asthmatic Kitty Records)
July 5, 2005

Sunny Day Real Estate
The Rising Tide (Time Bomb Records)
June 20, 2000

Superchunk
No Pocky for Kitty—Original Recording
Remastered (Merge Records)
1991

Talking Heads
Talking Heads: 77 (Warner Bros.
Records)
September 16, 1977

Tapes 'n Tapes
The Loon (XL Recordings)
April 4, 2006

TV On The Radio
Desperate Youth Blood Thirsty Babes
(Touch and Go Records)
March 9, 2004

The White Stripes
White Blood Cells—Original Recording
Reissued (V2 Records)
July 3, 2001

Yeah Yeah Yeahs
Fever to Tell (Interscope Records)
April 29, 2003

Frank Zappa
Hot Rats—Original Recording
Remastered (Zappa Records)
October 10, 1969

Frank Zappa
Joe's Garage: Acts I, II & III—Original
Recording Remastered (Zappa Records)
November 19, 1979

Resource Guide

Books

Abbey, Eric James. *Garage Rock and Its Roots: Musical Rebels and the Drive for Individuality*. Jefferson, NC: McFarland & Company, 2006.

Adams, Chris. *Turquoise Days: The Weird World of Echo & the Bunnymen*. New York: Soft Skull Press, 2002.

Andersen, Mark, and Mark Jenkins. *Dance of Days: Two Decades of Punk in the Nation's Capital*. New York: Soft Skull Press, 2001.

Anderson, Kyle. *Accidental Revolution: The Story of Grunge*. New York: St. Martin's Griffin, 2007.

Artsrunik, Nicholas. *Franz Ferdinand*. London: Artnik, 2005.

Azerrad, Michael. *Come As You Are*. London: Virgin Publishing, 1994.

————. *Our Band Could Be Your Life: Scenes from the American Indie Underground 1981–1991*. New York: Back Bay Books, 2002.

Bacon Tony. *London Live: From the Yardbirds to Pink Floyd to the Sex Pistols*. Milwaukee, WI: Backbeat Books, 1999.

Beall, Eric. *Making Music Make Money: An Insider's Guide to Becoming Your Own Music Publisher*. Boston: Berklee Press, 2003.

Beck. *Online Diaries: The Lollapalooza Tour Journals of Beck, Courtney Love, Stephen Malkmus, Thurston Moore, Lee Ranaldo, and Mike Watt*. New York: Soft Skull Press, 2001.

Berger, Harris M. *Metal, Rock, and Jazz: Perception and the Phenomenology of Musical Experience (Music Culture)*. Hanover, NH: Wesleyan University Press, 1999.

Biafra, Jello, Camille Paglia, and Ursula Owen. *Index on Censorship: Smashed Hits the Book of Banned Music*. London: Index on Censorship, 1998.

Biafra, Jello, Lawrence Ferlinghetti, Billy Childish, and Henry Rollins. *Real Conversations, No. 1 (Henry Rollins, Jello Biafra, Lawrence Ferlinghetti, Billy Childish)*. San Francisco: Re/Search Publications, 2001.

Biafra, Jello, Lawrence Ferlinghetti, and Christian Parenti. *Mob Action against the State: Collected Speeches from the Bay Area Anarchist Bookfair (AK Press Audio)*, (Audio CD). Oakland, CA: AK Press, 2002.

Black, Johnny. *Reveal: The Story of R.E.M.* Milwaukee, WI: Backbeat Books, 2004.

Blackman, Nicole, and Juliette Torrez. *Revival: Spoken Work from Lollapalooza 94*. San Francisco: Manic D Press, 1995.

Blandford, James R. *PJ Harvey: Siren Rising*. London: Omnibus Press, 2004.

Bond, Sherry. *The Songwriter's and Musician's Guide to Nashville*. New York: Allworth Press, 2000.

Boot, Adrian, and Chris Salewicz Boot. *Punk—Illustrated History of a Music Revolution—Sex Pistols, The Clash, Patti Smith, The Chelsea Hotel, CBGB' s, Kurt Kobain & Nirvana, Green Da , & more . . . illustrated with photographs*. New York: Penguin Studio, 1997.

Borg, Bobby. *The Musician's Handbook: A Practical Guide to Understanding the Music Business*. New York: Billboard Books, 2003.

Brend, Mark. *Strange Sounds: Offbeat Instruments and Sonic Experiments in Pop*. Milwaukee, WI: Backbeat Books, 2005

Brown, Rodger Lyle. *"Party Out Of Bounds: The B-52's, R.E.M., and the Kids Who Rocked Athens, Georgia*. Atlanta, GA: Everthemore Books, 2003.

Brown, Roger James, and Martin Griese. *Electronica Dance Music Programming Secrets*. Upper Saddle River, NJ: Prentice-Hall, Dec. 1999.

Brunning, Bob. *1960s Pop*. New York: Peter Bedrick, 2001.

Budnick, Dean. *Jambands: The Complete Guide to the Players, Music, and Scene*. Milwaukee, WI: Backbeat Books, 2003.

Butcher, Jim. *Fool Moon (The Dresden Files, Book 2)*. Cincinnati, OH: Roc, 2001.

———. *Death Masks (The Dresden Files, Book 5)*. Cincinnati, OH: Roc, 2005.

Byrne, David, and Hilly Kristal. *CBGB and OMFUG: Thirty Years from the Home of Underground Rock*. New York: Harry N. Abrams, Inc., 2005.

Callwood, Brett. *MC5, Sonically Speaking*. London: Independent Music Press, 2007.

Carr, Daphne, and Mary Gaitskill. *Da Capo Best Music Writing 2006*. Cambridge, MA: De Capo Press, 2006.

Carson, Mina, Tisa Lewis, and Susan M. Shaw. *Girls Rock!: Fifty Years of Women Making Music*. Lexington: University Press of Kentucky, 2004.

Childerhose, Buffy, and Sarah McLachlan. *From Lilith to Lilith Fair: The Authorized Story*. New York: St. Martin's Griffin, 1998.

Cleveland, Barry. *Creative Music Production: Joe Meek's Bold Techniques*. Florence, KY: Artistpro, 2001.

Cobain, Kurt. *Journals*. Reissue ed. New York: Riverhead Trade, 2003.

Connolly, Cynthia (photographer), Sharon Cheslow (photographer), and Leslie Clague (photographer). *Banned in D C: Photos and Anecdotes from the DC Punk Underground*. 1st ed. Washington, DC: Sun Dog Propaganda, 1988.

Cooper, Kim. *The Aeroplane Over the Sea*. London: Continuum International Publishing Group, 2005.

Corgan, Billy. *Blinking with Fists: Poems*. London: Faber & Faber, 2006.

Cross, Charles R. *Heavier than Heaven: A Biography of Kurt Cobain*. New York: Hyperion, 2002.

Derogatis, Jim. *Let It Blurt: The Life & Times of Lester Bangs, America's Greatest Rock Critic*. New York: Broadway, 2000.

Diehl, Matt. *My So-Called Punk: Green Day, Fall Out Boy, The Distillers, Bad Religion—How Neo-Punk Stage-Dived into the Mainstream.* New York: St. Martin's Griffin, 2007.

Doherty, Jacqueline. *Pete Doherty: My Prodigal Son.* London: Headline Book Publishing, 2006.

Domini, John. *Talking Heads: 77.* Granada Hills, CA: Red Hen Press, 2003.

Donwood, Stanley, and Dr. Tchock. *Dead Children Playing: A Picture Book (Radiohead).* London: Verso, 2007.

Dresden Dolls, The. *The Dresden Dolls Companion.* New York: Cherry Lane Music, 2006.

Emond, Steve. *Emo Boy Volume 1: Nobody Cares About Anything Anyway, So Why Don't We All Just Die?* San Jose, CA: SLG Publishing, 2006.

Erlewine, Stephen Thomas. *Afghan Whigs.* 4th ed. Ann Arbor, MI: All Music Guide, 2001.

Erlewine, Stephen Thomas, Vladimir Bogdanov, and Chris Woodstra. *All Music Guide: The Expert's Guide to the Best Recordings (All Music Guides),* 4th ed. Milwaukee, WI: Backbeat Books, 2001.

Farinella, David. *Producing Hit Records: Secrets from the Studio.* New York: Schirmer Books, 2006.

Fitzgerald, F-Stop, and Marian Kester. *Dead Kennedys: The Unauthorized Version.* San Francisco: Last Gasp, 2004.

Foege, Alec. *Confusion Is Next: The Sonic Youth Story.* New York: St. Martin's Griffin, 1994.

Foranow, Wendy. *Empire of Dirt: The Aesthetics and Rituals of British Indie Music.* Middletown, CT: Wesleyan University Press, 2006.

Frank, Josh. *Fool the World: The Oral History of a Band Called Pixies* New York: St. Martin's Griffin, 2006.

Freedman, Estelle. *No Turning Back: The History of Feminism and the Future of Women.* New York: Ballantine Books, 2003.

Friskics-Warren, Bill. *I'll Take You There: Pop Music and the Urge for Transcendence.* London: Continuum International Publishing Group, 2006.

Gaar, Gillian G. *She's a Rebel: The History of Women in Rock & Roll.* Jackson, TN: Seal Press, 1992.

Gaar, Gillian G., and Yoko Ono. *She's a Rebel: The History of Women in Rock & Roll.* Jackson, TN: Seal Press, 2002.

Gaines, Donna. *A Misfit's Manifesto: The Spiritual Journey of a Rock-and-Roll Heart.* New York: Villard, 2003.

Gaitskill, Mary, and Daphne Carr. *Da Capo Best Music Writing 2006.* Cambridge, MA: Da Capo Press, 2006.

George-Warren, Holly, Patricia Romanowski, and Jon Pareles. *The Rolling Stone Encyclopedia of Rock & Roll (Revised and Updated for the 21st Century).* Forest City, NC: Fireside, 2001.

Gimarc, George. *Post Punk Diary: 1980–1982.* New York: St. Martin's Griffin, 1997.

Goddard, Simon. *The Smiths: Songs That Saved Your Life*. 3rd ed. London: Reynolds & Hearn, 2006.

Goldberg, Justin. *Ultimate Survival Guide for the New Music Industry: A Handbook for Hell*. Los Angeles: Lone Eagle, 2004.

Goldsher, Alan. *Modest Mouse: A Pretty Good Read*. New York: St. Martin's Griffin, 2006.

Goode, Michael I. *Stage Fright in Music Performance and Its Relationship to the Unconscious*. Burbank, CA: 1st Impression Publishing, 2003.

Graham, Ben. *Maximum White Stripes: The Unauthorised Biography of the White Stripes (Maximum series)*. Abridged ed. London: Chrome Dreams, 2003.

Gray, Michael. *The Bob Dylan Encyclopedia*. London: Continuum International Publishing Group, 2006.

Greenwald, Andy. *Nothing Feels Good*. New York: St. Martin's Griffin, 2003.

Greer, James. *Guided by Voices: A Brief History: Twenty-One Years of Hunting Accidents in the Forests of Rock and Roll*. New York: Grove Press, Black Cat, 2005.

Grossberger, Lewis. *Turn That Down! A Hysterical History of Rock, Roll, Pop, Soul, Punk, Funk, Rap, Grunge, Motown, Metal, Disco, Techno & Other Forms of Musical Aggression over the Ages*. Cincinnati, OH: Emmis Books, 2005.

Haenfler, Ross. *Straight Edge: Clean-Living Youth, Hardcore Punk, and Social Change*. Chapel Hill, NC: Rutgers University Press, 2006.

Hale, Jonathan. *Radiohead: From a Great Height*. Toronto: ECW Press, 1999.

Hal Leonard Corp. *Grunge Guitar Bible*. Milwaukee, WI: Hal Leonard Corp., 2003.

———. *Pop/Rock Piano Hits for Dummies: A Reference for the Rest of Us!* Milwaukee, WI: Hal Leonard Corporation, 2006.

———. *VH1's 100 Greatest Songs of Rock and Roll: Piano/Vocal/Guitar Edition*. Milwaukee, WI: Hal Leonard Corporation, 2003.

Handyside, Chris. *Fell in Love with a Band: The Story of The White Stripes*. New York: St. Martin's Griffin, 2004.

Hannaford, Alex. *Pete Doherty: Last of the Rock Romantics*. London: Random House UK, 2007.

———. *The White Stripes*. London: Artnik, 2005.

Hanson, Amy. *Smashing Pumpkins: Tales of a Scorched Earth*. London: Helter Skelter Publishing, 2004.

Harcourt, Nick. *Music Lust: Recommended Listening for Every Mood, Moment, and Reason*. Seattle, WA: Sasquatch Books, 2005.

Harvey, Hamilton. *Franz Ferdinand: And the Pop Renaissance*. London: Reynolds & Hearn, 2006.

Heatley, Michael. *Ryan Adams*. London: Omnibus Press, 2003.

Heylin, Clinton. *Babylon's Burning: From Punk to Grunge*. Edinburgh, Scotland, United Kingdom: Canongate Books, 2007.

Huxley, Martin. *Nine Inch Nails*. New York: St. Martin's Griffin, 1997.

Javanovic, Rob. *Perfect Sound Forever: The Story of Pavement*. Boston: Charles Justin and Co., 2004.

Jay, Richard. *How to Get Your Music in Film and TV.* New York: Schirmer Books, 2005.

Johnstone, Nick. *Melody Maker History of 20th Century Popular Music.* North Pomfret, VT: Trafalgar Square Publishing, 1999.

Joy, Camden. *The Last Rock Star Book: Or Liz Phair, a Rant.* Portland, OR: Verse Chorus Press, 1998.

Kalmar, Veronika. *Label Launch: A Guide to Independent Record Recordings, Promotion and Distribution.* New York: St. Martin's Griffin, 2002.

Kapranos, Alex. *Sound Bites: Eating on Tour with Franz Ferdinand.* New York: Penguin, 2006.

Kauffman, Ronen. *New Brunswick, New Jersey, Goodbye: Bands, Dirty Basements, and the Search for Self.* Van Nuys, CA: Hopeless Records, 2007.

Keithley, Joe, and Jack Rabid. *I Shithead: A Life in Punk.* Vancouver, BC, Canada: Arsenal Pulp Press, 2004.

Kendall, Katherine. *Kate Moss: Model of Imperfection.* New York: Chamberlain Bros., 2004.

Kielty, Martin. *Big Noise: The History of Scottish Rock 'n' Roll as Told by the People Who Made It.* Edinburgs, United Kingdom: Black & White Publishing, 2007.

Klosterman, Chuck. *Sex, Drugs, and Cocoa Puffs: A Low Culture Manifesto.* New York: Scribner, 2004.

Kosser, Michael. *How Nashville Became Music City, U.S.A.: 50 Years of Music Row.* Milwaukee, WI: Hal Leonard, 2006.

Koster, Rick. *Texas Music.* New York: St. Martin's Griffin, 2000.

Leblanc, Lauraine. *Pretty in Punk: Girls' Gender Resistance in a Boys' Subculture.* Rutgers, NJ: Rutgers University Press, 1999.

Lim, Dennis, ed. *The Village Voice Film Guide: 50 Years of Movies from Classics to Cult Hits.* Holboken, NJ: Hits. Holboken, NJ: Wiley, 2006.

Lornell, Kip, and Linda Ronstadt. *The NPR Curious Listener's Guide to American Folk.* New York: Perigee Trade, 2004.

MacKaye, Ian, Susie Horgan, and Henry Rollins. *Punk Love.* Riverside, NJ: Universe, 2007.

Malloy, Merrit. *The Great Rock 'N' Roll Quote Book.* New York: St. Martin's Griffin, 1995.

Manning, Sean. *The Show I'll Never Forget: 50 Writers Relive Their Most Memorable Concertgoing Experience.* Cambridge, MA: De Capo Press, 2007.

Marcus, Greil. *In the Fascist Bathroom: Punk in Pop Music, 1977–1992.* Cambridge, MA: Harvard University Press, 1999.

Marten, Nevelle, and Jeff Hudson. *Kinks.* San Marcos, TX: Bobcat Books, 2007.

Martin, Bill. *Listening to the Future: The Time of Progressive Rock, 1968–1978.* Chicago: Open Court Publishing Company, 1997.

McAleer, Dave. *The Book of Hit Singles 4 Ed: Top 20 Charts from 1954 to the Present Day.* Milwaukee, WI: Backbeat Books, 2001.

McAuliffe, Kevin Michael. *The Great American Newspaper The Rise and Fall of the Village Voice.* New York: Charles Scribner's Sons, 1978.

Mcdonough, Jimmy. *Shakey: Neil Young's Biography*. New York: Anchor, 2003.

McGuirk, Mike, and Jon Pruett. *The Music Festival Guide: For Music Lovers and Musicians*. Chicago: Chicago Review Press, 2004.

McNeil, Legs, and Gillian McCain. *Please Kill Me: The Uncensored Oral History of Punk*. New York: Penguin, 1997.

Melendez, Benjamin, Daphne Carr, Drew Daniel, and Franklin DukeBurno. *Listen Again: A Momentary History of Pop Music (Experience Music Project)*. Durham, NC: Duke University Press, 2007.

Mendelsshon, John. *The Pixies and Frank Black* London: Omnibus Press, 2005.

Mewton, Conrad. *All You Need to Know About Music & The Internet Revolution*. London: Sanctuary, 2005.

Moore, Thurston. *Mix Tape*. Riverside, NJ: Universe Publishing, 2005.

Morthland, John, and Lester Bangs. *Main Lines, Blood Feasts, and Bad Taste: A Lester Bangs Reader*. New York: Anchor, 2003.

Myers, Ben. *Green Day: American Idiot and the New Punk Explosion*. New York: Disinformation Company, 2006.

Novoselic, Krist. *Of Grunge and Government: Let's Fix This Broken Democracy*. New Providence, NJ: Rdv Books, 2004.

Nugent, Benjamin. *Elliott Smith and the Big Nothing*. Cambridge, MA: Da Capo Press, 2005.

Ogg, Alex. *The Men Behind Def Jam: The Radical Rise of Russell Simmons and Rick Rubin*. London: Omnibus Press, 2002.

Osborne, Roger. *Thirty Years of "NME" Album Charts*. London: Pan Macmillan, 1993.

Paytress, Mark. *Radiohead: The Complete Guide To Their Music*. London: Omnibus Press, 2005.

Pruett, Jon, and Mike McGuirk. *The Music Festival Guide: For Music Lovers and Musicians*. Chicago: Chicago Review Press, 2004.

Quirino, Raffaele. *Ani DiFranco: Righteous Babe Revisited* New York: Fox Music Books, 2004.

Raha, Maria. *Cinderella's Big Score: Women of the Punk and Indie Underground (Live Girls)*. Jackson, TN: Seal Press, 2004.

Ramone, Dee Dee. *Chelsea Horror Hotel: A Novel by Dee Dee Ramone*. New York: Thunder's Mouth Press, 2001.

Ramone, Dee Dee, Veronica Kofman, and Legs McNeil. *Lobotomy: Surviving the Ramones*. 2nd ed. New York: Thunder's Mouth Press, 2000.

Rappaport, Doreen. *John's Secret Dreams: The Life of John Lennon*. New York: Hyperion, 2004.

Reynolds, Simon. *Rip It Up and Start Again: Postpunk 1978–1984*. New York: Penguin, 2006.

Roach, Martin. *Morphing the Blues: The White Stripes and the Strange Relevance of Detroit*. London: Chrome Dreams, 2004.

Roach, Martin, and *New Musical Express*. *NME Top 100 Singles: The Definitive Chart of the UKs Best-Selling Songs*. London: Chrysalis, 2002.

Robbins, Ira A. *The Trouser Press Guide to 90's Rock*. 5th ed. Forest City, NC: Fireside, 1997.

Rock, Mick, and Iggy Pop. *Raw Power: Iggy & The Stooges*. London: Omnibus Press, 2005.

Rodgers, Jeffrey Pepper. *Rock Troubadours: Conversations on the Art and Craft of Songwriting with Jerry Garcia, Ani DiFranco, Dave Matthews, Joni Mitchell, Paul Simon, and More*. San Anselmo, CA: String Letter Publishing, 2000.

Rolling Stone Magazine. *The Rolling Stone Illustrated History of Rock and Roll: The Definitive History of the Most Important Artists and Their Music*. 3rd ed. New York: Random House, 1992.

Rollins, Henry. *Get in the Van: On the Road With Black Flag*. 2nd ed. Los Angeles: 2.13.61 Publications, 2004.

Rough Guides. *The Rough Guide to Cult Pop (Rough Guide Sports/Pop Culture)*. London: Rough Guides, 2004.

Rudder, Randy, and Roseanne Cash. *Country Music Reader*. Nashville, TN: Music City Book Pub., 2006.

Rudsenske, J. S., and J. P. Denk. *Music Business Made Simple: Start An Independent Record Label (Music Business Made Simple)*. New York: Schirmer Books, 2005.

Sabin, Roger. *Punk Rock: So What? The Cultural Legacy of Punk*. New York: Routledge, 1999.

Salyers, Christopher D., and Richard Hell. *CBGB: Decades of Graffiti*. New York: Mark Batty Publisher, 2006.

Samson, Pete, and Nathan Yates. *Pete Doherty: On the Edge: The True Story of a Troubled Genius*. London: John Blake, 2006.

Schmeling, Paul. *Berklee Music Theory Book 1*. Boston: Berklee Press, 2005.

Schwartz, Daylle Deanna. *I Don't Need a Record Deal! Your Survival Guide for the Indie Music Revolution*. New York: Billboard Books, 2005.

Sellers, John. *Perfect from Now On: How Indie Rock Saved My Life*. New York: Simon & Schuster, 2007.

Simmons, Michael, and John Sinclair. *Guitar Army: Rock & Revolution with the MC5 and the White Panther Party* Los Angeles: Process, 2007.

Sinker, Daniel. *We Owe You Nothing, Punk Planet: The Collected Interviews*. New York: Akashic Books, 2001.

Slaven, Neil. *Electric Don Quixote: The Story Of Frank Zappa*. 2nd ed. London: Omnibus Press 2003.

Southall, Brian. *The A–Z of Record Labels*. London: Sanctuary Publishing, Ltd., 2000.

Southall, Brian, and Chris Wright. *A–Z of Record Labels*. 2nd ed. London: Sanctuary Publishing, Ltd., 2003.

Souvignier, Todd. *Sampling: The Real Sound Revolution*. Milwaukee, WI: Hal Leonard, 2006.

Spellman, Peter.*The Musician's Internet: Online Strategies for Success in the Music Industry (Music Business)*. Boston: Berklee Press Publications, 2002.

———. *The Self-Promoting Musician (Music Business)*. Boston: Berklee Press, 2000.

Spencer, Amy. *DIY: The Rise of Lo-Fi Culture*. London: Marion Boyars Publishers, Ltd., 2005.

Spitz, Marc. *Nobody Likes You: Inside the Turbulent Life, Times, and Music of Green Day*. New York: Hyperion, 2006.

Strong, Martin C. *The Great Indie Discography*. 2nd ed. Edinburgh, Scotland, United Kingdom: Canongate Books, 2003.

Sullivan, Denise. *Rip It Up! Rock 'n' Roll Rulebreakers*. Milwaukee, WI: Backbeat Books, 2001.

———. *The White Stripes: Sweethearts of the Blues*. Milwaukee, WI: Backbeat Books, 2004.

Taormino, Tristan, Karen Green, and Ann Magnuson. *Girls Guide to Taking Over the World: Writings From The Girl Zine Revolution*. New York: St. Martin's Griffin, 1997.

Tate, Joseph. *Music and Art of Radiohead*. London: Ashgate Pub. Ltd., 2005.

Thompson, Dave. *Alternative Rock*. San Francisco: Miller Freeman Books, 2000.

Tobler, John. *"NME" Rock 'n' Roll Years*. London: Hamlyn, 1992.

True, Everett. *Hey Ho Let's Go: The Story of the Ramones*. London: Omnibus Press, 2005.

———. *The White Stripes and the Sound of Mutant Blues*. London: Omnibus Press, 2004.

Trynka, Paul. *Iggy Pop: Open Up and Bleed*. New York: Broadway Books, 2007.

Turner, Cherie. *Everything You Need to Know about the Riot Grrrl Movement: The Feminism of a New Generation*. New York: Rosen Publishing Group, 2001.

Turofsky, Diane. *CMJ 10: The First Decade 1979–1989*. New York: Robert K. Haber/College Media Inc, 1989.

Udo, Tommy. *Nine Inch Nails*. San Marcos, TX: Bobcat Books, 2007.

Unteberger, Richie. *The Rough Guide to Music USA*. London: Rough Guides, 1999.

Warhol, Andy. *The Philosophy of Andy Warhol: (From A to B and Back Again)*. Fort Washington, PA: Harvest Books, 1977.

Warner, Jay. *On This Day in Music History: Over 2,000 Popular Music Facts Covering Every Day of the Year*. Milwaukee, WI: Hal Leonard, 2004.

Weinstein, Deena. *Heavy Metal: The Music and Its Culture*. Cambridge, MA: Da Capo Press, 2000.

Weissman, Dick. *Which Side Are You On? An Inside History of the Folk Music Revival in America*. London: Continuum International Publishing Group, 2006.

Welsh, Pete. *Kids in the Riot: High and Low with The Libertines*. London: Music Sales, 2006.

Whitelaw, Paul. *Belle and Sebastian: Just a Modern Rock Story*. New York: St. Martin's Griffin, 2005.

Wimble, David. *The Indie Bible 7th Edition (Indie Bible)*, 7th ed. Ottawa, ON, Canada: Big Meteor Publications, 2005.

Wolff, Carlo. *Cleveland Rock & Roll Memories*. Cleveland, OH: Gray & Company Publishers, 2006.

Woods, Paul A. *Morrissey in Conversation: The Essential Interviews*. London: Plexus Publishing, 2007.

Wrekk, Alex. *Stolen Sharpie Revolution: A DIY Zine Resource*. Bloomington, IN: Microcosm, 2003.

Young, Rob. *Warp (Labels Unlimited)*. London: Black Dog Publishing, 2005.

———. *Rough Trade: Labels Unlimited*. London: Black Dog Publishing, 2006.

Zappa, Frank. *Real Frank Zappa Book*. New York: Simon & Schuster, 1990.

Zimmerman, Keith, and Kent Zimmerman. *Sing My Way Home: Voices of the New American Roots Rock*. Milwaukee, WI: Backbeat Books, 2004.

Zinner, Nick. *I Hope You Are All Happy Now* (book of photography). New York: St. Martin's Griffin, 2005.

Zummer, Thomas, Michael Sarff, and Carol Stakenas. *Lo-Fi Baroque*. New York: Thread Waxing Space, 1998.

Newspapers/Magazines

Baltin, Steve. "Afghan Whigs Say Goodnight." *Rolling Stone,* February 2001 (http://www.rollingstone.com/artists/afghanwhigs/articles/story/5919257/afghan_whigs_say_goodnight).

Collis, Clark. "More Justin Time." *Entertainment Weekly,* February 2, 2007.

Drozdowski, Ted. "Burmese Days: Thurston Moore, Rick Harte, Rob Dickinson, and More Speak Out." *Boston Phoenix,* January 10–17, 2002, music review.

Dverden, Nick. "The Next Big Thing! Art Brut." *BLENDER* magazine, December 2004.

Falwell, Rev. Jerry. "Parents Alert." *National Liberty Journal,* June 1999.

Freedom du Lac, J. "The 'Song Doctor' Is In: From Audioslave to Neil Diamond, Recording Artists Know Producer Rick Rubin's Touch Is a Powerful Tonic." *Washington Post,* January 15, 2006.

Gordinier, Jeff. "Message in a Battle." *Entertainment Weekly,* no. 442, July 24, 1998.

Harrington, Jim. "Bauhaus in Concert; Goth Rock at Its Best." *Oakland Tribune,* October 26, 2005.

Web Sites/Blogs/Non-Print Sources

"About Us." www.aboutus.org/Pitchforkmedia.

"Arctic Monkeys in Concert," *NPR.org,* March 27, 2006. www.npr.org/templates/story/story.php?storyId=5293452.

Basham, David. "Got Charts? No Doubt's Christmas Gift; Nirvana Ain't No Beatles." December 20, 2001, http://www.mtv.com/news/articles/1451583/20011220/nirvana.jhtml.

BBC News online, "NME: Still Rocking at 50," February 24, 2002.

Biography: Sebadoh. www.allmusic.com.

Carr, David. "Garage Rock Meets Garage Critics," August 29, 2005. http://www.nytimes.com/2005/08/29/business/media/29carr.html?pagewanted=all.

Cohen, Johathan. "Cat Power Cancels Spring Tour." February 6, 2006. http://www.billboard.com/bbcom/news/article_display.jsp?vnu_content_id= 1001958060.

Corcoran, Monica. "A Night Out With—Earlimart; Facing the Beer-Dark Sea. September 5, 2004. http://query.nytimes.com/gst/fullpage.html?res= 9905E4DC1331F936A3575AC0A9629C8B63.

Devenish, Colin. "Sire Boxes Madonna, Heads," August 5, 2005. http://www. rollingstone.com/news/story/7524661/sire_boxes_madonna_heads.

Diaz, Cesar. "Dig Your Own Hole." May 20, 2005. www.popmatters.com.

DiCrescenzo, Brent. "Radiohead: Kid A" (album review). http://www. pitchforkmedia.com/article/record_review/21226-kid-a.

DuBrowa, Corey. "Modest Mouse 20,000 Leagues Under Normalcy," *PASTE* magazine, March 28, 2007.

Freedom du Lac, J. "Giving Indie Acts a Plug, or Pulling It, April 30, 2006. http://www.washingtonpost.com/wp-dyn/content/article/2006/04/28/ AR2006042800457.html.

Fricke, David. "Meat Puppets: Out My Way (Album Review)," *Rolling Stone,* October 23, 1986. http://www.rollingstone.com/artists/meatpuppets/albums/ album/97116/review/5941046/out_my_way.

"Galaxie 500." www.rykodistribution.com.

"The Gossip Announce One-Off London Date." http://www.nme.com/news/ the-gossip/34307.

"Green Day—Dookie," About.com: Top 40/Pop. http://top40.about.com/od/ artistsdk/gr/greendaydookie.htm.

Grose, Jessica. "Artist of the Day: Say Hi to Your Mom," June 8, 2005. http:// www.spin.com/articles/say-hi-your-mom.

———. "Artist of the Day: Dirty on Purpose." August 17, 2005. http:// spinmagazine.com/articles/dirty-purpose.

Gundersen, Edna. "Emo Bands' Titles Are a Lot Longer Than This." July 28, 2006. http://www.usatoday.com/life/music/news/2006-07-27-emo-songs_x.htm.

Handler, Shane. "The New Pornographers: Canadian Blockbuster." November 1, 2005. http://www.glidemagazine.com/articles/47784/the-new-pornographers-canadian-blockbuster.html.

Harris, Chris. "Nightwatchman, Rage Reunion Have Morello Fired Up for Political Fights." February 6, 2007. http://www.vh1.com/news/articles/1551733/ 20070206/morello_tom.jhtml.

Hermes, Will. "Psych Out: The Do-It-Yourself Psychedelica of the Elephant 6 Bands." *Rolling Stone* April 2, 1998.

"The History of the NME Awards." http://www.nme.com/awardshistory.

"The Insider's Guide to Beth Ditto." http://www.cnn.com/2006/SHOWBIZ/ Music/11/24/tbr.ditto/index.html.

"In Utero." www.amazon.com.uk.

Itzkoff, Dave. "The Pitchfork Effect," September 2006. http://www.wired.com /wired/archive/14.09/pitchfork.html.

"The Killers Get a New Feud," September 27, 2005. http://www.nme.com /news/the-killers/21090.

"The Killers 'Offended' by Green Day," October 13, 2006. http://www. nme.com/news/the-killers/24702.

Kirschling, Gregory. "Natalie Portman Sounds Off." *Entertainment Weekly,* No. 962, October 24, 2007.

"Libertines Reunite on Stage." April 13, 2007. http://news.bbc.co.uk.

Lilith Fair Performers, Attendees Achieve Largest-Ever Synchronized Ovulation," August 26, 1998. http://www.theonion.com/content/node/28925.

Lorenzo, Dan. "Glenn Danzig" interview. February 22, 2005. http://www. music-news.com.

MacKaye, Ian, Richard Kern, Mike Watt, and Jim Rose. *D.I.Y. or Die: How to Survive as an Independent Artist.* documentary, 2002.

Mitchell, Elvis. "MC5 A True Testimonial (2002): Film Review," April 23, 2004. http://movies.nytimes.com/movie/review?res=9E02E0DC143AF930-A15757C0A9629C8B63.

Montgomery, James. "The Vanilla Thrilla! The Killers Vs. The Bravery." 1995. www.mtv.com.

Moss, Corey. "Liz Phair Wants Recognition for Being Cute *and* Deep," September 3, 2003. http://www.mtv.com/news/articles/1477719/20030828/phair_liz.jhtml.

"New Pornographers." www.rollingstone.com.

Nine Inch Nails: Biography. www.rollingstone.com.

Norris, Michele. "CAKE's McCrea Talks About New Album. November 26, 2004. www.npr.org/templates/story/story.php?storyId=4188448.

Paine, André. "The Southern Bell Has Her Own Bawl," February 26, 2007. http://www.thisislondon.co.uk/music/gig-23354363-details/Gossip/gigReview.do ?reviewId=23386894.

Philbrook, Erik, with Jon Bahr and Jin Moon. "Artists To Be on the Lookout For in 2005." http://www.ascap.com/playback/2005/winter/rockfuture.html.

Phillips, Amy. "Exclusive: The Decemberists Sign to Capitol Records." Pitchfork Media, December 12, 2005. http://www.pitchforkmedia.com/article/news/35595-exclusive-the-decemberists-sign-to-capitol-records.

"PJ Harvey Interview." *SPIN* magazine. 1996. http://room509.net/sr/articles/ interview/spin96.html.

Powers, Ann. "Joey Ramone, Punk's Influential Yelper, Dies at 49," September 16, 2001. http://query.nytimes.com/gst/fullpage.html?res=9405EFDC1E31-F935A25757C0A9679C8B63&n=Top%2fReference%2fTimes%20Topics%2fPeople%2fR%2fRamone%2c%20Joey.

"Rock/Pop Titles at Aquarius Records." www.aquariusrecords.com.

Ross, Jodi. "Ryan Adams, 'Golden Boy.' " February 15, 2002. www.cnn.com.

Rule, Dan. "Unassuming Star," February 22, 2008. http://www.theage.com.au /news/music/unassuming-star/2008/02/21/1203467229623.html.

Schreiber, Ryan, and Eric Carr. "Interview: Out Hud," June 1, 2003, http://www.pitchforkmedia.com/article/feature/31409-interview-out-hud.

SPIN Staff. "Death Cab for Cutie: Transatlanticism." October 8, 2003. www.spin.com.

Takemoto, Neil. "Ani Difranco and Her Church-Turned-Concert Hall," November 5, 2007. http://www.cooltownstudios.com/mt/archives/001174.html.

Vowell, Sarah. "Throwing Ovaries," July 11, 1997. www.theonion.com.

Wiederhorn, Jon. "Cake Singer So Not Excited About Touring, Admits His Band Is Irrelevant. November 4, 2004. http://www.mtv.com/news/articles/1493442/20041104/cake.jhtml.

blog.americangirlproductions.com/.

blogs.guardian.co.uk.

http://blogsarefordogs.com.

http://onepoorcorrespondent.blogspot.com.

http://www.indierockreviews.com/.

http://www.threeimaginarygirls.com/.

indierockweekly.podomatic.com/.

tirck.blogspot.com/.

whatwouldjb.blogspot.com/.

www.artistlaunch.com/indierock.

www.bagelradio.com/.

www.deadkennedysnews.com.

www.indierockbaseball.com.

www.indierockcafe.com/.

www.mackenzieland.com/.

www.pitchforkmedia.com/.

www.prefixmag.com.

www.radioindierock.com/.

www.sirius.com/leftofcenter.

www.stereogum.com/.

www.thedelimagazine.com/.

www.wornrecords.ca/steamroller/.

www.nme.com.

Index

About the Author

KERRY L. SMITH is a Boston-based music journalist who has written for *Rolling Stone,* Rolling Stone online, Vh1.com, MTV.com, the Associated Press, *Time Out New York,* Allmusic.com, Music.com, *Alternative Press* magazine, the *New York Sun,* and the *Boston Phoenix.*